CW00697024

# THE WEST YORKSHIRE WOODS PART II

## The Aire Valley

# THE WEST YORKSHIRE WOODS PART II

## The Aire Valley

by Christopher Goddard

*Rufus the Airedale (or Bingley) Terrier*

For Rufus, Dolly, Eric
and all the naughty dogs.
You are an inspiration to us all.

Published by Gritstone Publishing Co-operative
Birchcliffe Centre, Hebden Bridge, West Yorkshire, HX7 8DG

**www.gritstonepublishing.co.uk**

First Edition – 2021

Printed in Halifax by Had-Print



ISBN 978-1-913625-02-3

## ACKNOWLEDGEMENTS

With thanks to everyone who helped make this book possible:

Nick Goddard, Alison Ford and Phil Cross, Heather Woodstock and Stebben Bracewell, Alex Neilson, Tom Coxhead and Leeds Coppice Workers, Pete Rolls, Anthony Child, my colleagues at Gritstone Publishing Co-operative (Andrew Bibby, Andrew McCloy, Chiz Dakin, Colin Speakman, Laurence Rose and Eileen Jones), as well as all the helpful staff at Bradford and Leeds Local Studies Libraries.

As well as my partner, editor and general sounding board Caroline, I'd like to thank my parents for their continued support and assistance. In addition to instilling in me from an early age a love of the outdoors, they have supported me so much in all my endeavours, including checking routes, distributing books and proofreading this book. I'm eternally grateful xx

P.S. In the history section, the headings are all Neil Young song titles, just because...

# THE WEST YORKSHIRE WOODS PART II

## CONTENTS

# THE WOODS OF THE AIRE VALLEY - Overview Map

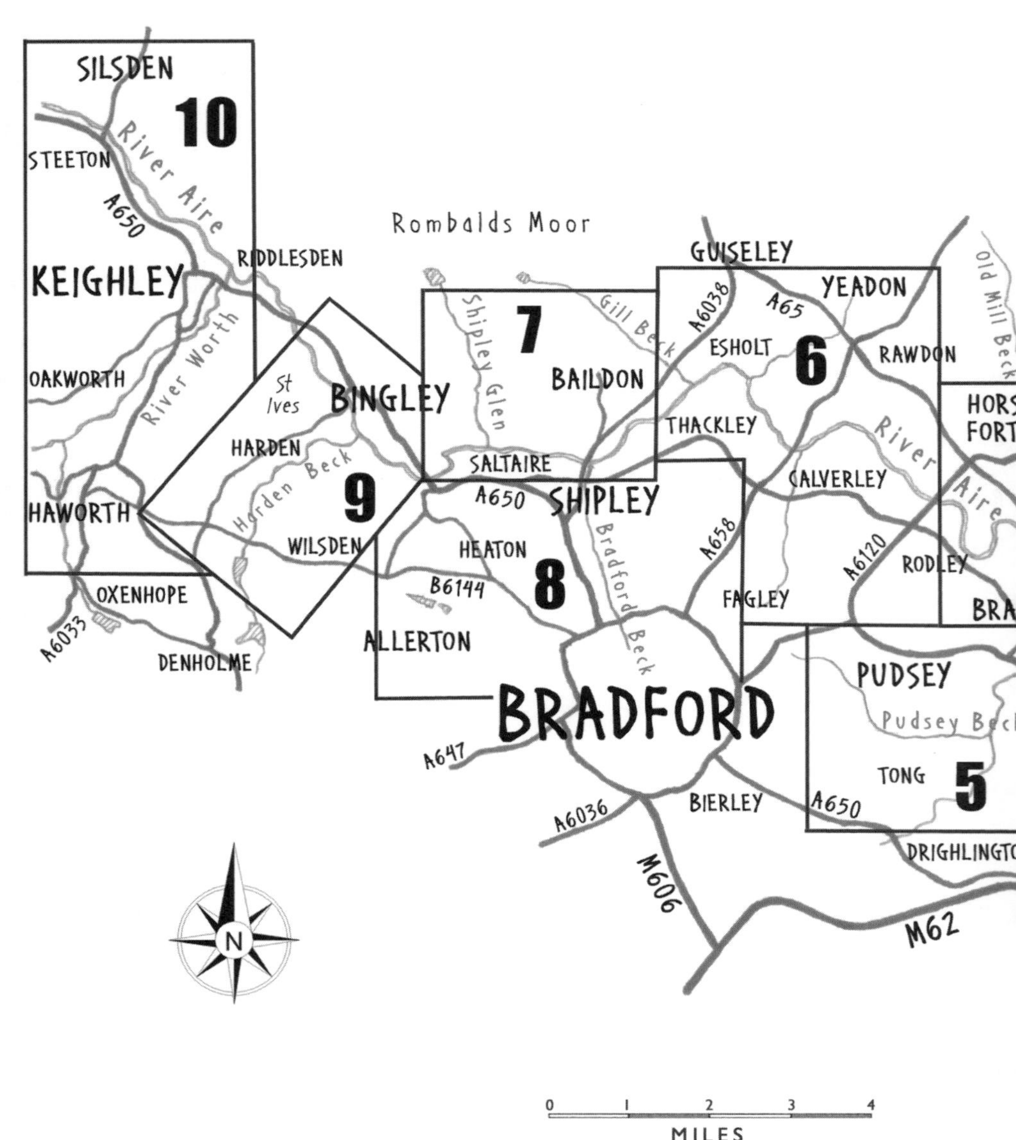

SILSDEN
10
STEETON
River Aire
A650
KEIGHLEY
RIDDLESDEN
River Worth
OAKWORTH
HAWORTH
OXENHOPE
A6033
DENHOLME
St Ives
BINGLEY
HARDEN
Harden Beck
9
WILSDEN
Rombalds Moor
7
Shipley Glen
Gill Beck
BAILDON
SALTAIRE
A650
SHIPLEY
HEATON
B6144
8
ALLERTON
Bradford Beck
A658
FAGLEY
BRADFORD
A647
A6036
BIERLEY
M606
M62
GUISELEY
A6038
A65
YEADON
ESHOLT
6
RAWDON
Old Mill Beck
THACKLEY
River Aire
CALVERLEY
A6120
RODLEY
PUDSEY
TONG
5
A650
0
1
2
3
4
MILES
N

# THE MAGIC OF THE WOODS

*In the woods too, a man casts off his years, as the snake his slough, and at what period soever of life, is always a child. In the woods, is perpetual youth. Within these plantations of God, a decorum and sanctity reign, a perennial festival is dressed, and the guest sees not how he should tire of them in a thousand years.*

(from 'Nature' by Ralph Waldo Emerson)

Believe it or not the English were once thought of by southern Europeans to be rather whimsical and prone to flights of fancy, such was our belief in fairies, fauns, dryads, nymphs, pixies, goblins, trolls and demons. I'm not sure what happened, but if this sense of magic still resides in us I think it is most likely to be brought out by the woods. It is easy to find yourself wanting to skip when walking through leafy bowers between twisted oak trees or crossing a carpet of bright bluebells. The woods can excite the child in all of us, make us want to spend all day building dens and tree houses, chasing each other with spears or bows and arrows or playing silly hide-and-seek games as we used to before we brought too many thoughts into the wood with us.

I have always thought it easier to imagine a god in the woods than in a stuffy church. The Druids were famous for their veneration of sacred groves, particularly oak, yew and ash, but they were just one of a number of our Celtic and pre-Celtic ancestors for whom trees were hallowed. The Anglo-Saxons also brought with them a German version of tree worship, which existed alongside these Celtic cults until Christianity swept it all aside from the 7th century. This religion of the book, as opposed to the largely undocumented religions that preceded it, may be largely responsible us losing our connection with the magic of the woods, though many of the non-conformist sects that were particularly popular in West Yorkshire in the 18th and 19th centuries were forced to meet in secret locations in the woods. Our old gods are the sacred trees that are alive with spirits should we wish to find them.

Until surprisingly recently superstitions about many of our most common trees were widely held. The Toothache Tree in Buck Wood near Bradford was used in the early 20th century to transfer the pain of toothache onto a tree by driving nails into its bark. Similarly warts could be passed to an ash tree by rubbing them with bacon and leaving this in the tree, or pricking them with a pin that was then plunged into the tree. Holly, rowan and birch all kept witches at bay, though a witches broom was made of birch. A piece of elder in your pocket helped you sleep and even guarded against adultery, and yet could be possessed by witches. The hawthorn was the fairies' meeting place and should never be removed from the forest. Willow was a tree of sorrow and prophecy. Ash sap had the power to heal, and ill children passed through a cleft ash would be imbued with the ash tree's great strength. Alder leaves were used to soothe travellers' feet and the tree thought to connect to the other world, so permission should be asked of the tree before cutting it. The slow-growing venerated yew was most powerful of all; dark, deadly poisonous and bad luck to chop down or even carry, it transported you to the underworld if you fell asleep beneath it.

Perhaps part of the enduring excitement of the woods is the way light and dark meet there, both literally and metaphorically. It is just as easy to imagine the devil, monsters and ghosts as it is benign forces. In the Middle Ages, large woods were seen as dangerous, impassable, dark and the realm of highwaymen. There is a reason for the enduring appeal of the story of Robin Hood and he perhaps best illustrates our ambivalent relationship with the woods. Woods on the edge of the city or down remote lanes are still likely to be the site of nefarious activities that we'd rather keep away from, particularly at dusk and beyond. There is a reason so many of the best horror films – *The Evil Dead,*

*The Blair Witch Project*, *The Witch*, *The Last House on the Left*, *Eden Lake*, *The Cabin in the Woods*, *Friday the 13th* and *Antichrist* among the finest – are set in the woods because the setting itself forms an integral part of the uneasiness these films inspire. Walking in woods in the mist or as darkness falls, there is always the possibility of something lurking just beyond that tree. I find this particularly true in conifer plantations, where the darkness and monotony of the trees is so disquieting. Before much of it was felled recently, Rivock Plantation above Keighley was associated with sightings of spectral hooded figures, thought to be the ghosts of miners killed in the nearby pits. Chatterchains, a spectral black dog with rattling chains around its neck, was said to live in the woods under Baildon Bank, and the Gabble Ratchets were a pack of huge hounds with human heads that roamed the woods – around Leeds these were said to represent the souls of unbaptised children.

a maiden chestnut in Beeston Wood, Oulton Park

Researching this book I have come across numerous school and community projects in the woods of the Aire Valley, where fairy villages have been created with miniature doors, signs and figures pinned to the poor trees, and my first thought has been that this is vandalism. Why are we not teaching our children about the real history of the woods? But, though I would like to see more biodegradable materials used, perhaps I ought to respect it as a way of connecting with an important part of our history and passing on the wonder of the woods to future generations. Countless times I have used the word 'magical' to describe my favourite parts of walks in this book, places where I am transported to some primordial or fairytale world, so why shouldn't we encourage our children to let their imagination run wild in the woods?

I hadn't picked up on forest bathing until researching this book, but it is now fashionable around the world. In Japan it is known as *shinrin yoku*, a term created in 1982 by the Minister of Agriculture, Forestry and Fisheries, and doctors regularly prescribe a walk in the woods as therapy for various ailments. In Norwegian tradition it is called *skogluft* (meaning 'forest air'), in Kneipp therapy (a German alternative medicine) it is one of the five core curative methods, and it is advocated as a means of improving mental health by English journalist Isabel Hardman in her book *The Natural Health Service*. These ideas have proved particularly important during the Covid-19 pandemic, when all we have as an escape other than Zoom and Netflix is our immediate local landscape, whether this is escaping mental health issues or just incapacitating boredom. In much of West Yorkshire we are fortunate that many of our urban areas have good access to plenty of woodlands and, even in the centre of Leeds, you don't have to walk too far to reach a landscape of trees.

The effect of trees on us is starting to be better understood, though they remain almost as much of a mystery as the human mind. Some trees, including pine, yew and hornbeam, release antimicrobial chemicals called phytoncides. These contain similar terpenes to those found in CBD and lower our pulse rate and blood pressure and improve our immune system. Sap is not just a pleasant smell, it actively calms us. However, trees only emit these phytoncides when in places they are comfortable growing, and can have an opposite negative chemical effect when they are not – perhaps this is why some plantations have such a disquieting effect on us. The woods also can have an obvious cooling effect on us in the height of summer, when the shade and the moisture stored in mosses keeps the air cool and can be a relief from the hot sun. Trees act as natural air purifiers, not just on the larger scale of making our planet habitable, but locally by absorbing a lot of air pollution, which is important when many of West Yorkshire's woods are close to urban areas.

Trees are not as passive as we might assume. We tend to see them as helpless victims we need to cosset but, for all we have done to them and their natural environment, they will be here long after us. The complexity of the networks of mycorrhizal fungi that sustain trees is just coming to light. Mycorrhiza literally means 'fungus root' and refers to a symbiotic relationship between plant and fungus, with the networks of fungal roots that exist beneath the mushrooms and toadstools of the forest wrapping themselves around the roots of a tree and in some cases working deep into them. A single mycorrhizal organism can cover many hectares and connect all the trees in a large wood, providing a co-dependency without which species like the beech cannot survive. The fungus feeds on sugars that the tree produces by photosynthesis, and in return breaks down the leaf and wood matter on the forest floor to make nutrients available to the trees. Its filaments also allow the trees to communicate with each other by emitting chemical signals, as well as share nutrients and water to sustain those that are in poor health. Trees can warn each other about weather events, insect infestations and other imminent dangers, reacting by producing more tannins to make their leaves unpalatable to large mammals or releasing terpenes to attract or repel certain insects. Each species has its own mycorrhizal network and its ability to colonise a new area is often dependent upon these developing sufficiently. In fact the oak acorn's inability to germinate in woods, relying instead on the forgetful jay to bury them elsewhere, is thought to be the result of a quirk in its mycorrhizal fungi.

The vibrations that trees emit through these networks can be felt by us, whether we are aware of it or not. I think it is awe-inspiring to lay on the ground in the wood and imagine the activity going on beneath me, to think that the trees can sense us and are communicating about us that very moment. Trees have adapted to us far more adeptly than we have to them – for example trees closer to roads have thicker bark to account for the subtle pulsation of passing traffic – but we are not even trying to listen back. Trees are one of our best memories of time – they can live through many generations, surviving the pollution and climate change that we are apparently insensitive to – and it is all there etched in their rings, which contain dead wood from each year of a tree's life.

It's not that trees don't operate on our timescale, it's that we don't operate on theirs. Perhaps getting closer to trees can help us to become a little more like them.

# THE RIVER AIRE AND ITS WOODLANDS

*'The river runs by, the colour of flesh,*
*That wondrous river that runs from my mum to my breast.*
*I whispered its name, the majestic Aire,*
*And sang as it surfaced the secrets of all*
*who'd been there.'*

(from *Wide Majestic Aire* by Trembling Bells)

Aire Head Springs

The River Aire has its source high on the limestone pavement of the Yorkshire Dales in the form of several small streams that flow into Malham Tarn. Half a mile below the tarn, it sinks deep into the rocks and primarily emerges, not in the stream at the foot of the 260ft face of Malham Cove, but at Aire Head Springs half a mile downstream of Malham village. Here the river gushes up out of the field to be joined by Malham Beck and Gordale Beck and start its 90-mile course down through the heart of the old West Riding. At the other end it reaches the River Ouse near the village of Airmyn, a name derived from an Old Scandinavian word *mynni* for a river mouth.

Although the whole of the river was once contained within or along the boundary of the old West Riding, now only just over half of its course runs through the modern county of West Yorkshire. However, it is this middle section of the river that is most characterised by woodland. The limestone landscape of the Dales is largely treeless and sheep-mown, with just a few trees along the river bank, while the lazy meanders across the flat marshes downstream of Knottingley have even fewer wooded areas. In between the two, the industrial heartland of West Yorkshire that developed along the Aire and its tributaries contains more woodland than the more rural areas at either end. Though during the 19th century the Aire came to resemble an open sewer, full of greasy sludge, lanolin and dyestuffs and supporting very little plant or animal life (it was described by the writer Edmund Bogg in 1902 as 'the dark, turbid river of Hades'), around it were preserved great areas of trees that still characterise significant stretches of the valley, particularly from Kirkstall to Bingley.

The Aire is a river of great contrasts, even along its course through West Yorkshire. Sometimes it looks like a damp grey splodge at the bottom of an overgrown bank, in other places it has the majestic and timeless sweep that Alex Nielsen describes in his lyrics above. In Leeds it is front and centre, the river that bore the city, while elsewhere it is overshadowed by the imposing sweep of the Leeds and Liverpool Canal, which mirrors its course as far as Gargrave. Downstream its flow is disrupted by weirs, shortcuts and re-routings. It once heaved with watercraft, tugs towing lines of containers, known as Tom Puddings, full of coal to the power stations at Ferrybridge and beyond, and bodies washed up on its banks with alarming frequency. So often now it looks benign and tamed, it is easy to forget that this silent snake of water shaped half the county and defined most of its history.

First recorded as Yr in the 10th century, the origin of River Aire's name is very hard to trace with any certainty. It may derive from an Old Norse word for an island, referring to the islands originally created by its various courses in its lower section. It may also, like most rivers, have retained its Celtic name, here possibly meaning 'strong flowing' like the River Ure, or from the Welsh *aer* for 'slaughter'. However, it may also be that the name Leeds itself was derived from the Celtic word for the river, with Aire being a later Anglian interpretation of this.

The Aire is a very different river from the Calder, which I covered in *The West Yorkshire Woods: Part I.* The Calder has its entire course within the county of West Yorkshire, rising on its gritstone and joining the Aire before reaching the East Riding's flatlands. The area I covered in that book was solely the River Calder's upper course, characterised by steep-sided valleys with woodlands clinging to their rocky edges. By the time the Aire reaches West Yorkshire near Silsden it is already a significant river that meanders generously across the broad valley floor. During the last ice age the Airedale ice sheet carved out this great U-shaped valley and continued downstream almost all the way into the centre of Leeds, whereas the Calder was deeply cut by glacial meltwater and doesn't have this same width. Consequently the Aire does not have the continuous string of woodland that the Calder has above Mirfield, though it does have a broader mix of woods. There are still some steep wooded ravines further up the valley (Shipley Glen, Harden Beck and Holden Gill), and also large areas of ancient woodland arranged around the suburbs of the cities of Leeds and Bradford, such as Buck Wood, Calverley Wood, Bramley Fall and Middleton Wood. Further downstream the wetlands are covered in willow, birch and alder, much of it replanted following extensive mining and quarrying in the 20th century.

There may not be much woodland cover across this area, and West Yorkshire as a whole, but what there is forms a striking backdrop to the Aire. Figures vary greatly, but the county is thought to have approximately 16,000 hectares of woodland, representing 7.9%[1] of the total area. This is well below the UK average of 13% and far from the EU average of 37%, but closer to the figure for England of 10%. Though woodland cover is below 4% in some parts of Bradford[2], north-west Leeds is the county's most wooded area with 16.8% cover. However, woodland is notoriously hard to define and may not include scrub woodland or newly-planted areas. Total tree canopy cover is increasingly seen as a more useful measure of the impact of trees on the overall landscape. With this measure, Bradford has 11.2% tree canopy (equivalent to 5,300 hectares), Leeds has 17.1% (over 10,000 hectares) and Bingley as much as 20.8%. However, the most significant aspect of this is that both woodland and tree canopy cover are increasing across the whole area and indeed the country.

As usual I have produced detailed maps of all significant areas of woodland in the Aire Valley that have some public access, as well as plenty of green spaces linking these areas. I have mapped the trees using the same tree symbols as in Part 1, representing the dominant tree type in each small area with a generic symbol of ash, beech, birch, chestnut, conifer, holly, lime, oak, sycamore and willow to add some character[3]. Mapping woods is inherently folly, as it treats trees as fixed entities, rather than acknowledging the slow but continuous process of change. But I see it as a snapshot of the woods as they are at this particular point in time. In certain sites, trees were being felled to make way for construction as I worked on the book, but I left my original maps as they were, to capture what was once there, and also because I didn't know what was going to replace them, other than diggers and cranes.

I've devised 22 new routes through these woodland areas, usually choosing less obvious pathways and linking several wooded areas together. There are not enough trees to create entirely wooded walks, but this ensures the walks remain pleasantly varied and hopefully in all seasons trees and woods form a significant part of the landscape. Each route is accessible by public transport and in most cases from a railway station, plus there are a couple of linear or longer routes which require (or can be shortened) by public transport. This means there are necessarily urban parts of these routes, but I think there is something very satisfying about walking straight out of the centre of Keighley, Bradford, Headingley or Castleford to the woods and it is usually surprising how quickly

[1] Considerably more than the 4% I quoted in Part 1. Though it will have increased in the intervening four years I suspect that figure was on the low side, perhaps based on old data or a different definition of woodland.

[2] Though Bradford has less woodland, far more of it is ancient woodland (including Shipley Glen, Buck Wood, Park Wood and Goit Stock Woods, compared to that of Leeds (where it is only 20%).

[3] By the end I did wish I'd added a poplar symbol, as this tree and the related aspen are far more common in the Aire Valley than the Calder Valley.

the towns and cities recede.

What I found most striking about the woods along the Aire Valley was just how well trodden they are. Many form natural playgrounds for the suburbs of Leeds and Bradford, so there is barely a corner where a path hasn't been worn. Buck Wood, Calverley Wood, Hirst Wood, Middleton Wood, Bramley Fall, Meanwood and Adel Woods are warrens of trackways that I found dizzying to map, often deciding it would be easier to advise the walker to make their own way to the far end of the wood than to attempt to trace a route through the maze. I also found there are refreshingly few private woods; only in the more rural areas at either end of the county did I find signs to keep out or keep to the path. Former industrial sites and scrubland around the edges of settlements have been reclaimed both by nature and people, albeit sometimes with our more antisocial activities. However, older scrub woods that were once used for flytipping and motor-biking are now being renovated by community groups, so this can all be seen as part of our rewilding process. The woodland landscapes of the Aire Valley have inspired many writers and artists[4], and continue to provide a striking backdrop to this highly populated region.

Adel Crags

### Access

Roughly half of the woodlands in the Aire Valley are owned by the local council or another public body, though in Bradford it is even higher. These woods can generally be assumed to be Open Access, where you can walk anywhere under most circumstances. Of the remaining privately owned woods, some are very definitely private, with signs making this clear (e.g. those in Methley Park or Park Wood in Tong). There is also no way to access several other appealing areas of woodland without trespassing, though I have mapped some of these in this book for the sake of giving a fuller picture of the valley's woodlands. There are many other private woods that have public routes through them – in some cases it is made clear that you should stick on the path, in others there is a network of well used informal paths. You'll also find various paths into and through areas of woodland on the edge of urban areas that are obviously frequented by local dog walkers. I have mapped these paths and in plenty of cases used them for my recommended routes. It is hoped that these paths will remain accessible but, within five years of publication of *Part I* of this series, two of my routes have been legally blocked off through private woodland. Where I can envisage this happening again, I have included an alternative route, but it is not always possible to predict which landowner may suddenly decide to string barbed wire across previously well used local routes. Do be aware of this and always try to have an Ordnance Survey map to hand (whether printed or on your phone) to navigate round these potential problems.

It can often be hard to tell where you are or are not supposed to be in the woods, especially if exploring off the paths or hunting for historical features. Generally follow local signage, don't damage walls or fences, and don't interfere with any management practices (such as stacks of logs or equipment) within the woods. Otherwise, happy exploring!

[4] Arthur Ransome was brought up in Far Headingley, while J.R.R. Tolkien also lived in this part of Leeds while working at the university and was inspired by the rich woodland of The Hollies. The sculpted stones of Weetwood also inspired the work of Henry Moore, who was born in Castleford and studied at Leeds School of Art. David Hockney and landscape painter Margaret Firth were brought up and studied in Bradford, while TS Eliot also spent time in Weetwood in the early 1960s, meeting a young Alan Bennett who had grown up in Far Headingley.

# THE GEOLOGY OF THE AIRE VALLEY

Most of the rocks underlying the Aire Valley were laid down in the Carboniferous period 360-300 million years ago. The oldest rocks form the limestone plateaux of the Yorkshire Dales but, by the time the River Aire reaches West Yorkshire, it cuts through the millston grit of the South Pennines, which underlies the uplands of Baildon Moor, Rombalds Moor, Keighley Moor, Harden Moor and the Chevin. During a period of fluctuating sea levels caused by tectonic movements, the gritstone was laid down on a vast river delta, formed from alternating layers of sandstone (formed of coarser material) and mudstone/shale (formed of finer material). The millstone grit is a particularly coarse sandstone, containing feldspar and quartz, and its highest (youngest) layer is the Rough Rock, which is exposed and quarried at Shipley Glen, Baildon Bank and Bramley Fall. The latter was famed for bein particularly hard-wearing and used in York Castle, Dover, Millwall and Grimsby Docks, the abutments of many London bridges, and many local buildings, including Kirkstall Abbey.

The Elland Flags form a layer of highly valued sandstone above the millstone grit and this has been exposed at Calverley Woods and Bolton Woods. Much of the bedrock in the valley bottom is masked by glacial deposits from the retreating Aire ice sheet, which also deposited most of the gritstone blocks found in the woods downstream.

In the late Carboniferous period much of Europe became a subtropical swamp with grea forests and rich amphibian life. As sea levels fluctuated, dense tropical vegetation was repeatedly submerged and covered with layers of mud and clay, forming the coal measures that overlay the sandstone across the eastern part of West Yorkshire, with rich coal seams where this vegetation was squashed over millennia and subject to the action of water and bacteria. Subsequent movement of the earth's surface after the Carboniferous period caused local faulting, adding further complications to this overall picture; these include the Keighley (or Aire Valley), Rivock, Denholme, Billing Hill, Calverley, Farsley-Scarcroft, Horsforth-Tinshill, Bramley, Tong, Lawnswood, Roundhay Park, Cross Gates, and Gledhow Faults. Harden Beck and Deep Cliff ravine were both formed by a cross fault which runs through Harden Moor and across Wilsden Beck.

The lower coal measures cover most of Bradford and Leeds and reach up the Aire Valle as far as Northcliffe, Wilsden, Denholme and High Bank near Shipley, with outlying seams exposed by local faulting on Baildon Moor, in Keighley's Park Wood and on Rough Holden (near Silsden). However, the seams at this end of the valley are only a few feet thick and the coal of poor quality, suitable only for small-scale extraction. The middle coal measures that make up the heartland of the Yorkshire Coalfield around Wakefield, Barnsley and Rotherham are much richer and less fractured by faulting, but are also harder to reach, being largely buried beneath a great quantity of alluvial clay and gravel brought downstream and deposited across the lower Pennine valleys. It was said that larger clover leaves were found growing on the clay deposited above these coal seams, and this was a way of discerning where seams ran. These measures cover a relatively small part of the Aire Valley around Castleford and Rothwell, as well as in Middleton Woods.

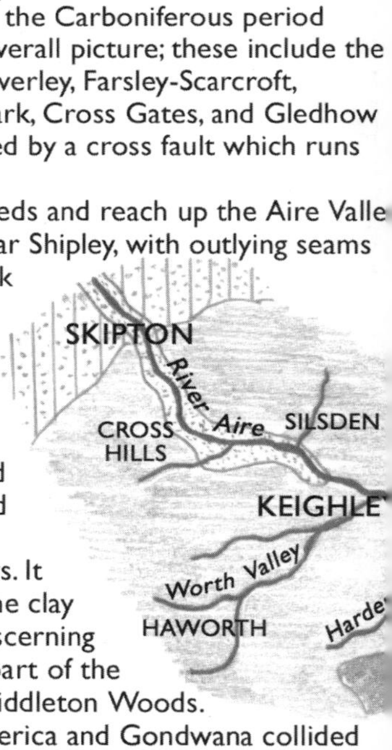

Around 300,000 years ago the great continents of Euramerica and Gondwana collided to form a single land mass called Pangea, causing great folds in the earth's surface. What was to become Britain was uplifted from the sea and folded to form mountains including the Pennines, which is a fairly regular anticline with the oldest rocks exposed in the centre of the country. The Pennine tableland was gradually eroded over subsequent millennia to form its valleys, though the Aire's course is relatively recent. The headwaters of the river would have flowed south-west into the Irish Sea via the Ribble prior to the las

Ice Age, which occurred during the Pleistocene and ended around 11,700 years ago. The Airedale ice sheet, like the Wharfedale ice sheet, originated high in the Dales and forged a course south-east, creating the Aire Gap as it inched its way almost as far as what is now the centre of Leeds. Ice also extended up side valleys like Shipley Glen, Harden Beck and Gill Beck, while a glacial lake formed in Moseley Bottoms above Horsforth.

Gill Beck is unique in that the ice here had pushed across the watershed from the Wharfedale ice sheet via Guiseley Gap. When this melted and retreated during a milder inter-glacial period, the coarser material it was carrying was deposited in large quantities near Tong Park at a time before the Airedale ice sheet had advanced this far. It contained a lot of limestone carried from the Yorkshire Dales and the area consequently has rich soil and an abundance of wild flowers, including wild angelica, meadowsweet, saxifrage, celandine, hellebore and cuckoo pint. Though much of the deposited material (or moraine) has since been eroded, glacial mounds are still evident around Tong Park and Gill Beck. When the ice finally retreated for good at the end of the last Ice Age, a huge lake was held up by the moraine spread across the Aire Valley here. Several low mounds along the Aire Valley were deposited at the bottom of this lake, including those at Hirst Wood and Bailey Hills, and the valley was filled with glacial till composed of blue clay and stones up to six hundred feet deep in places.

The Bailey Hills moraine formed a long ridge on which Bingley now stands and forced the River Aire into a new overflow channel to its west. Bingley Bog was the river's old course, and this moraine necessitated the building of the Five Rise Locks on the canal and the partial filling in of the bog to build the railway through Bingley. Harden and Bingley remain a botanist's delight and are renowned for their primroses. Moraine deposited at the foot of Shipley Glen deflected the lower course of Loadpit Beck to the east, while the glen itself was cut by meltwater from the north. Glacial clay had been deposited beneath a lake in the bottom of the glen and the beck's circuitous route is caused by the meltwater seeking a way around this moraine. Many smaller hills to the north-east of Leeds were also formed by similar glacial deposits.

To the east of the coal measures a narrow corridor of Magnesian limestone (from the Permian period, which followed the Carboniferous period) extends along the county's eastern boundary. This is a softer yellowish limestone that outcrops less, but is nonetheless exposed near the River Aire around Kippax, Great Preston and Fryston and forms the White Wall of Fryston Park. It was widely quarried for building stone and agricultural lime, and gives the warm colour to the stone of villages like Ledston, Ledsham and Fairburn.

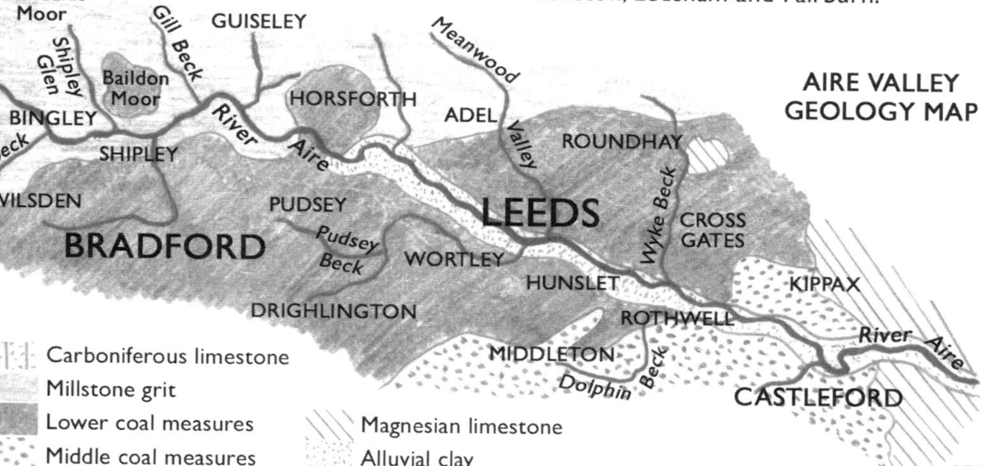
AIRE VALLEY
GEOLOGY MAP
Rombalds Moor
Gill Beck
GUISELEY
Meanwood
Shipley Glen
Baildon Moor
HORSFORTH
ADEL
Valley
BINGLEY
River Aire
ROUNDHAY
SHIPLEY
Wyke Beck
VILSDEN
PUDSEY
LEEDS
CROSS GATES
BRADFORD
Pudsey Beck
WORTLEY
HUNSLET
KIPPAX
DRIGHLINGTON
ROTHWELL
River Aire
MIDDLETON
Beck
Dolphin
CASTLEFORD
Carboniferous limestone
Millstone grit
Lower coal measures
Middle coal measures
Magnesian limestone
Alluvial clay

# THE HISTORY OF THE AIRE VALLEY AN ITS WOODLANDS

*'Worthy a poet's muse, thou grand old wood!*
*For generations thou hast proudly stood.*
*A forest once wert thou of kingly pride,*
*Stretching thy noble borders far and wide.*
*Within thy sylvan glades the wild boar rang'd;*
*On stealthy pinions glided birds of prey;*
*But, oh, since then how greatly art thou changed!'*

(from *Brown's Wood* by Reverend Lowther E. Ellis)

The history of the woodlands is particularly hard to uncover as it is often only mentioned in passing in the better-told histories of neighbouring settlements and landed estates. This is particularly true in the north of England, with most of the books on woodland focusing almost exclusively on the woods of the south-east, such as the Weald and the Chilterns. Although many patterns of landscape change and woodland use are applicable across the whole country, there remain great local variations, not least because of the varied distribution of tree species. It is hard to get a really good picture of how these national patterns apply to the Aire Valley, particularly in a year when Covid-19 has limited my access to the invaluable resources of the local history libraries. I am aware that this is a slightly different historical overview to that presented in *The West Yorkshire Woods: Part 1* on the woods of the Calder Valley, though this is partly because I am keen not to replicate my observations – it is worth reading *Part 1* for more on the Normans' Forest Laws, woodland crafts and charcoal burning, as well as the pages on individual tree species that are dotted through that book.

The history I've been able to write about the Aire Valley has depended on the material available and necessarily incorporates a degree of educated guesswork. This is particularly true when it comes to estimating the percentage of woodland cover – we struggle to agree on a current figure for West Yorkshire, so what chance is there of establishing one for the Bronze Age? Figures in this book contradict figures in the first book, but are based on the best estimates I've seen. However, I think two broad patterns and points are consistently demonstrated; firstly, that most of the damage to what we consider our ancient wildwood occurred earlier than we might assume (i.e. before the arrival of the Romans); and, secondly, that the primary driving force behind woodland clearance has always been agriculture and not industry, which relied upon the resources of the woods until the 19th century and often preserved those ancient woods that do still remain. With that in mind, let us begin…

### Down By The River

After the glaciers retreated at the end of the last Ice Age around 9700 BCE, birch, hazel, oak and pine returned to the barren landscape, with damp-loving alder establishing itself on the wetter low-lying areas. As the climate improved and trees slowly covered most of Britain, people returned from the continent via the land bridge that still connected us. These Mesolithic (Middle Stone Age) people slowly spread across the country, occupying the lower Aire Valley (flints being found at Skelton Grange and Thorpe Stapleton near Temple Newsam) and the high ground upstream (with flint flakes and arrowheads found on Bracken Hall Green, as well as widely across Baildon Moor and Rombalds Moor). These hunter gatherers made temporary clearings in the wood for seasonal camps, but moved on regularly, probably spreading widely the fruit and nut trees they favoured for food.

Sessile oak and birch dominated on the steep valley sides and the higher ground, which had acidic soils and were generally more exposed. Pedunculate oak, holly, ash and elm grew on the more sheltered and less acidic sites, including places like Buck Wood. Alder[1], willow and wych elm thrived on the wettest ground, forming carr woodland in the low-lying areas, like the broad swamp that surrounded the Aire downstream of Leeds. This was what we call the wildwood[2], though much of it was likely made up of open wood pasture rather than dense forest. It was a sustainable Eden that briefly existed while humans were still greatly outnumbered by wild animals. Although the hippos, lions and mammoths did not survive the last ice age, Britain was awash with bears, wolves, aurochs (wild cattle), lynx, bison, elk, beavers and boar. The tooth of a bison was unearthed when digging out Milner Field's fishpond in the woods near Shipley Glen, and the bones of bears and lynx have been found across the area, alongside those of earlier beasts. Herds of bison and elk were hunted with spears by the early settlers, who sometimes cleared woodland to attract prey.

Rising sea levels cut off the land bridge to Europe and created the island of Great Britain sometime around 6000 BCE. The beech is thought to have been the last tree to make the journey across from Europe, arriving just a few hundred years earlier to become one of Britain's 27 species of native trees. Now thought to be native only to the south of England, the beech did naturally reach West Yorkshire and further north before the climate deteriorated in the Bronze Age.

The Neolithic Revolution, which began in the Middle East around 10000 BCE, did not reach Britain until around 4000 BCE, possibly with the arrival of Mediterranean settlers, who introduced methods of farming, animal husbandry and pottery-making. This precipitated a great change for the wild forests; trees were cut down, pigs and cattle were domesticated to graze the new clearings, and wheat was planted further south. In other parts of the world the forests could be easily cleared through burning, but in Britain they were generally too moist and had to be cleared the hard way. The Sweet Track dates from this period, a 2km timber trackway across the Somerset Levels that was made from poles too regular to have been produced without coppicing. The importance of wood as a resource for buildings, boats, fuel, fodder and fencing had led to the introduction of coppicing, and so the woodlands were managed for the first time. Despite these incursions, the overall tree cover is thought to have increased to a peak during the early Neolithic period as it spread further up the hills to cover all but the highest peaks of the Pennines, a high water mark that slowly began to recede as the population grew.

The Bronze Age began with the arrival of Beaker people from the continent via the Humber Estuary between 2000-1800 BCE, bringing new metals and new breeds of domesticated animals. The introduction of the metal axe and plough greatly increased the rate of change, with trees more easily chopped down and grubbed out (dug out by the roots). People covered the whole of the British Isles and cultivated every corner of the land for the first time. Sheep became populous, as wolves began to decline and the auroch (a species of wild cattle), elk and walrus were all hunted to extinction by settlers with the aid of dogs. Wood was now vital for firing kilns to produce tools, largely in the form of charcoal, which burned hotter and more predictably than wood. Charcoal was widely used to smelt bronze from tin and copper, with the result that a lot of wood was needed to produce everyday bronze items. The Scots pine, its straight trunks so useful for building, quickly disappeared from England. Relative peace and consistent population growth, including a likely further colonisation from the continent, reduced the tree cover

[1] The number of Allertons around Leeds and Bradford is testament to the proliferation of the alder tree in the area; aller, oller and owler all refer to this.

[2] The term 'wildwood' was coined by woodland historian Oliver Rackham to refer to the virgin forest that developed after the last Ice Age, though there is much debate about its composition and whether this really existed as a great swathe of trees covering the whole land. The name is thought to have come from the Wild Wood that features so prominently in Kenneth Grahame's *Wind In The Willows.*

to below 50%. The largest remaining forests were located in areas that were difficult to plough, mainly on clay soils and steep hillsides. Tree cover also retreated naturally as the climate became milder and wetter during the late Bronze Age, with moorland bogs forming on the higher ground and the number of elm trees declining dramatically.

The Aire Valley appears to have been widely settled during the Bronze Age as it formed an important trade route across the Aire Gap, the easiest crossing point over the Pennines. Jet from Whitby and amber from across the Baltic Sea went west, while gold and bronze headed east from Ireland. Bronze tools have been found in Buck Wood, Roundhay, Hunslet, Chapel Allerton and a beaker[3] was unearthed at Tinshill near Leeds. A Bronze Age quern stone used for grinding corn was found on Bracken Hall Green, a Beaker settlement uncovered while building a housing estate in Middleton, and flint tools and weapons have been found across Baildon and Rombalds Moors. There are also several burial mounds (or barrows) across the county's high ground, including on Woodhouse Moor near the centre of Leeds, while cup and ring markings are scattered throughout the woods and moors of the area. These designs, varying from simple cups to intricate arrangements, remain a mystery, but are often linked with the planets and stars. Particularly good examples can be found in Cottingley Wood, Buck Wood and Gab Wood (near Cookridge).

cup- and ring-marked stone in Gab Wood, near Cookridge

Celtic languages and culture arrived from Western Europe in the late Bronze Age, when there was a flourishing international trade. Moving into the Iron Age, a particular British Celtic culture and family of languages developed across the whole country. The iron plough brought further areas of woodland under cultivation as it became yet simpler to remove trees, the clearance moving further down the hillsides of the Aire Valley. With iron smelted on a large scale, coppicing and charcoal production was widespread by 500 BCE. The large extended family farms of the Bronze Age developed into the first towns, largely constructed from wood. Iron Age settlement sites have been found in Hirst Wood, Cookridge Wood, Castle Stead near Denholme, and near Ledston, with lynchet banks and furrows from Celtic strip farming evident on the Hawksworth side of Gill Beck and in Parkinson's Park near Guiseley. A Celtic stone head was found in a stream by Ireland Wood when it was cleared for housing in 1954 and a Romano-British carving can be seen in Adel Woods depicting the Celtic deity Cocidius.

It has been estimated that by the end of the Iron Age there could have been 3-4 million people in Britain and the landscape would have been primarily agricultural. After so much of the woodland was cleared to make way for farming, most of the remaining woods were to be found in steep-sided rocky valleys, such as Shipley Glen and the Meanwood Valley, as well as the boggy swamps that still lay along most of the Aire Valley. Elsewhere, only its value for iron production and fuel preserved woodland; indeed much of the damage had already been done by the time the Romans arrived and little semblance of the ancient wildwood remained.

### Everybody Knows This Is Nowhere

The Romans first reached Britain in 55 BCE under Julius Caesar, establishing important trading links. However, despite several planned and attempted invasions, they did not occupy Britain until 43 CE. It was seen as a land rich in untapped minerals, one of which was wood – deforestation being even more advanced in the Mediterranean, and the

[3] The Beaker people acquired their name for the pottery beakers and other artefacts they buried with their dead. They migrated from Eurasia to Central Europe and eventually Britain, bringing paler skin, blonde hair and blue eyes to a population that was once much darker.

south-east of England, where they landed, was particularly richly wooded. However, much of the country may have been a disappointment, and the Elmet Project have estimated that the woodland cover in West Yorkshire was only around 30% when the Romans reached the region in 70 CE. They had marched north to quell the rebellious Brigantes tribe who occupied the bulk of northern England, and there are several defensive structures around Leeds that may have been built by British tribes to repel Roman invasion – in Gipton Wood near Oakwood, on Woodhouse Moor, at Hawcaster Rigg in Chapel Allerton, and the substantial works at Aberford Dykes and Grim's Ditch. Becca Banks (the largest of the Aberford Dykes[4]) runs for three miles along a ridge of land south of Aberford that became a Roman road, while Grim's Ditch *(see p23)* runs 5 miles from the River Aire near Temple Newsam to Seacroft.

The Romans laid out a series of roads to make it easier to subdue and control the unruly north, and established forts at Castleford, Adel and possibly Leeds. Castleford, then known as Lagentium, stood beside an important ford over the River Aire, but there is debate over the relative significance of Adel and Leeds. The settlement of Cambodunum (meaning 'fort by the bend in the river') is recorded by the Venerable Bede as standing on the road between York (Eboracum) and Manchester (Mancunium) via Tadcaster (Calcaria), and was generally thought to have been at Quarry Hill, near the centre of Leeds, where various Roman finds have been made. The site stands near another early ford over the River Aire, one formed by silt from the Meanwood Valley's stream and Hol Beck pouring into the river.

The existence of an Iron Age township, the Roman fort and a large associated *vicus* (a civilian settlement) near Adel Mill is well established. It stood on a key trans-Pennine route from Tadcaster via the fort at Ilkley (Olicana), a road that also ran through Moor Allerton along the line of Street Lane. Traditionally thought to have been Burgodunum, there are now those who suggest that Adel was actually the site of Cambodunum. It stands at a junction of Roman roads, with another route heading south via the Long Causeway to cross the Aire near Kirkstall Bridge and pass through Bramley, Farnley and Gildersome Street. It is now suggested that this may have been the main route from York to Manchester, as its length tallies more accurately with the mileage recorded by Bede.

Further west, a Roman road crossed Harden Moor between Manchester and Ilkley. However, the paved route that can be seen here near the Guide Inn is part of another lesser Roman route through Harden village, possibly linking with Tong Street on the other side of Bradford and leading on to the fort in Wakefield. A Roman crossing of the River Aire between Marley and Riddlesden was known as Longlands Ford, and a Roman coin hoard was discovered in a military chest at nearby Elam Grange. Another Roman road crossed Silsden Moor between Addingham and Skipton, while the most obvious route in the area leads due north from Castleford (now the A656). A Roman urn has been found next to Brown's Wood in Thackley and further coin hoards uncovered in North Bierley, Silsden, Alwoodley, Beeston and Allerton Bywater.

The Romans introduced the sweet chestnut and possibly the sycamore, felled some of the Druids' sacred groves and brought more intensive coppicing methods, but they did not transform the woodland landscape as much as might be expected. In the north Brigantia struck an alliance, becoming part of the Roman Empire to maintain autonomy under their queen Cartimundia. Brigantia was a federation of several tribes across the north of England and it soon fell apart as many opposed this treaty. Elmet was among the newly formed kingdoms that broke away from Brigantia in the 2nd century. A Latin name possibly referring to an elm forest or meaning 'full of leaves', the Forest of Elmet covered the northern part of what is now West Yorkshire, following the River Aire west from the River Ouse to Bingley, the land beyond being part of Craven, another of these new Celtic

[4] Further ditches here were dug later against the advancing Angles, as they were at Adel and possibly Grim's Ditch.

kingdoms. Elmet was a Christianised kingdom with its royal seat at Barwick, north-east of Leeds, and its people were known as the Elmedsetan. They remained Roman allies until the Romans withdrew from Britain in 410 CE, and thereafter kept a strong grip on this harsh territory by retaining a link with the tribe's Celtic brethren in Cumbria and North Wales.

The inhospitable land of Elmet was largely by-passed by the various invaders who filled the power vacuum after the Romans' departure. After the Picts and Scots invaded northern England from Scotland and Ireland respectively, the Jutes, Saxons and Angles arrived from mainland Europe in the 5th and 6th centuries. The north and midlands were largely conquered by the Angles, who came from northern Germany and gave their name to England. It was not until 616 that Elmet was invaded by King Edwin of Deira (an Anglian kingdom to the east between Tees and Humber) to take control of the Aire Gap route to the west.

After Elmet's King Ceretic (or Ceredig ap Gwallog) was defeated, St Paulinus introduced Christianity by establishing a substantial church and palace at what had been the Roman settlement of Cambodunum in 627. This was destroyed within six years by the avowedly anti-Christian King Penda of Mercia, who briefly reinstated the kingdom of Elmet, creating a new alliance. In 655 the Elmedsetan fought for King Penda against the Northumbrians at the Battle of the Winwaed, thought to be near Whinmoor north-east of Leeds. Following his defeat and death, they became subsumed in the vast kingdom of Northumbria and a new place of Christian worship was established in Leeds. Many of the details of this period are unknown, but it has inspired tales like that of an army camping at Soldier's Trench above Shipley Glen *(see p88)* before an unknown Dark Age battle, and Harden Moor's mysterious Fairfax Entrenchment *(see p119)*, which is now thought to date from this era.

Although vestiges of the Celts and their culture remained in the more remote parts of the Aire Valley before finally being wiped away by the Normans, little of their language remains in the area's place names. Apart from the rivers (Aire, Calder, Derwent, Ouse), only a few other features have a Celtic origin, including the Chevin (related to the Welsh word *cefn* for a ridge), the Billing (in Rawdon), Eccleshill, Pen-y-Ffynnnon (in Meanwood), Airmyn, and Leeds itself. Another remnant is the common Cat Steps, which indicates a footpath or steps on a woody brow and comes from the same root as the Welsh *coed* – examples are found in Buck Wood, Heaton Woods, Silsden, Clayton, Oxenhope, Horsforth and North Beck in Keighley.

The great number of battles and invasions that characterised the Dark Ages led to an associated decline in population, with the woods making a partial return during this period. Anglian settlers, though, soon began further assarting (clearing of the woodland for farming) and all the land became owned for the first time. Anglo-Saxon (or Old English as it came to be known) place names dominate the landscape, many the name of Anglian settlers with a common suffix like -ley, -worth, -ton, -den, -hope or -ham (e.g. Bingley is 'Binna's clearing', Keighley is 'Cyhha's clearing', Silsden is 'Siggel's valley', Chellow is 'Ceol's hill', Guiseley is 'Gislic's clearing', Cullingworth is 'Cula's enclosure', Cottingley is 'Cotta's clearing', Eccup is 'Ecca's hope or valley', Armley is 'Earma's clearing' and Cookridge is 'Cwica's ridge'). Locally familiar suffixes like -royd, -ley, -field, -hey and stubb (or stubbing) refer directly to land newly cleared of woodland. As well as common words like bridge, field, ford, ridge, bury, hall, burn, hill, moor, cliff and croft, we inherited several woodland terms from the Anglo-Saxons – hurst, greave, shaw, holt and the word 'wood' itself, as well as the tree-names linden (lime), elder and holly.

The Vikings, made up of Danes, Swedes and Norse, reached England in 787, desecrating Lindisfarne and laying waste to the country with intermittent raids. They took York in 867 and invaded the rest of Yorkshire in 876, eventually colonising rather than simply plundering the rich agricultural land they found. York became the centre of

Scandinavian interest in England, but the limited number of Viking place names in West Yorkshire compared to East Yorkshire and the Vale of York suggest they didn't settle as extensively in this hill country. Giant's Hill near the River Aire at Armley was thought to be a Danish camp, but is now seen more likely to have been a Norman motte and bailey. The Anglians and Vikings were closely related and understood enough of each other's languages that a great deal of mixing of people and language took place. Names with Viking origins include kirk, gate, thorpe, wick, holme, thwaite, borough, mire, scar, rake, nab, scout, storth, how, garth, gill, beck, holme, carr, dale, tong, fold, and cross, as well as the tree names ash, birch, owler and busk (for bush).

The Vikings introduced wapentakes instead of hundreds[5] and divided the area by its rivers. On the south side of the Aire were Agbrigg and Morley Wapentakes, with Skyrack and Staincliffe Wapentakes lying between the Wharfe and Aire. Agbrigg lay at the eastern edge of the West Riding, with its assembly place near Wakefield, while Morley Wapentake had its ancient assembly place at Tingley (on high ground above Morley), its name derived from a word for 'assembly place'. Staincliffe included Keighley as well as most of Craven and met at a place west of Skipton, while Skyrack was a well wooded region whose traditional meeting place was in Headingley. The name Skyrack may have meant 'bright oak', but came to be taken as 'shire oak' (hence the names Shire Oak Road and Shire Oak Street in Headingley). Headingley's Shire Oak was a sapling during the Roman occupation and was possibly planted intentionally at the heart of a small settlement here around 300 CE. Certainly it was a majestic and sacred tree and time-honoured meeting place long before the Vikings established it as the centre of their wapentake. It stood opposite St Michael and All Angels' Church and the Skyrack Inn, and was described by Headingley resident Arthur Ransome as a 'ruin of remains enclosed in an iron paling' until it collapsed in a gale on 26th May 1941, having stood for over 1,600 years. It is now commemorated by the Original Oak pub, with a new sapling planted on the same spot, and from its wood a Madonna and child was carved and placed in the church.

the Shire Oak in Headingley before its collapse

In 937 Athelstan beat the Vikings and Scots at the Battle of Brunanburh (thought to have taken place at Bromborough on the Wirral) and the Kingdom of Northumbria became part of the English kingdom. There would be further Viking attacks and attempts at settlement in the north during the following century, but despite this Christianity began to spread more widely across the country. By the time the Normans arrived, the violent struggle of the Dark Ages had taken its toll on Britain's population, which is estimated to have been reduced to 1.5-2 million, less than half what it had been under Roman occupation. Woodland cover had diminished to 15%, not far above what it is today, and the last brown bear in Britain had been killed. Most settlements and roads remained on high ground, with the valleys being more wooded and swamp-filled, apart from the few settlements that developed around fords across the River Aire and its tributaries.

[5] A hundred was an administrative area consisting of around a hundred households; first used in Britain in the 10th century, it is thought to have been an ancient Saxon measure.

## The Losing End

After the Norman Conquest in 1066, the north continued to rebel against the new rulers and, following a massacre in 1069, William the Conqueror marched his army north. After being held up for three weeks by the waterlogged marshes of Brotherton and Fairburn in the lower Aire Valley, he laid siege to York and established a garrison there, before laying waste to much of the land north of the Humber in revenge for their siding with the enemy. The Harrying of the North saw crops destroyed, livestock killed and large populations left to starve or become displaced. It is estimated that half of the settlements in Yorkshire were destroyed, becoming waste land that was considered almost without value. Bramley, Allerton, Beeston, Halton and Garforth were completely destroyed, Headingley, Newsam and Colton were greatly diminished, but somehow Leeds itself survived relatively unscathed. Leeds had a mill at the time of the Domesday Book in 1086, when most manors in the region were recorded as 'all is waste', though in some cases, particularly in the uplands around Bradford, this was because the land was undeveloped rather than destroyed by William. Most of the existing settlement names were retained though and their sites soon resettled.

The Normans imposed a new feudal manorial system, based on that in place in parts of France. Manorialism had existed since the Romans, with landowners granting small plots of land and protection to peasants while gaining economic control over their labours. However, this was now all linked directly to the king and established a clear class system. William I now owned all the land and could grant it to barons who had been loyal to him. Most of the West Riding became the Honour of Pontefract, which was composed of 161 individual manors (in Bradford only the ancient manor of Eccleshill was not included) and granted to Ilbert de Lacy for his support at Hastings and during the Harrying of the North. The new Baron of Pontefract built Pontefract Castle and, when the Honour of Clitheroe was given to the de Lacy family by Henry I in 1102, they came to control an unbroken strip of land across the Pennines via the Aire Valley. Though the Honour of Pontefract would be taken from the de Lacys by Richard I, it was returned by King John before being passed to John o' Gaunt, the Duke of Lancaster and father of Henry IV, in 1361. Many of the families who came to dominate the area gained land during this period as these large estates were broken up; the Paynols in Leeds and Adel, the Calverley family settling first near Bradford and later around Rothwell, and the Saviles in Thornhill and later in the Aire Valley.

The Domesday Book was the result of a detailed survey of the whole country's land and its value. It also recorded the woodland, which covered approximately 15% of the country (though this varied locally, with the manor of Bingley recorded as being as much as a quarter wood pasture). There were no bridges across the River Aire at this time, just a series of fords upstream (at Utley, Bingley, Baildon Green, Baildon Bridge, Buck Mill, Apperley Bridge, Horsforth, Newlay, Kirkstall, Leeds and Woodlesford) and ferries downstream (at Allerton, Fairburn and Ferrybridge). The name Ferrybridge only dates from the time when the first bridge was built over the river there in 1198. Previously it had been Ferry Fryston with a ferry on the main route north from Pontefract, its site now beneath Ferrybridge Power Station, where cooling towers dwarf the original settlement's 12th-century graveyard.

The Normans asserted royal control over many of the woodlands, which were valued for hunting. Trees that once served as early boundary markers or meeting places became status symbols of landedness. Boundary ditches were created to keep livestock out of woods so hunting could be continued. The only parks that existed were deer enclosures, which served both as hunting grounds and status symbols. They were expensive to lay out and maintain – for example, Roundhay Park had six miles of boundary ditch and palisade fencing. Other deer parks were established at Farnley Park, Kippax Park, Fryston Park, Methley Park, Thackley Park, Denholme Park, Holden Park near Silsden, and

New Park in Kirkstall. Their lodges were usually temporary wooden huts, like a modern shooting hut, within the park, and were only later built in stone. Venison from these parks was highly sought after, but during hard times the parks would have been filled with domesticated animals, which were far cheaper to corral. Woods in these parks and other estates were doubtless retained purely for hunting and stayed in a wilder state since a dense under-storey[6] was perfect cover for pheasants, deer, foxes and badgers. Predators like lynx and wolves did not fare so well, marked as vermin and hunted to extinction around the 16th century. Wild boar lasted a little longer, but were considered a nuisance, not least the famous boar of Cliff Wood that terrorised the town of Bradford in the 14th century *(see p107)*.

*remains of deer park boundary in Holden Park, near Silsden*

The Normans brought church and state far closer and new churches were built at Adel, Leeds, Bradford, Bingley, Keighley, Guiseley, Calverley and Kippax. St John the Baptist's Church in Adel is particularly well preserved, with intricate carvings around its door and chancel, and is evidence of Adel's importance in the area prior to Leeds developing as a trading centre. Monasticism was revived, with many of Yorkshire's eight great Cistercian abbeys granted land in the Aire Valley. Rievaulx Abbey had monastic granges at Harden Grange and Faweather Grange, Selby Abbey held Chellow Grange near Bradford, and Fountains Abbey held plenty of land upriver in Craven, while land in Cottingley and Bingley[7], as well as what was to become Temple Newsam, was granted to the Knights Templar.

It was the foundation of Kirkstall Abbey at a former hermitage by the River Aire in 1152 that changed the region most significantly. Land was granted by Henry de Lacy to build this new Cistercian house and to establish monastic granges further afield at Elam Grange, Moor Grange, Roundhay Grange, New Grange (now Beckett's Park) and Whitecote[8] in Bramley. These large farms were worked by lay brothers for rearing cattle and sheep. Roundhay Grange was a vaccary (or cow pasture) and the monks were granted access to the strongly defended woods in the deer park itself for fuel, building and making fences. They profited greatly from the woollen industry, shipping many of their wares directly to Italian merchants and by-passing the growing cloth market in Leeds. By the end of the 13th century, they were weaving, dying and fulling cloth, smelting iron, lead and copper, and selling leather, pottery, tiles and grain. Involvement in the leather and iron industries required a healthy supply of wood, which the monks managed for charcoal and oak bark in Hawksworth Wood, Bramley Fall and Roundhay *(see p46)*. Kirkstall Abbey lost Roundhay Grange after its near bankruptcy in 1288, with Old Park in Headingley created as a deer park to replace it in providing venison to the monks.

[6] In the 18th century this would lead to the widespread introduction of the rhododendron, which became a pest species that gives great character to our woods but tends to take over at the expense of other undergrowth.
[7] It has been suggested that what is now St Ives was one of the mysterious Knights Templar's most significant sites in the country and an important early Masonic meeting place. There are many symbols and reminders of this across the oldest buildings in Bingley, including All Saints Church, the White Horse Inn, Beck Foot Farm and Beckfoot Mill. A Gothic screen added to Harden Hall in the early 19th century by Walker Ferrand is covered in pinnacles and crosses related to the Knights' Templars and subsequent ownership by the Knights Hospitallers (or Order of St John).
[8] Fleeter Pastures on a large bend in the River Aire west of Newlay was grazed by sheep from the grange across the river at Whitecote. This required a bridge to be built a hundred yards west of the current Newlay Bridge and some of it can still be seen when the river is low. Although there was an ancient ford, it could only be used by horses and cattle as it wasn't shallow enough to drive smaller animals across.

Part of the manorial system was a requirement for all tenants to take their corn and cloth to soke mills, soke being the right of local jurisdiction granted to the lord of the manor. These rights were fiercely protected as they were very profitable[9]. Each manor had its own corn mill, mostly water-driven mills on the River Aire and its tributaries, where every tenant had to take their corn for grinding and pay the appropriate toll. There were mills on the Aire at Calverley Bridge and Buck Mill, on the Meanwood Beck at Wood Mills, on the Holden Beck at Silsden Mill, on the River Worth at Ingrow, and many others besides. There was also a windmill on Windmill Hill in Silsden (where Keighley Golf Course now stands, its name corrupted to William Hill) until the late 16th century, and later windmills in Scott Hall and Potternewton near Leeds.

The other common manorial mill was the fulling mill, with many corn mills later converted to fulling. Fulling was an intensive part of the process of woollen cloth-making, the woven cloth being soaked in water and pounded (originally by feet – hence the term 'walk mills') to knit the fibres together. An early technological advance enabled this to be done by hammers in water-powered mills; the first recorded in England being near Temple Newsam in 1185. Fulling mills were widely used from the 13th century across the region and were profitable as all clothiers came to rely on them.

Fulling and corn mills both required regularly maintained dams to provide a continuous flow of water and timber was used in large quantity in early dams. Many of the region's older sunken paths were worn by people and packhorses following these routes to the manorial mills for centuries. The monopoly on corn and fulling lasted in some places until the 18th century, when the water-powered mills were replaced with steam-driven ones and new systems were in place.

### Old Ways

The Forest Laws introduced by William I established the king as owner of all the forests, though the term forest was not used exclusively for wooded land but applied more generally to hunting grounds. These forests covered large areas and had strict laws, with some relatively minor offences punishable by death. They were hugely unpopular and, by 1217, a couple of years after the Magna Carta, King John was forced to sign the Carta de Foresta, which asserted the rights of commoners to access all woods to forage for food, feed livestock on the woodland mast (the right of pannage) and gather wood for fuel, hedging, building and tool-making (the right of estovers). It re-established many of the older common woods as valuable resources for the villages. With the commoners' rights closely regulated, these woods were retained and carefully looked after for the common good for centuries. Common woods were often smaller parcels of woodland which were of less value commercially, like Shaw Wood in Guiseley, though Meanwood (which is Old English for 'common wood') was a far larger expanse of woodland.

Food was another important use of the common woods, and there were dedicated nut woods and orchards, though fewer of these in the north. The common wastes and moors, such as Black Moor and Alwoodley Moss to the north of Leeds, were valuable sources of peat for fuel where there was no coal locally. Commoners could also hunt rabbits, gather fruit and berries and harvest bracken, which had many uses – as animal bedding and fuel, or for use in making soap and candles, fulling, and burning lime. These manorial commons were enclosed to prevent livestock straying into adjacent manors, and the names Greengates, Alwoodley Gates and Cross Gates relate to these ancient boundaries, with fines levied on anyone who left gates open.

The woods and waste generally lay beyond a village's fields and common meadow. Though some woodlands (often known as 'outwoods') were retained by landowners to preserve their right to timber and underwood (scrub and younger growth beneath the

[9] Lady Anne Clifford's mill at Holden was bankrupted by a lawsuit with those who ran neighbouring Silsden Mill that rumbled on for fifteen years during the Civil War.

main canopy), many were leased out for valuable income. Strict agreements were drawn up for use of the woods, specifying quantities of timber, cordwood and bark that could be removed annually, how they were to be removed, how much brushwood could be gathered for fuel, how many pigs could be fed on its mast, how many sods of turf could be taken up for covering charcoal burns, and even the amount of moss that could be gathered for roofing. The court rolls are full of tenants who had unlawfully felled trees or cut branches that were not marked for such (on royal estates like Roundhay these were said to be 'marked by the King's axe'). Often a medieval tenant wasn't allowed to cut any wood from a tree except to repair fences or waterways. It was often referred to as 'waste of timber' such was the value of these trees to the manorial landowner. The lord of the manor of Roundhay was even prosecuted for felling a tree on his own land along the high road by the lord of the adjacent manor.

All of the larger woods would have been managed commercially and widely coppiced, with fences and ditches created to keep out livestock and allow regrowth. On the whole woodland in West Yorkshire was managed in a similar way as it was across the whole country, though tree species would have varied locally depending on soil, light, water and altitude. Coppicing was based on the simple premise that any cut tree will quickly spring back to life, the new shoots growing very straight for the first few years. The practice is evident in the many Spring Woods, as well as Bull Coppy Wood near Gilstead, Coppy Lanes in Bramley and Newsholme Dean, Coppy Close in Cottingley, Coppy Farm near Steeton, the Coppice Wood estate in Yeadon and Guiseley, Coppice View in Idle, Coppice Way in Oakwood, the Coppice at St Ives, and Coppice Wood at Temple Newsam.

Coppiced wood (known as cordwood) was measured in cords, with four cords needed for a single charcoal burn. Coppicing cycles (how often the trees were cut back) varied locally and depended on its intended use, but generally increased as demand for larger charcoal wood grew with the burgeoning iron industry, doubling on average from 7 years in the 14th century to 15 years in the 18th century, with some as long as 21 years. One common practice was known as 'coppicing with standards', with a handful of trees retained for timber and sold as 'black barks' as opposed to the coppiced 'spring wood'. There may also have been periods within the long history of coppicing when coppice woods were neglected, particularly when the population fell dramatically, but as woodlands became more scarce they were worked more and more intensively as coppice. There is still plenty of evidence of coppicing across the region, though many of the tell-tale multi-trunked trees have since been singled out or clear-felled[10].

coppiced oak tree in Wrose Brow Plantation

[10] Medusoid trees are a form of growth associated with neglected coppice, including sprawling corkscrew branches growing from a single stem. They have a deformed look that is often associated with Druidic groves.

The woodlands supported a whole phalanx of professions, with many people working in the woods, often living in temporary shelters there during the summer. Barkers stripped bark from the trees to be felled, sniggers hauled timber out of the woodland by pony and sawyers cut wood to size, before turners, bodgers, joiners, cartwrights, cordwainers (leather-workers) and heald/bobbin makers worked the wood and bark into finished products. Most numerous of all were the charcoal burners, known as colliers until coal became widely used. Carefully cut and stacked poles were partially burnt in covered mounds for up to two days, with limited oxygen producing a fuel that would burn at a far higher temperature than untreated wood. Radio-carbon dating by the Celebrating our Woodland Heritage Project recently discovered evidence of charcoal burning in Hirst Wood dating back to 1290.

Having acquired the manor of Headingley, the monks of Kirkstall Abbey negotiated rights of turbary in all their newly acquired woods, allowing them to cover charcoal burns in air-tight turf, a process known in the West Riding as 'hilling'. It demonstrates how important woodland rights were to business interests in the area, with most of the coppiced woods geared primarily towards supplying the iron industry with charcoal[11]. Many of the ancient woods of the Aire Valley possess the tell-tale circular flattened hearths on which charcoal was burned, though there are fewer obvious examples than the Calder Valley – the slopes above the Aire are generally more gentle and the extensive felling and replanting of woodlands in the 19th and 20th centuries, as well as the creation of tracks, roads, railways, canals, and quarries may have destroyed much of the evidence of charcoal production. Brent Wood in Eccleshill is a corruption of 'burnt wood', referring to charcoal burning, and there is a Charcoal Wood at Temple Newsam.

Assarting continued through the Middle Ages where there were still sufficient common grounds remaining, usually single farmsteads built in or around the woods. Good timber was sold, with bushes and roots burned, ash spread over the ground, then drains cut and new fields enclosed by a fences, hedge or bank. Stone was not used as a building material until the 13th century and not widespread until the 17th century, until when paupers lived in basic wooden cots, with larger longhouses for the wealthier peasants. Medieval buildings were a mix of post-and-truss and cruck type, their timber frames filled in with wattle and daub or posts encased in clay.

This continued incursion into the woods was, as ever, driven by agriculture, predominantly sheep farming in the West Riding. The wool industry grew from the 13th century and, by the 15th century, the county was producing more than the rest of the country put together. It isn't entirely clear why the industry thrived in this area, though the soft water from the Pennine gritstone was greatly valued for working cloth. The wool trade was easy to get into, requiring only the purchase of a relatively cheap loom to produce cloth at home. It is possible that the partible division of inheritance among offspring reduced farmland to such small units in areas of poor land that an alternative income was needed by many families, hence the popularity of the dual economy of sheep farming and wool spinning. Leeds was becoming a centre of the clothing trade, with a weekly cloth market and two annual fairs, although Bradford was still relatively small; in 1311 it was recorded as having a corn mill, a fulling mill, market, church, manor house, dye house and tanneries, but little else.

Much of the remaining woodland was protected through the Middle Ages, thanks to its importance for the early iron and tanning industries. Early industry tended to be located where the raw materials existed, often in the woods where there was quarried stone and charcoal, leaving the villages themselves free from industrial activity. From the 12th century iron was smelted in bloomeries at Roundhay, Weetwood and Kirkstall by the monks of the newly founded Kirkstall Abbey, making tools like axes, nails and chisels to

[11] The charcoal burners' dozen was twelve horse loads of coal (wool was also measured in dozens, thus the name of northern dozens cloth which Leeds became renowned for).

clear the land and build their monastery. A smithy called Munkes Milne was first recorded on Meanwood Beck in 1238, with rights to burn charcoal and dig turf in the adjacent woods, as well as meadow land to graze the horses needed to work the woods. By this time bloomeries were using water-powered bellows and hammers, technology that had been brought to Yorkshire from France by the Cistercian monks.

The name Cinder Hills (found near Fagley, Shipley and Silsden, and in Seacroft along Wyke Beck) refers to the waste slag from this iron smelting process. Some of the iron ore came from near Seacroft, some from areas south of the River Aire and some was brought in from further afield[12]. For every tonne of ironstone, six tonnes of charcoal was needed to smelt it in primitive furnaces at temperatures over 1000C, so it was cheaper to transport ironstone to bloomeries in or near the woods where the charcoal was produced. Charcoal was also used in glassmaking, gunpowder production and woolcombing (the combs being heated on charcoal fires).

In the 14th century rats arrived in Britain, bringing the Black Death to England for the first time in 1348. A wave of plagues over the next couple of centuries probably reduced the population by half and resulted in a temporary recovery of the woodlands. Indeed some communities took refuge in the woods to try to avoid the plague, particularly around London. But the reprieve was only brief. From the 1470s, it became harder to import iron, so poorer-quality iron produced in Britain was in high demand. Iron smelting continued at Roundhay and Seacroft by the de Lacy family after the land was surrendered by Kirkstall Abbey. Smithies were also recorded at Weetwood, Hazel Well in Meanwood, Ravenscliffe Wood, Faweather near Baildon, Heaton Royds, Chellow Dean, Harden, Windhill Crag near Shipley, Cockersdale near Farnley and in Hunslet, with a new smithy established at Esholt in the 1570s.

*water-driven hammer at Kirkstall Forge*

It was in this decade that the first blast furnaces in Yorkshire were built at Wadsley (near Sheffield) and Rievaulx, providing a continuous supply of crude (pig) iron that could be worked up in large forges. All the existing bloomeries failed before the end of the century, with Weetwood Smithies last recorded as being operational in 1553. New forges were created on sites with greater water power, including notably Kirkstall Forge, which was built in the 1610s and operated by experts from the Weald and France. Both the new furnaces and forges needed large amounts of charcoal until the coke-fired blast furnaces that were developed in the second half of the 18th century. Such was its voracious consumption of wood that, in 1558, Elizabeth I passed 'An Act that Timber shall not be Felled to make Coals for the burning of Iron' to allow mature oak timber to grow and supply the Navy for shipbuilding.

The outright loss of woodland generally occurred only when demand for charcoal slowed. Possibly in response to the 1558 Act, the western part of Weetwood was grubbed out for pasture in the 16th century before becoming the estate of Weetwood Hall. The Civil Wars had an adverse impact on woodland, as demand reduced yet further and Kirkstall Forge had to be closed. Even when the demand was high, the ironmasters controlled pricing and took advantage of the long-term nature of the woodland economy to exploit woodland owners who relied almost entirely on them for their income.

[12] Iron was what the Scots were primarily after when they raided the Wharfe and Aire Valleys in 1318 as they had little natural ironstone. They plundered Calverley, Horsforth, Guiseley, Bingley and Keighley and ransacked churches other than those dedicated to their patron saint, Andrew.

Cookridge Wood was sold and broken into four areas in 1705[13], but these smaller parcels of woodland were less financially viable and the tenant created a series of enclosures in the woodland that is mirrored today in the shape of the housing estates of Ireland Wood and Tinshill. A glut of imported Swedish and Russian iron in the 1720s and 30s reduced demand and profit yet further and the woods began to be unviable. Affordable Scandinavian softwoods and the use of stone in buildings also greatly reduced the demand for oak timber. Grimewell Banks and further parts of Cookridge Wood were stubbed, evidence that the maintenance of large woodlands was tied very closely to the demands of the iron industry.

Another industrial activity that rarely resulted in the loss of woodland was coal mining. Though coal was discovered and burned in blacksmiths' furnaces by the Romans, who prized it as ornate black jewellery and used it in worshipping their gods, it was ignored again during subsequent centuries[14]. The first mention of coal being dug in the Aire Valley was in the 12th century, when the monks of Kirkstall Abbey worked in Middleton Wood. In the 14th century the lord of the manor was recorded digging coal and clay on Baildon Moor and Rough Holden above Keighley. These areas and many other woods and moors along the valley display the marks of these workings, hundreds of shallow pits evident almost anywhere the ground hasn't since been changed.

Shallow surface seams in the Lower Coal Measures could be accessed by digging simple bell pits, working a very small area before they became unstable and were filled in. A bell pit had an entrance about six feet wide, with the coal worked by candle or rush light and brought out by ladder. Coal was used locally in the brewing, salt-making and lime-burning industries, as well as for fuel, but little coal was transported far in the Middle Ages. It was hard to move and the short, fractured surface seams were of poor quality compared to the Middle Coal Measures that would later be accessed further below ground, so charcoal was favoured by most industries. After surface coal was worked out, day holes were dug into the hillsides along horizontal seams, some of which had stone-built entrances and horse gins to haul the coal out of the pits – the remains of some of these can be seen in Middleton Wood and Heaton Woods.

### Revolution Blues

By the early 17th century the manorial system was no longer predominant, with yeomen and the new merchant gentry on the rise. This shift of the power base was consolidated during the English Civil War, which was the most notable in a series of political disturbances in the 17th century. Areas linked to trade were usually more Puritan and supported the Parliamentarians against Charles I, who was thought to have Catholic sympathies. Bradford, Leeds, Bingley and Keighley supported the Parliamentarian cause, but there were Royalist strongholds nearby, at the castles in Skipton and Pontefract and a garrison in Wakefield.

Skipton Castle was besieged from 1642-45, in reply to which the Royalists successfully raided the Parliamentary garrison at Keighley. However, it was Bradford that came closest to falling, its church twice defended against the king's Whitecoats in 1642. In December

[13] Boundary and land ownership disputes over Cookridge Wood ran back to the early 17th century, when the woods were an important source of charcoal for the manors of both Headingley and Adel-cum-Eccup. After the wood was split into four sections in the 18th century to resolve these issues, attempts were made by the Ordnance Survey during their first survey of the area to simplify place names, so that there were no overlapping or duplicated appellations. Cookridge Wood was lost entirely from the map, though it is the most historic name in the area. Instead Captain Tucker gave new names to these relatively new parcels of woodland in his survey for the first series maps in 1847-48; Iveson Wood (the area owned by Alderman Iveson in the 18th century), Ireland Wood (the area still in Cookridge parish), Spring Wood, Daffy Wood and Clayton Wood.

[14] Coal was first rediscovered outcropping on the North Sea coast, and consequently it was known until the 17th century as 'sea coal' to distinguish it from 'wood coal'.

the Earl of Newcastle, William Calverley, is said to have been on the verge of breaking through in the Siege of Bradford and massacring its inhabitants. Staying with the Tempests at Bolling Hall, an apparition appeared, urging him to 'pity poor Bradford!' In reality, it probably had more to do with the arrival of Sir Thomas Fairfax's army, who were camped on Harden Moor while the Parliamentary commander in chief stayed at Harden Grange (where he wrote dispatches on a stone table that became known as Fairfax Table). There is conjecture as to whether a raid by Royalist solders from Skipton Castle took place on Harden Moor; bullets have been found but no bodies, despite part of the moor being known as Soldiers' Graves *(see p119)*.

After securing Bradford, Fairfax marched on Leeds, which had been taken by the Royalists under Sir William Savile. The bridge at Kirkstall having been intentionally destroyed, the Battle of Leeds took place on 23rd January 1643 and centred on Leeds Bridge, the last crossing over the Aire. Leeds fell to the Roundheads, with part of the battle fought in Batty's Wood by Meanwood Beck, and 460 Royalist prisoners were taken.

The Earl of Newcastle's forces retaliated and routed the Parliamentarians first at the Battle of Seacroft Moor (north-east of Leeds) in March and then at Adwalton Moor (near Drighlington, south-east of Bradford) in June 1643. The Royalists then controlled the region until the decisive Battle of Marston Moor the following June, when Cromwell and his troops marched north to take York and seize control of northern England. Skipton Castle fell in 1645 and was partially destroyed, and there were three sieges of Pontefract Castle, with several fights on Brotherton Marsh near Castleford (where many relics have since been found). The castle held out each time and remained the last Royalist stronghold to survive until it was finally destroyed in 1649. Some of the defeated Cavaliers hid out in Farnley Wood for some time, although within twenty years it had become renowned as the meeting place of a group of Parliamentarians. The 1663 Farnley Wood Plot sought to overthrow Charles II by attacking Royalist strongholds in Leeds, but the paltry gang were quickly undone by informants and twenty-one of them were hanged.

Added to the casualties of war, the population was ravaged by poor harvests and plague, with Leeds losing 20% of the population over a six-month period in 1644-45 and resorting to holding its markets out in Bramley, while Bradford was badly affected later on in 1645. The textile trade struggled to recover until the advent of turnpikes and the canal system nearly a century later.

### Weld

Though the area had long been busy, industrial activity in the Aire Valley really took off from the 18th century, transforming a relatively rural landscape into the urban region it is today. Though Leeds had developed into a large town, Daniel Defoe's observed in the 1720s that 'Leeds may not be much inferior to Halifax', and similar could have been said of Wakefield. Meanwhile Bradford was still a relatively minor market town in 1750; well wooded until the 17th century, Bradford Dale did not have a major river and was largely insular and self-sufficient due to poor transport and communications.

The most important development was the canal network, with the Aire and Calder Navigation cut in the 1770s, partly by French prisoners of war during the Napoleonic Wars. This made the River Aire navigable as far upstream as Leeds and established an important trade link to the Humber, North Sea and Europe; the city of Leeds never looked back. At the same time, the first sections of the Leeds and Liverpool Canal from Leeds to Gargrave were opening and the Bradford Canal was constructed to feed into it. Bradford was suddenly connected to the rest of the country and beyond, becoming the UK's fastest-growing industrial town, its population increasing by 50% every decade in the 19th century. By the 1820s, the canal was completed to Liverpool, providing trade links with Ireland and the Americas.

The canal provided a new form of transportation for many types of cargo, including coal, lead, iron, flax, alum, yarn, wool, woollens, linen, hemp, cutlery, groceries, dyewares, mahogany, salt, Burslem-ware, wine, spirits, corn, butter, cheese and Irish yarn. Timber, charcoal, quarried stone, iron and coal could now be shipped further afield from the woods. Limestone from Skipton and the Yorkshire Dales was traded with coal from downstream, lime being essential for lowering the pH of the acidic soil that is found in much of the West Riding. The Leeds and Liverpool Canal is lined with kilns where limestone was burned with charcoal to produce quicklime for the nearby fields.

The late 18th century also saw the widespread development of the road network, with the creation of new turnpike roads. Prior to this, the only way to transport most cargo had been via packhorse routes, which were often steep, narrow and badly maintained, particularly in the hills where they could be impassable for weeks during the winter. The Kirkstall, Otley and Shipley Turnpike was created in 1825, the Leeds and Selby Turnpike opened in 1740, the Keighley and Bradford Turnpike and the Keighley and Kendal Turnpike were both set up in 1753, the Blue Bell and Toller Lane Turnpike from Bradford to Colne via Haworth and the Leeds and Otley Turnpike opened in 1755, and dozens of others followed. These were all toll routes financed by private investment, and were unpopular with those who now had to pay to use them. There were riots in Leeds, where the tolls were among the highest in the country, and toll gates were destroyed at Beeston, Halton and along the new route between Leeds and Bradford (now the A647). Although some old routes were intentionally damaged to force people to use the new roads, many packhorse routes remained well used by those trying to avoid the tolls. A number of these passed through the woods, where they are still evident today.

Many of the new roads were laid out during the Parliamentary Enclosure Acts that were enacted across the whole country, mostly after the Inclosure Act of 1773. The first parish in the region to pass an enclosure act was Calverley in 1755, with other parishes following suit over the next 80 years. During this time most of the common moors, wastes and woods were lost, with rights of grazing and gathering wood, peat and bracken all surrendered forever. Straight line walls, roads and enclosures were imposed on the landscape, and any area of woodland or farmland with eccentric shapes almost certainly predates this. Some vestigial common land was retained, probably to allow cloth to be hung out on tenters, and became important green spaces in the growing cities; Woodhouse Moor in Leeds is a good example of this.

At around the same time, plantation forestry became popular. It was not a new idea; the practice of planting trees of the same species and age, treating trees as raw materials to be grown in the most efficient way to maximise yield, had been around since the 17th century. Plantations were sometimes created for aesthetic reasons as well as for profit. They came to be fashionable on estates, used to create a screen between the gentry in their homes and the working countryside. By the early 19th century Sir Henry Steuart (in his unfortunately titled *A Practical Essay on the Best Method of Giving Immediate Effect to Wood*) even advocated transplanting large nursery trees into plantations along with shrub layers, to replicate well-established woodland. Beech, sycamore and conifers were the most popular plantation trees in the north, though the woods that were created were nothing like the ancient flowing beech woods of the south or the Caledonian pine forests.

In recent years a lot of energy has gone into trying to undo this industrialisation of the woods. Those involved in countryside management nowadays understand more about trees, and know that different species need different nutrients and grow far better with a variety of other species around them.

Woollen cloth production in the West Riding of Yorkshire grew eight-fold in the 18th century, by the end of which its share of the national market had grown from 20% to 60% and worsted had come to dominate the local textile industry. Worsted yarn was subtly different from ordinary wool; its shorter fibres were combed out to produce a smooth, even yarn of long fibres. While ordinary wool had to be fulled, scribbled and dressed before it could be used for weaving, worsted was far simpler to work with. It did, however, rely on greater capital to turn raw wool, which was largely brought from Lincolnshire and the East Riding, into finished worsted cloth. Wool was brought here as there was an excellent supply of soft water for dyeing and finishing, as well as access to coal and iron for powering machinery. The industry was reliant on foreign markets, and by the 1780s 80% of the region's produce was sold abroad, particularly to America, where changing fashions required frequent adaptations in production methods. Yorkshire's merchants were renowned for their gift of the gab, successfully selling their wares to new places around the world. In the early 19th century cotton cloth was popular, as it was cheaper, lighter and more fashionable, even if it did rely on imported cotton and its end product was less hard-wearing, but by the 1830s cloth manufacture was almost entirely with wool. Some of this was also imported, most notably the alpaca and angora wool that Sir Titus Salt popularised, turning it into fashionable high-end cloth.

Within the space of fifty years, the process of worsted spinning grew from hand-weavers working in their homes, to small water-powered mills, to vast steam-powered weaving sheds. There were riots in the 1820s when new machinery was introduced, followed by the Plug Riots in 1842, where workers went on strike across the country to protest against wage cuts and the fact that the Chartist cause was being largely ignored. The Chartists were factory workers, craftsmen and hand-workers who demanded the vote. Their continued rebellion was quelled in the West Riding by the army's arrival in 1848, and its failure killed off the last vestiges of handloom weaving. Samuel Cunliffe Lister had invented the first successful combing machine in 1845 and huge mill complexes were developed in new sites at Saltaire, Manningham and Queensbury. By the mid 19th century, Bradford had 40% of the looms and a third of the workforce in the UK's worsted industry and was known as Worstedopolis.

Until its closure in 1817 Wakefield's cloth market was a regional centre for wool fairs. Meanwhile smaller manufacturers took their finished woollen goods to the markets in Halifax and Leeds, but during the 19th century these declined as Bradford's central market expanded, while the new larger manufacturers established their own showrooms. Leeds specialised in a coarse broadcloth known as northern dozens, but its industry was more diverse than Bradford's, as it was renowned for leather working, printing and coal mining as well as cloth.

Brick making became an important industry in Leeds by the late 18th century, when Leeds and Castleford were also becoming renowned for pottery. The fireclay needed was found in mudstones alongside the coal measures and the kilns were fired by readily available coal. The first building made from brick in West Yorkshire was Temple Newsam House, built in the mid 17th century, with Tong Hall one of the first near Bradford to import materials from Leeds' brick district. Bradford had relatively little suitable clay, as it often contained a lot of shale, so bricks were only used for lining flues and the inner skin of buildings, the rest of which were constructed of the more readily available gritstone. Initially brick making was carried out on a small scale across the area with handmade bricks produced wherever clay could be sourced. By the 19th century the process was mechanised, with the manufacturer's name stamped on the bricks. There were brickworks in the woods of Baildon Green, Heaton and a Brick Kiln Close in Frizinghall, while Whitakers had several sites around Leeds, including Horsforth whose bricks were made from clay dug in Hawksworth Wood.

WHITAKER
LEEDS
*a Whitaker's brick made in Horsforth*

Most of the region's newly wealthy clothiers were non-conformists – mainly Quakers, Methodists or Baptists – and traditionally stayed out of politics and the military, which were considered the realm of old money. They created a new network among themselves, and by the 19th century many had become MPs and were prominent in local politics. Poor labourers and colliers in pit villages, mill towns and farming communities were Primitive Methodists and belonged to other non-conformist denominations. They favoured open-air preaching, not necessarily always out of choice, and often held services in woodland locations, including Wesley's Pulpit near Woodhall and Buckstone Rock near Rawdon.

The rapidly growing settlements of the West Riding became very unsanitary by the early 19th century. Haworth had one of the worst life expectancies in the country because its wells were polluted by the overflowing graveyard. There was a cholera epidemic around Calverley in the 1830s, thought to have been caused by people washing their raw wool in the town's wells. While those who drank from woodland and moorland wells were largely unaffected, cholera and typhoid epidemics were common in the urban population until reliable piped water was supplied in the early 20th century. Throughout the 19th century, Bradford Beck and the River Aire were little more than open sewers, made worse by the lanolin grease scraped from all of the wool that was treated in the region. Leeds first water supply was provided by small reservoirs above the city, to which water was pumped from the polluted River Aire. Eccup Reservoir was built in the 1840s, fed by pipelines from the River Ouse and reservoirs in the Washburn Valley, and supplying Leeds via the fine Seven Arches Aqueduct in Adel Woods. Although Leeds had a sewerage system from the 1850s, it was not until 1899 that it was made compulsory for all houses to be connected to a sewer. Bradford opened its first sewage works at Frizinghall in 1874, before having to create the vast works at Esholt *(see p82)* in the early 20th century, a feature that still dominates one of the most beautifully wooded parts of the Aire Valley.

The relationship of the new industrial cities with their surrounding woodland is fascinating. The importance of woodland products for various aspects of industrial processes remained high, though increasingly wood was imported from Ireland and Scandinavia. The demand for bobbins, shuttles, rollers and clogs rose so quickly that it was cheaper to source wood in bulk from elsewhere. Even by the 17th century, the growing city of Leeds was supplied not with charcoal from nearby woods but increasingly with coal imported by sea from Newcastle.

The construction of the Middleton Railway *(see p20)* in 1758 by Charles Brandling, himself a Geordie, provided a cheaper local source of coal. By the early 19th century, ventilation, drainage and pumping engines were in place to allow access to the rich deep coal seams beneath the lower Aire Valley. Pillar-and-stall mining developed along the extensive seams around Castleford, Methley and Rothwell. Waggonways ran down to the River Aire from the collieries and coal was transported along the navigation by tugs pulling barges (known as Tom Puddings) full of coal. A tug could pull up to nineteen of these, each laden with around eighty tonnes of coal, and they were common until the 1950s. Downstream, the Aire's water was used for cooling the power stations dotted across the flat landscape; Ferrybridge Power Station used thirteen million gallons of water a day, as well as 8,000 tonnes of coal from the adjacent collieries.

Though charcoal continued to be produced until the late 19th century, the primary commercial value of a tree during the industrial era probably lay in its bark. There was a shortage of oak bark in the 1790s, resulting in a spike in its price and a search for local sources. The tanning industry thrived along the tributaries of the Aire, where soft water filtered through the gritstone. Tanneries were recorded at Esholt, Horsforth Woodside, Bingley, Cottingley, Cullingworth, Wilsden, Oulton, Burley, Hewenden and Silsden.

Cottingley and Bingley were particular centres of leatherwork, and in the 18th and 19th centuries Leeds became the second leather producer after London. The tanneries along Meanwood Beck were central to this, its valley lined with tan pits (known as 'bark pits' or 'ouse pits') and stacks of drying oak bark, and reeking of the foul odours of the trade. Skinners, tanners and woolcombers were seen as the lowest of the low, doubtless partly because they smelt so bad after work. Treated as outsiders, some lived in their own enclave, like the community of woolcombers at Harden Beck. Woolcombing was a significant industry until the late 19th century, with fifteen recorded in Thackley in the 1841 Census. Quarrymen were little different, many being itinerant and moving from quarry to quarry while living in squatted hovels around the (often wooded) sites where they worked.

overgrown tan pits in the Meanwood Valley

There was relatively little change in overall woodland cover during the 19th century, though the vast Farnley Wood *(see p62)* is notable for its loss. However, extensive quarrying and mining resulted in many existing woodlands being replanted or changing character to become secondary woodland, full of sycamore or beech instead of oak, birch and hazel. Parts of Gledhow Valley Woods, Bramley Fall and Esholt Woods were replanted in the 19th century to meet industrial needs. When the railway line was built along the Aire Valley between Leeds and Bradford in the 1840s[16], it cut through several woodland areas like Swaine Wood and Thackley Wood, while Hirst Wood was greatly reduced by the line to Skipton. The Brown's Wood that Reverend Ellis mourns in his poem *(see page xvi)* disappeared shortly before the first series of OS maps, sacrificed for the railway lines between Thackley and Windhill. Though many photos from the turn of the 20th century and beyond show a very thin covering of trees in areas that are now healthily wooded, much of it was due to the debilitating effect of the smoke that hung over Leeds, Bradford and much of the Aire Valley during the industrial era. Pollution significantly inhibited woodland growth and lowered the pH of the soil, leaving unhealthy and stunted trees clinging to the hillsides.

As their commercial value diminished, woodlands and trees increasingly became cherished for their aesthetic and amenity value. This romantic view of trees had begun in the late 18th century, with Romantic poets and artists venerating them for their naturalness, overlooking the fact that the woods had been worked by peasants for centuries and this was largely responsible for the shape of the woodlands. Many of the pollards that were often found on wooded common land to provide fuel for the poor were destroyed in the 18th and 19th century for being ugly and not fitting with new ideas about what trees should be. This impulse to order and tidy up nature, even if working to a template of wildness, has been called 'an increasingly fussy paternalism towards trees' by the nature writer Richard Mabey, and is seen in much of the landscaping of the great parks like those at Temple Newsam, Roundhay and Milner Field.

By the mid 19th century some of the finest woods were being eyed up by entrepreneurial landowners for exclusive housing schemes. Roads and plots were laid out through Rawdon Cragg Wood by Nathaniel Briggs in the 1850s, attracting many of Bradford's nouveau riche to build mansions here, and there is now very little open woodland left here. Calverley Wood, which was similarly laid out by Thomas Thornhill, only avoided the same fate because of a lack of interest, perhaps because it was on a north-facing slope. In Leeds, new suburbs for the wealthy were laid out in Roundhay, Headingley and Woodhouse. These new commercial estates resulted in the loss of some

[16] Interestingly William Rookes Crompton Stansfield, who famously lost his Esholt estate to Bradford Corporation's sewage works after complaining about the smell of the untreated filth in the River Aire (see p80), earlier complained as strongly about the railways. Two lines were laid through his estate and he ended up buying Frimley Park in Surrey for some peace and quiet.

public rights of way through the woods, and the caretakers for the Thornhill Estate prevented people from trespassing in Calverley and Fagley Woods or accessing the wells there, even after the plans to build an estate had been shelved.

There was a growing recognition that public access had to be safeguarded and public spaces provided for the growing populations of the valley's towns and cities. In 1839 an Act of Parliament required the provision of open spaces for exercise and recreation, though those that were provided tended to be tiny areas of green. In Europe, the first forest reserves were created in the 1830s in Czechoslovakia, with France following suit in the early 1850s. Back home the Commons, Open Spaces and Footpaths Preservation Society was formed in 1865 and the city corporations were authorised to purchase wastes and commons. Woodhouse Moor had been purchased by Leeds Corporation in 1855 and Woodhouse Ridge was appended in 1876, with Batty's Wood given to the council by Mr John Warburton, creating a large green space close to the centre of Leeds. Further out, Roundhay Park was purchased by the council in 1872, becoming one of Europe's finest public parks. Bradford Corporation opened Peel Park in 1863, Lister Park in 1870 and Bowling Park in 1880, with Roberts Park created by Sir Titus Salt in 1871. The city also inherited Buck Wood and Esholt Woods as part of the Esholt estate when the council compulsorily purchased it in 1906, and the woods were opened to the public soon after. In addition, the Estate Duty tax introduced in 1894 caused many of the landed gentry to sell their estates as they could not afford to hang on to them, with several becoming public parks (i.e. Temple Newsam, Beckett's Park and Bingley St Ives). Others were compulsorily purchased to make way for new housing estates, with the old houses either demolished or used as hospitals, asylums or special schools.

The advent of trams and omnibuses in the late 19th century provided cheap transport for more people to live in or visit places further out of the cities. Europe's first electric tramway operated between Oakwood and Leeds from May 1891, running along what is now a grass strip alongside Roundhay Road[17]. Trams to Far Headingley in 1873 and later Lawnswood gave access to the Meanwood Valley and Adel Woods. People flocked out of the cities on bank holidays, particularly Easter and Whitsun, and tea shops and pleasure gardens with simple rides sprang up to cash in. Shipley Glen, a name first coined in the 1840s, became hugely popular from the late 1870s, its sprawling pleasure grounds and new tramway said to have attracted 100,000 people on Easter Monday 1910. Happy Valley Pleasure Grounds in Goit Stock Woods thrived in the 1920s, while Golden Acre Park near Adel was popular in the 1930s, though the lack of public transport was its eventual undoing. Many of the wealthy locals in these areas complained of noise, vandalism and litter. In Adel the moor was set on fire, rare wild flowers like St John's wort and buckbean were picked and people camped out in the woods and stayed up half the night. In 1913 a few landowners here tried to get visitors to stay only on public rights of way and off the commons, employing a gamekeeper to enforce this, but they were swimming against the tide of public opinion.

Bespoke holiday homes sprang up around Alwoodley in the early 20th century, a collection of temporary chalets, huts, railway carriages and caravans that were cleared in the 1950s as they were deemed to be unsanitary.

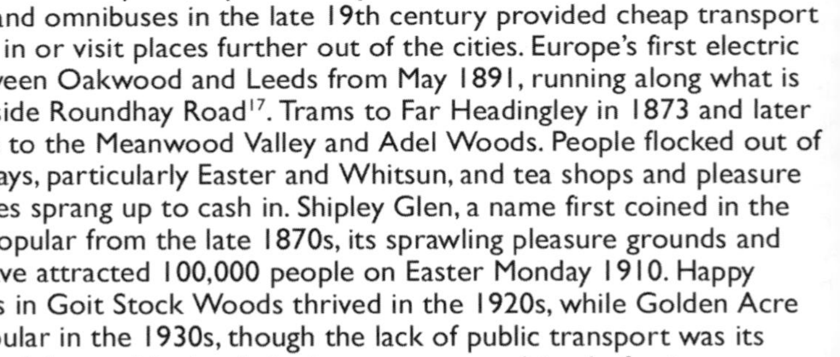

*Seven Arches Aqueduct in Adel Woods*

[17] There had been earlier plans for an elevated railway similar to that in Chicago, but it found little support.

## Living with War

Both World Wars had a significant impact on the region's woods, with national timber shortages resulting in many being clear-felled and replanted, and some of our finest and oldest trees being lost. Moseley Wood was replanted in World War I, woods in Allerton Bywater were clear-felled in the 1920s, and Holme Wood near Tyersal was clear-felled and grubbed out in World War II. The Forestry Commission was established in 1919 to replant trees on a large scale across the country. In the 1930s parts of Buck Wood were replanted by the council, with native broadleaves replaced with conifers as a cash crop, though local opposition limited the plan and the trees were never harvested. Though grown since the 17th and 19th centuries respectively, species like Norway spruce and Douglas fir were planted in huge swathes, though West Yorkshire suffered relatively little mass conifer planting compared to the valleys of Wales and the Scottish Borders. The largest plantations covered in this book are found in Cottingley Woods and the St Ives estate, although at least the larch and Scots pine that were planted here after World War I have far more character than the usual dark lines of spruce.

During World War I practice trenches were dug in Heaton Woods and near East Ardsley. A great shortage of meat towards the end of the war also resulted in a rise in poaching in the woods. During World War II the woods were used for rifle ranges, tank exercises, grenade practices and ammunition stores, many of these sites still evident. Everyone had to chip in, even the proprietors of golf courses reluctantly dug ditches across the fairways to prevent enemy planes landing and planted vegetables on any available ground. Bradford was bombed on August 31st 1940, with some German bombs accidentally dropped in Heaton Woods, and Leeds was blitzed most damagingly on March 14th and 15th 1941. Anti-aircraft guns and searchlights were placed on the high ground, including Baildon Moor, Rawdon Billing and Post Hill near Farnley. The most important site locally was Avro's giant aeroplane factory at what is now Leeds-Bradford Airport near Yeadon. It was camouflaged by film industry experts, who covered the roof with turf, field patterns and fake animals that were moved each day, so as not to look suspiciously static on aerial photos. Yeadon Tarn and the lake at Golden Acre Park were both drained so they couldn't be used as landmarks for bombers to locate the factory. Though Golden Acre suffered bomb damage, the factory remained untouched and built more than five thousand planes during the course of the war

Towards the end of the war sites in or around the woods were used to house large numbers of captured German and Italian soldiers. The largest prisoner-of-war camp in West Yorkshire was at Butcher Hill near Horsforth, and there were numerous other satellites, including at Post Hill near Farnley, Middleton Wood and Calverley Woods (where the buildings' outlines are still preserved). Rather than punishing the enemy, they were seen as places for rehabilitation, with prisoners set to work locally, including laying the foundations for the housing estates of Greengates and Fagley. After the end of the war, it took up to eighteen months to repatriate many of these former prisoners and they began to mingle more in the local community, particularly the Italians who had little or no loyalty to Hitler. Although banned from public transport and some establishments, they could go to church, visit the cinema and fraternise with locals.

Following both wars there was a significant surge in house-building as the squalid inner-city slums were cleared. The Homes Fit for Heroes programme was a response to the country's failing housing stock and partly sought to prevent the possibility of a revolution similar to that in Russia. Two and a half million houses were built across the country between 1919-1934 for soldiers returning from World War I. Garden estates and new villages sprang up in mock-Tudor and other fanciful architectural styles to appeal to families moving out of the city to the clean air of these new suburbs. Leeds slum clearances took place in the late 1920s, with large populations from the city moved out of the city centre to Ravenscliffe and Lower Grange in the 1930s and Fagley,

Greengates and Buttershaw immediately after World War II. However, a large proportion of these new houses were sold by private enterprise and ended up in the hands of more affluent workers rather than the working-class people they were originally designed to benefit. Cookridge Village, created from 1927 as a 'Village of Youth', had lots of different plots and builders and was developed in a haphazard way, driven largely by economics. Though the council did preserve large parts of the woodland they acquired to provide recreational areas around these estates, including Middleton Wood, Hawksworth Wood and Gipton Wood, they also built houses on former woodlands. Housing development after World War II made further encroachment into the wooded valleys north-west of Leeds, including Ireland Wood, the Iveson estate, Holt Park near Adel, Tinshill, Silk Mill and Moseley Wood (eradicating the last vestiges of a once substantial historical woodland – *see p54*).

The building of new roads also threatened the woods. When the M62 opened in the 1970s, there was a plan to build an Aire Valley Motorway, a dual carriageway along the length of Airedale that would pass through many of its ancient woods. An enquiry into the route was disrupted by a series of protests from local people who realised the value of this green corridor through the urban heart of West Yorkshire. This and a planned road up Shipley Glen were mercifully shelved, along with proposed reservoirs in Shipley Glen and Newsholme Dean. Now it is the shadow of the planned HS2 railway that looms large over tracts of unspoilt countryside and recently redeveloped woodland parks east of Leeds.

In the lower Aire Valley opencast coal mining laid waste to what remained of the surface of this mining landscape. Beginning in 1943 around Temple Newsam (where it barely stopped short of the mansion and removed several areas of former woodland) this process for getting the last of the area's diminishing coal reserves spread south-east along the valley to St Aidan's. Opening gaping holes up to 84m deep, it cut down through three coal seams that had already been worked by shafts and exposed many old, collapsed mining tunnels. As well as coal, sand and gravel were extracted, having been liberally deposited on this area of flood plain near the meeting of the Aire and Calder rivers. Coal was taken by rail to Ferrybridge Power Station and spoil was used to support the M62 and tipped widely around Newsam Green, St Aidan's and Fairburn Ings. Tipping started to be restricted on Fairburn Ings in the 1960s and, where pools formed due to subsidence, an RSPB reserve was designated in 1968. Opencasting continued until 2002 around St Aidan's, which itself is now established as an RSPB nature park.

### Fork in the Road

The end of World War I marked the low point for Britain's woodlands, with only 5% of the land remaining wooded. Since then this has increased to more than 13% due to rewilding and new planting, though this is still very low compared to the EU average of 37% (a figure that has surely risen with the UK's departure from the Union) and West Yorkshire comes in at a lowly 7.9%. Ancient woodland, which is defined as that which has been continuously wooded since 1600, only accounts for 2% of the nation's land cover, though West Yorkshire performs better on this front. Even then only half of our ancient woodland is in its semi-natural state, the rest having been felled and replanted since 1600.

Since World War II there has been a resurgent interest in the countryside, with the Ramblers' Association and National Trust being formed soon after the war. By the 1970s this enthusiasm was compounded by a sense of guilt about the state of our environment, with tree-planting programmes established in an attempt to redress the balance. The Woodland Trust was founded in 1972, in part to combat widespread planting of conifers at the expense of native species[18]. As Dutch Elm Disease was finishing off the English elm population, government grants in 1973 and 1974 drove the 'Plant a Tree in 73' and 'Plant Some More in 74' campaigns. Schools and local communities were involved in these and later projects, generating greater engagement with our local environment. In recent years local groups have been formed to protect and promote individual areas of woodland, removing litter, researching history and improving access and interpretation. Locally, these include the Friends of Buck Wood, Park Wood, Calverley Wood, Meanwood Park, Bracken Hall, Middleton Park, Adel Woods, and Hirst Wood Regeneration Group. Forest schools are now widespread and it is not uncommon to come across small clearings with paraphernalia associated with traditional woodland crafts.

The Forest of Leeds project was initiated by Leeds City Council to enhance the city's woodland and urban green spaces, including the creation of Water Haigh Park on a former pit site, where alder, birch, oak, rowan, larch and Corsican pine have been planted. Similarly, proposals for the Forest of Bradford project include planting woodland on former mining areas at Rough Holden and on bare slopes at Windhill and Wrose. After declaring a climate emergency in March 2019, Leeds made a commitment to become carbon neutral by 2030, leading the way in the UK on increasing tree canopy cover to 33% to offset its greenhouse gas emissions. Woodland and tree cover figures are increasing all the time and are now thought to be close to their levels at the time of the Norman Conquest.

While all these efforts are commendable, we continue to plant trees rather than allow woods to naturally develop, largely because we want to see the results of our efforts during our lifetime. Left alone, a field would become wooded in fifty years, but in the process would go through a phase of thorny scrub that we find unpalatable, so we tend to plant trees where they don't necessarily want to grow. Though we have got better at planting the right sort of trees for the local climate and topography, we still tend to plant far too close together to create anything approaching natural woodland.

About 50% of woodland is privately owned and 50% public, though public ownership is no guarantee of a wood's protection. In 2011, a plan was mooted by Whitehall to sell off all publicly owned forests to raise money and was only shelved after a public outcry. Of the woodland that is publicly owned, much is still held by local councils, many of whom have stated aims to improve the biodiversity of existing woodland by reducing the density of trees to improve the ground layers and under-storeys and leaving fallen trees to rot to encourage wildlife and regeneration. However, Bradford and Leeds councils admit that they can't afford to pay for any active thinning or coppicing of their woodlands other than removing trees that might be considered dangerous[19]. As a result there is little in the way of dead wood, younger trees or scrub beneath the dense cloak of older trees, and over 70% of plantations on sites of ancient woodland are now considered to be under threat.

Leeds Coppice Workers, a workers' cooperative operating since 2012, are working on several neglected woods around the city to bring them back to their former glory, including Townclose Hills, Middleton Wood, Post Hill and East Ardsley Fall. As well as working to selectively thin over-shaded woods and encourage different layers of growth, they produce sustainable local charcoal and coppice products and provide training and education. This sort of small-scale coppice restoration work has been funded by limited Woodland Improvement Grants, and there is hope that Defra's new Environmental Land Management Scheme may deliver more subsidies for smaller landowners and allow similar schemes to be supported. It is a good start, but a drop in the ocean. Unfortunately the timescale by which woodland needs managing both in order to thrive and to yield profits is so out of step with the way our government, and indeed our society, functions.

[18] In a remarkably short-sighted program between the wars, the Forestry Commission had felled, poisoned and even blown up areas of ancient woodland to be able to plant quick growing conifers. However, the soil that remained on these sites meant that it has been possible to reverse this trend and re-establish semi-natural broadleaf woodland in some of these places.

[19] Trees are too often today seen as dangerous to health and safety. The sad plight of so many of Sheffield's wonderful roadside trees between 2012-18 is a reminder that our councils' short-term attitude to tree management is driven by box-ticking and cost-cutting.

# A GLOSSARY OF WOODLAND TERMS

**arborglyphs** = tree graffiti
**birks** = birches
**bywash** = flagged overflow from canal into river
**canker** = rust *(Yorkshire dialect)*
**carr** = marsh
**clap** = self-closing gate *(Yorkshire dialect)*
**coven-tree** = a guelder rose
**dib** = hollow *(Yorkshire dialect)*
**eller/owler** = alder
**fall** = coppiced wood
**fleet** = secondary stream or channel, possibly a mill stream
**garth** = yard or enclosure
**gate** = road
**gled** = kite
**hanging** = describes a steep wooded slope
**hearth** (or **stance**) = flattened circular area where charcoal was burned
**hebble** = bridge
**hey/haigh** = enclosure
**hirst/hurst** = copse or wooded hill
**holme** = water meadow
**holt** = wood
**hope** = valley
**hove** = ground ivy
**ing** = meadow
**intake** = land taken in from the waste
**laithe** = barn
**laund** = glade
**ley** = forest glade or clearing
**ling** = heather
**lister** = dyer
**lound/lund** = small wood (thought originally to have referred to a sacred grove)
**moss** = swamp or bog
**nab** = knoll
**rein** = boundary strip (usually of woodland)
**royd** = clearing in the trees
**shaw/shay** = copse (e.g. Heaton Shay)
**shroggs** = bushes or thicket
**slaughter** = sloe tree
**smout hole** = hole in bottom of drystone wall for letting sheep or hares through
**spring** = plantation for coppicing
**stag-headed** = tree whose crown includes dead branches
**staithe** = landing place
**stangs** = wooden bars across early gate stoops
**stoop** = stone post, whether used as a waymarker or for a gatepost
**stubb/stubbing** = clearing (where stumps have been grubbed out)
**syke/sike** = small beck
**throstle** = thrush
**thwaite** = clearing
**tong** = fork in a river
**turnbye** = stone drains across packhorse tracks leading water into the drains alongside
**twitter** = unevenly spun thread
**whin/winny** = gorse
**worth** = enclosure

# CHAPTER 1 - CASTLEFORD & ROTHWELL

**Map Sheet:** Explorer 289 (Leeds)

**Public Transport:** Railway stations at Castleford & Woodlesford on Leeds to Hull line.

**Parking:** Various car parks at Fairburn Ings & St Aidan's Nature Reserves (some pay, some free).

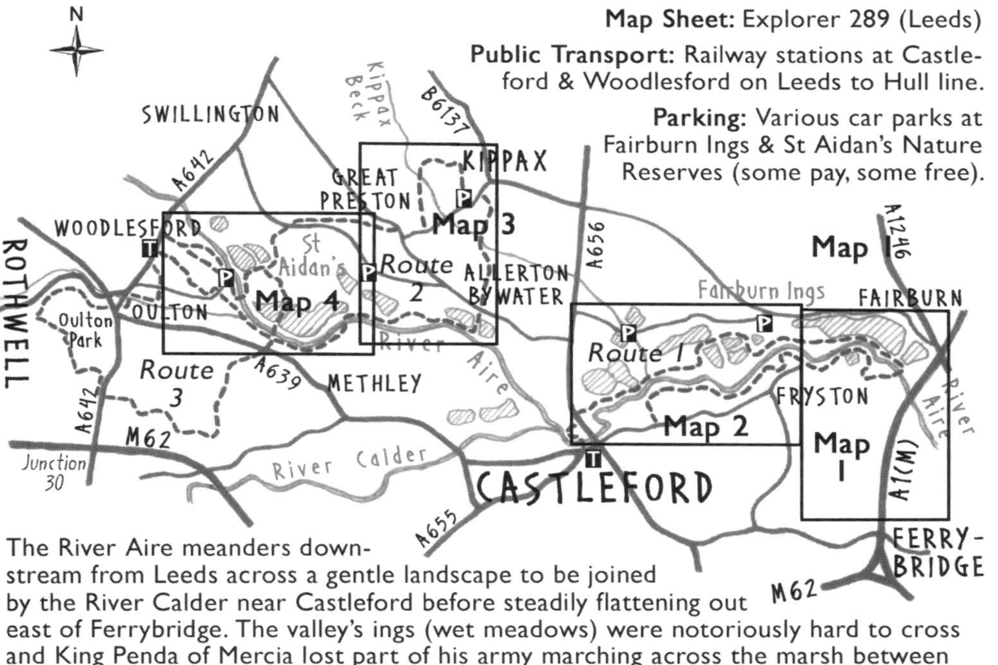
N
SWILLINGTON
Kippax Beck
B6137
KIPPAX
GREAT PRESTON
A642
WOODLESFORD
ROTHWELL
St Aidan's
Map 4
Map 3
Route 2
ALLERTON BYWATER
A656
Map 1
A1246
Fairburn Ings
FAIRBURN
OULTON
Oulton Park
Route 3
A639
METHLEY
River Aire
Route 1
FRYSTON
Map 2
Map 1
A1(M)
River Aire
A642
M62
Junction 30
River Calder
CASTLEFORD
A655
FERRY-BRIDGE
M62

The River Aire meanders downstream from Leeds across a gentle landscape to be joined by the River Calder near Castleford before steadily flattening out east of Ferrybridge. The valley's ings (wet meadows) were notoriously hard to cross and King Penda of Mercia lost part of his army marching across the marsh between Castleford and Ferrybridge in the 7th century. The land was only drained in the 17th century, but still operates as a washland safety valve to prevent flooding upstream.

Until the mid 19th century, this part of the Aire was dominated by large houses and their estates, with pockets of woodland dotted across a rural landscape that can still be seen around Ledston, Lotherton, Parlington and Potterton Halls just to the north. Those houses still standing largely lie on a belt of Magnesian limestone, whereas the land along the Aire itself was underlain by coal measures and consequently was ravaged by 150 years of mining activities. After the era of the great collieries, when many new pit villages sprang up, opencast mining and spoil dumping reshaped the landscape, and the great halls at Methley, Kippax and Fryston were lost due to subsidence.

Since all this industry ended in the 1990s, remarkable changes have taken place and it is now possible to travel through this landscape oblivious of its recent history. Spoil heaps at Fairburn Ings, opencast quarries at St Aidan's and former pits at Water Haigh and Fryston have been transformed into nature reserves and country parks. As this is part of a trans-Pennine flyway used by migrating birds following the Aire to the sea from high in the Pennines, the lakes and reedbeds that have formed here are rich in birdlife and a twitcher's delight. Though some ancient woodland remains, most of the trees are inevitably young and still establishing their imprint on the landscape.

Castleford forms the focal point of the area, an important Roman settlement which was transformed from a small village into an industrial centre in the mid 19th century by the burgeoning glass and coal-mining industries. Rothwell, centred around its 14th-century castle, was once more important than Castleford or Leeds, and has now merged into the villages of Oulton and Woodlesford, each of which provides a starting points for exploring the valley's green corridor.

# MAP 1: FAIRBURN INGS EAST & FRYSTON WOODS

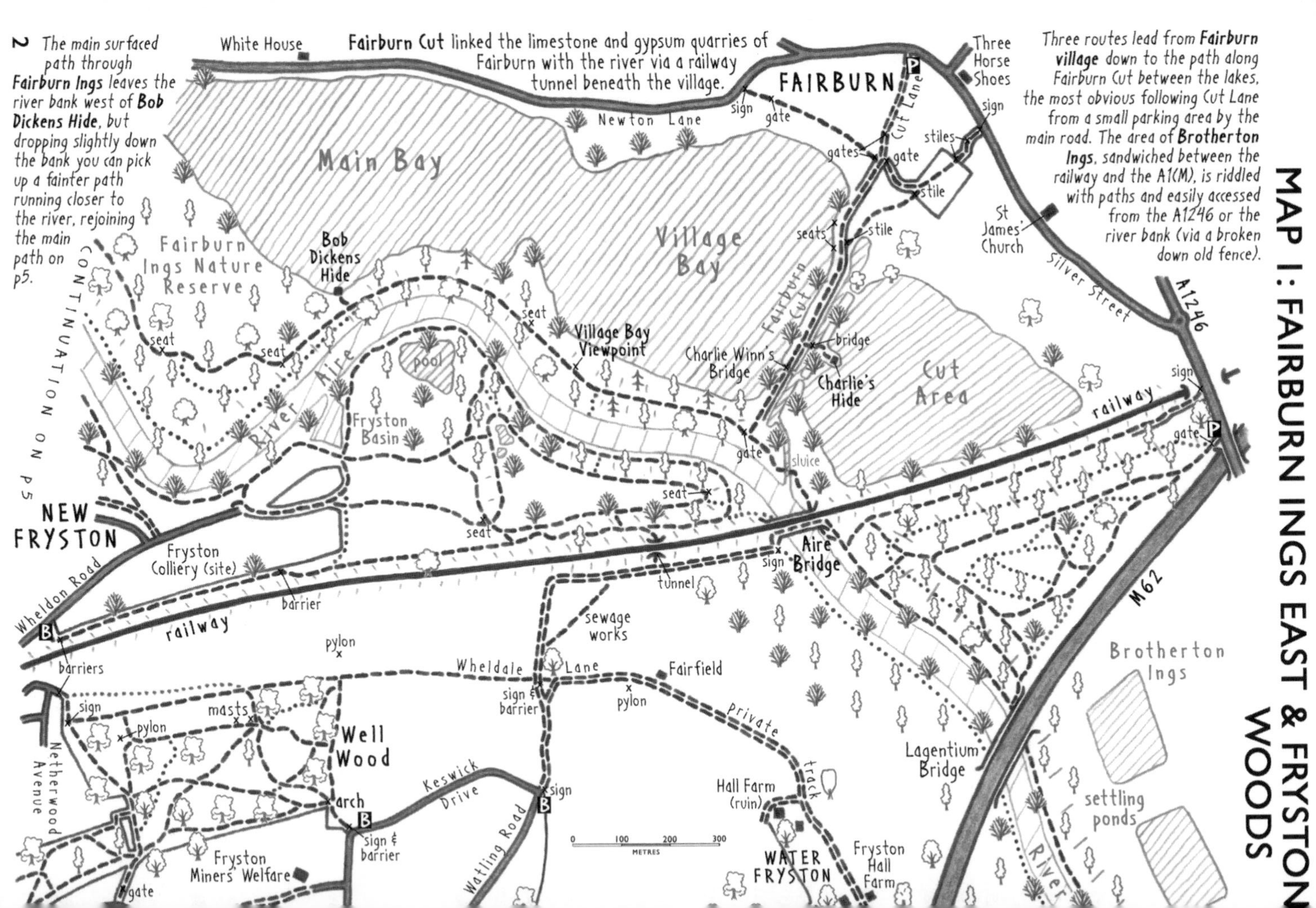

The main surfaced path through Fairburn Ings leaves the river bank west of Bob Dickens Hide, but dropping slightly down the bank you can pick up a fainter path running closer to the river, rejoining the main path on p5.
White House
Fairburn Cut linked the limestone and gypsum quarries of Fairburn with the river via a railway tunnel beneath the village.
FAIRBURN
Three Horse Shoes
Three routes lead from Fairburn village down to the path along Fairburn Cut between the lakes, the most obvious following Cut Lane from a small parking area by the main road. The area of Brotherton Ings, sandwiched between the railway and the A1(M), is riddled with paths and easily accessed from the A1246 or the river bank (via a broken down old fence).
P
Cut Lane
sign
gate
Newton Lane
sign
stiles
gates
gate
stile
Main Bay
Village Bay
seats
stile
St James' Church
Silver Street
A1246
Fairburn Ings Nature Reserve
Bob Dickens Hide
seat
Village Bay Viewpoint
Fairburn Cut
bridge
Charlie Winn's Bridge
Charlie's Hide
Cut Area
sign
seat
seat
pool
River Aire
Fryston Basin
railway
gate
P
gate
sluice
seat
seat
NEW FRYSTON
Fryston Colliery (site)
tunnel
sign
Aire Bridge
M62
Wheldon Road
B
barrier
railway
sewage works
pylon
barriers
Wheldale
Lane
Fairfield
Brotherton Ings
sign
sign & barrier
pylon
masts
pylon
Well Wood
Private
Lagentium Bridge
Netherwood Avenue
Keswick Drive
sign
B
arch
B
track
Hall Farm (ruin)
settling ponds
sign & barrier
Watling Road
0
100
200
300
METRES
Fryston Miners' Welfare
gate
WATER FRYSTON
Fryston Hall Farm
River


CONTINUATION ON P5

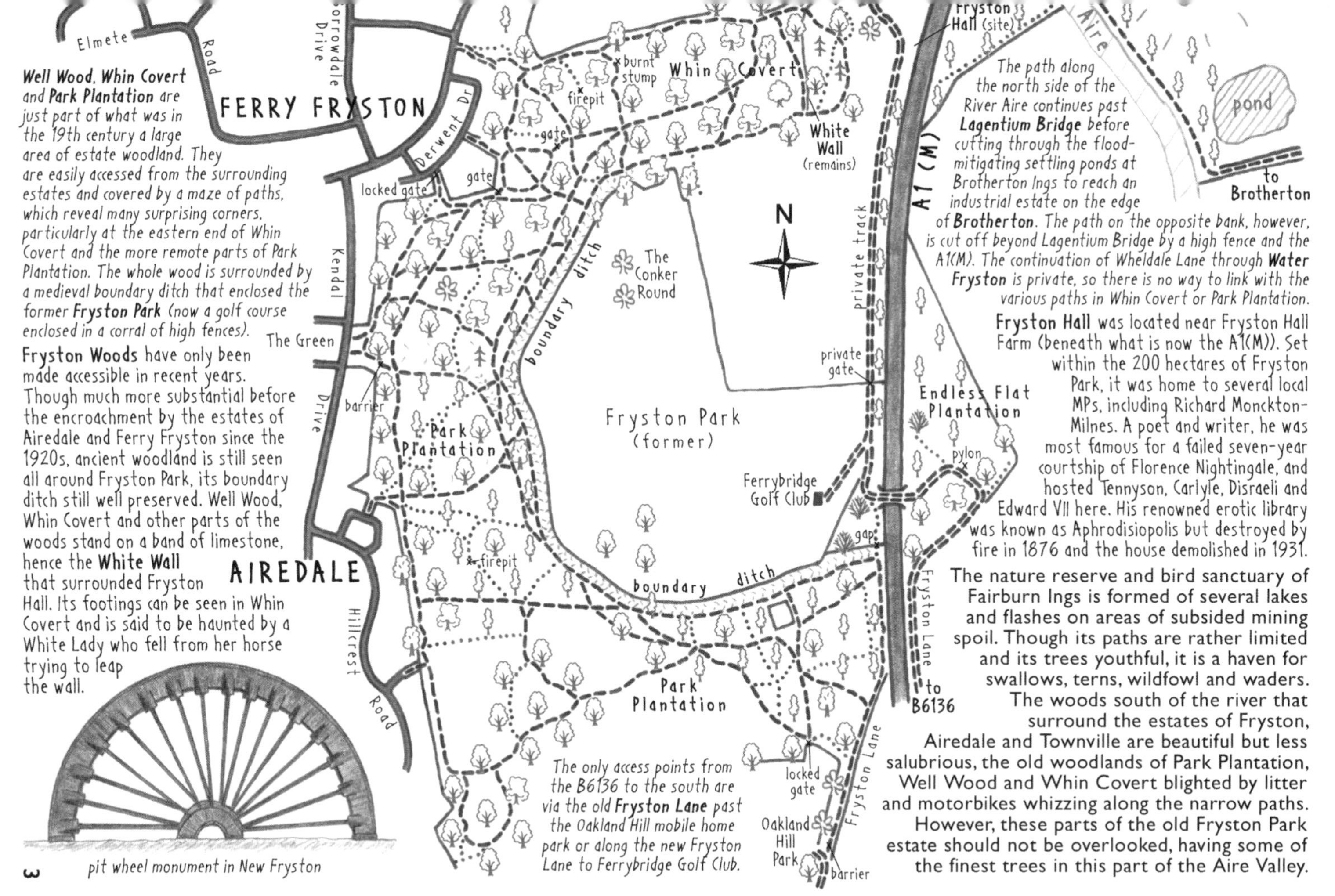

Elmete
Road
Borrowdale Drive
FERRY FRYSTON
Derwent Dr
locked gate
gate
gate
firepit
burnt stump
Whin Covert
White Wall (remains)
Fryston Hall (site)
Aire
pond
to Brotherton
A1 (M)
N
The Conker Round
private track
private gate
boundary ditch
Kendal Drive
The Green
barrier
Park Plantation
Fryston Park (former)
Ferrybridge Golf Club
Endless Flat Plantation
pylon
gap
firepit
AIREDALE
Hillcrest Road
boundary ditch
Park Plantation
Fryston Lane
to B6136
locked gate
Oakland Hill Park
Fryston Lane
barrier


***Well Wood*, *Whin Covert* and *Park Plantation*** are just part of what was in the 19th century a large area of estate woodland. They are easily accessed from the surrounding estates and covered by a maze of paths, which reveal many surprising corners, particularly at the eastern end of Whin Covert and the more remote parts of Park Plantation. The whole wood is surrounded by a medieval boundary ditch that enclosed the former ***Fryston Park*** (now a golf course enclosed in a corral of high fences).

**Fryston Woods** have only been made accessible in recent years. Though much more substantial before the encroachment by the estates of Airedale and Ferry Fryston since the 1920s, ancient woodland is still seen all around Fryston Park, its boundary ditch still well preserved. Well Wood, Whin Covert and other parts of the woods stand on a band of limestone, hence the **White Wall** that surrounded Fryston Hall. Its footings can be seen in Whin Covert and is said to be haunted by a White Lady who fell from her horse trying to leap the wall.

*The path along the north side of the River Aire continues past **Lagentium Bridge** before cutting through the flood-mitigating settling ponds at Brotherton Ings to reach an industrial estate on the edge of **Brotherton**. The path on the opposite bank, however, is cut off beyond Lagentium Bridge by a high fence and the A1(M). The continuation of Wheldale Lane through **Water Fryston** is private, so there is no way to link with the various paths in Whin Covert or Park Plantation.*

**Fryston Hall** was located near Fryston Hall Farm (beneath what is now the A1(M)). Set within the 200 hectares of Fryston Park, it was home to several local MPs, including Richard Monckton-Milnes. A poet and writer, he was most famous for a failed seven-year courtship of Florence Nightingale, and hosted Tennyson, Carlyle, Disraeli and Edward VII here. His renowned erotic library was known as Aphrodisiopolis but destroyed by fire in 1876 and the house demolished in 1931.

The nature reserve and bird sanctuary of Fairburn Ings is formed of several lakes and flashes on areas of subsided mining spoil. Though its paths are rather limited and its trees youthful, it is a haven for swallows, terns, wildfowl and waders.

The woods south of the river that surround the estates of Fryston, Airedale and Townville are beautiful but less salubrious, the old woodlands of Park Plantation, Well Wood and Whin Covert blighted by litter and motorbikes whizzing along the narrow paths. However, these parts of the old Fryston Park estate should not be overlooked, having some of the finest trees in this part of the Aire Valley.

*The only access points from the B6136 to the south are via the old **Fryston Lane** past the Oakland Hill mobile home park or along the new Fryston Lane to Ferrybridge Golf Club.*

*pit wheel monument in New Fryston*

# MAP 2: FAIRBURN INGS WEST & FRYSTON

The former colliery sites and spoil heaps that dominated this part of the Aire Valley until relatively recently have been revitalised as Fairburn Ings Nature Reserve and the Fryston Trails network. Though there are signs of industry at every turn – old railways, spoil heaps and winding wheels – it is amazing to see how quickly nature re-establishes itself on sites like these. Fairburn Ings Centre and Newton Lane Pond are the obvious bases for exploring north of the river, and New Fryston is also surrounded by some lovely paths and the whole area is close to Castleford.

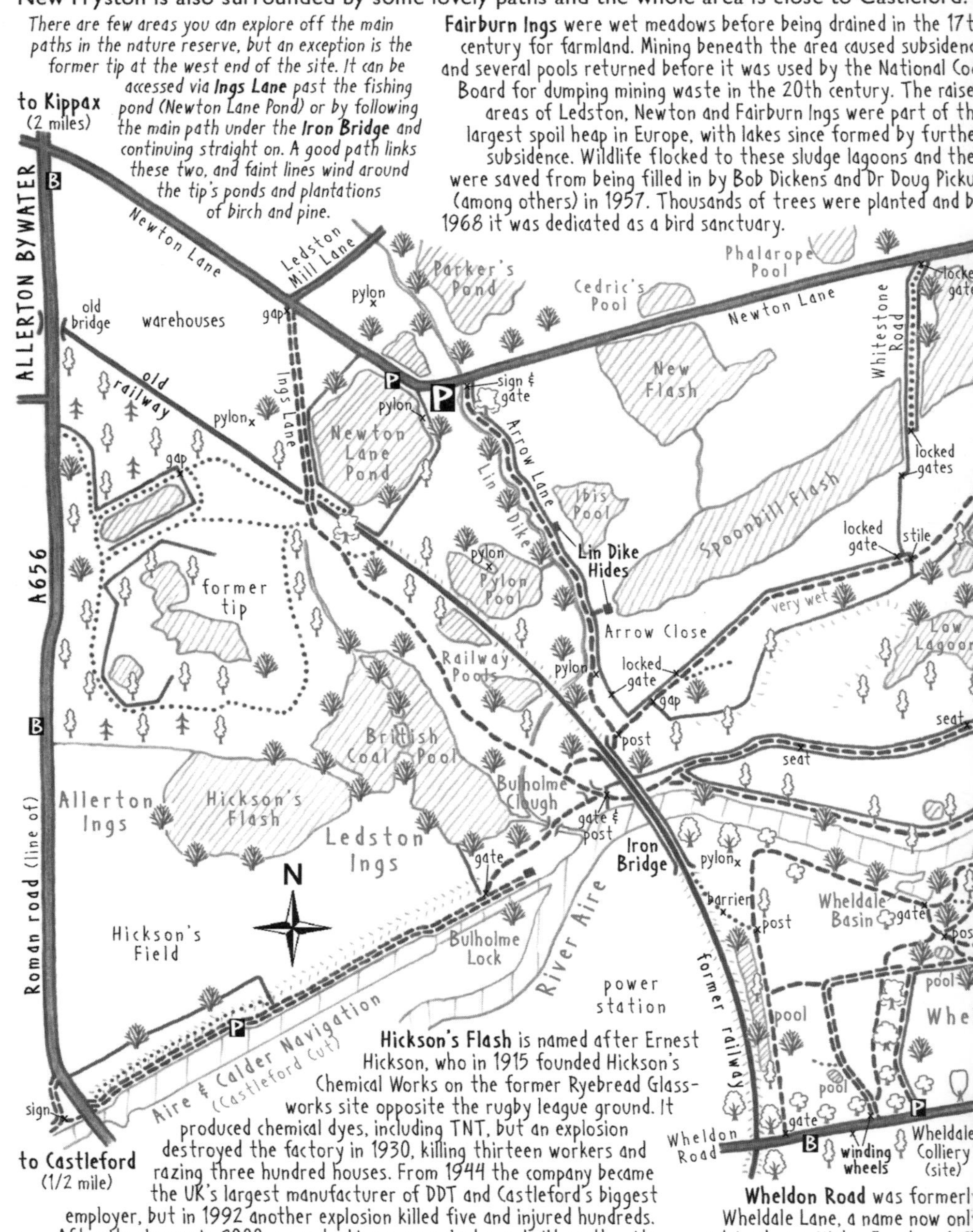

to Kippax
(2 miles)
ALLERTON BYWATER
Newton Lane
Ledston Mill Lane
Parker's Pond
Cedric's Pool
Phalarope Pool
Newton Lane
Whitestone Road
locked gate
old bridge
warehouses
gap
pylon
old railway
Ings Lane
sign & gate
New Flash
Newton Lane Pond
Arrow Lane
Lin Dike
Ibis Pool
Spoonbill Flash
locked gates
locked gate
stile
gap
former tip
A656
Pylon Pool
Lin Dike Hides
Arrow Close
very wet
Low Lagoon
Railway Pools
locked gate
post
seat
British Coal Pool
Bulholme Clough
Allerton Ings
Hickson's Flash
Ledston Ings
gate & post
Iron Bridge
gate
barrier
Wheldale Basin
Roman road (line of)
N
Hickson's Field
Bulholme Lock
River Aire
power station
former railway
pool
Aire & Calder Navigation
(Castleford Cut)
sign
to Castleford
(1/2 mile)
Wheldon Road
winding wheels
Wheldale Colliery (site)


There are few areas you can explore off the main paths in the nature reserve, but an exception is the former tip at the west end of the site. It can be accessed via **Ings Lane** past the fishing pond (Newton Lane Pond) or by following the main path under the **Iron Bridge** and continuing straight on. A good path links these two, and faint lines wind around the tip's ponds and plantations of birch and pine.

**Fairburn Ings** were wet meadows before being drained in the 17t century for farmland. Mining beneath the area caused subsidenc and several pools returned before it was used by the National Co Board for dumping mining waste in the 20th century. The raise areas of Ledston, Newton and Fairburn Ings were part of th largest spoil heap in Europe, with lakes since formed by furthe subsidence. Wildlife flocked to these sludge lagoons and the were saved from being filled in by Bob Dickens and Dr Doug Picku (among others) in 1957. Thousands of trees were planted and b 1968 it was dedicated as a bird sanctuary.

**Hickson's Flash** is named after Ernest Hickson, who in 1915 founded Hickson's Chemical Works on the former Ryebread Glass-works site opposite the rugby league ground. It produced chemical dyes, including TNT, but an explosion destroyed the factory in 1930, killing thirteen workers and razing three hundred houses. From 1944 the company became the UK's largest manufacturer of DDT and Castleford's biggest employer, but in 1992 another explosion killed five and injured hundreds. After its closure in 2000, a gas turbine power plant was built on the site.

**Wheldon Road** was formerl Wheldale Lane, a name now onl retained near Water Fryston (p2

What is left of **Newton Abbey** on dry land is barely visible, most of its pale stones submerged by mining subsidence in the 1960s. Though it may later have been used as a convent, there was nothing monastic about the moated manor house that was home to the Wallis family from the 12th to 14th century. What is most striking about **The Moat** (or Priory Pond) are the dozens of cormorants who nest in the submerged willows.

*Be aware that the lovely path across the meadows from **Newton** to the **Iron Bridge** can be very wet (wellies only) in one short section past Spoonbill Flash during the winter months. Though the abbey is hard to make out, it is worth venturing here to see the cormorants nesting in the trees. Unfortunately the worn lines that lead from this path towards the visitor centre reach only locked gates.*

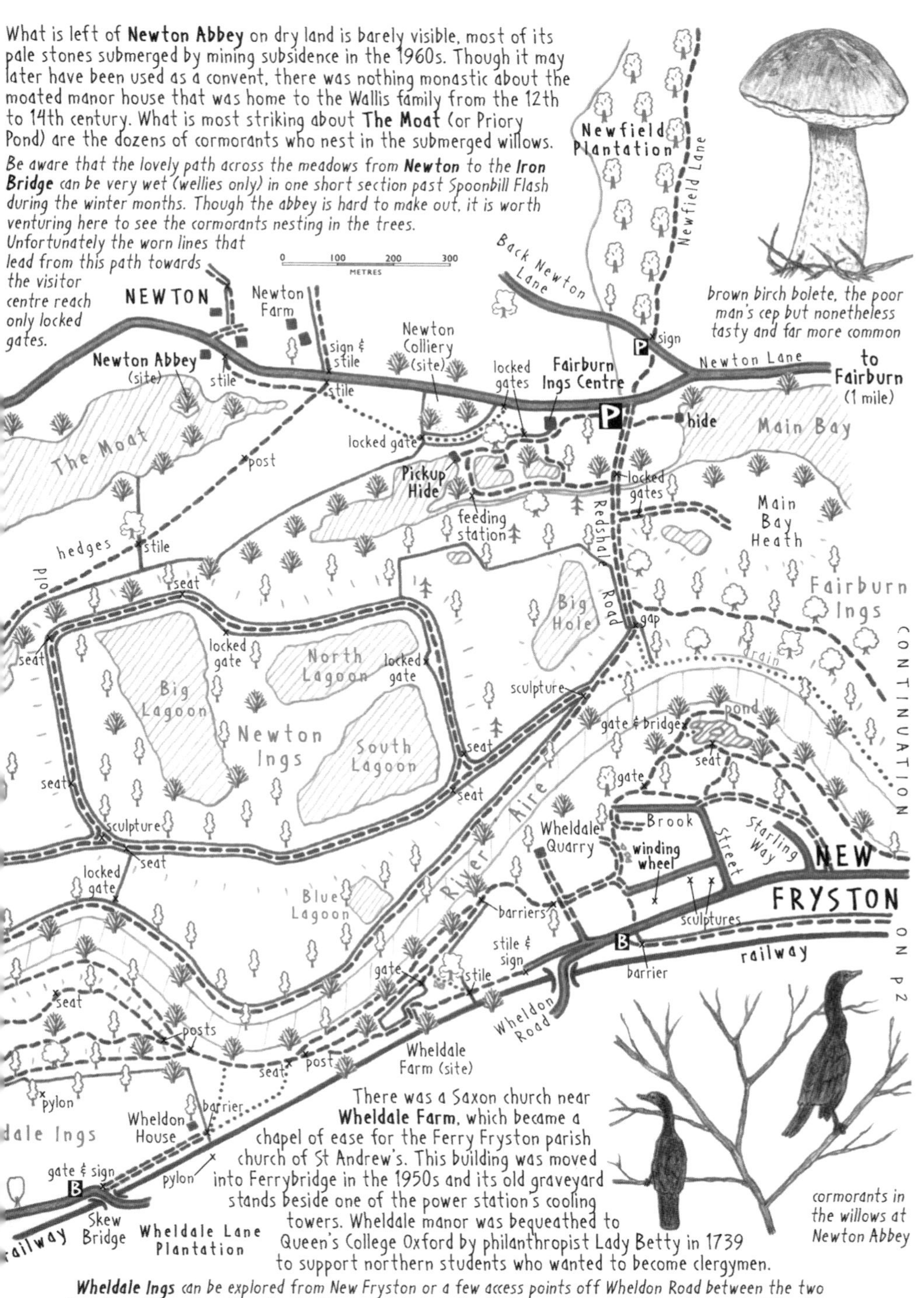

0 100 200 300
METRES
NEWTON
Newton Farm
Newton Abbey (site)
stile
sign & stile
stile
Newton Colliery (site)
locked gates
Fairburn Ings Centre
Newfield Plantation
Newfield Lane
Back Newton Lane
sign
Newton Lane
to Fairburn (1 mile)
hide
Main Bay
The Moat
post
locked gate
Pickup Hide
feeding station
locked gates
Main Bay Heath
Redshale Road
hedges
stile
old
seat
Big Hole
Fairburn Ings
gap
drain
seat
locked gate
North Lagoon
locked gate
Big Lagoon
sculpture
Newton Ings
South Lagoon
seat
seat
gate & bridge
pond
seat
gate
seat
River Aire
sculpture
seat
Wheldale Quarry
Brook
winding wheel
Street
Starling Way
NEW FRYSTON
locked gate
Blue Lagoon
barriers
sculptures
stile & sign
railway
barrier
gate
stile
Wheldon Road
seat
posts
seat
post
Wheldale Farm (site)
pylon
barrier
Wheldon House
dale Ings
gate & sign
pylon
Skew Bridge
railway
Wheldale Lane Plantation


CONTINUATION ON P2

brown birch bolete, the poor man's cep but nonetheless tasty and far more common

There was a Saxon church near **Wheldale Farm**, which became a chapel of ease for the Ferry Fryston parish church of St Andrew's. This building was moved into Ferrybridge in the 1950s and its old graveyard stands beside one of the power station's cooling towers. Wheldale manor was bequeathed to Queen's College Oxford by philanthropist Lady Betty in 1739 to support northern students who wanted to become clergymen.

cormorants in the willows at Newton Abbey

***Wheldale Ings** can be explored from New Fryston or a few access points off Wheldon Road between the two railway lines. The main path is the furthest west, but plenty of other routes cross the spoil ground of the former **Wheldale Colliery**. The only part of the river bank that is not accessible is around Wheldale Quarry in **New Fryston**, but a lovely path leaves the end of Brook Street and descends round the pond at the next bend of the river.*

# ROUTE 1: FAIRBURN INGS FROM CASTLEFORD

**Distance:** 9 miles (14.3km)

**Ascent:** 90m

**Parking:** Pay & display parking at Castleford railway station and other central car parks. Free parking off A656 opposite the Griffin Inn.

**Public Transport:** Castleford is on the Hallam and Pontefract railway lines, as well as being well served by local bus services.

**Character:** Castleford is not on first glance an obvious walking destination, but this route provides a fine exploration from this historic settlement through the nature reserves established along the River Aire in former collieries and spoil heaps. As well as Fairburn Ings, the walk explores the Fryston Country Trails and Lock Lane Bird Garden. The route is on good, largely flat paths throughout.

**Castleford**'s name refers to the existence of a Roman fort here beside an important ford across the River Aire. Watling Street met other major Roman roads nearby and its line is clearly seen along the A656 north of the town. The Romans called the large town here Lagentium, which translates as 'place of the bottles', so Castleford's glassmaking industry has a long history. It was pottery though that defined the town in the 18th and early 19th centuries, making use of the clay that lay just beneath the surface and could be fired using local coal to make tiles, bricks and high-quality fineware. **Glassmaking** became Castleford's staple trade in the mid 19th century, making it one of the fastest growing towns in the country.

There is a well preserved Roman milestone in **Castleford Museum**, as well as the Iron Age chariot that was found almost complete near Water Fryston when the A1(M) was created. This was buried with its owner in the 4th century BC and offerings continued to be left at the burial mound during the Roman era.

**2** Follow the flood bank alongside **Castleford Cut** until forced to join the adjacent tarmac track. At Bulholme Lock turn left back up the embankment, soon joining the bank of the River Aire. Keep right to pass beneath **Iron Bridge**, then fork left away from the river bank on a fenced path through the former spoil heaps that make up **Fairburn Ings Nature Reserve** *(see p4)*. Turn left at the first junction and loop around a trio of large lagoons with good views over the rest of the reserve and towards Ledston Hall. At the far end, turn left again to descend back towards the river bank.

seat
Big Lagoon
North Lagoon
seat
Low Lagoon
seat
sculpture
seat
seat
gate & post
Ledston Ings
Iron Bridge
seat
pylon
pylon
gate
post
Wheldale Basin
gate
0 200 400
METRES
2
Bulholme Lock
River Aire
former railway
post
pool
A656
Castleford Cut
River Calder
Junction Houses
sign
N
power plant
Griffin Inn
gate
bridges
sports field
Boot Room
6
Castleford Tigers RLFC
Lock Lane
Lock Lane Bird Garden
River Aire
Mill Lane
footbridge
Wheldon Road
Allinson's Flour Mill (Queen's Mill)
Castleford Museum
A6032
Bank St
Carlton St
CASTLEFORD
to bus station
1
Picture House
railway
Castleford railway station

**6** Turn right on **Wheldon Road** and pass the rugby league ground that is the town's prime focus. Reaching a roundabout turn left then immediately right along **Carlton Street**, Castleford's main shopping street. At the far end of the pedestrianised section turn left to rejoin the outward route back to **Castleford railway station** or, if parked elsewhere turn right along Bank Street to continue the circular route.

**1** Turn right out of **Castleford railway station** and follow the approach to join Station Road opposite the old Picture House. Carry straight on along Bank Street and turn right at its end. Beyond **Allinson's Flour Mill** (now Queen's Mill), turn left across the curving Millennium Bridge over the River Aire. Go left on a path along the far river bank, passing Lock Lane Bird Garden. At the junction with **Castleford Cut**, it is sometimes possible to cross the bridges to the track the other side; otherwise staying on the right bank brings you to the A656 near the Griffin Inn. Cross the bridge over the cut, then turn left to rejoin it, heading under the road before bearing immediately left up onto the flood bank.

❸ Bear left back up the slope, then turn right onto a lovely path (the 'Riverbank Trail') that winds through the trees to reach **Bob Dickens Hide**, a fine vantage point across Main Bay, part of the largest of the lakes at Fairburn Ings. Continue along the high embankment between the lake and the river until it ends by a gate, then carry straight on to reach **Aire Bridge**. On the far side, steps lead up to allow pedestrians to cross the bridge alongside the railway.

**Aire Bridge** (known locally as Three Bridges for its three-arch design) posed huge problems for the builders of the York & North Midland Railway. Due to issues with the foundations, its brickwork was constructed in five weeks to be completed just in time for the line to open in 1840. The catwalk alongside it was built with funds given by local miners and is still the only footway across the river between Castleford and Ferrybridge. Until then a rowing boat ferry had crossed from a landing staithe at the end of Ings Lane (now beneath Main Bay).

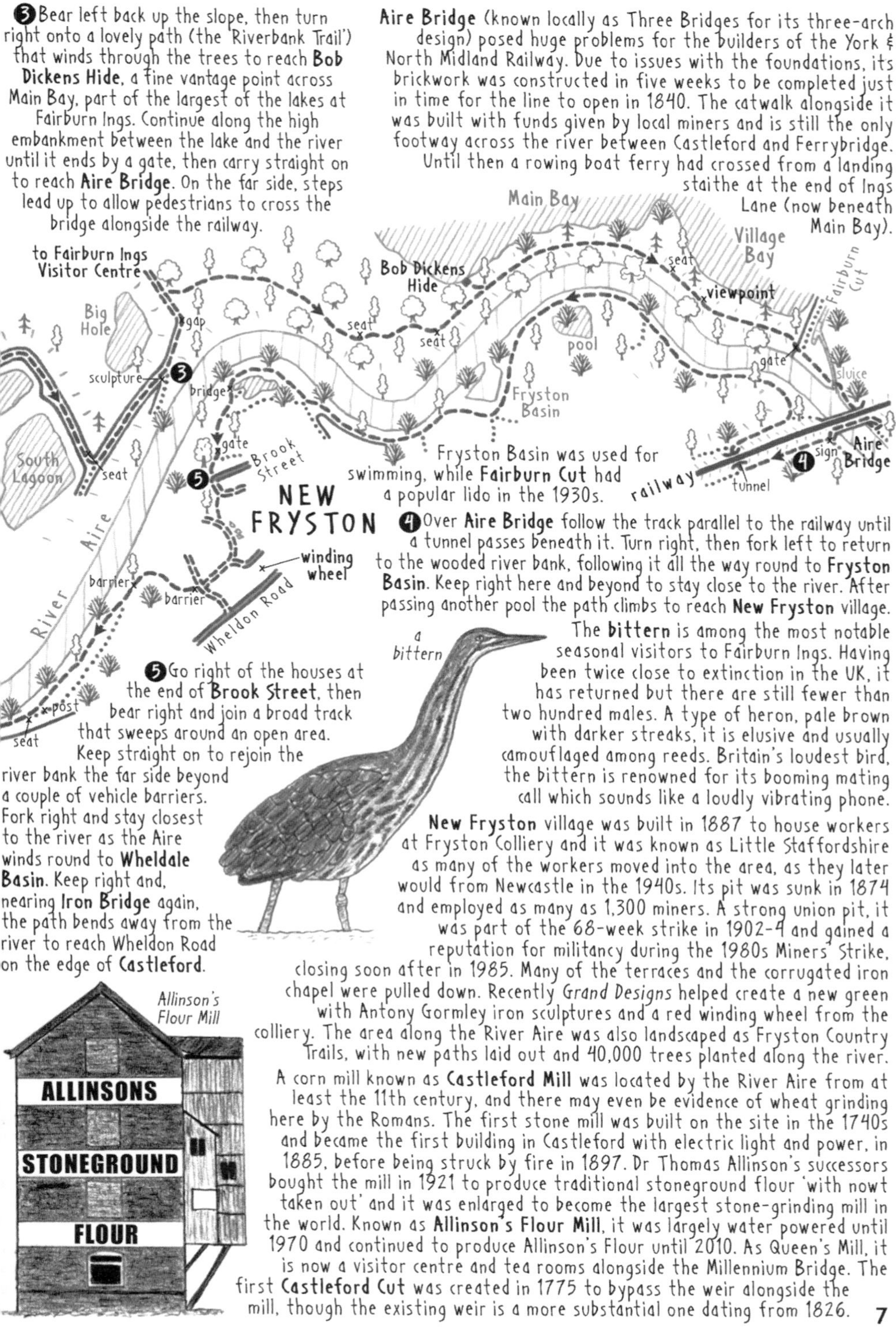
Main Bay
Village Bay
Fairburn Cut
to Fairburn Ings Visitor Centre
Bob Dickens Hide
seat
viewpoint
Big Hole
gap
seat
seat
pool
gate
sluice
sculpture
3
bridge
Fryston Basin
gate
Brook Street
5
South Lagoon
seat
Aire Bridge
4
sign
railway
tunnel
NEW FRYSTON
winding wheel
River Aire
barrier
barrier
Wheldon Road
post
seat

Fryston Basin was used for swimming, while **Fairburn Cut** had a popular lido in the 1930s.

❹ Over **Aire Bridge** follow the track parallel to the railway until a tunnel passes beneath it. Turn right, then fork left to return to the wooded river bank, following it all the way round to **Fryston Basin**. Keep right here and beyond to stay close to the river. After passing another pool the path climbs to reach **New Fryston** village.

❺ Go right of the houses at the end of **Brook Street**, then bear right and join a broad track that sweeps around an open area. Keep straight on to rejoin the river bank the far side beyond a couple of vehicle barriers. Fork right and stay closest to the river as the Aire winds round to **Wheldale Basin**. Keep right and, nearing **Iron Bridge** again, the path bends away from the river to reach Wheldon Road on the edge of **Castleford**.

*a bittern*

The **bittern** is among the most notable seasonal visitors to Fairburn Ings. Having been twice close to extinction in the UK, it has returned but there are still fewer than two hundred males. A type of heron, pale brown with darker streaks, it is elusive and usually camouflaged among reeds. Britain's loudest bird, the bittern is renowned for its booming mating call which sounds like a loudly vibrating phone.

**New Fryston** village was built in 1887 to house workers at Fryston Colliery and it was known as Little Staffordshire as many of the workers moved into the area, as they later would from Newcastle in the 1940s. Its pit was sunk in 1874 and employed as many as 1,300 miners. A strong union pit, it was part of the 68-week strike in 1902-4 and gained a reputation for militancy during the 1980s Miners' Strike, closing soon after in 1985. Many of the terraces and the corrugated iron chapel were pulled down. Recently *Grand Designs* helped create a new green with Antony Gormley iron sculptures and a red winding wheel from the colliery. The area along the River Aire was also landscaped as Fryston Country Trails, with new paths laid out and 40,000 trees planted along the river.

*Allinson's Flour Mill*

ALLINSONS
STONEGROUND
FLOUR

A corn mill known as **Castleford Mill** was located by the River Aire from at least the 11th century, and there may even be evidence of wheat grinding here by the Romans. The first stone mill was built on the site in the 1740s and became the first building in Castleford with electric light and power, in 1885, before being struck by fire in 1897. Dr Thomas Allinson's successors bought the mill in 1921 to produce traditional stoneground flour 'with nowt taken out' and it was enlarged to become the largest stone-grinding mill in the world. Known as **Allinson's Flour Mill**, it was largely water powered until 1970 and continued to produce Allinson's Flour until 2010. As Queen's Mill, it is now a visitor centre and tea rooms alongside the Millennium Bridge. The first **Castleford Cut** was created in 1775 to bypass the weir alongside the mill, though the existing weir is a more substantial one dating from 1826.

# MAP 3: KIPPAX & ALLERTON BYWATER

This area stretches from the Aire-side marshes of St Aidan's Nature Park to Townclose Hills on the edge of Kippax, taking in several separate wooded enclaves linked by former coal railways (including the Lines Way). Hollinhurst Wood and Owl Wood are the finest ancient woods, while Kippax Meadows Park and Townclose Wood are younger plantations on former industrial sites, but all of them are now managed as local nature reserves by the Yorkshire Wildlife Trust.

*There is no public access to the fine beech trees of* ***Preston Wood****, but a path runs around* ***Peasecroft Wood*** *from Fleakingley Lane and others link to Wood Lane and the village hall.*

**Townclose Hills**, **Preston Hill** and **Kippax Meadows** are formed from bluffs of limestone, which is exposed on the White Hills above Oxford Drive and in the railway cutting west of Townclose Hills and was widely quarried for stone and sand. and Townclose Hills are still covered in ash trees, as well as a wide array of wildflowers, including primroses, orchids, cowslips and harebell. It is better known locally as Billy Wood (possibly a shortening of an earlier William Wood), hence one of Medhurst Colliery's two shafts being **Billywood Pit**. The pit closed at the turn of the 20th century, but the site of the adjacent cottages can still be seen.

Kippax Park Hall's facade

**Butt Hill**'s name refers to where archery was once practised in Kippax.

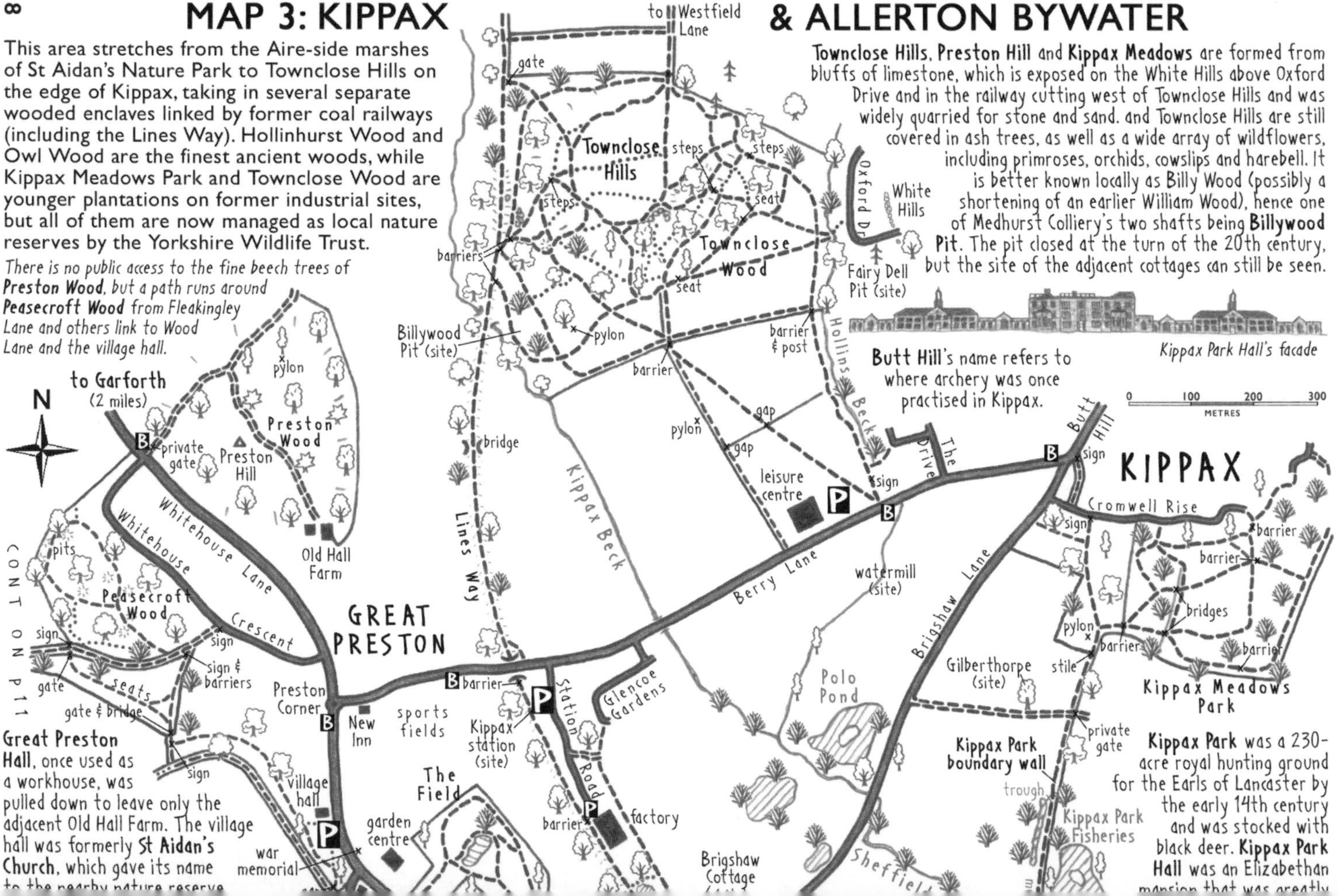

**Great Preston Hall**, once used as a workhouse, was pulled down to leave only the adjacent Old Hall Farm. The village hall was formerly **St Aidan's Church**, which gave its name to the nearby nature reserve

**Kippax Park** was a 230-acre royal hunting ground for the Earls of Lancaster by the early 14th century and was stocked with black deer. **Kippax Park Hall** was an Elizabethan mansion that was greatly

CONT ON P11

A **watermill** at Kippax was mentioned in the Domesday Book, driven by the tiny Hollins Beck. Until the 15th century it was the manorial soke mill for milling corn, as well as Kippax Mill, a windmill east of the village.

***Hollinhurst Wood*** *is a fine oak wood with a maze of paths that can be easily accessed from the roads on all sides.*

**Glow worms** can be seen at Townclose Hills, one of only two such sites in West Yorkshire. A type of beetle, they feed primarily on snails that love limestone soil.

*The main path along the* ***River Aire*** *follows the flood bank around the meanders of its old course. The direct path along its current bank is generally useable on the western* ***oxbow lake****, but overgrown and almost impassable on the eastern oxbow lake.*

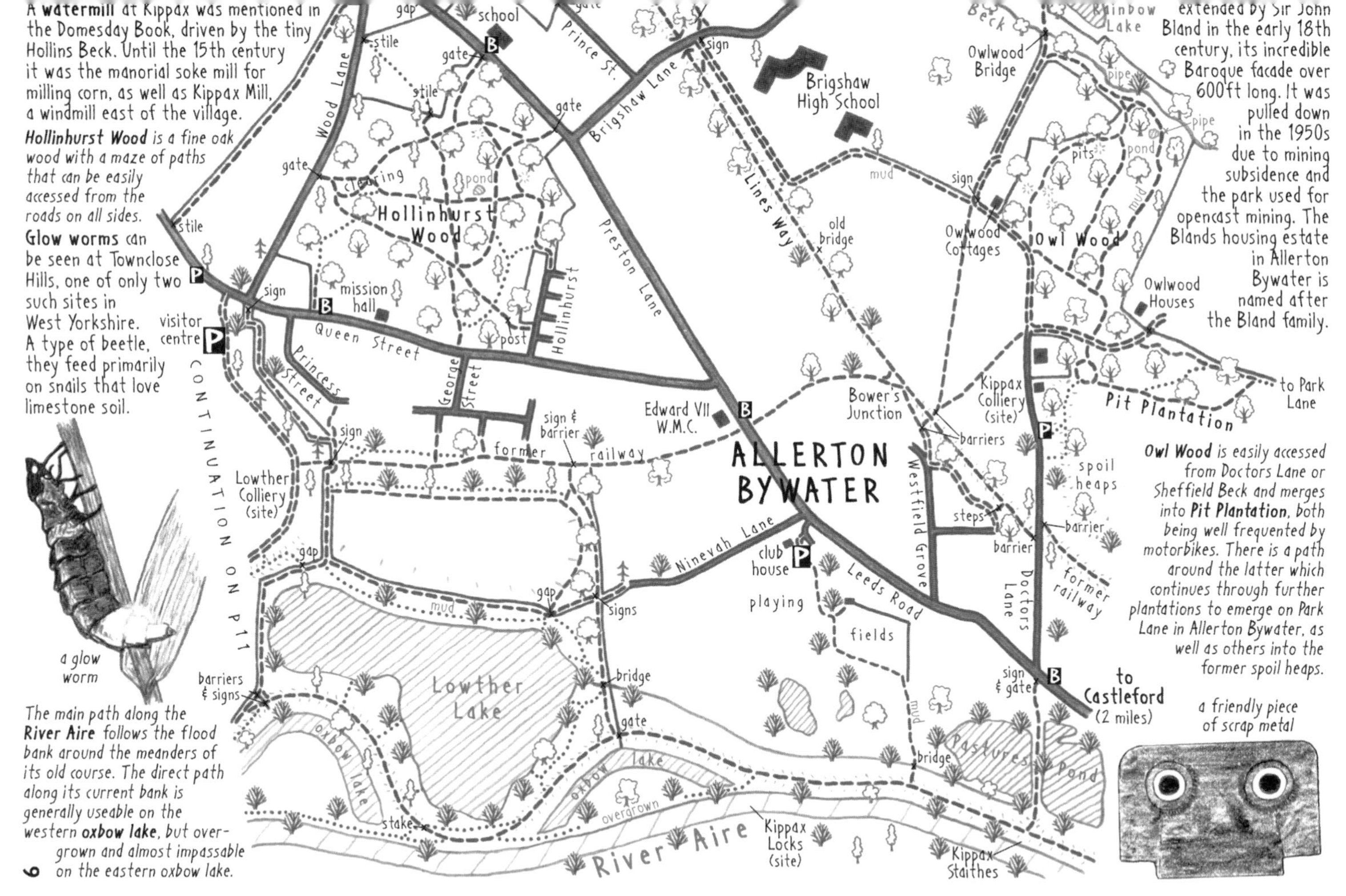

Wood Lane
gap
stile
gate
school
B
Prince St.
Brigshaw Lane
sign
Brigshaw High School
clearing
pond
Hollinhurst Wood
mission hall
post
Hollinhurst
Queen Street
Princess Street
George Street
Preston Lane
P
visitor centre
Lines Way
old bridge
mud
Owlwood Bridge
Owlwood Cottages
Owl Wood
pits
pipe
Rainbow Lake
Beck
Owlwood Houses
Kippax Colliery (site)
Pit Plantation
to Park Lane
Bower's Junction
barriers
Edward VII W.M.C.
sign & barrier
former railway
ALLERTON BYWATER
Westfield Grove
steps
barrier
Doctors Lane
spoil heaps
former railway
Lowther Colliery (site)
Ninevah Lane
club house
playing fields
Leeds Road
signs
bridge
gate
Lowther Lake
oxbow lake
overgrown
stake
barriers & signs
River Aire
Kippax Locks (site)
Kippax Staithes
Pastures Pond
sign & gate
to Castleford (2 miles)
a glow worm
a friendly piece of scrap metal


CONTINUATION ON P11

extended by Sir John Bland in the early 18th century, its incredible Baroque facade over 600ft long. It was pulled down in the 1950s due to mining subsidence and the park used for opencast mining. The Blands housing estate in Allerton Bywater is named after the Bland family.

***Owl Wood*** *is easily accessed from Doctors Lane or Sheffield Beck and merges into* ***Pit Plantation****, both being well frequented by motorbikes. There is a path around the latter which continues through further plantations to emerge on Park Lane in Allerton Bywater, as well as others into the former spoil heaps.*

# MAP 4: ST AIDAN'S

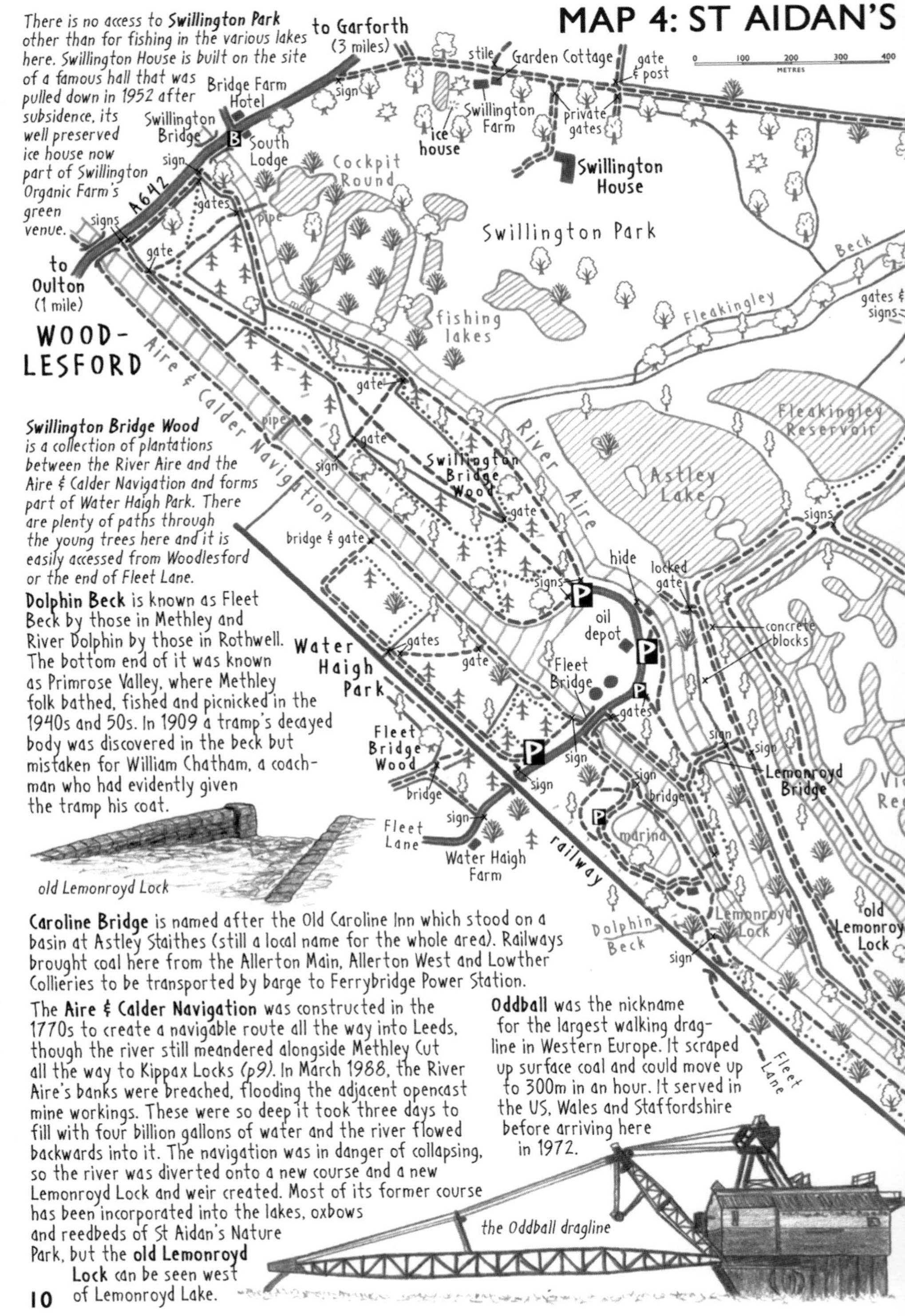

to Garforth
(3 miles)
stile
Garden Cottage
gate & post
0 100 200 300 400
METRES
sign
Bridge Farm Hotel
Swillington Bridge
B
South Lodge
ice house
Swillington Farm
private gates
Swillington House
Cockpit Round
sign
A642
gates
pipe
signs
Swillington Park
Beck
gate
to Oulton
(1 mile)
fishing lakes
Fleakingley
gates & signs
WOOD-
LESFORD
Aire & Calder Navigation
gate
River Aire
Fleakingley Reservoir
pipe
gate
sign
Swillington Bridge Wood
Astley Lake
gate
signs
bridge & gate
hide
locked gate
signs
P
oil depot
concrete blocks
gates
Water Haigh Park
gate
Fleet Bridge
P
gates
sign
sign
Fleet Bridge Wood
sign
Lemonroyd Bridge
bridge
sign
sign
bridge
sign
Fleet Lane
P
marina
railway
Water Haigh Farm
old Lemonroyd Lock
Dolphin Beck
Lemonroyd Lock
sign
Fleet Lane
old Lemonroyd Lock
the Oddball dragline


There is no access to **Swillington Park** other than for fishing in the various lakes here. Swillington House is built on the site of a famous hall that was pulled down in 1952 after subsidence, its well preserved ice house now part of Swillington Organic Farm's green venue.

**Swillington Bridge Wood** is a collection of plantations between the River Aire and the Aire & Calder Navigation and forms part of Water Haigh Park. There are plenty of paths through the young trees here and it is easily accessed from Woodlesford or the end of Fleet Lane.

**Dolphin Beck** is known as Fleet Beck by those in Methley and River Dolphin by those in Rothwell. The bottom end of it was known as Primrose Valley, where Methley folk bathed, fished and picnicked in the 1940s and 50s. In 1909 a tramp's decayed body was discovered in the beck but mistaken for William Chatham, a coachman who had evidently given the tramp his coat.

**Caroline Bridge** is named after the Old Caroline Inn which stood on a basin at Astley Staithes (still a local name for the whole area). Railways brought coal here from the Allerton Main, Allerton West and Lowther Collieries to be transported by barge to Ferrybridge Power Station.

The **Aire & Calder Navigation** was constructed in the 1770s to create a navigable route all the way into Leeds, though the river still meandered alongside Methley Cut all the way to Kippax Locks *(p9)*. In March 1988, the River Aire's banks were breached, flooding the adjacent opencast mine workings. These were so deep it took three days to fill with four billion gallons of water and the river flowed backwards into it. The navigation was in danger of collapsing, so the river was diverted onto a new course and a new Lemonroyd Lock and weir created. Most of its former course has been incorporated into the lakes, oxbows and reedbeds of St Aidan's Nature Park, but the **old Lemonroyd Lock** can be seen west of Lemonroyd Lake.

**Oddball** was the nickname for the largest walking dragline in Western Europe. It scraped up surface coal and could move up to 300m in an hour. It served in the US, Wales and Staffordshire before arriving here in 1972.

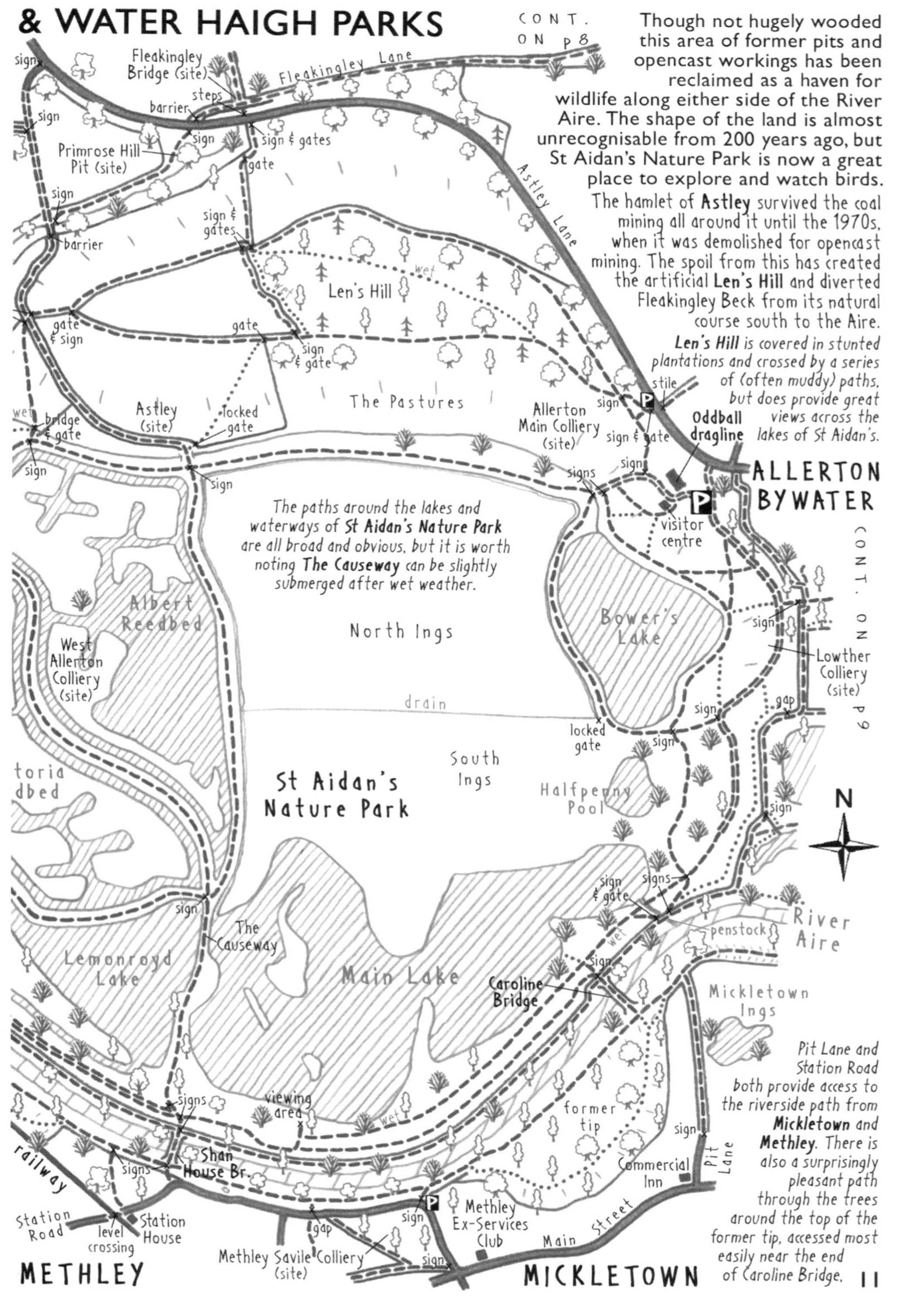

& WATER HAIGH PARKS
CONT. ON p8
Though not hugely wooded this area of former pits and opencast workings has been reclaimed as a haven for wildlife along either side of the River Aire. The shape of the land is almost unrecognisable from 200 years ago, but St Aidan's Nature Park is now a great place to explore and watch birds.
The hamlet of Astley survived the coal mining all around it until the 1970s, when it was demolished for opencast mining. The spoil from this has created the artificial Len's Hill and diverted Fleakingley Beck from its natural course south to the Aire.
Len's Hill is covered in stunted plantations and crossed by a series of (often muddy) paths, but does provide great views across the lakes of St Aidan's.
The paths around the lakes and waterways of St Aidan's Nature Park are all broad and obvious, but it is worth noting The Causeway can be slightly submerged after wet weather.
Pit Lane and Station Road both provide access to the riverside path from Mickletown and Methley. There is also a surprisingly pleasant path through the trees around the top of the former tip, accessed most easily near the end of Caroline Bridge.
Fleakingley Bridge (site)
Fleakingley Lane
steps
barrier
sign
sign & gates
Primrose Hill Pit (site)
gate
sign & gates
barrier
Astley Lane
Len's Hill
wet
gate & sign
gate
sign & gate
The Pastures
Astley (site)
locked gate
bridge & gate
Allerton Main Colliery (site)
stile
sign & gate
Oddball dragline
ALLERTON BYWATER
signs
visitor centre
CONT. ON p9
Albert Reedbed
West Allerton Colliery (site)
North Ings
Bower's Lake
Lowther Colliery (site)
gap
drain
locked gate
South Ings
St Aidan's Nature Park
Halfpenny Pool
toria dbed
N
The Causeway
Lemonroyd Lake
Main Lake
River Aire
penstock
Caroline Bridge
Mickletown Ings
viewing area
former tip
Shan House Br.
railway
Commercial Inn
Pit Lane
Station Road
level crossing
Station House
Methley Savile Colliery (site)
Methley Ex-Services Club
Main Street
METHLEY
MICKLETOWN

# ROUTE 2: ST AIDAN'S NATURE PARK &

**Distance:** 10 miles (16km) *(or 7½ miles (12km) without the loop into Woodlesford)*

**Ascent:** 160m

**Parking:** Free parking in Woodlesford on Eshald Lane and along Fleet Lane. Other parking at Kippax Leisure Centre or the site of the old station.

**Public Transport:** Woodlesford railway station is on the Pontefract Line from Leeds & Wakefield and the Hallam Line between Leeds & Sheffield.

**Character:** A broad exploration of the gentle landscape between Rothwell and Castleford, mixing nature reserves and plantations on former industrial sites with ancient woods and broad arable fields. Good paths throughout, though the mud can be very claggy in winter months.

❶ Turn left out of **Woodlesford railway station** to reach the main road, following it left beneath the railway. Crossing the **Aire & Calder Navigation**, turn right along its far bank for 100m then turn left through a gate. Follow the right-hand path between the plantations of **Swillington Bridge Wood**, then fork left of an artificial hill (a former spoil heap) to enter the trees at a gate and follow a path along the River Aire to the parking area at the end of **Fleet Lane**. Join the road briefly, then bear left onto the riverside embankment by a wooden hide with good views across **St Aidan's Nature Park**. Follow the river bank for another quarter of a mile before crossing **Lemonroyd Bridge**.

❷ Over **Lemonroyd Bridge** turn left and follow a broad track between the reedbeds and lakes of **St Aidan's Nature Park**. Beyond Astley Lake follow the main track left and bear left over a bridge at the next bend, climbing diagonally across the field beyond. At the top turn left on a broad fenced track down to **Fleakingley Beck**, where you turn right (signed 'Fleakingley Bridge'). Head straight across Astley Lane and follow the path of **Fleakingley Lane** straight on up a gentle hill.

**Woodlesford** is a corruption of Wridelsford, from the Old English *wrid* for a bush or thicket.

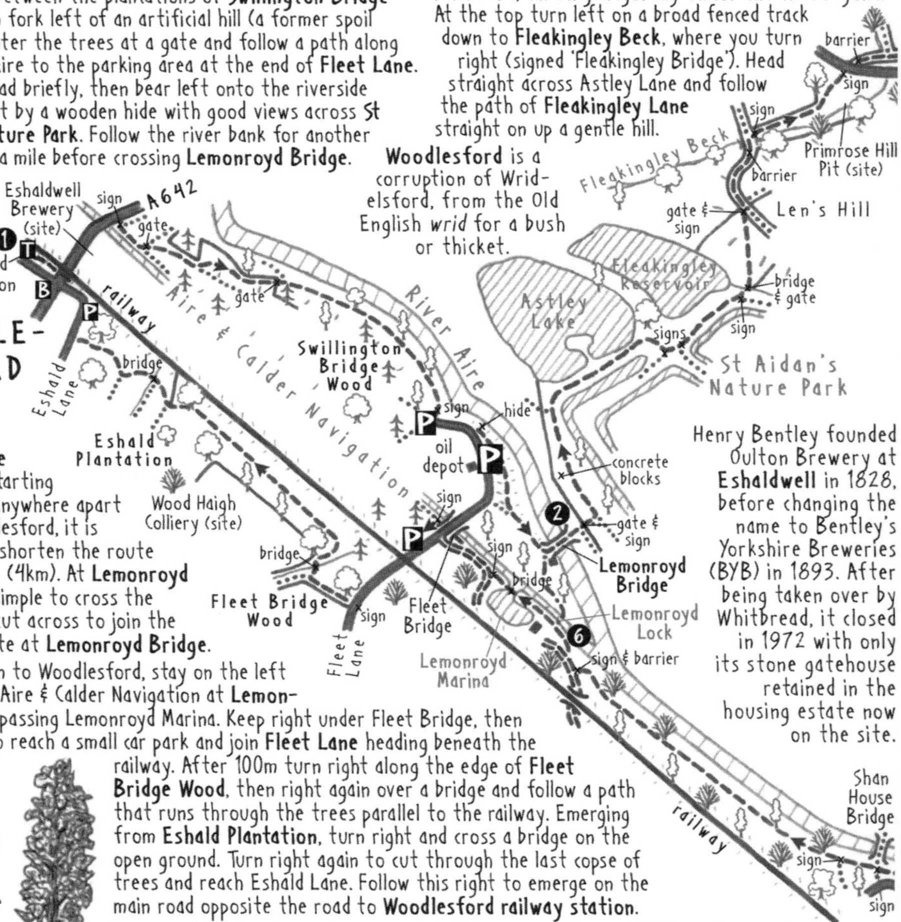

**Alternative route:** If starting the route anywhere apart from Woodlesford, it is possible to shorten the route by 2½ miles (4km). At **Lemonroyd Lock**, it is simple to cross the bridge and cut across to join the onward route at **Lemonroyd Bridge**.

❻ To return to Woodlesford, stay on the left side of the Aire & Calder Navigation at **Lemonroyd Lock**, passing Lemonroyd Marina. Keep right under Fleet Bridge, then turn left to reach a small car park and join **Fleet Lane** heading beneath the railway. After 100m turn right along the edge of **Fleet Bridge Wood**, then right again over a bridge and follow a path that runs through the trees parallel to the railway. Emerging from **Eshald Plantation**, turn right and cross a bridge on the open ground. Turn right again to cut through the last copse of trees and reach Eshald Lane. Follow this right to emerge on the main road opposite the road to **Woodlesford railway station**.

Henry Bentley founded Oulton Brewery at **Eshaldwell** in 1828, before changing the name to Bentley's Yorkshire Breweries (BYB) in 1893. After being taken over by Whitbread, it closed in 1972 with only its stone gatehouse retained in the housing estate now on the site.

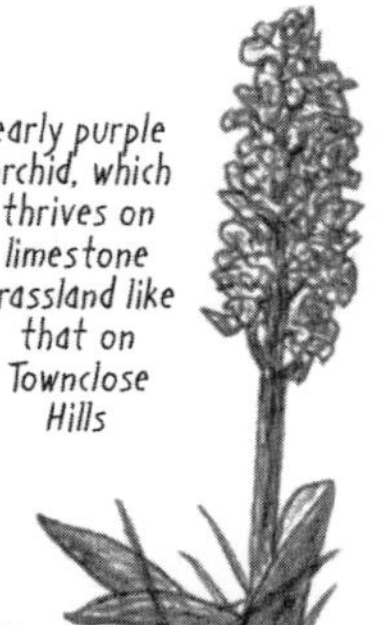

*early purple orchid, which thrives on limestone grassland like that on Townclose Hills*

Deep **coal mining** begun in earnest in this area in the mid 19th century and reshaped the whole landscape, but both Astley and Lowther Collieries were already in operation by then. Water Haigh Pit was sunk in 1901 and the resulting development joined the previously distinct villages of Woodlesford and Oulton. Swillington Bridge Wood covers a colliery spoil tip (or pit stack) that gave off heat for many years. The mines of Allerton Bywater Colliery (to the east of the village) reached across a vast underground area to the A1 and were the last deep mines in the area, closing in 1992.

# TOWNCLOSE HILLS FROM WOODLESFORD

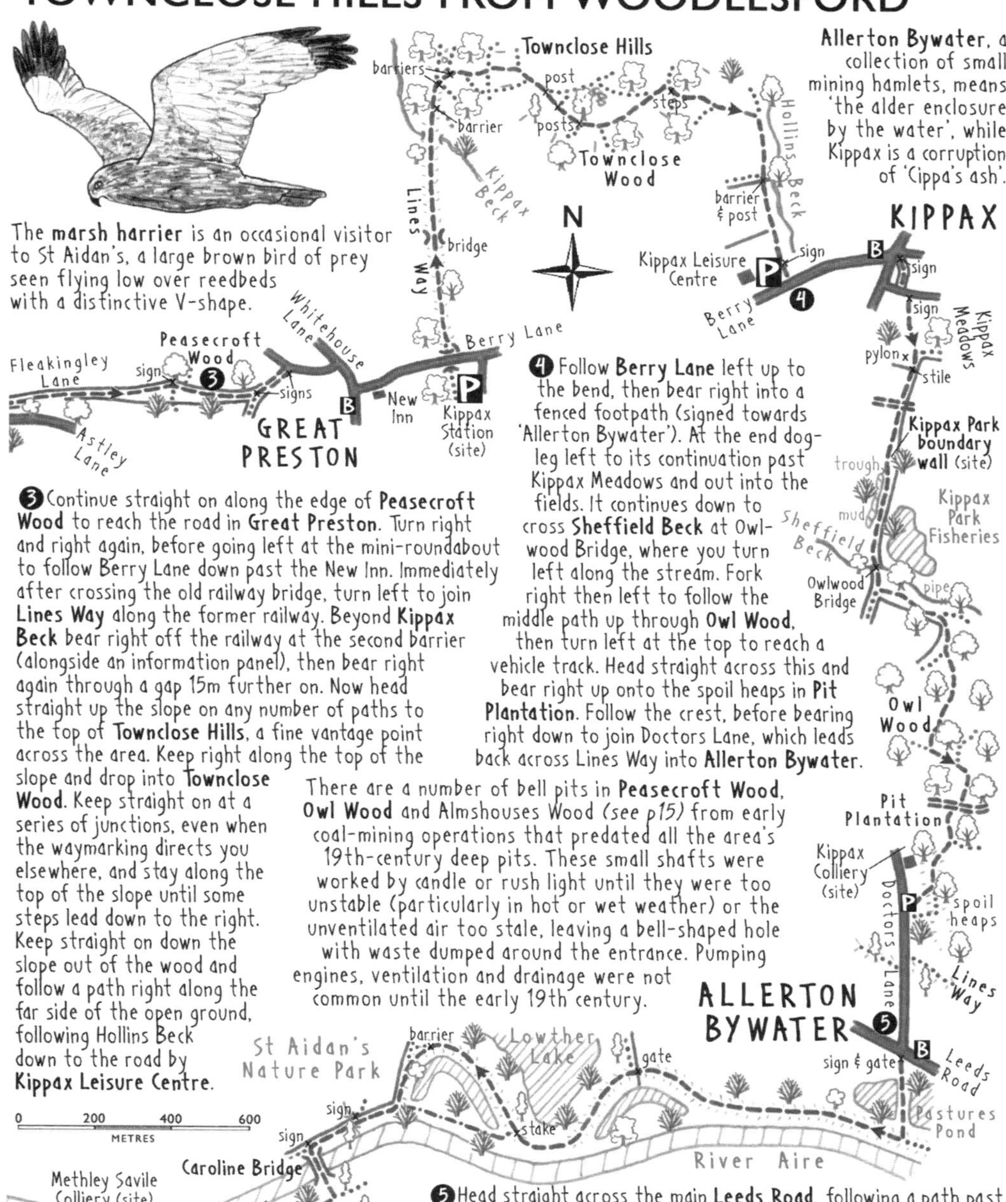

Townclose Hills
barriers
barrier
post
posts
steps
Townclose Wood
Kippax Beck
Lines Way
bridge
N
Hollins Beck
barrier & post
Kippax Leisure Centre
sign
KIPPAX
Berry Lane
sign
Kippax Meadows
pylon
stile
Kippax Park boundary wall (site)
trough
mud
Kippax Park Fisheries
Sheffield Beck
Owlwood Bridge
pipe
Owl Wood
Pit Plantation
Kippax Colliery (site)
spoil heaps
Doctors Lane
Lines Way
ALLERTON BYWATER
Leeds Road
sign & gate
Pastures Pond
River Aire
Lowther Lake
gate
barrier
stake
St Aidan's Nature Park
sign
sign
Caroline Bridge
former tip
Methley Savile Colliery (site)
Station Rd.
sign
MICKLETOWN
0 200 400 600
METRES
Fleakingley Lane
sign
Peasecroft Wood
signs
Whitehouse Lane
Astley Lane
GREAT PRESTON
New Inn
Kippax Station (site)
Berry Lane


The **marsh harrier** is an occasional visitor to St Aidan's, a large brown bird of prey seen flying low over reedbeds with a distinctive V-shape.

**Allerton Bywater**, a collection of small mining hamlets, means 'the alder enclosure by the water', while Kippax is a corruption of 'Cippa's ash'.

❸ Continue straight on along the edge of **Peasecroft Wood** to reach the road in **Great Preston**. Turn right and right again, before going left at the mini-roundabout to follow Berry Lane down past the New Inn. Immediately after crossing the old railway bridge, turn left to join **Lines Way** along the former railway. Beyond **Kippax Beck** bear right off the railway at the second barrier (alongside an information panel), then bear right again through a gap 15m further on. Now head straight up the slope on any number of paths to the top of **Townclose Hills**, a fine vantage point across the area. Keep right along the top of the slope and drop into **Townclose Wood**. Keep straight on at a series of junctions, even when the waymarking directs you elsewhere, and stay along the top of the slope until some steps lead down to the right. Keep straight on down the slope out of the wood and follow a path right along the far side of the open ground, following Hollins Beck down to the road by **Kippax Leisure Centre**.

❹ Follow **Berry Lane** left up to the bend, then bear right into a fenced footpath (signed towards 'Allerton Bywater'). At the end dog-leg left to its continuation past Kippax Meadows and out into the fields. It continues down to cross **Sheffield Beck** at Owlwood Bridge, where you turn left along the stream. Fork right then left to follow the middle path up through **Owl Wood**, then turn left at the top to reach a vehicle track. Head straight across this and bear right up onto the spoil heaps in **Pit Plantation**. Follow the crest, before bearing right down to join Doctors Lane, which leads back across Lines Way into **Allerton Bywater**.

There are a number of bell pits in **Peasecroft Wood**, **Owl Wood** and Almshouses Wood *(see p15)* from early coal-mining operations that predated all the area's 19th-century deep pits. These small shafts were worked by candle or rush light until they were too unstable (particularly in hot or wet weather) or the unventilated air too stale, leaving a bell-shaped hole with waste dumped around the entrance. Pumping engines, ventilation and drainage were not common until the early 19th century.

❺ Head straight across the main **Leeds Road**, following a path past Pastures Pond to the **River Aire**. Turn right along the riverside embankment and follow it for over a mile round a pair of oxbow lakes from the river's former course. It is possible to bear left before the second of these and follow the river bank, but this faint path can be overgrown in late summer. The main path continues along the river to **Caroline Bridge**; cross here and turn right by the mound of a former tip. Stay along the river for over a mile, passing **Shan House Bridge** and eventually reaching a vehicle track. Turn right and keep right to emerge by **Lemonroyd Lock**.

The original course of the **River Aire** is evident in places through the oxbow lakes of its meanders, which were artificially by-passed by the Methley Cut in the 1770s to improve the Aire & Calder Navigation, which had made the river navigable all the way to Leeds by 1704.

# ROUTE 3: OULTON & METHLEY PARKS

❶ From **Woodlesford railway station** follow Station Lane left, then turn right along the A642 into the village. Opposite the Co-op turn left to reach a gap into **Water Haigh Park** and go straight on between the plantations. Bear right over a bridge and join Eshald Lane at the far corner of the park. At the T-junction go straight over into a footpath, then turn right before the bridge over **Dolphin Beck**. Follow the stream into **Oulton** and turn left along the road. Go straight on by the New Masons Arms, then cross the A639 by the Three Horse Shoes (there is a crossing 200m left if needed). Just to the right go through the ornate gateway to **St John's Church** and pass to the right of the building before following a vehicle track to reach Oulton Hall's main drive.

Clay was extracted from **Robin Hood's Quarry** for brick-making. It is now part of **Water Haigh Park**, made up of former pits and spoil heaps on either side of the railway and canal.

**Oulton** is a corruption of Out-ton, referring to land on the edge of Rothwell manor. Its common was enclosed by Royal Assent in 1809 to create **Oulton Park**, but **Oulton Hall** was not built until the 1850s by John Blayds after a fire at the former expanded farmhouse. It was used as a convalescent home and hospital in the 20th century, but fell into ruin before being restored in the 1990s as a hotel with a 27-hole golf course.

❷ To see **Oulton Hall** you need to follow the drive left for quarter of a mile, but the onward route bears right across the drive onto a path that initially runs alongside the A654. After it pulls away from the road, fork right at a waymark post through the fine trees of **Beeston Wood** – there are some particularly beautiful sweet chestnut trees. At the next junction continue straight on, then turn left to follow the far edge of **Oulton Park**, which is mostly taken up by a golf course. Keep straight on and, 200m after passing the end of Muirfield Drive, turn right to stay in the trees and join a path alongside **Royds Lane**. By Keepers Cottage go straight across the track, then bear right into the trees before turning next left in the delightfully named **Dick Haste Wood**. Follow the edge of the park, then keep right to emerge on the A642 through an old gravel pit.

This area will be greatly affected by **HS2** if it ever materialises, with the Leeds and York lines cutting straight across Methley Park, Water Haigh Park and Swillington Bridge Wood, including the ancient woodland of Moss Carr Wood and the Site of Ecological and Geological Importance at Cockpit Round.

Intriguingly named **Cheesecake Hall** was an early 16th-century timber-framed house of which nothing now remains.

The **Iron Age settlement** near Moss Carr was excavated in 2001, when it was under threat from planned opencast mining operations. Though barely detectable in the open field, three ditched enclosures and six roundhouses were found and are part of a site that likely extends under Moss Carr Wood.

❸ Follow the **A642** right to a signed path leading left opposite the next road junction. Follow the left edge of the field, then turn right at the end, following a broad grassy path as it bends round to the left. At the end turn left and skirt along the edge of the mixed ancient wood of **Moss Carr Wood** (to which there is sadly no access). After half a mile turn left to stay alongside the trees and descend to **Hungate Lane**.

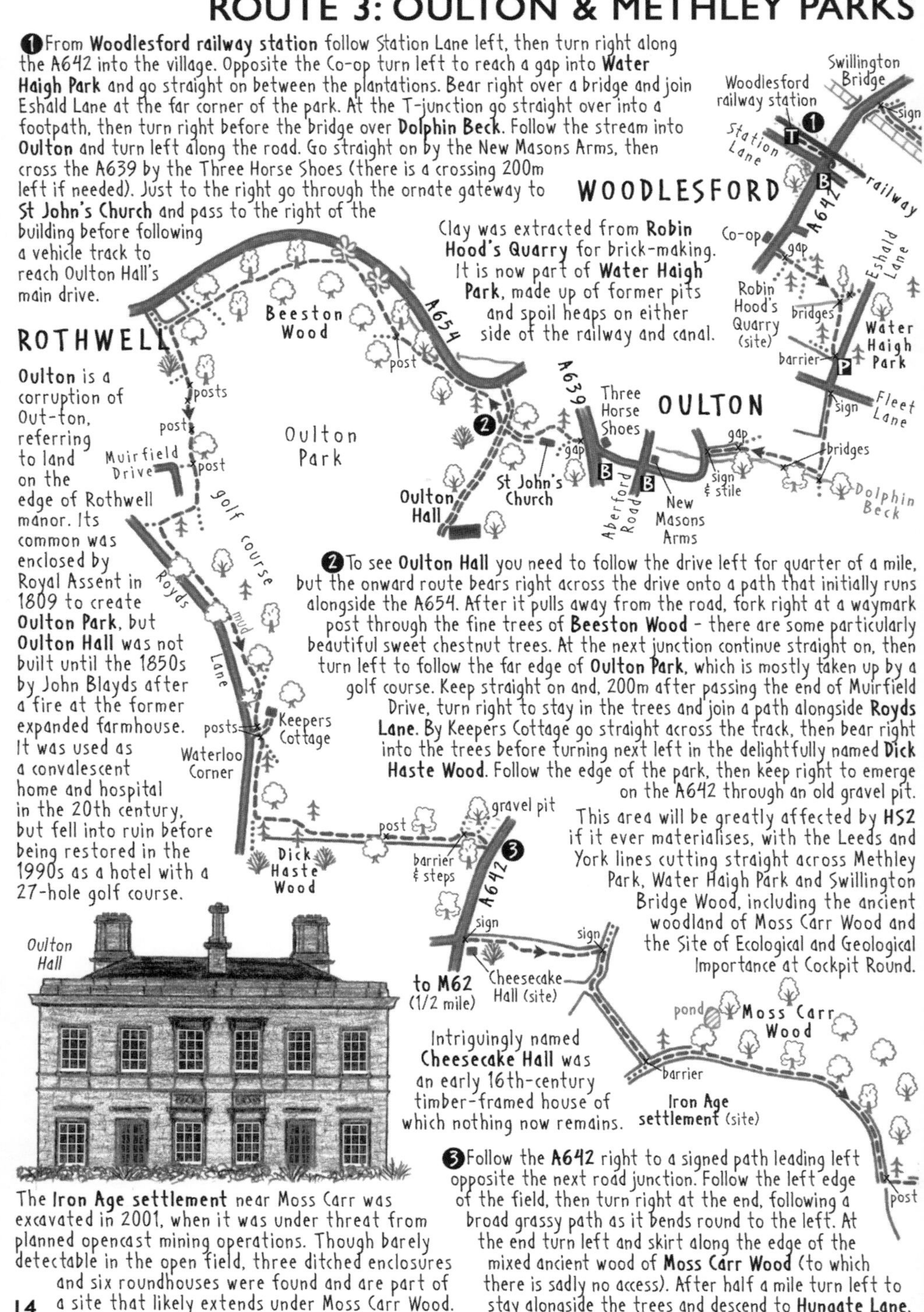

Swillington Bridge
Woodlesford railway station
sign
Station Lane
railway
WOODLESFORD
A642
Co-op
gap
Robin Hood's Quarry (site)
bridges
Eshald Lane
Water Haigh Park
barrier
Fleet Lane
sign
OULTON
A639
Three Horse Shoes
gap
bridges
sign & stile
Dolphin Beck
St John's Church
Oulton Hall
Aberford Road
New Masons Arms
A654
Beeston Wood
post
ROTHWELL
posts
post
Muirfield Drive
post
Oulton Park
golf course
Royds Lane
mud
Keepers Cottage
posts
Waterloo Corner
Dick Haste Wood
post
gravel pit
barrier & steps
A642
sign
sign
Cheesecake Hall (site)
to M62 (1/2 mile)
pond
Moss Carr Wood
barrier
Iron Age settlement (site)
post
Oulton Hall

# FROM WOODLESFORD

**Distance:** 9 miles (14.5km)

**Ascent:** 130m

**Parking:** Free parking on Eshald Lane and Fleet Lane in Woodlesford/Oulton.

**Public Transport:** Woodlesford railway station is on the Pontefract Line between Leeds and Wakefield, and the Hallam Line between Leeds and Sheffield.

**Character:** A gentle route linking the woods of Oulton and Methley Parks with St Aidan's Nature Park. Though you see neither great house (Methley Hall because it was pulled down), the landscape is full of varied woodland, and there are many chances to spot wildlife.

**4** Follow **Hungate Lane** left for 200m, then turn left on a well signed path through **Methley Park**. Join a fenced path past the trees of The Rookery, then cut right through a gate to join a track near the site of **Methley Hall** (of its few remains only the ice house is publicly accessible near the kitchen garden). Follow the track left along the edge of the wood, passing to the left of the large red brick kitchen garden. Stay on the track through the giant beeches of **Almshouses Wood** to emerge past the lodge and former almshouses. Where the track bends left, continue straight on across the field and join another track by Melwood House Farm to reach the **A639**.

**5** Follow the A639 right into **Methley**, bearing second left along Station Road. Over the level crossing by the former station house, turn immediately left into the trees then right to reach **Shan House Bridge**. Cross the River Aire and continue straight on into **St Aidan's Nature Park**, dropping down to follow a causeway between Lemonroyd and Main Lakes. Carry straight on at the first junction and bear left then immediately right at the second, passing Astley Lake and some large concrete blocks. Turn right just before a sign and recross the river at **Lemonroyd Bridge**.

**Alternative Route:** If the causeway is too flooded or you want to shorten the route a little, it is simple to follow one of the paths alongside the river between Shan House and Lemonroyd Bridges.

**6** Keep right beyond **Lemonroyd Bridge** and follow the river to join Fleet Lane by a hide. At the car park at its end, head up the middle path through **Swillington Bridge Wood** (another part of Water Haigh Park). Turn left just before a gate, then keep right to follow a fenceline across the slope until a path leads down to the **Aire & Calder Navigation**. Follow this right to reach the A642, following the road left over Swillington Bridge back into **Woodlesford**.

Victoria and Albert Reedbeds are named after pits at nearby Allerton Main Colliery, though they cover ground where West Allerton Colliery once stood.

**Methley Hall** was rebuilt in grand style on an ancient manorial seat by Sir John Savile in 1588. The woods have all been managed for coppicing and, while Dutch elm disease saw to the elm trees that once lined the driveway, there are still some wonderful ancient oak trees standing in the open parkland. The 60-room mansion was in poor condition when Sir Titus Salt chose to lease it for his family home in 1856, adorning it with mock castellations and turrets, and building glasshouses and vineries to cultivate fruit and flowers. He moved to Crow Nest in 1865 and, though **Methley Park** is still owned by the Mexborough Estate, the run-down hall was requisitioned by the army during both world wars before being pulled down in 1963 after suffering subsidence due to mining. Only its cellars and a few outbuilding walls remain.

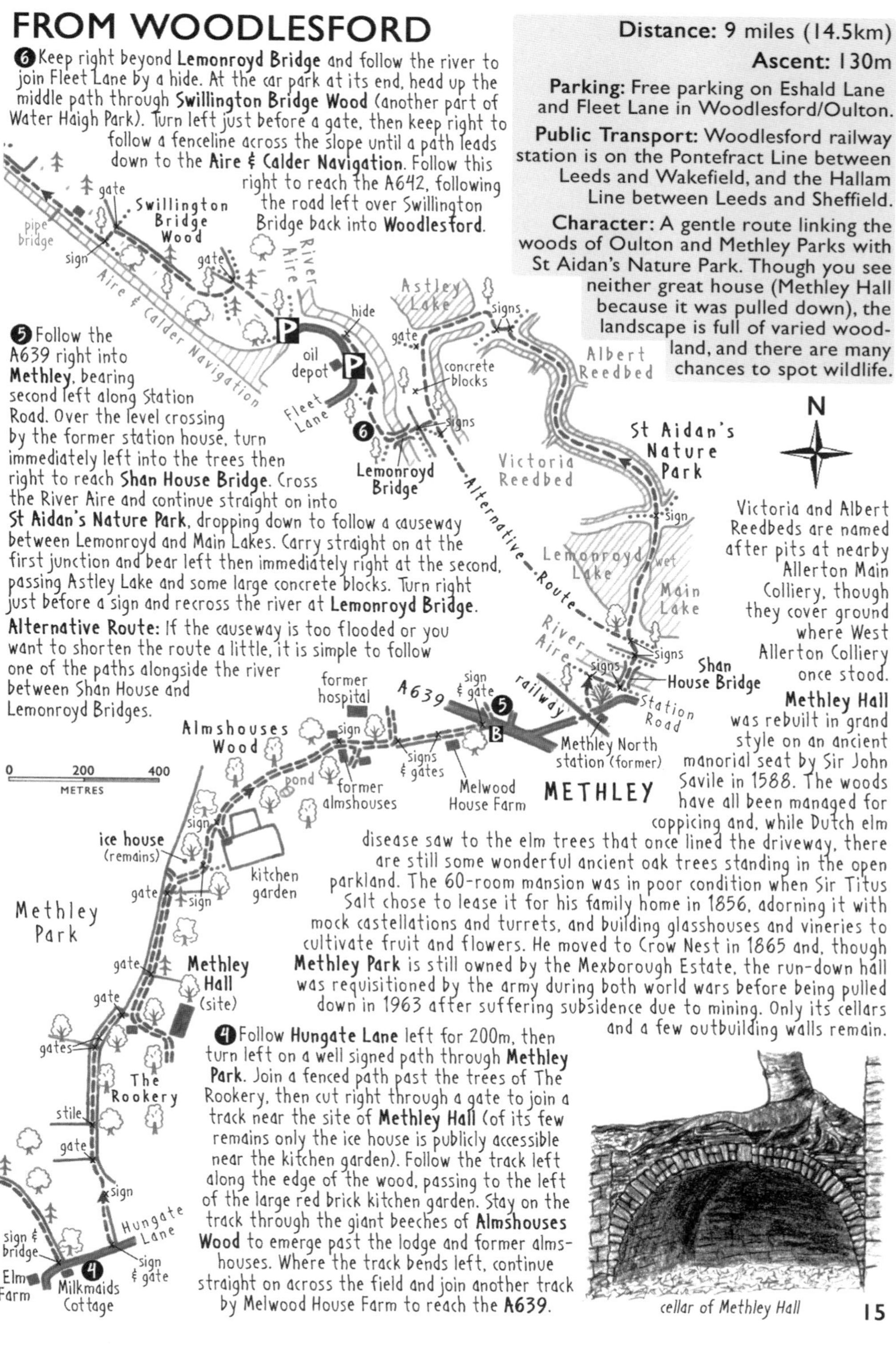

Swillington Bridge Wood
gate
pipe bridge
sign
Aire & Calder Navigation
River Aire
hide
oil depot
Fleet Lane
Astley Lake
signs
concrete blocks
Albert Reedbed
Lemonroyd Bridge
Alternative Route
Victoria Reedbed
St Aidan's Nature Park
N
Lemonroyd Lake
wet
Main Lake
Shan House Bridge
Station Road
railway
Methley North station (former)
A639
sign & gate
former hospital
Almshouses Wood
former almshouses
signs & gates
Melwood House Farm
METHLEY
pond
0 200 400
METRES
ice house (remains)
kitchen garden
Methley Park
Methley Hall (site)
gates
The Rookery
stile
Hungate Lane
sign & bridge
Elm Farm
Milkmaids Cottage


*cellar of Methley Hall*

# TAWNY OWLS

The tawny owl (which has also been known as the brown, wood, beech and ivy owl) is the most common and widespread owl in the UK, but is rarely seen because of its camouflage and nocturnal habits. It nests in trees, making its long-term home in woodland and older trees around settlements. The tawny owl has brown streaked plumage that is paler on the underside, big black eyes and a large rounded head. Its tail is very short due to its small wings that make it very adept at moving quickly through woodland. The female is slightly larger than the male.

Hunting almost exclusively by night, all owls are remarkably evolved, deadly predators. Their feathers are particularly soft so as not to make a noise when in flight, and those on their head are designed to funnel the slightest noise to their ears, which are on slightly different levels to allow them to accurately triangulate the sound. With an ability to silently swivel its head in any direction, not much escapes an owl's notice. The tawny has the most varied diet of any owl, but is still reliant on catching small mammals, birds, frogs, insects or worms.

The tawny owl breeds early in the year, so is most likely seen or heard in the autumn, when the young are driven from the nest to seek out new territories and a mate. Around 75% do not make it, eaten by foxes or starved if they fail to find a suitable nest. Its distinctive 'twit-twoo' call is the combination of a call by the female being answered immediately by the male (whose eerie hoot was once thought to be an omen of bad luck or even death). It is most often heard on a cloudy evening; on a clear night, owls are more likely to be hunting. The tawny owl generally nests in holes in mature broadleaf trees (or sometimes in provided owl boxes) and a mating pair will stay together for life in the same nest. Its typical lifespan is four to five years, but some ringed birds have been known to live for over twenty years.

There are thought to be anywhere between 20,000-50,000 pairs of tawny owls in the UK, but they are notoriously hard to count. As they don't like flying over water, tawnies are not present on many islands, nor indeed Ireland. It is thought their numbers have declined this century, possibly as a result of loss of habitats and prey, or light pollution, which hinders its ability to hunt efficiently. It was put on the Amber List of Birds of Conservation Concern in 2015.

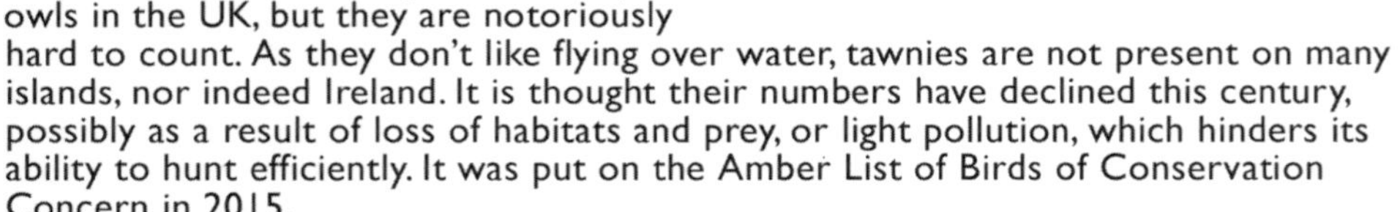

Usually assumed to be wise birds because of their large bespectacled eyes, owls are now thought not to be particularly intelligent, certainly compared to corvids and parrots, which are far more social creatures. In India owls are traditionally considered stupid, but our reverence may be because the Greek goddess of wisdom, Athena, often had an owl on her shoulder.

In Leeds it is the European eagle owl that became an important symbol on the city's first coat of arms in 1626, despite this species not being present in the country at the time. This imagery was directly inherited from the Savile family's coat of arms, as Sir John Savile was the borough's first alderman; the owls on the Calverley family's coat of arms, and the name's proliferation around Rodley, derived from the same source. Leeds Town Hall once had a three-foot high owl on its apex, but as many as twenty-four remain around the city, with several visited by the Leeds Owl Trail.

# CHAPTER 2 - LEEDS

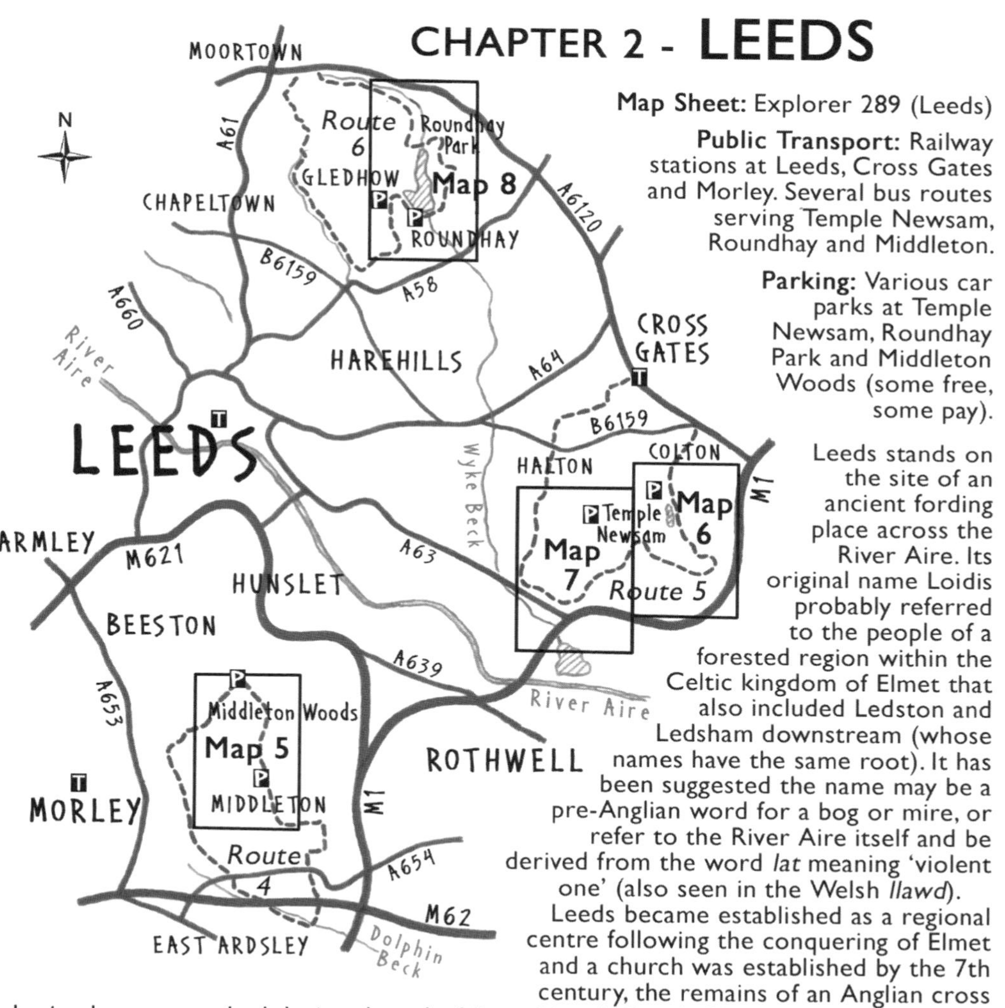
N
MOORTOWN
A61
Route 6
Roundhay Park
GLEDHOW
Map 8
CHAPELTOWN
ROUNDHAY
A6120
B6159
A58
A660
River Aire
HAREHILLS
CROSS GATES
A64
LEEDS
B6159
HALTON
COLTON
Wyke Beck
Temple Newsam
Map 6
Map 7
Route 5
M1
ARMLEY
M621
A63
HUNSLET
BEESTON
A639
River Aire
A653
Middleton Woods
Map 5
MIDDLETON
MORLEY
ROTHWELL
M1
Route 4
A654
M62
EAST ARDSLEY
Dolphin Beck

**Map Sheet:** Explorer 289 (Leeds)

**Public Transport:** Railway stations at Leeds, Cross Gates and Morley. Several bus routes serving Temple Newsam, Roundhay and Middleton.

**Parking:** Various car parks at Temple Newsam, Roundhay Park and Middleton Woods (some free, some pay).

Leeds stands on the site of an ancient fording place across the River Aire. Its original name Loidis probably referred to the people of a forested region within the Celtic kingdom of Elmet that also included Ledston and Ledsham downstream (whose names have the same root). It has been suggested the name may be a pre-Anglian word for a bog or mire, or refer to the River Aire itself and be derived from the word *lat* meaning 'violent one' (also seen in the Welsh *llawd*).

Leeds became established as a regional centre following the conquering of Elmet and a church was established by the 7th century, the remains of an Anglian cross having been unearthed during the rebuilding of Leeds Parish Church in 1837. Referred to as Ledes in the Domesday Book, it prospered where other settlements were diminished after the Normans laid waste to much of the region. Having received its first charter in 1207, the new town centred around Briggate grew to be significant enough to receive a Royal Charter in 1626 to regulate its growing cloth trade. Leeds borough originally lay entirely on the north side of the River Aire, but its parish later extended to include Armley, Hunslet and Holbeck. During the 19th century, Leeds' population grew eight-fold to over 400,000 to become the city we know today.

Though the city is not greatly wooded, industry having removed any greenery along the River Aire itself, it has some fantastic woodland and parkland areas scattered around its suburbs. This chapter does not include the Meanwood Valley, Bramley Fall and the woods of Horsforth and Ireland Wood, as these are covered in separate chapters, instead focusing on Middleton Woods, Temple Newsam Park and Roundhay Park. Middleton Woods is a wonderful ancient woodland with great views over the city centre. Temple Newsam, the largest of Leeds' parks at 935 acres, is named after the Knights Templar and centres on its 17th-century mansion. Roundhay Park, once a Norman deer park, is a beautiful area of parkland that has been the flagship of Leeds' public spaces since its acquisition in 1872.

# MAP 5: MIDDLETON PARK & WOODS

Middleton Park is a remnant of the manorial estate of Middleton Hall and is now owned by the City of Leeds. Land was acquired in Middleton and Belle Isle from the Middleton Estate & Colliery Co. to house the population cleared from the city's slums in the 1920s, and the woodlands were retained as a recreational space. It remains a rare green enclave in south Leeds that is easily accessed from all sides. The ancient oak woodlands of Middleton and Beeston Park are riddled with bell pits, shafts and tramways from early coal mining, while the areas of colliery spoil on either side have been reclaimed and planted with trees.

After a messy boundary dispute in the early 13th century between Adam de Beeston and William de Gramary, **Park Wood** was partitioned between Beeston and Middleton Parks. Local knights dug a ditch and bank to demarcate this, a line still clearly evident.

***Park Wood*** *(also known as Beeston Woods) is difficult to navigate as some of the most obvious tracks are mountain bike trails that it would be unwise to walk on. Most of these are near the top of the wood and well signed as bike routes. Lower down near the barely visible stream there are several routes across the slope and a whole series of well preserved* ***bell pits****, while halfway up the slope a faint path* follows the line of the 13th-century ***boundary ditch***.

**Ring Road** was built by navvies in the 1920s, cutting through an area of colliery waste between Beeston and Middleton.

*The western edge of the park is now taken up with* ***Leeds Urban Bike Park****. Though there are many tracks here, you are wise to stick to the footpaths in the woods. A wide track leads from the car park to the* ***Rose Garden****, while another skirts left of the centre to join up with* ***Balkcliffe Lane****.*

to Crossflats Park
Southleigh Drive
barrier
BEESTON PARK SIDE
bell pits
bike
Cockburn School
bridge & sign
bell pits
Park Wood
to Beeston (1 mile)
Gipsy Lane
barrier
bridge
boundary ditch
bike trails
The
barriers
sign
golf course
bell pits
bike trails
South Leeds Golf Club
Wood Pit (site)
seat
sign
barrier
signs
sign
ice house (footings)
sign
Balkcliffe Lane
barrier
Middleton Lodge (site)
sign
bike trails
sign
old fairways
Rose Garden
Nick's View
lake
Bodmin Road
barrier
seat
visitor centre
barrier
Leeds Urban Bike Park
Middleton Park
tennis courts
P
Ring Road
bike trails
old fairways
barrier
Hall Pond
seat
barrier
seat
Middleton Water Tower
barrier
sign
Town St
to Middleton Circus
Middleton Hall (site)


*shaft mound in Middleton Wood*

*Middleton Water Tower*

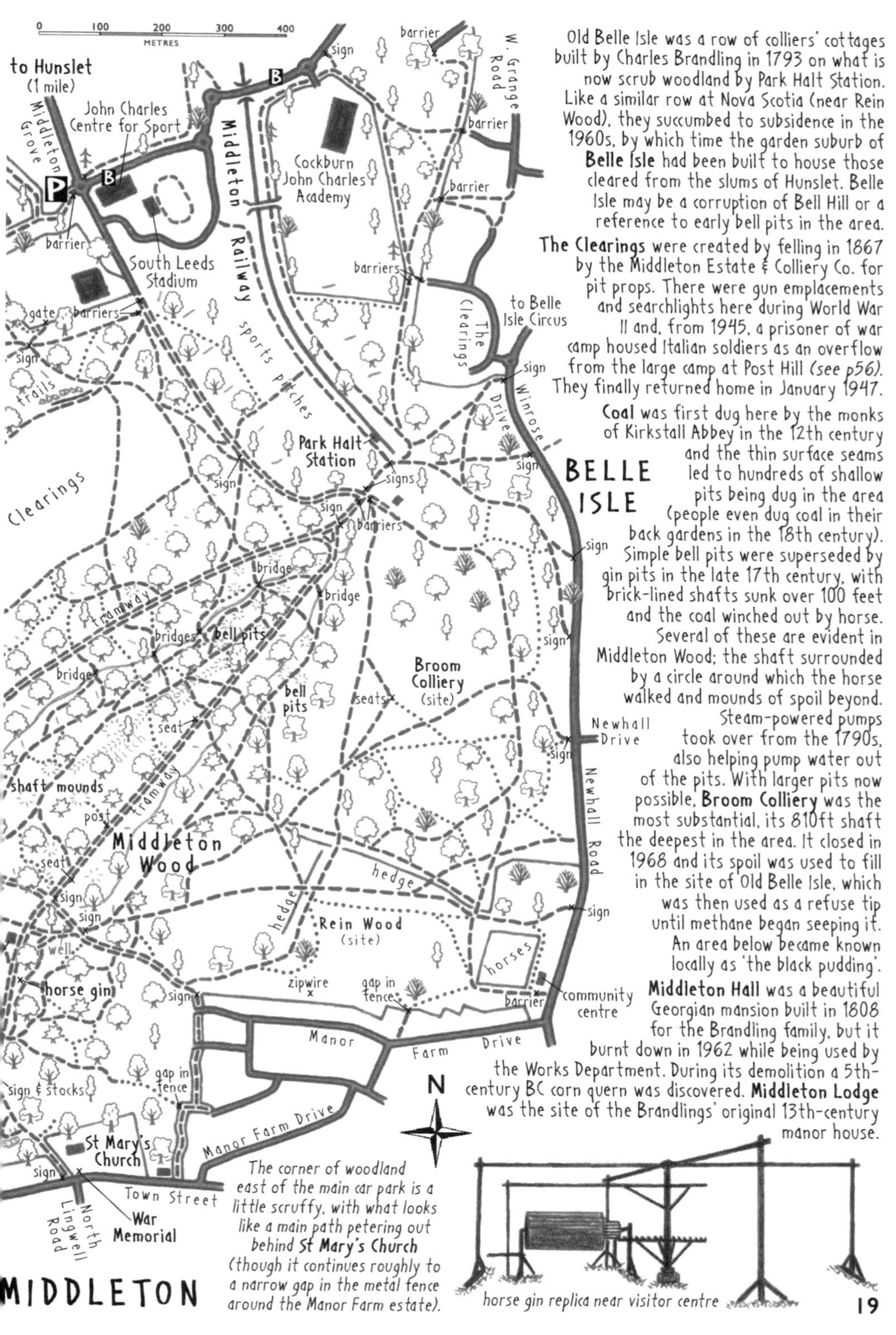
0 100 200 300 400
METRES
to Hunslet
(1 mile)
Middleton Grove
John Charles Centre for Sport
B
P
barrier
South Leeds Stadium
Middleton Railway
Cockburn John Charles Academy
barrier
sign
W. Grange Road
barrier
barrier
barriers
The Clearings
to Belle Isle Circus
sign
Winrose Drive
gate
barriers
sign
trails
sports pitches
Park Halt Station
signs
sign
sign
barriers
Clearings
BELLE ISLE
sign
bridge
bridge
tramway
bridges
bell pits
bridge
sign
Broom Colliery
(site)
seats
bell pits
seat
ditch
Newhall Drive
sign
Newhall Road
shaft mounds
tramway
post
Middleton Wood
seat
sign
sign
hedge
hedge
sign
Rein Wood
(site)
well
horses
horse gin
sign
zipwire
gap in fence
barrier
community centre
Manor Farm Drive
gap in fence
sign & stocks
Manor Farm Drive
St Mary's Church
N
sign
Town Street
North Lingwell Road
War Memorial
MIDDLETON

Old Belle Isle was a row of colliers' cottages built by Charles Brandling in 1793 on what is now scrub woodland by Park Halt Station. Like a similar row at Nova Scotia (near Rein Wood), they succumbed to subsidence in the 1960s, by which time the garden suburb of **Belle Isle** had been built to house those cleared from the slums of Hunslet. Belle Isle may be a corruption of Bell Hill or a reference to early bell pits in the area.

**The Clearings** were created by felling in 1867 by the Middleton Estate & Colliery Co. for pit props. There were gun emplacements and searchlights here during World War II and, from 1945, a prisoner of war camp housed Italian soldiers as an overflow from the large camp at Post Hill *(see p56)*. They finally returned home in January 1947.

**Coal** was first dug here by the monks of Kirkstall Abbey in the 12th century and the thin surface seams led to hundreds of shallow pits being dug in the area (people even dug coal in their back gardens in the 18th century). Simple bell pits were superseded by gin pits in the late 17th century, with brick-lined shafts sunk over 100 feet and the coal winched out by horse. Several of these are evident in Middleton Wood; the shaft surrounded by a circle around which the horse walked and mounds of spoil beyond. Steam-powered pumps took over from the 1790s, also helping pump water out of the pits. With larger pits now possible, **Broom Colliery** was the most substantial, its 810ft shaft the deepest in the area. It closed in 1968 and its spoil was used to fill in the site of Old Belle Isle, which was then used as a refuse tip until methane began seeping it. An area below became known locally as 'the black pudding'.

**Middleton Hall** was a beautiful Georgian mansion built in 1808 for the Brandling family, but it burnt down in 1962 while being used by the Works Department. During its demolition a 5th-century BC corn quern was discovered. **Middleton Lodge** was the site of the Brandlings' original 13th-century manor house.

*The corner of woodland east of the main car park is a little scruffy, with what looks like a main path petering out behind* **St Mary's Church** *(though it continues roughly to a narrow gap in the metal fence around the Manor Farm estate).*

*horse gin replica near visitor centre*

# ROUTE 4: MIDDLETON PARK & ARDSLEY FALL FROM MIDDLETON

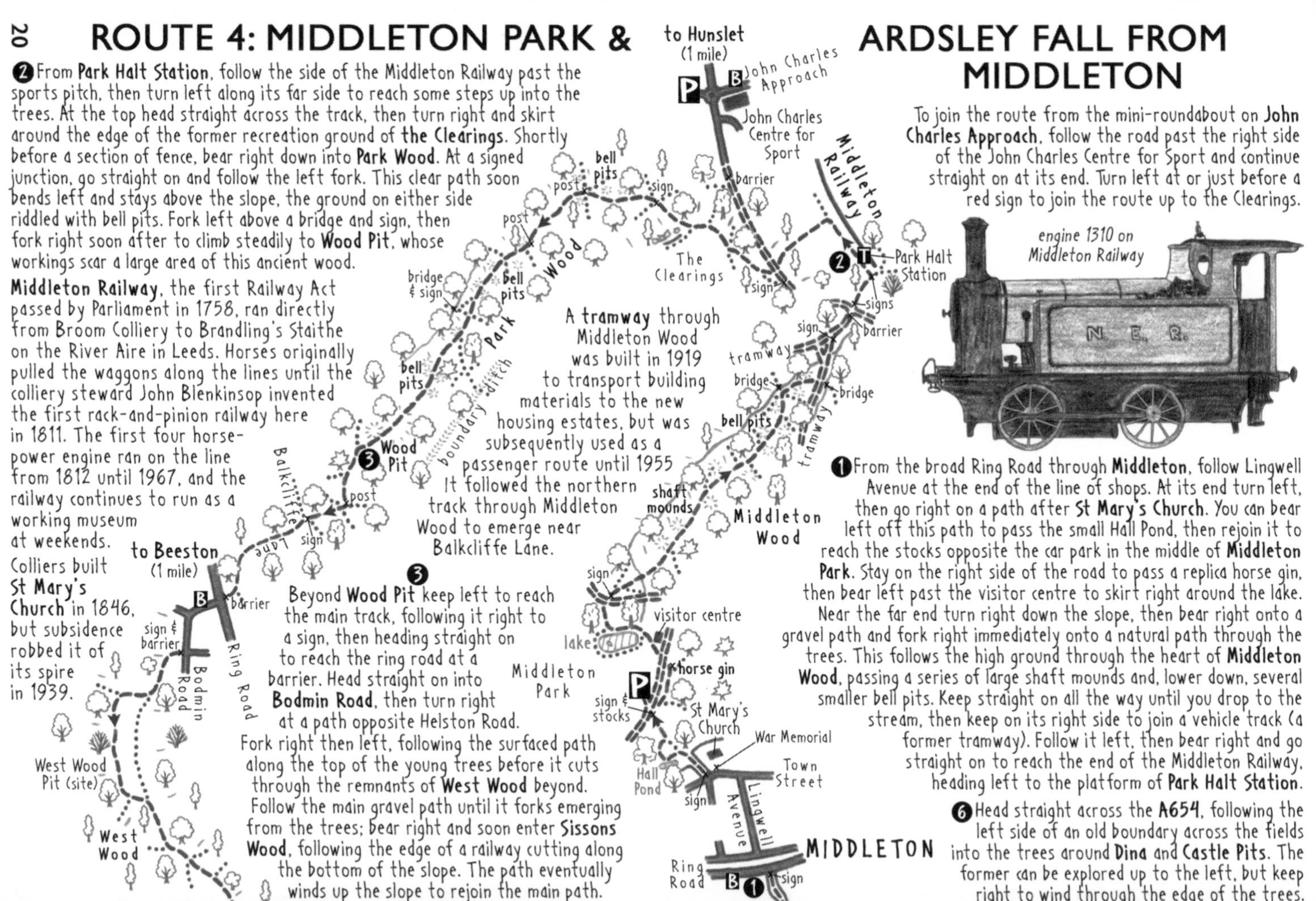
to Hunslet
(1 mile)
John Charles Approach
John Charles Centre for Sport
Middleton Railway
barrier
sign
Park Halt Station
signs
barrier
bell pits
post
The Clearings
Wood
Park
bridge & sign
bell pits
boundary ditch
Wood Pit
post
Balkcliffe Lane
sign
to Beeston
(1 mile)
barrier
Ring Road
sign & barrier
Bodmin Road
West Wood Pit (site)
West Wood
tramway
bridge
bell pits
shaft mounds
Middleton Wood
visitor centre
lake
horse gin
Middleton Park
sign & stocks
St Mary's Church
War Memorial
Town Street
Hall Pond
Lingwell Avenue
MIDDLETON
Ring Road
engine 1310 on Middleton Railway

To join the route from the mini-roundabout on **John Charles Approach**, follow the road past the right side of the John Charles Centre for Sport and continue straight on at its end. Turn left at or just before a red sign to join the route up to the Clearings.

**1** From the broad Ring Road through **Middleton**, follow Lingwell Avenue at the end of the line of shops. At its end turn left, then go right on a path after **St Mary's Church**. You can bear left off this path to pass the small Hall Pond, then rejoin it to reach the stocks opposite the car park in the middle of **Middleton Park**. Stay on the right side of the road to pass a replica horse gin, then bear left past the visitor centre to skirt right around the lake. Near the far end turn right down the slope, then bear right onto a gravel path and fork right immediately onto a natural path through the trees. This follows the high ground through the heart of **Middleton Wood**, passing a series of large shaft mounds and, lower down, several smaller bell pits. Keep straight on all the way until you drop to the stream, then keep on its right side to join a vehicle track (a former tramway). Follow it left, then bear right and go straight on to reach the end of the Middleton Railway, heading left to the platform of **Park Halt Station**.

**2** From **Park Halt Station**, follow the side of the Middleton Railway past the sports pitch, then turn left along its far side to reach some steps up into the trees. At the top head straight across the track, then turn right and skirt around the edge of the former recreation ground of **the Clearings**. Shortly before a section of fence, bear right down into **Park Wood**. At a signed junction, go straight on and follow the left fork. This clear path soon bends left and stays above the slope, the ground on either side riddled with bell pits. Fork left above a bridge and sign, then fork right soon after to climb steadily to **Wood Pit**, whose workings scar a large area of this ancient wood.

**Middleton Railway**, the first Railway Act passed by Parliament in 1758, ran directly from Broom Colliery to Brandling's Staithe on the River Aire in Leeds. Horses originally pulled the waggons along the lines until the colliery steward John Blenkinsop invented the first rack-and-pinion railway here in 1811. The first four horse-power engine ran on the line from 1812 until 1967, and the railway continues to run as a working museum at weekends.

Colliers built **St Mary's Church** in 1846, but subsidence robbed it of its spire in 1939.

A **tramway** through Middleton Wood was built in 1919 to transport building materials to the new housing estates, but was subsequently used as a passenger route until 1955. It followed the northern track through Middleton Wood to emerge near Balkcliffe Lane.

**3** Beyond **Wood Pit** keep left to reach the main track, following it right to a sign, then heading straight on to reach the ring road at a barrier. Head straight on into **Bodmin Road**, then turn right at a path opposite Helston Road. Fork right then left, following the surfaced path along the top of the young trees before it cuts through the remnants of **West Wood** beyond. Follow the main gravel path until it forks emerging from the trees; bear right and soon enter **Sissons Wood**, following the edge of a railway cutting along the bottom of the slope. The path eventually winds up the slope to rejoin the main path.

**6** Head straight across the **A654**, following the left side of an old boundary across the fields into the trees around **Dina** and **Castle Pits**. The former can be explored up to the left, but keep right to wind through the edge of the trees.

**4** Follow the path right along the top of the slope behind the houses before dropping down to the **A654**. Follow this left for a few yards, then turn right down an uninviting track through the industrial estate. Many dogs will bark at you, but continue to the bottom, where you turn left alongside the railway line. Continue right all the way through the **rubble yard**, which can be very muddy in places. Reaching a locked gate below the motorway at the far end, skirt left along the fenceline to emerge on **Station Lane**.

This area south of Middleton is part of Yorkshire's famous **Rhubarb Triangle**. Its reputation developed in the 19th century, with night soil and shoddy (nitrogen-rich waste from the woollen industry) used as fertiliser to grow forced rhubarb in the winter. The rhubarb is grown in heated barns and still picked by candlelight. Until the 1960s special trains ran regularly from here to London markets.

**Alternative route:** If you want to avoid the muddy section through the rubble yard, you can cut the route short by continuing along the **A654**. Beyond the **Falconers Rest** turn left on a tarmac path beside Martingale Drive. This continues across several small roads to join **Towcester Avenue** at the top of Throstle Carr Beck.

Emerging near a sign turn left across the field, then left at the end to cross **Throstle Carr Beck**. A path follows the far side of the stream left past Sharp Lane Plantations, winding all the way up to the road at its head. Turn right briefly on **Towcester Avenue**, then left on Throstle Road. Opposite Throstle Close turn right on a footway between the houses that continues all the way to the ring road through **Middleton**.

**Distance:** 7½ miles (12.5km)

**Ascent:** 210m

**Parking:** Free parking in Middleton Park or at John Charles Centre for Sport near Hunslet.

**Public Transport:** Middleton is served by the regular buses 74 & 75 from Leeds, as well as bus 118 between Leeds and Wakefield. Alternatively on weekends and Bank Holidays you can park at Moor Road Station in Hunslet and catch the historic Middleton Railway to Park Halt.

**Character:** As well as Middleton Park's fascinating ancient woods, this route takes in several other wooded areas (both new and old) as it loops around the hill on which Middleton perches. It can be significantly shortened to avoid the barking dogs and potentially muddy splosh through the rubble yard by Dolphin Beck, but variety is brought to the route by the section through the younger woodland in East Ardsley Fall and along Throstle Carr Beck.

**5** Follow **Station Lane** right over the railway, then bear left into the trees. You soon pick up a larger path running the length of **East Ardsley Fall** parallel to the railway line. Before the tunnel beneath the road at the far end, bear right up to join Fall Lane. Follow it left up to **Thorpe on the Hill**, turning right at the mini-roundabout then bearing left to cross a footbridge over the motorway. Head left at the end, then left again at a sign, following a path across the field to the **A654**.

tuning fork beech tree in Middleton Wood

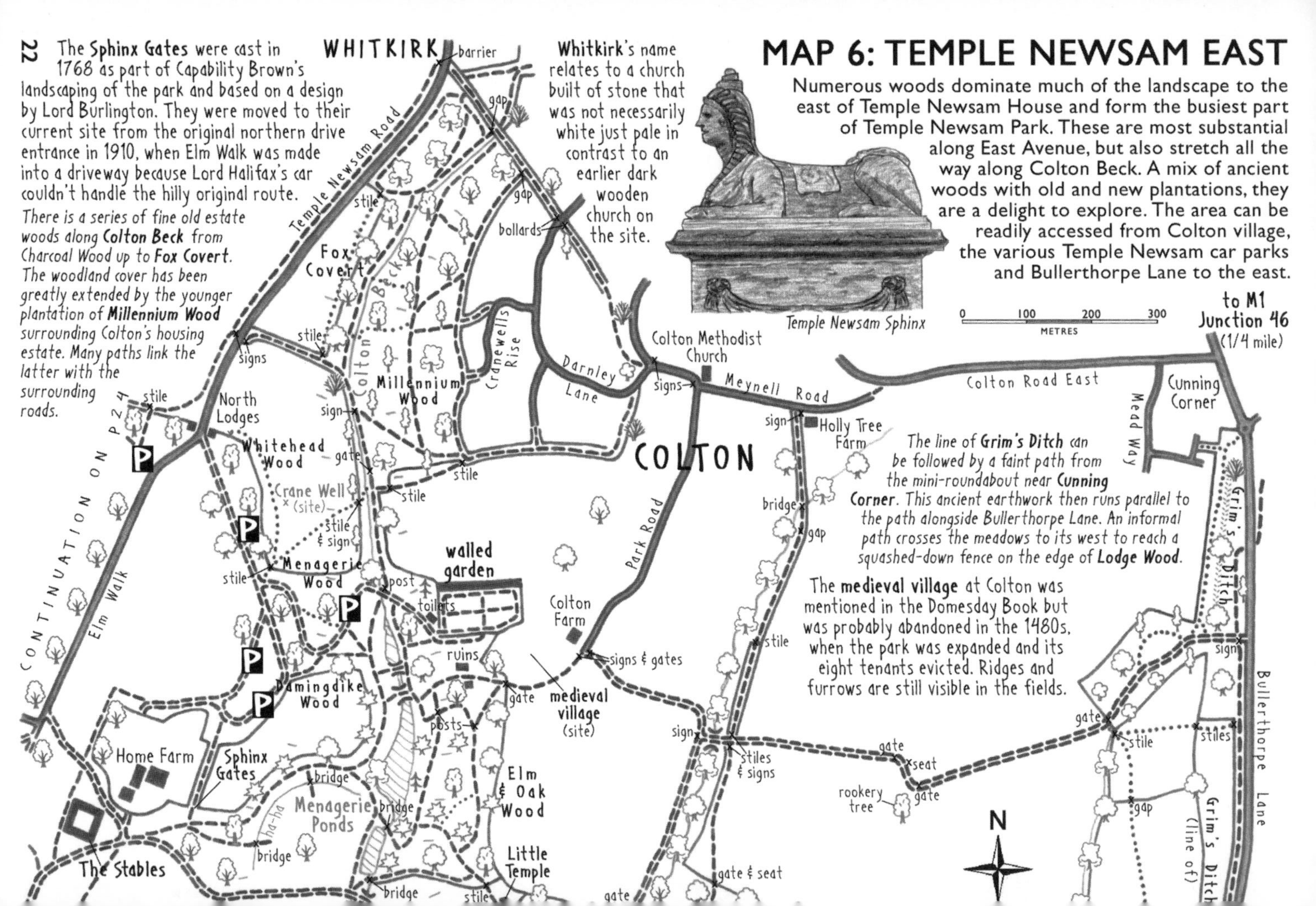
22
MAP 6: TEMPLE NEWSAM EAST
Numerous woods dominate much of the landscape to the east of Temple Newsam House and form the busiest part of Temple Newsam Park. These are most substantial along East Avenue, but also stretch all the way along Colton Beck. A mix of ancient woods with old and new plantations, they are a delight to explore. The area can be readily accessed from Colton village, the various Temple Newsam car parks and Bullerthorpe Lane to the east.
The Sphinx Gates were cast in 1768 as part of Capability Brown's landscaping of the park and based on a design by Lord Burlington. They were moved to their current site from the original northern drive entrance in 1910, when Elm Walk was made into a driveway because Lord Halifax's car couldn't handle the hilly original route.
There is a series of fine old estate woods along Colton Beck from Charcoal Wood up to Fox Covert. The woodland cover has been greatly extended by the younger plantation of Millennium Wood surrounding Colton's housing estate. Many paths link the latter with the surrounding roads.
Whitkirk's name relates to a church built of stone that was not necessarily white just pale in contrast to an earlier dark wooden church on the site.
Temple Newsam Sphinx
The line of Grim's Ditch can be followed by a faint path from the mini-roundabout near Cunning Corner. This ancient earthwork then runs parallel to the path alongside Bullerthorpe Lane. An informal path crosses the meadows to its west to reach a squashed-down fence on the edge of Lodge Wood.
The medieval village at Colton was mentioned in the Domesday Book but was probably abandoned in the 1480s, when the park was expanded and its eight tenants evicted. Ridges and furrows are still visible in the fields.
0 100 200 300
METRES
to M1 Junction 46 (1/4 mile)
WHITKIRK
barrier
Temple Newsam Road
COLTON
Colton Methodist Church
Meynell Road
Colton Road East
Cunning Corner
Mead Way
Holly Tree Farm
Darnley Lane
Cranewells Rise
Park Road
Colton Farm
Fox Covert
Colton Beck
Millennium Wood
North Lodges
Whitehead Wood
Crane Well
x (site)
Menagerie Wood
walled garden
toilets
post
ruins
medieval village (site)
signs & gates
Damingdike Wood
Home Farm
Sphinx Gates
Menagerie Ponds
ha-ha
Elm & Oak Wood
Little Temple
The Stables
Elm Walk
CONTINUATION ON P24
Grim's Ditch
Grim's Ditch (line of)
Bullerthorpe Lane
rookery tree
N
gap
stile
bollards
signs
sign
gate
stile & sign
bridge
posts
gap
stiles & signs
gate & seat
seat
stiles

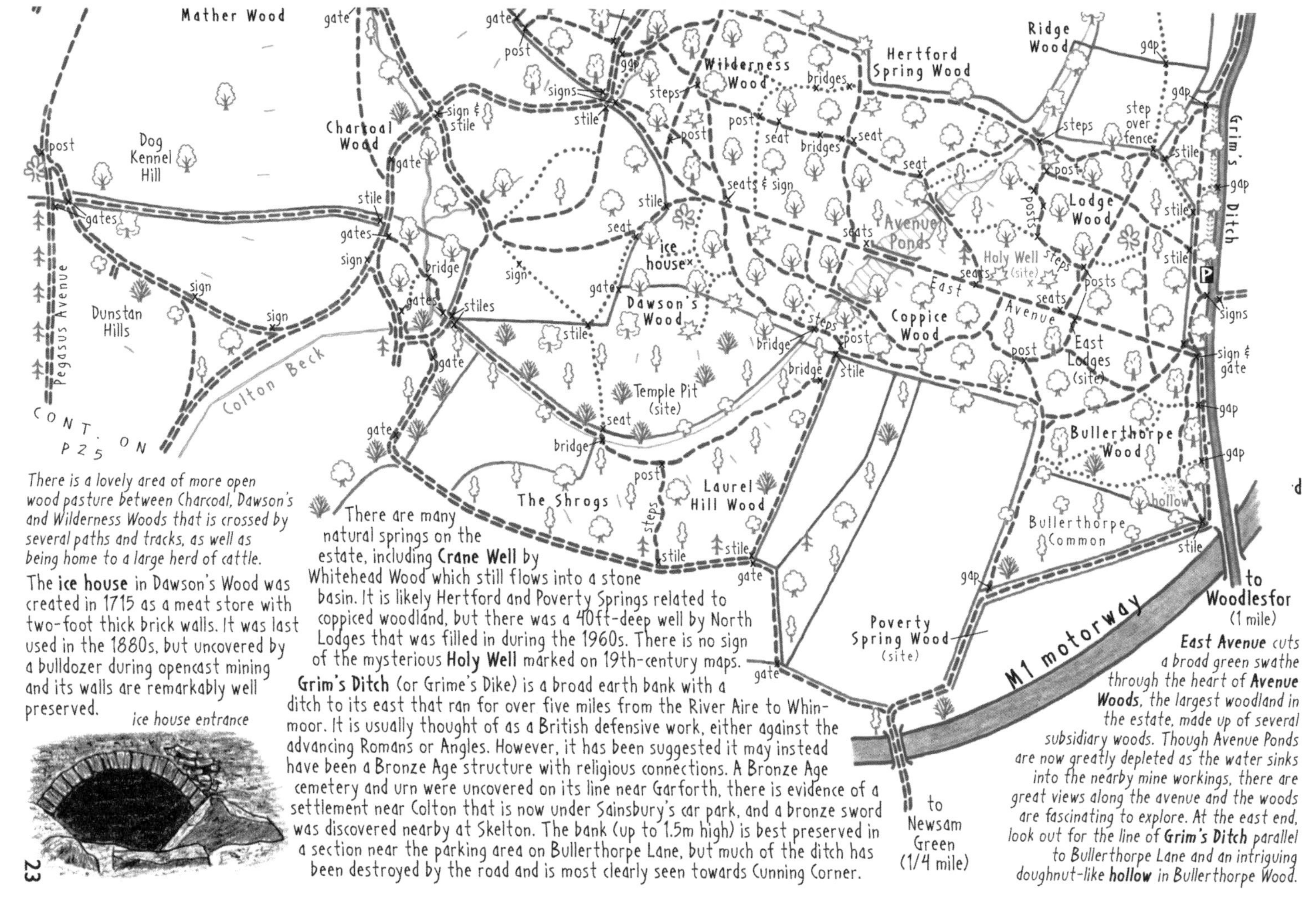

Mather Wood
Dog Kennel Hill
Dunstan Hills
Pegasus Avenue
Charcoal Wood
Colton Beck
CONT. ON P25
Wilderness Wood
Hertford Spring Wood
Ridge Wood
Lodge Wood
ice house
Dawson's Wood
Temple Pit (site)
Avenue Ponds
Holy Well (site)
East Avenue
Coppice Wood
East Lodges (site)
Bullerthorpe Wood
Bullerthorpe Common
hollow
The Shrogs
Laurel Hill Wood
Poverty Spring Wood (site)
Grim's Ditch
M1 motorway
to Woodlesfor (1 mile)
to Newsam Green (1/4 mile)
post
gates
gate
stile
sign
signs
sign & stile
sign & gate
bridge
stiles
seat
seats
seats & sign
steps
bridges
posts
step over fence
gap
P
ice house entrance


*There is a lovely area of more open wood pasture between Charcoal, Dawson's and Wilderness Woods that is crossed by several paths and tracks, as well as being home to a large herd of cattle.*

The **ice house** in Dawson's Wood was created in 1715 as a meat store with two-foot thick brick walls. It was last used in the 1880s, but uncovered by a bulldozer during opencast mining and its walls are remarkably well preserved.

There are many natural springs on the estate, including **Crane Well** by Whitehead Wood which still flows into a stone basin. It is likely Hertford and Poverty Springs related to coppiced woodland, but there was a 40ft-deep well by North Lodges that was filled in during the 1960s. There is no sign of the mysterious **Holy Well** marked on 19th-century maps.

**Grim's Ditch** (or Grime's Dike) is a broad earth bank with a ditch to its east that ran for over five miles from the River Aire to Whinmoor. It is usually thought of as a British defensive work, either against the advancing Romans or Angles. However, it has been suggested it may instead have been a Bronze Age structure with religious connections. A Bronze Age cemetery and urn were uncovered on its line near Garforth, there is evidence of a settlement near Colton that is now under Sainsbury's car park, and a bronze sword was discovered nearby at Skelton. The bank (up to 1.5m high) is best preserved in a section near the parking area on Bullerthorpe Lane, but much of the ditch has been destroyed by the road and is most clearly seen towards Cunning Corner.

***East Avenue** cuts a broad green swathe through the heart of **Avenue Woods**, the largest woodland in the estate, made up of several subsidiary woods. Though Avenue Ponds are now greatly depleted as the water sinks into the nearby mine workings, there are great views along the avenue and the woods are fascinating to explore. At the east end, look out for the line of **Grim's Ditch** parallel to Bullerthorpe Lane and an intriguing doughnut-like **hollow** in Bullerthorpe Wood.*

# MAP 7: TEMPLE NEWSAM WEST

To the west of Temple Newsam House, there is a collection of small woods scattered around the golf course. Those close to the road are easily accessed and full of paths, while others are lost between the fairways. I have also included a wooded area around Skelton Lake on the former spoil heaps the other side of the motorway.

**Halton Colliery**, first recorded in 1660, is among the earliest coal workings on the estate, with several bell pits discernible among the brambles at the north end of **Halton Moor Wood**. There were three deeper shafts sunk in Halton by the late 18th century, while small pits (some as deep as 12 feet) were dug in these woods by mining families, using only picks and shovels, during the 1926 General Strike.

***Halton Moor Wood*** *has some lovely old trees (those that haven't been burnt) but is not the most salubrious corner of the estate. A maze of paths has been created by kids on motorbikes and all seem to emerge in a bracken-filled clearing at the heart of the wood.*

***North Plantation*** *is beautifully varied and full of paths and bike tracks. It is easily accessed from car parks on the site of Lawn Pond and by the lodges at the north end of Elm Walk (where there used to be a miniature railway).*

**Jacob's Well** provided Temple Newsam House with water until a water tower was built in Halton in the 1870s. A 300m conduit emerged beneath the servants' quarters, driven uphill slightly by an hydraulic ram. Filled in 1910, this pipe has been linked to the legendary tunnel of Kirkstall Abbey (see p46).

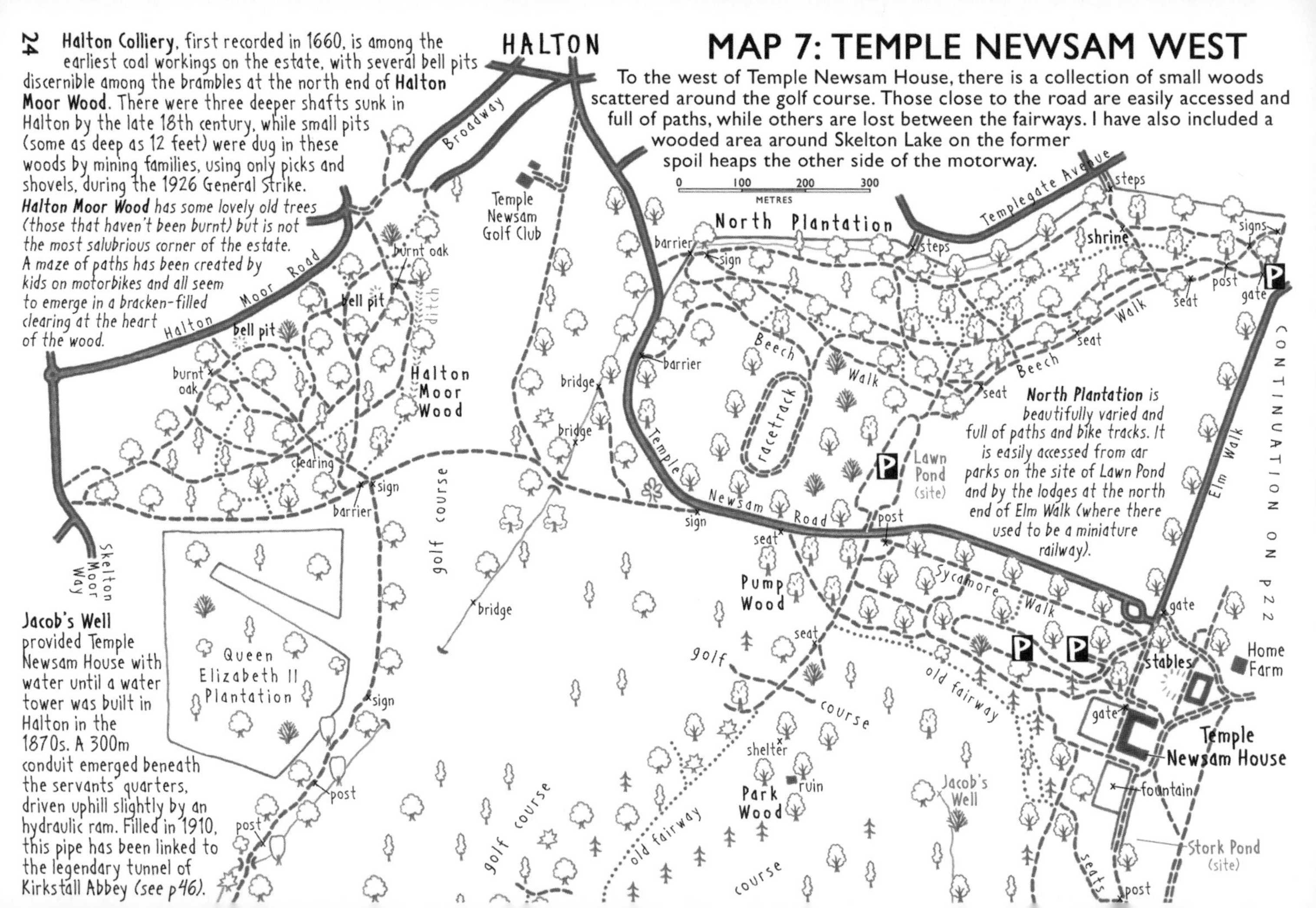
HALTON
Broadway
Temple Newsam Golf Club
Halton Moor Road
burnt oak
bell pit
bell pit
ditch
Halton Moor Wood
burnt oak
clearing
sign
barrier
Skelton Moor Way
Queen Elizabeth II Plantation
sign
post
post
golf course
bridge
bridge
bridge
golf course
old fairway
course
barrier
sign
North Plantation
0 100 200 300 METRES
Templegate Avenue
steps
steps
shrine
signs
post
seat
gate
Walk
seat
Beech
Beech
Walk
seat
barrier
racetrack
Lawn Pond (site)
Temple Newsam Road
sign
seat
post
Pump Wood
Sycamore Walk
seat
golf
course
old fairway
shelter
ruin
Park Wood
Jacob's Well
Elm Walk
gate
stables
Home Farm
gate
Temple Newsam House
fountain
Stork Pond (site)
seats
post
CONTINUATION ON p22

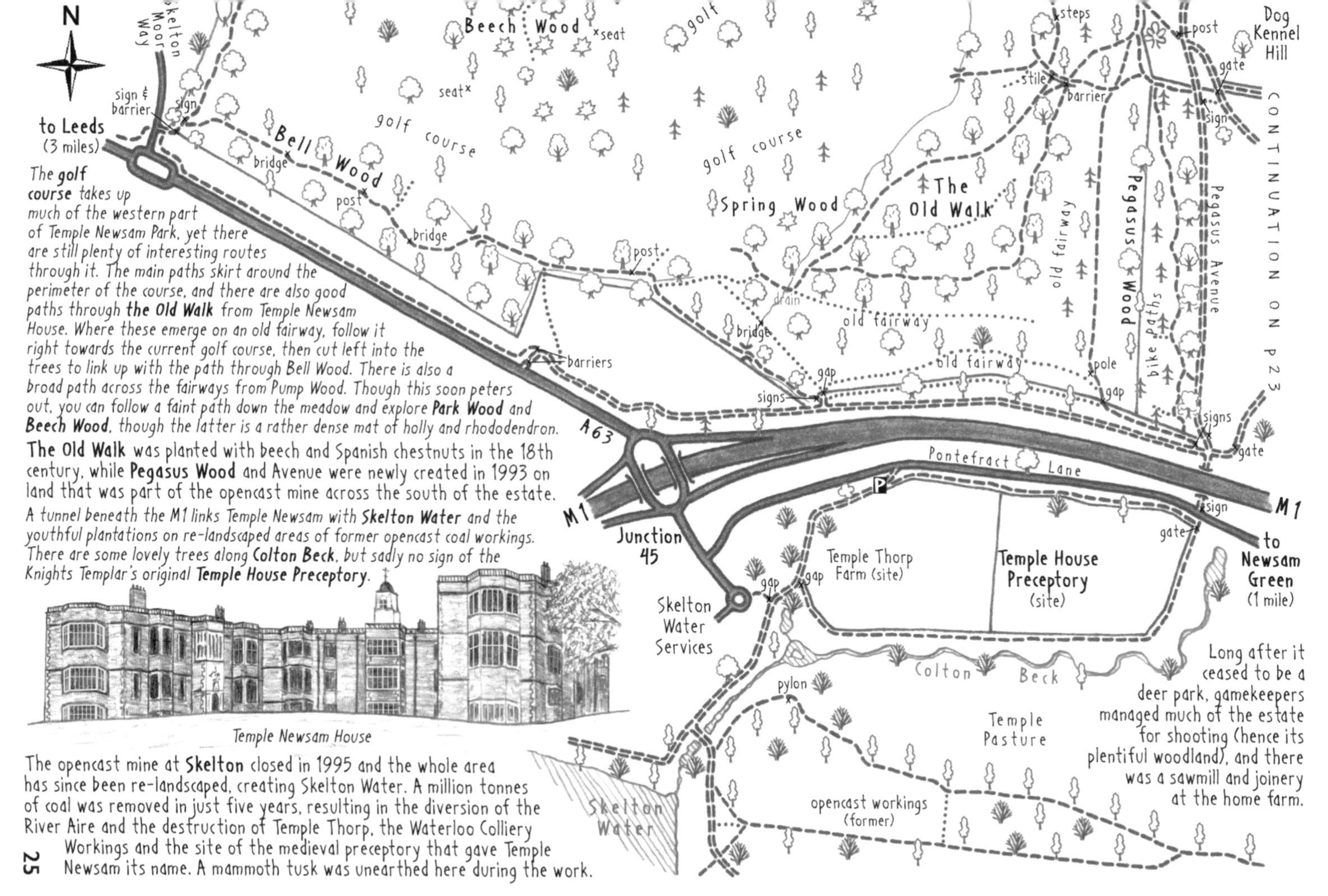
N
Skelton Moor Way
sign & barrier
sign
to Leeds (3 miles)
Bell Wood
bridge
post
bridge
golf course
seat×
Beech Wood
×seat
golf
golf course
Spring Wood
The Old Walk
post
drain
bridge
old fairway
old fairway
barriers
gap
signs
A63
M1
Junction 45
Skelton Water Services
gap
gap
Temple Thorp Farm (site)
P
Pontefract Lane
Temple House Preceptory (site)
pole
gap
Pegasus Wood
bike paths
Pegasus Avenue
signs
gate
sign
gate
M1
to Newsam Green (1 mile)
steps
stile
barrier
post
sign
gate
Dog Kennel Hill
CONTINUATION ON p23
Colton Beck
pylon
Temple Pasture
opencast workings (former)
Skelton Water

The **golf course** takes up much of the western part of Temple Newsam Park, yet there are still plenty of interesting routes through it. The main paths skirt around the perimeter of the course, and there are also good paths through **the Old Walk** from Temple Newsam House. Where these emerge on an old fairway, follow it right towards the current golf course, then cut left into the trees to link up with the path through Bell Wood. There is also a broad path across the fairways from Pump Wood. Though this soon peters out, you can follow a faint path down the meadow and explore **Park Wood** and **Beech Wood**, though the latter is a rather dense mat of holly and rhododendron.

**The Old Walk** was planted with beech and Spanish chestnuts in the 18th century, while **Pegasus Wood** and Avenue were newly created in 1993 on land that was part of the opencast mine across the south of the estate.

*A tunnel beneath the M1 links Temple Newsam with **Skelton Water** and the youthful plantations on re-landscaped areas of former opencast coal workings. There are some lovely trees along **Colton Beck**, but sadly no sign of the Knights Templar's original **Temple House Preceptory**.*

*Temple Newsam House*

The opencast mine at **Skelton** closed in 1995 and the whole area has since been re-landscaped, creating Skelton Water. A million tonnes of coal was removed in just five years, resulting in the diversion of the River Aire and the destruction of Temple Thorp, the Waterloo Colliery Workings and the site of the medieval preceptory that gave Temple Newsam its name. A mammoth tusk was unearthed here during the work.

Long after it ceased to be a deer park, gamekeepers managed much of the estate for shooting (hence its plentiful woodland), and there was a sawmill and joinery at the home farm.

# ROUTE 5: TEMPLE NEWSAM FROM CROSS GATES

**Distance:** 8 miles (13km)

**Ascent:** 160m

**Parking:** Various free car parks at Temple Newsam or street parking in Cross Gates.

**Public Transport:** Cross Gates is on the main railway line between Leeds and York.

**Character:** A thorough tour of the woods and features of Temple Newsam Park, including the house, Little Temple, walled garden and its many ponds. The circuit is completed via Primrose Valley Park and Colton Beck, with relatively little road walking around Cross Gates.

**Primrose Valley** was a 19th-century beauty spot, a farmhouse pub of the same name standing on the south side of the railway bridge at Halton Dene. It later became the Bird in Hand, serving the miners at Killingbeck Pit and named after the canary they would traditionally have taken down the mine. The former colliery site was used for landfill until the 1980s and is now Primrose Valley Park.

**St Wilfrid's Church** was built in the 1930s, when most of the new housing estates sprang up around Halton. It was designed by noted Arts & Crafts architect, Albert Randall Wells, and has a striking timber-gabled spire.

St Wilfrid's Church spire

**Whinny Wood**'s name refers to *whin*, meaning furze or gorse; it was part of the open common of Halton Moor before the garden suburb was built here in the 1930s.

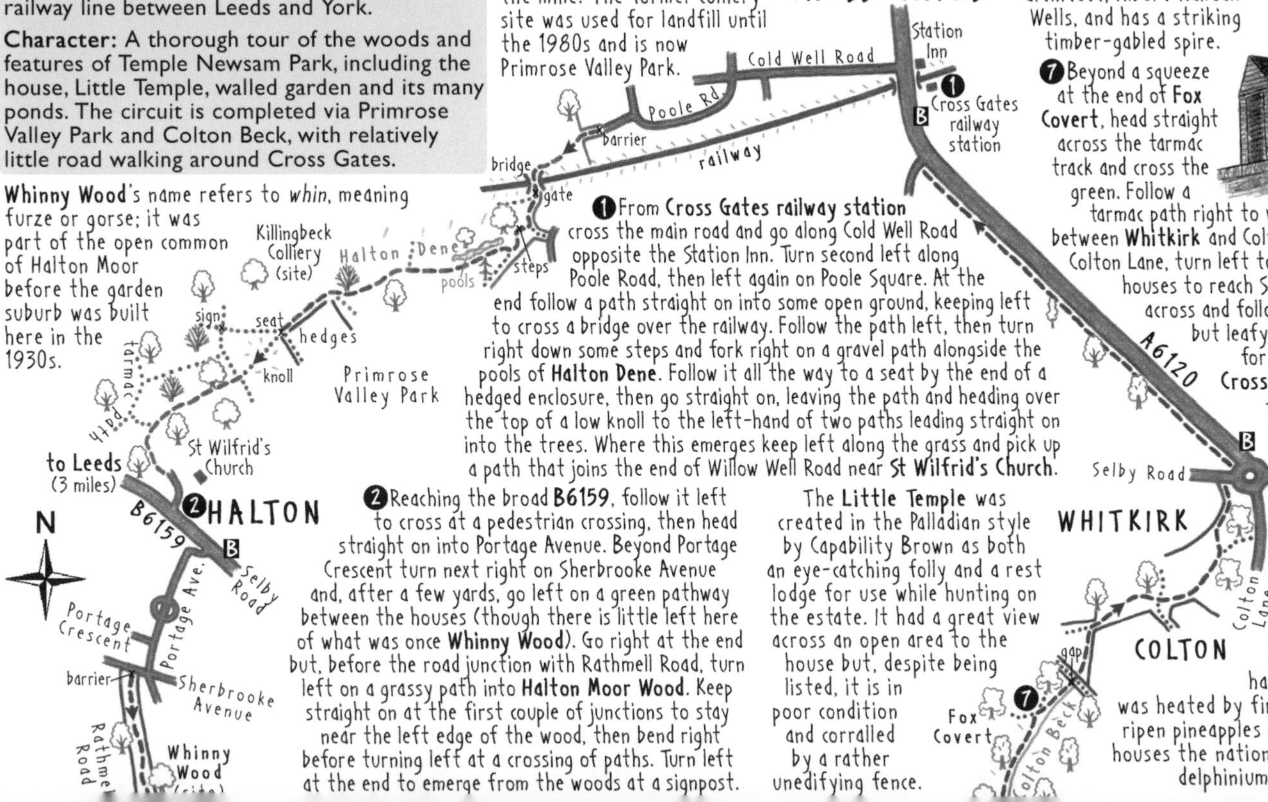

**1** From **Cross Gates railway station** cross the main road and go along Cold Well Road opposite the Station Inn. Turn second left along Poole Road, then left again on Poole Square. At the end follow a path straight on into some open ground, keeping left to cross a bridge over the railway. Follow the path left, then turn right down some steps and fork right on a gravel path alongside the pools of **Halton Dene**. Follow it all the way to a seat by the end of a hedged enclosure, then go straight on, leaving the path and heading over the top of a low knoll to the left-hand of two paths leading straight on into the trees. Where this emerges keep left along the grass and pick up a path that joins the end of Willow Well Road near **St Wilfrid's Church**.

**2** Reaching the broad **B6159**, follow it left to cross at a pedestrian crossing, then head straight on into Portage Avenue. Beyond Portage Crescent turn next right on Sherbrooke Avenue and, after a few yards, go left on a green pathway between the houses (though there is little left here of what was once **Whinny Wood**). Go right at the end but, before the road junction with Rathmell Road, turn left on a grassy path into **Halton Moor Wood**. Keep straight on at the first couple of junctions to stay near the left edge of the wood, then bend right before turning left at a crossing of paths. Turn left at the end to emerge from the woods at a signpost.

The **Little Temple** was created in the Palladian style by Capability Brown as both an eye-catching folly and a rest lodge for use while hunting on the estate. It had a great view across an open area to the house but, despite being listed, it is in poor condition and corralled by a rather unedifying fence.

**7** Beyond a squeeze at the end of **Fox Covert**, head straight across the tarmac track and cross the green. Follow a tarmac path right to wind across the parkland between **Whitkirk** and Colton. Entering trees near Colton Lane, turn left to follow the edge of the houses to reach Selby Road. Head straight across and follow the side of the broad but leafy boulevard of the A6120 for over half a mile back to **Cross Gates railway station**.

The name **Cross Gates** referred to a crossing point onto the common, its gates preventing livestock straying.

The **walled kitchen garden** was laid out by Capability Brown in the 18th century. It had its own firewall that was heated by fireplaces and a boiler to ripen pineapples and other fruit. It now houses the national collection of asters, delphiniums and chrysanthemums.

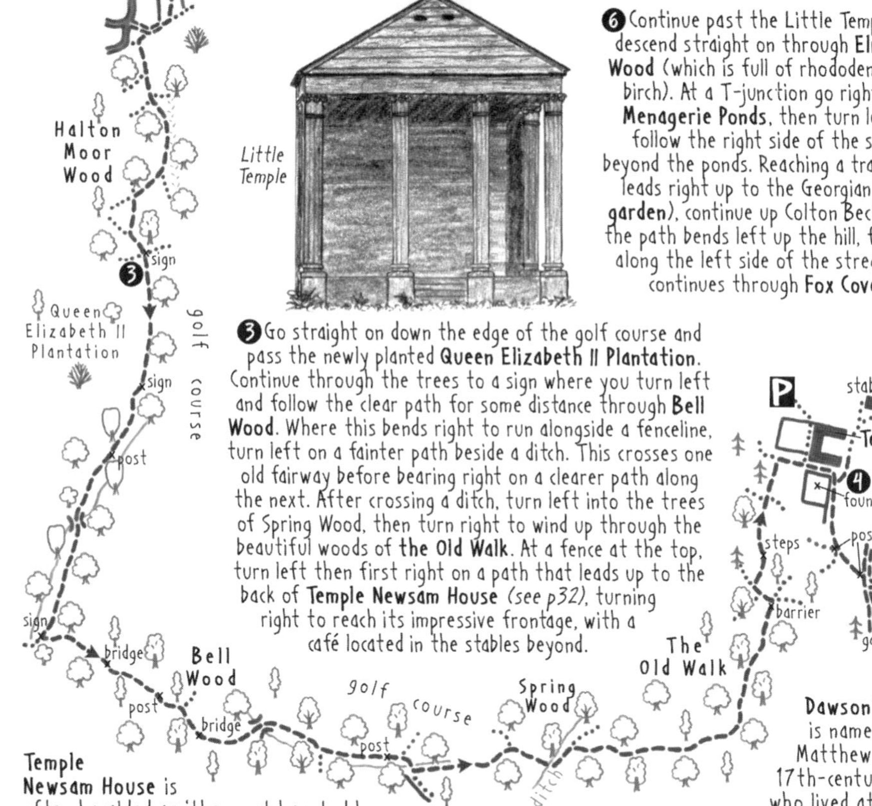

Halton Moor Wood
Little Temple
Queen Elizabeth II Plantation
sign
golf course
post
bridge
Bell Wood
Spring Wood
ditch
The Old Walk
steps
barrier
stables
Temple Newsam House
fountain
posts
gate
Dog Kennel Hill
0 200 400
METRES
stile
Colton Beck
Dawson's Wood
Laurel Hill Wood
Coppice Wood
seats
Avenue Ponds
East Avenue
seat
Lodge Wood
Hertford Spring Wood
Wilderness Wood
gap
gates
Little Temple
Elm & Oak Wood
Menagerie Ponds
walled garden
Millennium Wood


**3** Go straight on down the edge of the golf course and pass the newly planted **Queen Elizabeth II Plantation**. Continue through the trees to a sign where you turn left and follow the clear path for some distance through **Bell Wood**. Where this bends right to run alongside a fenceline, turn left on a fainter path beside a ditch. This crosses one old fairway before bearing right on a clearer path along the next. After crossing a ditch, turn left into the trees of Spring Wood, then turn right to wind up through the beautiful woods of **the Old Walk**. At a fence at the top, turn left then first right on a path that leads up to the back of **Temple Newsam House** *(see p32)*, turning right to reach its impressive frontage, with a café located in the stables beyond.

**4** At the front of the house double back and follow the tarmac path past the hedged Italianate garden. Keep straight on at a couple of waymarkers, then turn left along a hedge-lined path just before a gate. At the bottom bear right through a gate opposite and cross **Colton Beck** (if locked, follow the track right then keep left to reach the same point). Continue straight on across the next track on a path alongside another stream. Cross at a bridge then keep left to a stile at the end of **Laurel Hill Wood**. Bear left then right, before turning right by **Avenue Ponds** to climb up through Coppice Wood and emerge on **East Avenue**.

**5** Follow **East Avenue** left briefly towards the distant house, then turn right by some seats to descend across **Avenue Ponds** (rather a disappointment). By a seat at the next junction turn right, then keep left to join the far edge of **Hertford Spring Wood**. Turn right at the next junction to stay along the edge of the wood. At the end turn left then bear immediately right, descending to cross the stream. Head straight across the track beyond to climb through the beech trees to reach the sad-looking **Little Temple**.

**6** Continue past the Little Temple and descend straight on through **Elm & Oak Wood** (which is full of rhododendron and birch). At a T-junction go right above **Menagerie Ponds**, then turn left and follow the right side of the stream beyond the ponds. Reaching a track (which leads right up to the Georgian **walled garden**), continue up Colton Beck. Where the path bends left up the hill, fork right along the left side of the stream as it continues through **Fox Covert**.

**Dawson's Wood** is named after Matthew Dawson, a 17th-century head servant who lived at Newton Grange.

**Temple Newsam House** is often heralded as 'the most haunted house in Yorkshire'. The Blue Lady has been seen on many occasions and is thought to be Mary Ingram, who died at 14 in 1651. Her carriage was attacked by highwaymen who stole her possessions and left her terrified, dying only a few weeks later. She now haunts the house in a blue dress searching for her favourite necklace. She has been joined by a monk in a brown habit, a boy in a cupboard and Phoebe Gray, a maid who in 1704 was suffocated and thrown down a well by an estate worker as he tried to kiss her after a party in 1704.

# MAP 8: ROUNDHAY PARK

Roundhay Park (the People's Park) is a popular urban playground covering over 700 acres. Its northern and eastern parts are covered in ancient plantation woodland of oak and beech, interspersed with areas of holly around Upper Lake, Elmet Hall and Braim Wood. The map extends to quieter areas west along Great Heads Beck and south along Wyke Beck, but focuses on the busy park and its many features, including the Mansion House, Castle, Arboretum and Specialist Gardens. All car parking is free.

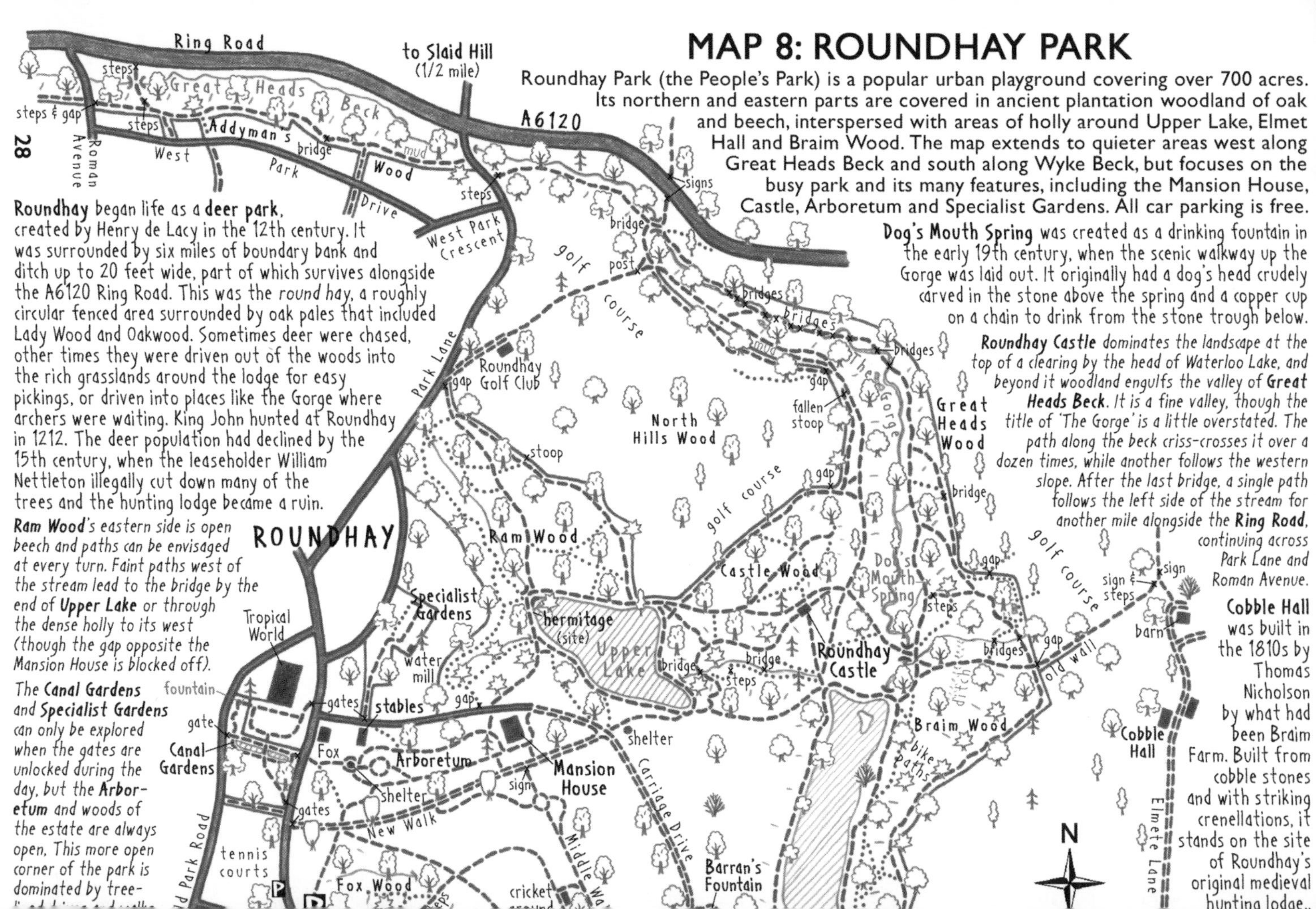

Ring Road
to Slaid Hill
(1/2 mile)
A6120
steps
steps & gap
Great Heads Beck
steps
Addyman's
bridge
mud
Wood
West
Park
Drive
Roman Avenue
steps
West Park Crescent
signs
bridge
post
golf course
Park Lane
Roundhay Golf Club
gap
bridges
bridges
mud
bridges
The Gorge
gap
fallen stoop
North Hills Wood
Great Heads Wood
stoop
gap
golf course
bridge
ROUNDHAY
Ram Wood
Castle Wood
Dog's Mouth Spring
gap
golf course
sign & steps
sign
steps
Specialist Gardens
hermitage (site)
Upper Lake
bridge
bridge
steps
Roundhay Castle
bridges
gap
old wall
barn
Tropical World
water mill
ditch
fountain
gates
stables
gap
gate
Canal Gardens
Fox
Arboretum
shelter
Mansion House
Braim Wood
Cobble Hall
bike paths
shelter
sign
Carriage Drive
gates
New Walk
Middle Walk
Elmete Lane
tennis courts
Park Road
Fox Wood
cricket
Barran's Fountain
N


**Roundhay** began life as a **deer park**, created by Henry de Lacy in the 12th century. It was surrounded by six miles of boundary bank and ditch up to 20 feet wide, part of which survives alongside the A6120 Ring Road. This was the *round hay*, a roughly circular fenced area surrounded by oak pales that included Lady Wood and Oakwood. Sometimes deer were chased, other times they were driven out of the woods into the rich grasslands around the lodge for easy pickings, or driven into places like the Gorge where archers were waiting. King John hunted at Roundhay in 1212. The deer population had declined by the 15th century, when the leaseholder William Nettleton illegally cut down many of the trees and the hunting lodge became a ruin.

***Ram Wood****'s eastern side is open beech and paths can be envisaged at every turn. Faint paths west of the stream lead to the bridge by the end of* ***Upper Lake*** *or through the dense holly to its west (though the gap opposite the Mansion House is blocked off).*

The **Canal Gardens** and **Specialist Gardens** *can only be explored when the gates are unlocked during the day, but the* ***Arboretum*** *and woods of the estate are always open. This more open corner of the park is dominated by tree-*

**Dog's Mouth Spring** was created as a drinking fountain in the early 19th century, when the scenic walkway up the Gorge was laid out. It originally had a dog's head crudely carved in the stone above the spring and a copper cup on a chain to drink from the stone trough below.

***Roundhay Castle*** *dominates the landscape at the top of a clearing by the head of Waterloo Lake, and beyond it woodland engulfs the valley of* ***Great Heads Beck****. It is a fine valley, though the title of 'The Gorge' is a little overstated. The path along the beck criss-crosses it over a dozen times, while another follows the western slope. After the last bridge, a single path follows the left side of the stream for another mile alongside the* ***Ring Road****, continuing across Park Lane and Roman Avenue.*

**Cobble Hall** was built in the 1810s by Thomas Nicholson by what had been Braim Farm. Built from cobble stones and with striking crenellations, it stands on the site of Roundhay's original medieval hunting lodge

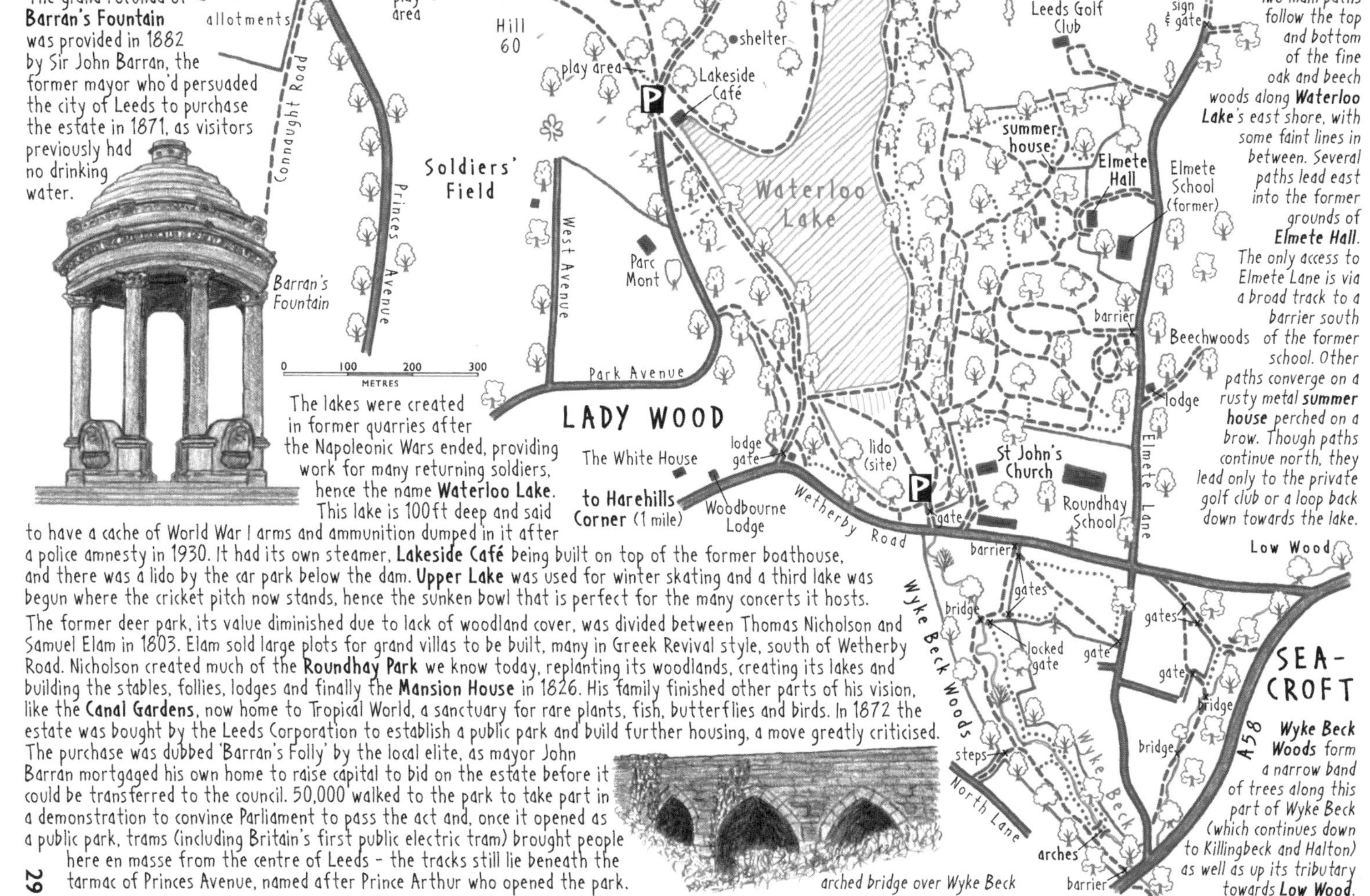

allotments
Connaught Road
play area
Hill 60
Princes Avenue
Soldiers' Field
Barran's Fountain
West Avenue
Park Avenue
0 100 200 300
METRES
shelter
play area
Lakeside Café
P
Parc Mont
Waterloo Lake
LADY WOOD
The White House
lodge gate
Woodbourne Lodge
to Harehills Corner (1 mile)
lido (site)
P
gate
Wetherby Road
St John's Church
Roundhay School
Leeds Golf Club
summer house
Elmete Hall
Elmete School (former)
barrier
Beechwoods
lodge
sign & gate
Elmete Lane
Low Wood
barrier
gates
bridge
locked gate
gate
gates
gate
bridge
bridge
Wyke Beck Woods
Wyke Beck
steps
North Lane
arches
barrier
A58
SEA-CROFT


The grand rotunda of **Barran's Fountain** was provided in 1882 by Sir John Barran, the former mayor who'd persuaded the city of Leeds to purchase the estate in 1871, as visitors previously had no drinking water.

Two main paths follow the top and bottom of the fine oak and beech woods along **Waterloo Lake**'s east shore, with some faint lines in between. Several paths lead east into the former grounds of **Elmete Hall**. The only access to Elmete Lane is via a broad track to a barrier south of the former school. Other paths converge on a rusty metal **summer house** perched on a brow. Though paths continue north, they lead only to the private golf club or a loop back down towards the lake.

**Wyke Beck Woods** form a narrow band of trees along this part of Wyke Beck (which continues down to Killingbeck and Halton) as well as up its tributary towards **Low Wood**.

The lakes were created in former quarries after the Napoleonic Wars ended, providing work for many returning soldiers, hence the name **Waterloo Lake**. This lake is 100ft deep and said to have a cache of World War I arms and ammunition dumped in it after a police amnesty in 1930. It had its own steamer, **Lakeside Café** being built on top of the former boathouse, and there was a lido by the car park below the dam. **Upper Lake** was used for winter skating and a third lake was begun where the cricket pitch now stands, hence the sunken bowl that is perfect for the many concerts it hosts.

The former deer park, its value diminished due to lack of woodland cover, was divided between Thomas Nicholson and Samuel Elam in 1803. Elam sold large plots for grand villas to be built, many in Greek Revival style, south of Wetherby Road. Nicholson created much of the **Roundhay Park** we know today, replanting its woodlands, creating its lakes and building the stables, follies, lodges and finally the **Mansion House** in 1826. His family finished other parts of his vision, like the **Canal Gardens**, now home to Tropical World, a sanctuary for rare plants, fish, butterflies and birds. In 1872 the estate was bought by the Leeds Corporation to establish a public park and build further housing, a move greatly criticised. The purchase was dubbed 'Barran's Folly' by the local elite, as mayor John Barran mortgaged his own home to raise capital to bid on the estate before it could be transferred to the council. 50,000 walked to the park to take part in a demonstration to convince Parliament to pass the act and, once it opened as a public park, trams (including Britain's first public electric tram) brought people here en masse from the centre of Leeds – the tracks still lie beneath the tarmac of Princes Avenue, named after Prince Arthur who opened the park.

*arched bridge over Wyke Beck*

# ROUTE 6: ROUNDHAY PARK & GLEDHOW VALLEY WOODS FROM OAKWOOD

**Distance:** 7½ miles (12.2km)

**Ascent:** 220m

**Parking:** Free car parks by Oakwood Clock (off Princes Avenue) and in Roundhay Park (at the end of Park Avenue and on Wetherby Road).

**Public Transport:** Buses 2, 12, X98 and X99 run regularly from Leeds city centre to Oakwood Clock and Harehills Corner. Bus 2 also runs along Street Lane in Moortown, presenting a possible shortcut.

**Character:** A simple route that makes the most of the green corridors of north-east Leeds, following Gledhow Valley and Great Heads Beck through the suburbs, as well as exploring the most wooded parts of Roundhay Park and taking in Waterloo Lake, Elmete Hall and the Castle. The route can be started in Oakwood, Harehills Corner or Moortown.

**3** Turn right at **Roundhay Castle**, then bear left to stay high above Great Heads Beck's narrow gorge. Follow the main path until it bends left towards the golf course; turn right down towards the stream, but keep left alongside it to reach Park Lane. A few yards to the right a path continues into **Addyman's Wood** opposite, winding through this narrow strip of trees beside the roar of the Ring Road. Stay along the top of the woods and continue straight across Roman Avenue, the path persisting all the way through **Long Bottom Wood**. Stay high until you are eventually forced down to join the **Ring Road**.

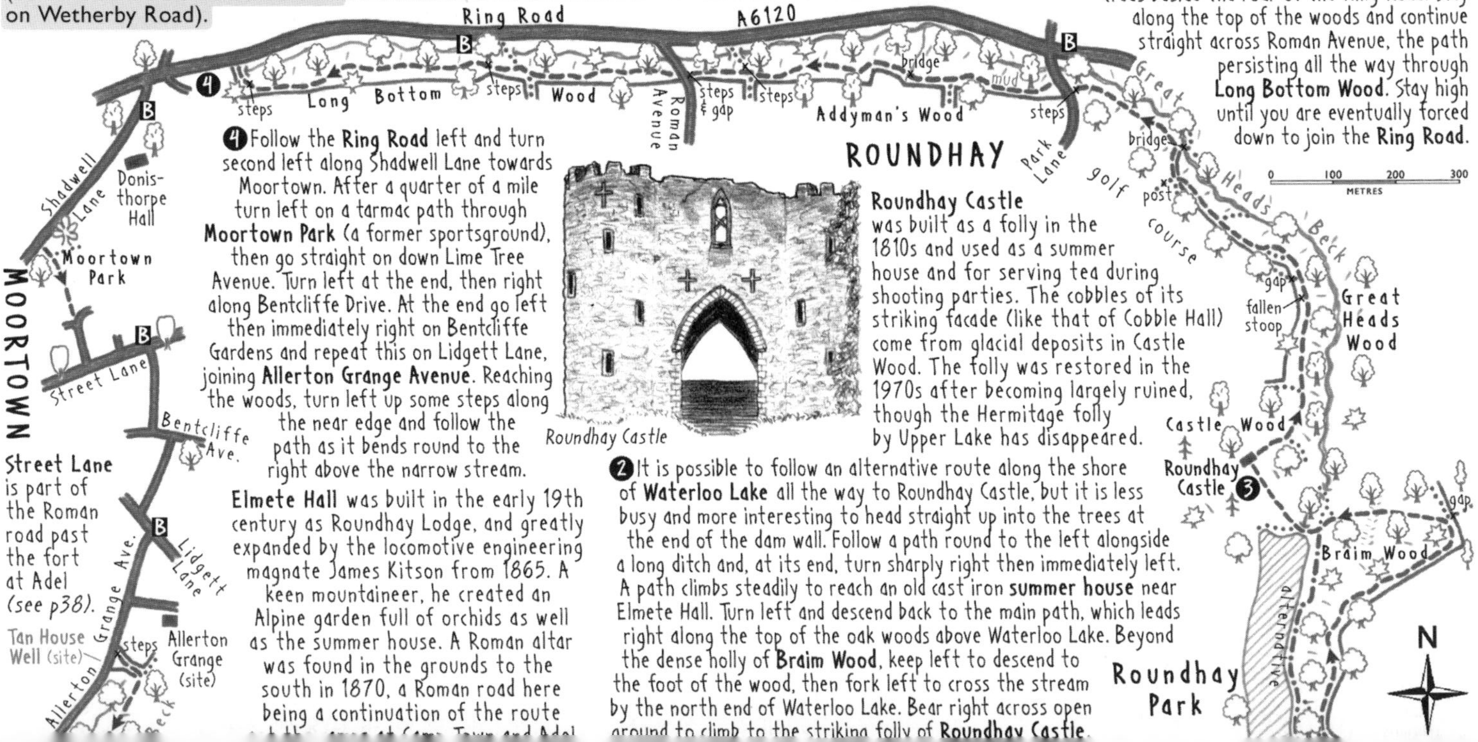

**4** Follow the **Ring Road** left and turn second left along Shadwell Lane towards Moortown. After a quarter of a mile turn left on a tarmac path through **Moortown Park** (a former sportsground), then go straight on down Lime Tree Avenue. Turn left at the end, then right along Bentcliffe Drive. At the end go left then immediately right on Bentcliffe Gardens and repeat this on Lidgett Lane, joining **Allerton Grange Avenue**. Reaching the woods, turn left up some steps along the near edge and follow the path as it bends round to the right above the narrow stream.

Roundhay Castle

**Roundhay Castle** was built as a folly in the 1810s and used as a summer house and for serving tea during shooting parties. The cobbles of its striking facade (like that of Cobble Hall) come from glacial deposits in Castle Wood. The folly was restored in the 1970s after becoming largely ruined, though the Hermitage folly by Upper Lake has disappeared.

**Street Lane** is part of the Roman road past the fort at Adel (see p38).

**Elmete Hall** was built in the early 19th century as Roundhay Lodge, and greatly expanded by the locomotive engineering magnate James Kitson from 1865. A keen mountaineer, he created an Alpine garden full of orchids as well as the summer house. A Roman altar was found in the grounds to the south in 1870, a Roman road here being a continuation of the route

**2** It is possible to follow an alternative route along the shore of **Waterloo Lake** all the way to Roundhay Castle, but it is less busy and more interesting to head straight up into the trees at the end of the dam wall. Follow a path round to the left alongside a long ditch and, at its end, turn sharply right then immediately left. A path climbs steadily to reach an old cast iron **summer house** near Elmete Hall. Turn left and descend back to the main path, which leads right along the top of the oak woods above Waterloo Lake. Beyond the dense holly of **Braim Wood**, keep left to descend to the foot of the wood, then fork left to cross the stream by the north end of Waterloo Lake. Bear right across open ground to climb to the striking folly of **Roundhay Castle**.

Ring Road
A6120
B
Long Bottom Wood
steps
Roman Avenue
steps & gap
Addyman's Wood
bridge
mud
Park Lane
Great Heads Beck
golf course
post
fallen stoop
gap
Great Heads Wood
Castle Wood
Roundhay Castle
Braim Wood
alternative
Roundhay Park
ROUNDHAY
Shadwell Lane
Donisthorpe Hall
Moortown Park
MOORTOWN
Street Lane
Bentcliffe Ave.
Lidgett Lane
Grange Ave.
Allerton Grange (site)
Tan House Well (site)
Allerton
0 100 200 300 METRES
N

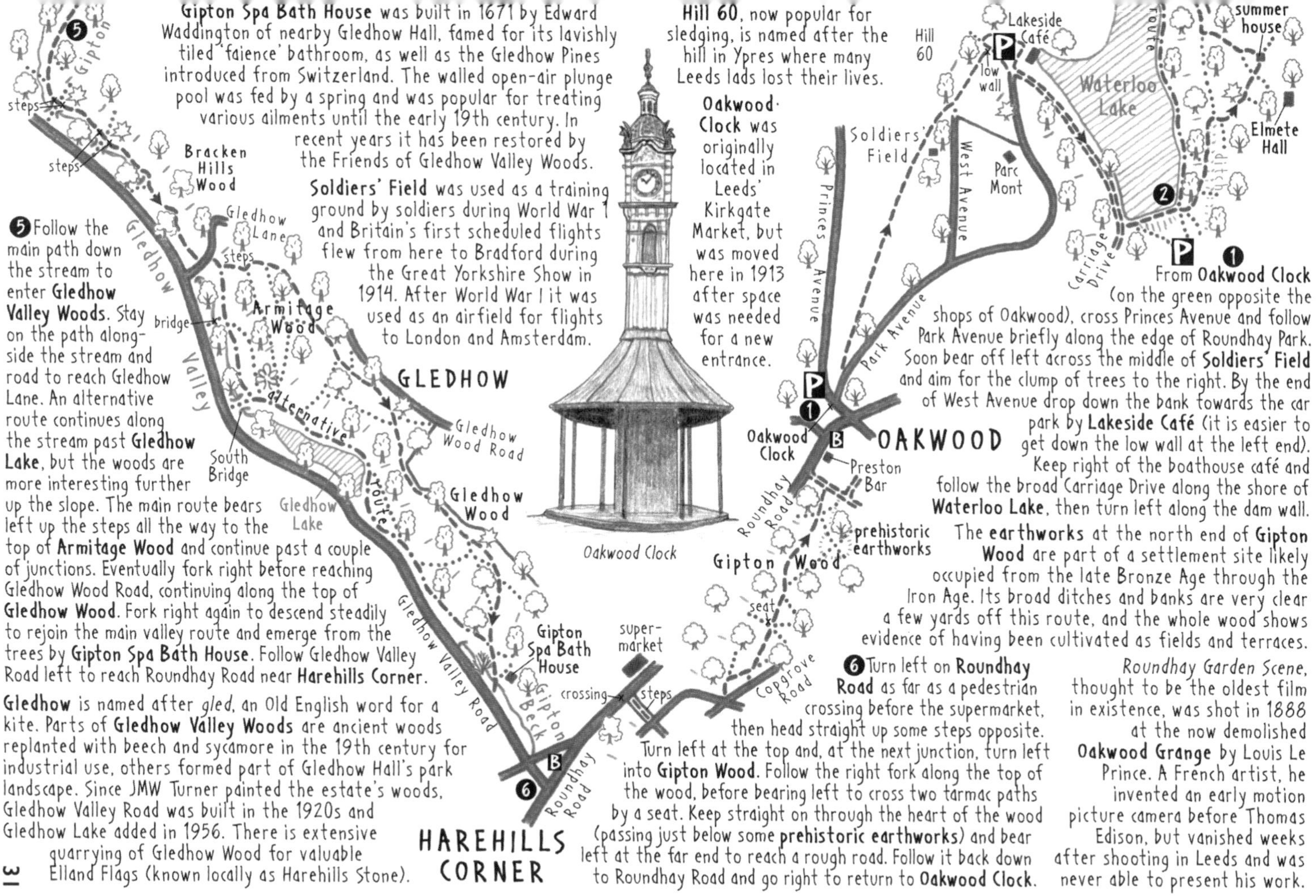

**Gipton Spa Bath House** was built in 1671 by Edward Waddington of nearby Gledhow Hall, famed for its lavishly tiled 'faience' bathroom, as well as the Gledhow Pines introduced from Switzerland. The walled open-air plunge pool was fed by a spring and was popular for treating various ailments until the early 19th century. In recent years it has been restored by the Friends of Gledhow Valley Woods.

**Soldiers' Field** was used as a training ground by soldiers during World War I and Britain's first scheduled flights flew from here to Bradford during the Great Yorkshire Show in 1914. After World War I it was used as an airfield for flights to London and Amsterdam.

**5** Follow the main path down the stream to enter **Gledhow Valley Woods**. Stay on the path alongside the stream and road to reach Gledhow Lane. An alternative route continues along the stream past **Gledhow Lake**, but the woods are more interesting further up the slope. The main route bears left up the steps all the way to the top of **Armitage Wood** and continue past a couple of junctions. Eventually fork right before reaching Gledhow Wood Road, continuing along the top of **Gledhow Wood**. Fork right again to descend steadily to rejoin the main valley route and emerge from the trees by **Gipton Spa Bath House**. Follow Gledhow Valley Road left to reach Roundhay Road near **Harehills Corner**.

**Gledhow** is named after *gled*, an Old English word for a kite. Parts of **Gledhow Valley Woods** are ancient woods replanted with beech and sycamore in the 19th century for industrial use, others formed part of Gledhow Hall's park landscape. Since JMW Turner painted the estate's woods, Gledhow Valley Road was built in the 1920s and Gledhow Lake added in 1956. There is extensive quarrying of Gledhow Wood for valuable Elland Flags (known locally as Harehills Stone).

**Hill 60**, now popular for sledging, is named after the hill in Ypres where many Leeds lads lost their lives.

**Oakwood Clock** was originally located in Leeds' Kirkgate Market, but was moved here in 1913 after space was needed for a new entrance.

*Oakwood Clock*

**1** From **Oakwood Clock** (on the green opposite the shops of Oakwood), cross Princes Avenue and follow Park Avenue briefly along the edge of Roundhay Park. Soon bear off left across the middle of **Soldiers' Field** and aim for the clump of trees to the right. By the end of West Avenue drop down the bank towards the car park by **Lakeside Café** (it is easier to get down the low wall at the left end). Keep right of the boathouse café and follow the broad Carriage Drive along the shore of **Waterloo Lake**, then turn left along the dam wall.

The **earthworks** at the north end of **Gipton Wood** are part of a settlement site likely occupied from the late Bronze Age through the Iron Age. Its broad ditches and banks are very clear a few yards off this route, and the whole wood shows evidence of having been cultivated as fields and terraces.

**6** Turn left on **Roundhay Road** as far as a pedestrian crossing before the supermarket, then head straight up some steps opposite. Turn left at the top and, at the next junction, turn left into **Gipton Wood**. Follow the right fork along the top of the wood, before bearing left to cross two tarmac paths by a seat. Keep straight on through the heart of the wood (passing just below some **prehistoric earthworks**) and bear left at the far end to reach a rough road. Follow it back down to Roundhay Road and go right to return to **Oakwood Clock**.

*Roundhay Garden Scene*, thought to be the oldest film in existence, was shot in 1888 at the now demolished **Oakwood Grange** by Louis Le Prince. A French artist, he invented an early motion picture camera before Thomas Edison, but vanished weeks after shooting in Leeds and was never able to present his work.

# TEMPLE NEWSAM HOUSE & ESTATE

The Knights Templar were granted land known as 'New Houses' around 1152 and founded a preceptory near what was later Temple Thorp Farm. As well as a chapel, there was a farm, fulling and corn mills, tan pits, a dairy and a brewhouse. When the order was dissolved in 1308, the estate was confiscated by Edward II and eventually passed to the Darcy family as the Manor of Temple Newsam, with free warren within the park's bounds for country pursuits. The estate was extended in the 1480s, a further forty acres being enclosed at the expense of eight households in Colton who were moved to a new village half a mile away. The first Temple Newsam House was built by Thomas Darcy in 1518, before he was hanged for treason and his estates seized.

Henry Stuart, Lord Darnley, was born here in 1546; his marriage to Mary Queen of Scots prompted another seizure of the estate. In 1622 Sir Arthur Ingram purchased the estate, which had been extended further to create a large deer park and pasture. Ingram demolished most of the original house, rebuilding the north and south wings on the same courtyard plan and retaining the west wing that included the King's Chamber where Darnley was born. The east wing burnt down in 1636 and was never replaced, creating the open front seen today. It was West Yorkshire's first brick building, a stately Jacobean mansion with the striking inscription in stonework on the battlement. Ingram also created formal gardens, a banqueting house, bowling green, dog kennels and the great barn of Home Farm.

Landscaping in the 1710s by William Etty for Viscount Irwin created the main avenue to the north, the ice house and the three-tiered Avenue Ponds with an ornate bridge on East Avenue. Carp and tench were introduced to the ponds, with oak, beech and elm planted around them and the hill to the east being partially levelled. The stable block and North Lodges were built in 1742, along with the wall around the estate using stones from Halton Quarry. In the 1760s Irwin redeveloped the house's interior and employed Capability Brown to re-landscape the park. Brown set about creating a pastoral landscape around the house; North Plantation and several other new beech woodlands were created, as well as many ha-has (fences sunk in ditches to keep livestock out but remain invisible from the house).The stable was extended, the Little Temple built, and Menagerie Ponds created. The East Lodges were built near the end of East Avenue, though this beautiful approach to the house only became the main drive in 1847 with the opening of Woodlesford railway station. These Gothic lodges were abandoned after the nearby spring failed due to mining work and demolished in 1946.

The house gardens were redesigned in an Italianate style around 1875 for Emily Meynell-Ingram, with rhododendrons and azaleas planted in the woods to provide cover for gamebirds. The last deer was shot in the park in 1918 and Edward Wood handed the estate to the Leeds Corporation in 1922, with 20,000 visitors flocking there on its opening day. Ponds were cleared, bridges rebuilt, the stable block converted into refreshment rooms and a zoo installed in the kitchen garden. The golf course opened in 1923 and a model railway opened in North Plantation in 1960, but closed in the late 1970s and was re-installed at Eggborough Power Station.

During World War II a third of the estate was requisitioned for opencast coal mining as six seams lay beneath it. There had been coal pits in the park since the 17th century and Waterloo Colliery was opened by Sir Arthur Ingram in 1815, with Temple Pit's shaft sunk between Dawson's Wood and the Shrogs in the early 20th century. Now, however, most of the land to the south of the house and East Avenue was excavated, removing more than 200,000 tonnes of coal by 1948. Opencast workings destroyed much of the vista imagined by Capability Brown in front of the house and removed features like the gibbet, grotto and Stork Pond. Mining continued until 1976, when the ground was landscaped with trees planted on many of the previously wooded areas.

statue in Temple Newsam's Italianate Garden

# CHAPTER 3 - MEANWOOD VALLEY

**Map Sheet:** Explorer 289 (Leeds) & 297 (Lower Wharfedale)

**Public Transport:** Railway stations at Leeds, Burley Park and Headingley, and several bus routes serving Meanwood, Adel and Bramhope.

**Parking:** Various free car parks at Meanwood Park, Golden Acre Park, The Hollies, Adel Woods, Adel Church and Alwoodley Village Green.

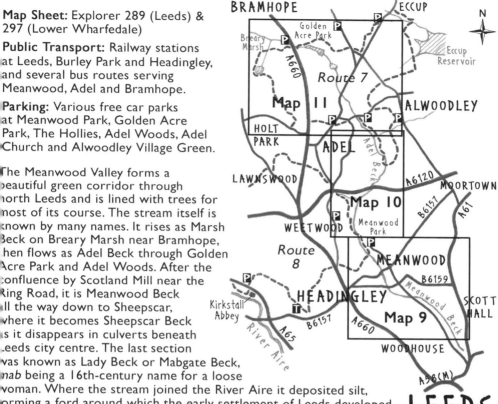

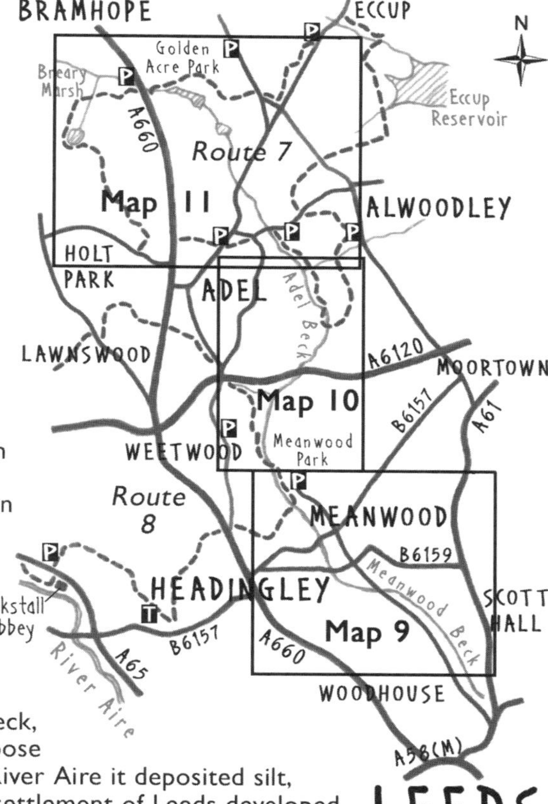

BRAMHOPE
ECCUP
N
Golden
Acre Park
Breary
Marsh
A660
Eccup
Reservoir
Route 7
Map 11
ALWOODLEY
HOLT
PARK
ADEL
Adel Beck
LAWNSWOOD
A6120
MOORTOWN
Map 10
B6157
A61
Meanwood
Park
WEETWOOD
Route
8
MEANWOOD
B6159
Meanwood Beck
Kirkstall
Abbey
HEADINGLEY
SCOTT
HALL
Map 9
B6157
A660
A65
River Aire
WOODHOUSE
A58(M)
LEEDS


The Meanwood Valley forms a beautiful green corridor through north Leeds and is lined with trees for most of its course. The stream itself is known by many names. It rises as Marsh Beck on Breary Marsh near Bramhope, then flows as Adel Beck through Golden Acre Park and Adel Woods. After the confluence by Scotland Mill near the Ring Road, it is Meanwood Beck all the way down to Sheepscar, where it becomes Sheepscar Beck as it disappears in culverts beneath Leeds city centre. The last section was known as Lady Beck or Mabgate Beck, *mab* being a 16th-century name for a loose woman. Where the stream joined the River Aire it deposited silt, forming a ford around which the early settlement of Leeds developed.

Meanwood, its name being Old English for a common wood, once referred to the woods on both sides of the stream, including Weetwood and possibly Lawn Wood. These three woods were divided between the parishes of Chapel Allerton, Headingley and Adel-cum-Eccup. Lawn Wood, the smallest of these, was opened as Lawnswood Cemetery in 1875 after Leeds Parish Church's burial ground was overflowing. Weetwood was first referred to in 1238 as the site of an iron bloomery and smithy, operated by the monks of Kirkstall Abbey on the site of what was to become Smithy Mills (now Valley Farm). This wood was greatly reduced in the 16th century and, like Meanwood, has been extensively quarried in the last 200 years.

The original settlement of Meanwood was at Meanwood Hill Top, with Meanwoodside (also known as Weetwood-side or simply Woodside) straddling the beck below. However, Adel was the most important ancient settlement in the whole of Leeds after the Romans built a fort and settlement there. Its name likely refers to a boggy place and was often spelt Addle (as it is pronounced) until the early 19th century. Headingley is similarly ancient, its Shire Oak an important meeting place since the Dark Ages.

The valley remains one of the richest woodland landscapes around Leeds and a rewarding place to explore. Accessible from so much of the city, it is unsurprisingly popular.

*the Whale Stone in Weetwood*

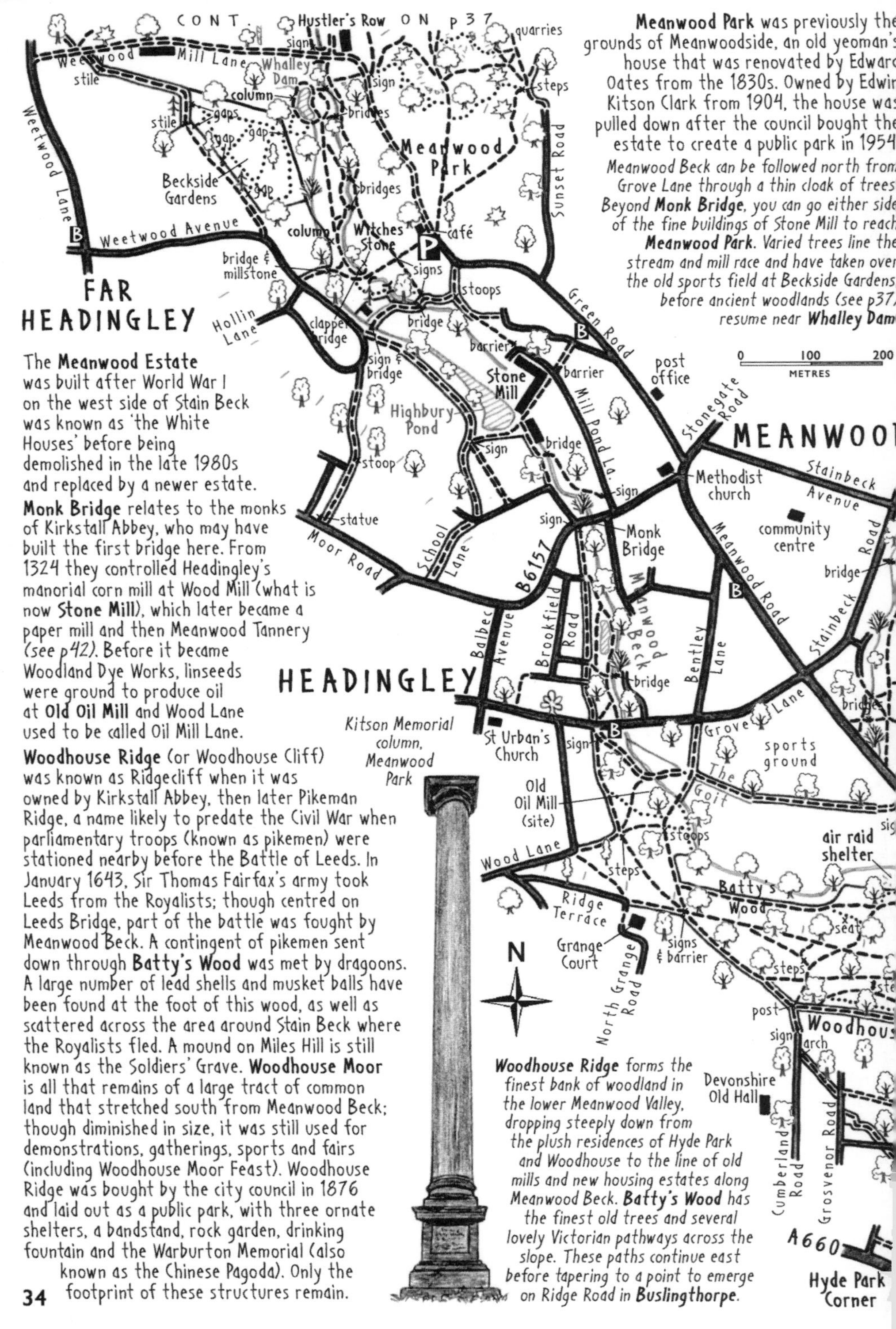
CONT. Hustler's Row ON p37
sign
quarries
Weetwood Mill Lane
Whalley Dam
stile
column
sign
steps
bridges
stile
gaps
gap
gaps
Meanwood Park
Weetwood Lane
Beckside Gardens
gap
bridges
Sunset Road
B
Weetwood Avenue
column
Witches Stone
P
café
bridge & millstone
signs
FAR HEADINGLEY
Hollin Lane
clapper bridge
stoops
bridge
Green Road
B
barrier
sign & bridge
Stone Mill
barrier
post office
0 100 200
METRES
Highbury Pond
Mill Pond La.
Stonegate Road
MEANWOOD
stoop
sign
bridge
Methodist church
Stainbeck Avenue
statue
sign
community centre
Moor Road
School Lane
B6157
Monk Bridge
Meanwood Road
Road
bridge
B
Balbec Avenue
Brookfield Road
Meanwood Beck
Bentley Lane
Stainbeck
HEADINGLEY
bridge
Grove Lane
bridge
St Urban's Church
sign
B
sports ground
The Goit
Old Oil Mill (site)
stoops
air raid shelter
Wood Lane
steps
Batty's Wood
Ridge Terrace
Grange Court
signs & barrier
seat
steps
N
North Grange Road
post
Woodhouse
sign
arch
Devonshire Old Hall
Cumberland Road
Grosvenor Road
A660
Hyde Park Corner

**Meanwood Park** was previously the grounds of Meanwoodside, an old yeoman's house that was renovated by Edward Oates from the 1830s. Owned by Edwin Kitson Clark from 1904, the house was pulled down after the council bought the estate to create a public park in 1954.

*Meanwood Beck can be followed north from Grove Lane through a thin cloak of trees. Beyond* ***Monk Bridge****, you can go either side of the fine buildings of Stone Mill to reach* ***Meanwood Park****. Varied trees line the stream and mill race and have taken over the old sports field at Beckside Gardens before ancient woodlands (see p37) resume near* ***Whalley Dam****.*

The **Meanwood Estate** was built after World War I on the west side of Stain Beck was known as 'the White Houses' before being demolished in the late 1980s and replaced by a newer estate. **Monk Bridge** relates to the monks of Kirkstall Abbey, who may have built the first bridge here. From 1324 they controlled Headingley's manorial corn mill at Wood Mill (what is now **Stone Mill**), which later became a paper mill and then Meanwood Tannery *(see p42)*. Before it became Woodland Dye Works, linseeds were ground to produce oil at **Old Oil Mill** and Wood Lane used to be called Oil Mill Lane.

**Woodhouse Ridge** (or Woodhouse Cliff) was known as Ridgecliff when it was owned by Kirkstall Abbey, then later Pikeman Ridge, a name likely to predate the Civil War when parliamentary troops (known as pikemen) were stationed nearby before the Battle of Leeds. In January 1643, Sir Thomas Fairfax's army took Leeds from the Royalists; though centred on Leeds Bridge, part of the battle was fought by Meanwood Beck. A contingent of pikemen sent down through **Batty's Wood** was met by dragoons. A large number of lead shells and musket balls have been found at the foot of this wood, as well as scattered across the area around Stain Beck where the Royalists fled. A mound on Miles Hill is still known as the Soldiers' Grave. **Woodhouse Moor** is all that remains of a large tract of common land that stretched south from Meanwood Beck; though diminished in size, it was still used for demonstrations, gatherings, sports and fairs (including Woodhouse Moor Feast). Woodhouse Ridge was bought by the city council in 1876 and laid out as a public park, with three ornate shelters, a bandstand, rock garden, drinking fountain and the Warburton Memorial (also known as the Chinese Pagoda). Only the footprint of these structures remain.

*Kitson Memorial column, Meanwood Park*

***Woodhouse Ridge*** *forms the finest bank of woodland in the lower Meanwood Valley, dropping steeply down from the plush residences of Hyde Park and Woodhouse to the line of old mills and new housing estates along Meanwood Beck.* ***Batty's Wood*** *has the finest old trees and several lovely Victorian pathways across the slope. These paths continue east before tapering to a point to emerge on Ridge Road in* ***Buslingthorpe****.*

# MAP 9: MEANWOOD VALLEY SOUTH
## (Woodhouse Ridge, Sugarwell Hill & Meanwood Park)

The Meanwood Valley reaches a long green arm into the heart of Leeds, ending just outside the city centre. Between Buslingthorpe and Headingley, Woodhouse Ridge forms a thick wooded cloak along the south of the valley, while the younger Sugarwell Hill Park climbs the slope to the north. Though there is a narrow section around Monk Bridge, the greenery returns at Meanwood Park and Beckside Gardens, and any walk along the beck remains dominated by trees. It is easily accessed from the suburbs on all side and is closest to Burley Park railway station.

**Sugar Well** was a rag (or clootie) well, where rags were tied to trees as offerings to symbolically shed ailments up to the 1960s. The clear water here was noticeably sweet (in many other wells sugar was added to the water to make it palatable) and the name of nearby **Miles Hill** is thought to relate to a Celtic word for 'honey water'.

*air raid shelter, Batty's Wood*

**Sugarwell Hill Windmill** (now known as the Round House) dates from 1789, while **Scott Hall Windmill** was built in 1776 by Thomas Garforth, the owner of Wood Mills (some distance away, now the site of Stone Mill). Both were marked as 'old windmills' on the 1850s map and used as residences from the 1880s, though Scott Hall Windmill was pulled down in the late 1930s.

***Stain Beck** and **Miles Hill** form further green corridors through the estates of north Leeds, but the trees quickly disappear. Miles Hill, the high point of Sugarwell Hill, has fine views over Leeds city centre.*

The **Destructor Chimney** on Meanwood Road was a striking landmark below Woodhouse Ridge from 1895 until its demolition in 1978. Standing 240-feet high, it served the city's refuse incinerator.

***Sugarwell Hill Park** is comprised of a lot of young woodland on the slope between Meanwood Beck and Scott Hall Road, with **Meanwood Valley Urban Farm** in the middle. There are open areas along the beck and on the top of the hill, but the steepest part of the hill is dense with trees. **Scott Wood Lane** and Low Wood Lane are older thoroughfares, while a couple of smaller paths cross the slope higher up from a rough gap on Buslingthorpe Lane.*

At Buslingthorpe, **Meanwood Beck** becomes corralled in a small brick channel before disappearing beneath the city centre (apart from short sections behind Mabgate) to emerge in the River Aire opposite Leeds Dock.

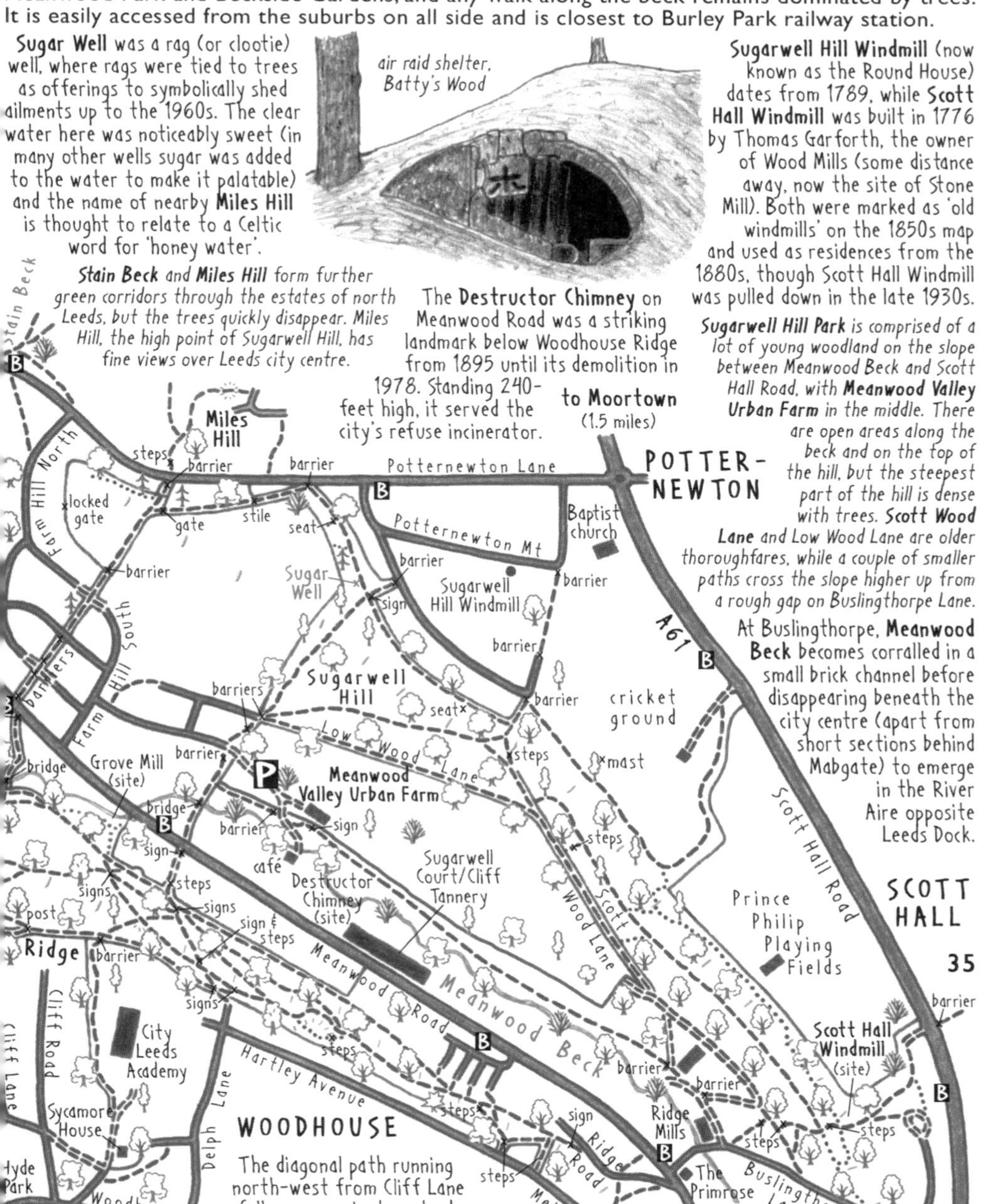

Stain Beck
to Moortown
(1.5 miles)
Miles Hill
steps
barrier
Potternewton Lane
POTTER-NEWTON
locked gate
gate
stile
seat
Potternewton Mt
Baptist church
Farm Hill North
Sugar Well
sign
Sugarwell Hill Windmill
A61
Farm Hill South
barriers
Sugarwell Hill
cricket ground
Low Wood Lane
mast
bridge
Grove Mill (site)
Meanwood Valley Urban Farm
café
Destructor Chimney (site)
Sugarwell Court/Cliff Tannery
Scott Hall Road
Scott Wood Lane
Prince Philip Playing Fields
SCOTT HALL
signs
post
sign & steps
Ridge
Meanwood Road
Meanwood Beck
Cliff Road
Cliff Lane
City Leeds Academy
Hartley Avenue
Sycamore House
Delph Lane
WOODHOUSE
Ridge Road
Ridge Mills
The Primrose
Scott Hall Windmill (site)
Buslingthorpe Lane
gap
Hyde Park
Woodhouse St
Woodhouse Moor
Melville Place
BUSLINGTHORPE
The diagonal path running north-west from Cliff Lane follows an ancient route down to Headingley's manorial corn mill.

# MAP 10: MEANWOOD VALLEY CENTRAL (Weetwood, Meanwood & Adel)

The heart of the Meanwood Valley is abundantly wooded and one of Leeds' finest natural treasures. Weetwood (now known as The Hollies) is full of dense rhododendron, holly and many exotic species. Meanwood is more open, a rock-filled expanse of oak whose tentacles reach around the modern estate of the Woodleas. North of the Ring Road, Scotland Wood's pines open out into the rich oak, birch and holly of Adel Woods, home to the Buck Stone, Seven Arches Aqueduct and Slabbering Baby Well. All these areas are covered in pathways and full of interest.

**Eastmoor School** opened in 1857 as Leeds Reformatory for Boys, providing healthy outdoor activities like wood cutting, carpentry, gardening and swimming. It operated under various guises until 1991, though its eerie listed buildings remain.

**Slabbering Baby Well** (known locally as Slavering Sal) was created in 1901 by Ben Verity for Mill Fall Cottage, which once stood opposite and was the site of the popular **Verity's Tea Shop** until the 1950s (run by the indomitable Mrs Francis Verity). It had been a small flax mill in the 1840s, but all that remains of either are a potato store and the nearby stone toilet block the council insisted was built. Spring water once gushed from the baby's mouth, though it now dribbles underneath more like the name suggests. **St Helen's Lane** in Adel is named after St Helen's Well, a pre-Christian holy well.

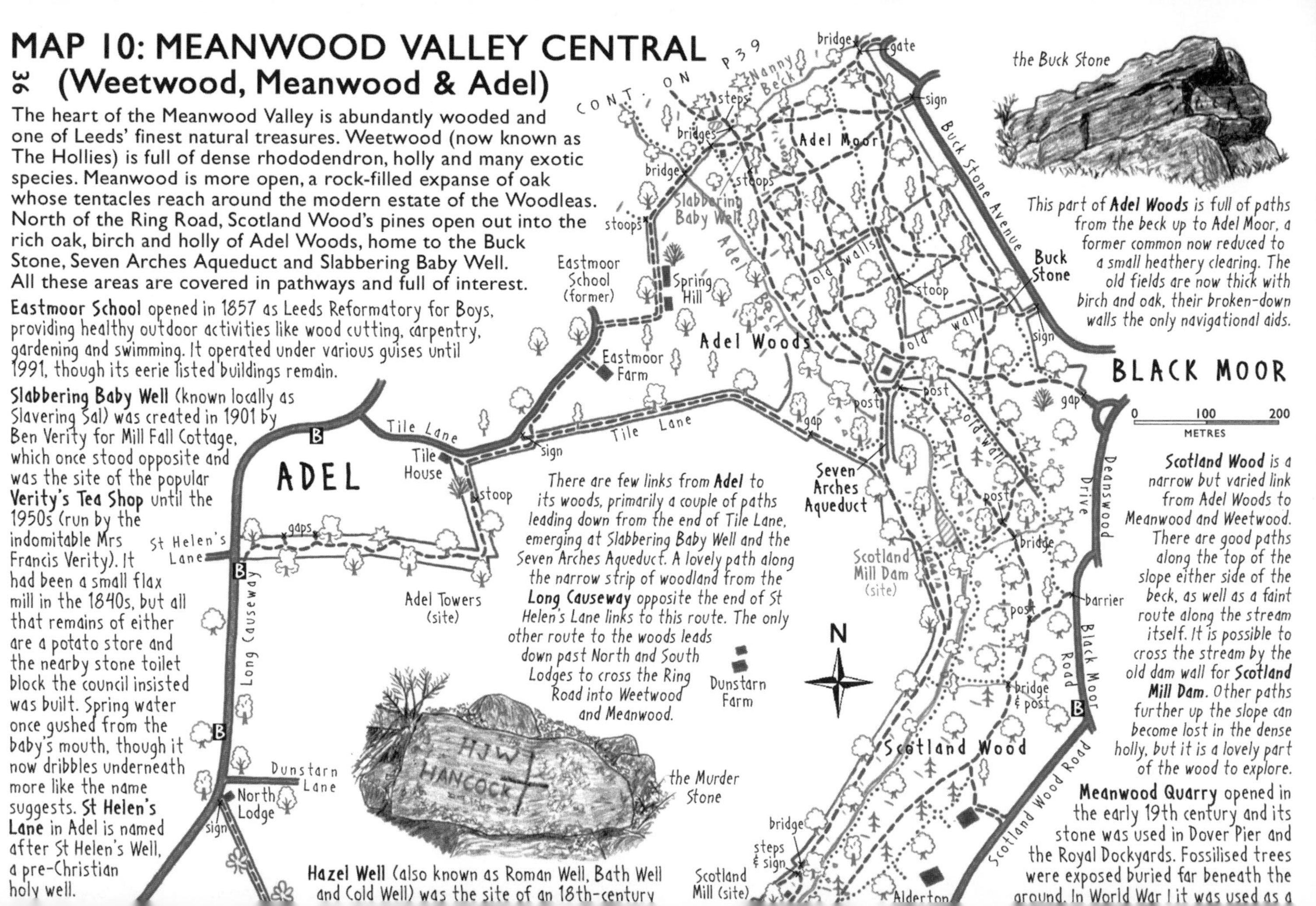

the Buck Stone
CONT. ON P39
bridge
gate
sign
Nanny Beck
steps
bridges
bridge
stoops
Adel Moor
Buck Stone Avenue
Slabbering Baby Well
Adel Beck
stoops
old walls
stoop
old wall
Buck Stone
sign
Eastmoor School (former)
Spring Hill
Eastmoor Farm
Adel Woods
post
post
gap
BLACK MOOR
0 100 200
METRES
Tile Lane
Tile Lane
sign
Tile House
ADEL
stoop
Seven Arches Aqueduct
old wall
post
bridge
Deanswood Drive
St Helen's Lane
gaps
Long Causeway
Adel Towers (site)
Scotland Mill Dam (site)
barrier
post
N
Black Moor Road
Dunstarn Farm
bridge & post
Scotland Wood
Dunstarn Lane
North Lodge
sign
HJW HANCOCK
the Murder Stone
Scotland Wood Road
bridge
steps & sign
Scotland Mill (site)
Alderton


There are few links from **Adel** to its woods, primarily a couple of paths leading down from the end of Tile Lane, emerging at Slabbering Baby Well and the Seven Arches Aqueduct. A lovely path along the narrow strip of woodland from the **Long Causeway** opposite the end of St Helen's Lane links to this route. The only other route to the woods leads down past North and South Lodges to cross the Ring Road into Weetwood and Meanwood.

This part of **Adel Woods** is full of paths from the beck up to Adel Moor, a former common now reduced to a small heathery clearing. The old fields are now thick with birch and oak, their broken-down walls the only navigational aids.

**Scotland Wood** is a narrow but varied link from Adel Woods to Meanwood and Weetwood. There are good paths along the top of the slope either side of the beck, as well as a faint route along the stream itself. It is possible to cross the stream by the old dam wall for **Scotland Mill Dam**. Other paths further up the slope can become lost in the dense holly, but it is a lovely part of the wood to explore.

**Hazel Well** (also known as Roman Well, Bath Well and Cold Well) was the site of an 18th-century

**Meanwood Quarry** opened in the early 19th century and its stone was used in Dover Pier and the Royal Dockyards. Fossilised trees were exposed buried far beneath the ground. In World War I it was used as a bath house attached to the Well House Inn (which had spells as the Woodcock, Woodpecker and Long Taproom). Parkside Road was known as Dunny Hill by locals after one of its landlords Isaac Dunbar.

gun-testing range, before being filled with household rubbish from the 1940s. The main site, now grazed by horses, is largely invisible.

***The Woodleas** housing estate is surrounded by a ring of predominantly beech woodland, with the ancient Park Bottom Wood covering the slope down towards Meanwood Beck, linking into adjacent Meanwood and Scotland Wood.*

**Meanwood Hall** was built in the 1760s by Thomas Denison. The city acquired the Meanwood Park estate in 1919 and established Meanwood Park Colony for those with learning disabilities. It had 841 patients at its peak and closed in 1997, when it was converted to housing and **the Woodleas** estate sprung up around it. A beech tree in front of the hall is said to predate the building.

The **Murder Stone** is a misleadingly titled memorial stone to Henry Trevor Wheeler Handcock, a 26-year-old Londoner who shot himself here in 1892, possibly after being spurned by a local girl. It is carved with a cross and his misspelt name, and lodged in an old stone wall.

***Weetwood** is a dark but rather magical expanse of mostly planted yet often exotic woodland on several quarried sites near the former mansions of **The Hollies** and Moorlands School. Its maze of paths is a joy to explore and lead steeply down to a mill race for Weetwood Mill, at the north end of which a bridge crosses the beck into **Meanwood**.*

**Moorlands School** was built in 1863 as Fox Hill, an opulent mansion with its own spire, by Francis Tetley (whose father Joshua founded Tetley's Brewery).

*It can be hard to trace any paths through **Meanwood**, as the rocky ground beneath its oaks is so open you can walk anywhere. The rock has been widely quarried, most obviously behind Myrtle Tavern, though the deepest part of **Meanwood Quarry** is now filled in. The most obvious paths lead along the river, linking south into Meanwood Park or north to **Parkside Road**.*

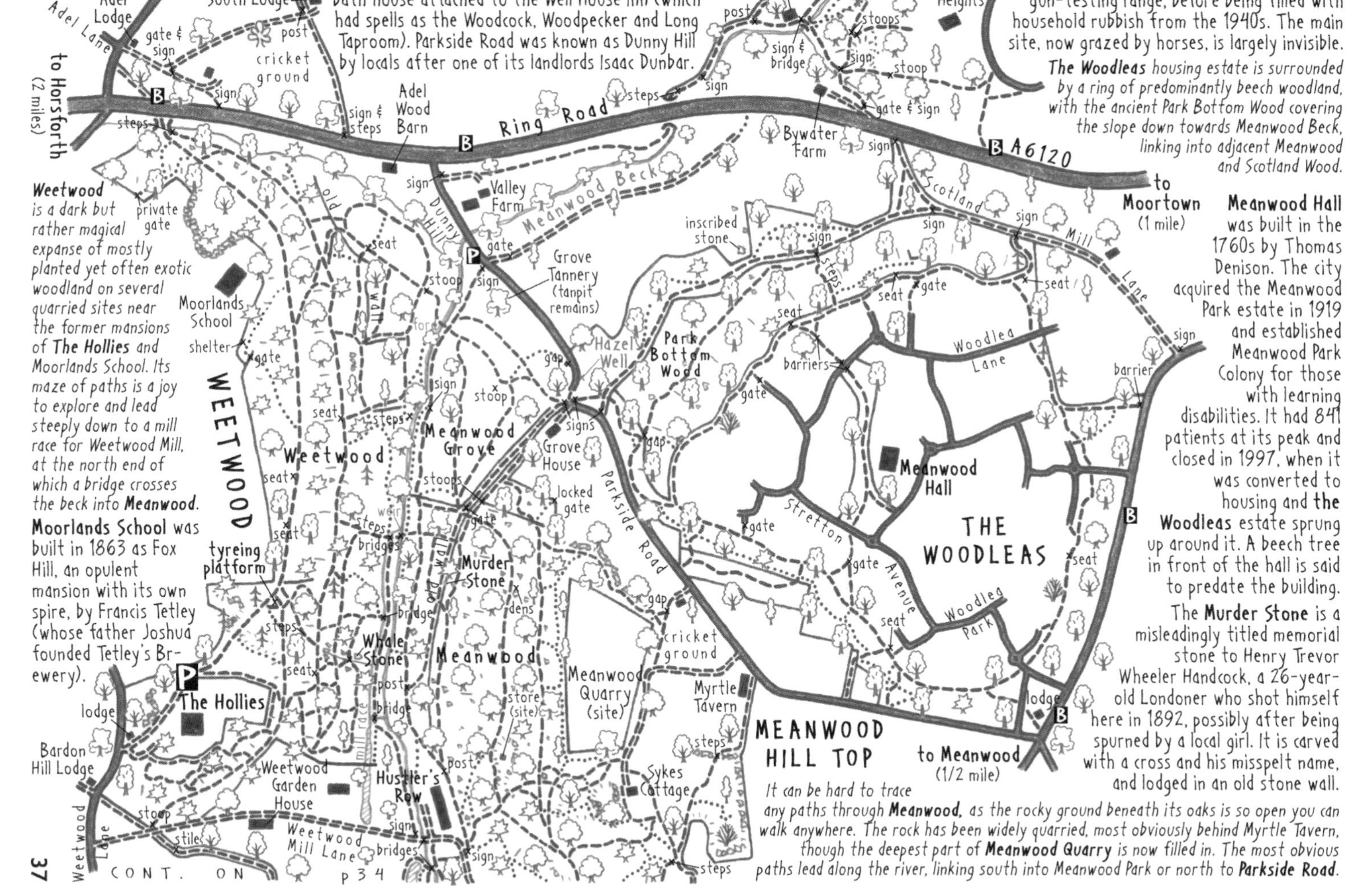
Adel Lodge
Adel Lane
to Horsforth
(2 miles)
South Lodge
post
cricket ground
Adel Wood Barn
Ring Road
A6120
to Moortown
(1 mile)
Bywater Farm
Heights
Valley Farm
Meanwood Beck
Dunny Hill
Grove Tannery
(tanpit remains)
inscribed stone
Scotland
Mill
Lane
Park Bottom Wood
Hazel Well
Woodlea Lane
Meanwood Hall
THE WOODLEAS
Stretton
Avenue
Woodlea Park
barrier
barriers
lodge
to Meanwood
(1/2 mile)
Parkside Road
Grove House
locked gate
Meanwood Grove
Weetwood
WEETWOOD
Moorlands School
shelter
private gate
tyreing platform
Murder Stone
old wall
dens
Whale Stone
Meanwood
cricket ground
Meanwood Quarry
(site)
store
(site)
Myrtle Tavern
MEANWOOD HILL TOP
Sykes Cottage
Hustler's Row
mill race
Weetwood Garden House
Weetwood Mill Lane
The Hollies
lodge
Bardon Hill Lodge
Weetwood Lane
stile
stoop
steps
seat
gate
sign
bridges
CONT. ON p34

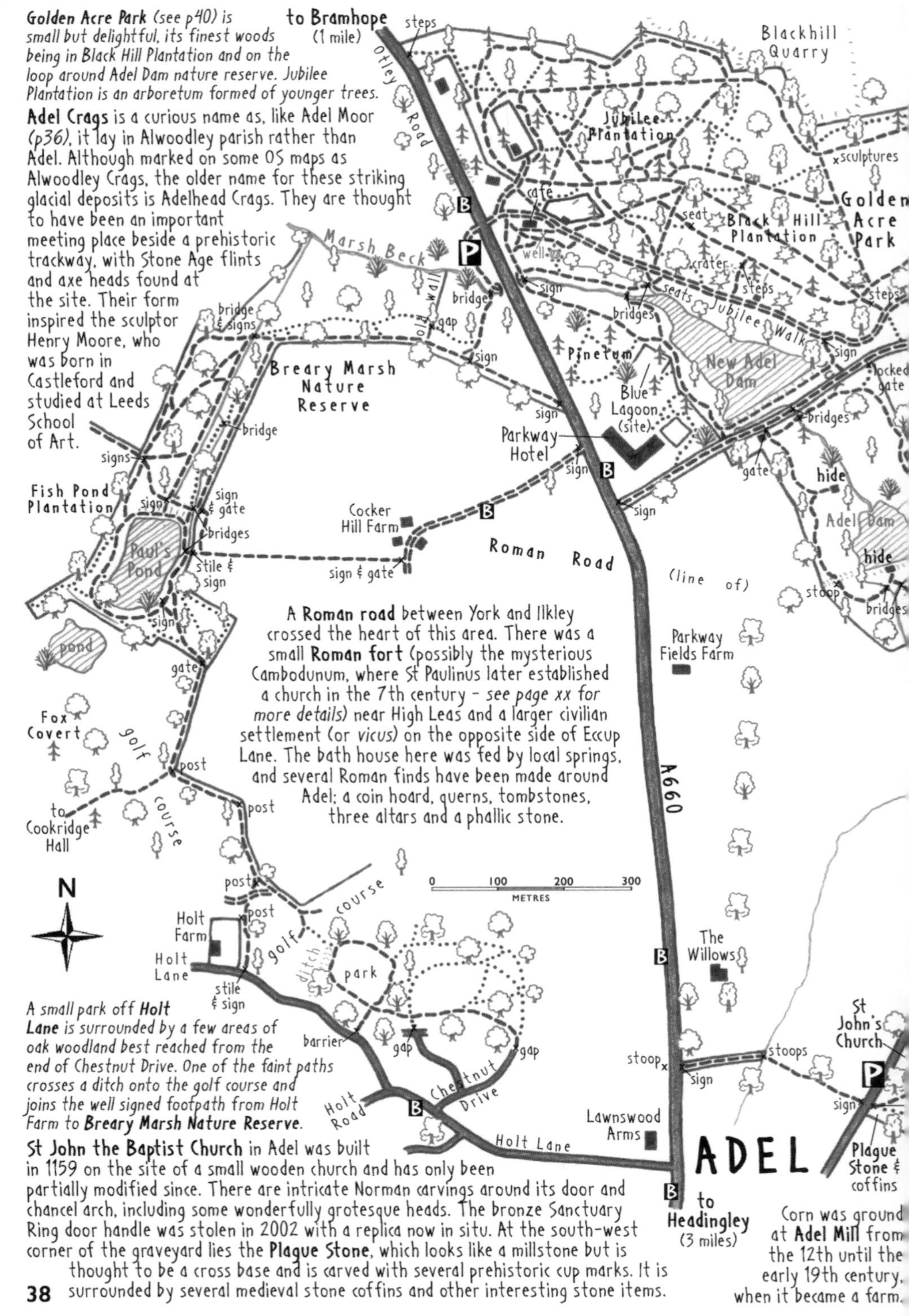
to Bramhope
(1 mile)
steps
Otley Road
Blackhill
Quarry
Jubilee
Plantation
xsculptures
cafe
B
P
Marsh Beck
well
seat
Black Hill
Plantation
Golden
Acre
Park
crater
steps
steps
sign
bridge
old wall
gap
bridges
seats
Jubilee Walk
sign
bridge & signs
Pinetum
New Adel
Dam
locked
gate
sign
Breary Marsh
Nature
Reserve
Blue
Lagoon
(site)
sign
bridges
bridge
Parkway
Hotel
sign
B
gate
hide
signs
Fish Pond
Plantation
sign
sign & gate
bridges
Cocker
Hill Farm
B
sign
Adel Dam
Paul's
Pond
stile & sign
sign & gate
Roman Road
(line of)
hide
stoop
bridges
sign
pond
gate
Parkway
Fields Farm
Fox
Covert
golf
course
post
to
Cookridge
Hall
post
A660
N
post
post
course
0 100 200 300
METRES
Holt
Farm
golf
Holt
Lane
ditch
park
The
Willows
B
stile
& sign
barrier
gap
gap
Chestnut
Drive
stoop
sign
stoops
St
John's
Church
P
sign
Holt
Road
B
Holt Lane
Lawnswood
Arms
ADEL
Plague
Stone &
coffins
B
to
Headingley
(3 miles)

**Golden Acre Park** *(see p40) is small but delightful, its finest woods being in Black Hill Plantation and on the loop around Adel Dam nature reserve. Jubilee Plantation is an arboretum formed of younger trees.*

**Adel Crags** is a curious name as, like Adel Moor *(p36)*, it lay in Alwoodley parish rather than Adel. Although marked on some OS maps as Alwoodley Crags, the older name for these striking glacial deposits is Adelhead Crags. They are thought to have been an important meeting place beside a prehistoric trackway, with Stone Age flints and axe heads found at the site. Their form inspired the sculptor Henry Moore, who was born in Castleford and studied at Leeds School of Art.

A **Roman road** between York and Ilkley crossed the heart of this area. There was a small **Roman fort** (possibly the mysterious Cambodunum, where St Paulinus later established a church in the 7th century - *see page xx for more details)* near High Leas and a larger civilian settlement (or *vicus*) on the opposite side of Eccup Lane. The bath house here was fed by local springs, and several Roman finds have been made around Adel; a coin hoard, querns, tombstones, three altars and a phallic stone.

*A small park off* ***Holt Lane*** *is surrounded by a few areas of oak woodland best reached from the end of Chestnut Drive. One of the faint paths crosses a ditch onto the golf course and joins the well signed footpath from Holt Farm to* ***Breary Marsh Nature Reserve****.*

**St John the Baptist Church** in Adel was built in 1159 on the site of a small wooden church and has only been partially modified since. There are intricate Norman carvings around its door and chancel arch, including some wonderfully grotesque heads. The bronze Sanctuary Ring door handle was stolen in 2002 with a replica now in situ. At the south-west corner of the graveyard lies the **Plague Stone**, which looks like a millstone but is thought to be a cross base and is carved with several prehistoric cup marks. It is surrounded by several medieval stone coffins and other interesting stone items.

Corn was ground at **Adel Mill** from the 12th until the early 19th century, when it became a farm.

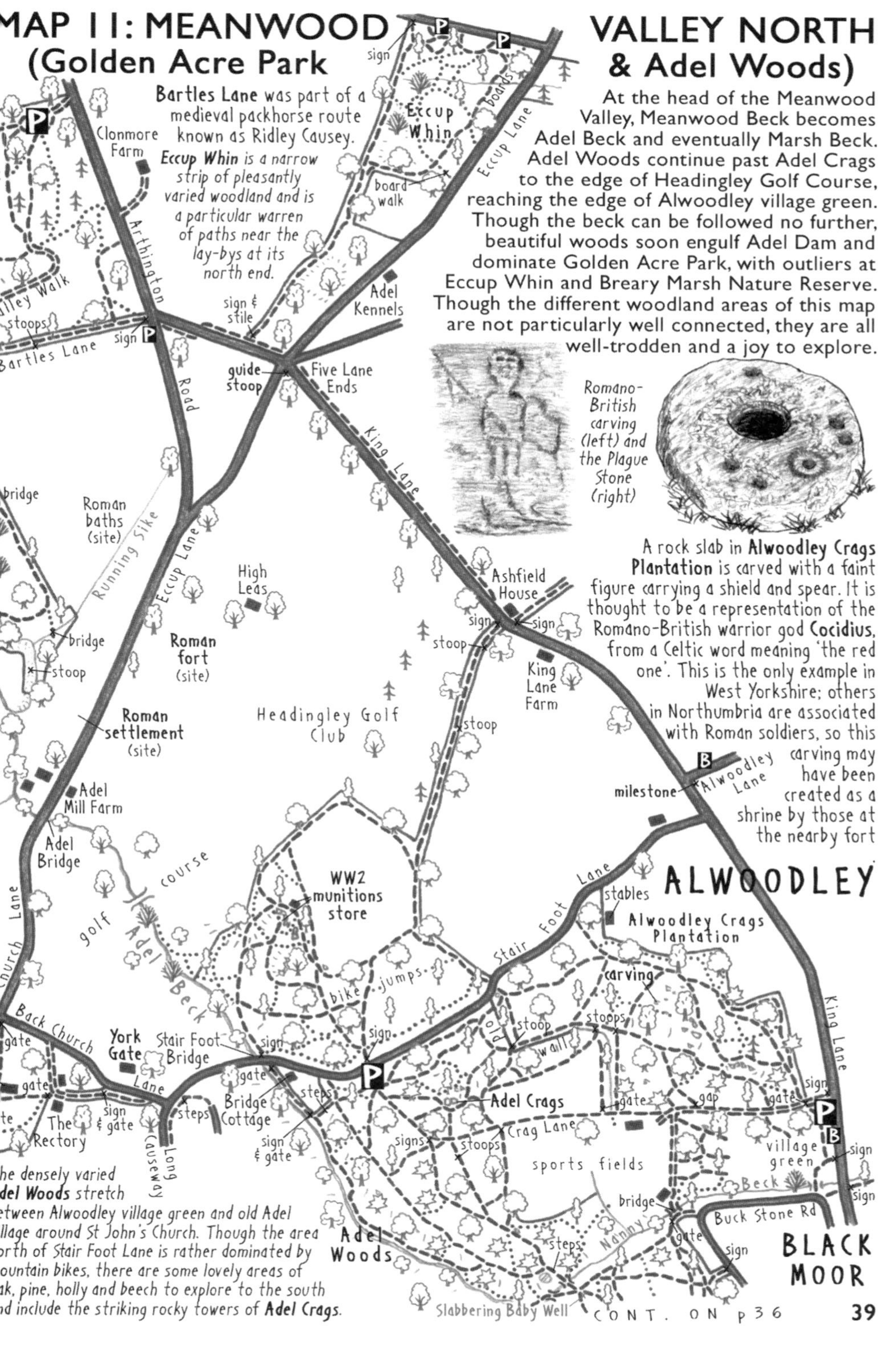
MAP 11: MEANWOOD VALLEY NORTH
(Golden Acre Park & Adel Woods)
At the head of the Meanwood Valley, Meanwood Beck becomes Adel Beck and eventually Marsh Beck. Adel Woods continue past Adel Crags to the edge of Headingley Golf Course, reaching the edge of Alwoodley village green. Though the beck can be followed no further, beautiful woods soon engulf Adel Dam and dominate Golden Acre Park, with outliers at Eccup Whin and Breary Marsh Nature Reserve. Though the different woodland areas of this map are not particularly well connected, they are all well-trodden and a joy to explore.
Bartles Lane was part of a medieval packhorse route known as Ridley Causey.
Eccup Whin is a narrow strip of pleasantly varied woodland and is a particular warren of paths near the lay-bys at its north end.
Romano-British carving (left) and the Plague Stone (right)
A rock slab in Alwoodley Crags Plantation is carved with a faint figure carrying a shield and spear. It is thought to be a representation of the Romano-British warrior god Cocidius, from a Celtic word meaning 'the red one'. This is the only example in West Yorkshire; others in Northumbria are associated with Roman soldiers, so this carving may have been created as a shrine by those at the nearby fort
he densely varied
del Woods stretch
etween Alwoodley village green and old Adel
llage around St John's Church. Though the area
orth of Stair Foot Lane is rather dominated by
ountain bikes, there are some lovely areas of
ak, pine, holly and beech to explore to the south
nd include the striking rocky towers of Adel Crags.
sign
Eccup Whin
boards
Eccup Lane
board walk
Clonmore Farm
Arthington Road
alley Walk
stoops
Bartles Lane
sign
sign & stile
Adel Kennels
guide stoop
Five Lane Ends
King Lane
bridge
Roman baths (site)
Running Sike
Eccup Lane
High Leas
Ashfield House
sign
sign
stoop
King Lane Farm
bridge
stoop
Roman fort (site)
Roman settlement (site)
Headingley Golf Club
stoop
Adel Mill Farm
Adel Bridge
milestone
Alwoodley Lane
golf course
WW2 munitions store
ALWOODLEY
stables
Alwoodley Crags Plantation
Church Lane
Adel Beck
Stair Foot Lane
bike jumps
carving
stoops
stoop
wall
Old
Back Church Lane
gate
York Gate
Stair Foot Bridge
sign
sign
gate
Bridge Cottage
steps
Adel Crags
gate
gap
gate
sign
gate
The Rectory
sign & gate
steps
Long Causeway
signs
stoops
Crag Lane
sign & gate
sports fields
village green
sign
Beck
sign
bridge
Buck Stone Rd
Adel Woods
steps
Nanny
gate
sign
BLACK MOOR
Slabbering Baby Well
CONT. ON p36
39

# GOLDEN ACRE PARK

What is now Golden Acre Park was for most of its history a largely ignored boggy wasteland, forming part of Bramhope Bog or Breary Marsh (meaning 'overgrown with briars'). On the slopes above stood Blackhill Well Farm (occupied until 1930s, its site near the Blenheim Courtyard and café) and Blackhill Well (which still flows through the rockery). New Adel Dam (later known as Black Hill Dam and Wormald's Dam) was created on the site in 1825 by a consortium of mill owners further down the valley. Its dam burst on July 11th 1829 and what became known as Adel Beck Flood flooded the whole Meanwood Valley down to Leeds and destroyed bridges, mills and some tenement homes around Scotland Mill.

The name Golden Acre was coined in the 1920s by Herbert Thompson because of the colour of the sandstone quarried here. His Golden Acre Estate was to be a new housing development, but it proved too far from Leeds to attract buyers and only a few houses were built along Otley Road near the park entrance. His son Frank Thompson inherited the estate in 1928 and set about creating an amusement park modelled on Coney Island. The dam, intentionally cut in the 1880s, was repaired and a new boating lake formed the centrepiece. A miniature railway ran round the lake with several stations, and a music tower in the middle broadcast swing music around the park. Attractions included hoverplanes (similar to Bayou swamp boats), the Mountain Glide, a helter skelter, playship, lighthouse, monorail, circus, pitch and putt and the largest dancehall in Yorkshire. Golden Acre Park opened on Good Friday 1932, with the Blue Lagoon swimming pool added in 1934, a zoo in 1937 and the Parkway Hotel in 1938. The latter was a Tudorbethan building featuring a ballroom known as the Cocoanut Grove and kennels for the guests' dogs known as the Barkway.

However, the 1930s was not a good time to launch such an ambitious project and Golden Acre Park was overshadowed by Roundhay Park, which was far easier for people to reach without a car. It did not reopen for the new season in 1939, and Thompson tried to sell it off for housing before offering it to the council in 1943. Little remains of the amusement park; a small section of railway and a platform near the café; and parts of the Blue Lagoon, which continued in use through the 1950s as part of the Parkway Hotel before being demolished in 1965.

During World War II the lake was drained after the park was bombed, a crater still visible near the foot of Black Hill Plantation. This wood was also used for tank exercises and volunteer training, with some shell pits still evident. Flyash and rubble from slum clearance were subsequently dumped at the western end of the lake, so when it was reinstated it was a significantly smaller feature.

After the war the council set about creating 'the Kew Gardens of the North', with various botanical gardens laid out by Ted Snell and trees planted round site. The Pinetum (an arboretum of conifers) was planted in 1953 on boggy ground, with the arboretum of the Jubilee Plantation created the same decade. Many of the mature beeches of Blackhill Plantation, planted around 1815 by Sir John Sheffield of Cookridge Hall, were felled by storms in February 1962 and replaced with birch and pine. Golden Acre quickly became renowned for its ornamental gardens, whose colourful displays changed every year and became home to several national plant collections (including lilac, hosta and deutzia). Former farmland and plantations to the east were purchased by the council in 1982. Previously part of Cookridge Hall's estate, Breary Marsh was appended in 1983, its rare alder carr woodland home to marsh violet, figwort and angelica. Adel Dam, dating from the 18th century, was restored after being taken over by the Yorkshire Wildlife Trust in 1968. It has a wealth of birdlife, including bats, warblers, blackcap and chiffchaff, and many exotic plant species that were introduced by Edwin Eddison.

*the remains of Golden Acre Park's railway and platform*

# THE TANNING INDUSTRY

The Aire Valley was a nationally important centre of the tanning industry, Leeds being second only to London as a leather producer in the 19th century, when it knocked out over 100,000 pairs of boots a week. This was particularly true along the Meanwood Valley, whose soft water flowing from the millstone grit to the north-west of the city was attractive to fullers and paper-makers as well as tanners. Tanneries required plentiful woods (to supply tannin-rich oak bark), relatively flat ground for their tan pits and a steady flow of water to drive waterwheels for grinding the oak bark and filling the tan pits. They also needed a source of the hides themselves, which meant being close to butchers in large centres of population. Most tanneries were located on the furthest reaches of settlements like Leeds, though, because of their foul odours, and the Meanwood Valley was a perfect location on all these counts.

The process of leather tanning has changed little since the Middle Ages. Fellmongers first prepared the animal hides for tanning (*fell* here being an Old English word for skin). The skins were then soaked in lime solution to remove hair and fat from the hide, before being soaked in a liquor of tannin-rich oak bark and water at increasing strengths to preserve and toughen it to leather. The oak bark was supplied by barkers (often women) working in the nearby woods, stripping the fresher bark from the trees before drying it in stacks for a few weeks. The crude leather produced was passed to curriers, who softened, dressed and coloured the material to make it ready for use by the various leatherworkers (shoemakers, saddlers and glove-makers). One of its major uses locally was in the leather picker straps widely used in textile mills. As demand grew, the local woods could no longer supply all of the necessary bark and much of it was imported from Ireland or beyond.

*overgrown tanpits at Exley's Tannery, Meanwood*

Early tanning was generally done on a small scale, often just a cottage industry, but many monasteries realised the industry's economic value. Tanning pits have been found at Rievaulx, Tintern and other major abbeys, and are thought to have existed at Kirkstall Abbey. Larger tanneries with mill structures, dams and waterwheels were developed during the 18th century. Whalley Tannery (now the site of Holmes Farm near Meanwoodside) was the oldest tannery in the Meanwood Valley. Established in the mid 17th century by Thomas Whalley, it was supplied with water via a goit still present that leads to Highbury Pond. Geldard's Tannery was a small but profitable operation set up by John Geldard opposite Hustler's Row, while Exley's (Grove) Tannery was a more substantial 19th-century enterprise by Parkside Road. The latter was pulled down around 1927, but its tan pits are still obvious in the trees behind the picnic site.

The lower part of the Meanwood Valley was home to several larger leatherworks, tanneries and dyeworks, the scale of these operations still evident at Sugarwell Court (once Cliff Tannery) and Stone Mill. After a fire in 1852 the latter was rebuilt as Meanwood Tannery by Samuel Smith to become one of the largest tanneries in the country. Meanwood's most important employer, its three hundred tan pits covered five acres and could handle 70,000 hides at any one time. Smith's son, another Samuel, left to run the family's brewery in Tadcaster, but the mill (then known as Highbury Works) was used by fellmongers well into the 20th century. Its listed buildings were renovated in 1994 as housing now known as Stone Mill and Tannery Park.

Tanneries were notoriously rough places, as the foul smell tended to put off anyone who had the choice of working elsewhere. Meanwood was full of tanners and quarrymen and was consequently renowned for drunken and immoral behaviour. Leeds' tanning industry declined dramatically around the turn of the 20th century due to foreign competition. With the end of quarrying, the Meanwood Valley became a quiet backwater; though some cloth mills had reached it, the lack of a canal or rail network limited the sort of larger mills that were built there.

# ROUTE 7: ADEL WOODS & GOLDEN ACRE PARK FROM ALWOODLEY

**Distance:** 8½ miles (13.5km)

**Ascent:** 150m

**Parking:** Free car parks at Alwoodley village green, by St John's Church in Adel and at Golden Acre Park.

**Public Transport:** Buses 7A & X7 run from Leeds to King Lane in Alwoodley and buses 8, X84 & 85 from Leeds stop on the A660 in Adel.

**Character:** A varied walk around the gentle landscape at the top end of the Meanwood Valley. It explores Eccup Whin, Golden Acre Park and Breary Marsh, as well as a loop through the rich scenery of Adel Woods, taking in Slabbering Baby Well, Seven Arches Aqueduct and the Buck Stone. The walk can also be started in Adel and there are a couple of obvious shortcuts, with paths running alongside King Lane and Stair Foot Lane.

**2** The path soon follows the left edge of the fields, before turning left over a stile towards the plantations around **Eccup Reservoir**. You barely glimpse the water as the path cuts down the left edge of the trees and across the broad field beyond. Reaching **Eccup Moor Road** turn right and then keep left on a short loop of mostly quiet lanes. Only Eccup Lane requires caution, but you soon turn right on Black Hill Lane (unsigned) then bear left into the trees of **Eccup Whin** at the first opportunity. Reaching a larger path, double back left over a section of boardwalk and stay on this clear path as it eventually bends round to the right. Turn left at the end to follow the edge of the trees back to **King Lane**.

**3** Turn right alongside **King Lane** and, at its end, head straight on into the path of Bartles Lane, the start of **Golden Acre Park**. Just before it bends left, cut through to the right to a vehicle track and head straight on up some steps opposite. Turn left at the top and wind through the holly and pine of **Black Hill Plantation**. Fork left by a seat and continue across the slope to emerge from the trees, bearing left at another cluster of seats to descend to the park's famous ornamental gardens. Keep to the left of these and turn left at the end to reach a subway leading beneath the main road. On the other side, the main car park is just to the right but you turn left over a bridge into **Breary Marsh Nature Reserve**.

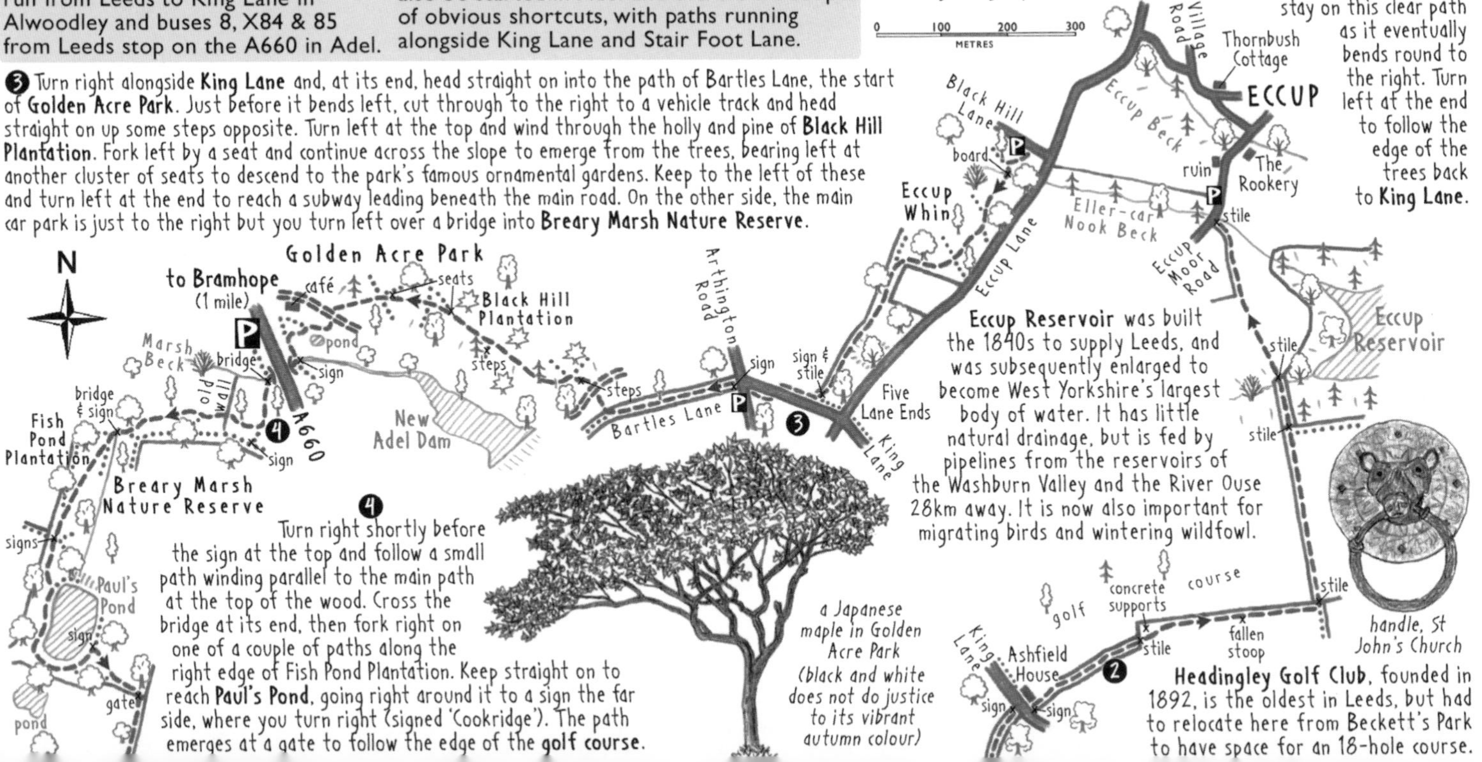

**Eccup Reservoir** was built the 1840s to supply Leeds, and was subsequently enlarged to become West Yorkshire's largest body of water. It has little natural drainage, but is fed by pipelines from the reservoirs of the Washburn Valley and the River Ouse 28km away. It is now also important for migrating birds and wintering wildfowl.

**4** Turn right shortly before the sign at the top and follow a small path winding parallel to the main path at the top of the wood. Cross the bridge at its end, then fork right on one of a couple of paths along the right edge of Fish Pond Plantation. Keep straight on to reach **Paul's Pond**, going right around it to a sign the far side, where you turn right (signed 'Cookridge'). The path emerges at a gate to follow the edge of the **golf course**.

*a Japanese maple in Golden Acre Park (black and white does not do justice to its vibrant autumn colour)*

*handle, St John's Church*

**Headingley Golf Club**, founded in 1892, is the oldest in Leeds, but had to relocate here from Beckett's Park to have space for an 18-hole course.

**1** From the entrance to the car park by **Alwoodley village green**, follow Crag Lane left into the woods and turn first right by a gate across the track. Stay around the edge of **Alwoodley Crags Plantation** at first, then head straight on across the top of the woods until you bear right by a large stone to cross **Stair Foot Lane**. Keep right along the edge of the trees to emerge on a path leading right up the edge of a meadow. Keep straight on to reach **King Lane** again opposite Ashfield House, a path continuing to its right.

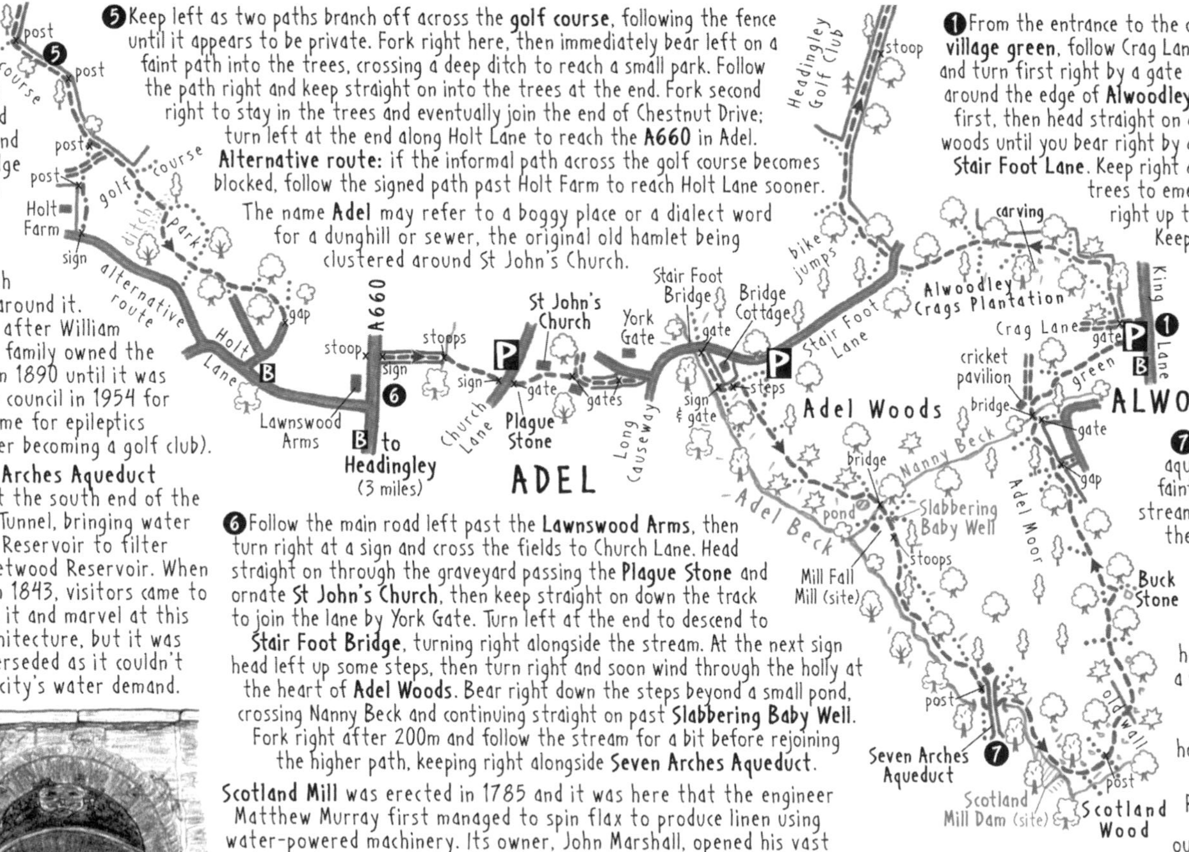

**5** Keep left as two paths branch off across the **golf course**, following the fence until it appears to be private. Fork right here, then immediately bear left on a faint path into the trees, crossing a deep ditch to reach a small park. Follow the path right and keep straight on into the trees at the end. Fork second right to stay in the trees and eventually join the end of Chestnut Drive; turn left at the end along Holt Lane to reach the **A660** in Adel.

**Alternative route:** if the informal path across the golf course becomes blocked, follow the signed path past Holt Farm to reach Holt Lane sooner.

The name **Adel** may refer to a boggy place or a dialect word for a dunghill or sewer, the original old hamlet being clustered around St John's Church.

**Paul's Pond** was created as a fishpond for Cookridge Hall around 1820 by Richard Wormald, with a beech plantation around it. It is named after William Paul, whose family owned the estate from 1890 until it was sold to the council in 1954 for use as a home for epileptics (before later becoming a golf club).

The **Seven Arches Aqueduct** was built at the south end of the Blackmoor Tunnel, bringing water from Eccup Reservoir to filter beds at Weetwood Reservoir. When it opened in 1843, visitors came to walk across it and marvel at this feat of architecture, but it was quickly superseded as it couldn't handle the city's water demand.

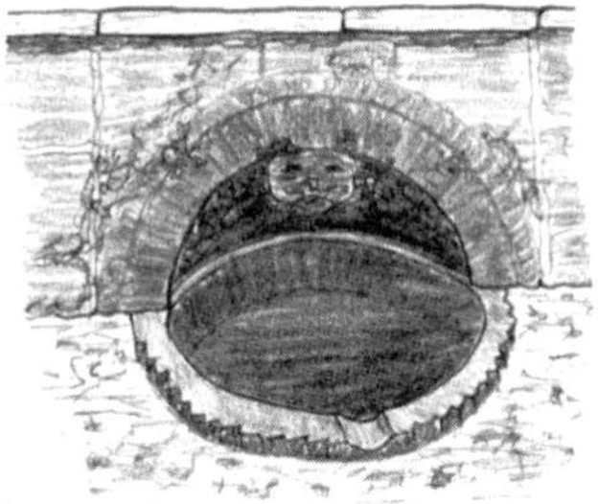

**6** Follow the main road left past the **Lawnswood Arms**, then turn right at a sign and cross the fields to Church Lane. Head straight on through the graveyard passing the **Plague Stone** and ornate **St John's Church**, then keep straight on down the track to join the lane by York Gate. Turn left at the end to descend to **Stair Foot Bridge**, turning right alongside the stream. At the next sign head left up some steps, then turn right and soon wind through the holly at the heart of **Adel Woods**. Bear right down the steps beyond a small pond, crossing Nanny Beck and continuing straight on past **Slabbering Baby Well**. Fork right after 200m and follow the stream for a bit before rejoining the higher path, keeping right alongside **Seven Arches Aqueduct**.

**Scotland Mill** was erected in 1785 and it was here that the engineer Matthew Murray first managed to spin flax to produce linen using water-powered machinery. Its owner, John Marshall, opened his vast Mill A in Holbeck on the same principles and helped launch Leeds' industrial revolution. **Mill Fall Mill**, built by Miles Potter in 1838, was less successful; the flow of Nanny Beck was affected by the creation of Eccup Reservoir and it was necessary to build the tiny but rather ineffective dam on the opposite side of the stream. Scotland Mill burned down in 1906, with Mill Fall Mill being demolished in the 1950s.

**7** In the middle of the aqueduct, turn left on a faint path and follow the stream's left bank down to the old wall of **Scotland Mill Dam**. Leave the bank here and soon fork left up through the beech trees, heading straight on at a waymarker on a path that winds through the oak, rocks and holly. Keep straight on across another main path, then fork right as the trees thin out to reach the **Buck Stone**. Double back left to rejoin the lower path and stay straight on along the top edge of Adel Woods and Moor. At the far end bear right then left to recross **Nanny Beck**. Turn right on any of the small paths near the cricket pavilion and wind through the trees to emerge on **Alwoodley village green** with the car park at the far left corner.

*Slabbering Baby Well*

# ROUTE 8: MEANWOOD PARK & KIRKSTALL ABBEY FROM HEADINGLEY

**Distance:** 8 miles (12.8km) **Ascent:** 220m

**Parking:** Free car parks at Kirkstall Abbey and Meanwood Park, plus plenty of street parking.

**Public Transport:** Headingley is on the Wharfedale railway line from Leeds.

**Character:** A route that manages to link together many parcels of woodland to create a surprisingly green course through the suburbs of Leeds. It takes in Beckett's Park, Meanwood Park, the Hollies, Lawns Wood, Clayton Wood, Hawksworth Wood and finishes past the magnificent ruins of Kirkstall Abbey.

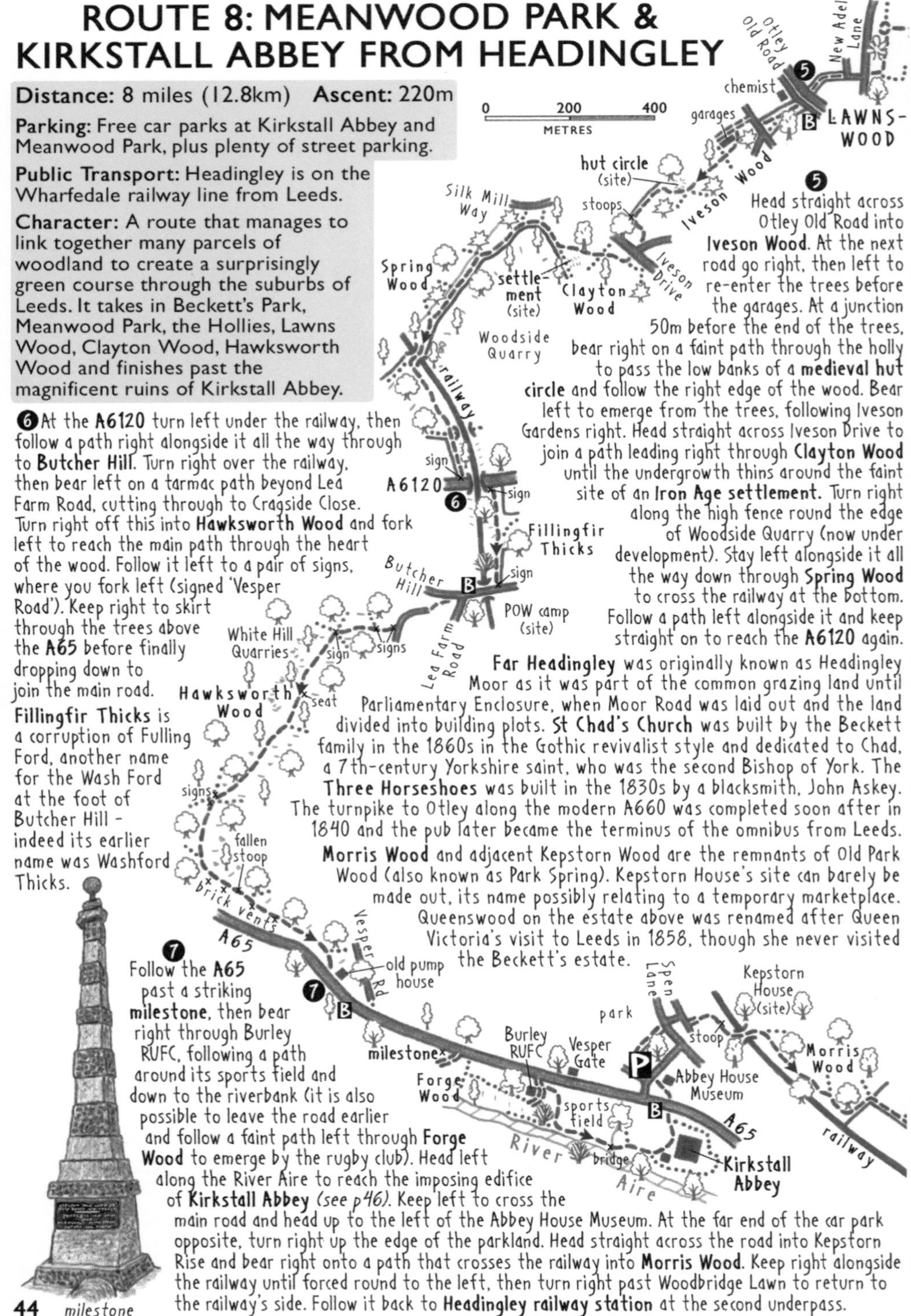

0
200
400
METRES
Otley Old Road
New Adel Lane
chemist
garages
LAWNSWOOD
hut circle (site)
stoops
Iveson Wood
Iveson Drive
Silk Mill Way
Spring Wood
settlement (site)
Clayton Wood
Woodside Quarry
railway
sign
A6120
sign
Fillingfir Thicks
Butcher Hill
sign
POW camp (site)
Lea Farm Road
White Hill Quarries
sign
signs
Hawksworth Wood
seat
signs
fallen stoop
brick vents
A65
Vesper Rd
old pump house
Spen Lane
Kepstorn House (site)
park
stoop
milestone
Burley RUFC
Vesper Gate
Abbey House Museum
Morris Wood
Forge Wood
sports field
A65
River Aire
bridge
Kirkstall Abbey
railway


**5** Head straight across Otley Old Road into **Iveson Wood**. At the next road go right, then left to re-enter the trees before the garages. At a junction 50m before the end of the trees, bear right on a faint path through the holly to pass the low banks of a **medieval hut circle** and follow the right edge of the wood. Bear left to emerge from the trees, following Iveson Gardens right. Head straight across Iveson Drive to join a path leading right through **Clayton Wood** until the undergrowth thins around the faint site of an **Iron Age settlement.** Turn right along the high fence round the edge of Woodside Quarry (now under development). Stay left alongside it all the way down through **Spring Wood** to cross the railway at the bottom. Follow a path left alongside it and keep straight on to reach the **A6120** again.

**6** At the **A6120** turn left under the railway, then follow a path right alongside it all the way through to **Butcher Hill**. Turn right over the railway, then bear left on a tarmac path beyond Lea Farm Road, cutting through to Cragside Close. Turn right off this into **Hawksworth Wood** and fork left to reach the main path through the heart of the wood. Follow it left to a pair of signs, where you fork left (signed 'Vesper Road'). Keep right to skirt through the trees above the **A65** before finally dropping down to join the main road.

**Fillingfir Thicks** is a corruption of Fulling Ford, another name for the Wash Ford at the foot of Butcher Hill – indeed its earlier name was Washford Thicks.

**Far Headingley** was originally known as Headingley Moor as it was part of the common grazing land until Parliamentary Enclosure, when Moor Road was laid out and the land divided into building plots. **St Chad's Church** was built by the Beckett family in the 1860s in the Gothic revivalist style and dedicated to Chad, a 7th-century Yorkshire saint, who was the second Bishop of York. The **Three Horseshoes** was built in the 1830s by a blacksmith, John Askey. The turnpike to Otley along the modern A660 was completed soon after in 1840 and the pub later became the terminus of the omnibus from Leeds. **Morris Wood** and adjacent Kepstorn Wood are the remnants of Old Park Wood (also known as Park Spring). Kepstorn House's site can barely be made out, its name possibly relating to a temporary marketplace. Queenswood on the estate above was renamed after Queen Victoria's visit to Leeds in 1858, though she never visited the Beckett's estate.

**7** Follow the **A65** past a striking **milestone**, then bear right through Burley RUFC, following a path around its sports field and down to the riverbank (it is also possible to leave the road earlier and follow a faint path left through **Forge Wood** to emerge by the rugby club). Head left along the River Aire to reach the imposing edifice of **Kirkstall Abbey** *(see p46)*. Keep left to cross the main road and head up to the left of the Abbey House Museum. At the far end of the car park opposite, turn right up the edge of the parkland. Head straight across the road into Kepstorn Rise and bear right onto a path that crosses the railway into **Morris Wood**. Keep right alongside the railway until forced round to the left, then turn right past Woodbridge Lawn to return to the railway's side. Follow it back to **Headingley railway station** at the second underpass.

*milestone*

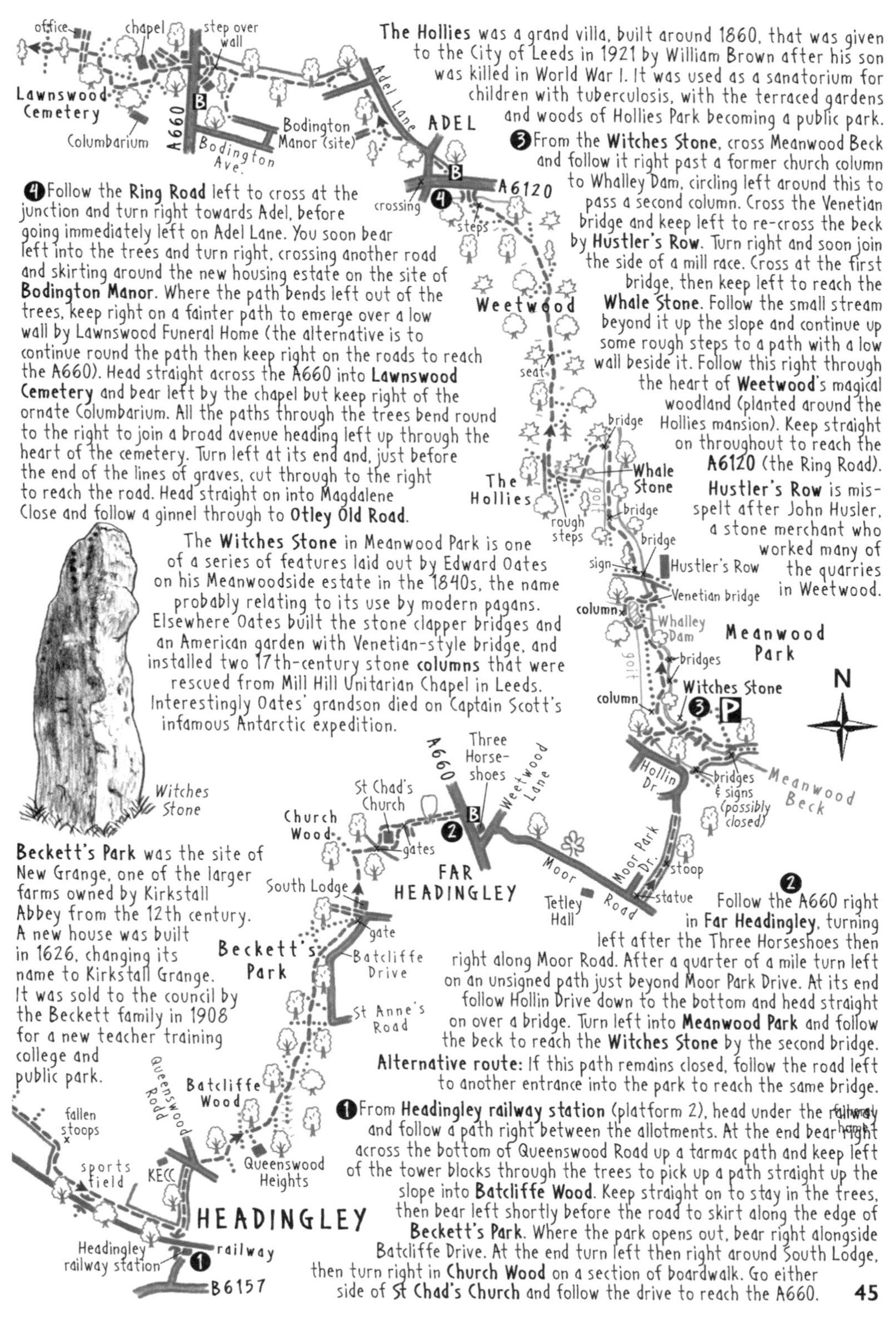

office
chapel
step over wall
Lawnswood Cemetery
Columbarium
A660
B
Bodington Ave.
Bodington Manor (site)
Adel Lane
ADEL
B
A6120
crossing
4
steps
Weetwood
seat
bridge
The Hollies
Whale Stone
goit
rough steps
bridge
bridge
sign
Hustler's Row
Venetian bridge
column
Whalley Dam
goit
bridges
Meanwood Park
column
Witches Stone
3
P
N
Hollin Dr.
bridges & signs (possibly closed)
Meanwood Beck
Moor Park Dr.
stoop
statue
Moor Road
Tetley Hall
A660
Three Horse-shoes
Weetwood Lane
St Chad's Church
Church Wood
2
B
gates
FAR HEADINGLEY
South Lodge
gate
Beckett's Park
Batcliffe Drive
St Anne's Road
Witches Stone
Batcliffe Wood
Queenswood Road
fallen stoops
sports field
KECC
Queenswood Heights
HEADINGLEY
Headingley railway station
1
railway
B6157
funeral home


**The Hollies** was a grand villa, built around 1860, that was given to the City of Leeds in 1921 by William Brown after his son was killed in World War I. It was used as a sanatorium for children with tuberculosis, with the terraced gardens and woods of Hollies Park becoming a public park.

**3** From the **Witches Stone**, cross Meanwood Beck and follow it right past a former church column to Whalley Dam, circling left around this to pass a second column. Cross the Venetian bridge and keep left to re-cross the beck by **Hustler's Row**. Turn right and soon join the side of a mill race. Cross at the first bridge, then keep left to reach the **Whale Stone**. Follow the small stream beyond it up the slope and continue up some rough steps to a path with a low wall beside it. Follow this right through the heart of **Weetwood**'s magical woodland (planted around the Hollies mansion). Keep straight on throughout to reach the **A6120** (the Ring Road).

**Hustler's Row** is misspelt after John Husler, a stone merchant who worked many of the quarries in Weetwood.

**4** Follow the **Ring Road** left to cross at the junction and turn right towards Adel, before going immediately left on Adel Lane. You soon bear left into the trees and turn right, crossing another road and skirting around the new housing estate on the site of **Bodington Manor**. Where the path bends left out of the trees, keep right on a fainter path to emerge over a low wall by Lawnswood Funeral Home (the alternative is to continue round the path then keep right on the roads to reach the A660). Head straight across the A660 into **Lawnswood Cemetery** and bear left by the chapel but keep right of the ornate Columbarium. All the paths through the trees bend round to the right to join a broad avenue heading left up through the heart of the cemetery. Turn left at its end and, just before the end of the lines of graves, cut through to the right to reach the road. Head straight on into Magdalene Close and follow a ginnel through to **Otley Old Road**.

The **Witches Stone** in Meanwood Park is one of a series of features laid out by Edward Oates on his Meanwoodside estate in the 1840s, the name probably relating to its use by modern pagans. Elsewhere Oates built the stone clapper bridges and an American garden with Venetian-style bridge, and installed two 17th-century stone **columns** that were rescued from Mill Hill Unitarian Chapel in Leeds. Interestingly Oates' grandson died on Captain Scott's infamous Antarctic expedition.

**Beckett's Park** was the site of New Grange, one of the larger farms owned by Kirkstall Abbey from the 12th century. A new house was built in 1626, changing its name to Kirkstall Grange. It was sold to the council by the Beckett family in 1908 for a new teacher training college and public park.

**2** Follow the A660 right in **Far Headingley**, turning left after the Three Horseshoes then right along Moor Road. After a quarter of a mile turn left on an unsigned path just beyond Moor Park Drive. At its end follow Hollin Drive down to the bottom and head straight on over a bridge. Turn left into **Meanwood Park** and follow the beck to reach the **Witches Stone** by the second bridge. **Alternative route:** If this path remains closed, follow the road left to another entrance into the park to reach the same bridge.

**1** From **Headingley railway station** (platform 2), head under the railway and follow a path right between the allotments. At the end bear right across the bottom of Queenswood Road up a tarmac path and keep left of the tower blocks through the trees to pick up a path straight up the slope into **Batcliffe Wood**. Keep straight on to stay in the trees, then bear left shortly before the road to skirt along the edge of **Beckett's Park**. Where the park opens out, bear right alongside Batcliffe Drive. At the end turn left then right around South Lodge, then turn right in **Church Wood** on a section of boardwalk. Go either side of **St Chad's Church** and follow the drive to reach the A660.

# KIRKSTALL ABBEY & FORGE

Kirkstall Abbey was founded in 1152 on a remote wooded site alongside the River Aire by Abbot Alexander and a small group of Cistercian monks. A hermitage had been established here 50 years earlier by a shepherd called Seleth and the land was granted to them by Henry de Lacy. The Cistercians, a breakaway from the Benedictine Order (in this case those at Fountains Abbey), preferred remote sites to practise austere piety. The new monastery was built within 30 years with stone quarried from the surrounding woods, particularly Bramley Fall. Most of this structure, dedicated to St Mary, remains; the few later additions include the lofty church tower.

*the ruins of Kirkstall Abbey*

Choir monks lived on site, with lay brothers working the land and woods nearby. They cleared the higher ground for livestock farms at Moor Grange, New Grange (now Beckett's Park), Elam Grange and Roundhay Grange, but didn't touch the large tract of Hawksworth Wood, recognising the importance of charcoal and oak bark. As well as the productive wool trade, they oversaw iron smelting, tanning and stone quarrying. Corn mills were established at Troy in Horsforth, at Wood Mill on Meanwood Beck and near the abbey itself, with Abbey Mill Race in Hawksworth Wood created from Oil Mill Beck to the latter. By 1300 they were weaving, dyeing and fulling cloth, as well as selling leather, pottery, iron tools and grain. Despite narrowly avoiding bankruptcy in 1288, the abbey became one of the region's wealthiest local landowners, with profitable assets across West Yorkshire.

Kirkstall Abbey's dissolution in 1539 was peaceful, with the abbot allowed to retire in the gatehouse and many monks retaining occupation of former monasterial operations. Instead of being plundered, the partially ruined building remained in use by local farmers for storage and keeping livestock. In the 1890s it was purchased by Colonel John North, who presented the grounds to the Leeds Corporation as a public park. It is one of the finest preserved abbeys in the country, with a large part of its walls, mosaic floors and cloisters remaining, including the abbot's lodging and gatehouse that now forms the Abbey House Museum. It is free to visit and open daily except Mondays.

One of the abbey's longest running mysteries is the escape tunnel the monks are rumoured to have built from the abbey, though no-one knows where this led. There is a blocked up tunnel in the cellar of Hollybush Farm a quarter of a mile away, or a tunnel in the grounds of the now-demolished Newlaithes Hall (which turned out to lead only 100m from Bank Well to the kitchen garden). Similar tales exist about Bramley Old Hall, New Grange and even Temple Newsam House several miles away. There are also many stories about the monks of Kirkstall Abbey desperately hiding gold from the authorities at the Dissolution, but searches in Newlaithes House, Moseley Wood and other sites have yet to unearth anything.

Iron production began at Kirkstall Forge in the early 17th century on the site of an earlier fulling mill. Having acquired large woodlands at Hawksworth Wood, Bramley Fall, Cookridge Wood and Farnley Wood to supply his new forge, Sir John Savile created a new blast furnace, as well as a weir across the Aire near Newlay Bridge to supply the extra power required via Kirkstall Forge Goit. The forge was abandoned during the Civil Wars, after which the Saviles' estates were seized. It was only re-established in 1658, becoming one of the earliest slitting mills, where iron bars were slitted into thin rods to be made into nails. Charcoal was used in the blast furnaces until around 1740, when it was replaced by coal. Business boomed after the canal was built, even though the forge was on the opposite bank of the river and a ferry took cargo for loading on the canal. In the 19th century the forge became renowned for axles and had the world's largest steam hammer. It continued to operate until 1995, with most of its buildings demolished for new developments in recent years.

# CHAPTER 4 - HORSFORTH & BRAMLEY

**Map Sheet:** Explorer 288 (Bradford & Huddersfield)

**Public Transport:** Railway stations at Kirkstall Forge, Horsforth & Bramley.

**Parking:** Free car parks at Bramley Fall and Kirkstall Abbey.

The twin sentinels of Bramley and Horsforth stand on hills either side of the Aire Valley west of Leeds. Horsforth is a corruption of 'horse ford', though it is unclear whether this referred to the ancient ford over the Aire at Newlay (which was only passable for large animals), another shallow crossing near Calverley Bridge, or a smaller ford on Oil Mill Beck that is far nearer to the original settlement. Horsforth was originally further down the hillside towards Oil Mill Beck and centred on Batchelor Lane, but after the plague its survivors moved up the hill for healthier air. It was declared a town only in 1999, having had the distinction of being the largest village in England in the late 19th century, and retains a somewhat Arcadian air.

Bramley is an ancient settlement whose historic core was sadly destroyed by clumsy 1960s developments. Its name means 'clearing overgrown with broom' and the town was renowned for its boot-makers, the Bramley Chukka boot being a type of footwear worn by the British Army in the desert. Though there is little woodland in the town itself, Bramley Fall leads down from its northern edge to the Aire.

Kirkstall Abbey was founded here in the 12th century because of its remote setting in a steep valley surrounded by woodland. The monks worked these woods extensively for charcoal, stone and timber and doubtless helped ensure they were preserved. Oil Mill Beck in particular remains a richly wooded valley, its ancient woodlands weaving between the modern housing estates of Hawksworth, Ireland Wood and Tinshill. Although all of Moseley Wood and large parts of Hawksworth and Cookridge Woods tragically made way for some of these 20th-century developments, it is still one of the greenest corners of Leeds, with the new Kirkstall Forge station sited right in the middle of it.

*the Hoop Stone in Horsforth*

# MAP 12: HORSFORTH & COOKRIDGE WOOD

To the east of Horsforth and the mills along Oil Mill Beck is a great swathe of once unbroken woodland. Today the estate roads of Ireland Wood and Tinshill break up what was Cookridge Wood into smaller parcels, but ancient oak woods quickly take over behind the houses, schools and former hospitals, and it is a fascinating area to explore. There are several Iron Age and medieval settlement sites (some more evident than others) that highlight its former importance.

A medieval manorial corn mill serving Horsforth, Rawdon and Tinshill stood on a site by the weir just south of the railway station. It had many later uses but was still known as **Troy Corn Mill** until its demolition in the 1960s. The 18th-century spinning mill at Troy Mills remains, and **Brookfoot Mill** stands alongside the clapper bridge on an old packhorse route across Oil Mill Beck and has some original 17th-century buildings.

***Backhouse Wood** is a damp mass of holly and is the one part of these woods that is not well trodden. **Spring Wood** in particular is a maze of paths and bike jumps that is hard to navigate, the railway and a long shallow drain running down from **Silk Mill Way** being the main navigational markers.*

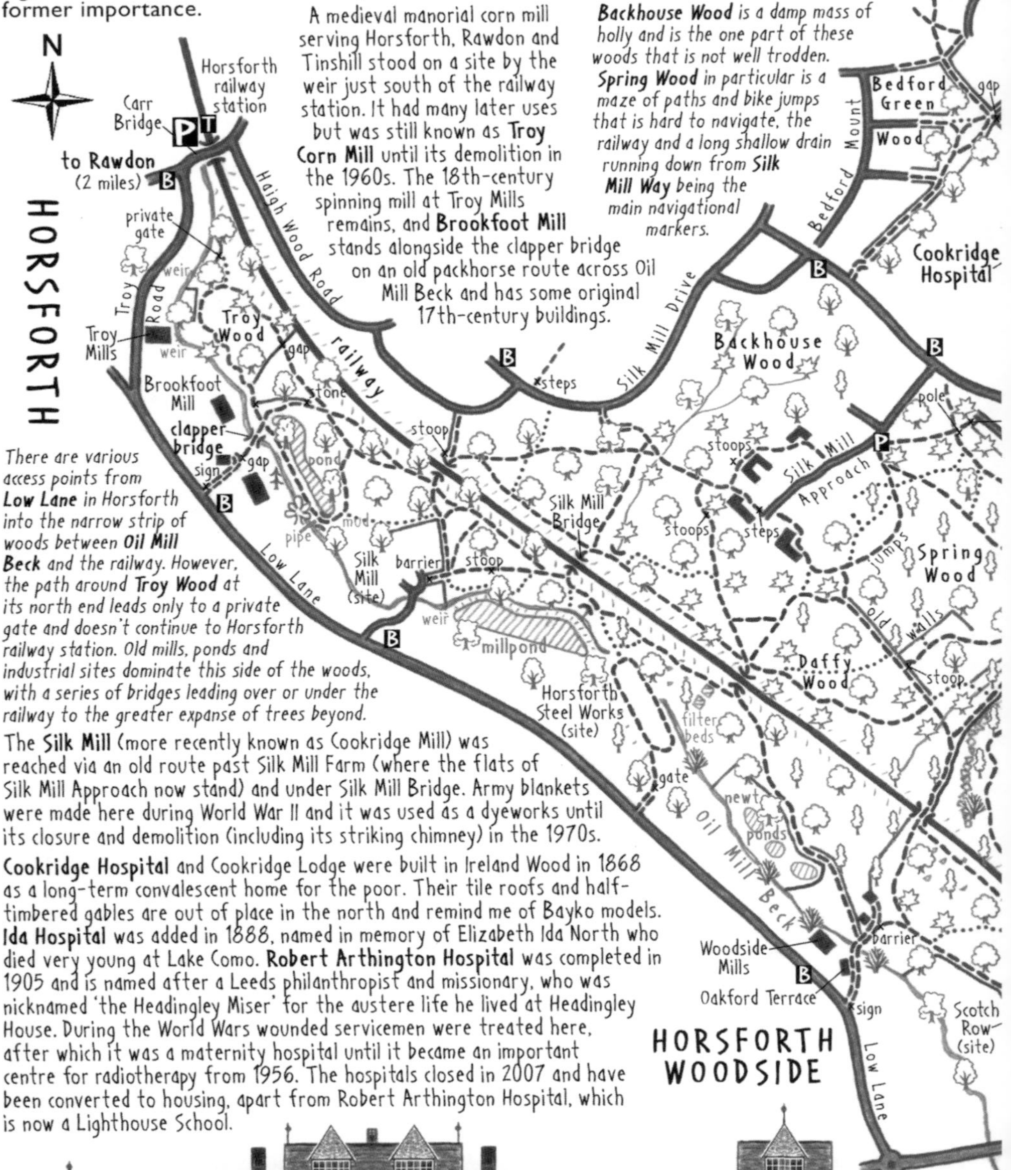

*There are various access points from **Low Lane** in Horsforth into the narrow strip of woods between **Oil Mill Beck** and the railway. However, the path around **Troy Wood** at its north end leads only to a private gate and doesn't continue to Horsforth railway station. Old mills, ponds and industrial sites dominate this side of the woods, with a series of bridges leading over or under the railway to the greater expanse of trees beyond.*

The **Silk Mill** (more recently known as Cookridge Mill) was reached via an old route past Silk Mill Farm (where the flats of Silk Mill Approach now stand) and under Silk Mill Bridge. Army blankets were made here during World War II and it was used as a dyeworks until its closure and demolition (including its striking chimney) in the 1970s.

**Cookridge Hospital** and Cookridge Lodge were built in Ireland Wood in 1868 as a long-term convalescent home for the poor. Their tile roofs and half-timbered gables are out of place in the north and remind me of Bayko models. **Ida Hospital** was added in 1888, named in memory of Elizabeth Ida North who died very young at Lake Como. **Robert Arthington Hospital** was completed in 1905 and is named after a Leeds philanthropist and missionary, who was nicknamed 'the Headingley Miser' for the austere life he lived at Headingley House. During the World Wars wounded servicemen were treated here, after which it was a maternity hospital until it became an important centre for radiotherapy from 1956. The hospitals closed in 2007 and have been converted to housing, apart from Robert Arthington Hospital, which is now a Lighthouse School.

*Cookridge Hospital*

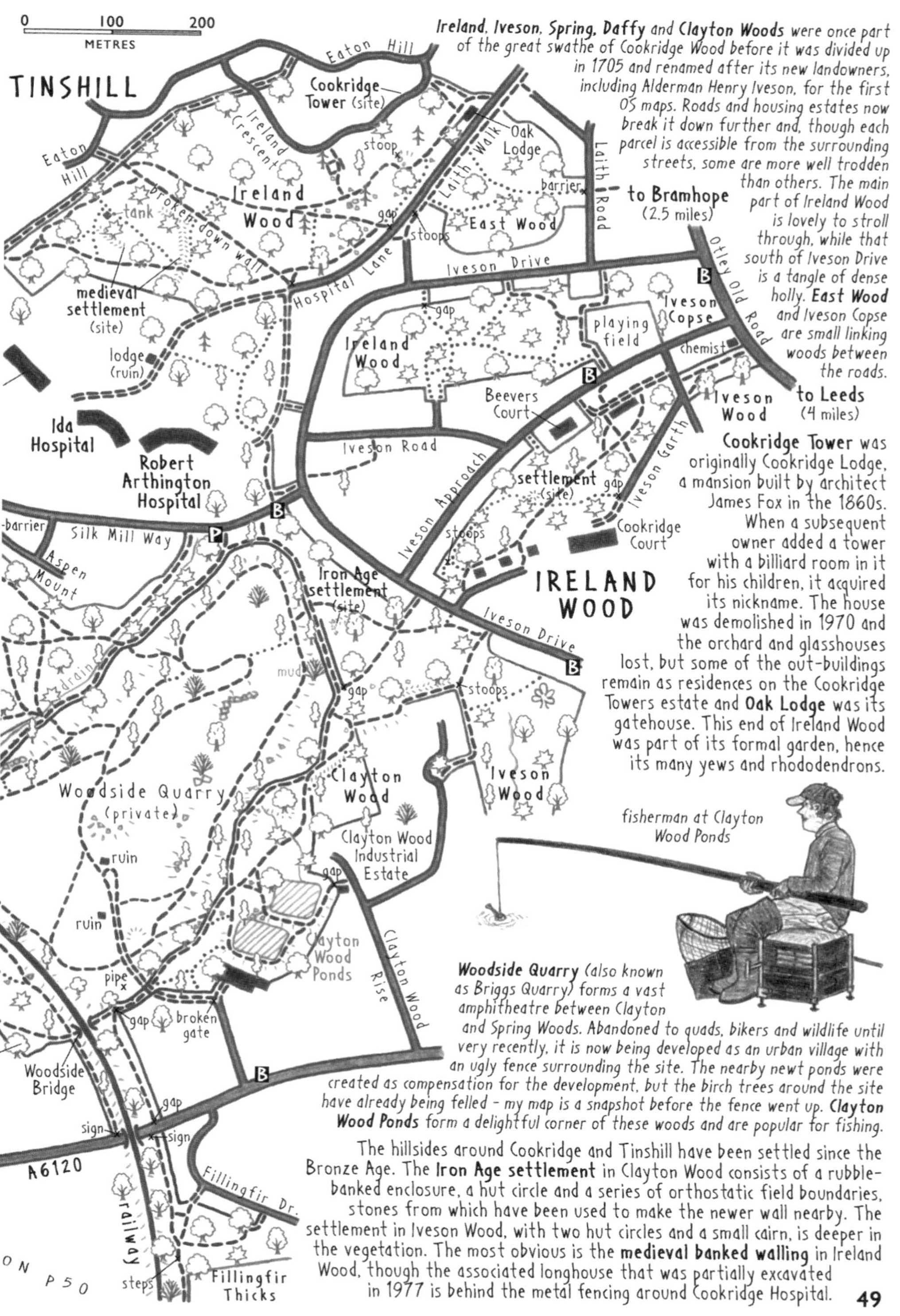

0
100
200
METRES
TINSHILL
Eaton Hill
Cookridge Tower (site)
Ireland Crescent
Oak Lodge
Laith Walk
Laith Road
stoop
barrier
to Bramhope (2.5 miles)
Ireland Wood
tank
broken-down wall
gap
stoops
East Wood
medieval settlement (site)
Hospital Lane
Iveson Drive
Otley Old Road
Iveson Copse
playing field
chemist
lodge (ruin)
Ireland Wood
Beevers Court
Iveson Wood
to Leeds (4 miles)
Ida Hospital
Robert Arthington Hospital
Iveson Road
Iveson Approach
Iveson Garth
settlement (site)
barrier
Silk Mill Way
Aspen Mount
Cookridge Court
Iron Age settlement (site)
IRELAND WOOD
Iveson Drive
drain
mud
stoops
Woodside Quarry (private)
Clayton Wood
Iveson Wood
fisherman at Clayton Wood Ponds
ruin
Clayton Wood Industrial Estate
Clayton Wood Ponds
Clayton Wood Rise
pipe
broken gate
Woodside Bridge
sign
A6120
Fillingfir Dr.
railway
steps
Fillingfir Thicks

ON P50

**Ireland, Iveson, Spring, Daffy** and **Clayton Woods** were once part of the great swathe of Cookridge Wood before it was divided up in 1705 and renamed after its new landowners, including Alderman Henry Iveson, for the first OS maps. Roads and housing estates now break it down further and, though each parcel is accessible from the surrounding streets, some are more well trodden than others. The main part of Ireland Wood is lovely to stroll through, while that south of Iveson Drive is a tangle of dense holly. **East Wood** and Iveson Copse are small linking woods between the roads.

**Cookridge Tower** was originally Cookridge Lodge, a mansion built by architect James Fox in the 1860s. When a subsequent owner added a tower with a billiard room in it for his children, it acquired its nickname. The house was demolished in 1970 and the orchard and glasshouses lost, but some of the out-buildings remain as residences on the Cookridge Towers estate and **Oak Lodge** was its gatehouse. This end of Ireland Wood was part of its formal garden, hence its many yews and rhododendrons.

**Woodside Quarry** (also known as Briggs Quarry) forms a vast amphitheatre between Clayton and Spring Woods. Abandoned to quads, bikers and wildlife until very recently, it is now being developed as an urban village with an ugly fence surrounding the site. The nearby newt ponds were created as compensation for the development, but the birch trees around the site have already being felled - my map is a snapshot before the fence went up. **Clayton Wood Ponds** form a delightful corner of these woods and are popular for fishing.

The hillsides around Cookridge and Tinshill have been settled since the Bronze Age. The **Iron Age settlement** in Clayton Wood consists of a rubble-banked enclosure, a hut circle and a series of orthostatic field boundaries, stones from which have been used to make the newer wall nearby. The settlement in Iveson Wood, with two hut circles and a small cairn, is deeper in the vegetation. The most obvious is the **medieval banked walling** in Ireland Wood, though the associated longhouse that was partially excavated in 1977 is behind the metal fencing around Cookridge Hospital.

# MAP 13: BRAMLEY FALL & HAWKSWORTH WOOD

Hawksworth Wood is a great stretch of ancient woodland and, with the smaller pockets of Cragg Wood, Little Hawksworth Wood and the Outwood, forms a continuation of the woods around Horsforth along Oil Mill Beck. Bramley Fall is a popular area of quarried woods on the opposite side of the River Aire, further cut off by the railway, canal and main road. This is all part of the wooded landscape that surrounded Kirkstall Abbey and was worked extensively by the monks.

***The Outwood*** *is a wild overgrown wood with a couple of paths along its lower side. Beware the stile at the junction of Rein Road, as the faint path it promises peters out in the jumbled rocks and holly at the heart of the wood.* ***Cragg Wood*** *is similarly impassable away from the well defined paths.*

The **Abbey Inn** was used as a mortuary, with drinkers passing coffins on the way to the toilets. It was later purchased by the adjacent dyeworks to control its workers' drinking.

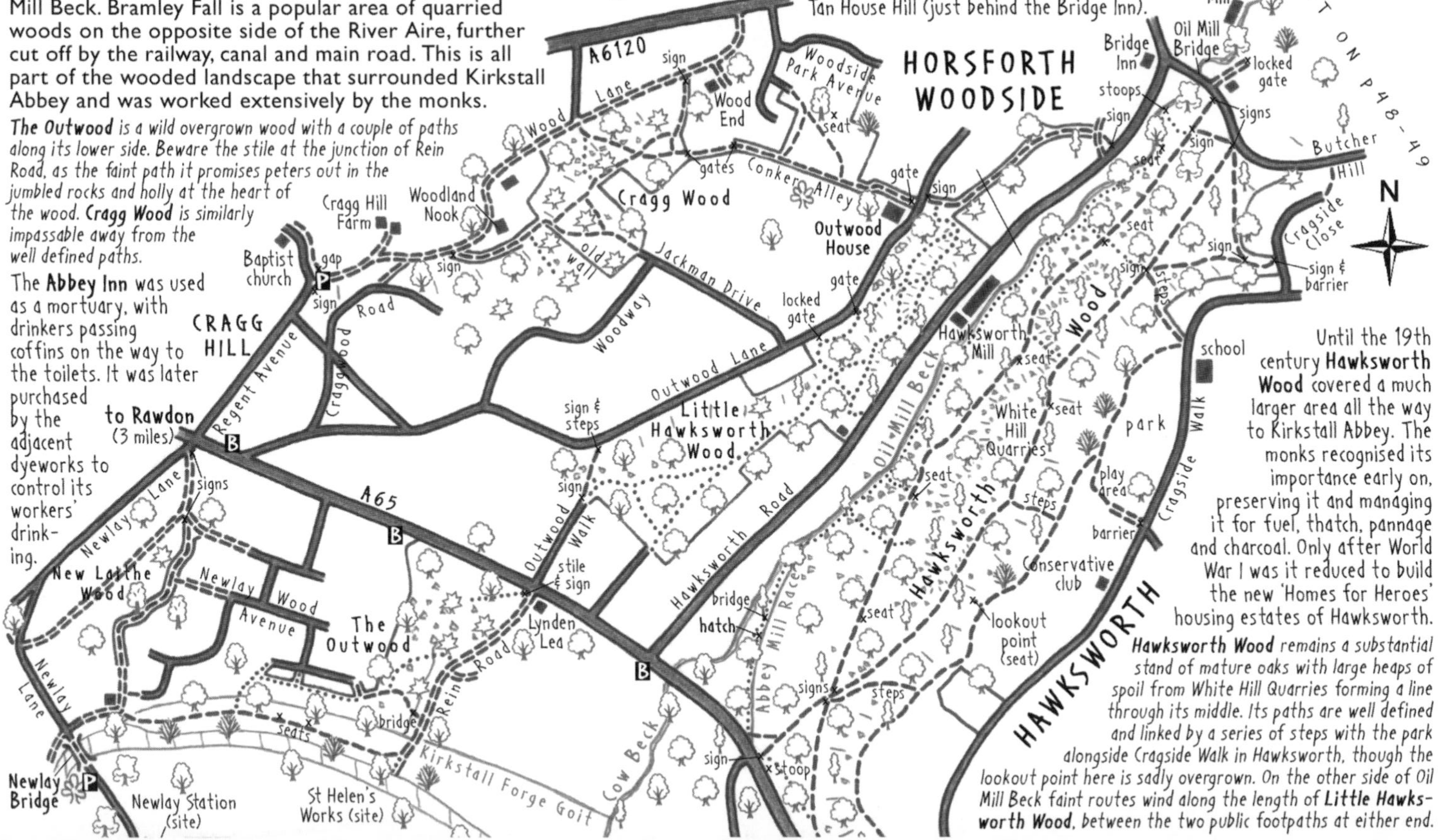

**Hawksworth Mill** was an early paper mill at the foot of Hawksworth Wood, which was later used as a twine works, with ropewalks across Oil Mill Beck. **Horsforth Mill** was only built in 1903 by the site of an 18th-century corn mill. The woods here are dominated by oaks that would have supplied bark for the tannery that operated from 1816 to 1968 on Tan House Hill (just behind the Bridge Inn).

Until the 19th century **Hawksworth Wood** covered a much larger area all the way to Kirkstall Abbey. The monks recognised its importance early on, preserving it and managing it for fuel, thatch, pannage and charcoal. Only after World War I was it reduced to build the new 'Homes for Heroes' housing estates of Hawksworth.

***Hawksworth Wood*** *remains a substantial stand of mature oaks with large heaps of spoil from White Hill Quarries forming a line through its middle. Its paths are well defined and linked by a series of steps with the park alongside Cragside Walk in Hawksworth, though the lookout point here is sadly overgrown. On the other side of Oil Mill Beck faint routes wind along the length of* ***Little Hawksworth Wood****, between the two public footpaths at either end.*


HORSFORTH WOODSIDE
HAWKSWORTH
CRAGG HILL
N
A6120
A65
Wood Lane
Woodside Park Avenue
Wood End
Cragg Wood
Conker Alley
Outwood House
Cragg Hill Farm
Woodland Nook
Baptist church
Cragg Wood Road
Regent Avenue
Jackman Drive
Woodway
Outwood Lane
Little Hawksworth Wood
Outwood Walk
Hawksworth Road
to Rawdon (3 miles)
Newlay Lane
New Laithe Wood
Newlay Wood Avenue
The Outwood
Lynden Lea
Rein Road
Kirkstall Forge Goit
Cow Beck
St Helen's Works (site)
Newlay Station (site)
Newlay Bridge
Hawksworth Mill
Oil Mill Beck
Abbey Mill Race
Hawksworth Wood
White Hill Quarries
park
play area
Conservative club
lookout point (seat)
school
Cragside Walk
Cragside Close
Butcher Hill
Bridge Inn
Oil Mill Bridge
Horsforth Mill
locked gate


CONT ON P48–49

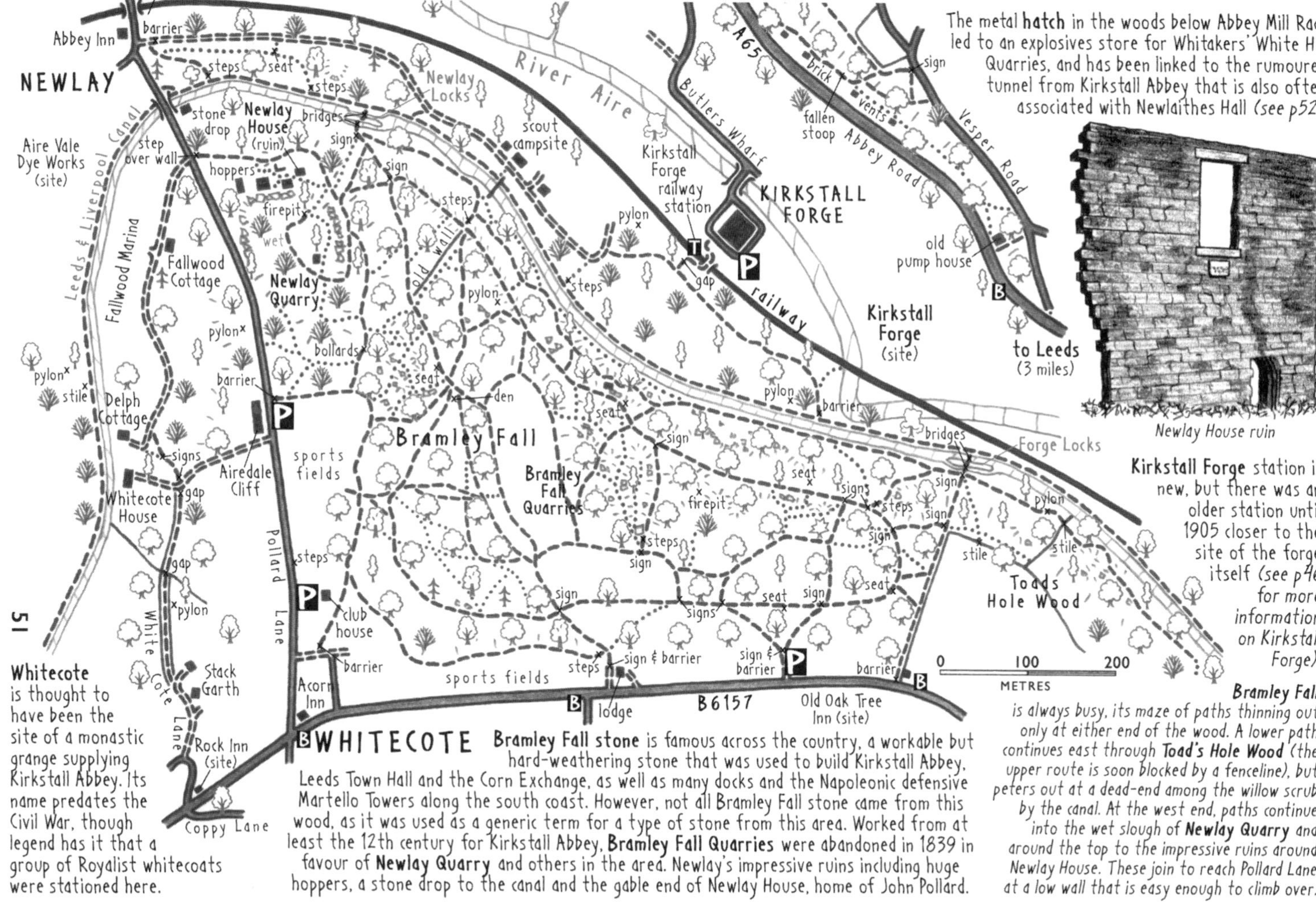

NEWLAY
Abbey Inn
barrier
steps
seat
steps
Newlay Locks
River Aire
stone drop
Newlay House (ruin)
bridges
sign
scout campsite
Aire Vale Dye Works (site)
Leeds & Liverpool Canal
Fallwood Marina
step over wall
hoppers
firepit
wet
sign
steps
old wall
Newlay Quarry
Fallwood Cottage
pylon
bollards
seat
den
pylon
Bramley Fall
Bramley Fall Quarries
barrier
Delph Cottage
stile
signs
Airedale Cliff
gap
Whitecote House
sports fields
Pollard Lane
steps
club house
barrier
Acorn Inn
WHITECOTE
White Cote Lane
Stack Garth
Rock Inn (site)
Coppy Lane
sports fields
steps
sign & barrier
lodge
B6157
sign & barrier
Old Oak Tree Inn (site)
barrier
sign
signs
seat
firepit
steps
sign
seat
signs
steps
stile
Toads Hole Wood
pylon
Forge Locks
bridges
railway
gap
Kirkstall Forge railway station
KIRKSTALL FORGE
Butlers Wharf
A65
brick
fallen stoop
vents
Abbey Road
Vesper Road
old pump house
Kirkstall Forge (site)
to Leeds (3 miles)
0 100 200 METRES


The metal **hatch** in the woods below Abbey Mill Race led to an explosives store for Whitakers' White Hill Quarries, and has been linked to the rumoured tunnel from Kirkstall Abbey that is also often associated with Newlaithes Hall (see p52).

*Newlay House ruin*

**Kirkstall Forge** station is new, but there was an older station until 1905 closer to the site of the forge itself (see p46 for more information on Kirkstall Forge).

***Bramley Fall*** *is always busy, its maze of paths thinning out only at either end of the wood. A lower path continues east through* ***Toad's Hole Wood*** *(the upper route is soon blocked by a fenceline), but peters out at a dead-end among the willow scrub by the canal. At the west end, paths continue into the wet slough of* ***Newlay Quarry*** *and around the top to the impressive ruins around Newlay House. These join to reach Pollard Lane at a low wall that is easy enough to climb over.*

**Bramley Fall stone** is famous across the country, a workable but hard-weathering stone that was used to build Kirkstall Abbey, Leeds Town Hall and the Corn Exchange, as well as many docks and the Napoleonic defensive Martello Towers along the south coast. However, not all Bramley Fall stone came from this wood, as it was used as a generic term for a type of stone from this area. Worked from at least the 12th century for Kirkstall Abbey, **Bramley Fall Quarries** were abandoned in 1839 in favour of **Newlay Quarry** and others in the area. Newlay's impressive ruins including huge hoppers, a stone drop to the canal and the gable end of Newlay House, home of John Pollard.

**Whitecote** is thought to have been the site of a monastic grange supplying Kirkstall Abbey. Its name predates the Civil War, though legend has it that a group of Royalist whitecoats were stationed here.

# ROUTE 9: COOKRIDGE, HAWKSWORTH & BRAMLEY FALL WOODS FROM HORSFORTH

**Distance:** 9 miles (14.6km) **Ascent:** 330m

**Parking:** Pay parking at Horsforth and Kirkstall Forge railway stations. Free parking at Bramley Fall and Calverley Bridge.

**Public Transport:** Horsforth is on the Harrogate railway line from Leeds, and Kirkstall Forge is on the Leeds to Bradford railway line.

**Character:** An intricate but rewarding route through the numerous woods around Oil Mill Beck and along the Aire between Horsforth and Bramley. Hawksworth Wood, Bramley Fall and the various remnants of Cookridge Wood are fine ancient woods, while Hunger Hills Woods provide a great vantage point over the city.

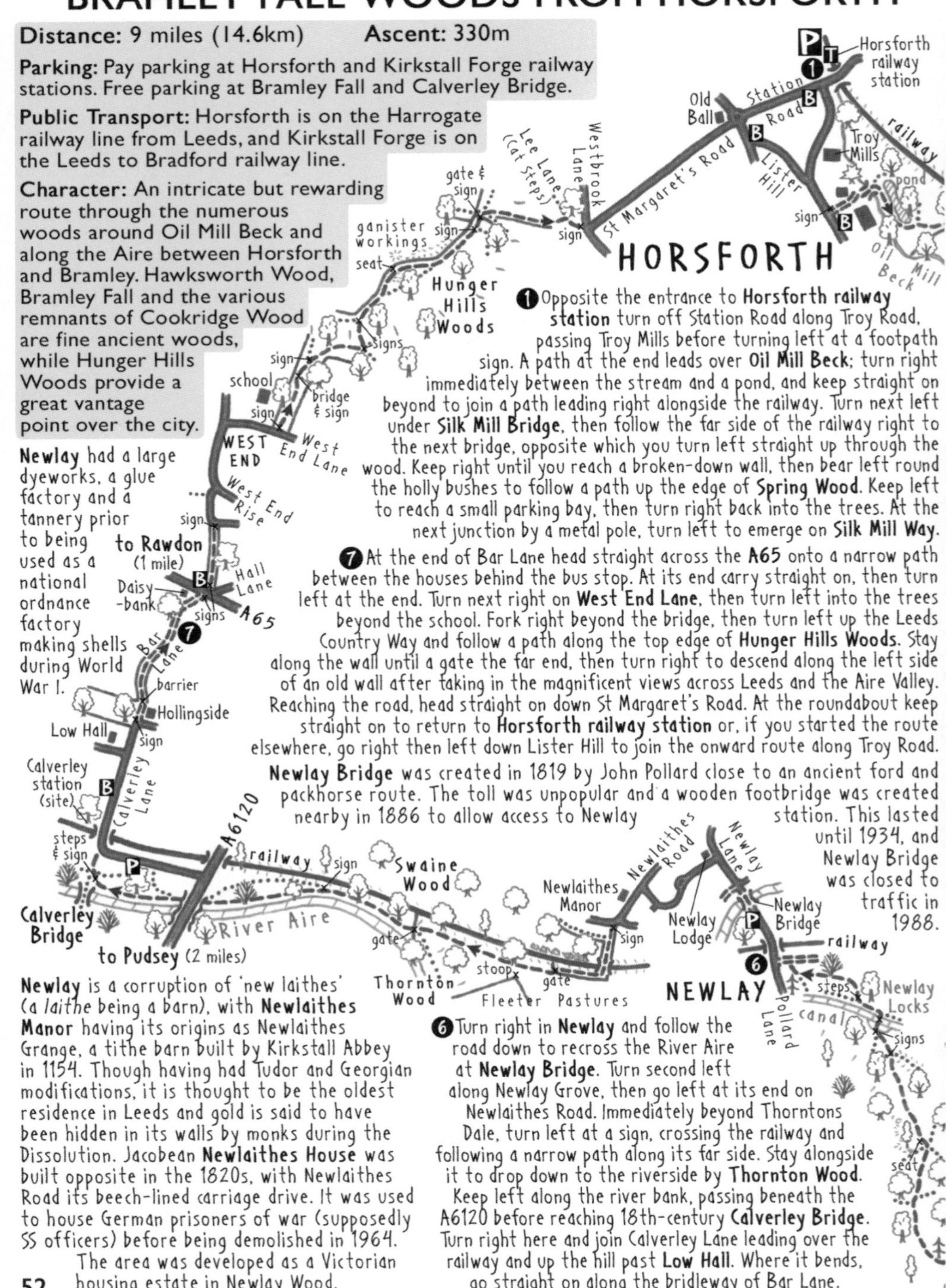
Horsforth railway station
Station Road
Old Ball
Westbrook Lane
Lee Lane (Cat Steps)
St Margaret's Road
Lister Hill
Troy Mills
railway
pond
sign
Oil Mill Beck
HORSFORTH
gate & sign
ganister workings
seat
Hunger Hills Woods
signs
school
bridge & sign
WEST END
West End Lane
West End Rise
to Rawdon (1 mile)
Daisy-bank
Hall Lane
A65
Bar Lane
barrier
Hollingside
Low Hall
Calverley station (site)
Calverley Lane
steps & sign
A6120
Calverley Bridge
River Aire
to Pudsey (2 miles)
Swaine Wood
gate
Thornton Wood
stoop
Fleeter Pastures
Newlaithes Manor
Newlaithes Road
Newlay Lane
Newlay Lodge
Newlay Bridge
NEWLAY
Pollard Lane
canal
steps
Newlay Locks
seat

**Newlay** had a large dyeworks, a glue factory and a tannery prior to being used as a national ordnance factory making shells during World War I.

❶ Opposite the entrance to **Horsforth railway station** turn off Station Road along Troy Road, passing Troy Mills before turning left at a footpath sign. A path at the end leads over **Oil Mill Beck**; turn right immediately between the stream and a pond, and keep straight on beyond to join a path leading right alongside the railway. Turn next left under **Silk Mill Bridge**, then follow the far side of the railway right to the next bridge, opposite which you turn left straight up through the wood. Keep right until you reach a broken-down wall, then bear left round the holly bushes to follow a path up the edge of **Spring Wood**. Keep left to reach a small parking bay, then turn right back into the trees. At the next junction by a metal pole, turn left to emerge on **Silk Mill Way**.

❼ At the end of Bar Lane head straight across the **A65** onto a narrow path between the houses behind the bus stop. At its end carry straight on, then turn left at the end. Turn next right on **West End Lane**, then turn left into the trees beyond the school. Fork right beyond the bridge, then turn left up the Leeds Country Way and follow a path along the top edge of **Hunger Hills Woods**. Stay along the wall until a gate the far end, then turn right to descend along the left side of an old wall after taking in the magnificent views across Leeds and the Aire Valley. Reaching the road, head straight on down St Margaret's Road. At the roundabout keep straight on to return to **Horsforth railway station** or, if you started the route elsewhere, go right then left down Lister Hill to join the onward route along Troy Road.

**Newlay Bridge** was created in 1819 by John Pollard close to an ancient ford and packhorse route. The toll was unpopular and a wooden footbridge was created nearby in 1886 to allow access to Newlay station. This lasted until 1934, and Newlay Bridge was closed to traffic in 1988.

**Newlay** is a corruption of 'new laithes' (a *laithe* being a barn), with **Newlaithes Manor** having its origins as Newlaithes Grange, a tithe barn built by Kirkstall Abbey in 1154. Though having had Tudor and Georgian modifications, it is thought to be the oldest residence in Leeds and gold is said to have been hidden in its walls by monks during the Dissolution. Jacobean **Newlaithes House** was built opposite in the 1820s, with Newlaithes Road its beech-lined carriage drive. It was used to house German prisoners of war (supposedly SS officers) before being demolished in 1964.

The area was developed as a Victorian housing estate in Newlay Wood.

❻ Turn right in **Newlay** and follow the road down to recross the River Aire at **Newlay Bridge**. Turn second left along Newlay Grove, then go left at its end on Newlaithes Road. Immediately beyond Thorntons Dale, turn left at a sign, crossing the railway and following a narrow path along its far side. Stay alongside it to drop down to the riverside by **Thornton Wood**. Keep left along the river bank, passing beneath the A6120 before reaching 18th-century **Calverley Bridge**. Turn right here and join Calverley Lane leading over the railway and up the hill past **Low Hall**. Where it bends, go straight on along the bridleway of Bar Lane.

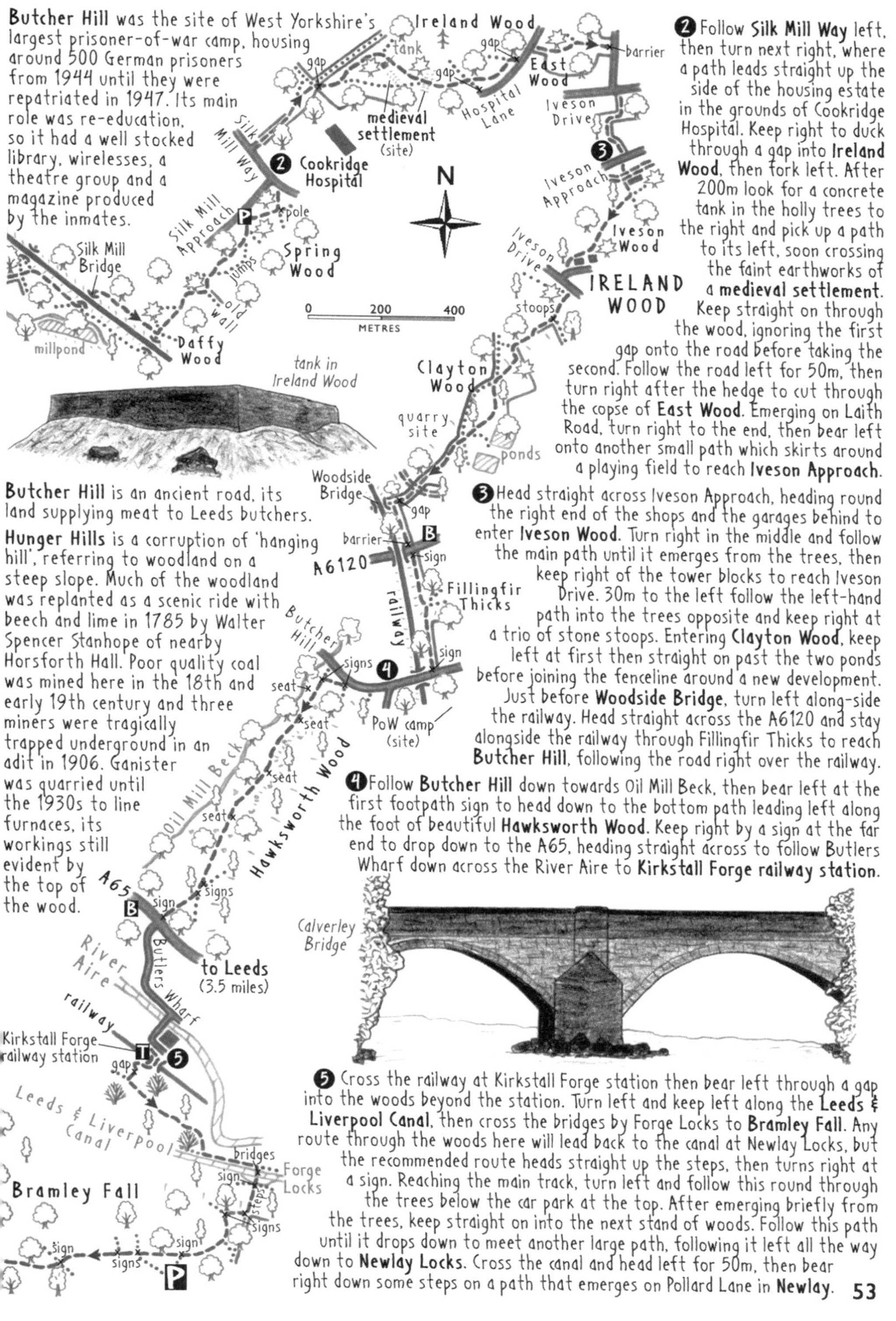
Ireland Wood
tank
gap
gap
gap
barrier
East Wood
Hospital Lane
Iveson Drive
Silk Mill Way
medieval settlement (site)
Cookridge Hospital
2
3
N
Iveson Approach
Silk Mill Approach
P
pole
Spring Wood
Iveson Wood
Iveson Drive
Silk Mill Bridge
jumps
old wall
IRELAND WOOD
0 200 400 METRES
stoops
Daffy Wood
millpond
tank in Ireland Wood
Clayton Wood
quarry site
ponds
Woodside Bridge
gap
barrier
B
sign
A6120
railway
Fillingfir Thicks
Butcher Hill
signs
4
sign
seat
seat
PoW camp (site)
seat
Oil Mill Beck
Hawksworth Wood
seat
A65
signs
B
sign
Butlers Wharf
to Leeds (3.5 miles)
River Aire
railway
Calverley Bridge
Kirkstall Forge railway station
5
gap
Leeds & Liverpool Canal
bridges
sign
Forge Locks
Bramley Fall
steps
signs
sign
sign
signs
P

**Butcher Hill** was the site of West Yorkshire's largest prisoner-of-war camp, housing around 500 German prisoners from 1944 until they were repatriated in 1947. Its main role was re-education, so it had a well stocked library, wirelesses, a theatre group and a magazine produced by the inmates.

**Butcher Hill** is an ancient road, its land supplying meat to Leeds butchers.

**Hunger Hills** is a corruption of 'hanging hill', referring to woodland on a steep slope. Much of the woodland was replanted as a scenic ride with beech and lime in 1785 by Walter Spencer Stanhope of nearby Horsforth Hall. Poor quality coal was mined here in the 18th and early 19th century and three miners were tragically trapped underground in an adit in 1906. Ganister was quarried until the 1930s to line furnaces, its workings still evident by the top of the wood.

❷ Follow **Silk Mill Way** left, then turn next right, where a path leads straight up the side of the housing estate in the grounds of Cookridge Hospital. Keep right to duck through a gap into **Ireland Wood**, then fork left. After 200m look for a concrete tank in the holly trees to the right and pick up a path to its left, soon crossing the faint earthworks of a **medieval settlement**. Keep straight on through the wood, ignoring the first gap onto the road before taking the second. Follow the road left for 50m, then turn right after the hedge to cut through the copse of **East Wood**. Emerging on Laith Road, turn right to the end, then bear left onto another small path which skirts around a playing field to reach **Iveson Approach**.

❸ Head straight across Iveson Approach, heading round the right end of the shops and the garages behind to enter **Iveson Wood**. Turn right in the middle and follow the main path until it emerges from the trees, then keep right of the tower blocks to reach Iveson Drive. 30m to the left follow the left-hand path into the trees opposite and keep right at a trio of stone stoops. Entering **Clayton Wood**, keep left at first then straight on past the two ponds before joining the fenceline around a new development. Just before **Woodside Bridge**, turn left along-side the railway. Head straight across the A6120 and stay alongside the railway through Fillingfir Thicks to reach **Butcher Hill**, following the road right over the railway.

❹ Follow **Butcher Hill** down towards Oil Mill Beck, then bear left at the first footpath sign to head down to the bottom path leading left along the foot of beautiful **Hawksworth Wood**. Keep right by a sign at the far end to drop down to the A65, heading straight across to follow Butlers Wharf down across the River Aire to **Kirkstall Forge railway station**.

❺ Cross the railway at Kirkstall Forge station then bear left through a gap into the woods beyond the station. Turn left and keep left along the **Leeds & Liverpool Canal**, then cross the bridges by Forge Locks to **Bramley Fall**. Any route through the woods here will lead back to the canal at Newlay Locks, but the recommended route heads straight up the steps, then turns right at a sign. Reaching the main track, turn left and follow this round through the trees below the car park at the top. After emerging briefly from the trees, keep straight on into the next stand of woods. Follow this path until it drops down to meet another large path, following it left all the way down to **Newlay Locks**. Cross the canal and head left for 50m, then bear right down some steps on a path that emerges on Pollard Lane in **Newlay**.

# THE DEMISE OF MOSELEY WOOD

Moseley Wood was first mentioned as a hazel wood in the 12th century, and once covered 400 acres north-east of Horsforth railway station on the slopes of Tinshill. It was likely used extensively for coppicing and charcoal production, possibly for the monks of Kirkstall Abbey, who are said to have regularly passed through the wood. Though there is said to be a Roman road through the wood, its course more likely stayed along the high 'rig' on which Cookridge stands as it traversed from the camp near Adel to the fort at Olicana (Ilkley). Moseley Wood's name relates to a boggy clearing and the nearby Moseley Farm is first mentioned in 1554. The woodland became part of Cookridge Hall's rural estate, to which it would remain attached until this was broken up in 1919.

In the late 17th century the landowner Thomas Kirk laid out a series of geometric pathways through the wood, which he called Moseley Wood Park. Twelve avenues converged at an oak tree in the middle of the wood, which became known as 'Jack and his 11 brothers' after a family who were said to have been turfed out of their cottage here at the Dissolution. Monks from Kirkstall Abbey are also said to have hidden treasure in the wood to prevent it from falling into the Crown's hands and planted this oak tree on top. The Leeds historian Ralph Thoresby visited in 1693, writing in his diary that he 'viewed the ingeniously contrived walks in Mr Kirk's wood, being the most curious of that nature that ever I beheld', and it gained fame with travellers from all over the country. Kirk died in 1706 and was buried beneath the chancel floor in St John's Church, Adel, and his ghost is said to have been seen on several occasions since.

One of the later features created for Thomas Kirk was a carved stone seat whose curious geometric shape seemed to mirror that of the wood itself. It was most commonly known as the Monk's Seat, but has had many alternative names over the years, including Roman Chair, Pilgrim's Seat and Wishing Chair. Moseley Wood was used for shooting rabbits, pheasants and partridges by subsequent owners and was a target for poaching. After briefly being restored to its former glory in 1817, further seats were crafted from natural boulders by navvies working on nearby Bramhope Tunnel in the 1840s. The railway brought many weekend visitors to the woods from Leeds and Headingley, particularly as it became renowned for nightingales, but by the end of the 19th century its pathways and trees were largely wild and uncared for.

During World War I large parts of the wood were felled due to a timber shortage, being replaced by pine, birch and other quicker-growing trees. It was also infested by a plague of green caterpillars in the summer of 1917, and a national meat shortage led to another spike in poaching. After the war, financial difficulties forced the Wormald family to sell off portions of the estate for residential development. In the 1920s Cecil Crowther built the first area of desirable semi-detached houses at Cookridge, naming Mavis Lane and Avenue after his daughter. A few other detached houses were built along Tinshill Lane, but more than half the wood remained public until the 1950s, with the rest retained but now part of private gardens.

The death knell was sounded for Moseley Wood when Leeds Council sold off the rest of the estate they'd acquired to make way for one of the city's many new garden suburbs. The inner city slums were cleared and its population rehoused in the leafy environs of Cookridge and Tinshill. All the remaining trees were felled and the wood's geometric avenues were not even retained in the new housing estate (the circle at the centre of the wood would have been close to the junction of Wrenbury Crescent and Green Lane). Six building firms developed the area, so it has little coherence architecturally or in terms of planning. Plans were being made to move the Monk's Seat to St John's Church in Adel, but it was destroyed by builders before this could happen, possibly now forming part of a rockery or foundation on Moseley Wood Walk or Moseley Wood Gardens. It was a sad end for one of Leeds' most interesting historic woods.

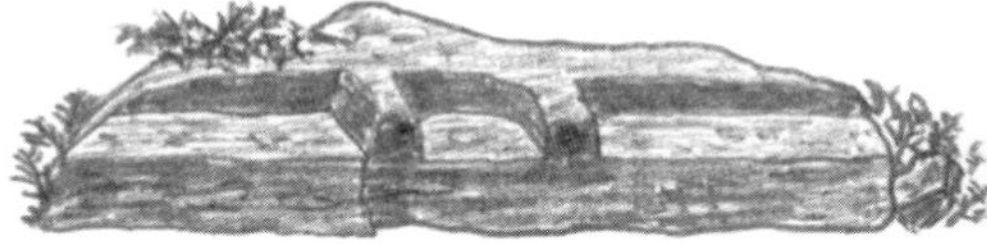

*the Monk's Seat*

# CHAPTER 5 - PUDSEY, FARNLEY & TONG BECKS

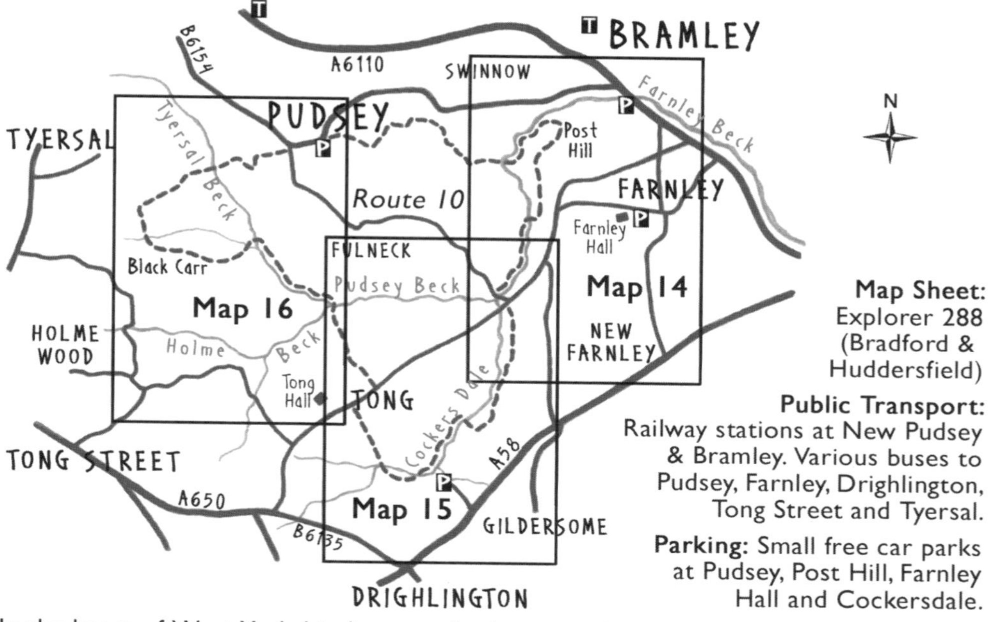
BRAMLEY
B6154
A6110
SWINNOW
Farnley Beck
PUDSEY
TYERSAL
Tyersal Beck
Post Hill
FARNLEY
Route 10
Farnley Hall
FULNECK
Black Carr
Pudsey Beck
Map 14
Map 16
NEW FARNLEY
HOLME WOOD
Holme Beck
Tong Hall
TONG
Cockers Dale
TONG STREET
A58
A650
Map 15
GILDERSOME
B6135
DRIGHLINGTON
N

**Map Sheet:** Explorer 288 (Bradford & Huddersfield)

**Public Transport:** Railway stations at New Pudsey & Bramley. Various buses to Pudsey, Farnley, Drighlington, Tong Street and Tyersal.

**Parking:** Small free car parks at Pudsey, Post Hill, Farnley Hall and Cockersdale.

In the heart of West Yorkshire's mass of urbanity, mid-way between Leeds and Bradford and just a couple of miles from the M62, lies this surprisingly rural landscape. A series of quiet wooded valleys forms a green oasis between the towns on all sides, their streams uniting at Union Bridge as Pudsey/Farnley Beck, before becoming Wortley Beck and following a circuitous route to join the River Aire near Leeds city centre as Hol Beck (whose course is culverted but for a short section alongside Water Lane). Each of the becks – Tong Beck (through Cockers Dale), Pudsey Beck, Holme Beck, Tyersal Beck and Farnley Beck – is lined with trees linking a string of small woodlands. The largest woods are at Post Hill, Park Wood and Black Carr, the latter one of the finest ancient oak woodlands in the county. Several others have disappeared in the past two centuries, including Holme Wood, North Wood and the vast Farnley Wood.

The lovely village of Tong stands on a limb of land at the heart of this area, an ancient manorial settlement on the site of a Saxon church. On a hilltop to the north is Pudsey, an island of high ground at the heart of the county – indeed it's name refers to 'Pudoc's island', meaning an island of fertile land belonging to a particular Anglian settler. Farnley (the 'fern clearing') developed around Farnley Hall, with New Farnley largely built in the 19th century. These manorial estates that helped preserve the rural nature of this area have also limited public access in places; while Post Hill, Black Carr and Cockers Dale are all readily accessible, Park Wood, Holme Beck and other large tracts are out of bounds.

witches broom in a birch tree - these are deformities caused by a fungus, leading to a mass of woody growth from a single point on the tree

# MAP 14: FARNLEY, TROYDALE & POST HILL

Troydale is the most beautifully wooded part of the Pudsey and Farnley Beck, the names somewhat interchangeable where it forms the boundary between the two parishes. The woods of Post Hill cloak the valley's eastern side and continue up the delightful stream to Union Bridge. On the hill above stands Farnley Park and the old village of Farnley itself, which has several fine wooded thoroughfares around Farnley Hall Park. Younger woodland has sprung up on former industrial sites around New Farnley and Ducky Hills, providing a rich variety of routes through this busy landscape.

**Post Hill** was the site of two anti-aircraft guns, a searchlight and a prisoner-of-war camp during World War II. A large mound where the guns were mounted is all that remains. After the war, the displaced persons, mostly Italian and German soldiers, were able to work and shop locally (wearing a yellow circle that signified their status) before returning home in 1947. The name Post Hill arose after it was acquired in 1926 by the *Yorkshire Evening Post* and presented to Leeds Motor Club, who ran scrambling (motocross) and stock car events. It was famed for having the world's steepest hill climb, with cobbles laid up the steepest part of the hill (known locally as Roman Hill), and up to 20,000 spectators flocking to watch. It was taken over by the city council as a park in 2002, but motorbike trials still take place occasionally.

*A substantial area of scrub willow and ash woodland has developed on the former quarries and landfill site of* ***Ducky Hills*** *(named after Duck Cote Farm that once stood here). Clear paths lead into it from the top of Swinnow Lane before becoming lost in a maze of smaller paths, one of which leads steeply down the quarry slopes to emerge on the bend at the bottom.*

**Park Quarries** produced paving and road stone from the early 18th century. The housing estates of Swinnow above were built after World War II on former rhubarb fields, this being the furthest reaches of the most broadly defined Rhubarb Triangle.

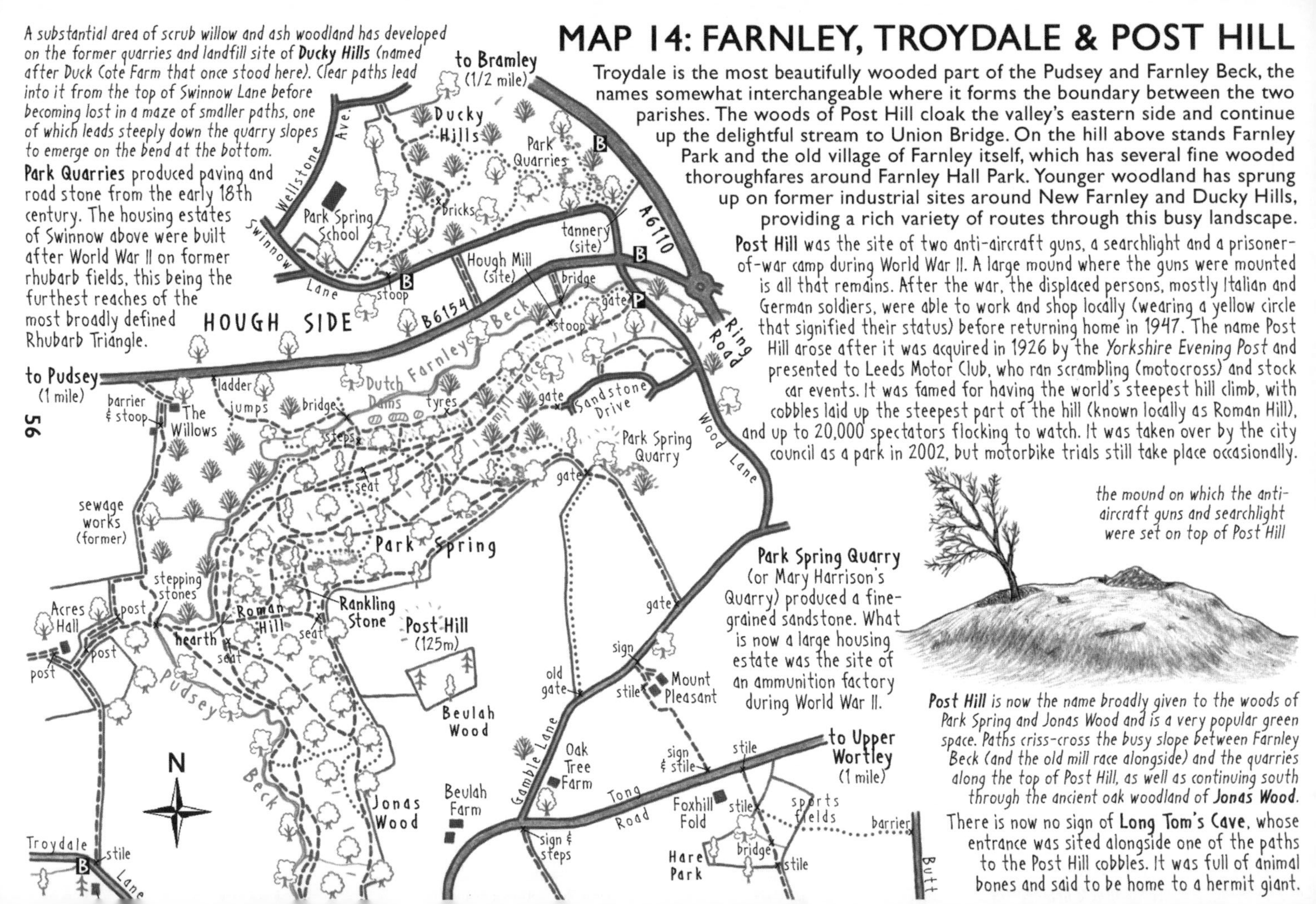

to Bramley
(1/2 mile)
Ducky Hills
Park Quarries
Wellstone Ave.
Park Spring School
bricks
Swinnow Lane
stoop
tannery (site)
A6110
Hough Mill (site)
bridge
gate
B6154
Farnley Beck
stoop
Ring Road
HOUGH SIDE
to Pudsey
(1 mile)
ladder
jumps
bridge
Dutch Dams
tyres
mill race
gate
Sandstone Drive
barrier & stoop
The Willows
steps
Park Spring Quarry
Wood Lane
seat
gate
sewage works (former)
Park Spring
stepping stones
Rankling Stone
Post Hill
(125m)
Acres Hall
post
Roman Hill
seat
hearth
seat
post
post
Pudsey Beck
gate
sign
old gate
stile
Mount Pleasant
Beulah Wood
Gamble Lane
Oak Tree Farm
sign & stile
stile
to Upper Wortley
(1 mile)
N
Jonas Wood
Beulah Farm
Tong Road
Foxhill Fold
stile
sports fields
barrier
sign & steps
bridge
Hare Park
stile
Butt
Troydale Lane
stile


**Park Spring Quarry** (or Mary Harrison's Quarry) produced a fine-grained sandstone. What is now a large housing estate was the site of an ammunition factory during World War II.

*the mound on which the anti-aircraft guns and searchlight were set on top of Post Hill*

***Post Hill*** *is now the name broadly given to the woods of Park Spring and Jonas Wood and is a very popular green space. Paths criss-cross the busy slope between Farnley Beck (and the old mill race alongside) and the quarries along the top of Post Hill, as well as continuing south through the ancient oak woodland of* ***Jonas Wood****.*

There is now no sign of **Long Tom's Cave**, whose entrance was sited alongside one of the paths to the Post Hill cobbles. It was full of animal bones and said to be home to a hermit giant.

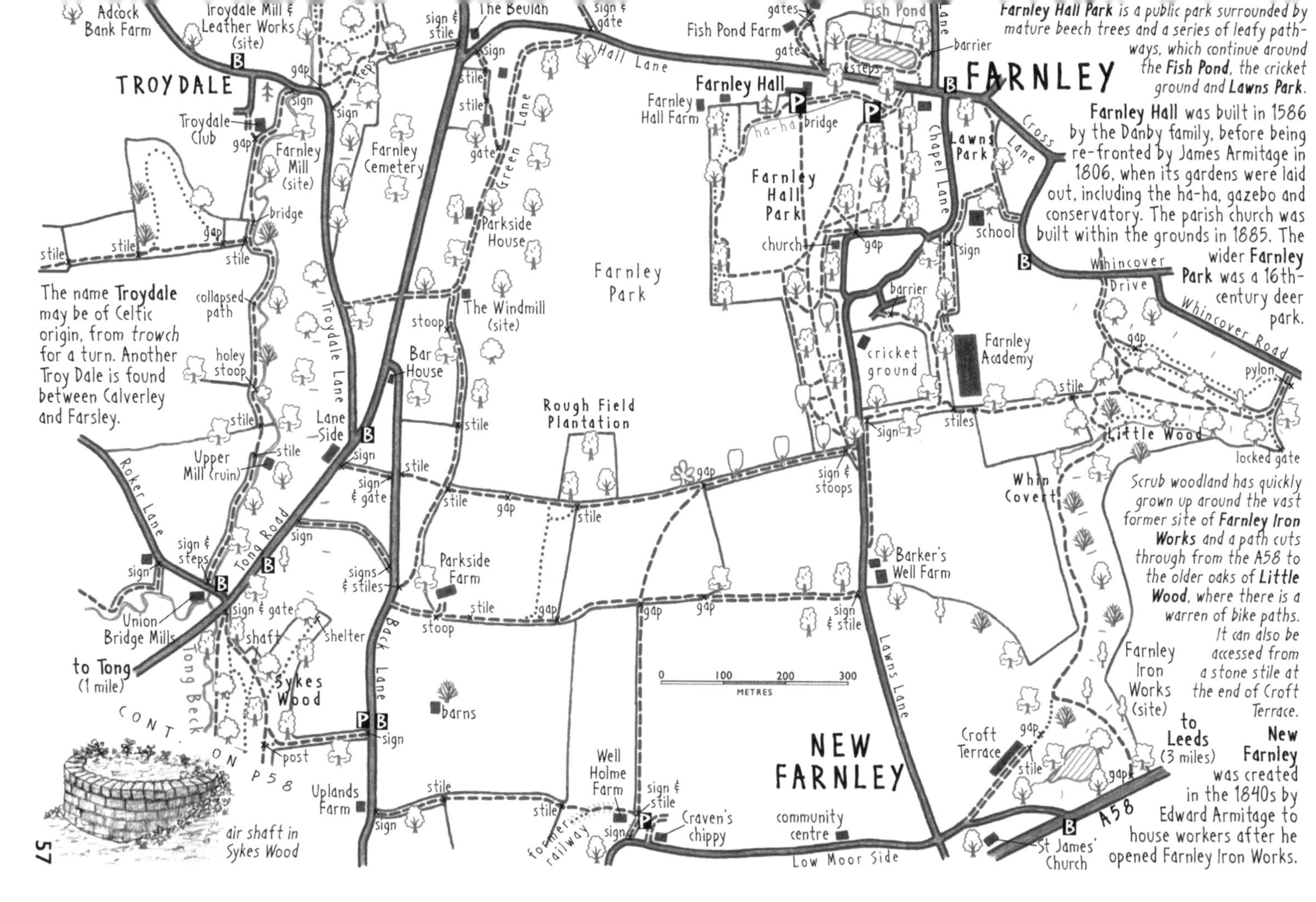
FARNLEY
**Farnley Hall Park** is a public park surrounded by mature beech trees and a series of leafy pathways, which continue around the **Fish Pond**, the cricket ground and **Lawns Park**.
**Farnley Hall** was built in 1586 by the Danby family, before being re-fronted by James Armitage in 1806, when its gardens were laid out, including the ha-ha, gazebo and conservatory. The parish church was built within the grounds in 1885. The wider **Farnley Park** was a 16th-century deer park.
Scrub woodland has quickly grown up around the vast former site of **Farnley Iron Works** and a path cuts through from the A58 to the older oaks of **Little Wood**, where there is a warren of bike paths. It can also be accessed from a stone stile at the end of Croft Terrace.
**New Farnley** was created in the 1840s by Edward Armitage to house workers after he opened Farnley Iron Works.
The name **Troydale** may be of Celtic origin, from *trowch* for a turn. Another Troy Dale is found between Calverley and Farsley.
TROYDALE
NEW FARNLEY
Farnley Park
Farnley Hall Park
Farnley Hall
Rough Field Plantation
Little Wood
Whin Covert
Sykes Wood
Farnley Iron Works (site)
Farnley Academy
cricket ground
Lawns Park
school
church
Fish Pond
Fish Pond Farm
Farnley Hall Farm
Farnley Cemetery
Parkside House
The Windmill (site)
Bar House
Lane Side
Parkside Farm
Barker's Well Farm
Well Holme Farm
Craven's chippy
community centre
Uplands Farm
Croft Terrace
St James' Church
Troydale Mill & Leather Works (site)
Adcock Bank Farm
The Beulah
Troydale Club
Farnley Mill (site)
Upper Mill (ruin)
Union Bridge Mills
Hall Lane
Green Lane
Chapel Lane
Cross Lane
Whincover Drive
Whincover Road
Lawns Lane
Low Moor Side
Back Lane
Troydale Lane
Tong Road
Roker Lane
Tong Beck
A58
former railway
to Leeds (3 miles)
to Tong (1 mile)
CONT. ON P58
air shaft in Sykes Wood
0 100 200 300 METRES

# MAP 15: TONG, FULNECK AND COCKERS DALE

The charming village of Tong stands on a ridge of farmland between the wooded valleys of Pudsey and Tong Becks. The latter is a particular delight, several paths exploring the woods alongside the beck, which has the strongest smell of wild garlic at the right time of year. To the south lies Drighlington, to the east New Farnley and to the north the historic village of Fulneck on the edge of Pudsey, yet this area is a peaceful rural oasis that is a pleasure to explore.

In 1743 members of the Moravian church (a separatist movement from Bohemia) established a new settlement at Fall Neck (meaning 'a woodland on a neck of land'). Initially known as Lamb's Hill, the new hamlet was renamed **Fulneck** to mirror Fulnek, one of their strongholds in Moravia. The church (known as Grace Hall) was built in 1748, with choir houses for single Sisters and Brethren on either side. These are now part of **Fulneck School**, a boarding school founded in the 1750s.

A tramway ran from **Far Tong Colliery** and other pits north of Tong to Bowling Iron Works in Bradford via Charlie Pit *(see p61)*. The **Alexandra Incline** was the steepest stretch, ending at an engine house east of Coney Wood. Its buttresses can still be seen crossing the foot of Keeper Lane.

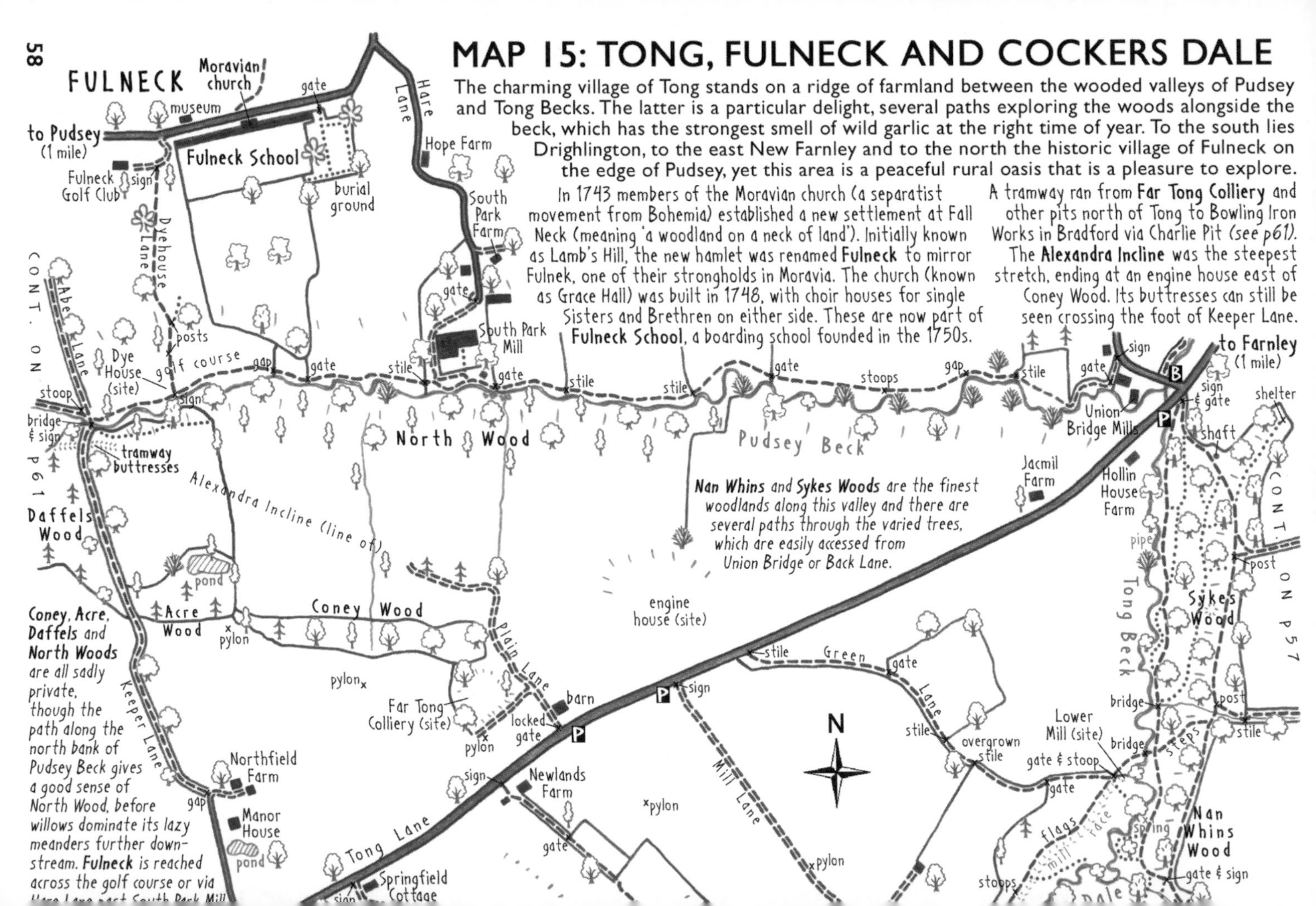
FULNECK
Moravian church
museum
gate
to Pudsey (1 mile)
Fulneck School
Fulneck Golf Club
sign
burial ground
Hare Lane
Hope Farm
South Park Farm
gate
South Park Mill
Dyehouse Lane
posts
Dye House (site)
golf course
gap
gate
stile
gate
stile
stile
gate
stoops
gap
stile
gate
sign
to Farnley (1 mile)
Union Bridge Mills
sign & gate
shelter
shaft
Hollin House Farm
Jacmil Farm
Pudsey Beck
North Wood
stoop
bridge & sign
sign
tramway buttresses
Alexandra Incline (line of)
Abe Lane
Daffels Wood
pond
Acre Wood
pylon
Coney Wood
Plain Lane
barn
locked gate
pylon
Far Tong Colliery (site)
engine house (site)
Nan Whins and Sykes Woods are the finest woodlands along this valley and there are several paths through the varied trees, which are easily accessed from Union Bridge or Back Lane.
stile
Green Lane
gate
stile
sign
Mill Lane
N
pylon
overgrown stile
Lower Mill (site)
gate & stoop
gate
bridge
bridge
steps
post
stile
post
Tong Beck
pipe
Sykes Wood
Nan Whins Wood
gate & sign
flags
mill race
spring
stoops
Dale
Keeper Lane
gap
Northfield Farm
Manor House
pond
sign
Newlands Farm
gate
Tong Lane
Springfield Cottage
pylon
pylon
CONT. ON p61
CONT. ON p57
Coney, Acre, Daffels and North Woods are all sadly private, though the path along the north bank of Pudsey Beck gives a good sense of North Wood, before willows dominate its lazy meanders further downstream. Fulneck is reached across the golf course or via

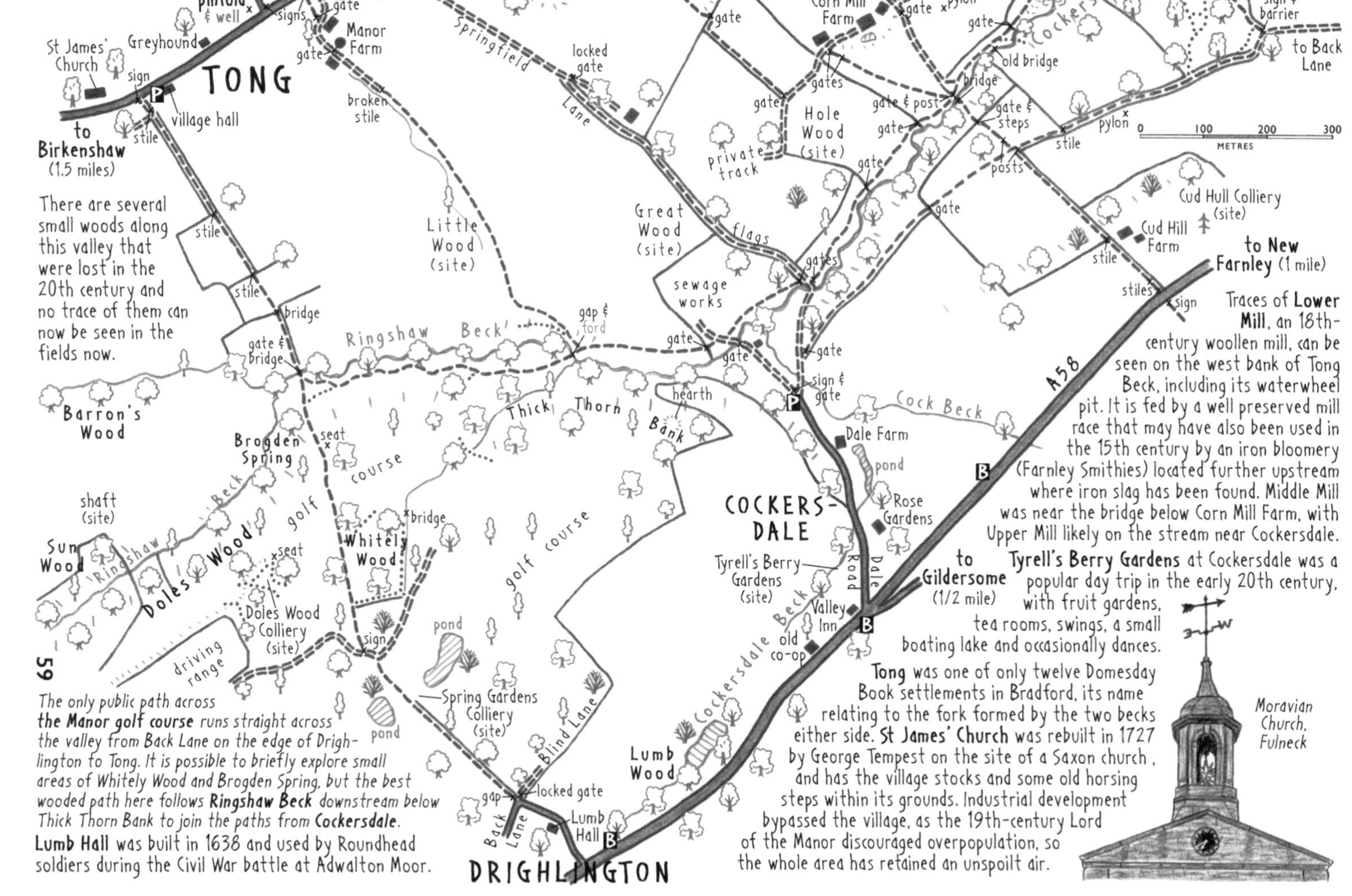
TONG
pintold & well
signs
gate
Manor Farm
St James' Church
Greyhound
sign
village hall
stile
to Birkenshaw (1.5 miles)
broken stile
Springfield
locked gate
Lane
Little Wood (site)
Great Wood (site)
flags
sewage works
private track
Hole Wood (site)
gates
gate & post
Corn Mill Farm
pylon
old bridge
bridge
gate & steps
posts
Cockers
sign & barrier
to Back Lane
0 100 200 300 METRES
Cud Hull Colliery (site)
Cud Hill Farm
stiles
sign
to New Farnley (1 mile)
A58
bridge
Ringshaw Beck
gap & ford
gate & bridge
Barron's Wood
Brogden Spring
seat
course
Thick Thorn Bank
hearth
sign & gate
Cock Beck
Dale Farm
pond
Rose Gardens
COCKERS-DALE
Dale Road
Tyrell's Berry Gardens (site)
Valley Inn
old co-op
to Gildersome (1/2 mile)
Cockersdale Beck
shaft (site)
Sun Wood
Ringshaw Beck
Doles Wood
golf
Whitely Wood
Doles Wood Colliery (site)
driving range
golf course
Spring Gardens Colliery (site)
Blind Lane
locked gate
gap
Back Lane
Lumb Hall
Lumb Wood
DRIGHLINGTON
B
Moravian Church, Fulneck

There are several small woods along this valley that were lost in the 20th century and no trace of them can now be seen in the fields now.

Traces of **Lower Mill**, an 18th-century woollen mill, can be seen on the west bank of Tong Beck, including its waterwheel pit. It is fed by a well preserved mill race that may have also been used in the 15th century by an iron bloomery (Farnley Smithies) located further upstream where iron slag has been found. Middle Mill was near the bridge below Corn Mill Farm, with Upper Mill likely on the stream near Cockersdale.

**Tyrell's Berry Gardens** at Cockersdale was a popular day trip in the early 20th century, with fruit gardens, tea rooms, swings, a small boating lake and occasionally dances.

**Tong** was one of only twelve Domesday Book settlements in Bradford, its name relating to the fork formed by the two becks either side. **St James' Church** was rebuilt in 1727 by George Tempest on the site of a Saxon church, and has the village stocks and some old horsing steps within its grounds. Industrial development bypassed the village, as the 19th-century Lord of the Manor discouraged overpopulation, so the whole area has retained an unspoilt air.

*The only public path across* ***the Manor golf course*** *runs straight across the valley from Back Lane on the edge of Drighlington to Tong. It is possible to briefly explore small areas of Whitely Wood and Brogden Spring, but the best wooded path here follows* ***Ringshaw Beck*** *downstream below Thick Thorn Bank to join the paths from* ***Cockersdale****.*

**Lumb Hall** was built in 1638 and used by Roundhead soldiers during the Civil War battle at Adwalton Moor.

# MAP 16: TYERSAL & HOLME BECKS

Pudsey Beck forks by the bottom of Keeper Lane and Abe Lane to form two tributaries. Holme Beck has limited accessible woodland, as Park Wood and what is left of Holme Wood are both private. Tyersal Beck is a more popular valley, the ancient oak woods of Black Carr, Spring Wood and the Rein facing younger woodland across the valley below Windmill Hill and Bankhouse. Sadly all of North Wood and most of Holme Wood were lost in the 20th century and other parts of this valley remain under ongoing threat from further expansion of the Holme Wood housing estate.

**Black Carr Wood** is considered one of the finest ancient woodlands in West Yorkshire as its sessile oak is unsullied by invasive species; though this can make it rather a monoculture, it is rich in wild flowers, woodpeckers and other birds. Oak was coppiced here, along with hazel and alder nearer the streams.

*Despite plenty of antisocial behaviour in the area,* ***Black Carr*** *is a treasure to explore, paths dropping into the top of its stunning oak woods from Tyersal Lane or Ned Lane or crossing into it from Tyersal Beck at the bottom. Carr Beck is particularly dense with paths.*

**to Tyersal Gate** (1/2 mile)

**Nesbit Hall** (a corruption of Nisbet) was built by Claud Nisbet in 1761 on the site of the ancient seat of Bank House.

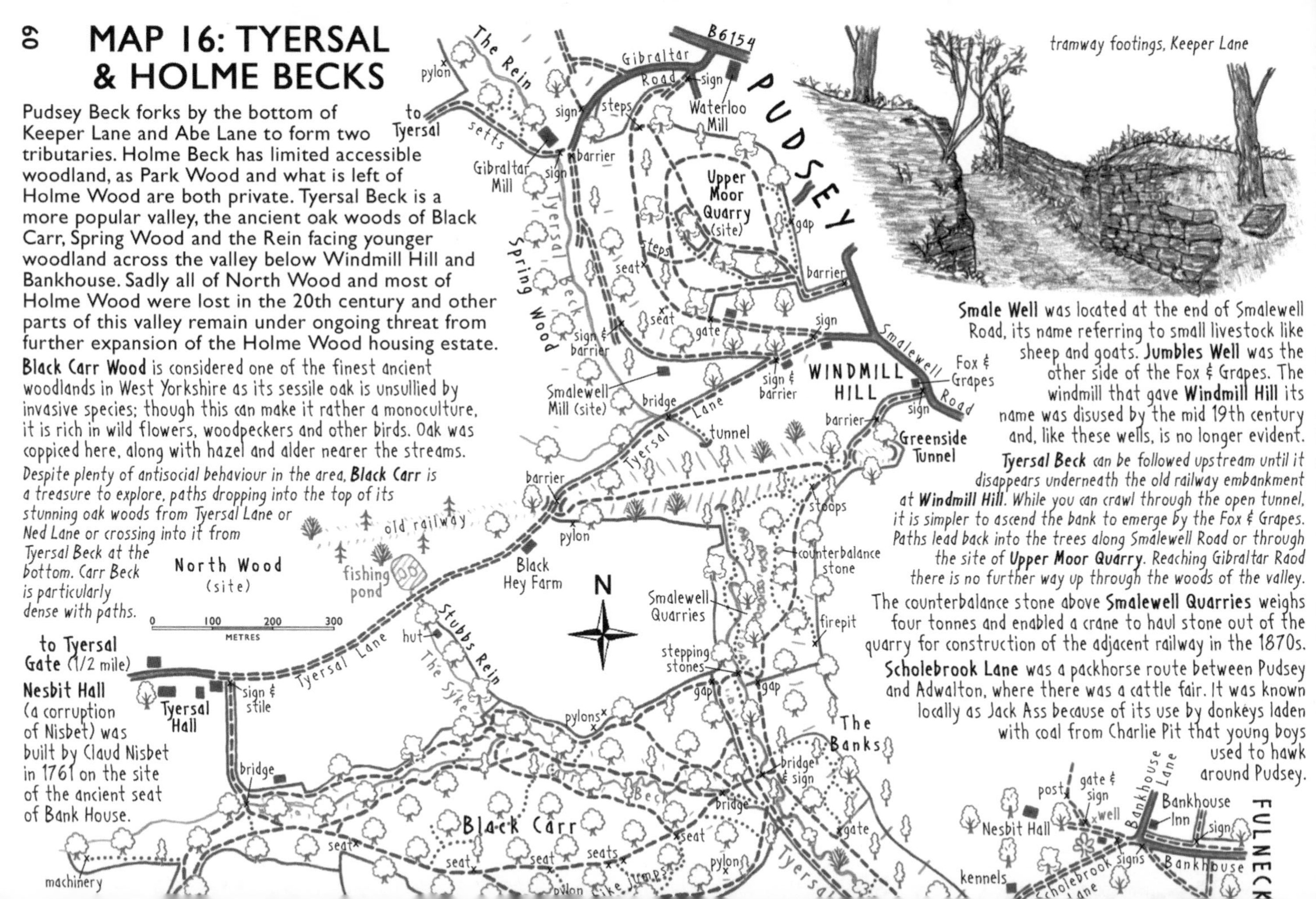

The Rein
pylon
to Tyersal
setts
Gibraltar Mill
sign
barrier
Gibraltar Road
B6154
sign
Waterloo Mill
steps
PUDSEY
Upper Moor Quarry (site)
gap
steps
seat
barrier
seat
gate
sign
Smalewell Road
Fox & Grapes
WINDMILL HILL
sign & barrier
sign & barrier
Tyersal Beck
Spring Wood
Smalewell Mill (site)
bridge
Tyersal Lane
tunnel
barrier
Greenside Tunnel
barrier
stoops
counterbalance stone
old railway
pylon
Black Hey Farm
North Wood (site)
fishing pond
N
Smalewell Quarries
firepit
0
100
200
300
METRES
hut
Stubbs Rein
The Syke
stepping stones
gap
gap
pylons
The Banks
Tyersal Lane
sign & stile
Tyersal Hall
bridge
bridge & sign
bridge
Carr Beck
Black Carr
seat
seat
seat
seats
seat
pylon
Sike Jumps
gate
machinery
post
gate & sign
well
Nesbit Hall
Bankhouse Lane
Bankhouse Inn
sign
signs
Bankhouse
Scholebrook Lane
kennels
FULNECK


tramway footings, Keeper Lane

**Smale Well** was located at the end of Smalewell Road, its name referring to small livestock like sheep and goats. **Jumbles Well** was the other side of the Fox & Grapes. The windmill that gave **Windmill Hill** its name was disused by the mid 19th century and, like these wells, is no longer evident.

***Tyersal Beck*** *can be followed upstream until it disappears underneath the old railway embankment at* ***Windmill Hill****. While you can crawl through the open tunnel, it is simpler to ascend the bank to emerge by the Fox & Grapes. Paths lead back into the trees along Smalewell Road or through the site of* ***Upper Moor Quarry****. Reaching Gibraltar Raod there is no further way up through the woods of the valley.*

The counterbalance stone above **Smalewell Quarries** weighs four tonnes and enabled a crane to haul stone out of the quarry for construction of the adjacent railway in the 1870s.

**Scholebrook Lane** was a packhorse route between Pudsey and Adwalton, where there was a cattle fair. It was known locally as Jack Ass because of its use by donkeys laden with coal from Charlie Pit that young boys used to hawk around Pudsey.

# HOLME WOOD

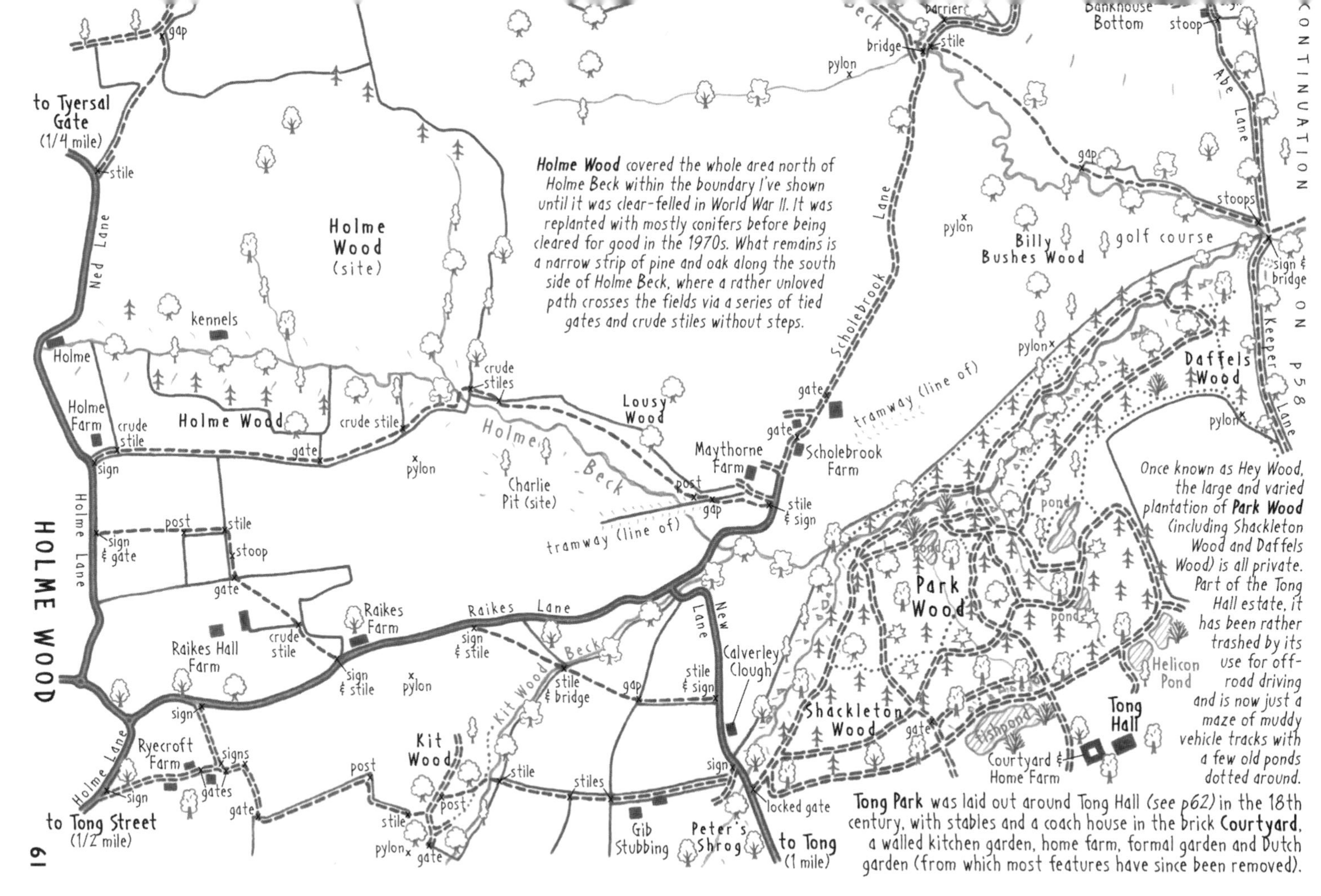

CONTINUATION ON P58
Holme Wood covered the whole area north of Holme Beck within the boundary I've shown until it was clear-felled in World War II. It was replanted with mostly conifers before being cleared for good in the 1970s. What remains is a narrow strip of pine and oak along the south side of Holme Beck, where a rather unloved path crosses the fields via a series of tied gates and crude stiles without steps.
Once known as Hey Wood, the large and varied plantation of Park Wood (including Shackleton Wood and Daffels Wood) is all private. Part of the Tong Hall estate, it has been rather trashed by its use for off-road driving and is now just a maze of muddy vehicle tracks with a few old ponds dotted around.
Tong Park was laid out around Tong Hall (see p62) in the 18th century, with stables and a coach house in the brick Courtyard, a walled kitchen garden, home farm, formal garden and Dutch garden (from which most features have since been removed).
to Tyersal Gate (1/4 mile)
gap
stile
Ned Lane
Holme Wood (site)
kennels
Holme
Holme Farm
crude stile
Holme Wood
crude stile
gate
crude stiles
sign
Holme Lane
post
stile
sign & gate
stoop
gate
pylon
Holme Beck
Charlie Pit (site)
Lousy Wood
tramway (line of)
Maythorne Farm
post
gap
stile & sign
gate
Scholebrook Farm
Scholebrook Lane
bridge
stile
barrier
pylon
Bankhouse Bottom
stoop
Abe Lane
gap
stoops
sign & bridge
Keeper Lane
Billy Bushes Wood
golf course
pylon
Daffels Wood
pylon
pond
Park Wood
Helicon Pond
Tong Hall
Courtyard & Home Farm
fishpond
gate
Shackleton Wood
locked gate
to Tong (1 mile)
Raikes Lane
Raikes Farm
Raikes Hall Farm
crude stile
sign & stile
New Lane
Calverley Clough
stile & sign
gap
Beck
stile & bridge
Kit Wood
sign
Ryecroft Farm
signs
gates
gate
post
stile
post
pylon
gate
stiles
Gib Stubbing
Peter's Shrog
to Tong Street (1/2 mile)

# ROUTE 10: BLACK CARR, TONG, COCKER'S DALE & POST HILL FROM PUDSEY

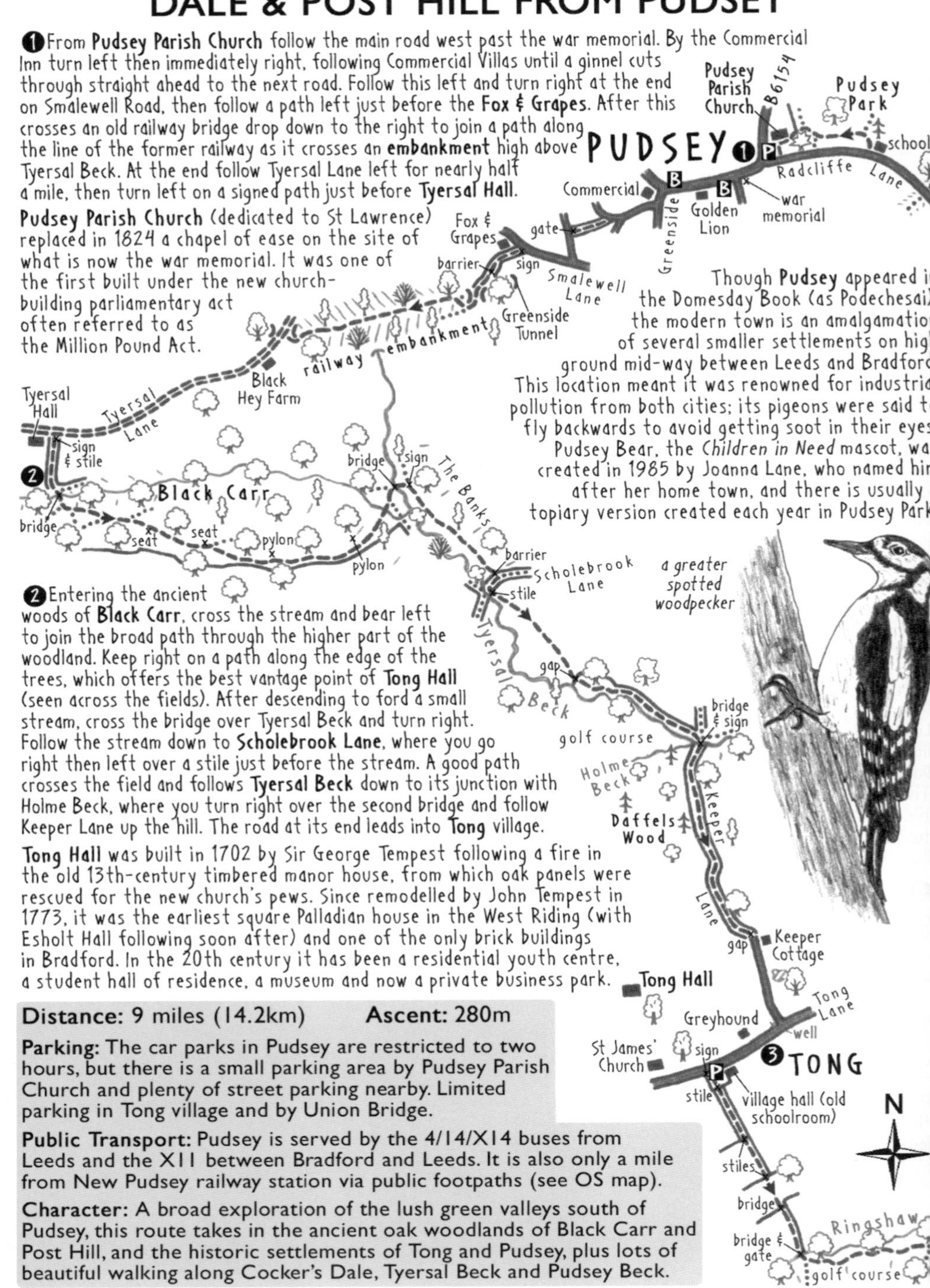

Pudsey Parish Church
B6154
Pudsey Park
school
PUDSEY
1
P
Radcliffe Lane
Commercial
B
B
Greenside
Golden Lion
war memorial
Fox & Grapes
gate
barrier
sign
Smalewell Lane
Greenside Tunnel
railway embankment
Black Hey Farm
Tyersal Hall
Tyersal Lane
sign & stile
2
Black Carr
bridge
seat
seat
pylon
pylon
bridge
sign
The Banks
barrier
Scholebrook Lane
stile
Tyersal Beck
gap
bridge & sign
golf course
Holme Beck
Daffels Wood
Keeper Lane
gap
Keeper Cottage
Tong Hall
Greyhound
Tong Lane
well
St James' Church
sign
3
TONG
P
stile
village hall (old schoolroom)
stiles
bridge
bridge & gate
Ringshaw
golf course
N
a greater spotted woodpecker


**1** From **Pudsey Parish Church** follow the main road west past the war memorial. By the Commercial Inn turn left then immediately right, following Commercial Villas until a ginnel cuts through straight ahead to the next road. Follow this left and turn right at the end on Smalewell Road, then follow a path left just before the **Fox & Grapes**. After this crosses an old railway bridge drop down to the right to join a path along the line of the former railway as it crosses an **embankment** high above Tyersal Beck. At the end follow Tyersal Lane left for nearly half a mile, then turn left on a signed path just before **Tyersal Hall**.

**Pudsey Parish Church** (dedicated to St Lawrence) replaced in 1824 a chapel of ease on the site of what is now the war memorial. It was one of the first built under the new church-building parliamentary act often referred to as the Million Pound Act.

Though **Pudsey** appeared i the Domesday Book (as Podechesai) the modern town is an amalgamatio of several smaller settlements on hig ground mid-way between Leeds and Bradford This location meant it was renowned for industria pollution from both cities; its pigeons were said t fly backwards to avoid getting soot in their eyes Pudsey Bear, the *Children in Need* mascot, wa created in 1985 by Joanna Lane, who named hi after her home town, and there is usually topiary version created each year in Pudsey Park

**2** Entering the ancient woods of **Black Carr**, cross the stream and bear left to join the broad path through the higher part of the woodland. Keep right on a path along the edge of the trees, which offers the best vantage point of **Tong Hall** (seen across the fields). After descending to ford a small stream, cross the bridge over Tyersal Beck and turn right. Follow the stream down to **Scholebrook Lane**, where you go right then left over a stile just before the stream. A good path crosses the field and follows **Tyersal Beck** down to its junction with Holme Beck, where you turn right over the second bridge and follow Keeper Lane up the hill. The road at its end leads into **Tong** village.

**Tong Hall** was built in 1702 by Sir George Tempest following a fire in the old 13th-century timbered manor house, from which oak panels were rescued for the new church's pews. Since remodelled by John Tempest in 1773, it was the earliest square Palladian house in the West Riding (with Esholt Hall following soon after) and one of the only brick buildings in Bradford. In the 20th century it has been a residential youth centre, a student hall of residence, a museum and now a private business park.

**Distance:** 9 miles (14.2km) **Ascent:** 280m

**Parking:** The car parks in Pudsey are restricted to two hours, but there is a small parking area by Pudsey Parish Church and plenty of street parking nearby. Limited parking in Tong village and by Union Bridge.

**Public Transport:** Pudsey is served by the 4/14/X14 buses from Leeds and the X11 between Bradford and Leeds. It is also only a mile from New Pudsey railway station via public footpaths (see OS map).

**Character:** A broad exploration of the lush green valleys south of Pudsey, this route takes in the ancient oak woodlands of Black Carr and Post Hill, and the historic settlements of Tong and Pudsey, plus lots of beautiful walking along Cocker's Dale, Tyersal Beck and Pudsey Beck.

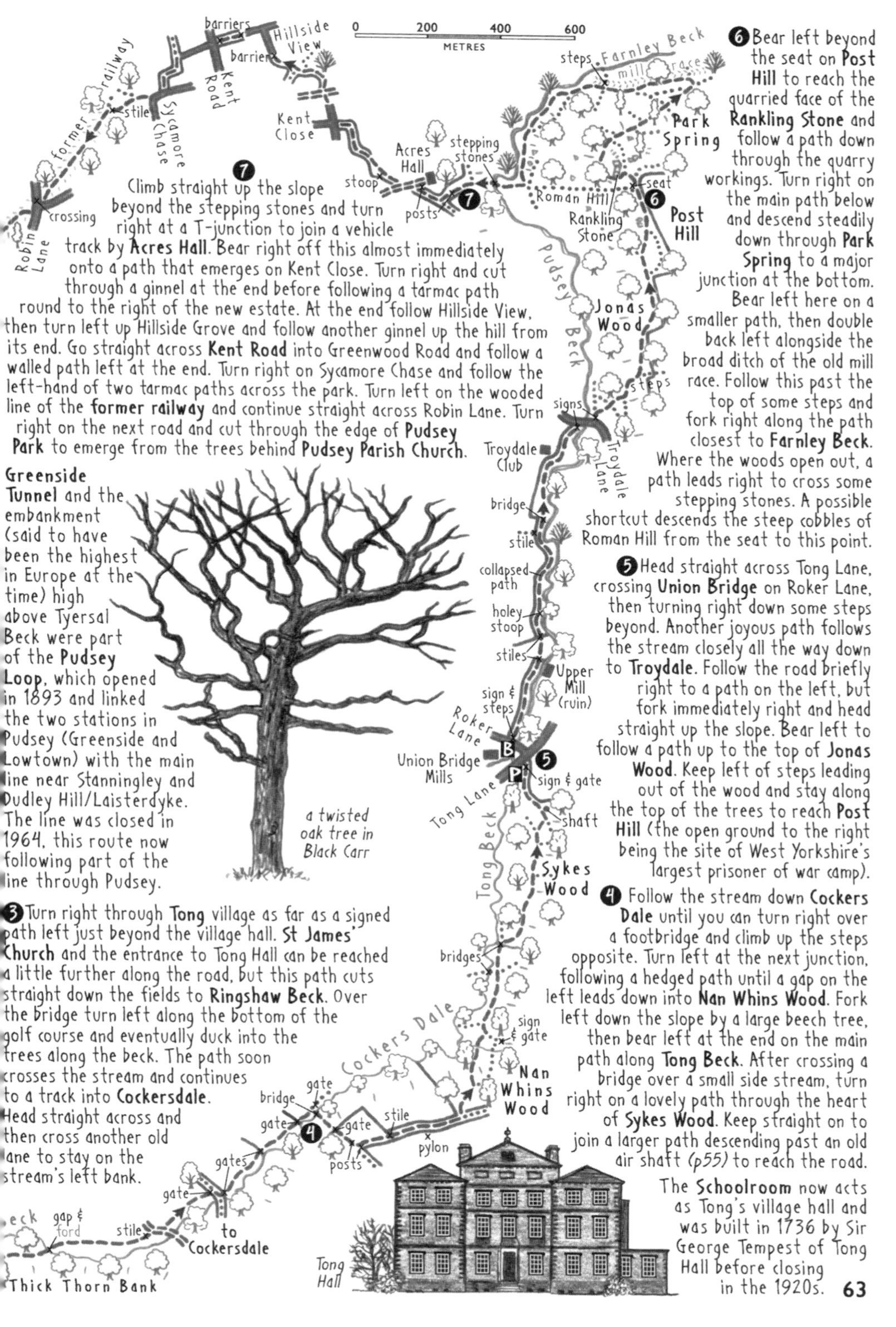

0 200 400 600
METRES
barriers
barriers
Hillside View
Kent Road
Sycamore Chase
former railway
stile
Kent Close
Acres Hall
stepping stones
stoop
posts
crossing
Robin Lane
steps
Farnley Beck
mill race
Park Spring
Roman Hill
seat
Rankling Stone
Post Hill
Pudsey Beck
Jonas Wood
steps
signs
Troydale Club
Troydale Lane
bridge
stile
collapsed path
holey stoop
stiles
Upper Mill (ruin)
sign & steps
Roker Lane
Union Bridge Mills
sign & gate
Tong Lane
shaft
Tong Beck
Sykes Wood
bridges
sign & gate
Nan Whins Wood
Cockers Dale
gate
bridge
gate
gate
stile
posts
pylon
gates
gate
gap & ford
stile
to Cockersdale
Thick Thorn Bank
Tong Hall
a twisted oak tree in Black Carr


**3** Turn right through **Tong** village as far as a signed path left just beyond the village hall. **St James' Church** and the entrance to Tong Hall can be reached a little further along the road, but this path cuts straight down the fields to **Ringshaw Beck**. Over the bridge turn left along the bottom of the golf course and eventually duck into the trees along the beck. The path soon crosses the stream and continues to a track into **Cockersdale**. Head straight across and then cross another old lane to stay on the stream's left bank.

**4** Follow the stream down **Cockers Dale** until you can turn right over a footbridge and climb up the steps opposite. Turn left at the next junction, following a hedged path until a gap on the left leads down into **Nan Whins Wood**. Fork left down the slope by a large beech tree, then bear left at the end on the main path along **Tong Beck**. After crossing a bridge over a small side stream, turn right on a lovely path through the heart of **Sykes Wood**. Keep straight on to join a larger path descending past an old air shaft *(p55)* to reach the road.

**5** Head straight across Tong Lane, crossing **Union Bridge** on Roker Lane, then turning right down some steps beyond. Another joyous path follows the stream closely all the way down to **Troydale**. Follow the road briefly right to a path on the left, but fork immediately right and head straight up the slope. Bear left to follow a path up to the top of **Jonas Wood**. Keep left of steps leading out of the wood and stay along the top of the trees to reach **Post Hill** (the open ground to the right being the site of West Yorkshire's largest prisoner of war camp).

**6** Bear left beyond the seat on **Post Hill** to reach the quarried face of the **Rankling Stone** and follow a path down through the quarry workings. Turn right on the main path below and descend steadily down through **Park Spring** to a major junction at the bottom. Bear left here on a smaller path, then double back left alongside the broad ditch of the old mill race. Follow this past the top of some steps and fork right along the path closest to **Farnley Beck**. Where the woods open out, a path leads right to cross some stepping stones. A possible shortcut descends the steep cobbles of Roman Hill from the seat to this point.

**7** Climb straight up the slope beyond the stepping stones and turn right at a T-junction to join a vehicle track by **Acres Hall**. Bear right off this almost immediately onto a path that emerges on Kent Close. Turn right and cut through a ginnel at the end before following a tarmac path round to the right of the new estate. At the end follow Hillside View, then turn left up Hillside Grove and follow another ginnel up the hill from its end. Go straight across **Kent Road** into Greenwood Road and follow a walled path left at the end. Turn right on Sycamore Chase and follow the left-hand of two tarmac paths across the park. Turn left on the wooded line of the **former railway** and continue straight across Robin Lane. Turn right on the next road and cut through the edge of **Pudsey Park** to emerge from the trees behind **Pudsey Parish Church**.

**Greenside Tunnel** and the embankment (said to have been the highest in Europe at the time) high above Tyersal Beck were part of the **Pudsey Loop**, which opened in 1893 and linked the two stations in Pudsey (Greenside and Lowtown) with the main line near Stanningley and Dudley Hill/Laisterdyke. The line was closed in 1964, this route now following part of the line through Pudsey.

The **Schoolroom** now acts as Tong's village hall and was built in 1736 by Sir George Tempest of Tong Hall before closing in the 1920s.

# FARNLEY WOOD

I only discovered Farnley Wood while poring over old Ordnance Survey maps to populate my list of lost woods of the Aire Valley *(see p152)*. Mostly these are small pockets of woodland that have disappeared since the first series in the 1840s, like Shaw Wood (once Guiseley's great common wood but already reduced to a copse by then), or large woods that have been greatly reduced for housing since World War II, like Hawksworth Wood or Moseley Wood. However, where the suburbs haven't encroached, the pattern of land is surprisingly consistent since the mid 19th century. So imagine my surprise when I came across a vast wood covering approximately 350 acres between Farnley, Lower Wortley and Gildersome. I pulled out the current map to see what I'd missed, yet where Farnley Wood had once stood there were just fields and a few scraps of conifer plantation around Beeston Royds.

Farnley Wood is not just any lost wood, though; it could be argued to be one of West Yorkshire's most famous woods, forever associated with the Farnley Wood Plot of 1663. During the Civil War a group of Royalist soldiers fleeing from the Battle of Marston Moor had sheltered in this wood for a time. Within a few years, with Charles II restored to the throne, a group of men from Farnley and Gildersome reconvened here to plot to overthrow the King, initially by attacking Royalist strongholds in Leeds. It was incredibly poorly thought out and, when 26 conspirators met in the wood on 12th October 1663, they had been informed on and were arrested. Twenty-one of them were executed in York, three after escaping and hiding in the pits of Gildersome. The leafy bowers of this ancient wood were coppiced for charcoal before and after this, providing an important supply to Farnley Smithies and later Kirkstall Forge.

Until the latter half of the 19th century Farnley Wood stood proudly on any map of West Yorkshire. On Saxton's 1577 map of Yorkshire, it is represented by a cluster of tree symbols as large as any in the Leeds area and, by Jefferys' map of 1771, it looks the single largest in the region, as it does on John Tuke's 1787 map of Yorkshire. Then, between 1850 and 1890, it just disappears completely from the maps. The clue to its scale is given by farm names like Wood End near the A58 and Wood Farm near the A62, with Farnley Wood, Farnley Wood Side and Wood Lane in between.

So what happened? It would be easy to assume that, as this area formed part of the rich Middle Coal Measures, the trees were cut down to make way for the many coal shafts sunk across the area. There were four pits here by 1890 – Simpson, Farnley Wood Lift, Tingle and Dixon Pits – all along the edge of the former woodland. Where this happened in other places though, particularly Middleton Wood, only the immediate area around the pit was felled, leaving the rest as a valuable resource for pit props or other things. There is a familiar pattern here of older small-scale coal workings in the wood itself, probably undertaken by very similar horse-drawn methods as those well documented in Middleton Wood. By 1905 the adjacent fireclay works, a quarry by Ochre House and a mineral railway to Farnley Iron Works, give clues to other resources being exploited in the area, but it remains a largely agricultural landscape. And that is what we find there today, a remarkably ordinary series of fields on a low ridge between Farnley Wood Beck and Wortley Beck, with an overgrown trig point at its east end overlooking the centre of Leeds.

The mystery of why we lost one of our finest woods is particularly perplexing as it is only around 150 years old. We know things change all the time, but there is something very sad about the loss of such a large area of woodland within relatively recent memory.

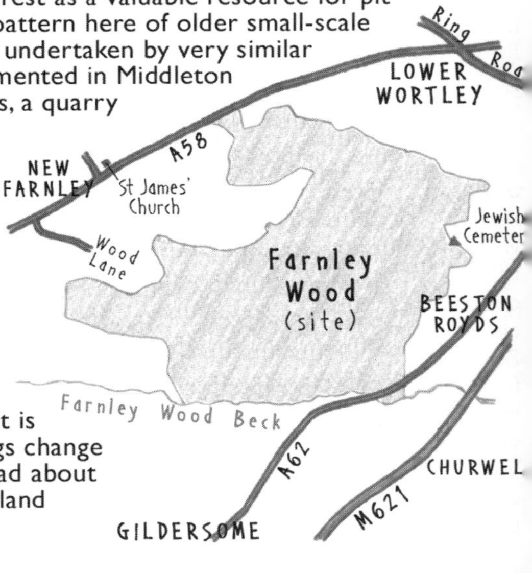

Ring Road
LOWER WORTLEY
A58
NEW FARNLEY
St James' Church
Wood Lane
Jewish Cemeter
Farnley Wood (site)
BEESTON ROYDS
Farnley Wood Beck
A62
CHURWEL
M621
GILDERSOME

# CHAPTER 6 - HEART OF THE AIRE

**Map Sheet:** Explorer 288 (Bradford & Huddersfield)

**Public Transport:** Railway stations at Apperley Bridge, Baildon and New Pudsey. Various bus routes to Calverley, Thackley, Guiseley, Yeadon and Rawdon.

**Parking:** Free car parks at Calverley Woods, Buck Wood and Apperley Bridge. Pay car park at Esholt.

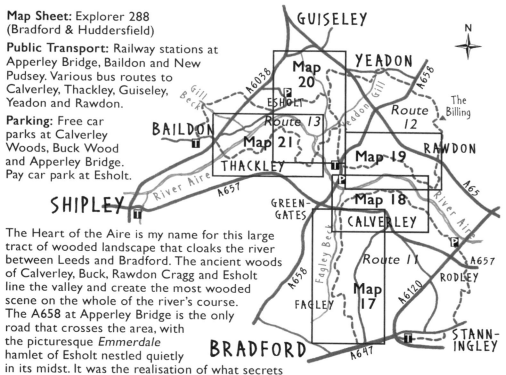

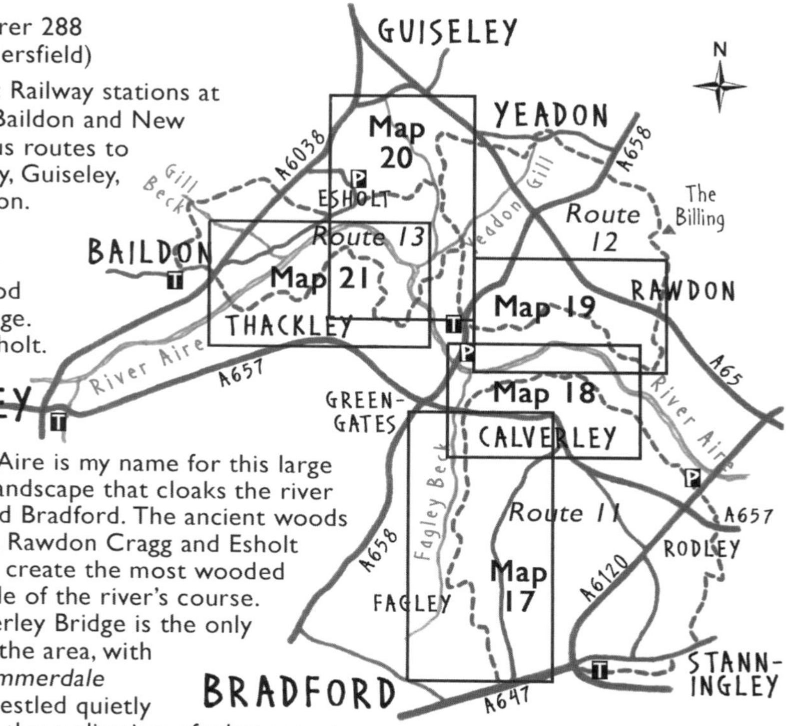

The Heart of the Aire is my name for this large tract of wooded landscape that cloaks the river between Leeds and Bradford. The ancient woods of Calverley, Buck, Rawdon Cragg and Esholt line the valley and create the most wooded scene on the whole of the river's course. The A658 at Apperley Bridge is the only road that crosses the area, with the picturesque *Emmerdale* hamlet of Esholt nestled quietly in its midst. It was the realisation of what secrets this surprising area holds that inspired me to start working on this book.

This jewel in the Aire's crown has not been free of interference, though, with exclusive housing estates for wealthy mill owners being laid out in the 19th century through Rawdon Cragg Wood and (to a lesser extent) Calverley Wood. The City of Bradford's vast waste water treatment works at Esholt is the greatest blight, covering a large part of the valley floor, overshadowing Esholt Hall and ensuring any pint at the Woolpack is accompanied by a distinctive aroma.

The Aire was once fordable in several places on this section of the valley – at Esholt, Thackley and Calverley – while the canal and railway have added further barriers, dividing woodlands and severing the old routes that once criss-crossed the valley. The woodlands continue up several feeder streams, where the hilltop urbanity of this part of the Aire Valley quickly closes in. Gill Beck is covered in the next chapter, while Fagley Beck's green arm reaches far into Bradford, and Guiseley Beck and Yeadon Gill fall steeply from the townships of Aireborough (which, as a modern appellation for Guiseley, Yeadon and Rawdon, was defined as 'the most average place in England and Wales' in the 2001 Census). Apperley Bridge lies at the centre of the region and makes a fine starting point for any exploration, whether by car or rail.

*the Toothache Tree in Buck Wood*

# MAP 17: FAGLEY WOODS & WOODHALL LAKE

The series of woods along the east side of Fagley Beck are collectively known locally as Fagley Woods, providing a natural playground for the housing estates of Fagley, Ravenscliffe and Greengates. These were built either side of World War II to house those cleared from the slums of Bradford, with the east side of Fagley Beck preserved as ancient woodland and for golf courses. There are further wooded enclaves around Woodhall Lake and Woodhall Quarries, an area that can be easily accessed from Woodhall Lane and the A647.

*__Ravenscliffe Road__ is an old packhorse route (known locally as the Jockey Path) through Harper's Spring, Sowden Wood and Ravenscliffe Wood along the eastern side of __Fagley Beck__. Various smaller paths (many cut by quads and motorbikes) branch off up into the trees and allow these dense holly and oak woods to be explored. They all end up leading back down to the main path, as most of the land outside the woods is a private golf course.*

**Low Rein Reservoir** was built by the Bradford Corporation and became popular for fishing and picnicking with the new estate's residents, with ice cream and sweets sold seasonally in the adjacent woods. After two people died trying to rescue children who got in difficulty swimming there (as it was too steep to climb out), it was fenced off. Others fished downstream in **Harper's Dam**, into which edible French frogs had been released. Ravenscliffe Mill's other millpond was famously stocked with goldfish and carp, and fenced off for the mill owner's sole use. I have used the old names for **Sowden Wood** (now Round Wood after the nearby glacial mounds of Round Hills) and **Harper's Spring** (now Bill Wood), the latter named after a local family who served as the minstrels for Roger de Calverley in the 13th century, before acquiring land in the area.

**Woodhall Road** was an ancient track known as Clay Lane, as there several clay pits dug along its length.

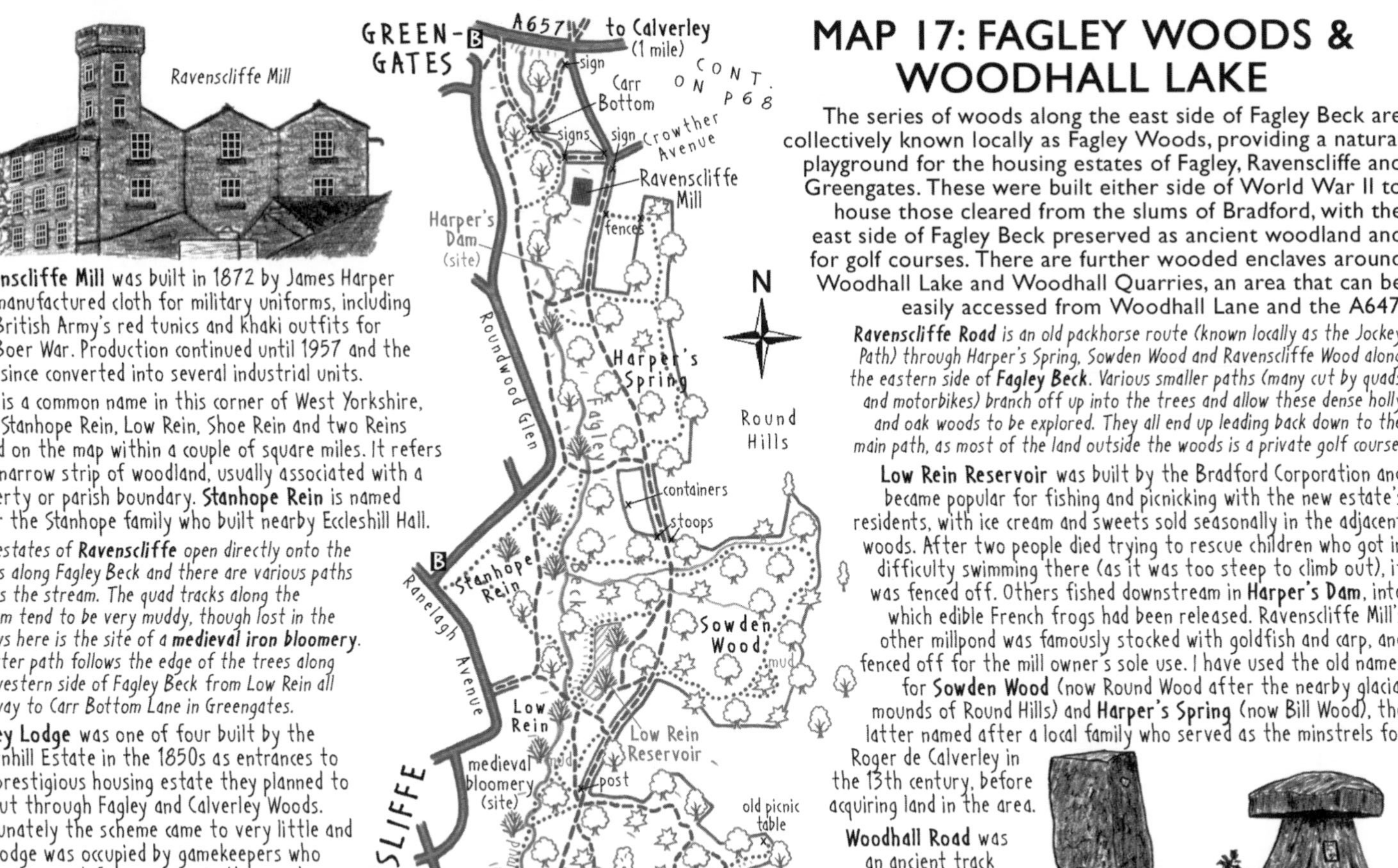
Ravenscliffe Mill
GREEN-GATES
A657
to Calverley (1 mile)
CONT. ON P68
sign
Carr Bottom
signs
sign
Crowther Avenue
Ravenscliffe Mill
fences
Harper's Dam (site)
Roundwood Glen
N
Harper's Spring
Fagley
Round Hills
containers
stoops
Stanhope Rein
Beck
Ranelagh Avenue
Sowden Wood
mud
Low Rein
Low Rein Reservoir
medieval bloomery (site)
post
old picnic table
RAVENSLIFFE
sign
steps
Ravenscliffe Rd
rifle range (site)
Shoe
Ravenscliffe
Woodhall Hills Golf Club
Priesthorpe Road
stoop and sculpture on Woodhall Golf Course

**Ravenscliffe Mill** was built in 1872 by James Harper and manufactured cloth for military uniforms, including the British Army's red tunics and khaki outfits for the Boer War. Production continued until 1957 and the mills since converted into several industrial units.

**Rein** is a common name in this corner of West Yorkshire, with Stanhope Rein, Low Rein, Shoe Rein and two Reins found on the map within a couple of square miles. It refers to a narrow strip of woodland, usually associated with a property or parish boundary. **Stanhope Rein** is named after the Stanhope family who built nearby Eccleshill Hall.

*The estates of __Ravenscliffe__ open directly onto the woods along Fagley Beck and there are various paths across the stream. The quad tracks along the stream tend to be very muddy, though lost in the willows here is the site of a __medieval iron bloomery__. A better path follows the edge of the trees along the western side of Fagley Beck from Low Rein all the way to Carr Bottom Lane in Greengates.*

**Fagley Lodge** was one of four built by the Thornhill Estate in the 1850s as entrances to the prestigious housing estate they planned to lay out through Fagley and Calverley Woods. Fortunately the scheme came to very little and the lodge was occupied by gamekeepers who kept an eye out for poachers in the wood.

Sand pits on the site of Ravenscliffe Avenue were used to fill sandbags during World War II, while the Home Guard made use of a small quarry at the top of **Ravenscliffe Wood** as a rifle range.

The **Blue Pig** at Lower Fagley was originally the Ravenscliffe Arms, but unlike other Blue Pigs wasn't named as a working men's club. Its nickname is thought to refer to a landlord who kept a variety of pig that was a cross between a white sow and a black boar. Its location on the boundary between Bradford and Leeds meant there was a 'whistling shop' here for selling illegal spirits. The law from either town could be evaded simply by crossing the stream that formed the boundary. The pub was lit by gaslight until after World War II, and was renowned for selling watercress that grew in abundance in Fagley Beck.

The name **Fagley** refers to a Yorkshire dialect word feg for coarse grass and *ley*, which relates to a woodland clearing. Lower Fagley was once a larger hamlet, but many of the cottages were abandoned when the large housing estate was built in the 1940s, leaving only a sawmill and the Blue Pig.

*The main route from* **Fagley** *to the woods is down Fagley Road to the dilapidated ruin of the old* **Blue Pig**, *and there is also a pleasant path along the former railway line. Its embankment is very obvious north-west of Woodhall Road but becomes invisible where the former cutting has been filled in heading south-west past* **Sunny Bank**. *The wasteland along the top of Fagley Beck is sadly lacking trees and dominated instead by the imposing presence of Morrisons' headquarters at Hilmore House.*

**Woodhall Lake** (known locally as the Blue Lagoon) was created in the 1840s as part of the Lower Woodhall estate by Daniel Peckover, a noted Bradford banker, merchant and Quaker. During a slump in the wool business, he kept his workers employed on his estate, building a summer house and boathouse by this new fishpond. Woodhall Lodge was the entrance to the estate.

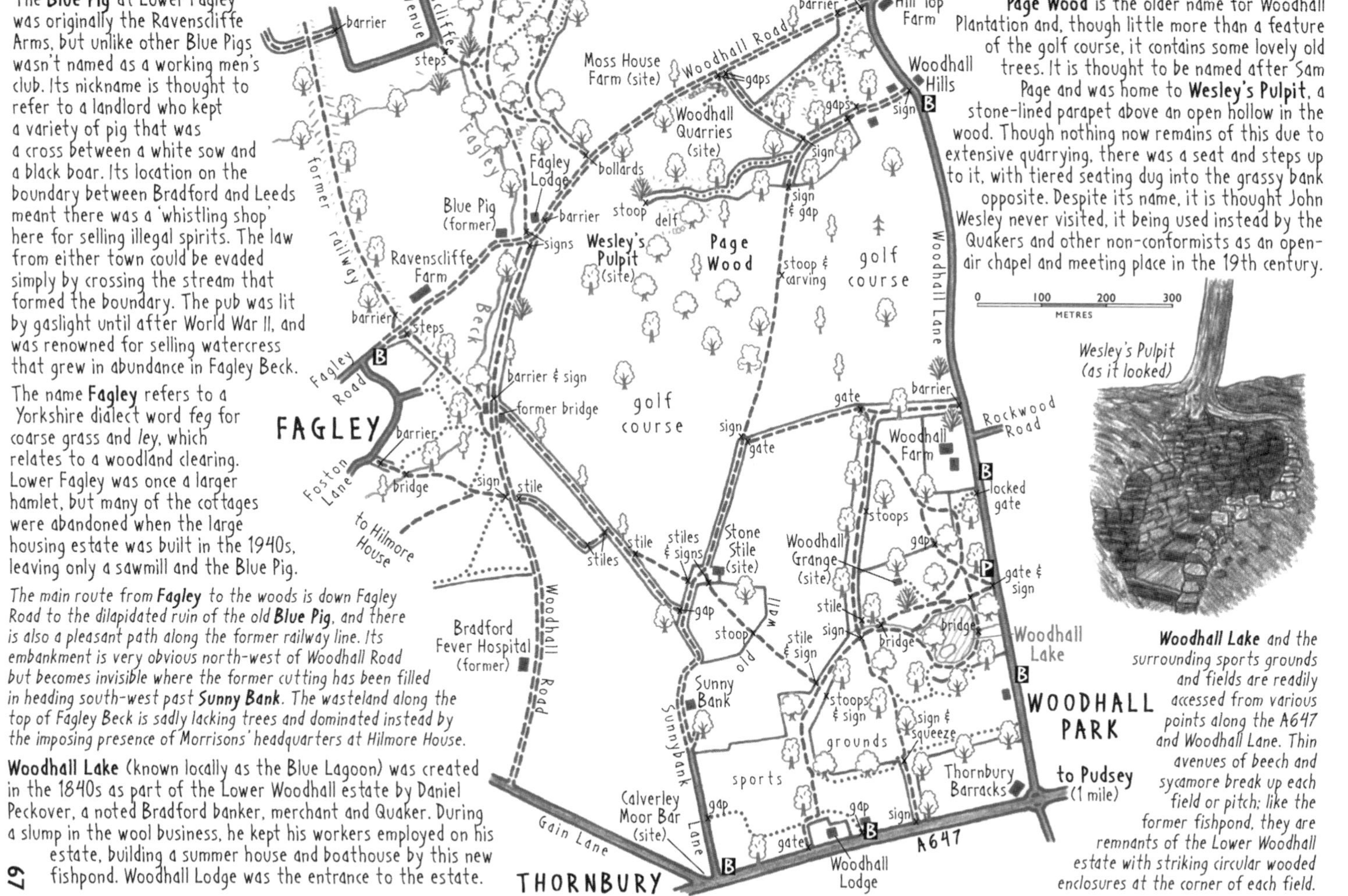

FAGLEY
THORNBURY
WOODHALL PARK
Page Wood
golf course
golf course
Wesley's Pulpit (site)
Woodhall Quarries (site)
Moss House Farm (site)
Hill Top Farm
Woodhall Hills
Woodhall Road
Woodhall Lane
Rockwood Road
Fagley Lodge
Blue Pig (former)
Ravenscliffe Farm
Ravenscliffe Avenue
Fagley Beck
former railway
Fagley Road
Foston Lane
to Hilmore House
Bradford Fever Hospital (former)
Woodhall Road
Stone Stile (site)
old wall
Sunny Bank
Sunnybank Lane
Calverley Moor Bar (site)
Gain Lane
Woodhall Farm
Woodhall Grange (site)
Woodhall Lake
Thornbury Barracks
Woodhall Lodge
sports grounds
A647
to Pudsey (1 mile)
barrier
steps
gaps
gap
sign
signs
bollards
stoop
delf
sign & gap
stoop & carving
barrier & sign
former bridge
bridge
stile
stiles
stiles & signs
gate
locked gate
stoops
gate & sign
stile & sign
stoops & sign
sign & squeeze
0 100 200 300 METRES


**Page Wood** is the older name for Woodhall Plantation and, though little more than a feature of the golf course, it contains some lovely old trees. It is thought to be named after Sam Page and was home to **Wesley's Pulpit**, a stone-lined parapet above an open hollow in the wood. Though nothing now remains of this due to extensive quarrying, there was a seat and steps up to it, with tiered seating dug into the grassy bank opposite. Despite its name, it is thought John Wesley never visited, it being used instead by the Quakers and other non-conformists as an open-air chapel and meeting place in the 19th century.

*Wesley's Pulpit (as it looked)*

***Woodhall Lake** and the surrounding sports grounds and fields are readily accessed from various points along the A647 and Woodhall Lane. Thin avenues of beech and sycamore break up each field or pitch; like the former fishpond, they are remnants of the Lower Woodhall estate with striking circular wooded enclosures at the corner of each field.*

# MAP 18: CALVERLEY WOODS

Calverley Woods is justifiably one of the most popular woodland areas in the Aire Valley, its ancient woodlands comprised largely of oak, holly and birch and full of interesting features. Fortunately much of the planned development of the wood as an upmarket housing estate never materialised, leaving only driveways and some entrance lodges. Among the dense trees are quarry ruins, wells, small pools, an arch folly and the layout of a prisoner-of-war camp to discover, as well as more paths than I can possibly map.

A series of avenues (named after the daughters of Thomas Thornhill) and plots for 'gentlemen's houses' were laid out across Calverley Woods in the 1850s by the Thornhill Estate. There were four lodges, the grandest being the **Needles Eye** gatehouse at the junction near Underwood Farm, but sadly this was demolished in the 1940s on safety grounds. Despite plenty of interest among Bradford's wealthy merchants, the only plot sold was Ferncliffe, built in 1857 and now a Leonard Cheshire nursing home.

**Tomlin Well**, possibly a corruption of Tumbling or Little Tom's Well, has part of its stone trough still in place. The small reservoir in the middle of the wood supplied Woodhouse Grove School in Rawdon with fresh water in the 19th century.

***West Wood*** *is a fine mix of oak, birch and holly, with beech planted along its avenues. It has several interesting features higher up the slope, including the folly arch, well and former pool, with many paths leading up to these. Paths either side of Carr Beck also head up the other side of the valley to the edge of* ***Greengates****.*

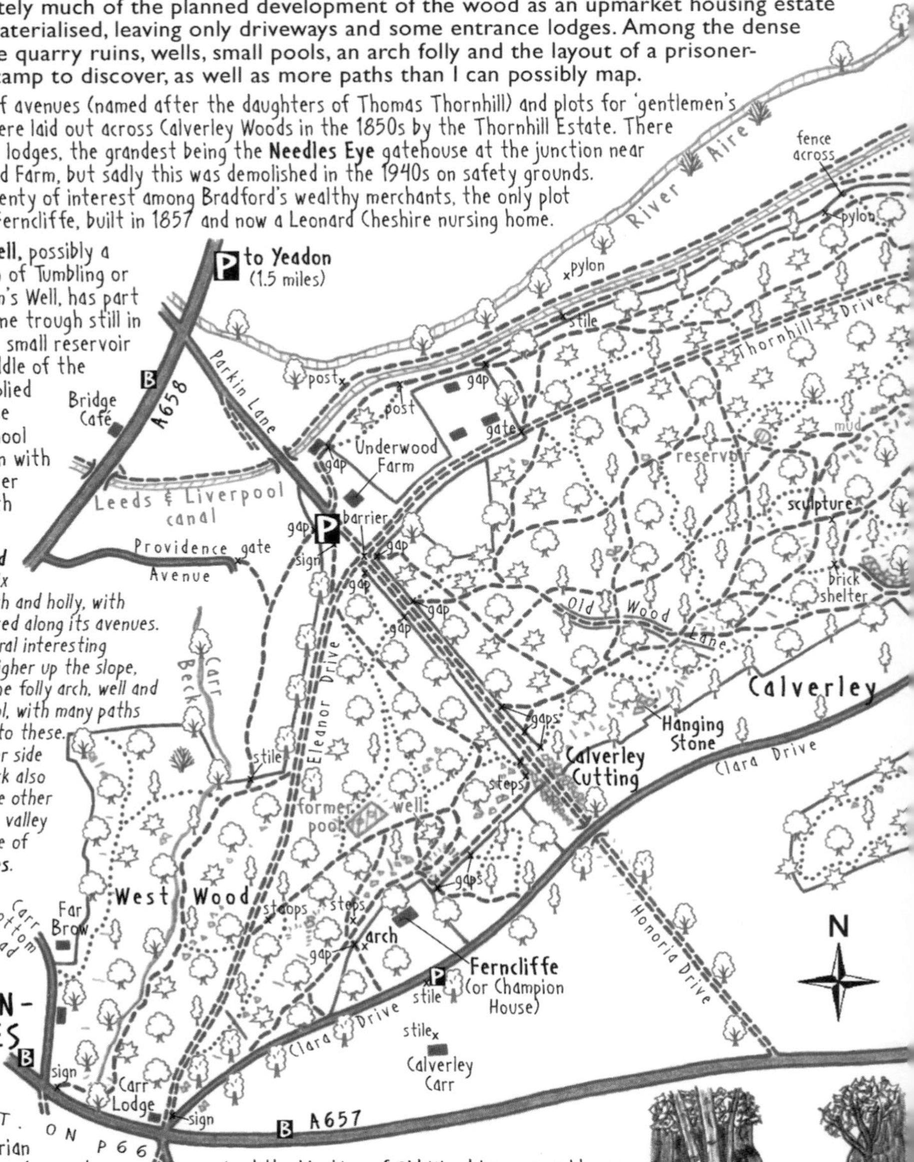

CONT. ON P66

The Victorian estate's development required the blocking of Old Wood Lane, a packhorse route through Calverley Wood, its walls still evident in places. An alternative was created through the newly blasted **Calverley Cutting**, a steep and crude route that looked more like a railway incline to the miffed locals. The public **well** in West Wood also became private, with drinking water provided to Calverley village as compensation, as well as a recreation ground. The well house still stands and once had an adjoining gardener's cottage from when it was used to water the garden of **Ferncliffe**. The arch, grottos, tennis court and former swimming pool were also part of the grounds of this grand house, renamed Champion House after its use in the BBC series of the same name.

*Calverley Cutting*

CONT. ON p72

On April 23rd 1605 Walter Calverley killed his two children and wounded his wife (who was saved only by her whalebone bodice) in Calverley Old Hall. He refused to enter a plea and weights were added to his chest until he died. His ghost was said to live in a cave near **Hanging Stone** and gallop the woods on his headless horse until an exorcist performed a ritual here, keeping the ghost away 'so long as hollies grow green in Calverley Wood'. Until the late 19th century local children played games and sang rhymes about raising Old Calverley.

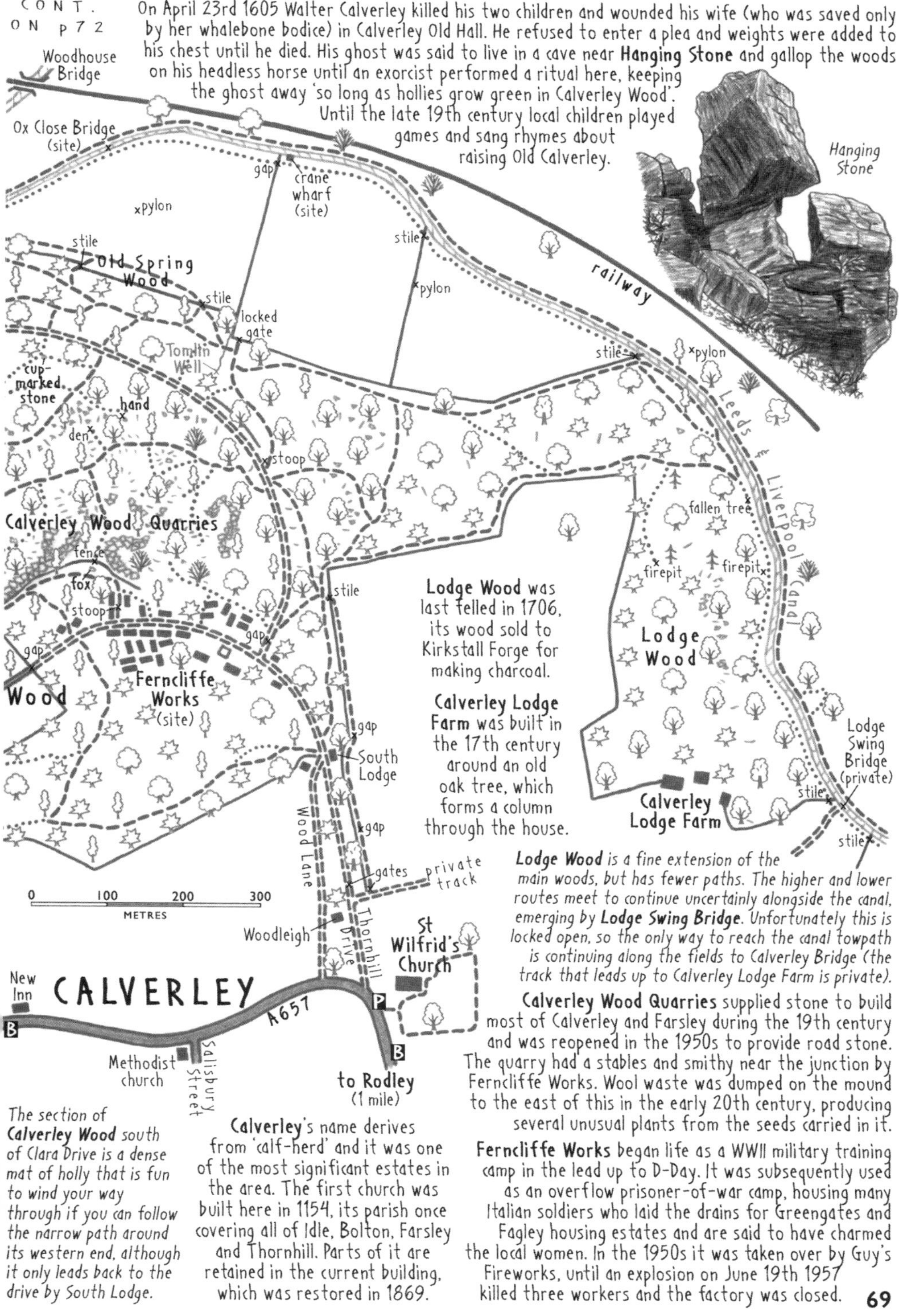
Woodhouse Bridge
Ox Close Bridge (site)
gap
crane wharf (site)
pylon
stile
Old Spring Wood
stile
locked gate
Tomlin Well
cup-marked stone
hand
den
stoop
pylon
stile
railway
stile
pylon
Hanging Stone
Leeds Liverpool Canal
fallen tree
firepit
firepit
Calverley Wood Quarries
fence
fox
stoop
gap
gap
stile
Wood
Ferncliffe Works (site)
Lodge Wood
gap
South Lodge
gap
Wood Lane
gates
private track
Woodleigh
Thornhill Drive
St Wilfrid's Church
Calverley Lodge Farm
Lodge Swing Bridge (private)
stile
stile
0 100 200 300
METRES
New Inn
CALVERLEY
A657
P
B
B
B
Methodist church
Salisbury Street
to Rodley (1 mile)

**Lodge Wood** was last felled in 1706, its wood sold to Kirkstall Forge for making charcoal.

**Calverley Lodge Farm** was built in the 17th century around an old oak tree, which forms a column through the house.

***Lodge Wood*** *is a fine extension of the main woods, but has fewer paths. The higher and lower routes meet to continue uncertainly alongside the canal, emerging by* ***Lodge Swing Bridge****. Unfortunately this is locked open, so the only way to reach the canal towpath is continuing along the fields to Calverley Bridge (the track that leads up to Calverley Lodge Farm is private).*

**Calverley Wood Quarries** supplied stone to build most of Calverley and Farsley during the 19th century and was reopened in the 1950s to provide road stone. The quarry had a stables and smithy near the junction by Ferncliffe Works. Wool waste was dumped on the mound to the east of this in the early 20th century, producing several unusual plants from the seeds carried in it.

**Ferncliffe Works** began life as a WWII military training camp in the lead up to D-Day. It was subsequently used as an overflow prisoner-of-war camp, housing many Italian soldiers who laid the drains for Greengates and Fagley housing estates and are said to have charmed the local women. In the 1950s it was taken over by Guy's Fireworks, until an explosion on June 19th 1957 killed three workers and the factory was closed.

*The section of* ***Calverley Wood*** *south of Clara Drive is a dense mat of holly that is fun to wind your way through if you can follow the narrow path around its western end, although it only leads back to the drive by South Lodge.*

**Calverley**'s name derives from 'calf-herd' and it was one of the most significant estates in the area. The first church was built here in 1154, its parish once covering all of Idle, Bolton, Farsley and Thornhill. Parts of it are retained in the current building, which was restored in 1869.

# ROUTE 11: CALVERLEY WOOD & FAGLEY BECK FROM NEW PUDSEY

**Distance:** 8 miles (12.9km)

**Ascent:** 200m

**Parking:** Free parking in Stanningley, Calverley Bridge, and along Clara Drive in Calverley Wood.

**Public Transport:** New Pudsey station is on the main Calder valley train line. Various bus stops along the route.

**Character:** A fine circuit of Fagley Beck and Calverley and Lodge Woods from New Pudsey or Stanningley that returns via Coal Hill and Farsley Beck. Although there are busy road sections at the beginning and end, the route largely picks a quiet line through urban areas. The section alongside the canal can be rough and muddy with frisky cattle or bulls in the fields, but the alternative is tedious.

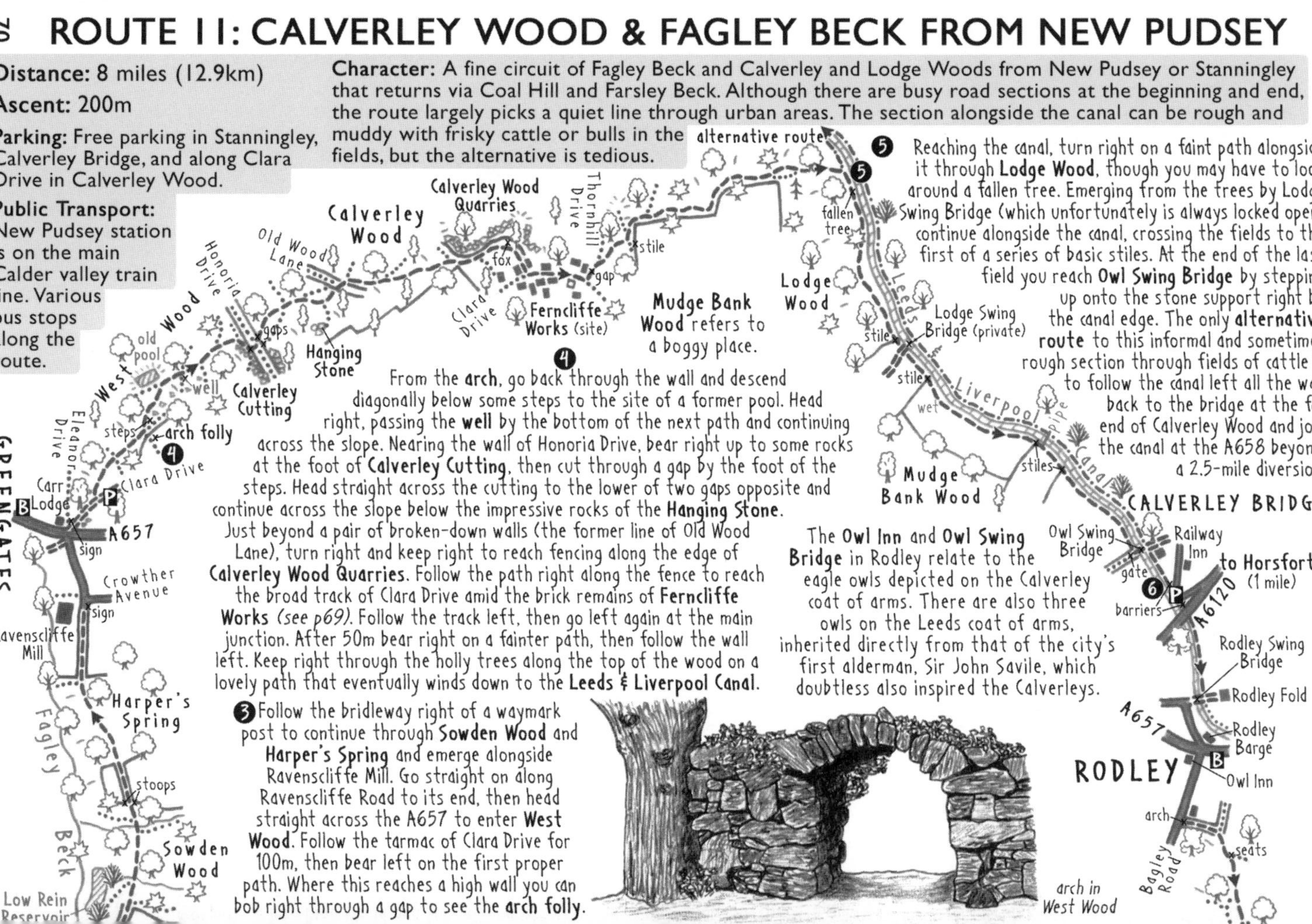

alternative route
Calverley Wood Quarries
Thornhill Drive
Calverley Wood
Old Wood Lane
Honoria Drive
stile
fox
gap
gaps
Clara Drive
Ferncliffe Works (site)
Hanging Stone
West Wood
old pool
well
Calverley Cutting
steps
arch folly
Eleanor Drive
Clara Drive
Carr Lodge
B
P
A657
sign
Crowther Avenue
sign
Ravenscliffe Mill
GREENGATES
Harper's Spring
Fagley
Beck
stoops
Sowden Wood
Low Rein Reservoir
Lodge Wood
fallen tree
Leeds
Lodge Swing Bridge (private)
stile
stile
wet
Liverpool
pipe
Canal
stiles
Mudge Bank Wood
CALVERLEY BRIDGE
Owl Swing Bridge
Railway Inn
gate
P
barriers
to Horsforth (1 mile)
A6120
Rodley Swing Bridge
Rodley Fold
A657
Rodley Barge
RODLEY
B
Owl Inn
arch
seats
Bagley Road
arch in West Wood


**3** Follow the bridleway right of a waymark post to continue through **Sowden Wood** and **Harper's Spring** and emerge alongside Ravenscliffe Mill. Go straight on along Ravenscliffe Road to its end, then head straight across the A657 to enter **West Wood**. Follow the tarmac of Clara Drive for 100m, then bear left on the first proper path. Where this reaches a high wall you can bob right through a gap to see the **arch folly**.

**4** From the **arch**, go back through the wall and descend diagonally below some steps to the site of a former pool. Head right, passing the **well** by the bottom of the next path and continuing across the slope. Nearing the wall of Honoria Drive, bear right up to some rocks at the foot of **Calverley Cutting**, then cut through a gap by the foot of the steps. Head straight across the cutting to the lower of two gaps opposite and continue across the slope below the impressive rocks of the **Hanging Stone**. Just beyond a pair of broken-down walls (the former line of Old Wood Lane), turn right and keep right to reach fencing along the edge of **Calverley Wood Quarries**. Follow the path right along the fence to reach the broad track of Clara Drive amid the brick remains of **Ferncliffe Works** *(see p69)*. Follow the track left, then go left again at the main junction. After 50m bear right on a fainter path, then follow the wall left. Keep right through the holly trees along the top of the wood on a lovely path that eventually winds down to the **Leeds & Liverpool Canal**.

**Mudge Bank Wood** refers to a boggy place.

**5** Reaching the canal, turn right on a faint path alongside it through **Lodge Wood**, though you may have to loop around a fallen tree. Emerging from the trees by Lodge Swing Bridge (which unfortunately is always locked open) continue alongside the canal, crossing the fields to the first of a series of basic stiles. At the end of the last field you reach **Owl Swing Bridge** by stepping up onto the stone support right by the canal edge. The only **alternative route** to this informal and sometimes rough section through fields of cattle is to follow the canal left all the way back to the bridge at the far end of Calverley Wood and join the canal at the A658 beyond, a 2.5-mile diversion.

The **Owl Inn** and **Owl Swing Bridge** in Rodley relate to the eagle owls depicted on the Calverley coat of arms. There are also three owls on the Leeds coat of arms, inherited directly from that of the city's first alderman, Sir John Savile, which doubtless also inspired the Calverleys.

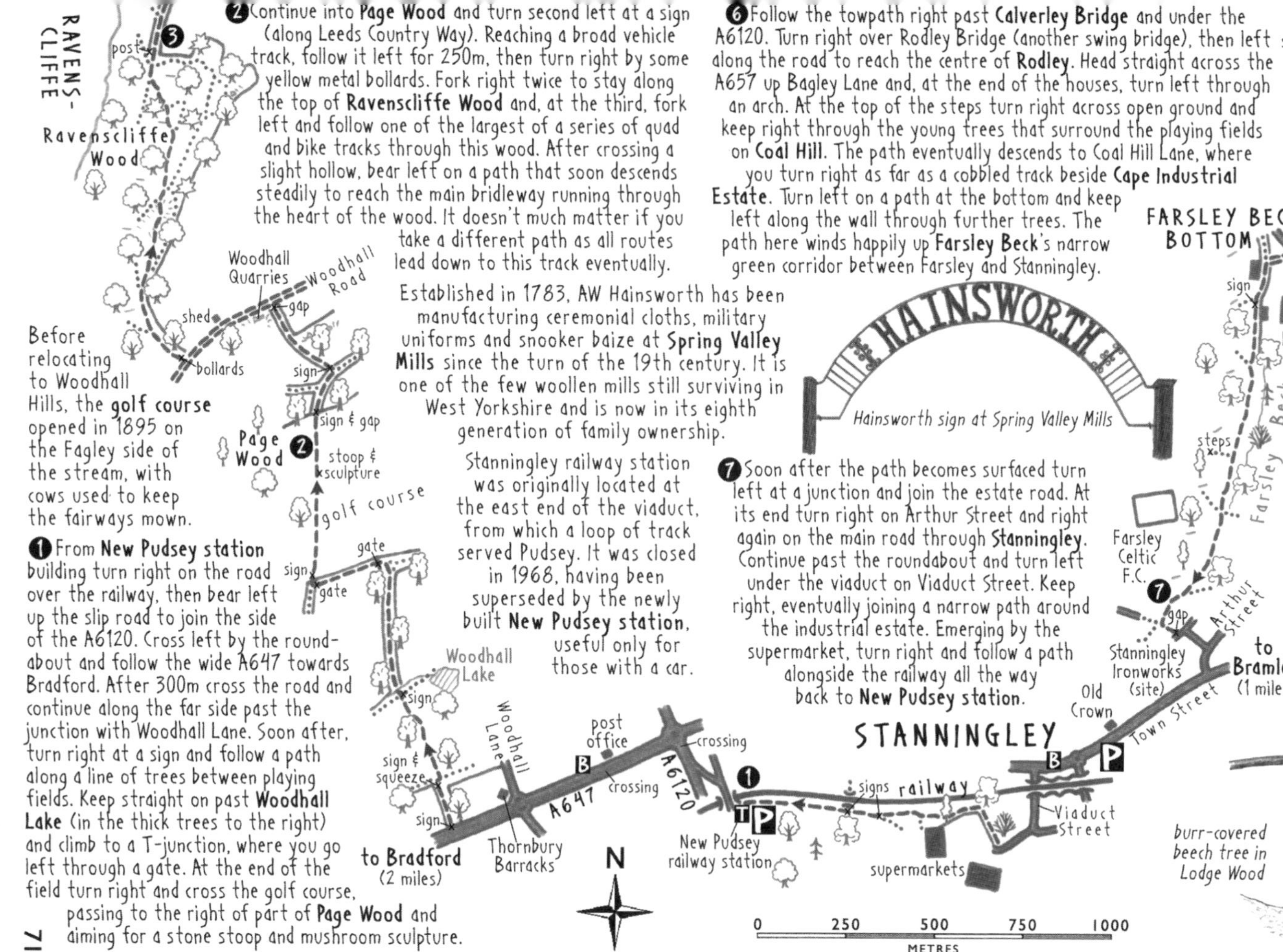

RAVENS-
CLIFFE
Ravenscliffe
Wood
post
3
shed
bollards
Woodhall
Quarries
Woodhall
Road
gap
sign
sign & gap
Page
Wood
2
stoop &
sculpture
golf course
gate
sign
gate
Woodhall
Lake
sign
sign &
squeeze
sign
to Bradford
(2 miles)
Woodhall
Lane
Thornbury
Barracks
post
office
B
crossing
A647
A6120
crossing
N
1
T
P
New Pudsey
railway station
signs
railway
supermarkets
STANNINGLEY
B
P
Viaduct
Street
Old
Crown
Town Street
to
Bramley
(1 mile)
Stanningley
Ironworks
(site)
gap
Arthur
Street
7
Farsley
Celtic
F.C.
steps
Farsley
Beck
sign
Cape
Industrial
Estate
FARSLEY BECK
BOTTOM
sign
Coal
Hill La.
stoops
playing
field
stoops
stoops
Coal
Hill
0
250
500
750
1000
METRES


Hainsworth sign at Spring Valley Mills

burr-covered beech tree in Lodge Wood

**1** From **New Pudsey station** building turn right on the road over the railway, then bear left up the slip road to join the side of the A6120. Cross left by the roundabout and follow the wide A647 towards Bradford. After 300m cross the road and continue along the far side past the junction with Woodhall Lane. Soon after, turn right at a sign and follow a path along a line of trees between playing fields. Keep straight on past **Woodhall Lake** (in the thick trees to the right) and climb to a T-junction, where you go left through a gate. At the end of the field turn right and cross the golf course, passing to the right of part of **Page Wood** and aiming for a stone stoop and mushroom sculpture.

**2** Continue into **Page Wood** and turn second left at a sign (along Leeds Country Way). Reaching a broad vehicle track, follow it left for 250m, then turn right by some yellow metal bollards. Fork right twice to stay along the top of **Ravenscliffe Wood** and, at the third, fork left and follow one of the largest of a series of quad and bike tracks through this wood. After crossing a slight hollow, bear left on a path that soon descends steadily to reach the main bridleway running through the heart of the wood. It doesn't much matter if you take a different path as all routes lead down to this track eventually.

Before relocating to Woodhall Hills, the **golf course** opened in 1895 on the Fagley side of the stream, with cows used to keep the fairways mown.

Established in 1783, AW Hainsworth has been manufacturing ceremonial cloths, military uniforms and snooker baize at **Spring Valley Mills** since the turn of the 19th century. It is one of the few woollen mills still surviving in West Yorkshire and is now in its eighth generation of family ownership.

Stanningley railway station was originally located at the east end of the viaduct, from which a loop of track served Pudsey. It was closed in 1968, having been superseded by the newly built **New Pudsey station**, useful only for those with a car.

**6** Follow the towpath right past **Calverley Bridge** and under the A6120. Turn right over Rodley Bridge (another swing bridge), then left along the road to reach the centre of **Rodley**. Head straight across the A657 up Bagley Lane and, at the end of the houses, turn left through an arch. At the top of the steps turn right across open ground and keep right through the young trees that surround the playing fields on **Coal Hill**. The path eventually descends to Coal Hill Lane, where you turn right as far as a cobbled track beside **Cape Industrial Estate**. Turn left on a path at the bottom and keep left along the wall through further trees. The path here winds happily up **Farsley Beck**'s narrow green corridor between Farsley and Stanningley.

**7** Soon after the path becomes surfaced turn left at a junction and join the estate road. At its end turn right on Arthur Street and right again on the main road through **Stanningley**. Continue past the roundabout and turn left under the viaduct on Viaduct Street. Keep right, eventually joining a narrow path around the industrial estate. Emerging by the supermarket, turn right and follow a path alongside the railway all the way back to **New Pudsey station**.

A 256-foot iron bridge was built inside **Stanningley Ironworks** before being transported all the way to Malaysia to span the River Langat in Selangor.

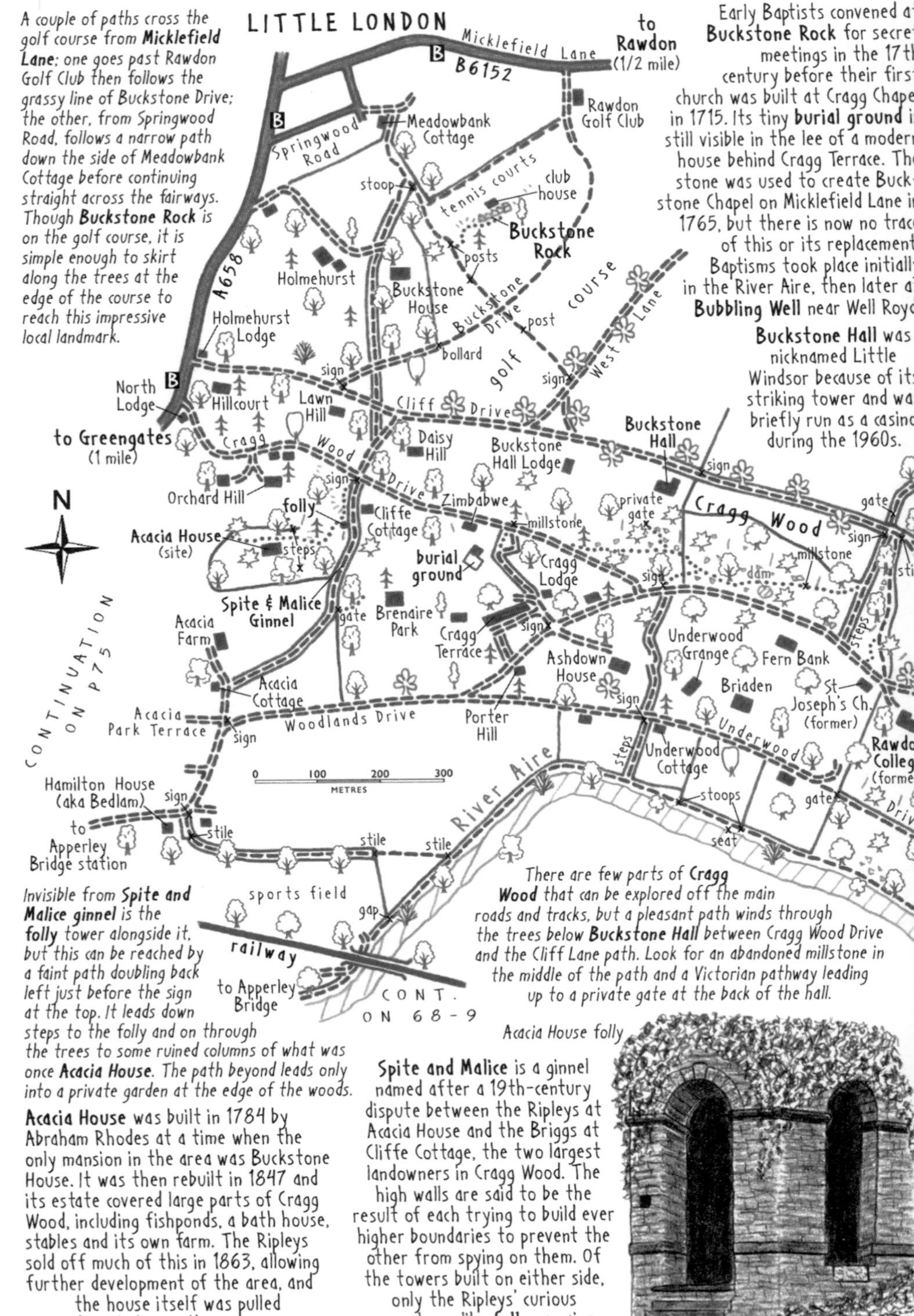

LITTLE LONDON
Micklefield Lane
B6152
to Rawdon (1/2 mile)
Rawdon Golf Club
Springwood Road
Meadowbank Cottage
stoop
tennis courts
club house
Buckstone Rock
posts
A658
Holmehurst
Buckstone House
Buckstone Drive
post
golf course
West Lane
Holmehurst Lodge
bollard
sign
North Lodge
Hillcourt
Lawn Hill
Cliff Drive
to Greengates (1 mile)
Cragg Wood Drive
Daisy Hill
Buckstone Hall Lodge
Buckstone Hall
Orchard Hill
folly
Cliffe Cottage
Zimbabwe
millstone
private gate
Cragg Wood
gate
N
Acacia House (site)
steps
burial ground
Cragg Lodge
dam
Spite & Malice Ginnel
gate
Brenaire Park
Cragg Terrace
Acacia Farm
Underwood Grange
Fern Bank
Ashdown House
Briaden
St. Joseph's Ch. (former)
Acacia Cottage
Porter Hill
Acacia Park Terrace
Woodlands Drive
Underwood
Underwood Cottage
Rawdon College (former)
CONTINUATION ON P75
0 100 200 300 METRES
River Aire
Hamilton House (aka Bedlam)
stoops
to Apperley Bridge station
stile
seat
sports field
gap
railway
to Apperley Bridge
CONT. ON 68-9


A couple of paths cross the golf course from **Micklefield Lane**; one goes past Rawdon Golf Club then follows the grassy line of Buckstone Drive; the other, from Springwood Road, follows a narrow path down the side of Meadowbank Cottage before continuing straight across the fairways. Though **Buckstone Rock** is on the golf course, it is simple enough to skirt along the trees at the edge of the course to reach this impressive local landmark.

Early Baptists convened at **Buckstone Rock** for secret meetings in the 17th century before their first church was built at Cragg Chapel in 1715. Its tiny **burial ground** is still visible in the lee of a modern house behind Cragg Terrace. The stone was used to create Buckstone Chapel on Micklefield Lane in 1765, but there is now no trace of this or its replacement. Baptisms took place initially in the River Aire, then later at **Bubbling Well** near Well Royd.

**Buckstone Hall** was nicknamed Little Windsor because of its striking tower and was briefly run as a casino during the 1960s.

There are few parts of **Cragg Wood** that can be explored off the main roads and tracks, but a pleasant path winds through the trees below **Buckstone Hall** between Cragg Wood Drive and the Cliff Lane path. Look for an abandoned millstone in the middle of the path and a Victorian pathway leading up to a private gate at the back of the hall.

*Invisible from* ***Spite and Malice ginnel*** *is the* ***folly*** *tower alongside it, but this can be reached by a faint path doubling back left just before the sign at the top. It leads down steps to the folly and on through the trees to some ruined columns of what was once* ***Acacia House****. The path beyond leads only into a private garden at the edge of the woods.*

Acacia House folly

**Acacia House** was built in 1784 by Abraham Rhodes at a time when the only mansion in the area was Buckstone House. It was then rebuilt in 1847 and its estate covered large parts of Cragg Wood, including fishponds, a bath house, stables and its own farm. The Ripleys sold off much of this in 1863, allowing further development of the area, and the house itself was pulled down between the wars.

**Spite and Malice** is a ginnel named after a 19th-century dispute between the Ripleys at Acacia House and the Briggs at Cliffe Cottage, the two largest landowners in Cragg Wood. The high walls are said to be the result of each trying to build ever higher boundaries to prevent the other from spying on them. Of the towers built on either side, only the Ripleys' curious mausoleum-like **folly** remains.

# MAP 19: RAWDON CRAGG WOOD

Rawdon Cragg Wood is a collection of woodlands on the north side of the River Aire that is dominated by the array of Victorian mansions laid out among the trees. Though there is very little open woodland left, there remains plenty of public access to this unique area. This is mostly along the arterial estate drives, many lined with magnificent chestnuts and beeches, but some pathways pick their way between the grand houses and give a fascinating glimpse into the lives of the wealthy then and now. Acacia House's ruin and fine folly and Buckstone Rock provide particular interest to an area that is easily reached from Rawdon, Apperley Bridge station or the new Horsforth Vale housing estate near Calverley Bridge.

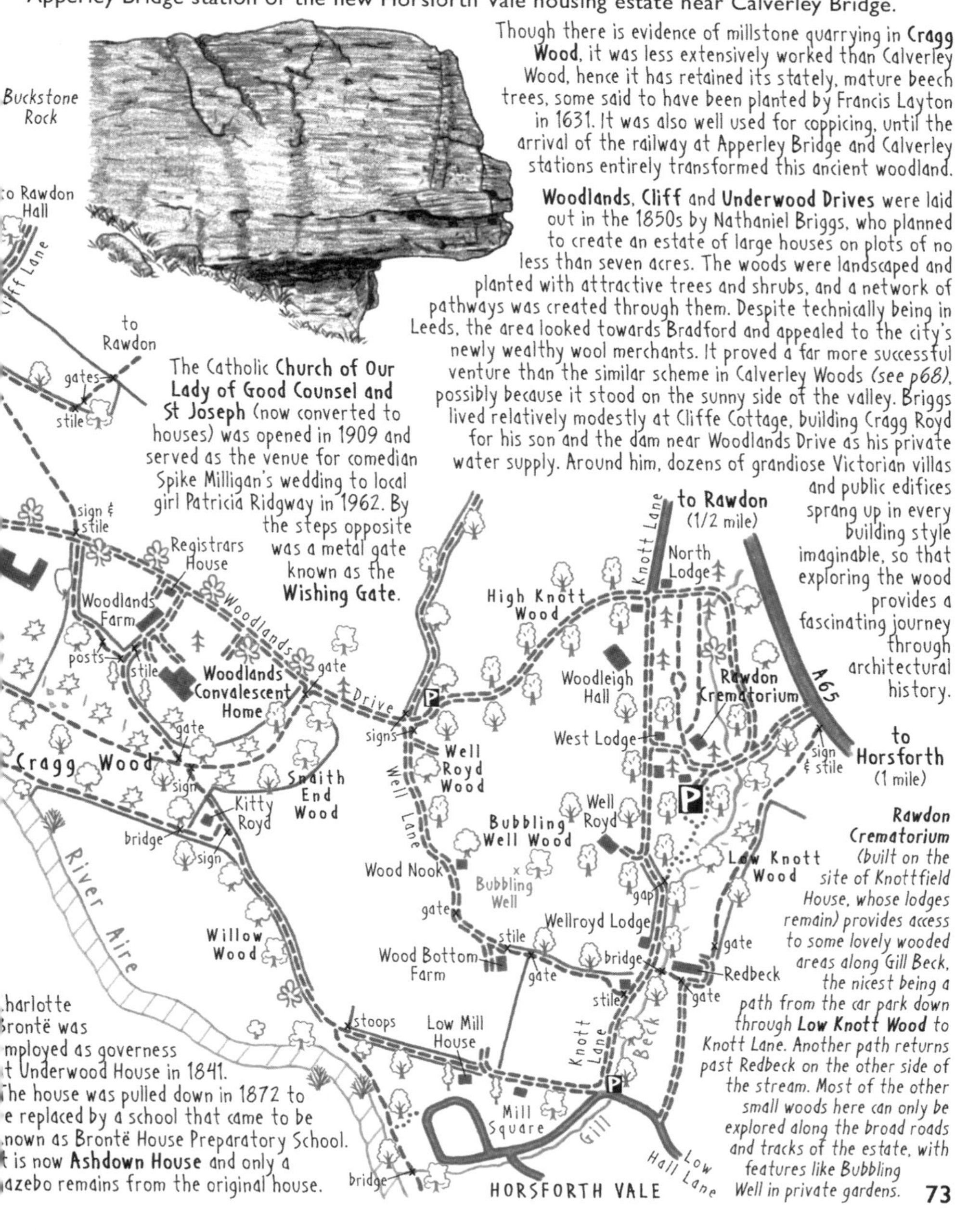
Buckstone Rock
o Rawdon Hall
Cliff Lane
to Rawdon
gates
stile
sign & stile
Registrars House
Woodlands Farm
posts
stile
Woodlands Drive
gate
Woodlands Convalescent Home
gate
signs
P
High Knott Wood
Woodleigh Hall
Knott Lane
to Rawdon (1/2 mile)
North Lodge
Rawdon Crematorium
A65
West Lodge
sign & stile
to Horsforth (1 mile)
Well Royd Wood
Well Lane
Cragg Wood
sign
Smaith End Wood
Kitty Royd
bridge
sign
River Aire
Bubbling Well Wood
Well Royd
Wood Nook
Bubbling Well
gate
Low Knott Wood
gap
Wellroyd Lodge
Willow Wood
stile
Wood Bottom Farm
gate
bridge
gate
Redbeck
gate
stile
stoops
Low Mill House
Knott Lane
Beck
Gill
Mill Square
Low Hall Lane
bridge
HORSFORTH VALE

Though there is evidence of millstone quarrying in **Cragg Wood**, it was less extensively worked than Calverley Wood, hence it has retained its stately, mature beech trees, some said to have been planted by Francis Layton in 1631. It was also well used for coppicing, until the arrival of the railway at Apperley Bridge and Calverley stations entirely transformed this ancient woodland.

**Woodlands**, **Cliff** and **Underwood Drives** were laid out in the 1850s by Nathaniel Briggs, who planned to create an estate of large houses on plots of no less than seven acres. The woods were landscaped and planted with attractive trees and shrubs, and a network of pathways was created through them. Despite technically being in Leeds, the area looked towards Bradford and appealed to the city's newly wealthy wool merchants. It proved a far more successful venture than the similar scheme in Calverley Woods *(see p68)*, possibly because it stood on the sunny side of the valley. Briggs lived relatively modestly at Cliffe Cottage, building Cragg Royd for his son and the dam near Woodlands Drive as his private water supply. Around him, dozens of grandiose Victorian villas and public edifices sprang up in every building style imaginable, so that exploring the wood provides a fascinating journey through architectural history.

The Catholic **Church of Our Lady of Good Counsel and St Joseph** (now converted to houses) was opened in 1909 and served as the venue for comedian Spike Milligan's wedding to local girl Patricia Ridgway in 1962. By the steps opposite was a metal gate known as the **Wishing Gate**.

**Rawdon Crematorium** *(built on the site of Knottfield House, whose lodges remain) provides access to some lovely wooded areas along Gill Beck, the nicest being a path from the car park down through* ***Low Knott Wood*** *to Knott Lane. Another path returns past Redbeck on the other side of the stream. Most of the other small woods here can only be explored along the broad roads and tracks of the estate, with features like Bubbling Well in private gardens.*

harlotte Brontë was mployed as governess t Underwood House in 1841. The house was pulled down in 1872 to e replaced by a school that came to be nown as Brontë House Preparatory School. t is now **Ashdown House** and only a azebo remains from the original house.

# MAP 20: ESHOLT WOODS

Though Esholt Sewage Works detract from this part of the valley, Esholt Woods are a fine collection of woodlands around Guiseley Beck and Yeadon Gill. Their character changes quickly, with areas of beech, pine, oak, birch and sycamore all easily accessed from the edge of Guiseley, Yeadon and Esholt. There are also various younger plantations around the settling tanks and filter beds to the south, which rather engulf Esholt Hall and its former parkland. Esholt village remains untouched, its name referring to ash woods.

The **Woolpack Inn** was originally the Combers Arms, then the Commercial Hotel before being renamed after its role in *Emmerdale*. The TV series was filmed in the village from 1976 to 1997, but the pub's interior layout is different from that on screen. A mocked-up version of the whole village now exists on the Harewood estate for exclusive use as a TV set.

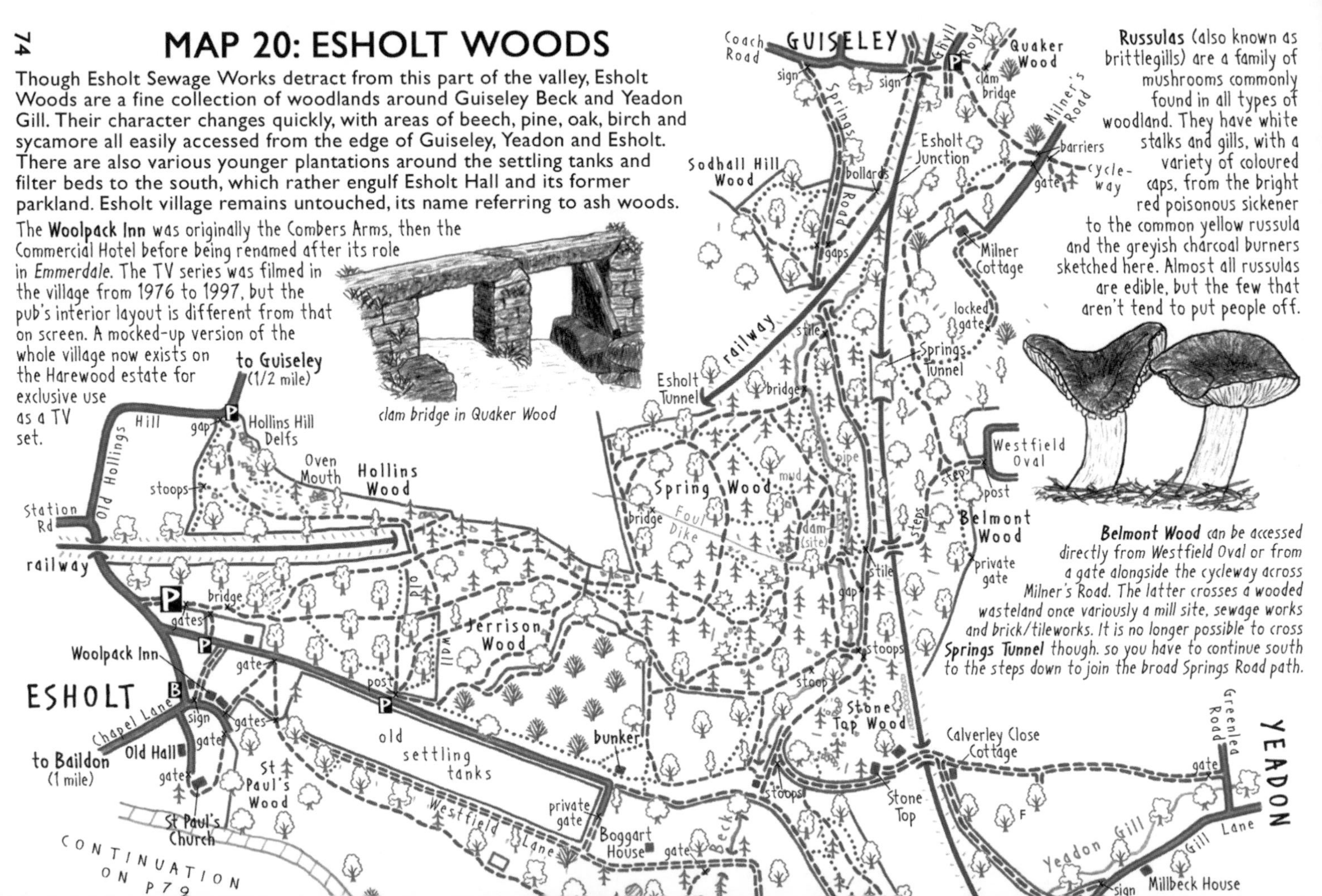
GUISELEY
Coach Road
sign
Springs Road
Ghyll Royd
Quaker Wood
clam bridge
Milner's Road
barriers
cycleway
gate
Esholt Junction
bollards
Sodhall Hill Wood
gaps
Milner Cottage
locked gate
Springs Tunnel
railway
stile
Esholt Tunnel
bridge
Westfield Oval
steps
post
Belmont Wood
private gate
Spring Wood
mud
pipe
dam (site)
Foul Dike
stoops
gap
stoop
Stone Top Wood
Calverley Close Cottage
Stone Top
YEADON
Greenlea Road
Yeadon Gill
Gill Lane
Millbeck House
to Guiseley (1/2 mile)
Hollins Hill Delfs
Old Hollings Hill
Oven Mouth
Hollins Wood
Station Rd
old
wall
Jerrison Wood
Woolpack Inn
ESHOLT
Chapel Lane
Old Hall
to Baildon (1 mile)
gates
St Paul's Wood
St Paul's Church
old settling tanks
bunker
Westfield Lane
Boggart House
Beck
CONTINUATION ON P79
clam bridge in Quaker Wood

**Russulas** (also known as brittlegills) are a family of mushrooms commonly found in all types of woodland. They have white stalks and gills, with a variety of coloured caps, from the bright red poisonous sickener to the common yellow russula and the greyish charcoal burners sketched here. Almost all russulas are edible, but the few that aren't tend to put people off.

***Belmont Wood*** *can be accessed directly from Westfield Oval or from a gate alongside the cycleway across Milner's Road. The latter crosses a wooded wasteland once variously a mill site, sewage works and brick/tileworks. It is no longer possible to cross* ***Springs Tunnel*** *though, so you have to continue south to the steps down to join the broad Springs Road path.*

*Esholt Hall is now used as a training and conference centre and, though it remains private, plenty of the woods around it are accessible. Most useful is a path from Esholt (picked up via a gate 50m beyond the Woolpack Inn) that runs through St Paul's Wood and eventually joins the main access road through the estate near Guiseley Beck. Paths also lead off the Avenue to Esholt Suspension Bridge and along Gill Lane.*

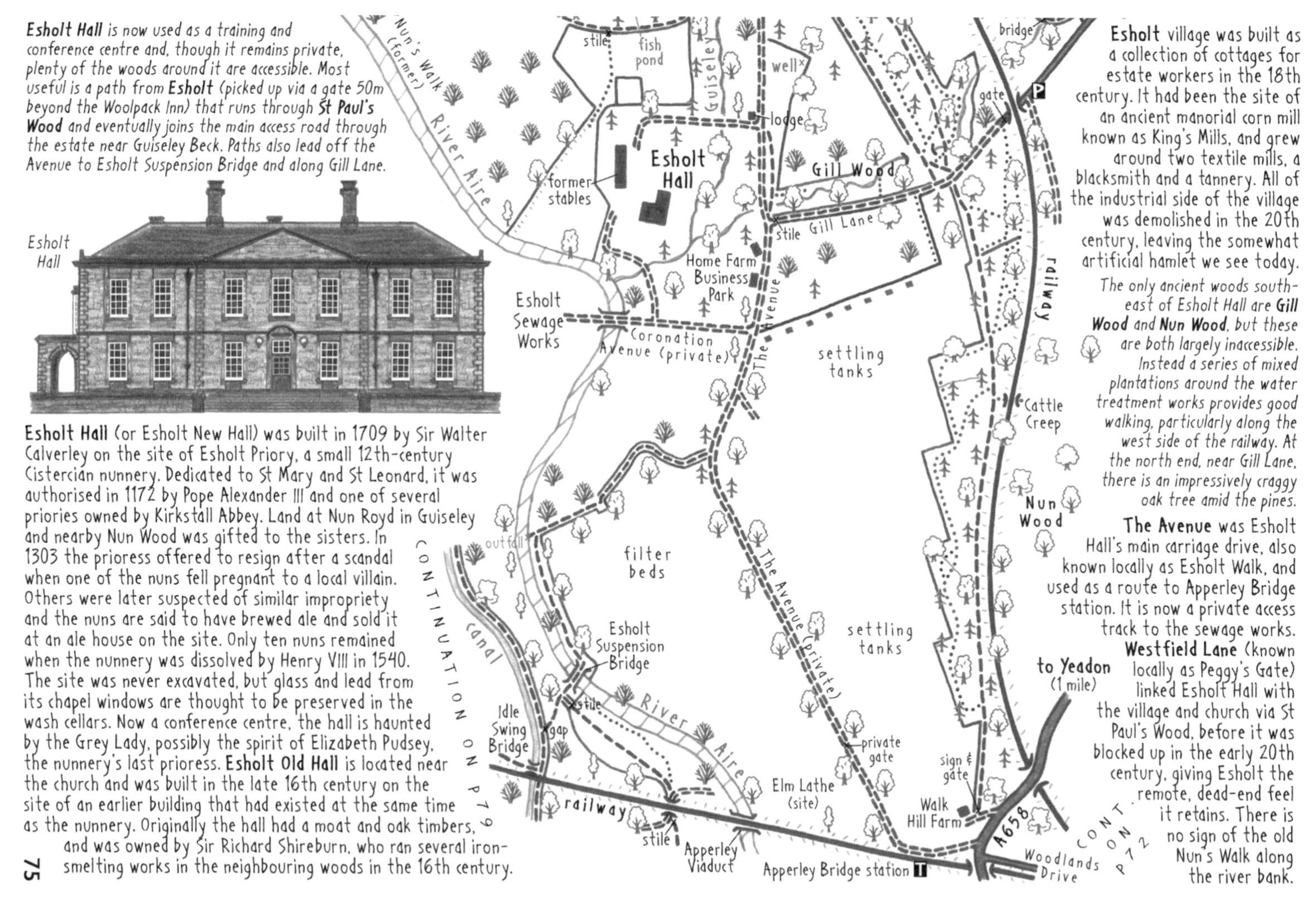

Esholt Hall
Nun's Walk (former)
River Aire
stile
fish pond
Guiseley
well
lodge
Esholt Hall
former stables
Gill Wood
Gill Lane
stile
Home Farm Business Park
Esholt Sewage Works
Coronation Avenue (private)
The Avenue
settling tanks
filter beds
outfall
canal
Esholt Suspension Bridge
stile
gap
Idle Swing Bridge
River Aire
railway
stile
Apperley Viaduct
Elm Lathe (site)
The Avenue (private)
private gate
settling tanks
Apperley Bridge station
Walk Hill Farm
sign & gate
A658
Woodlands Drive
CONT ON P72
to Yeadon (1 mile)
Nun Wood
Cattle Creep
railway
gate
bridge
P
CONTINUATION ON P79


**Esholt Hall** (or Esholt New Hall) was built in 1709 by Sir Walter Calverley on the site of Esholt Priory, a small 12th-century Cistercian nunnery. Dedicated to St Mary and St Leonard, it was authorised in 1172 by Pope Alexander III and one of several priories owned by Kirkstall Abbey. Land at Nun Royd in Guiseley and nearby Nun Wood was gifted to the sisters. In 1303 the prioress offered to resign after a scandal when one of the nuns fell pregnant to a local villain. Others were later suspected of similar impropriety and the nuns are said to have brewed ale and sold it at an ale house on the site. Only ten nuns remained when the nunnery was dissolved by Henry VIII in 1540. The site was never excavated, but glass and lead from its chapel windows are thought to be preserved in the wash cellars. Now a conference centre, the hall is haunted by the Grey Lady, possibly the spirit of Elizabeth Pudsey, the nunnery's last prioress. **Esholt Old Hall** is located near the church and was built in the late 16th century on the site of an earlier building that had existed at the same time as the nunnery. Originally the hall had a moat and oak timbers, and was owned by Sir Richard Shireburn, who ran several iron-smelting works in the neighbouring woods in the 16th century.

**Esholt** village was built as a collection of cottages for estate workers in the 18th century. It had been the site of an ancient manorial corn mill known as King's Mills, and grew around two textile mills, a blacksmith and a tannery. All of the industrial side of the village was demolished in the 20th century, leaving the somewhat artificial hamlet we see today.

*The only ancient woods south-east of Esholt Hall are **Gill Wood** and **Nun Wood**, but these are both largely inaccessible. Instead a series of mixed plantations around the water treatment works provides good walking, particularly along the west side of the railway. At the north end, near Gill Lane, there is an impressively craggy oak tree amid the pines.*

**The Avenue** was Esholt Hall's main carriage drive, also known locally as Esholt Walk, and used as a route to Apperley Bridge station. It is now a private access track to the sewage works.

**Westfield Lane** (known locally as Peggy's Gate) linked Esholt Hall with the village and church via St Paul's Wood, before it was blocked up in the early 20th century, giving Esholt the remote, dead-end feel it retains. There is no sign of the old Nun's Walk along the river bank.

# ROUTE 12: CRAGG WOOD, THE BILLING & GUISELEY BECK FROM YEADON

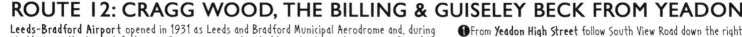

**Leeds-Bradford Airport** opened in 1931 as Leeds and Bradford Municipal Aerodrome and, during World War II, the largest factory in Europe was constructed here by Avro. It was camouflaged by film industry experts who covered the roof with turf, field patterns and fake animals that were moved each day. Yeadon Tarn was even drained so it couldn't be used as a landmark by German bombers. The factory survived and produced more than 5,000 planes during the war.

**1** From **Yeadon High Street** follow South View Road down the right side of the imposing **Town Hall**. At the end turn left up the main road, then bear first right on Harper Lane. A path continues between the houses at the end and emerges on Windmill Lane. Head straight on along Grange Avenue and, where the road bends left, keep straight on along another path. Turn right at the end on the **A658**, then left into Moorfield Drive, at the end of which a path leads out into the field. Head straight on to cross a fenced track, then bear slightly right to a stile at the top of the rise. Head straight down the field beyond to a gate and a path leading up onto **the Billing**.

The gun emplacement on **the Billing** was part of World War II defences to protect the nearby aerodrome. Its name is likely of Celtic origin as the hill was important for early settlers of the area, and a Bronze Age gold torque was discovered here in 1780.

**Yeadon** is Old English for 'steep hill' and part of its High Street is still known as the Steep. **Rawdon** means 'rough hill'.

*gun emplacement on the Billing*

**8** Head straight across **Milner's Road**, joining the line of a cycleway along the former railway line. Pass beneath three bridges before passing some factories, then turn left into **Engine Fields**. Bear right to cross the Yeadon Gill stream, then follow a path along the far side to pass a couple of millponds and emerge in **Yeadon** at a gate. Bear left along the road and turn soft right by the Robin Hood, heading up the hill into the town centre. Keep straight on up the cobbles of **the Steep**, then head straight on into the High Street.

**7** Head straight across Gill Lane, then bear right down the slope to cross the stream in **Yeadon Gill**. Climb straight up the other side and follow a path through the narrow strip of **Gill Wood** to reach a larger walled path. Follow this left, then continue up the side of **Guiseley Beck** before turning right up some steps over a railway bridge. Climb through **Belmont Wood** and turn left before the steps at the top, keeping left as you wind through the oak trees. The path skirts alongside the railway fence before bending right across some birch scrub to reach Milner's Road on the edge of **Guiseley**.

**2** At the top of **the Billing** you can head left a few yards to the trig point, a wonderful vantage point across Leeds and the Aire Valley. Then double back and head straight up to the true high point on the edge of the wood (the only glimpse of Leeds-Bradford's low-rise airport). Through the gate you can follow any route through the beech trees, but keeping straight on brings you past the concrete bases of some **WWII defences**. Keep left through the edge of the wood until you start climbing again, then turn right soon after and descend through the bracken. Keep straight on to pass left of **Billing Dam** and cross the playing field to reach **Rawdon** village by St Peter's School.

stile
gate
trig
WWII defences
The Billing
(231m)
Billing House
(site)
gate

**Distance:** 7½ miles (12.1km) **Ascent:** 270m

**Parking:** Free car parks in Yeadon by the Town Hall and on Well Lane, as well as various street parking.

**Public Transport:** Apperley Bridge is on the main Airedale railway line. Yeadon is on various bus routes from Leeds and Bradford.

**Character:** A varied route linking Rawdon Cragg Wood and Guiseley Beck with the nearby settlements. The high ground around Yeadon and Rawdon has little in the way of woods, but the walk takes in the small copse and fine vantage point of the Billing as well as woods at the head of Yeadon Gill. The route minimises road walking and is only awkward to follow where it seeks out some of the hidden corners of Cragg Wood.

The Tudor Gothic style **Rawdon College** was opened in 1859 by the Northern Baptist Education Society. It housed forty young men, preparing them for the evangelical life and university education. It was converted to flats in 1979.

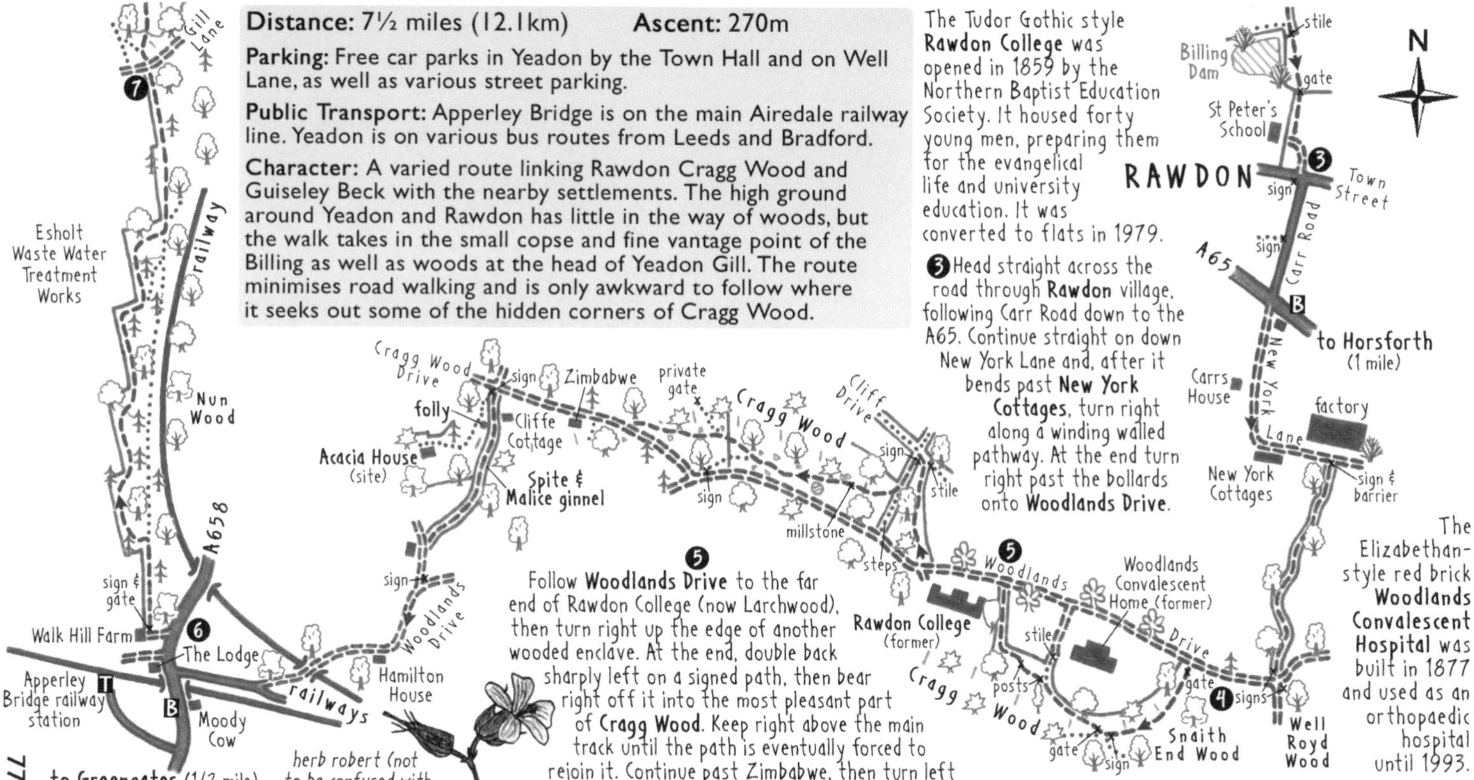

**3** Head straight across the road through **Rawdon** village, following Carr Road down to the A65. Continue straight on down New York Lane and, after it bends past **New York Cottages**, turn right along a winding walled pathway. At the end turn right past the bollards onto **Woodlands Drive**.

The Elizabethan-style red brick **Woodlands Convalescent Hospital** was built in 1877 and used as an orthopaedic hospital until 1993.

**4** It is possible to follow **Woodlands Drive** all the way through Cragg Wood, but this would miss most of this estate's interesting corners. Turn left at the first junction, passing through **Snaith End Wood** before turning right at the next junction. Follow a wall along the top of **Cragg Wood**, then bear left at a waymark post. This leads up the side of the former **Rawdon College** to return to Woodlands Drive, but if it is overgrown in summer it may be easier stay on the main path up the wall past the convalescent home.

**5** Follow **Woodlands Drive** to the far end of Rawdon College (now Larchwood), then turn right up the edge of another wooded enclave. At the end, double back sharply left on a signed path, then bear right off it into the most pleasant part of **Cragg Wood**. Keep right above the main track until the path is eventually forced to rejoin it. Continue past Zimbabwe, then turn left at a sign down **Spite & Malice Ginnel** *(see p72)*. It is possible to bear right off this immediately to pick up a rough path along the edge of the trees to reach a fine **folly** and, beyond, the ruined remains of **Acacia House**, but you must return the same way. Continue down the ginnel and bear left at the end to reach Woodlands Drive, following it right all the way to the A658 a few yards from **Apperley Bridge station**.

*herb robert (not to be confused with Herb Alpert!)*

**6** Follow the **A658** briefly up the hill, then turn left on the second track to a gate leading right into the woods by **Walk Hill Farm**. The main path can be followed parallel to the railway all the way, but it is nicer to bear left into the pine trees at the first opportunity. This winds along the edge of the sewage works, before rejoining the main path to reach **Gill Lane**.

# MAP 21: BUCK WOOD & DAWSON WOOD

Buck Wood is a fine ancient wood between Thackley and the Leeds & Liverpool Canal that provides a remarkable variety of wooded landscapes. It is linked to Dawson Wood by what were once just small parcels of woodland but now form a dense cover along the south side of the canal. Apart from the sewage works in its midst, it is a joy to explore and easily accessed from Thackley and Baildon.

**Buck Mill** was the site of Idle's manorial corn mill, as well as a fulling mill. In the 16th century the lease was held by the wealthy Buck family, who bought Thackley East Wood in 1620 and coppiced it extensively for charcoal. It has been known as Buck Wood since. Buck Mill was rebuilt as a scribbling mill around 1800, and was dynamited in 1923, its stone used to pave the track down to it.

**Buck Lane** was part of an ancient route from Bradford to Wharfedale via Idle.

**Tanhouse Field** predates the canal and was covered in tan pits between the site of a tannery and Brackendale Mills. A cup-marked stone was also discovered here when the canal was dug.

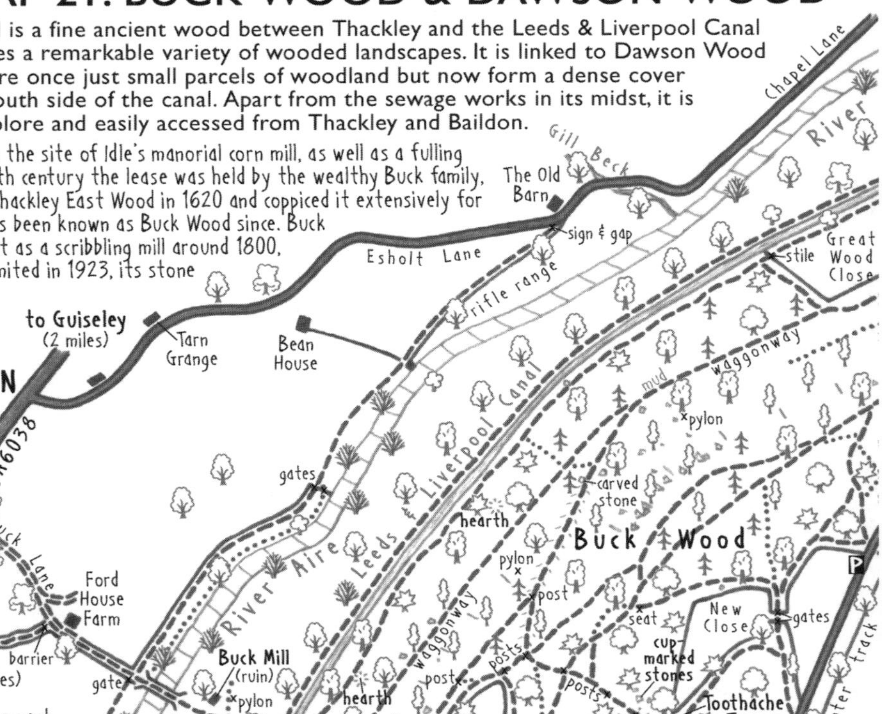

*ventilation shaft*

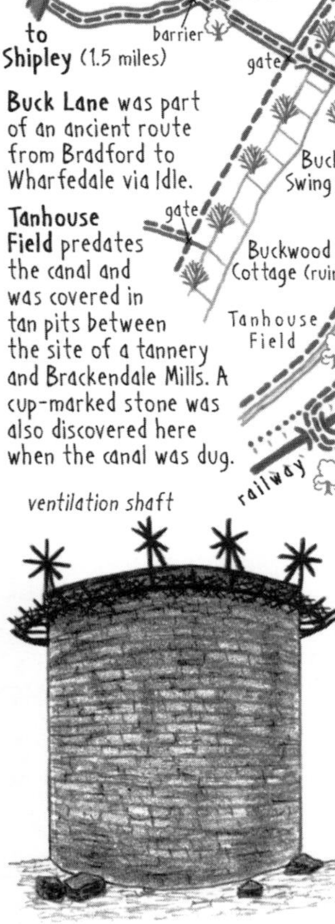

The **enclosure** in Buck Wood suggests Neolithic or early Bronze Age settlement of the area. Its low bank is hard to make out, but has a diameter of up to 90m and was likely reused during the Iron Age. There is a plethora of Bronze Age rock art found throughout the wood, with the most obvious being a series of **cup- and ring-marked stones** by the enclosure, though most of these are now covered in moss *(see sketch on p81)*. Some are laid on top of nearby sections of medieval orthostatic walling, others are used in newer stone walls. A network of sunken holloways is traceable through the wood, while the waggonway from Buckwood Cottage was used to transport quarried stone prior to the canal being built. Millstones were hewn in many of the smaller quarries and some partly worked examples can be seen discarded in parts of the wood.

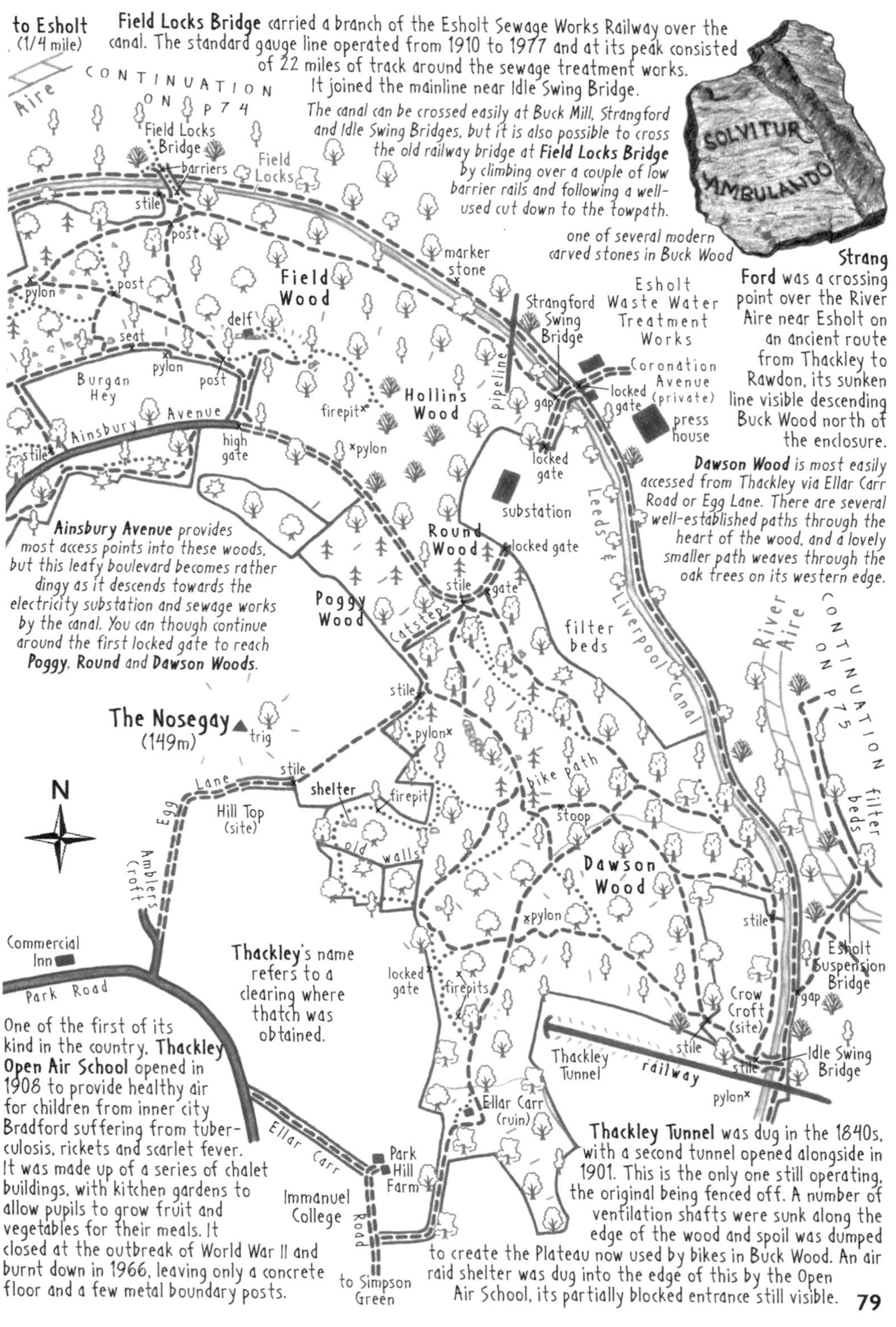
to Esholt
(1/4 mile)
Field Locks Bridge carried a branch of the Esholt Sewage Works Railway over the canal. The standard gauge line operated from 1910 to 1977 and at its peak consisted of 22 miles of track around the sewage treatment works. It joined the mainline near Idle Swing Bridge.
The canal can be crossed easily at Buck Mill, Strangford and Idle Swing Bridges, but it is also possible to cross the old railway bridge at Field Locks Bridge by climbing over a couple of low barrier rails and following a well-used cut down to the towpath.
SOLVITUR AMBULANDO
one of several modern carved stones in Buck Wood
Aire
CONTINUATION ON P74
Field Locks Bridge
barriers
Field Locks
stile
post
pylon
post
seat
pylon
post
delf
Field Wood
marker stone
Burgan Hey
Ainsbury Avenue
stile
high gate
firepit
Hollins Wood
pylon
pipeline
Strangford Swing Bridge
gap
locked gate
Esholt Waste Water Treatment Works
Coronation Avenue (private)
locked gate
press house
locked gate
substation
Strang Ford was a crossing point over the River Aire near Esholt on an ancient route from Thackley to Rawdon, its sunken line visible descending Buck Wood north of the enclosure.
Dawson Wood is most easily accessed from Thackley via Ellar Carr Road or Egg Lane. There are several well-established paths through the heart of the wood, and a lovely smaller path weaves through the oak trees on its western edge.
Ainsbury Avenue provides most access points into these woods, but this leafy boulevard becomes rather dingy as it descends towards the electricity substation and sewage works by the canal. You can though continue around the first locked gate to reach Poggy, Round and Dawson Woods.
Round Wood
locked gate
stile
gate
Poggy Wood
catsteps
filter beds
Leeds & Liverpool Canal
River Aire
CONTINUATION ON P75
stile
The Nosegay (149m)
trig
pylon
stile
Egg Lane
shelter
firepit
Hill Top (site)
bike path
stoop
old walls
Dawson Wood
filter beds
N
Amblers Croft
pylon
stile
Esholt Suspension Bridge
Commercial Inn
Park Road
Thackley's name refers to a clearing where thatch was obtained.
locked gate
firepits
Crow Croft (site)
gap
stile
stile
Idle Swing Bridge
Thackley Tunnel
railway
pylon
One of the first of its kind in the country, Thackley Open Air School opened in 1908 to provide healthy air for children from inner city Bradford suffering from tuberculosis, rickets and scarlet fever. It was made up of a series of chalet buildings, with kitchen gardens to allow pupils to grow fruit and vegetables for their meals. It closed at the outbreak of World War II and burnt down in 1966, leaving only a concrete floor and a few metal boundary posts.
Ellar Carr (ruin)
Ellar Carr Road
Park Hill Farm
Immanuel College
to Simpson Green
Thackley Tunnel was dug in the 1840s, with a second tunnel opened alongside in 1901. This is the only one still operating, the original being fenced off. A number of ventilation shafts were sunk along the edge of the wood and spoil was dumped to create the Plateau now used by bikes in Buck Wood. An air raid shelter was dug into the edge of this by the Open Air School, its partially blocked entrance still visible.

**Distance:** 7½ miles (12.1km)

**Ascent:** 310m

**Parking:** Limited free parking at Baildon railway station, as well as nearby street parking. Pay car park in Esholt.

**Public Transport:** Baildon railway station is on the Wharfedale Line between Bradford and Ilkley.

**Character:** A great exploration of this green oasis at the heart of the Aire Valley. The route picks its way through varied woods on either side of the River Aire before emerging in picturesque Esholt and returning via Gill Beck and Tong Park. The paths are generally good, though care is needed to find the right paths through the maze of routes in Buck Wood and Spring Wood.

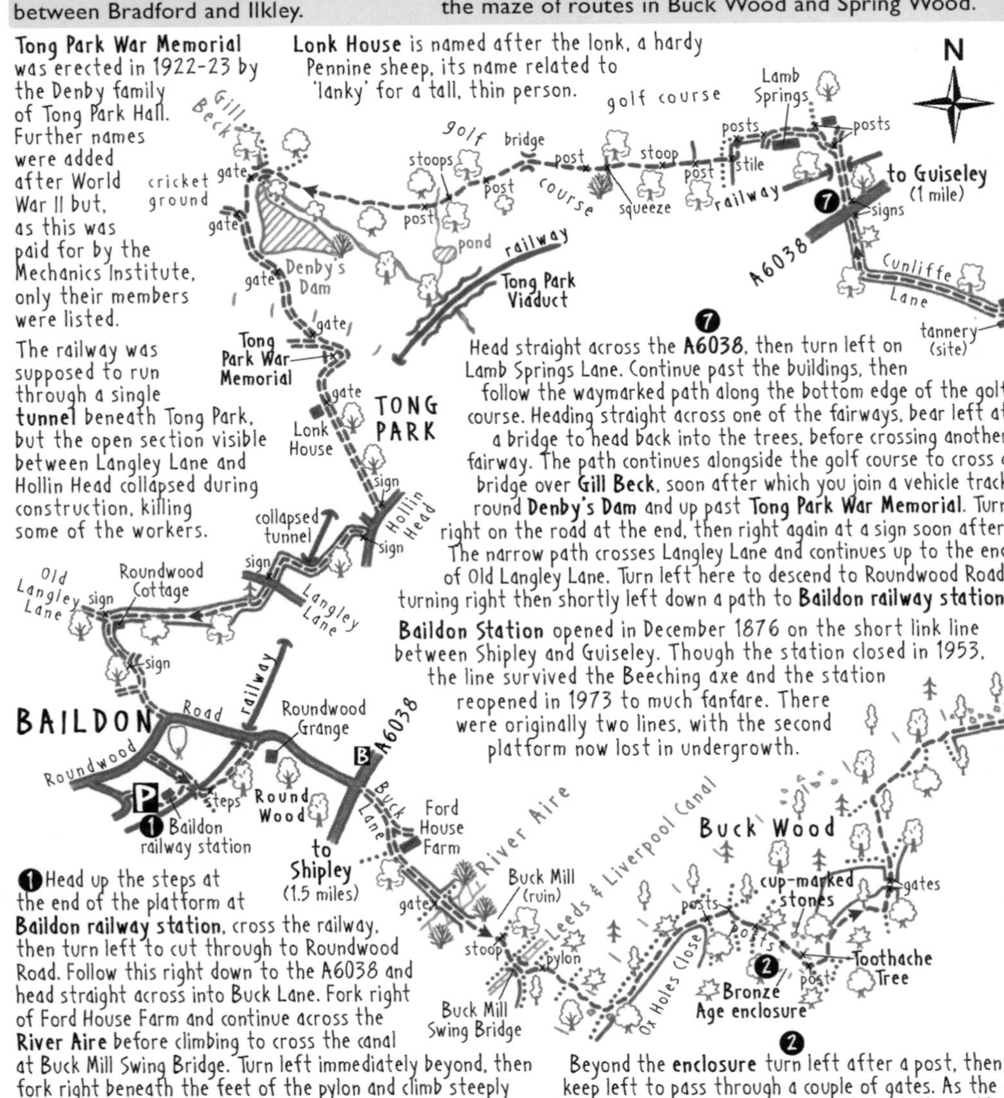
N
Gill Beck
gate
cricket ground
Denby's Dam
Tong Park War Memorial
TONG PARK
Lonk House
sign
Hollin Head
collapsed tunnel
Old Langley Lane
Roundwood Cottage
Langley Lane
BAILDON
Roundwood Road
railway
Roundwood Grange
A6038
Round Wood
steps
Baildon railway station
to Shipley (1.5 miles)
Buck Lane
Ford House Farm
River Aire
Buck Mill (ruin)
stoop
Leeds & Liverpool Canal
pylon
Buck Mill Swing Bridge
Ox Holes Close
Buck Wood
cup-marked stones
posts
Toothache Tree
Bronze Age enclosure
gates
post
golf course
stoops
bridge
stoop
squeeze
stile
Lamb Springs
to Guiseley (1 mile)
signs
Cunliffe Lane
tannery (site)
pond
Tong Park Viaduct

**Tong Park War Memorial** was erected in 1922-23 by the Denby family of Tong Park Hall. Further names were added after World War II but, as this was paid for by the Mechanics Institute, only their members were listed.

The railway was supposed to run through a single **tunnel** beneath Tong Park, but the open section visible between Langley Lane and Hollin Head collapsed during construction, killing some of the workers.

**Lonk House** is named after the lonk, a hardy Pennine sheep, its name related to 'lanky' for a tall, thin person.

**7** Head straight across the **A6038**, then turn left on Lamb Springs Lane. Continue past the buildings, then follow the waymarked path along the bottom edge of the golf course. Heading straight across one of the fairways, bear left at a bridge to head back into the trees, before crossing another fairway. The path continues alongside the golf course to cross a bridge over **Gill Beck**, soon after which you join a vehicle track round **Denby's Dam** and up past **Tong Park War Memorial**. Turn right on the road at the end, then right again at a sign soon after. The narrow path crosses Langley Lane and continues up to the end of Old Langley Lane. Turn left here to descend to Roundwood Road, turning right then shortly left down a path to **Baildon railway station**.

**Baildon Station** opened in December 1876 on the short link line between Shipley and Guiseley. Though the station closed in 1953, the line survived the Beeching axe and the station reopened in 1973 to much fanfare. There were originally two lines, with the second platform now lost in undergrowth.

**1** Head up the steps at the end of the platform at **Baildon railway station**, cross the railway, then turn left to cut through to Roundwood Road. Follow this right down to the A6038 and head straight across into Buck Lane. Fork right of Ford House Farm and continue across the **River Aire** before climbing to cross the canal at Buck Mill Swing Bridge. Turn left immediately beyond, then fork right beneath the feet of the pylon and climb steeply through the edge of **Buck Wood**. At the top turn left and then keep right along the edge of the wood until a blue waymarker directs you straight on. At the next post turn right and follow the main path for 300m up to a large open area between the holly trees where there is a faint bank of a **Bronze Age enclosure**. To the left of the path the larger mossy stones are covered in prehistoric rock art.

**2** Beyond the **enclosure** turn left after a post, then keep left to pass through a couple of gates. As the wood opens out, head straight on through the middle of the beech trees. Pick up a path heading right through the heart of **Buck Wood**, then keep left to join a wall along the top of the slope above Field Wood. Follow this round to the right to **Ainsbury Avenue**, keeping left of a high gate to follow this broad access road down into the dark woods by the sewage works.

# WOOD & ESHOLT WOODS FROM BAILDON

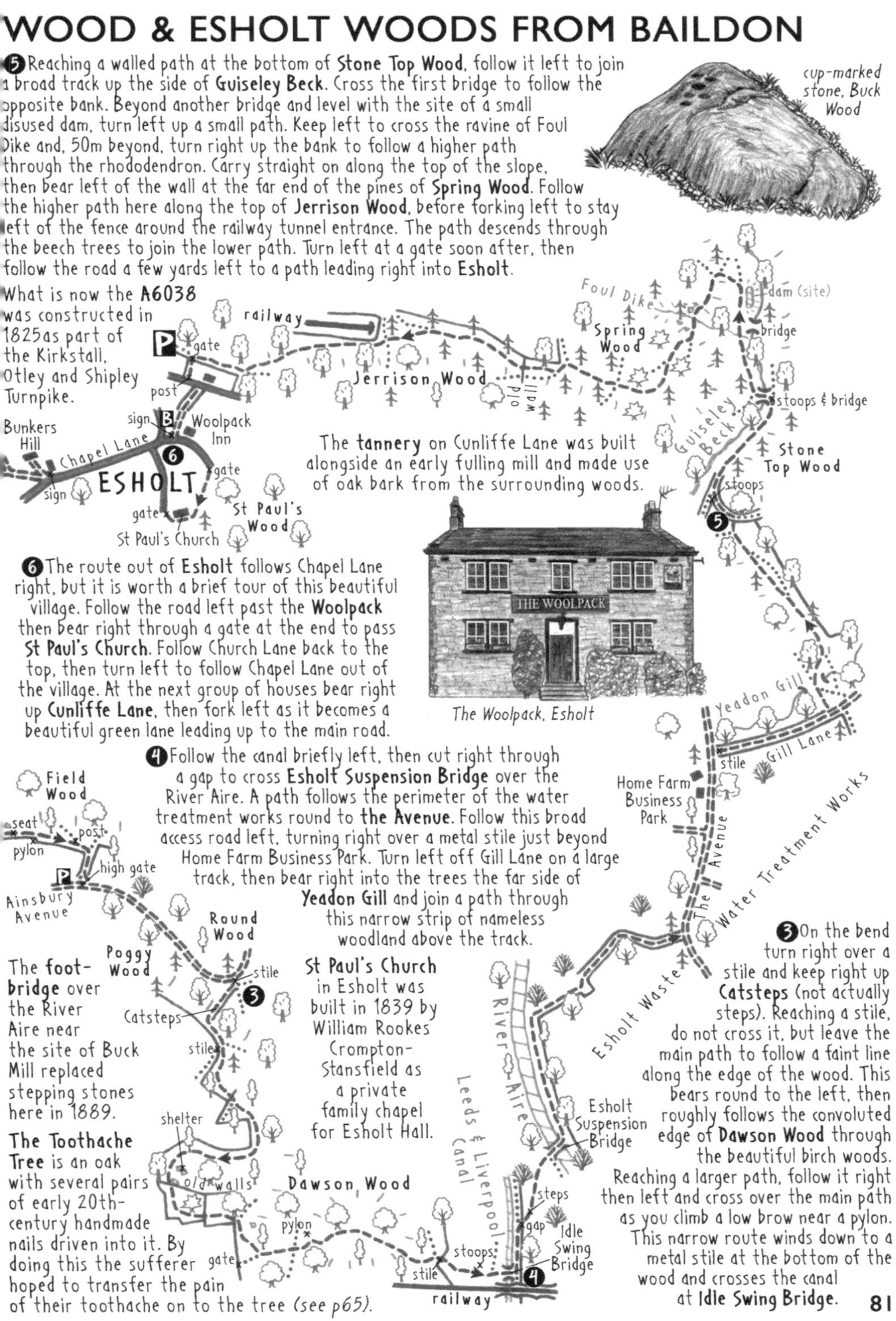

cup-marked stone, Buck Wood
Foul Dike
dam (site)
bridge
railway
gate
Spring Wood
Jerrison Wood
old wall
stoops & bridge
post
sign
Woolpack Inn
Guiseley Beck
Stone Top Wood
Bunkers Hill
Chapel Lane
ESHOLT
gate
stoops
sign
gate
St Paul's Wood
St Paul's Church
THE WOOLPACK
Yeadon Gill
Gill Lane
stile
Home Farm Business Park
The Avenue
Water Treatment Works
Field Wood
seat
post
pylon
high gate
Ainsbury Avenue
Round Wood
Poggy Wood
stile
Catsteps
stile
River Aire
Esholt Waste
Leeds & Liverpool Canal
shelter
Esholt Suspension Bridge
old walls
Dawson Wood
steps
pylon
gap
Idle Swing Bridge
stoops
gate
stile
railway


The Woolpack, Esholt

❺ Reaching a walled path at the bottom of **Stone Top Wood**, follow it left to join a broad track up the side of **Guiseley Beck**. Cross the first bridge to follow the opposite bank. Beyond another bridge and level with the site of a small disused dam, turn left up a small path. Keep left to cross the ravine of Foul Dike and, 50m beyond, turn right up the bank to follow a higher path through the rhododendron. Carry straight on along the top of the slope, then bear left of the wall at the far end of the pines of **Spring Wood**. Follow the higher path here along the top of **Jerrison Wood**, before forking left to stay left of the fence around the railway tunnel entrance. The path descends through the beech trees to join the lower path. Turn left at a gate soon after, then follow the road a few yards left to a path leading right into **Esholt**.

What is now the **A6038** was constructed in 1825as part of the Kirkstall, Otley and Shipley Turnpike.

The **tannery** on Cunliffe Lane was built alongside an early fulling mill and made use of oak bark from the surrounding woods.

❻ The route out of **Esholt** follows Chapel Lane right, but it is worth a brief tour of this beautiful village. Follow the road left past the **Woolpack** then bear right through a gate at the end to pass **St Paul's Church**. Follow Church Lane back to the top, then turn left to follow Chapel Lane out of the village. At the next group of houses bear right up **Cunliffe Lane**, then fork left as it becomes a beautiful green lane leading up to the main road.

❹ Follow the canal briefly left, then cut right through a gap to cross **Esholt Suspension Bridge** over the River Aire. A path follows the perimeter of the water treatment works round to **the Avenue**. Follow this broad access road left, turning right over a metal stile just beyond Home Farm Business Park. Turn left off Gill Lane on a large track, then bear right into the trees the far side of **Yeadon Gill** and join a path through this narrow strip of nameless woodland above the track.

The **foot-bridge** over the River Aire near the site of Buck Mill replaced stepping stones here in 1889.

**St Paul's Church** in Esholt was built in 1839 by William Rookes Crompton-Stansfield as a private family chapel for Esholt Hall.

❸ On the bend turn right over a stile and keep right up **Catsteps** (not actually steps). Reaching a stile, do not cross it, but leave the main path to follow a faint line along the edge of the wood. This bears round to the left, then roughly follows the convoluted edge of **Dawson Wood** through the beautiful birch woods. Reaching a larger path, follow it right then left and cross over the main path as you climb a low brow near a pylon. This narrow route winds down to a metal stile at the bottom of the wood and crosses the canal at **Idle Swing Bridge**.

**The Toothache Tree** is an oak with several pairs of early 20th-century handmade nails driven into it. By doing this the sufferer hoped to transfer the pain of their toothache on to the tree *(see p65)*.

# ESHOLT SEWAGE WORKS

The Esholt Waste Water Treatment Works dominate this part of the Aire Valley, with 300 acres of filter beds and settling tanks covering most of the valley floor between Apperley Bridge and Esholt. The main works are located between the river and canal, with the most prominent building being the modern incineration plant, though the old stone press house (now roofless) covers a far larger area near the canal.

In the mid 19th century Bradford's sewage was seen as being untreatable, so high was its grease content. Mills and woolcombers were dumping up to fifty tonnes of lanolin (grease from sheep's wool) straight into the city's becks every day, the filthy water flowing straight into Bradford Beck and Canal, which were treated as open sewers and renowned as the filthiest watercourses in the country. All of this fed into the River Aire and, although the first sewers in the city had been laid in the 1860s, in 1869 William Rookes Crompton Stansfield of Esholt Hall served an injunction against Bradford Corporation over the smell. As a mill owner in the city, they had little sympathy with him and tried to compulsorily purchase part of his estate for a new sewage works. After this was refused by the House of Lords as Esholt lay outside the city boundary, a decision that was greeted with great fanfare in Esholt village, the city began building a sewage treatment works at Frizinghall. This opened in 1874 and could treat 30,000 gallons an hour, yet quickly proved insufficient, as 20 million gallons of effluent were being produced by the city every day.

In 1897 the city's boundaries were extended to incorporate Esholt and the possibility of a far larger sewage works at Esholt was revived. The legal wrangle ended in 1906 when Bradford Corporation agreed to pay £239,742 for the whole estate to Stansfield's grand-daughters (the last male heir, another William Stansfield, had died in 1880). It would still take over twenty years to complete the new works, but the vast press house was in action by 1913, treating all the sludge that was pumped through a newly built three-mile tunnel from the existing works at Frizinghall. In 1926 the old works closed entirely, most of the site (filter beds, humus tanks, etc.) having been completed following a wartime interruption. The overall cost of the works was £3 million, with the land only a tiny fraction of this.

Sewage arriving at the works passed through a series of screens and primary settlement tanks, before being added to sulphuric acid to reduce its pH. The resulting acid-cracking removed the emulsified grease from the woollen industry's waste. The effluent was then treated in biological filter beds, before passing through humus tanks and clarification lakes to be suitable for discharge back into the river. The screen house on Gill Lane treated this water before discharge. The remaining sludge (about 45% of what arrived) was dewatered and then treated in the press house. Raw grease was recovered in 128 sludge presses, the residue producing 75 tonnes of press cake a day. After three to six months' maturation in open tips, this cake could be used as a fertiliser. Meanwhile the grease house treated the recovered grease, producing improved wool grease for making lubricants, paints, polishes and rust preventatives. The by-products plant also made soap, livestock marking fluids and a solvent extraction on site. Such were the quantities of these lucrative waste products and by-products that the council was making a profit from the works by the 1940s. By 1961 over £6 million had been raised, the works more than paying for themselves.

The waste water treatment works is now owned by Yorkshire Water and was recently modernised to incorporate hydroelectric and biogas power generation. The raw discharge emerging from the tunnel drives a screw generator, while the methane-rich effluent is used to produce biogas, which powers the whole site. This £34 million scheme also provides enough electricity for 7,000 homes.

LABOR OMNIA VINCIT
*Bradford's coat of arms on Esholt Sewage Works' press house*

# CHAPTER 7 - SHIPLEY & BAILDON

**Map Sheet:** Explorer 288 (Bradford & Huddersfield) & 297 (Lower Wharfedale)

**Public Transport:** Railway stations at Shipley, Saltaire and Baildon.

**Parking:** Free car parks at Shipley Glen, Hirst Wood and Baildon Moor. Pay car parks in Saltaire.

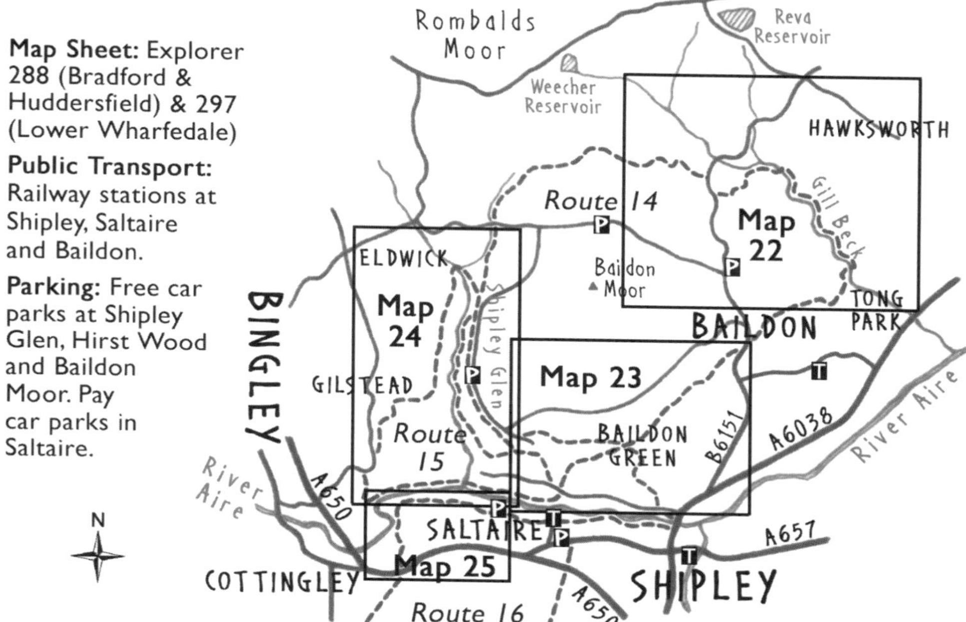
Rombalds Moor
Reva Reservoir
Weecher Reservoir
HAWKSWORTH
Route 14
Gill Beck
Map 22
Baildon Moor
ELDWICK
Map 24
Shipley Glen
BINGLEY
TONG PARK
BAILDON
GILSTEAD
Map 23
Route 15
BAILDON GREEN
B6151
A6038
River Aire
River Aire
A650
SALTAIRE
A657
Map 25
COTTINGLEY
SHIPLEY
A650
Route 16
N

Located high up on the slopes of Baildon Moor, Baildon is not your typical West Yorkshire mill town. Though mining and quarrying had a long history here, it only developed substantially as a town after its air and elevation were recommended as being healthy by some Bradford doctors in the late 19th century. Its name is of uncertain origin, possibly relating to the Celtic god Baal (from which we get Beltane), but probably more likely from the Old Norse word *bal* for a fire, suggesting a beacon fire was lit on the hill. Baildon remained fiercely independent and, like Shipley, resisted being subsumed into the city of Bradford until 1974 and has retained its own coat of arms.

Shipley was the 'clearing for sheep' near the junction of the River Aire and Bradford Beck and was mentioned in the Domesday Book. It remained a relatively small village until the arrival of the canals in the 1770s. As it was so well placed, industrial Shipley grew very quickly, but its lack of sewers and clean water meant it had a high mortality rate, particularly from scarlet fever. This contrasted strongly with its satellite, the model suburb of Saltaire built by Sir Titus Salt in the 1850s to house the workers at his new mill. While this has been preserved as a renowned World Heritage Site, many of Shipley's finest buildings were lost to post-war slum clearance and modern redevelopment.

Victorian and Edwardian tourists flocked to Saltaire railway station, alighting by the River Aire, with the woods and crags of Shipley Glen and Baildon Bank rising beyond. Though only the tramway remains from the days of Shipley Glen Pleasure Grounds, Saltaire is largely unchanged and remains the focal point for the woodlands of this area and the starting point for three walks in this book. The ancient woods of Shipley Glen and Hirst Wood are among the most popular in the valley and can be overcrowded in the summer. Gill Beck, which cradles the other side of Baildon Moor, offers equally delightful woodland but far more peace and quiet, the contrast demonstrated most clearly in Route 14.

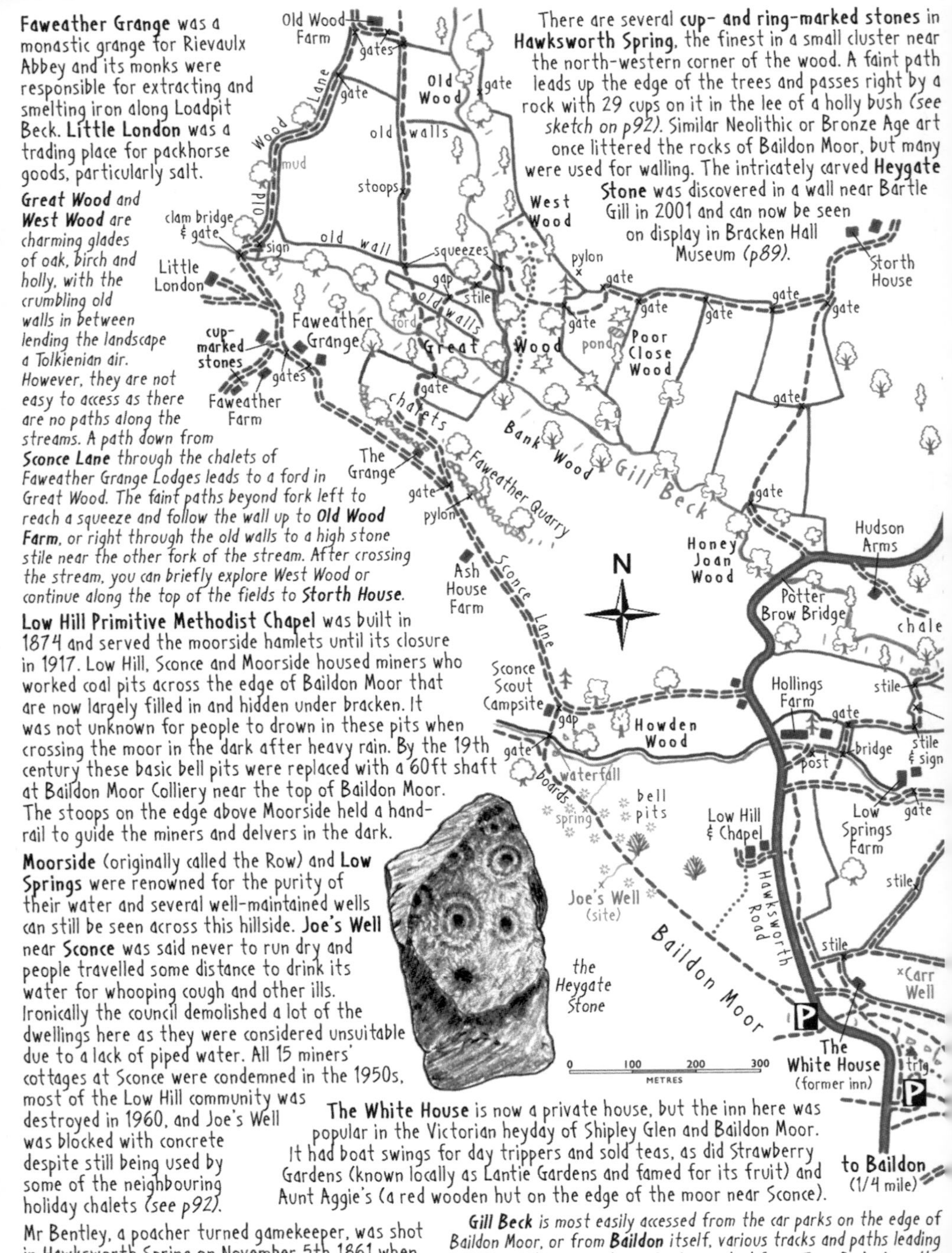
Old Wood Farm
gates
gate
Wood Lane
Old Wood
old walls
stoops
mud
Old
clam bridge & gate
sign
old wall
squeezes
West Wood
pylon
Little London
gap
stile
old walls
ford
Faweather Grange
cup-marked stones
gates
Great Wood
pond
Poor Close Wood
Faweather Farm
gate
chalets
Bank Wood
Gill Beck
The Grange
Faweather Quarry
pylon
Storth House
Hudson Arms
Honey Joan Wood
N
Ash House Farm
Sconce Lane
Potter Brow Bridge
chale
Sconce Scout Campsite
Hollings Farm
Howden Wood
bridge
post
stile & sign
waterfall
boards
bell pits
spring
Low Hill & Chapel
Low Springs Farm
Hawksworth Road
Joe's Well (site)
Baildon Moor
the Heygate Stone
Carr Well
The White House (former inn)
trig.
P
0 100 200 300 METRES
to Baildon (1/4 mile)

**Faweather Grange** was a monastic grange for Rievaulx Abbey and its monks were responsible for extracting and smelting iron along Loadpit Beck. **Little London** was a trading place for packhorse goods, particularly salt.

***Great Wood*** *and* ***West Wood*** *are charming glades of oak, birch and holly, with the crumbling old walls in between lending the landscape a Tolkienian air. However, they are not easy to access as there are no paths along the streams. A path down from* ***Sconce Lane*** *through the chalets of Faweather Grange Lodges leads to a ford in Great Wood. The faint paths beyond fork left to reach a squeeze and follow the wall up to* ***Old Wood Farm****, or right through the old walls to a high stone stile near the other fork of the stream. After crossing the stream, you can briefly explore West Wood or continue along the top of the fields to* ***Storth House****.*

There are several **cup- and ring-marked stones** in **Hawksworth Spring**, the finest in a small cluster near the north-western corner of the wood. A faint path leads up the edge of the trees and passes right by a rock with 29 cups on it in the lee of a holly bush (*see sketch on p92*). Similar Neolithic or Bronze Age art once littered the rocks of Baildon Moor, but many were used for walling. The intricately carved **Heygate Stone** was discovered in a wall near Bartle Gill in 2001 and can now be seen on display in Bracken Hall Museum (*p89*).

**Low Hill Primitive Methodist Chapel** was built in 1874 and served the moorside hamlets until its closure in 1917. Low Hill, Sconce and Moorside housed miners who worked coal pits across the edge of Baildon Moor that are now largely filled in and hidden under bracken. It was not unknown for people to drown in these pits when crossing the moor in the dark after heavy rain. By the 19th century these basic bell pits were replaced with a 60ft shaft at Baildon Moor Colliery near the top of Baildon Moor. The stoops on the edge above Moorside held a hand-rail to guide the miners and delvers in the dark.

**Moorside** (originally called the Row) and **Low Springs** were renowned for the purity of their water and several well-maintained wells can still be seen across this hillside. **Joe's Well** near **Sconce** was said never to run dry and people travelled some distance to drink its water for whooping cough and other ills. Ironically the council demolished a lot of the dwellings here as they were considered unsuitable due to a lack of piped water. All 15 miners' cottages at Sconce were condemned in the 1950s, most of the Low Hill community was destroyed in 1960, and Joe's Well was blocked with concrete despite still being used by some of the neighbouring holiday chalets (*see p92*).

**The White House** is now a private house, but the inn here was popular in the Victorian heyday of Shipley Glen and Baildon Moor. It had boat swings for day trippers and sold teas, as did Strawberry Gardens (known locally as Lantie Gardens and famed for its fruit) and Aunt Aggie's (a red wooden hut on the edge of the moor near Sconce).

Mr Bentley, a poacher turned gamekeeper, was shot in Hawksworth Spring on November 5th 1861 when challenging a former companion. The killer hid on Baildon Moor in the Dobrudden slag heaps (known locally as the Cinder Caves) and was fed by his wife until he was caught and hanged in York.

***Gill Beck*** *is most easily accessed from the car parks on the edge of Baildon Moor, or from* ***Baildon*** *itself, various tracks and paths leading down into the valley. It can also be reached from* ***Tong Park*** *along the setts of Tong Park Street. After it bends left, bear right down into the trees to pick up a path beneath* ***Tong Park Viaduct****. This bears left up to the edge of the field, or you can follow an old conduit straight on to reach Denby's Dam and a fisherman's path beside it to the bridge.*

# MAP 22: GILL BECK & TONG PARK

Gill Beck (originally known as Old Wood Beck until it was renamed after Nicholas Gill, the owner of Gill Mill) reaches up to the edge of Rombalds and Baildon Moors with a string of unspoilt ancient woodlands along its length. Only one road crosses the valley and there were fewer mills here than elsewhere, so Hawksworth Spring and Great Wood retain a primeval air. The only shame is the awkward (and often unsigned) footpath network that makes it hard to explore these woods, particularly at the top of the valley. The lower end, though, is easily reached from Baildon, Tong Park and the edge of Baildon Moor.

**Corn Mill Farm** is a recent conversion of Hawksworth Corn Mill, which had long stood derelict. It was burned down by a gang of Luddites in 1812, many of whom were executed for crimes around Rawdon, Yeadon and Guiseley.

The first mill at Tong Park was built in the 1770s, but this and its successor lay empty when William Denby acquired the site in the 1850s. He built **Tong Park Mills**, a series of dams (including Denby's Dam), and houses for his workers. In the 1880s he built Tong Park Hall, its site now covered by a modern housing development.

Tong Park Viaduct

*The path up the right side of **Gill Beck** from **Denby's Dam** is straightforward; those on the opposite side of the stream are less so. Though the track to the cricket ground is private, a path follows the other side of the wall from a gate by the dam and keeps right along the bottom of **Willy Wood**. Cross the wet hollow, then soon after start to climb the slope to emerge on **Sunny Brow**, to the west of which lies **Red Brick Dam**. A path continues along the edge of the trees, passing a pylon and crossing the main path down to the stepping stones. It soon reaches a dead end beyond the next pylon, frustratingly not quite linking up with the farm track along the top of **Birks Wood**.*

**Hawksworth** is named after the Hawk Stone east of Hollins Hall (*off map*).

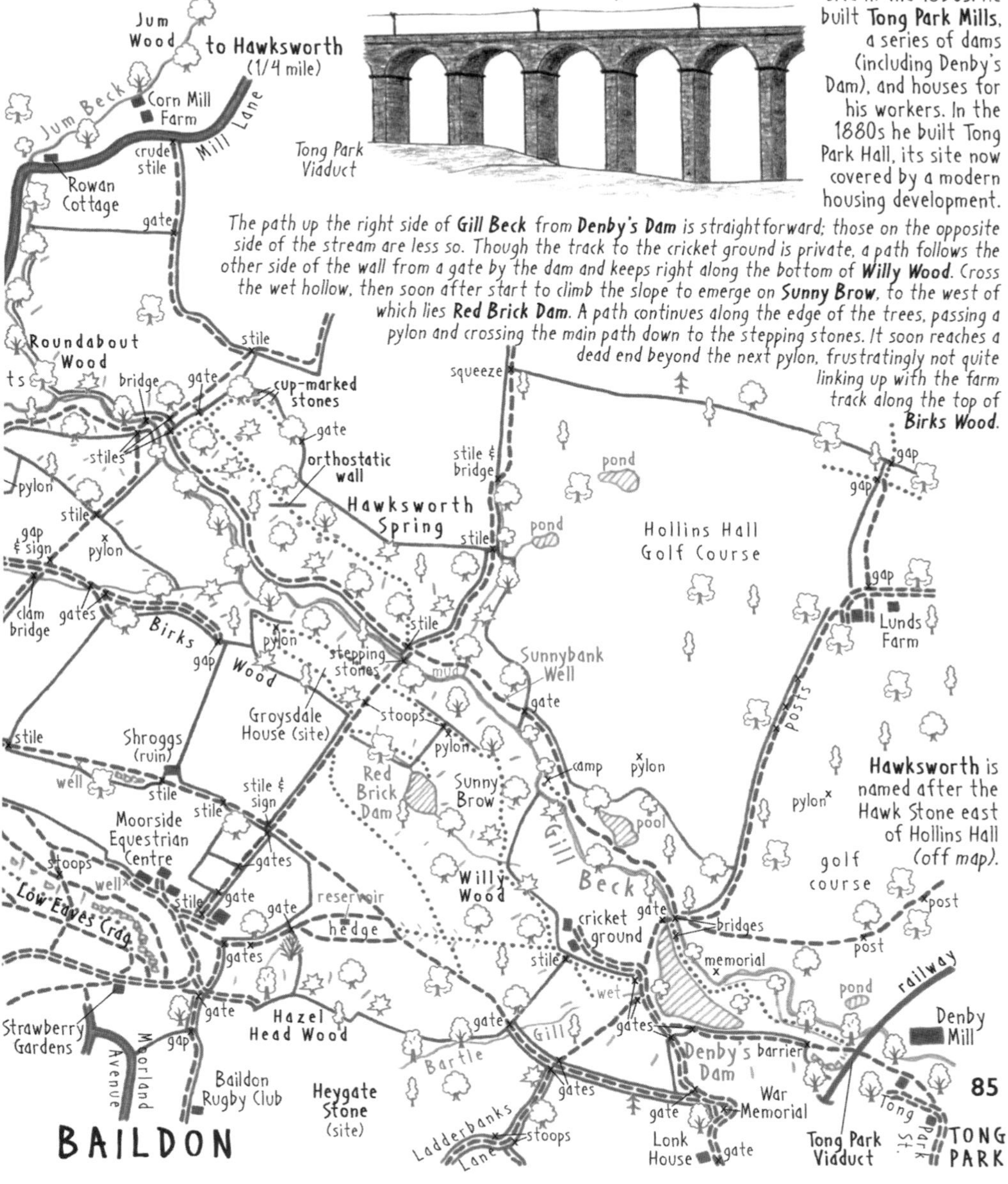

# MAP 23: BAILDON BANK, BAILDON GREEN

Baildon Bank (known locally as the Bank) is a steep rocky edge running all the way from the centre of Baildon to Shipley Glen. Its western end is densely wooded, with the old wall on the eastern edge of Midgeley Wood marking the boundary of the ancient woodland. Beyond this there were no trees as recently as the early 20th century, but since the quarries were abandoned it has become a richly treed landscaped. Together with the remnants of Baildon Wood and Fairbank Wood, there is plenty to explore around the housing estates of Baildon Green.

**Robin Hood's Chair** is one of a series of large boulders near the top of Shipley Glen Tramway, with a water-worn seat sculpted into its east side. Like **Robin Hood's House** (a natural shelter in a heap of boulders above Baildon Green), the outlaw's name has been fancifully attached to this feature.

Robin Hood's Chair

**Baildon Green** was once a much larger hamlet around the Cricketers Arms, with a brickworks as well as the large textile mill that remains below Robins Hood's House (Cloughs Mill). There was also a general store, mission church and two chapels. The pub name relates to the cricket field that used to stand on the green, with the quarry's backdrop known as 'the largest grandstand in England'. The common land of the green itself has been greatly reduced by the housing estates built around it. St Mary's Church was a tin church at the western end, its wall still preserved around the semi-detached houses now on the site.

*A good path runs along the top of* ***Walker*** *and* ***Midgeley Woods*** *from the end of Prod Lane, but there are plenty of smaller paths lower down. Entering the trees at the opposite corner from the building by the foot of the tramway, paths can be picked up running along the bottom of the slope or winding steeply up between the rocks to the higher path. They emerge on* ***Baildon Green*** *via a couple of faint paths above the overgrown brickworks site.*

*There are faint paths into the bottom parts of* ***Benson*** *and* ***Walker Woods*** *either side of the* ***Shipley Glen Tramway****. They peter out quickly but the holly and rock clogged slopes are still worth exploring.*

The **brickworks** at Baildon Green was operated by the Yorkshire Gannister Company, making firebricks using ganister clay quarried on Baildon Moor.

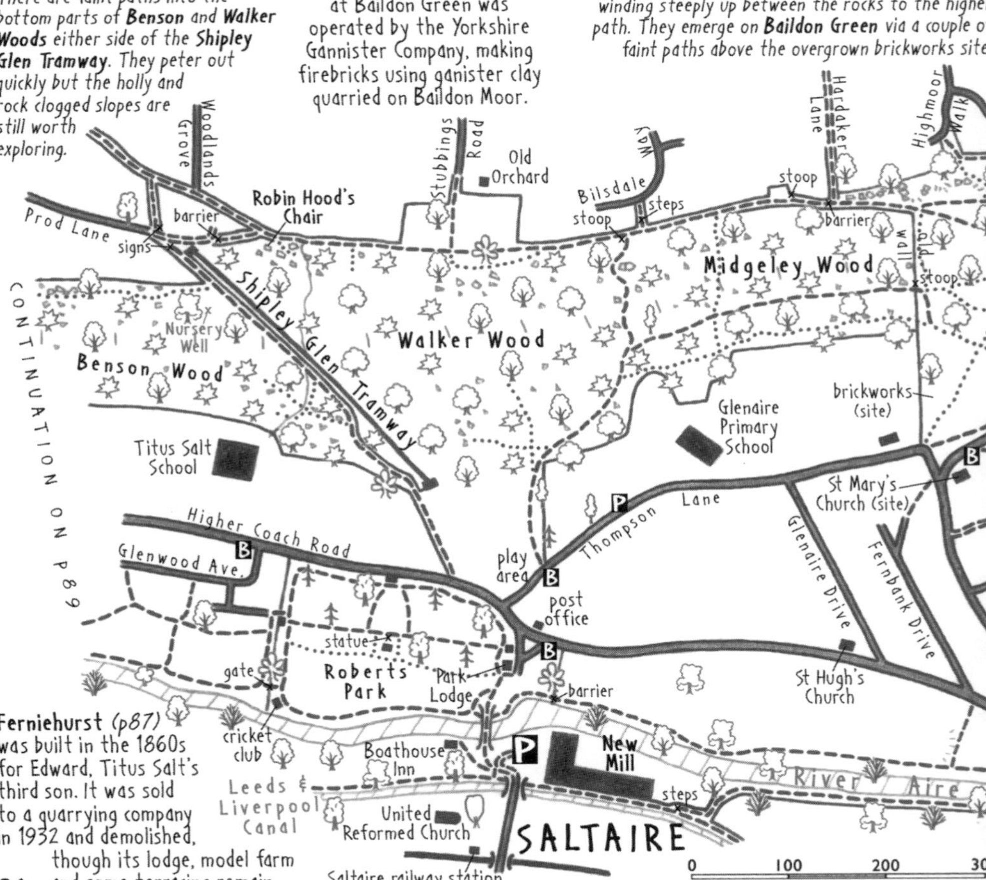

Woodlands Grove
Stubbings Road
Old Orchard
Bilsdale Way
Hardaker Lane
Highmoor Walk
Robin Hood's Chair
Prod Lane
barrier
signs
steps
stoop
barrier
old wall
Midgeley Wood
Shipley Glen Tramway
Nursery Well
Walker Wood
Benson Wood
brickworks (site)
Glenaire Primary School
Titus Salt School
St Mary's Church (site)
Thompson Lane
Glenaire Drive
Fernbank Drive
Higher Coach Road
Glenwood Ave.
play area
post office
statue
Roberts Park
Park Lodge
gate
barrier
St Hugh's Church
cricket club
Boathouse Inn
New Mill
River Aire
Leeds & Liverpool Canal
steps
United Reformed Church
SALTAIRE
Saltaire railway station
0
100
200
300
METRES


CONTINUATION ON p89


**Ferniehurst** *(p87)* was built in the 1860s for Edward, Titus Salt's third son. It was sold to a quarrying company in 1932 and demolished, though its lodge, model farm and some terracing remain.

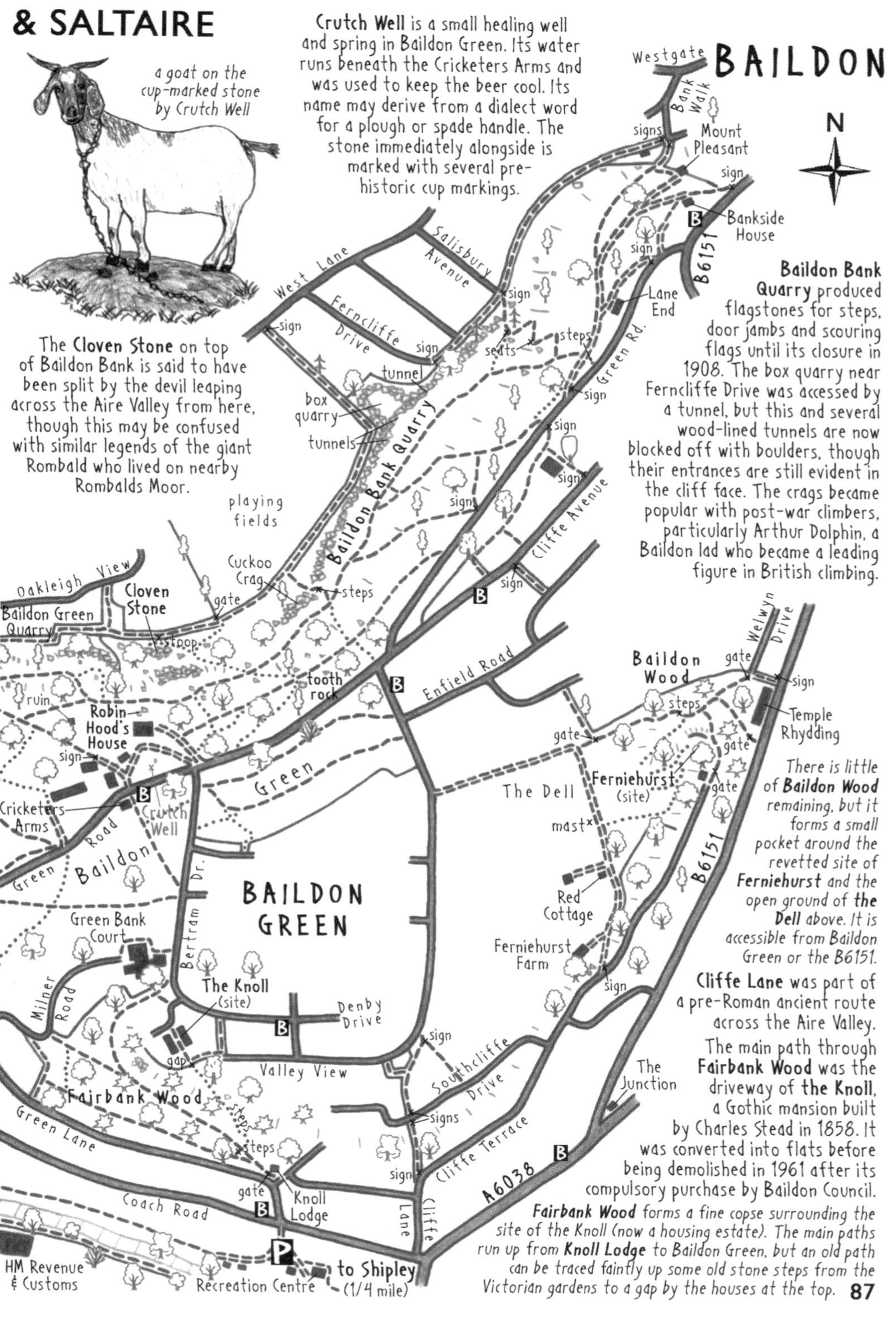
a goat on the cup-marked stone by Crutch Well
BAILDON
N
Westgate
Bank Walk
signs
Mount Pleasant
sign
Bankside House
B6151
Salisbury Avenue
West Lane
Ferncliffe Drive
sign
sign
seats
steps
Green Rd.
Lane End
tunnel
box quarry
tunnels
Baildon Bank Quarry
sign
Cliffe Avenue
playing fields
Cuckoo Crag
steps
Oakleigh View
Cloven Stone
gate
Baildon Green Quarry
stoop
tooth rock
Enfield Road
Baildon Wood
Welwyn Drive
gate
sign
steps
Temple Rhydding
ruin
Robin Hood's House
gate
gate
sign
Green
The Dell
Ferniehurst (site)
gate
Cricketers Arms
Crutch Well
mast
Green Road
Baildon
Bertram Dr.
BAILDON GREEN
Red Cottage
B6151
Green Bank Court
Ferniehurst Farm
The Knoll (site)
sign
Milner Road
Denby Drive
sign
gap
Valley View
Southcliffe Drive
The Junction
Fairbank Wood
signs
steps
Green Lane
steps
Cliffe Terrace
sign
gate
Knoll Lodge
A6038
Coach Road
Lane
Cliffe
HM Revenue & Customs
Recreation Centre
to Shipley (1/4 mile)

**Crutch Well** is a small healing well and spring in Baildon Green. Its water runs beneath the Cricketers Arms and was used to keep the beer cool. Its name may derive from a dialect word for a plough or spade handle. The stone immediately alongside is marked with several prehistoric cup markings.

The **Cloven Stone** on top of Baildon Bank is said to have been split by the devil leaping across the Aire Valley from here, though this may be confused with similar legends of the giant Rombald who lived on nearby Rombalds Moor.

**Baildon Bank Quarry** produced flagstones for steps, door jambs and scouring flags until its closure in 1908. The box quarry near Ferncliffe Drive was accessed by a tunnel, but this and several wood-lined tunnels are now blocked off with boulders, though their entrances are still evident in the cliff face. The crags became popular with post-war climbers, particularly Arthur Dolphin, a Baildon lad who became a leading figure in British climbing.

*There is little of* ***Baildon Wood*** *remaining, but it forms a small pocket around the revetted site of* ***Ferniehurst*** *and the open ground of* ***the Dell*** *above. It is accessible from Baildon Green or the B6151.*

**Cliffe Lane** was part of a pre-Roman ancient route across the Aire Valley.

The main path through **Fairbank Wood** was the driveway of **the Knoll**, a Gothic mansion built by Charles Stead in 1858. It was converted into flats before being demolished in 1961 after its compulsory purchase by Baildon Council.

***Fairbank Wood*** *forms a fine copse surrounding the site of the Knoll (now a housing estate). The main paths run up from* ***Knoll Lodge*** *to Baildon Green, but an old path can be traced faintly up some old stone steps from the Victorian gardens to a gap by the houses at the top.*

# MAP 24: SHIPLEY GLEN & MILNER FIELD

Shipley Glen is a narrow oak-clogged ravine that descends steeply from Baildon Moor. Its many low crags are popular with boulderers, while the open ground on Bracken Hall Green is covered in prehistoric sites and carvings. The woods continue west to Gilstead, where the site of Titus Salt Jr's mansion at Milner Field is lost in the dense trees. The whole area is easily accessed from Saltaire, Gilstead and Eldwick.

The name **Shipley Glen** is said to have been coined by Revd Peter Scott, a Shipley clergyman who brought his Sunday school class here for annual Whitsuntide excursions in the 1840s. The name stuck after featuring in the *Bradford Observer*, though it makes little geographical sense. The valley lies in Baildon not Shipley and is closest to Eldwick, while the stream is the Loadpit Beck. Its earliest name may have been Helwick Glen, Helwick being a corruption of High Eldwick (one of the earliest settlements in the area), and was referred to by locals as either Eldwick Glen or Brackenhall Glen depending on which side they lived.

Shipley Glen was shaped during the last Ice Age, but not cut by the tongue of ice which stretched up it. Instead this widened an existing gorge and deposited glacial moraine in the bottom of the glen beneath a lake somewhere above Crag Hebble Dam. The winding stream around Raygate Well was created by the water finding a way through this moraine. The mass of fallen rock in the glen is a result of the softer underlying shales having been eroded to allow the gritstone crags to collapse into the valley. Some of the rocks on Bracken Hall Crag include **No. 9 Rock** (beneath which a gambling school and courting couples are said to have met), **Sentinel Rock** (said to look like an old man's face), the **Blowberry Stone** (painted with the message 'God is Love' since at least the 1950s), and the Druid's Pulpit and Writing Desk.

Raygate (or Cloven Hoof) Well

The glen is full of fascinatingly named wells, including Sore Eyes Well, Judson Well, Raygate Well, Wood Well and Nursery Well. **Raygate Well** was known locally as Cloven Hoof Well and its name may relate to *rea*, a dialect word for an evil spirit. There is a mark on the stone by the well said to have been made by the devil – in leaping from here his hoofmark caused the water to rise from the ground. There is also a millstone in the middle of the small path nearby.

***Broadstone Wood** forms a fine oak cloak along the west side of Shipley Glen, but its steep slopes make it hard to cross Loadpit Beck between **Crag Hebble Dam** and the bridge at the top. The main path follows the top of the slope, and a faint path forks right north-east of **Broadstone House** to head down to the stream opposite Raygate Well, where a path follows the west bank briefly downstream. However, it is rough in places and crossing the stream is not always simple.*

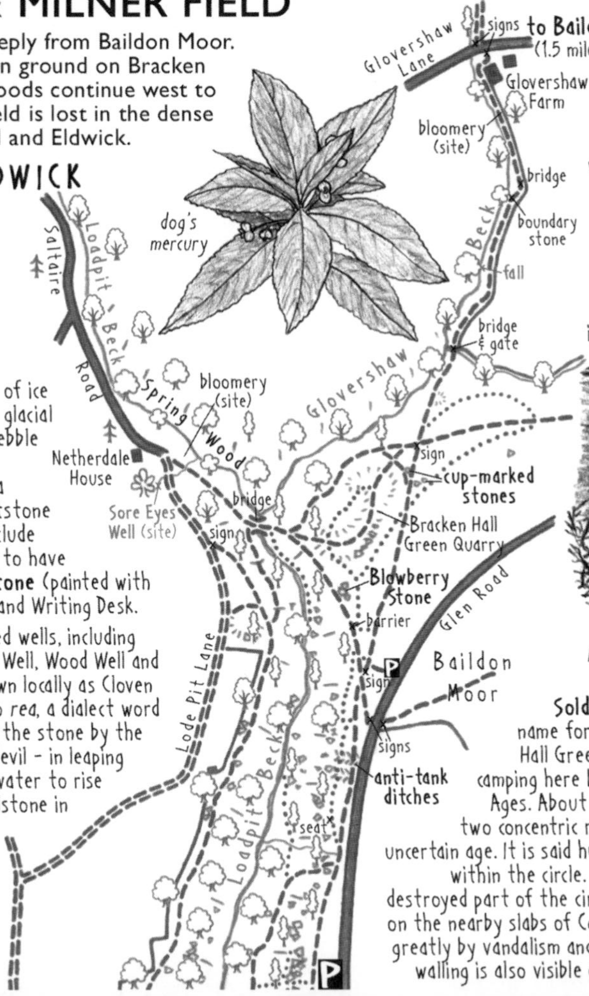

ELDWICK
Saltaire
Road
Loadpit Beck
Spring Wood
bloomery (site)
Netherdale House
Sore Eyes Well (site)
sign
bridge
dog's mercury
Gloversham Lane
signs
to Baildon (1.5 miles)
Gloversham Farm
bloomery (site)
bridge
boundary stone
Beck
fall
bridge & gate
Gloversham
sign
cup-marked stones
Bracken Hall Green Quarry
Blowberry Stone
barrier
Glen Road
Baildon Moor
sign
signs
anti-tank ditches
Lode Pit Lane
Loadpit Beck
seat

Two **bloomeries** on Gloversham and Loadpit Becks were used for iron smelting as late as the 19th century. The word 'load' (or lode) relates to a seam of ore, and ironstone was mined on the western side of Baildon Moor, particularly around Gloversham. Charcoal from the adjacent woods was used to heat the ore to high temperatures and separate the iron from its impurities, with slag still found in the soil of these sites.

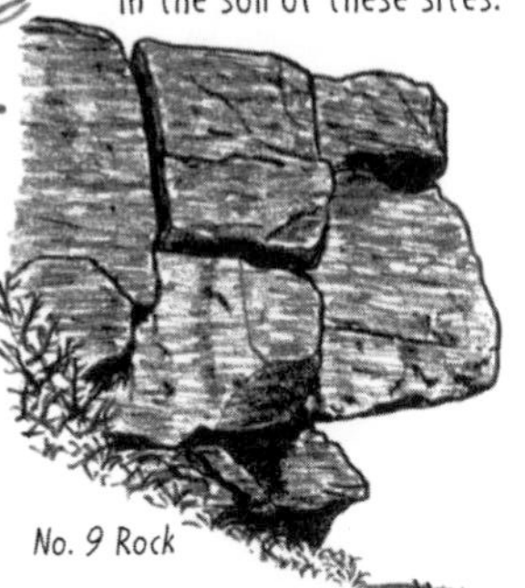

No. 9 Rock

**Soldier's Trench** is a local name for a large stone circle on Bracken Hall Green, inspired by a tale of soldiers camping here before a battle during the Dark Ages. About 50m in diameter, it consists of two concentric rings of stones on end and is of uncertain age. It is said huge Beltane fires used to be lit within the circle. The construction of Glen Road destroyed part of the circle, while much of the rock art on the nearby slabs of Catten Stones has been damaged greatly by vandalism and footfall. A section of Iron Age walling is also visible on the other side of Glen Road.

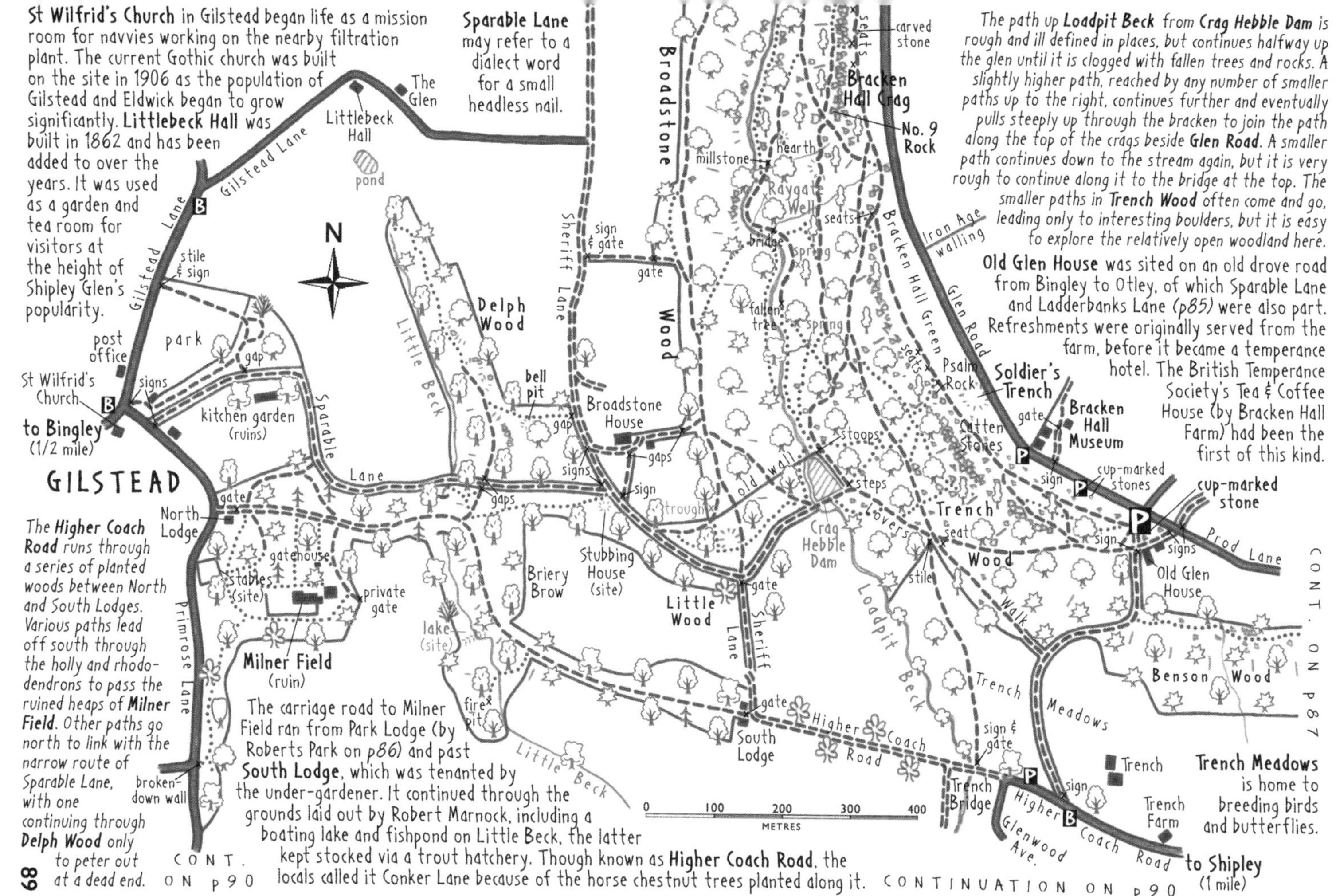

**St Wilfrid's Church** in Gilstead began life as a mission room for navvies working on the nearby filtration plant. The current Gothic church was built on the site in 1906 as the population of Gilstead and Eldwick began to grow significantly. **Littlebeck Hall** was built in 1862 and has been added to over the years. It was used as a garden and tea room for visitors at the height of Shipley Glen's popularity.
**Sparable Lane** may refer to a dialect word for a small headless nail.
*The path up **Loadpit Beck** from **Crag Hebble Dam** is rough and ill defined in places, but continues halfway up the glen until it is clogged with fallen trees and rocks. A slightly higher path, reached by any number of smaller paths up to the right, continues further and eventually pulls steeply up through the bracken to join the path along the top of the crags beside **Glen Road**. A smaller path continues down to the stream again, but it is very rough to continue along it to the bridge at the top. The smaller paths in **Trench Wood** often come and go, leading only to interesting boulders, but it is easy to explore the relatively open woodland here.*
**Old Glen House** was sited on an old drove road from Bingley to Otley, of which Sparable Lane and Ladderbanks Lane (*p85*) were also part. Refreshments were originally served from the farm, before it became a temperance hotel. The British Temperance Society's Tea & Coffee House (by Bracken Hall Farm) had been the first of this kind.
*The **Higher Coach Road** runs through a series of planted woods between North and South Lodges. Various paths lead off south through the holly and rhododendrons to pass the ruined heaps of **Milner Field**. Other paths go north to link with the narrow route of Sparable Lane, with one continuing through **Delph Wood** only to peter out at a dead end.*
The carriage road to Milner Field ran from Park Lodge (by Roberts Park on *p86*) and past **South Lodge**, which was tenanted by the under-gardener. It continued through the grounds laid out by Robert Marnock, including a boating lake and fishpond on Little Beck, the latter kept stocked via a trout hatchery. Though known as **Higher Coach Road**, the locals called it Conker Lane because of the horse chestnut trees planted along it.
**Trench Meadows** is home to breeding birds and butterflies.
GILSTEAD
The Glen
Littlebeck Hall
pond
Gilstead Lane
stile & sign
park
post office
gap
signs
St Wilfrid's Church
to Bingley (1/2 mile)
kitchen garden (ruins)
Sparable Lane
North Lodge
gate
gatehouse
stables (site)
private gate
Milner Field (ruin)
Primrose Lane
broken-down wall
Little Beck
Delph Wood
bell pit
gap
gaps
lake (site)
fire pit
Briery Brow
Sheriff Lane
sign & gate
gate
Broadstone Wood
Broadstone House
gaps
signs
sign
trough
Stubbing House (site)
Little Wood
South Lodge
Higher Coach Road
millstone
hearth
Raygate Well
bridge
fallen tree
spring
seats
carved stone
Bracken Hall Crag
No. 9 Rock
Bracken Hall Green
Psalm Rock
old wall
stoops
steps
Crag Hebble Dam
Loadpit Beck
Lovers' Walk
stile
seat
Trench Wood
Catten Stones
Soldier's Trench
Iron Age walling
Glen Road
Bracken Hall Museum
cup-marked stones
cup-marked stone
Prod Lane
Old Glen House
Benson Wood
Trench Meadows
sign & gate
Trench Bridge
Glenwood Ave.
Trench
Trench Farm
to Shipley (1 mile)
0 100 200 300 400
METRES
N

CONT. ON p87
CONT. ON p90
CONTINUATION ON p90

# MAP 25: HIRST WOOD & NAB WOOD

Part of a **prehistoric field system** is visible near the burial ground in Nab Wood, and a holloway at the east end of Hirst Wood is thought to be associated with the nearby site of an Iron Age **round house**.

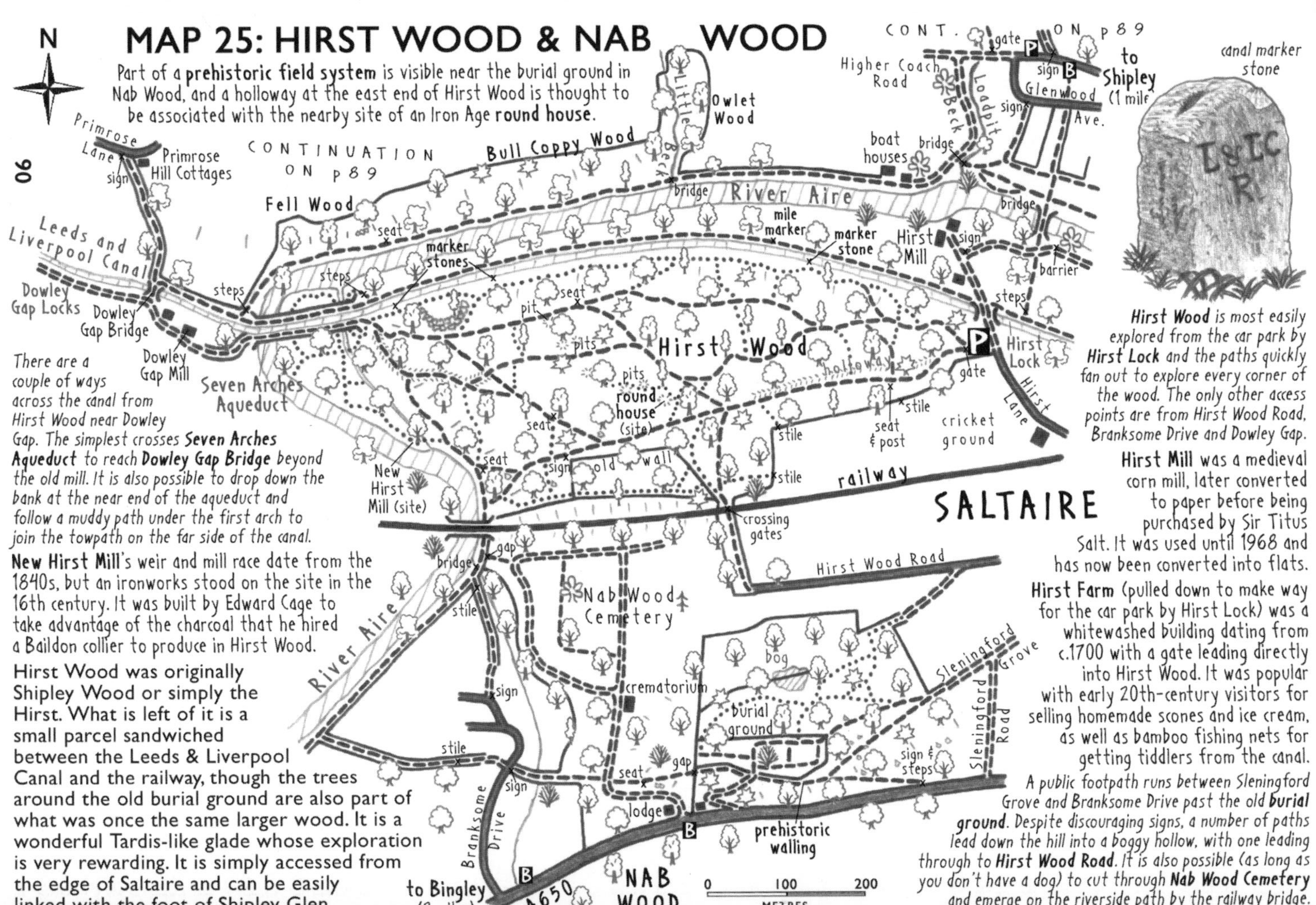
N
CONTINUATION ON p89
CONT. ON p89
canal marker stone
Primrose Lane
sign
Primrose Hill Cottages
Leeds and Liverpool Canal
Dowley Gap Locks
Dowley Gap Bridge
Dowley Gap Mill
steps
Fell Wood
seat
marker stones
steps
Seven Arches Aqueduct
Bull Coppy Wood
Little Beck
Owlet Wood
bridge
River Aire
mile marker
marker stone
boat houses
bridge
Hirst Mill
sign
Higher Coach Road
Loadpit Beck
gate
sign
Glenwood Ave.
to Shipley (1 mile
bridge
barrier
steps
Hirst Lock
Hirst Lane
gate
Hirst Wood
pit
seat
pits
pits
round house (site)
hollowway
seat
stile
stile
seat & post
stile
cricket ground
seat
sign
old wall
stile
railway
SALTAIRE
crossing gates
New Hirst Mill (site)
gap
bridge
stile
River Aire
Hirst Wood Road
Nab Wood Cemetery
crematorium
bog
burial ground
sign
stile
sign
seat
gap
lodge
prehistoric walling
Sleningford Grove
Sleningford Road
sign & steps
Branksome Drive
A650
to Bingley
NAB WOOD
0
100
200
METRES

There are a couple of ways across the canal from Hirst Wood near Dowley Gap. The simplest crosses **Seven Arches Aqueduct** to reach **Dowley Gap Bridge** beyond the old mill. It is also possible to drop down the bank at the near end of the aqueduct and follow a muddy path under the first arch to join the towpath on the far side of the canal.

**New Hirst Mill**'s weir and mill race date from the 1840s, but an ironworks stood on the site in the 16th century. It was built by Edward Cage to take advantage of the charcoal that he hired a Baildon collier to produce in Hirst Wood.

Hirst Wood was originally Shipley Wood or simply the Hirst. What is left of it is a small parcel sandwiched between the Leeds & Liverpool Canal and the railway, though the trees around the old burial ground are also part of what was once the same larger wood. It is a wonderful Tardis-like glade whose exploration is very rewarding. It is simply accessed from the edge of Saltaire and can be easily linked with the foot of Shipley Glen

**Hirst Wood** is most easily explored from the car park by **Hirst Lock** and the paths quickly fan out to explore every corner of the wood. The only other access points are from Hirst Wood Road, Branksome Drive and Dowley Gap.

**Hirst Mill** was a medieval corn mill, later converted to paper before being purchased by Sir Titus Salt. It was used until 1968 and has now been converted into flats.

**Hirst Farm** (pulled down to make way for the car park by Hirst Lock) was a whitewashed building dating from c.1700 with a gate leading directly into Hirst Wood. It was popular with early 20th-century visitors for selling homemade scones and ice cream, as well as bamboo fishing nets for getting tiddlers from the canal.

*A public footpath runs between Sleningford Grove and Branksome Drive past the old* ***burial ground****. Despite discouraging signs, a number of paths lead down the hill into a boggy hollow, with one leading through to* ***Hirst Wood Road****. It is also possible (as long as you don't have a dog) to cut through* ***Nab Wood Cemetery*** *and emerge on the riverside path by the railway bridge.*

# SHIPLEY GLEN PLEASURE GROUNDS

With the arrival of the railway to Shipley in 1847, Shipley Glen became accessible to people from Bradford and Leeds and quickly established itself as one of the most prominent local beauty spots. Saltaire railway station opened in 1856, from where it was only a short walk to the woods and crags. Many of the early visitors were church groups, taking trips on public holidays like May Day or Whit Sunday, so temperance hotels opened in former farm buildings in the 1850s to cater for them.

It wasn't until the 1870s that tourism at Shipley Glen started to change, with boat swings and donkey rides first introduced at the Old Glen Hotel. The area around Prod Lane was developed to take advantage of the people flocking past on their way up the busy bridleway to the glen. Vulcan House was built by the Voss family in 1879, the original tearoom soon being augmented with donkey rides, swings, dodgems, a paddling pool, a penny arcade and ice cream stalls. It marketed itself as Shipley Glen Pleasure Grounds, though this name became used generically for all of the rides and attractions that proliferated above Shipley Glen after the Royal Yorkshire Jubilee Exhibition put Saltaire firmly on the map.

The exhibition covered a twelve-acre site in Saltaire from May to September 1887, celebrating Queen Victoria's Silver Jubilee. As well as visitors, it brought a wide variety of rides and entertainments to the area, including one of the UK's first roller-coasters. The Ocean Switchback proved so popular that J.W. Waddington had it re-erected in 1888 in the fields behind Bracken Hall Farm and rebranded the Great Yorkshire Switchback. Local entrepreneur Sam Wilson created a horse-drawn tramway around the pond at Glen House, while others opened a camera obscura and a menagerie with monkeys on display close to Bracken Hall Farm. This ushered in an era of innovative and terrifying new rides. Halliday's Aerial Flight was constructed in 1889, a cable car-like rope-suspended ride running between stations for two hundred yards above the rocky edge of Shipley Glen. Sam Wilson's infamous Toboggan Slide opened in 1897, claiming to be the longest, widest and steepest slide in the country, its wooden sledges plummeting down the glen side at 60mph. However, it was dismantled after an accident on Whit Sunday 1900 when five people were badly injured. The Aerial Glide opened at the original Pleasure Grounds around 1900, suspending its riders and forcing them out sideways.

Thomas Hartley's Japanese Gardens on Prod Lane were inspired by a Japanese village at the Exhibition and opened around 1900. It had extravagant structures made out of ash and clinker and covered with white lime to look old, including a ruined castle on an island, small bridges, pergolas and archways. It was built in the gardens of Ivy House, allegedly to entertain Hartley's ailing mother, and visitors took a boat ride around the tiny lake or a ride on the miniature railway.

Shipley Glen Tramway opened on 18th May 1895, another of Sam Wilson's initiatives. Though it was shorter than originally planned, it saved people from having to walk up the steep path through the woods from Saltaire. The fare was 2d up and 1d down. It carried 17,000 visitors on Easter Monday 1910, but was still unable to cater for all the visitors that flooded here, said to reach around 100,000 at the Glen's peak. Originally the trams were hauled by ropes and powered by a gas engine, but it has been cable hauled and electrically operated since 1920.

Although some of these rides were short-lived, Shipley Glen Pleasure Grounds remained popular until the 1950s. The Japanese Gardens lasted until 1975, when the land was sold and used for a housing development, while Vulcan House's main fairground closed as recently as 2005 and the Aerial Glide was demolished despite being the oldest remaining ride of its type in the UK. Only the tramway remains to remind us of Shipley Glen's former glory.

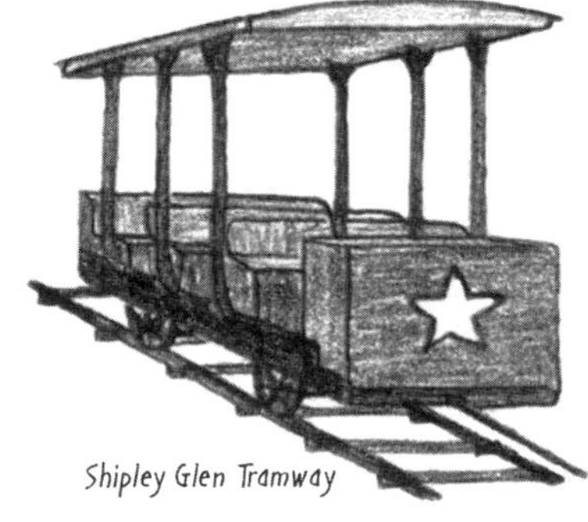

*Shipley Glen Tramway*

# ROUTE 14: SHIPLEY GLEN, GILL BECK &

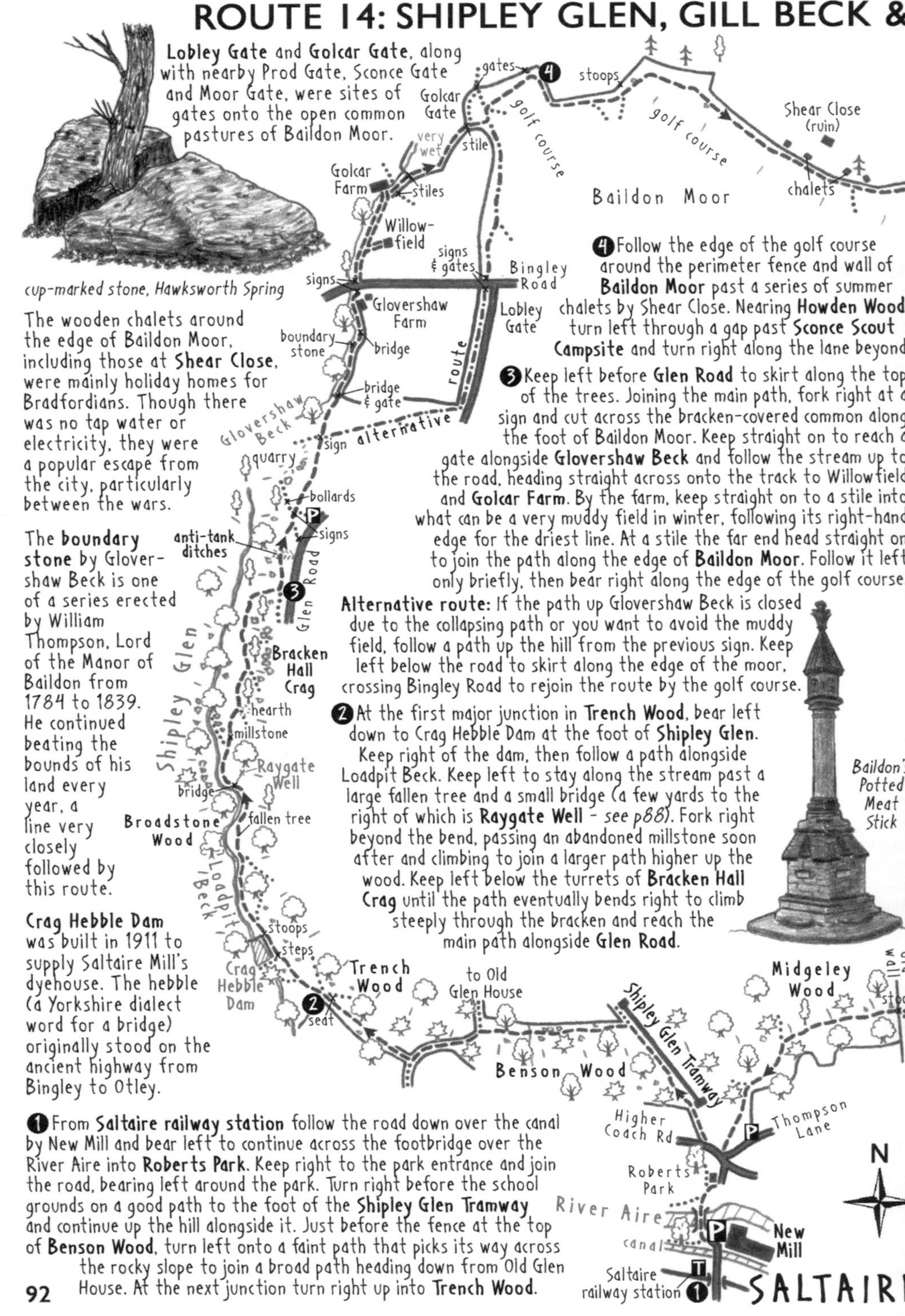

gates
stoops
Golcar Gate
golf course
Shear Close (ruin)
very wet
stile
Golcar Farm
stiles
chalets
Baildon Moor
Willow-field
signs & gates
Bingley Road
signs
Glovershaw Farm
Lobley Gate
boundary stone
bridge
route
bridge & gate
Glovershaw Beck
alternative
sign
quarry
bollards
P
signs
anti-tank ditches
Glen Road
Bracken Hall Crag
Shipley Glen
hearth
millstone
Raygate Well
bridge
Broadstone Wood
fallen tree
Loadpit Beck
stoops
steps
Crag Hebble Dam
Trench Wood
seat
to Old Glen House
Shipley Glen Tramway
Midgeley Wood
Benson Wood
Higher Coach Rd
Thompson Lane
Roberts Park
N
River Aire
canal
New Mill
Saltaire railway station
SALTAIRE
Baildon's Potted Meat Stick


*cup-marked stone, Hawksworth Spring*

**Lobley Gate** and **Golcar Gate**, along with nearby Prod Gate, Sconce Gate and Moor Gate, were sites of gates onto the open common pastures of Baildon Moor.

The wooden chalets around the edge of Baildon Moor, including those at **Shear Close**, were mainly holiday homes for Bradfordians. Though there was no tap water or electricity, they were a popular escape from the city, particularly between the wars.

The **boundary stone** by Glovershaw Beck is one of a series erected by William Thompson, Lord of the Manor of Baildon from 1784 to 1839. He continued beating the bounds of his land every year, a line very closely followed by this route.

**Crag Hebble Dam** was built in 1911 to supply Saltaire Mill's dyehouse. The hebble (a Yorkshire dialect word for a bridge) originally stood on the ancient highway from Bingley to Otley.

❹ Follow the edge of the golf course around the perimeter fence and wall of **Baildon Moor** past a series of summer chalets by Shear Close. Nearing **Howden Wood** turn left through a gap past **Sconce Scout Campsite** and turn right along the lane beyond.

❸ Keep left before **Glen Road** to skirt along the top of the trees. Joining the main path, fork right at a sign and cut across the bracken-covered common along the foot of Baildon Moor. Keep straight on to reach a gate alongside **Glovershaw Beck** and follow the stream up to the road, heading straight across onto the track to Willowfield and **Golcar Farm**. By the farm, keep straight on to a stile into what can be a very muddy field in winter, following its right-hand edge for the driest line. At a stile the far end head straight on to join the path along the edge of **Baildon Moor**. Follow it left only briefly, then bear right along the edge of the golf course.

**Alternative route:** If the path up Glovershaw Beck is closed due to the collapsing path or you want to avoid the muddy field, follow a path up the hill from the previous sign. Keep left below the road to skirt along the edge of the moor, crossing Bingley Road to rejoin the route by the golf course.

❷ At the first major junction in **Trench Wood**, bear left down to Crag Hebble Dam at the foot of **Shipley Glen**. Keep right of the dam, then follow a path alongside Loadpit Beck. Keep left to stay along the stream past a large fallen tree and a small bridge (a few yards to the right of which is **Raygate Well** - *see p88*). Fork right beyond the bend, passing an abandoned millstone soon after and climbing to join a larger path higher up the wood. Keep left below the turrets of **Bracken Hall Crag** until the path eventually bends right to climb steeply through the bracken and reach the main path alongside **Glen Road**.

❶ From **Saltaire railway station** follow the road down over the canal by New Mill and bear left to continue across the footbridge over the River Aire into **Roberts Park**. Keep right to the park entrance and join the road, bearing left around the park. Turn right before the school grounds on a good path to the foot of the **Shipley Glen Tramway** and continue up the hill alongside it. Just before the fence at the top of **Benson Wood**, turn left onto a faint path that picks its way across the rocky slope to join a broad path heading down from Old Glen House. At the next junction turn right up into **Trench Wood**.

# BAILDON BANK FROM SALTAIRE OR BAILDON

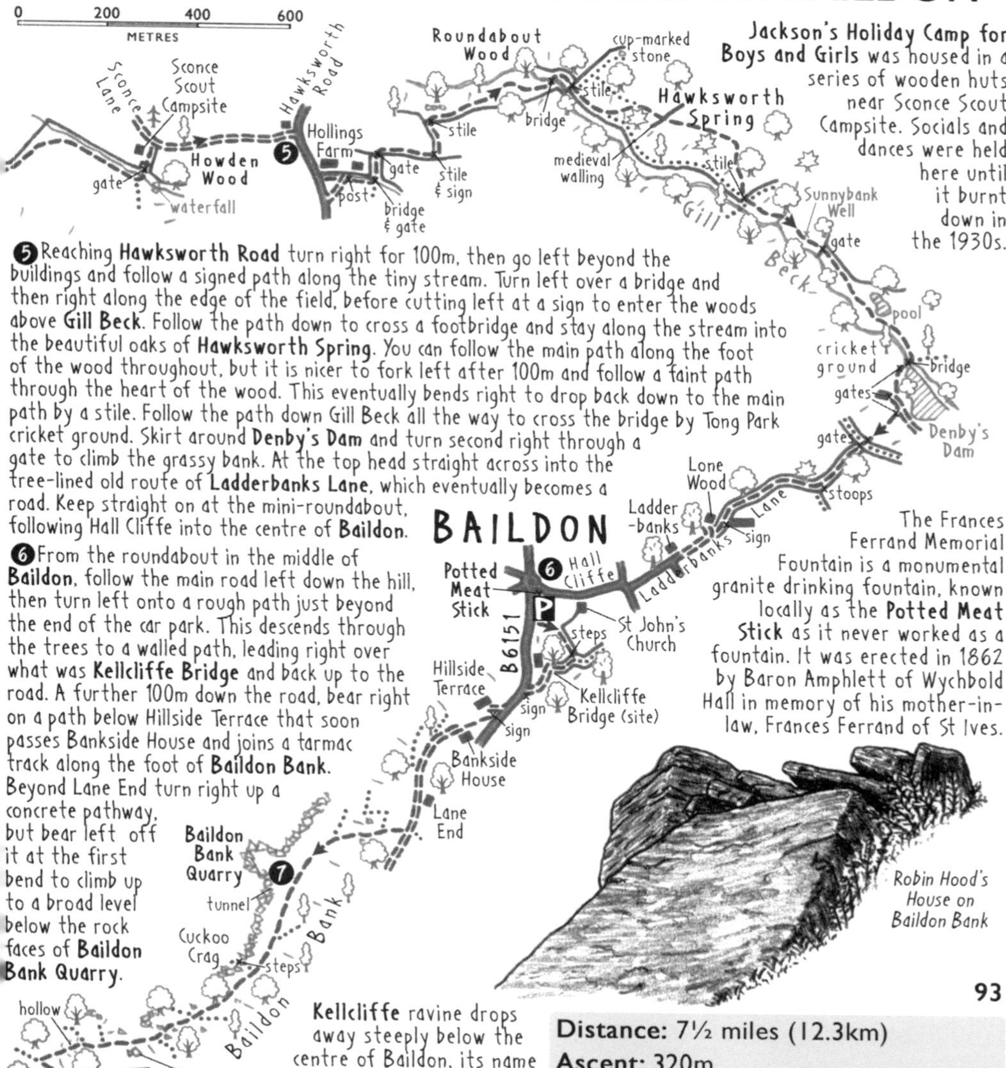
0
200
400
600
METRES
Sconce Lane
Sconce Scout Campsite
Hawksworth Road
Howden Wood
gate
waterfall
Hollings Farm
post
gate
bridge & gate
stile
stile & sign
Roundabout Wood
bridge
cup-marked stone
stile
Hawksworth Spring
medieval walling
stile
Gill Beck
Sunnybank Well
gate
pool
cricket ground
bridge
gates
gate
Denby's Dam
Lone Wood
stoops
Ladder-banks
Ladderbanks Lane
sign
BAILDON
Potted Meat Stick
Hall Cliffe
P
St John's Church
steps
B6151
Hillside Terrace
sign
sign
Kellcliffe Bridge (site)
Bankside House
Lane End
Baildon Bank Quarry
tunnel
Cuckoo Crag
steps
Baildon Bank
hollow
BAILDON GREEN
Robin Hood's House

**Jackson's Holiday Camp for Boys and Girls** was housed in a series of wooden huts near Sconce Scout Campsite. Socials and dances were held here until it burnt down in the 1930s.

❺ Reaching **Hawksworth Road** turn right for 100m, then go left beyond the buildings and follow a signed path along the tiny stream. Turn left over a bridge and then right along the edge of the field, before cutting left at a sign to enter the woods above **Gill Beck**. Follow the path down to cross a footbridge and stay along the stream into the beautiful oaks of **Hawksworth Spring**. You can follow the main path along the foot of the wood throughout, but it is nicer to fork left after 100m and follow a faint path through the heart of the wood. This eventually bends right to drop back down to the main path by a stile. Follow the path down Gill Beck all the way to cross the bridge by Tong Park cricket ground. Skirt around **Denby's Dam** and turn second right through a gate to climb the grassy bank. At the top head straight across into the tree-lined old route of **Ladderbanks Lane**, which eventually becomes a road. Keep straight on at the mini-roundabout, following Hall Cliffe into the centre of **Baildon**.

❻ From the roundabout in the middle of **Baildon**, follow the main road left down the hill, then turn left onto a rough path just beyond the end of the car park. This descends through the trees to a walled path, leading right over what was **Kellcliffe Bridge** and back up to the road. A further 100m down the road, bear right on a path below Hillside Terrace that soon passes Bankside House and joins a tarmac track along the foot of **Baildon Bank**. Beyond Lane End turn right up a concrete pathway, but bear left off it at the first bend to climb up to a broad level below the rock faces of **Baildon Bank Quarry**.

The Frances Ferrand Memorial Fountain is a monumental granite drinking fountain, known locally as the **Potted Meat Stick** as it never worked as a fountain. It was erected in 1862 by Baron Amphlett of Wychbold Hall in memory of his mother-in-law, Frances Ferrand of St Ives.

*Robin Hood's House on Baildon Bank*

**Kellcliffe** ravine drops away steeply below the centre of Baildon, its name referring to a spring.

❼ Follow the main path through **Baildon Bank Quarry** (with great views across the valley towards Idle Hill and Lister Mills) until it descends into the trees below Cuckoo Crag. Carry straight on, picking your way through another rocky quarried area, then continuing above the buildings of Baildon Green and rocks of **Robin Hood's House**. Soon after, bear left down a hollow to reach a larger path. Go left then immediately right down the slope, before turning right on a fainter path at the next junction. Continue across the slope, passing a tall stoop on the edge of **Midgeley Wood**. Keep left as this lovely path emerges from the dense holly on the edge of the open ground by the foot of **Shipley Glen Tramway**. It is simple to retrace the outward route back into **Saltaire**.



**Distance:** 7½ miles (12.3km)

**Ascent:** 320m

**Parking:** Pay car parks in Saltaire and Baildon (the latter cheaper), with some free street parking along the route.

**Public Transport:** Saltaire is on the main Airedale train and bus routes.

**Character:** A route of great variety, taking in the rugged woods of Shipley Glen and the verdant Gill Beck, with the more open landscape around Baildon Moor and Baildon Bank providing broader vistas. This is a slightly rougher walk than Route 15 and the section beyond Golcar Farm can be particularly wet in winter (though an alternative route is provided here).

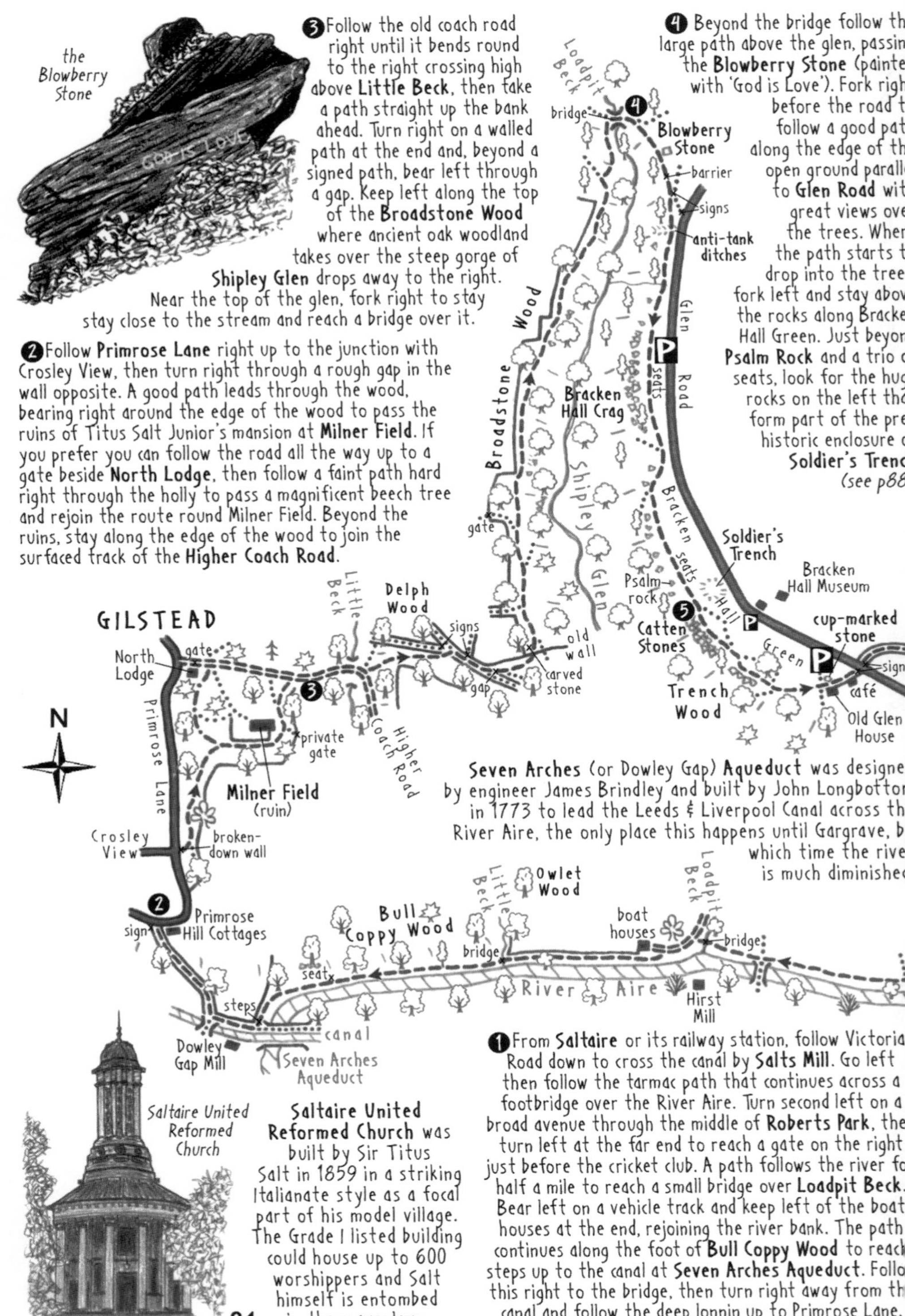

the Blowberry Stone
GOD IS LOVE
Loadpit Beck
bridge
4
Blowberry Stone
barrier
signs
anti-tank ditches
Glen Road
P
seats
Wood
Broadstone
Bracken Hall Crag
Shipley Glen
Bracken Hall Green
seats
gate
Soldier's Trench
Bracken Hall Museum
Psalm rock
5
Catten Stones
P
cup-marked stone
sign
café
Old Glen House
Trench Wood
old wall
carved stone
gap
signs
Delph Wood
Little Beck
GILSTEAD
North Lodge
gate
3
private gate
Higher Coach Road
Milner Field (ruin)
N
Primrose Lane
Crosley View
broken-down wall
2
sign
Primrose Hill Cottages
Owlet Wood
Little Beck
Loadpit Beck
Bull Coppy Wood
bridge
boat houses
bridge
seat
steps
River Aire
Hirst Mill
canal
Dowley Gap Mill
Seven Arches Aqueduct
Saltaire United Reformed Church


❸ Follow the old coach road right until it bends round to the right crossing high above **Little Beck**, then take a path straight up the bank ahead. Turn right on a walled path at the end and, beyond a signed path, bear left through a gap. Keep left along the top of the **Broadstone Wood** where ancient oak woodland takes over the steep gorge of **Shipley Glen** drops away to the right. Near the top of the glen, fork right to stay stay close to the stream and reach a bridge over it.

❹ Beyond the bridge follow th large path above the glen, passin the **Blowberry Stone** (painte with 'God is Love'). Fork righ before the road t follow a good pat along the edge of th open ground paralle to **Glen Road** wit great views ove the trees. Wher the path starts t drop into the trees fork left and stay abov the rocks along Bracke Hall Green. Just beyon **Psalm Rock** and a trio o seats, look for the hug rocks on the left tha form part of the pre historic enclosure o **Soldier's Trenc** (see p88

❷ Follow **Primrose Lane** right up to the junction with Crosley View, then turn right through a rough gap in the wall opposite. A good path leads through the wood, bearing right around the edge of the wood to pass the ruins of Titus Salt Junior's mansion at **Milner Field**. If you prefer you can follow the road all the way up to a gate beside **North Lodge**, then follow a faint path hard right through the holly to pass a magnificent beech tree and rejoin the route round Milner Field. Beyond the ruins, stay along the edge of the wood to join the surfaced track of the **Higher Coach Road**.

**Seven Arches** (or Dowley Gap) **Aqueduct** was designe by engineer James Brindley and built by John Longbotton in 1773 to lead the Leeds & Liverpool Canal across th River Aire, the only place this happens until Gargrave, b which time the rive is much diminishe

**Saltaire United Reformed Church** was built by Sir Titus Salt in 1859 in a striking Italianate style as a focal part of his model village. The Grade I listed building could house up to 600 worshippers and Salt himself is entombed in the mausoleum.

❶ From **Saltaire** or its railway station, follow Victoria Road down to cross the canal by **Salts Mill**. Go left then follow the tarmac path that continues across a footbridge over the River Aire. Turn second left on a broad avenue through the middle of **Roberts Park**, the turn left at the far end to reach a gate on the right just before the cricket club. A path follows the river fo half a mile to reach a small bridge over **Loadpit Beck**. Bear left on a vehicle track and keep left of the boat houses at the end, rejoining the river bank. The path continues along the foot of **Bull Coppy Wood** to reac steps up to the canal at **Seven Arches Aqueduct**. Follo this right to the bridge, then turn right away from th canal and follow the deep lonnin up to Primrose Lane.

# ROUTE 15: SHIPLEY GLEN FROM SALTAIRE

**Distance:** 6½ miles (10.3km)

**Ascent:** 180m

**Parking:** Pay car parks in Saltaire. Free parking at Baildon Green, Baildon Recreation Centre and along Glen Road.

**Public Transport:** Saltaire is on the main Airedale train and bus routes.

**Character:** A simple circuit of Shipley Glen that also takes in Baildon Green, the ruined mansion of Milner Field and some lovely walking along the River Aire. This route stays high above Shipley Glen itself, the woods opening out to offer great views and pass Bracken Hall Crag and Soldier's Trench. If you want to explore the gorge itself you are better off following the rougher Route 14, though this route has the benefit of passing a café and a couple of fine pubs.

❺ By **Soldier's Trench** fork right along the edge of Catten Stones, then keep right to dip into the edge of the trees of **Trench Wood**. You soon join a larger path along the top of wood, which can be followed to reach the **Old Glen House** pub, opposite which there is a fine cup-marked stone. Continue to the road and head straight across on a narrow footpath. At Rylstone Road head straight on, then fork left and continue past Woodlands Grove to reach the top of **Walker Wood.** Just down into the trees is **Robin Hood's Chair**, a basin sculpted into one of the rocks round to the right *(see sketch on p86)*.

**Baildon Carnival** was an important event for the British gypsy community, having been held in the town since the 17th century. Travellers camped on Baildon Green and Bracken Hall Green and many stayed through the summer, working at the Shipley Glen Pleasure Grounds *(see p96)*. The event remained popular locally and was revived in the late 1920s, but never returned after World War II.

**Alternative route:** A simple shortcut follows the line of **Shipley Glen Tramway** back down to Roberts Park, forking right off the route beyond Rylstone Road.

❻ Follow the path along the top of **Walker** and **Midgeley Woods**, passing a cycle barrier and descending beneath the quarries of Baildon Bank to emerge at the old hamlet of **Baildon Green**. On the green to the left just before the road is **Crutch Well** with another cup-marked stone just above it, but the route continues straight across the road to the left of the **Cricketers Arms**. Across the green, turn right up Bertram Drive and bear right on a path into the trees just before Knoll Park Drive. Follow the surfaced path down through the holly of **Fairbank Wood** to emerge on Green Lane by **Knoll Lodge**.

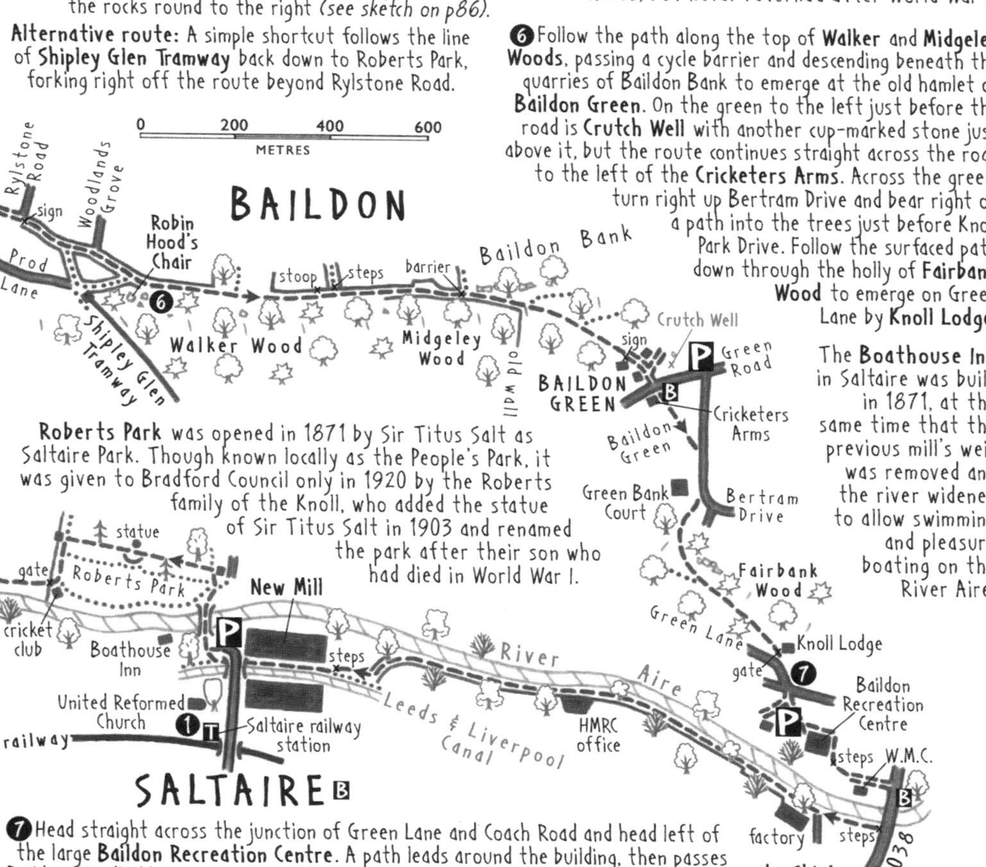

0
200
400
600
METRES
BAILDON
Rylstone Road
Woodlands Grove
sign
Robin Hood's Chair
Prod Lane
6
Shipley Glen Tramway
Walker Wood
stoop
steps
barrier
Baildon Bank
Midgeley Wood
old wall
Crutch Well
sign
Green Road
BAILDON GREEN
Cricketers Arms
Baildon Green
Green Bank Court
Bertram Drive
Fairbank Wood
Green Lane
Knoll Lodge
gate
7
Baildon Recreation Centre
steps
W.M.C.
statue
gate
Roberts Park
cricket club
Boathouse Inn
New Mill
steps
River Aire
Leeds & Liverpool Canal
HMRC office
United Reformed Church
1
Saltaire railway station
railway
SALTAIRE
factory
steps
A6038
to Shipley (1/4 mile)


**Roberts Park** was opened in 1871 by Sir Titus Salt as Saltaire Park. Though known locally as the People's Park, it was given to Bradford Council only in 1920 by the Roberts family of the Knoll, who added the statue of Sir Titus Salt in 1903 and renamed the park after their son who had died in World War I.

The **Boathouse Inn** in Saltaire was built in 1871, at the same time that the previous mill's weir was removed and the river widened to allow swimming and pleasure boating on the River Aire.

❼ Head straight across the junction of Green Lane and Coach Road and head left of the large **Baildon Recreation Centre**. A path leads around the building, then passes Baildon Woodbottom W.M.C. to reach the A6038. Turn right and cross the **River Aire**, then go right down steps beyond to join the riverside path, which has been made into the quirky Aire Sculpture Trail. Follow this all the way to join the Leeds & Liverpool Canal as it passes **Salts Mill**. After passing beneath the road bridge, turn right to return to **Saltaire** or continue along the route across a footbridge.

# THE SALT FAMILY & MILNER FIELD

Born in Morley in 1803, Sir Titus Salt was already in the woollen trade when he came across bales of alpaca wool in Liverpool in 1836. Having bought them cheap as no-one else wanted them, he incorporated the wool into worsted production on specially made machines and produced a fashionable dress fabric he called 'alpaca'. He successfully built up a business, using the canal to import Peruvian wool, including that of angora goats, via Liverpool. Charles Dickens nicknamed him 'the Great Yorkshire Llama' in *Household Words,* and Salt became Mayor of Bradford in 1848. He almost retired from business but, after failing to solve the city's pollution as a politician, he was inspired to build a model complex of mill and village. He bought land on the canal in Shipley, far from the smelly city, and created Saltaire, its American-style grid layout of streets designed to bring order to the new town. He housed all his workers, provided bath houses, allotments, a hospital, a park, playing fields for various sports associations and the Saltaire Club & Institute *(see p102).*

Saltaire Mill opened in 1853 on the site of Dixon's Mill, housing all aspects of cloth manufacture under one roof. It covered twelve acres, had 2,500 employees and cost £100,000. Salt originally flirted with the idea of incorporating into the building the great glass dome of the Crystal Palace, which he considered buying while it sat unloved in Hyde Park after the Great Exhibition of 1851. Like Bradford Town Hall, the mill was built in an Italianate style, incorporating Tuscan lantern towers and a campanile-inspired chimney stack. It included an infirmary, Turkish bath and wash house (a precursor of the laundrette). New Mill was added on the north side of the canal in 1868 to provide extra spinning capacity, its tower modelled on the campanile of Santa Maria Gloriosa Church in Venice. Salt briefly became an MP in 1859, but resigned the seat after two years and accepted his title only in 1869 after a long hesitation. In 1867 he left Methley Hall *(p15)* for Crow Nest Hall near Brighouse and died there in 1876.

Although the youngest of Sir Titus' five sons, Titus Salt Junior would go on to take over the family business after his father's death. He married Catherine Crossley in 1866 and purchased a 161-acre estate at Milner Field in 1869. The yeoman's house of Old Milner Field (built c.1603 by John Oldfield) was pulled down and a mansion described as a 'Wagnerian Gothic retreat' built 1871-73. Only the original gateposts were retained, the croquet lawn being created on the site of the original house to the north-west of the new mansion. Titus Junior was a great collector of exotic plants and an 81-foot conservatory was linked to the main house by an orangery; it housed eucalyptus trees, yuccas, palms, ferns and various fruit. A substantial kitchen garden was linked to the main house by a miniature railway and had several heated greenhouses for a winter garden of orchids, melons, mushrooms and vines. The parkland and woods were planted with yew, laurel and holly to create a 'gardenesque' feel.

Titus Junior became renowned for his lavish entertaining at Milner Field and hosted two Royal visits, by the Prince of Wales (and future Edward VII) in 1882 and Princess Beatrice in 1887. However, changes in fashions and US import duties affected the company's fortunes and he died of heart disease later that year, just a few days after the end of the costly Jubilee Exhibition *(see p91).* His wife and son lived in the house until 1903, when the whole estate and business was sold to Sir James Roberts and three other Bradford businessmen.

Many believed Milner Field was cursed, as tragedies befell several members of Roberts' family and other residents. From the late 1920s the house lay empty for over twenty years as no-one would buy it. It was used for grenade practice by the Home Guard during World War II and raided for materials, before being blown up for safety reasons around 1957, with most of the stone left for looting. The dark North Lodge was renovated in 2008, but little else remains – part of the entrance arch, the cellars, the conservatory's mosaic floor and several heaps of dressed stone from the drawing room's bay window.

Sir Titus Salt's statue in Roberts Park

# CHAPTER 8 - BRADFORD

**Map Sheet:** Explorer 288 (Bradford & Huddersfield)

**Public Transport:** Railway stations at Bradford, Frizinghall and Shipley. Various bus routes to Allerton, Heaton. and Sandy Lane.

**Parking:** Free car parks at Northcliffe Woods and Chellow Dene.

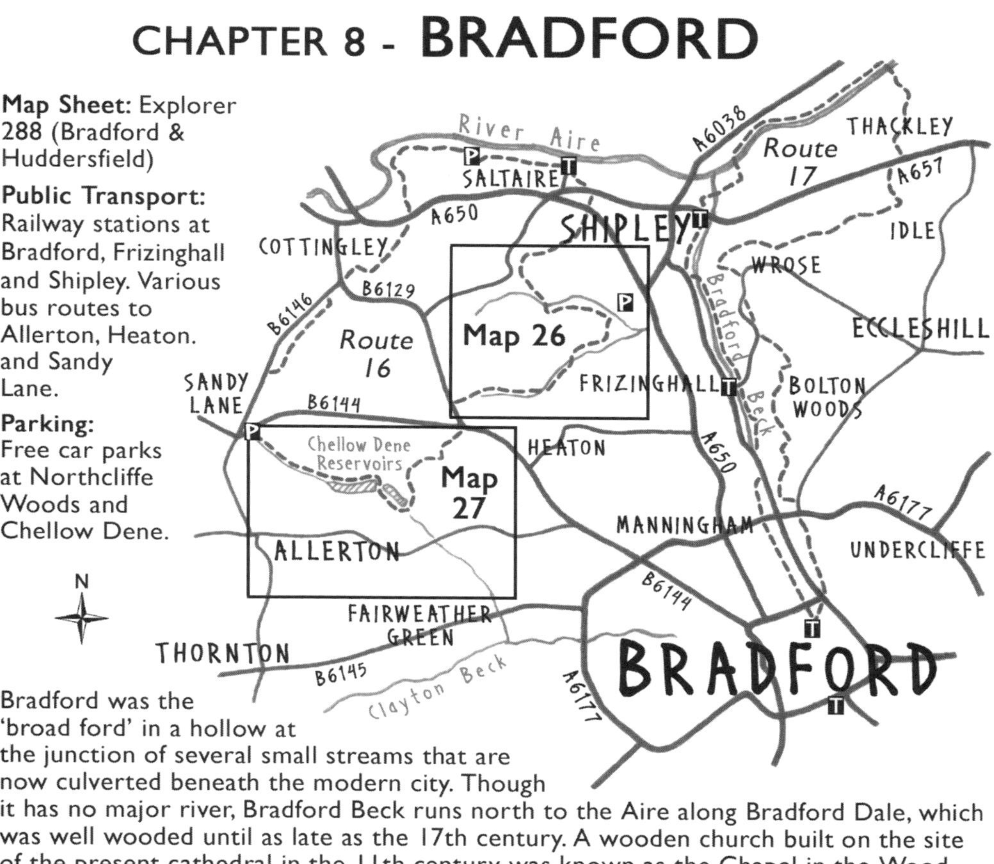
River Aire
SALTAIRE
A6038
THACKLEY
Route 17
A657
A650
SHIPLEY
IDLE
COTTINGLEY
WROSE
B6129
Bradford Beck
B6146
Route 16
Map 26
ECCLESHILL
SANDY LANE
FRIZINGHALL
BOLTON WOODS
B6144
Chellow Dene Reservoirs
HEATON
Map 27
A650
A6177
MANNINGHAM
ALLERTON
UNDERCLIFFE
N
B6144
FAIRWEATHER GREEN
THORNTON
BRADFORD
B6145
Clayton Beck
A6177

Bradford was the 'broad ford' in a hollow at the junction of several small streams that are now culverted beneath the modern city. Though it has no major river, Bradford Beck runs north to the Aire along Bradford Dale, which was well wooded until as late as the 17th century. A wooden church built on the site of the present cathedral in the 11th century was known as the Chapel in the Wood and Cliff Wood still reached from Bradford to the River Aire in the 14th century, when the Bradford Boar famously terrorised the area and obstructed routes through the wood *(see p107)*. As late as the mid 18th century Bradford was still a country town with a plantation at Hall Ings and a rookery behind Kirkgate. Though it was a late developer, Bradford's dramatic growth after the construction of the canals, to become Britain's centre of worsted production, came at the expense of much of this greenery.

What is left is rather piecemeal, Bradford Dale having suffered particularly as the focal point of industrial Bradford. I include a route here that traces the remnants of Cliff Wood, Bolton Woods and those of Wrose and Idle, before returning along the former line of the open sewer that the Bradford Canal was for so long. The woods to the east of the city are covered in previous chapters, while Royds Hall and Shelf Woods are included in my previous book on the Calder Valley, leaving a few pockets of ancient woodland to the north-west of the city. Though ravaged by mining and quarrying, Northcliffe and Heaton Woods, along with the woods around Chellow Dean Reservoirs, form richly wooded valleys where the city disappears completely. Each is looked after by its own community group, helping ensure there are still wooded landscapes to be enjoyed in the city.

*the Bradford Boar*

# MAP 26: NORTHCLIFFE & HEATON WOODS

Though only covering a small area between Shipley and Bradford, the ancient woodlands of Northcliffe, Royds Cliff and Old Spring Woods, as well as the younger parts of Heaton Woods, are full of mine workings and fascinating to explore. They are arranged around two small valleys, Red Beck and Northcliffe Dike, running down to Frizinghall and easily accessed from all sides.

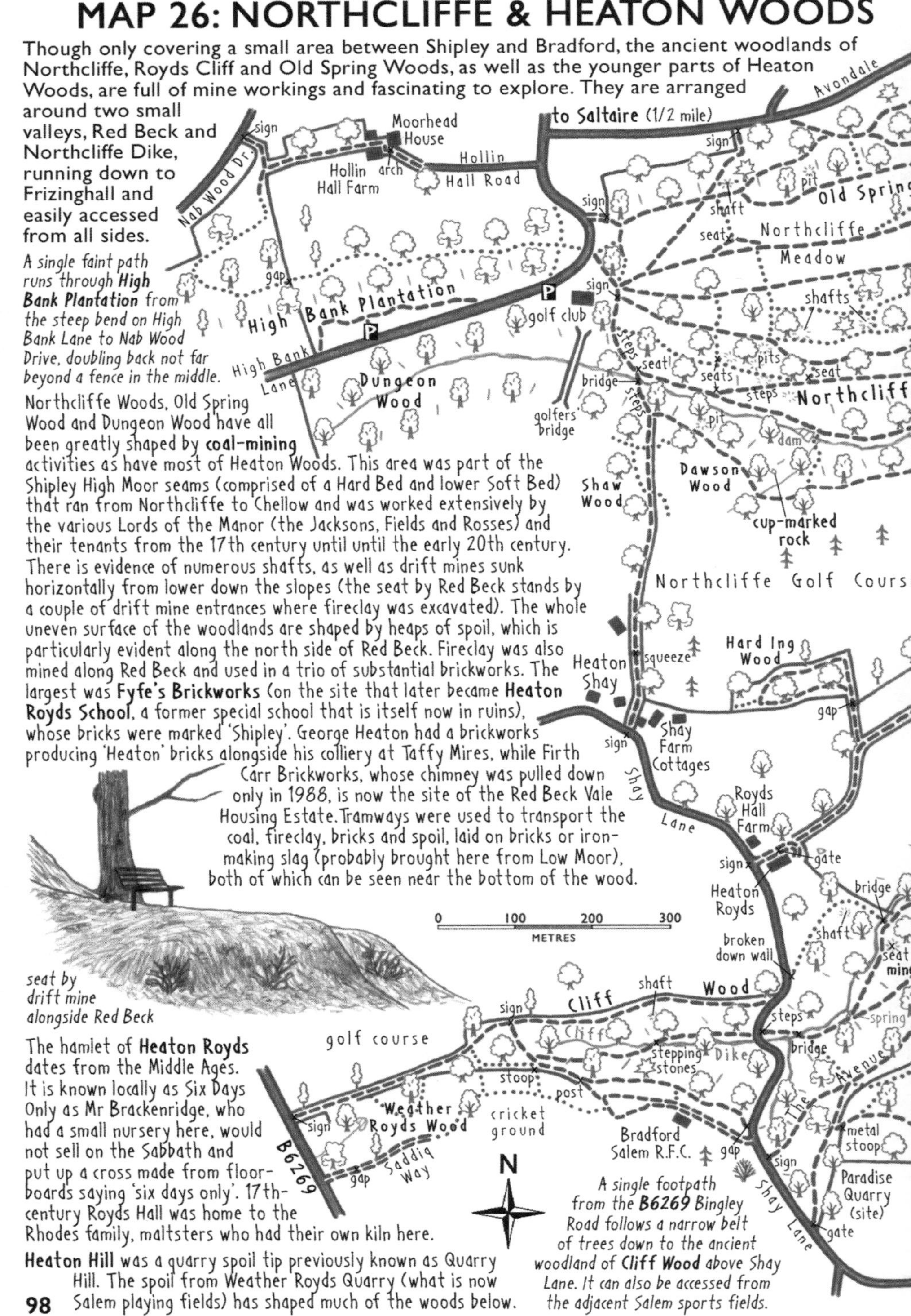

Avondale
to Saltaire (1/2 mile)
sign
Moorhead House
Hollin Hall Farm
arch
Hollin Hall Road
Nab Wood Dr.
sign
Old Spring
pit
shaft
seat
Northcliffe
Meadow
gap
sign
shafts
High Bank Plantation
golf club
High Bank Lane
steps
seat
pits
seats
seat
bridge
steps
Northcliffe
Dungeon Wood
golfers' bridge
pit
dam
Dawson Wood
Shaw Wood
cup-marked rock
Northcliffe Golf Course
Hard Ing Wood
Heaton Shay
squeeze
gap
sign
Shay Farm Cottages
Shay Lane
Royds Hall Farm
sign
gate
Heaton Royds
bridge
0 100 200 300
METRES
shaft
broken down wall
seat &
mine
seat by drift mine alongside Red Beck
shaft
Cliff Wood
sign
Cliff
steps
spring
golf course
stepping stones
Dike
bridge
The Avenue
stoop
post
Weather Royds Wood
cricket ground
sign
B6269
Saddia Way
gap
N
Bradford Salem R.F.C.
gap
sign
metal stoop
Paradise Quarry (site)
gate
Shay Lane


*A single faint path runs through* ***High Bank Plantation*** *from the steep bend on High Bank Lane to Nab Wood Drive, doubling back not far beyond a fence in the middle.*

Northcliffe Woods, Old Spring Wood and Dungeon Wood have all been greatly shaped by **coal-mining** activities as have most of Heaton Woods. This area was part of the Shipley High Moor seams (comprised of a Hard Bed and lower Soft Bed) that ran from Northcliffe to Chellow and was worked extensively by the various Lords of the Manor (the Jacksons, Fields and Rosses) and their tenants from the 17th century until until the early 20th century. There is evidence of numerous shafts, as well as drift mines sunk horizontally from lower down the slopes (the seat by Red Beck stands by a couple of drift mine entrances where fireclay was excavated). The whole uneven surface of the woodlands are shaped by heaps of spoil, which is particularly evident along the north side of Red Beck. Fireclay was also mined along Red Beck and used in a trio of substantial brickworks. The largest was **Fyfe's Brickworks** (on the site that later became **Heaton Royds School**, a former special school that is itself now in ruins), whose bricks were marked 'Shipley'. George Heaton had a brickworks producing 'Heaton' bricks alongside his colliery at Taffy Mires, while Firth Carr Brickworks, whose chimney was pulled down only in 1988, is now the site of the Red Beck Vale Housing Estate. Tramways were used to transport the coal, fireclay, bricks and spoil, laid on bricks or iron-making slag (probably brought here from Low Moor), both of which can be seen near the bottom of the wood.

The hamlet of **Heaton Royds** dates from the Middle Ages. It is known locally as Six Days Only as Mr Brackenridge, who had a small nursery here, would not sell on the Sabbath and put up a cross made from floorboards saying 'six days only'. 17th-century Royds Hall was home to the Rhodes family, maltsters who had their own kiln here.

**Heaton Hill** was a quarry spoil tip previously known as Quarry Hill. The spoil from Weather Royds Quarry (what is now Salem playing fields) has shaped much of the woods below.

*A single footpath from the* ***B6269*** *Bingley Road follows a narrow belt of trees down to the ancient woodland of* ***Cliff Wood*** *above Shay Lane. It can also be accessed from the adjacent Salem sports fields.*

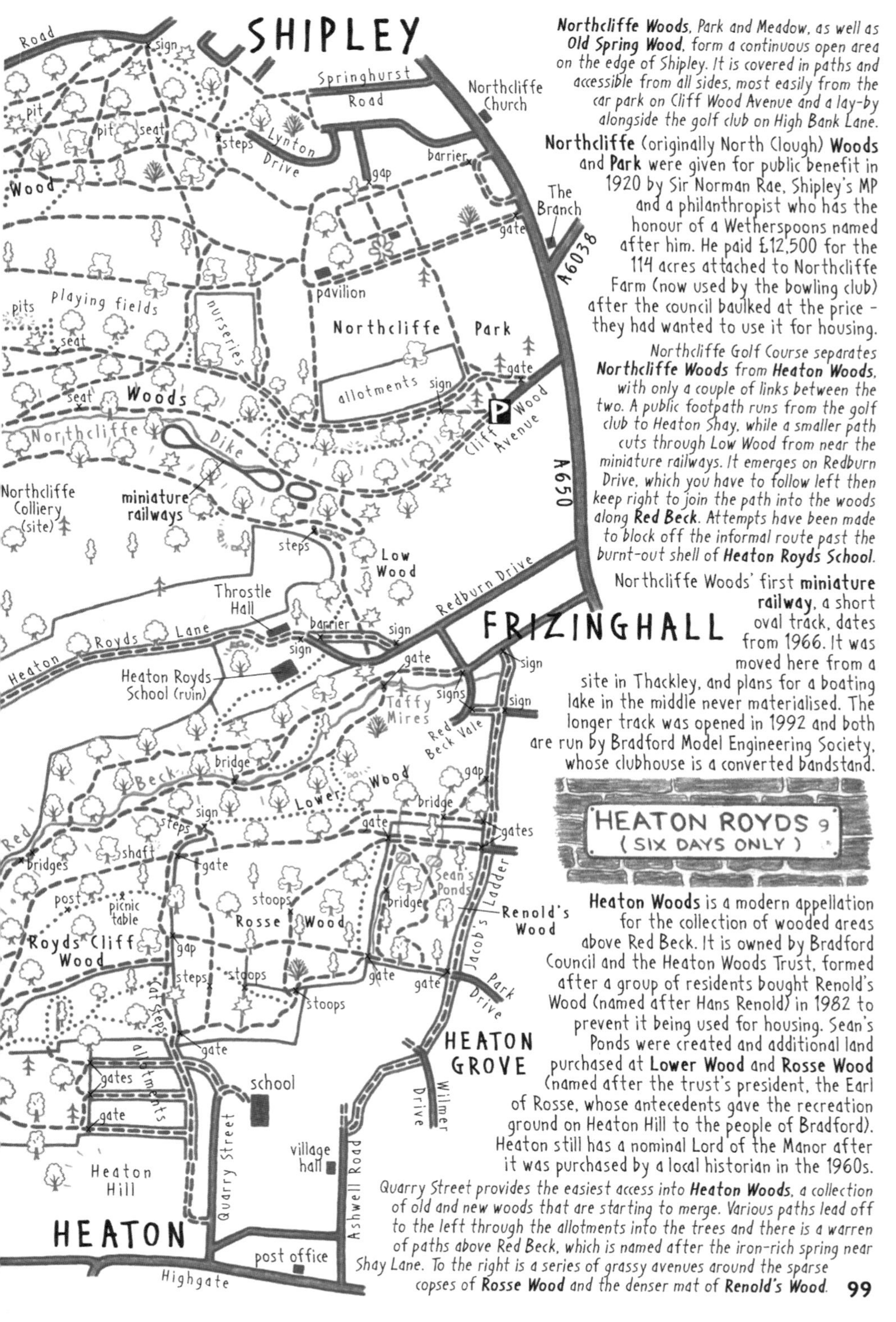

SHIPLEY
FRIZINGHALL
HEATON GROVE
HEATON
Road
sign
Springhurst Road
Northcliffe Church
Lynton Drive
pit
seat
steps
Wood
barrier
gap
The Branch
gate
A6038
pavilion
playing fields
pits
nurseries
Northcliffe Park
allotments
Woods
Cliff Wood Avenue
Northcliffe Dike
A650
Northcliffe Colliery (site)
miniature railways
Low Wood
Throstle Hall
Redburn Drive
Heaton Royds Lane
Heaton Royds School (ruin)
Taffy Mires
signs
Red Beck Vale
bridge
Red Beck
Lower Wood
shaft
bridges
post
picnic table
Royds Cliff Wood
Rosse Wood
stoops
Sean's Ponds
Renold's Wood
Jacob's Ladder
gates
Park Drive
Cat Steps
allotments
school
Quarry Street
village hall
Ashwell Road
Wilmer Drive
Heaton Hill
post office
Highgate
HEATON ROYDS 9
( SIX DAYS ONLY )


**Northcliffe Woods**, Park and Meadow, as well as **Old Spring Wood**, form a continuous open area on the edge of Shipley. It is covered in paths and accessible from all sides, most easily from the car park on Cliff Wood Avenue and a lay-by alongside the golf club on High Bank Lane.

**Northcliffe** (originally North Clough) **Woods** and **Park** were given for public benefit in 1920 by Sir Norman Rae, Shipley's MP and a philanthropist who has the honour of a Wetherspoons named after him. He paid £12,500 for the 114 acres attached to Northcliffe Farm (now used by the bowling club) after the council baulked at the price – they had wanted to use it for housing.

*Northcliffe Golf Course separates* ***Northcliffe Woods*** *from* ***Heaton Woods****, with only a couple of links between the two. A public footpath runs from the golf club to Heaton Shay, while a smaller path cuts through Low Wood from near the miniature railways. It emerges on Redburn Drive, which you have to follow left then keep right to join the path into the woods along* ***Red Beck****. Attempts have been made to block off the informal route past the burnt-out shell of* ***Heaton Royds School****.*

Northcliffe Woods' first **miniature railway**, a short oval track, dates from 1966. It was moved here from a site in Thackley, and plans for a boating lake in the middle never materialised. The longer track was opened in 1992 and both are run by Bradford Model Engineering Society, whose clubhouse is a converted bandstand.

**Heaton Woods** is a modern appellation for the collection of wooded areas above Red Beck. It is owned by Bradford Council and the Heaton Woods Trust, formed after a group of residents bought Renold's Wood (named after Hans Renold) in 1982 to prevent it being used for housing. Sean's Ponds were created and additional land purchased at **Lower Wood** and **Rosse Wood** (named after the trust's president, the Earl of Rosse, whose antecedents gave the recreation ground on Heaton Hill to the people of Bradford). Heaton still has a nominal Lord of the Manor after it was purchased by a local historian in the 1960s.

*Quarry Street provides the easiest access into* ***Heaton Woods****, a collection of old and new woods that are starting to merge. Various paths lead off to the left through the allotments into the trees and there is a warren of paths above Red Beck, which is named after the iron-rich spring near Shay Lane. To the right is a series of grassy avenues around the sparse copses of* ***Rosse Wood*** *and the denser mat of* ***Renold's Wood****.*

*Chellow Dean is most commonly accessed from the small car park at* ***Sandy Lane****, from where good paths head down through the varied woods and encircle both* ***Chellow Dean Reservoirs****.*

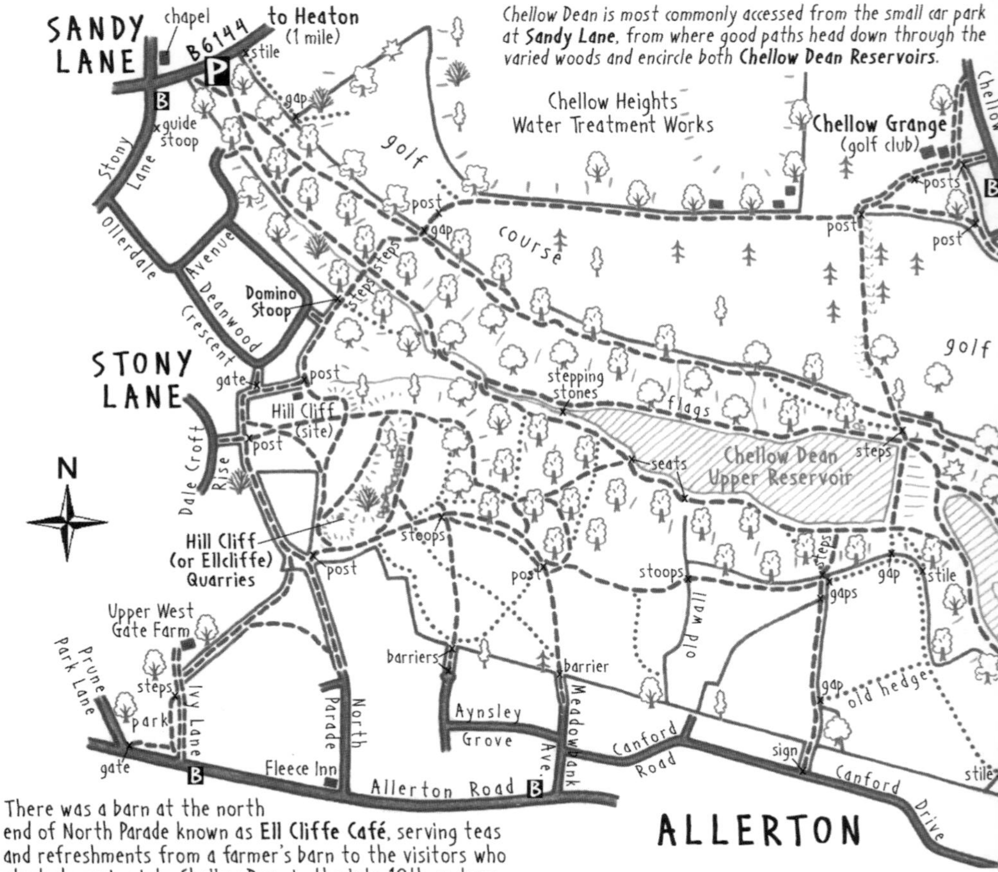

SANDY LANE
chapel
B6144
to Heaton (1 mile)
P
stile
B
guide stoop
Stony Lane
gap
golf
course
Chellow Heights Water Treatment Works
Chellow Grange (golf club)
Chellow
posts
post
B
Ollerdale Avenue
Deanwood Crescent
Domino Stoop
steps
post
gap
STONY LANE
gate
post
Hill Cliff (site)
stepping stones
flags
Chellow Dean Upper Reservoir
steps
seats
golf
Dale Croft Rise
post
N
Hill Cliff (or Ellcliffe) Quarries
stoops
post
stoops
steps
gap
stile
gaps
Upper West Gate Farm
Prune Park Lane
steps
park
Ivy Lane
gate
B
barriers
barrier
old wall
gap
old hedge
North Parade
Aynsley Grove
Meadowbank Ave.
Canford Road
sign
Canford Drive
stile
Fleece Inn
Allerton Road
B
ALLERTON


There was a barn at the north end of North Parade known as **Ell Cliffe Café**, serving teas and refreshments from a farmer's barn to the visitors who started pouring into Chellow Dean in the late 19th century.

*The meadows on the south side of Chellow Dean are all openly accessible and allow plenty of exploration above the treeline, particularly around* ***Ellcliffe Quarries****. There are many access points from* ***Allerton****, from the park at the top of the village all the way down to the roundabout at the bottom of the hill where Allerton Road meets Pearson Lane.*

The **Chellow Dean Reservoirs** were built as storage reservoirs by the Bradford Corporation after a water shortage in the city; the Upper Reservoir in 1844 and the Lower Reservoir in 1853. They no longer provide drinking water though, having failed to meet safety standards in 1975, and are now maintained solely for recreational use. The Lower Reservoir is notable as the only site in Yorkshire where the rare rusty-back fern is known to grow.

*Domino Stoop*

The **Chellow Heights Water Treatment Works** is the end of the Nidd Aqueduct, which transport over 20 million gallons of water a day from Scar House and Angram Reservoirs in Nidderdale and Chelker Reservoir near Addingham. The aqueduct crosses both Wharfedale and Airedale on its 30-mile journey to Bradford. The River Nidd was first dammed by the City of Bradford in the 1890s, such was the demand for water from a city that had little of its own natural supply. Water was originally piped from Manywells Spring near Cullingworth and the moorland reservoirs above Denholme, but these were insufficient to service this growing city. Chellow Heights now supplies water to all of Bradford and parts of Morley, Brighouse and Dewsbury.

**Chellow Dean Wetlands** were created in 2005 when Chellow Dean Beck was diverted to create several small ponds, improving biodiversity and attracting wildlife like dippers, herons and dragonflies.

*a grey heron*

# MAP 27: CHELLOW DEAN

Chellow Dean covers only a small area amid the north-western sprawl of Bradford, but it is a beautiful sanctuary within the city. Now an SSSI, the varied oak, beech and ash woodland forms a thin strip along the valley bottom and around the two Chellow Dean Reservoirs, and there are plenty of open areas to explore above the trees. The stream and thin belt of woodland continue downstream beyond Allerton Road to the newly created Chellow Dean Wetlands, providing a two-mile corridor of greenery that is easily accessed from Sandy Lane, Allerton, Daisy Hill and Fairweather Green.

*Chellow Dean can be accessed from **Daisy Hill Lane** by a couple of paths that cross some open meadows before skirting around either side of the **golf course**. Heading down the hill brings you to the lower reservoir via a lovely wooded corridor, while the path along the top edge of the golf course is less interesting.*

**Chellow Grange** was a Georgian manor house built in the 1720s by Edward Bolling of Bolling Hall. In the 19th century it was a boarding school, and it is now the clubhouse of West Bradford Golf Club. The name's origins lie in the Middle Ages, when there was a monasterial grange on this site owned by Selby Abbey – this sheep farm would have provided valuable income to the monks

The **workhouse** at **Daisy Hill** was built in 1913 to house paupers and now forms part of Lynfield Mount Psychiatric Hospital. Hill Top Cottages, arranged around a green the other side of Heights Lane, were built at a similar time for older paupers.

The mansion at **Wellwood** was pulled down to make way for a housing estate, leaving only its lodge.

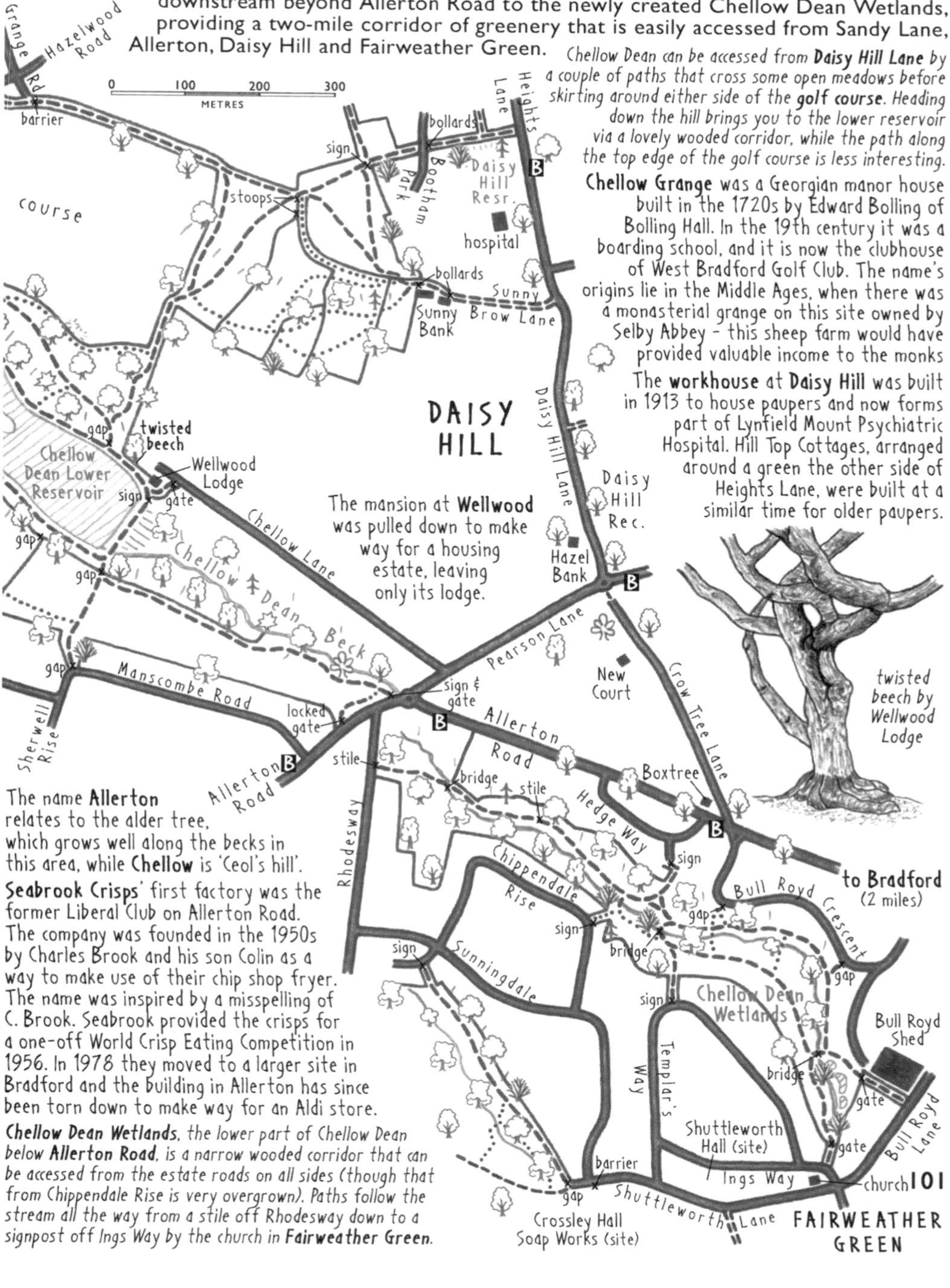

twisted beech by Wellwood Lodge

The name **Allerton** relates to the alder tree, which grows well along the becks in this area, while **Chellow** is 'Ceol's hill'.

**Seabrook Crisps**' first factory was the former Liberal Club on Allerton Road. The company was founded in the 1950s by Charles Brook and his son Colin as a way to make use of their chip shop fryer. The name was inspired by a misspelling of C. Brook. Seabrook provided the crisps for a one-off World Crisp Eating Competition in 1956. In 1978 they moved to a larger site in Bradford and the building in Allerton has since been torn down to make way for an Aldi store.

***Chellow Dean Wetlands**, the lower part of Chellow Dean below **Allerton Road**, is a narrow wooded corridor that can be accessed from the estate roads on all sides (though that from Chippendale Rise is very overgrown). Paths follow the stream all the way from a stile off Rhodesway down to a signpost off Ings Way by the church in **Fairweather Green**.*

# ROUTE 16: HIRST WOOD, CHELLOW DEAN & NORTHCLIFFE WOODS FROM SALTAIRE

**2** There are a myriad of ways through **Hirst Wood** and few landmarks, though it is neatly sandwiched between the railway and canal. If you fork right immediately through the gate into the wood, you will either end up alongside the canal or following a pleasant path parallel to it. If you reach a larger path, fork right and all routes lead down to the end of **Seven Arches Aqueduct**, carrying the canal over the River Aire. Bear left down the bank to the left of the aqueduct, cross the goit, then follow a faint path left along the river bank. Join a larger path to continue beneath the railway, then turn second left over a stile to emerge at the end of **Branksome Drive**.

The imposing **Victoria Hall** opened in 1871 as the Saltaire Club & Institute, a centre for recreation, culture and learning. Costing £25,000, it housed a library, lecture theatre, concert hall, gymnasium, billiard rooms and even a rifle range.

**3** Follow **Branksome Drive** left to its end, cross the main road and take the right-hand of two roads opposite, New Close Road. Turn immediately right at a sign and follow the tarmac footpath all the way round Cottingley Academy. It reaches the road on the edge of **Cottingley**, where you cross the B6146 and then turn right at the roundabout up **Cottingley Moor Road**. At the end of the school fence turn left through a gate and follow a path that bends round to run parallel to the road to reach North Bank Road. A few yards to the right, turn left on another path that joins a vehicle track to return to Cottingley Moor Road at the edge of **Sandy Lane**.

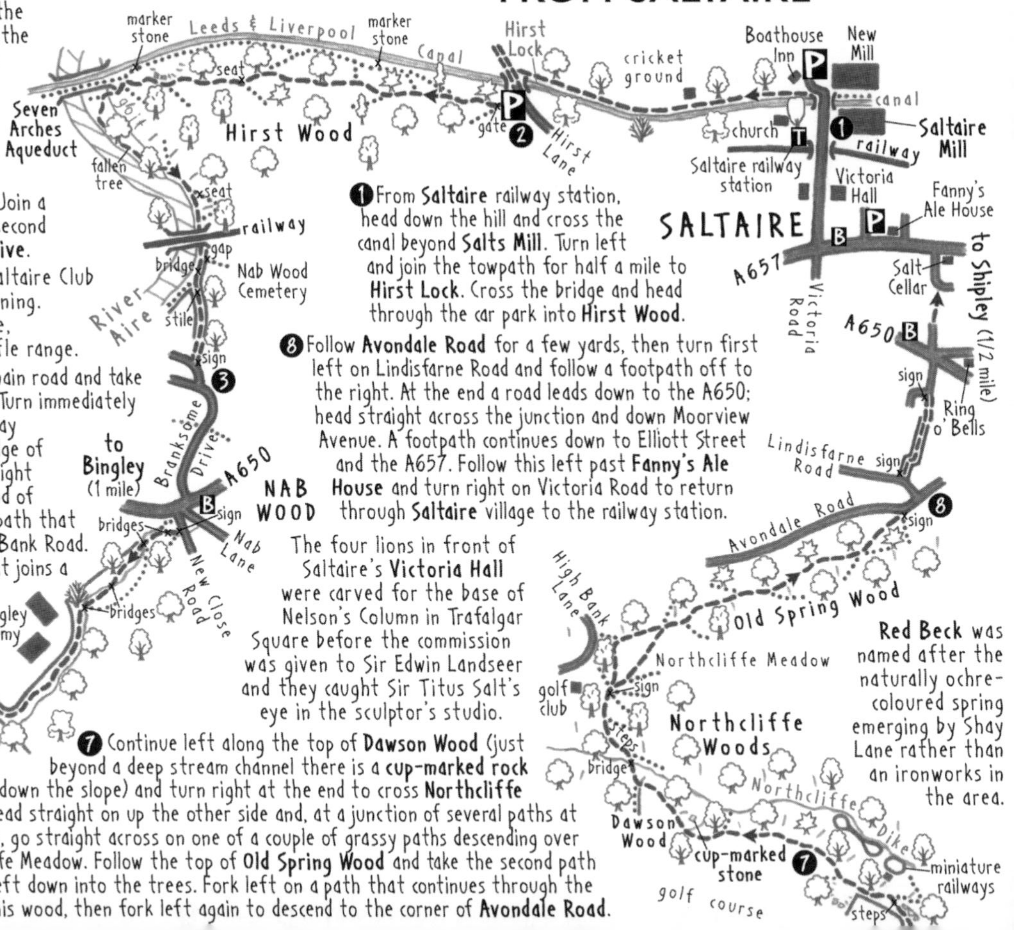

one of the Cottingley Fairies

**1** From **Saltaire** railway station, head down the hill and cross the canal beyond **Salts Mill**. Turn left and join the towpath for half a mile to **Hirst Lock**. Cross the bridge and head through the car park into **Hirst Wood**.

**8** Follow **Avondale Road** for a few yards, then turn first left on Lindisfarne Road and follow a footpath off to the right. At the end a road leads down to the A650; head straight across the junction and down Moorview Avenue. A footpath continues down to Elliott Street and the A657. Follow this left past **Fanny's Ale House** and turn right on Victoria Road to return through **Saltaire** village to the railway station.

The four lions in front of Saltaire's **Victoria Hall** were carved for the base of Nelson's Column in Trafalgar Square before the commission was given to Sir Edwin Landseer and they caught Sir Titus Salt's eye in the sculptor's studio.

**Red Beck** was named after the naturally ochre-coloured spring emerging by Shay Lane rather than an ironworks in the area.

**7** Continue left along the top of **Dawson Wood** (just beyond a deep stream channel there is a **cup-marked rock** down the slope) and turn right at the end to cross **Northcliffe Dike**. Head straight on up the other side and, at a junction of several paths at the top, go straight across on one of a couple of grassy paths descending over Northcliffe Meadow. Follow the top of **Old Spring Wood** and take the second path bearing left down into the trees. Fork left on a path that continues through the heart of this wood, then fork left again to descend to the corner of **Avondale Road**.


Leeds & Liverpool Canal
marker stone
marker stone
Hirst Lock
Hirst Lane
gate
seat
Seven Arches Aqueduct
goit
fallen tree
Hirst Wood
railway
gap
bridge
stile
River Aire
Nab Wood Cemetery
sign
Branksome Drive
to Bingley (1 mile)
A650
NAB WOOD
Nab Lane
New Close Road
bridges
Cottingley Academy
COTTINGLEY
Main St
sign
Sun Inn (former)
Cottingley Beck
school
Cottingley Moor Road
gate
hut
cricket ground
Boathouse Inn
New Mill
canal
Saltaire Mill
church
railway
Saltaire railway station
Victoria Hall
Fanny's Ale House
SALTAIRE
A657
Victoria Road
Salt Cellar
to Shipley (1/2 mile)
A650
Ring o' Bells
Lindisfarne Road
Avondale Road
Old Spring Wood
High Bank Lane
Northcliffe Meadow
golf club
Northcliffe Woods
steps
bridge
Dawson Wood
cup-marked stone
Northcliffe Dike
miniature railways
golf course
steps

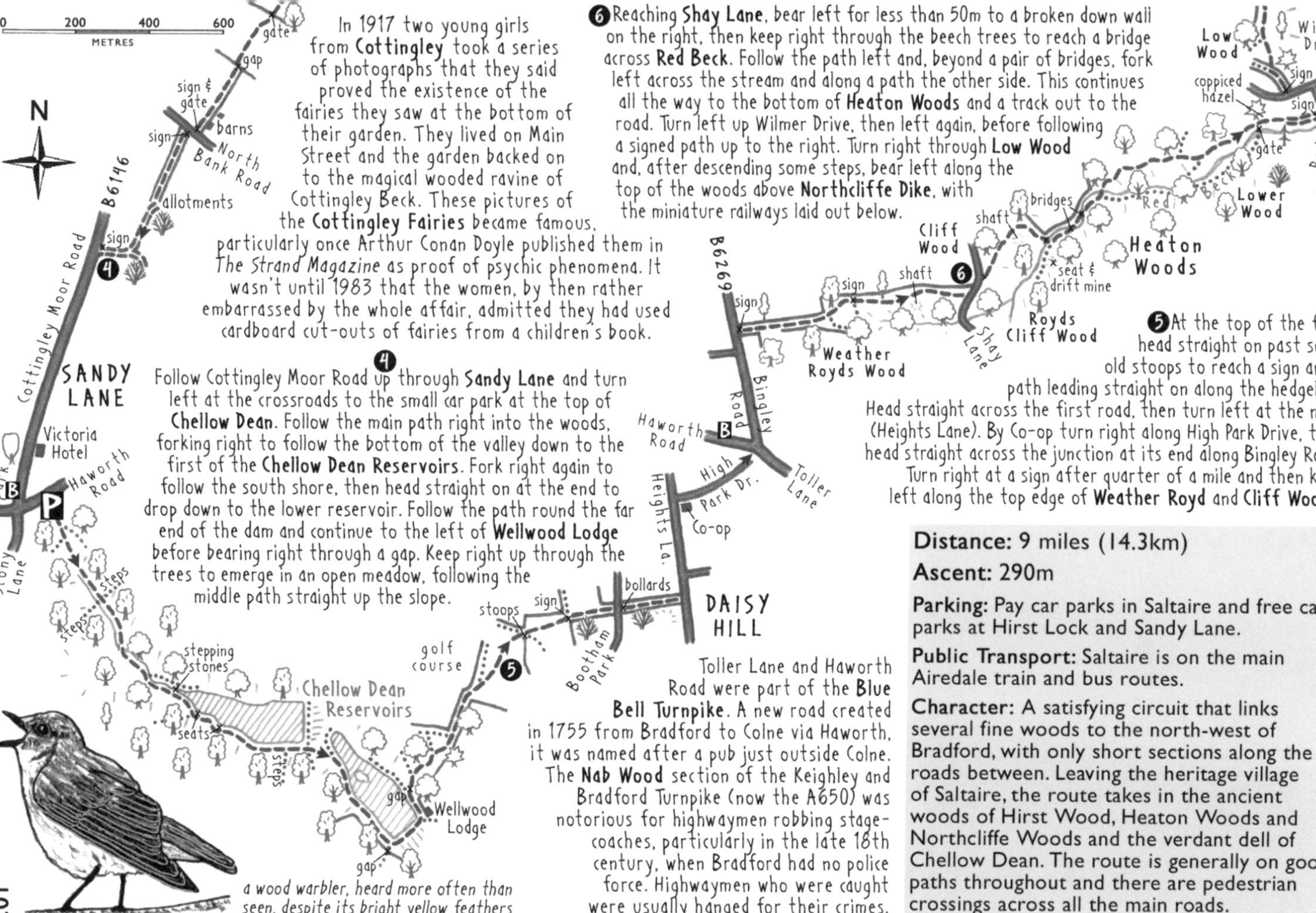
0 200 400 600
METRES
N
B6146
Cottingley Moor Road
SANDY LANE
Victoria Hotel
Park
B
P
Haworth Road
Stony Lane
sign
allotments
sign
barns
North Bank Road
sign & gate
gap
gate
steps
stepping stones
seats
Chellow Dean Reservoirs
steps
gap
Wellwood Lodge
gap
golf course
stoops
sign
bollards
Bootham Park
DAISY HILL
Heights La.
Co-op
High Park Dr.
Haworth Road
B
Bingley Road
Toller Lane
B6269
sign
Weather Royds Wood
sign
shaft
Cliff Wood
shaft
Shay Lane
Royds Cliff Wood
seat & drift mine
bridges
Heaton Woods
Red Beck
Lower Wood
gate
coppiced hazel
Low Wood
sign
sign
Wilmer Drive
Red Beck Vale

In 1917 two young girls from **Cottingley** took a series of photographs that they said proved the existence of the fairies they saw at the bottom of their garden. They lived on Main Street and the garden backed on to the magical wooded ravine of Cottingley Beck. These pictures of the **Cottingley Fairies** became famous, particularly once Arthur Conan Doyle published them in *The Strand Magazine* as proof of psychic phenomena. It wasn't until 1983 that the women, by then rather embarrassed by the whole affair, admitted they had used cardboard cut-outs of fairies from a children's book.

**4** Follow Cottingley Moor Road up through **Sandy Lane** and turn left at the crossroads to the small car park at the top of **Chellow Dean**. Follow the main path right into the woods, forking right to follow the bottom of the valley down to the first of the **Chellow Dean Reservoirs**. Fork right again to follow the south shore, then head straight on at the end to drop down to the lower reservoir. Follow the path round the far end of the dam and continue to the left of **Wellwood Lodge** before bearing right through a gap. Keep right up through the trees to emerge in an open meadow, following the middle path straight up the slope.

*a wood warbler, heard more often than seen, despite its bright yellow feathers*

**5** At the top of the field head straight on past some old stoops to reach a sign and a path leading straight on along the hedgeline. Head straight across the first road, then turn left at the next (Heights Lane). By Co-op turn right along High Park Drive, then head straight across the junction at its end along Bingley Road. Turn right at a sign after quarter of a mile and then keep left along the top edge of **Weather Royd** and **Cliff Woods**.

**6** Reaching **Shay Lane**, bear left for less than 50m to a broken down wall on the right, then keep right through the beech trees to reach a bridge across **Red Beck**. Follow the path left and, beyond a pair of bridges, fork left across the stream and along a path the other side. This continues all the way to the bottom of **Heaton Woods** and a track out to the road. Turn left up Wilmer Drive, then left again, before following a signed path up to the right. Turn right through **Low Wood** and, after descending some steps, bear left along the top of the woods above **Northcliffe Dike**, with the miniature railways laid out below.

Toller Lane and Haworth Road were part of the **Blue Bell Turnpike**. A new road created in 1755 from Bradford to Colne via Haworth, it was named after a pub just outside Colne. The **Nab Wood** section of the Keighley and Bradford Turnpike (now the A650) was notorious for highwaymen robbing stage-coaches, particularly in the late 18th century, when Bradford had no police force. Highwaymen who were caught were usually hanged for their crimes.

**Distance:** 9 miles (14.3km)

**Ascent:** 290m

**Parking:** Pay car parks in Saltaire and free car parks at Hirst Lock and Sandy Lane.

**Public Transport:** Saltaire is on the main Airedale train and bus routes.

**Character:** A satisfying circuit that links several fine woods to the north-west of Bradford, with only short sections along the roads between. Leaving the heritage village of Saltaire, the route takes in the ancient woods of Hirst Wood, Heaton Woods and Northcliffe Woods and the verdant dell of Chellow Dean. The route is generally on good paths throughout and there are pedestrian crossings across all the main roads.

# TREE PLAGUE & PESTILENCE

While we battle global pandemics, the plant kingdom is having its own reckoning with disease. Though tree plagues are nothing new – elms were first wiped out in Britain around 4,000 years ago – there is no doubt they are becoming increasingly common and widespread. Oliver Rackham has suggested that as many tree diseases have appeared since the 1970s as during the whole of Britain's history since it became an island. He places the blame on globalisation and the largely unrestricted movement of non-native plants and trees around the world, bringing fungi and insects with no predators, and which our native species are often not equipped to deal with. However, there is little doubt that climate change has also played a part; it is something trees can adapt to but not at the rate of change seen over the last few years.

Among the more benign infestations are oak galls, a fruit-like growth on oak leaves that allows gall wasp larvae to hatch and grow. Known as oak apples, they don't greatly harm the host tree, other than perhaps causing an early shedding of leaves. Tar spot is similarly benign, a fungus that produces black spots on the leaves of sycamores and maples, but doesn't pose a great threat to the tree's health.

an oak gall

However, the arrival of Dutch elm disease in Britain in the 1920s represented something far more dangerous. By the time it reached Yorkshire in the 1970s it had developed a particularly aggressive strain that wiped out almost the entire population of the English elm. A fungus spread by the elm bark beetle, it was first discovered in the Netherlands rather than necessarily originating there. There were once many elm woods in the Aire Valley, inspiring the names of Oak & Elm Wood and Elm Avenue at Temple Newsam, and the local Celtic kingdom of Elmet.

Ash dieback disease, caused by the fungus *Hymenoscyphus fraxineus*, was written about in the 1980s, but attention has only really been paid to it in the last decade, by which time it may be too late. It causes black spots on the leaves, wilting leaves and diamond lesions on the bark, and spreads with such ease that it is moving apace across the country from the south-east, threatening to wipe out the country's eighty million ash trees in a generation. The ash is also vulnerable to the emerald ash borer, an Asian beetle that has swept across the United States, prompting the release of millions of Chinese wasps to feed on it and slow its spread.

Acute oak decline is caused by changing environmental conditions, like waterlogging, drought and pollution, which can weaken the trees and make them susceptible to attack from a variety of insets, bacteria and fungi. It has been noticed in the UK since the 1990s, though it is more common in the warmer southern parts of England and Wales. It can cause a thinning crown and dark, weeping cracks running up the tree, and lead to death in less than five years, particularly in mature oaks. Oaks are also susceptible to sudden oak death, a bleeding canker on the trunk caused by the mould *Phytophthora ramorum*, which also affects firs, beech, rhododendrons and, most alarmingly, the larch. The larch is in real danger of being wiped out and, in Betty's Wood at St Ives near Bingley, a large infected area was recently felled to prevent its spread. A similar disease has greatly affected the horse chestnut in recent years, bleeding canker resulting in a dark liquid oozing from cracks in the bark.

Even the sycamore, that great survivor and probably the most populous tree in West Yorkshire, is under threat. Sooty bark disease is a fungus that lives in the wood of the sycamore and maple but only acts upon a tree when it is under strain. Recent hot, dry summers have put undue drought stress upon sycamores, leading to bark shedding, wilting and branches dying back. Interestingly it can also cause inflammation in humans' lungs, as can the oak processionary moth, which has begun to spread from London – the hairs of its caterpillar can cause nasty rashes and breathing difficulties.

However, it is not all doom and gloom. The Asian long-horned beetle, which is highly destructive to both oak and birch and thought to have been brought here in infested packaging, has recently been eradicated from the UK and it is hoped new bio-security rules will prevent further infestation by this and similar diseases.

# ROUTE 17: BRADFORD BECK, BOLTON WOODS & WROSE HILL FROM BRADFORD

This is a complicated but satisfying route that links several historical woods between Bradford city centre and Idle, before returning along the line of the former Bradford Canal. What might seem convoluted is actually a great walk that gives a different perspective on this grand city. It is spread over 3 pages, with a more detailed overview overleaf.

**5** Continue along the fence and straight on through **Wrose Brow Plantation**. Where the path eventually crosses the top of **Carr Mires Beck**, turn right up the steps, then go left along Low Ash Road. Turn left on a narrow path after the houses and descend to follow a good path through the heart of **Catstones Wood**. Beyond a gate at the far end contour across the slope to reach a stile in the far left corner of the field. Turn right on **High Busy Lane**, then go immediately right through a gap to wind through the young trees. Reaching High Busy Lane again on the edge of Idle, go through a gap to the left of **Carcase End Farm** and descend across the field to a gate above the new estate.

**6** Follow the path straight down through the housing estate, then turn right along the walled path of **Perkin Lane** at the bottom. Turn left at the end then head straight across a new road and follow the track through Cote to reach the A657 in **Thackley**. Follow it right for a few yards, then cut left on an unsigned path past Glebe House. Turn right at the end, then go left onto the former railway, turning right then left to join a road the other side. Turn second left along Brackendale and bear right at a sign to follow a path (signed Buck Mill Lane).

**7** Turn left along the edge of **Buck Wood** and descend to cross the Leeds & Liverpool Canal. Continue down and cross the **River Aire**, following a path left along its far bank. This continues for over a mile to the edge of Shipley, or you can explore the **Denso Marston Nature Reserve** as paths branch off right after the first gate. After going beneath a railway bridge cross the river via the next bridge and follow the road to its end by the canal. Follow the towpath right past Dockfield Mills and cross the second bridge (Gallows Bridge) to emerge opposite **Shipley**'s labyrinthine railway station. You can either get the train back to Bradford here or follow the onward route described overleaf.

An elm tree was planted on **Wrose**'s old village green in 1867 as the focal point of the village. When it succumbed to Dutch Elm Disease in 2000, a message in a bottle beneath it was uncovered.

A hoard of Roman coins was found at the top of **Catstones Wood** when during quarrying in the late 18th century. There is thought to have been a Roman station on Idle Hill, now the site of a transmitter mast, and possible a Roman Road running along what is now High Busy Lane. The name **Idle** probably relates to a piece of useless, uncultivable land.

CONTINUED OVERLEAF

# ROUTE 17 (continued)

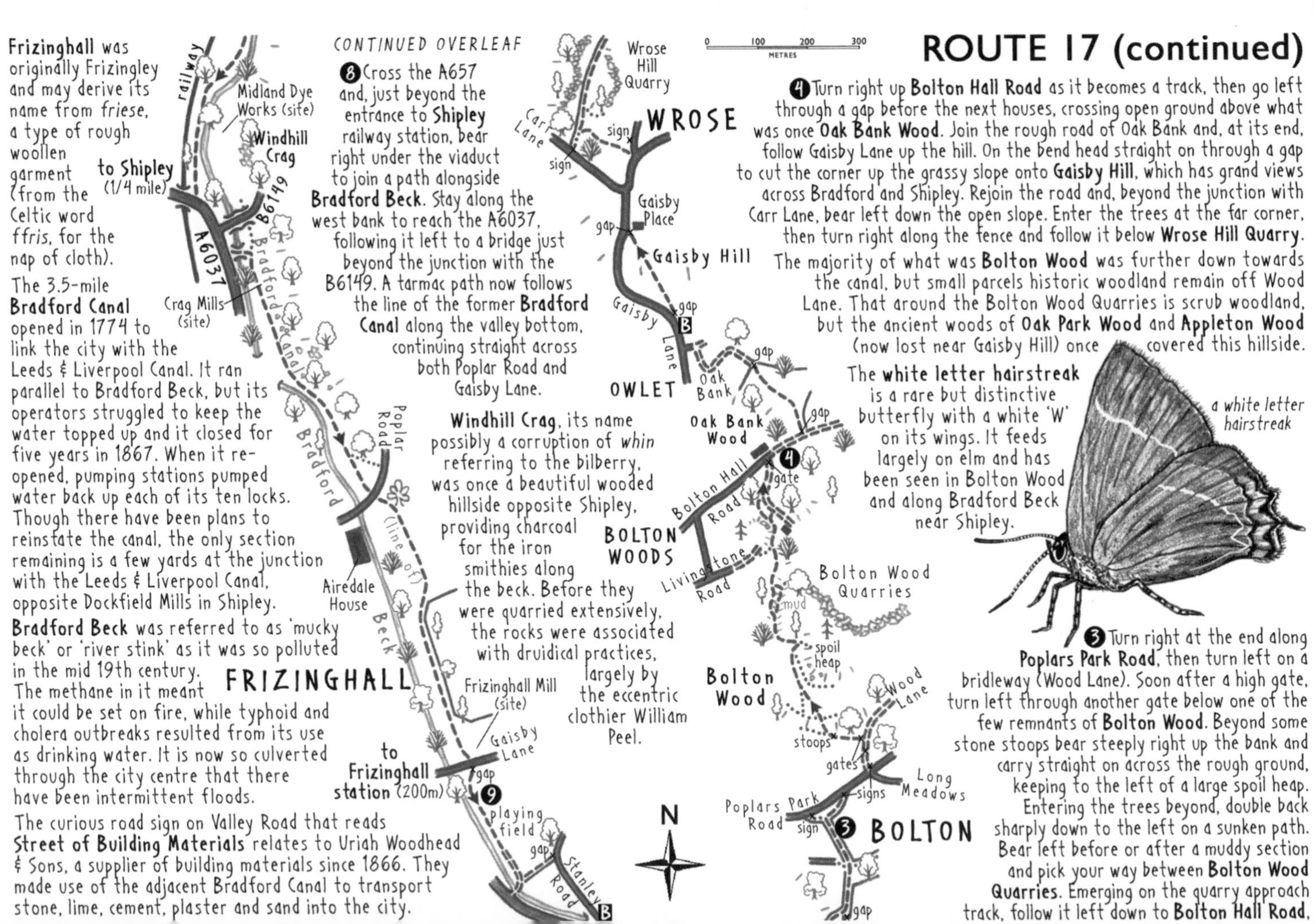
0 100 200 300
METRES
Wrose Hill Quarry
WROSE
Carr Lane
sign
sign
Gaisby Place
gap
Gaisby Hill
Gaisby Lane
gap
B
OWLET
Oak Bank
gap
Oak Bank Wood
gap
4
gate
Bolton Hall Road
BOLTON WOODS
Livingstone Road
Bolton Wood Quarries
mud
spoil heap
Bolton Wood
Wood Lane
stoops
gates
Long Meadows
signs
Poplars Park Road
sign
3
BOLTON
gap
N
railway
Midland Dye Works (site)
Windhill Crag
to Shipley (1/4 mile)
B6149
A6037
Bradford Canal
Crag Mills (site)
Poplar Road
Bradford Beck
(line of)
Airedale House
FRIZINGHALL
Frizinghall Mill (site)
Gaisby Lane
to Frizinghall station (200m)
gap
9
playing field
gap
Stanley Road
B
a white letter hairstreak

**4** Turn right up **Bolton Hall Road** as it becomes a track, then go left through a gap before the next houses, crossing open ground above what was once **Oak Bank Wood**. Join the rough road of Oak Bank and, at its end, follow Gaisby Lane up the hill. On the bend head straight on through a gap to cut the corner up the grassy slope onto **Gaisby Hill**, which has grand views across Bradford and Shipley. Rejoin the road and, beyond the junction with Carr Lane, bear left down the open slope. Enter the trees at the far corner, then turn right along the fence and follow it below **Wrose Hill Quarry**.

The majority of what was **Bolton Wood** was further down towards the canal, but small parcels historic woodland remain off Wood Lane. That around the Bolton Wood Quarries is scrub woodland, but the ancient woods of **Oak Park Wood** and **Appleton Wood** (now lost near Gaisby Hill) once covered this hillside.

The **white letter hairstreak** is a rare but distinctive butterfly with a white 'W' on its wings. It feeds largely on elm and has been seen in Bolton Wood and along Bradford Beck near Shipley.

**3** Turn right at the end along **Poplars Park Road**, then turn left on a bridleway (Wood Lane). Soon after a high gate, turn left through another gate below one of the few remnants of **Bolton Wood**. Beyond some stone stoops bear steeply right up the bank and carry straight on across the rough ground, keeping to the left of a large spoil heap. Entering the trees beyond, double back sharply down to the left on a sunken path. Bear left before or after a muddy section and pick your way between **Bolton Wood Quarries**. Emerging on the quarry approach track, follow it left down to **Bolton Hall Road**,

**Frizinghall** was originally Frizingley and may derive its name from *friese*, a type of rough woollen garment (from the Celtic word *ffris*, for the nap of cloth).

The 3.5-mile **Bradford Canal** opened in 1774 to link the city with the Leeds & Liverpool Canal. It ran parallel to Bradford Beck, but its operators struggled to keep the water topped up and it closed for five years in 1867. When it re-opened, pumping stations pumped water back up each of its ten locks. Though there have been plans to reinstate the canal, the only section remaining is a few yards at the junction with the Leeds & Liverpool Canal, opposite Dockfield Mills in Shipley.

**Bradford Beck** was referred to as 'mucky beck' or 'river stink' as it was so polluted in the mid 19th century. The methane in it meant it could be set on fire, while typhoid and cholera outbreaks resulted from its use as drinking water. It is now so culverted through the city centre that there have been intermittent floods.

The curious road sign on Valley Road that reads **Street of Building Materials** relates to Uriah Woodhead & Sons, a supplier of building materials since 1866. They made use of the adjacent Bradford Canal to transport stone, lime, cement, plaster and sand into the city.

*CONTINUED OVERLEAF*

**8** Cross the A657 and, just beyond the entrance to **Shipley** railway station, bear right under the viaduct to join a path alongside **Bradford Beck**. Stay along the west bank to reach the A6037, following it left to a bridge just beyond the junction with the B6149. A tarmac path now follows the line of the former **Bradford Canal** along the valley bottom, continuing straight across both Poplar Road and Gaisby Lane.

**Windhill Crag**, its name possibly a corruption of *whin* referring to the bilberry, was once a beautiful wooded hillside opposite Shipley, providing charcoal for the iron smithies along the beck. Before they were quarried extensively, the rocks were associated with druidical practices, largely by the eccentric clothier William Peel.

**9 Frizinghall railway station** is just a short distance from the route at Gaisby Lane. The onward route continues past the playing field beyond before turning left to reach Stanley Road. Follow it right to the end, then join the main **A6037**. Cross at the next pedestrian crossing, then turn right on Hillam Road soon after. At the end bear left up to Bolton Lane, following it right. Bear left across the A6177 and join Valley Road running parallel to the railway below **Bradford City's Valley Parade** ground. At the end turn right and carry straight on past Forster Square Retail Park to cross the A6181 and return to the mini-roundabout, where turning right leads back to **Bradford Forster Square** railway station.

**Boar Well** is something of a disappointing trickle today, but it was one of a pair of holy wells in Cliff Wood where the Bradford Boar was said to drink. This giant beast terrorised the town in the 14th century, killing livestock and scaring people from the wells. A reward was offered by John of Gaunt (Lord of the Manor and father of Henry VI) and the boar killed by John Northrop while it was drinking at **Spink Well**. He cut out its tongue as the head was too heavy to carry, but another man found the head and claimed the reward, before being exposed and run out of town. The boar has become the symbol of the city and features on its coat of arms *(p82)*.

*Spink Well*

**Distance:** 10 miles (15.9km) *(or 7½ miles (12km) if train caught back from Shipley)*

**Ascent:** 260m

**Parking:** Pay car parks by Bradford Forster Square and Shipley railway stations, and various street parking elsewhere.

**Public Transport:** Bradford Forster Square and Shipley stations are on the main Airedale Line, with the former only a short walk across the city centre from Bradford Interchange bus and railway station.

**Character:** Though this isn't a greatly wooded part of Bradford, there are remnants of historical woods along the hillside between the centre of Bradford and Idle. This route provides a lovely green way out of the city centre with great views throughout, before returning along the River Aire and Bradford Beck. The last 1¼ miles are along roads through the industrial estates, so you may prefer to shorten the route by taking the train from Shipley or Frizinghall back into Bradford. Navigation can be a little fiddly and some of the paths can be overgrown in summer.

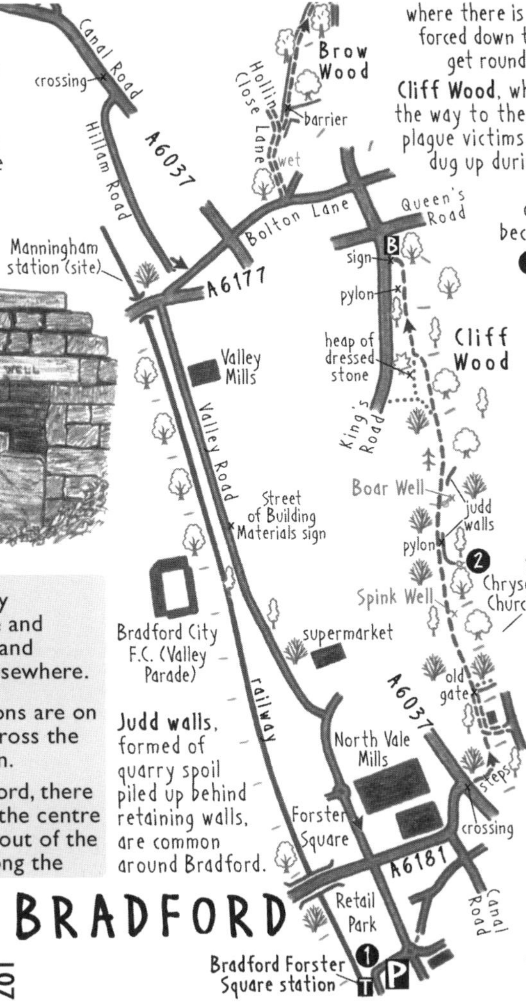

**Judd walls**, formed of quarry spoil piled up behind retaining walls, are common around Bradford.

# BRADFORD

where there is a gap to the right of the high gates. If forced down to the road sooner, simply keep right to get round to the same point on Bolton Hall Road.

**Cliff Wood**, which once stretched from Bradford all the way to the Aire, was the site of a hut built for plague victims in 1668, with their mass grave later dug up during quarry work. This quarry provided the stone for the carved monarchs on the City Hall. It has more recently become a rather sad-looking urban park.

**2** The path continues along the foot of **Cliff Wood**, once the haunt of the Bradford Boar's. You pass **Boar Well** soon after a pylon, the spring emerging unceremoniously into a waterlogged area by the path. Keep right to reach King's Road, following it right across a large junction before turning left down **Bolton Lane**. Turn right after 200m along the track of Hollin Close Lane. Bear right up a narrow path just before the house at the end and skirt along the bottom of **Brow Wood**. Turn left at the top and follow a wider path (soon tarmacked) between the housing estates.

**1** From **Bradford Forster Square** railway station, follow the approach road left past the car park to a mini-roundabout. Take the second exit, the blocked off end of Leeming Street, and follow it through the urban wasteland. Turn left at the end towards crumbling **North Vale Mills** then bear right along the main road. Where it meets the busy A6037, head straight across via a pedestrian crossing and up some steps opposite. Turn left at the top and briefly join a rough road before re-entering the trees on a path that soon passes the well-tended **Spink Well**.

# BRACKET FUNGI

Polypores are the fruit of fungi (collectively known as bracket or shelf fungi) whose mycelium feed on the heartwood of trees. All species of polypore have pores rather than gills, and they often grow very large, the giant polypore growing over 1m wide. While some are as tough as old boots as they accrete year on year, living for as long as fifty years, many of the softer annual growths are delicious to eat when young and fresh, and they have been long associated with alternative medicine. By the time these fruits appear it is too late to get rid of the fungus, which can often weaken a tree but can also serve a useful function by causing older trees to shed excess weight. Some trees, like oak and birch, defend themselves with a chemical barrier and contain the fungus within the heartwood, hence the rotten heart of many older oak trees. In other trees, like sycamore and ash, it is liable to spread through the whole tree and eventually kill it. It is thought that all ash trees contain the **shaggy bracket fungus**, an orange bracket with a hairy surface that is also found on apple trees, but it only springs to life when the tree allows it at a certain age to lighten its load.

**Birch polypore** (*Fomitopsis betulina*) is probably the UK's most common bracket fungus and is found on many birch trees. Though each fungus represents just one year's growth, older ones are often found still attached to the tree. Its legendary toughness meant it was also known as the razor strop bracket as razors could traditionally be sharpened on them.

artist's bracket

**Artist's bracket** (*Ganoderma applanatum*, or artist's conk) is a common fungus that grows mainly on dead or decaying beech or oak trees. It has distinctive annual growth rings and is brown on top, although its name relates to the white underside, which turns dark brown when scratched or written on; its Japanese name translates as 'powder-coated monkey's bench'. In the far east the newer growth is used as a flavouring and herbal remedy to benefit the immune system – indeed it is related to the 'mushroom of immortality', known as *reishi* in Japan and *lingzhi* in China.

**Dryad's saddle** (*Polyporus squamosus*, or pheasant back mushroom) is another common find, appearing in mottled brown clusters in spring and summer. They can grow very large and favour beech and sycamore. The fruit grows afresh each year rather than accumulating and its soft flesh, which smells like water melon, is edible when young. Its name relates to a tree spirit in the form of a young woman, most often associated with the oak, *drys* being oak in Greek.

**Chicken of the woods** (*Laetiporus sulphureus*, or sulphur shelf) is a bright sulphur-coloured polypore often found on decaying trees, particularly oak, sweet chestnut, willow and yew. Its texture is thought to resemble that of chicken and when fresh it is a lovely 'meaty' addition to stews, soups and stir fries.

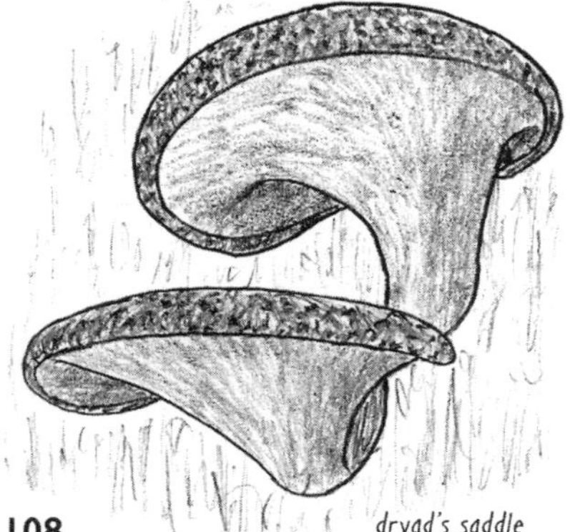
dryad's saddle

**Beefsteak fungus** (*Fistulina hepatica*, or ox tongue) is very distinctive, a rich red polypore that bleeds red when cut and looks remarkably like a raw steak. It is also delicious when cooked.

**Turkey tail** (*Trametes versicolor*) is a striking fan of colourful rings that mimics a turkey's feathers. It is thought to have medicinal properties.

**Tinder fungus** (*Fomes fomentarius* or horse's hoof fungus) ranges in colour from pale grey to black and is most likely seen on birch. Its name relates to its likely use by early people for lighting fires.

# CHAPTER 9 - BINGLEY & HARDEN BECK

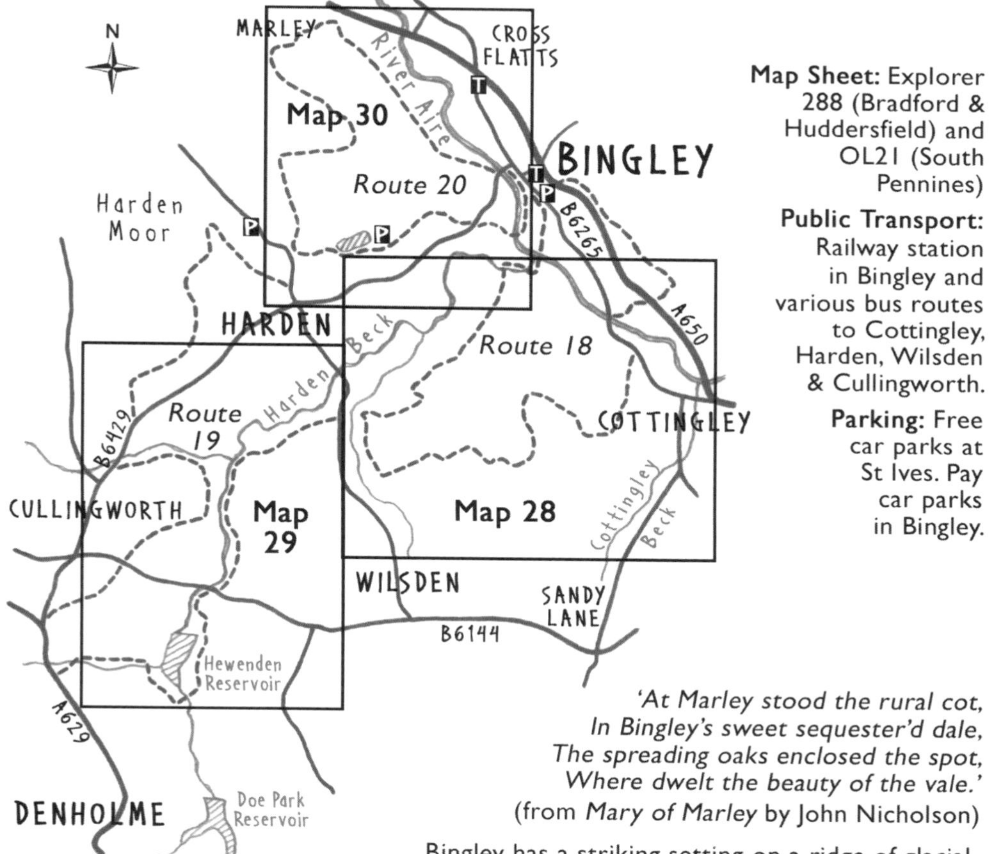
N
MARLEY
CROSS FLATTS
River Aire
Map 30
BINGLEY
Route 20
Harden Moor
B6265
A650
HARDEN
Harden Beck
Route 18
B6429
Route 19
COTTINGLEY
CULLINGWORTH
Map 29
Map 28
Cottingley Beck
WILSDEN
SANDY LANE
B6144
Hewenden Reservoir
A629
DENHOLME
Doe Park Reservoir

**Map Sheet:** Explorer 288 (Bradford & Huddersfield) and OL21 (South Pennines)

**Public Transport:** Railway station in Bingley and various bus routes to Cottingley, Harden, Wilsden & Cullingworth.

**Parking:** Free car parks at St Ives. Pay car parks in Bingley.

*'At Marley stood the rural cot,*
*In Bingley's sweet sequester'd dale,*
*The spreading oaks enclosed the spot,*
*Where dwelt the beauty of the vale.'*
(from *Mary of Marley* by John Nicholson)

Bingley has a striking setting on a ridge of glacial moraine above the River Aire, with the woods of St Ives and Cottingley laid out on the steep hillsides opposite. The A650 dual carriageway cuts rather crudely through the middle of this ancient market town, which was once known as 'the Throstle Nest of Old England' because thrushes were so abundant. A Domesday settlement, its name means 'Binna's clearing', and it is a fine place from which to explore the woods along Harden Beck.

Harden village was previously known as Halton ('hall enclosure') and was recorded as Hadelton in the Domesday Book, only later being corrupted to take the name of the valley below. Though Harden Beck is the name of the stream only below its confluence below Cullingworth (above which it is Hewenden or Hallas Beck), I use it to refer to the whole of this beautifully wooded tributary flowing from the moors above Denholme into the Aire at Beck Foot. Lined with mills from Beck Foot to Denholme, the valley was more heavily industrialised than Bingley itself, where the steep gorge of the Aire left little room for mill developments. Yet its woodlands were preserved and are particularly spectacular around the fine waterfalls in Goit Stock Woods. The estate woodlands of St Ives and Cottingley stand above either side of the valley, with large pine plantations interspersed with ancient oaks and birch.

# MAP 28: COTTINGLEY WOODS

Cottingley Woods are unique among the woods covered in this book; though composed of Scots pine and larch planted after World War II, they are forever linked to the fairies said to reside there and retain an other-worldly air. The Black Hills area, along with Wilsden Beck, Dark Wood and the tiny remnant of Fairbeards Wood, are native oak and birch woodland. Other than Blackhills Scout Campsite and the private track below Park Rocks, the woods are accessible and full of paths. They are easily explored from the edge of Cottingley, the bottom of Harden village or via Smithy Lane out of Wilsden. As well as a series of fine crags, the centrepiece is the 18th-century folly of St David's Ruin.

*the hedgehog mushroom, a pale cream and very tasty fungus that is also known as the bearded tooth or Pied du Mouton in France*

There was an early manorial corn mill for Harden near **Lawn**.

***Ruin Bank Wood** is easily accessed from Harden by forking left over Mytholme Bridge, then turning left before the bottom of the zigzags. Pass through a couple of gaps in the old walls to enter the pine plantation and follow the main path up the slope to reach **St David's Ruin**. Bearing left along the wall brings to you a couple of good paths through the heart of the wood, while a route along **Mytholme Beck** at the bottom is inaccessible without scrambling down across the stream.*

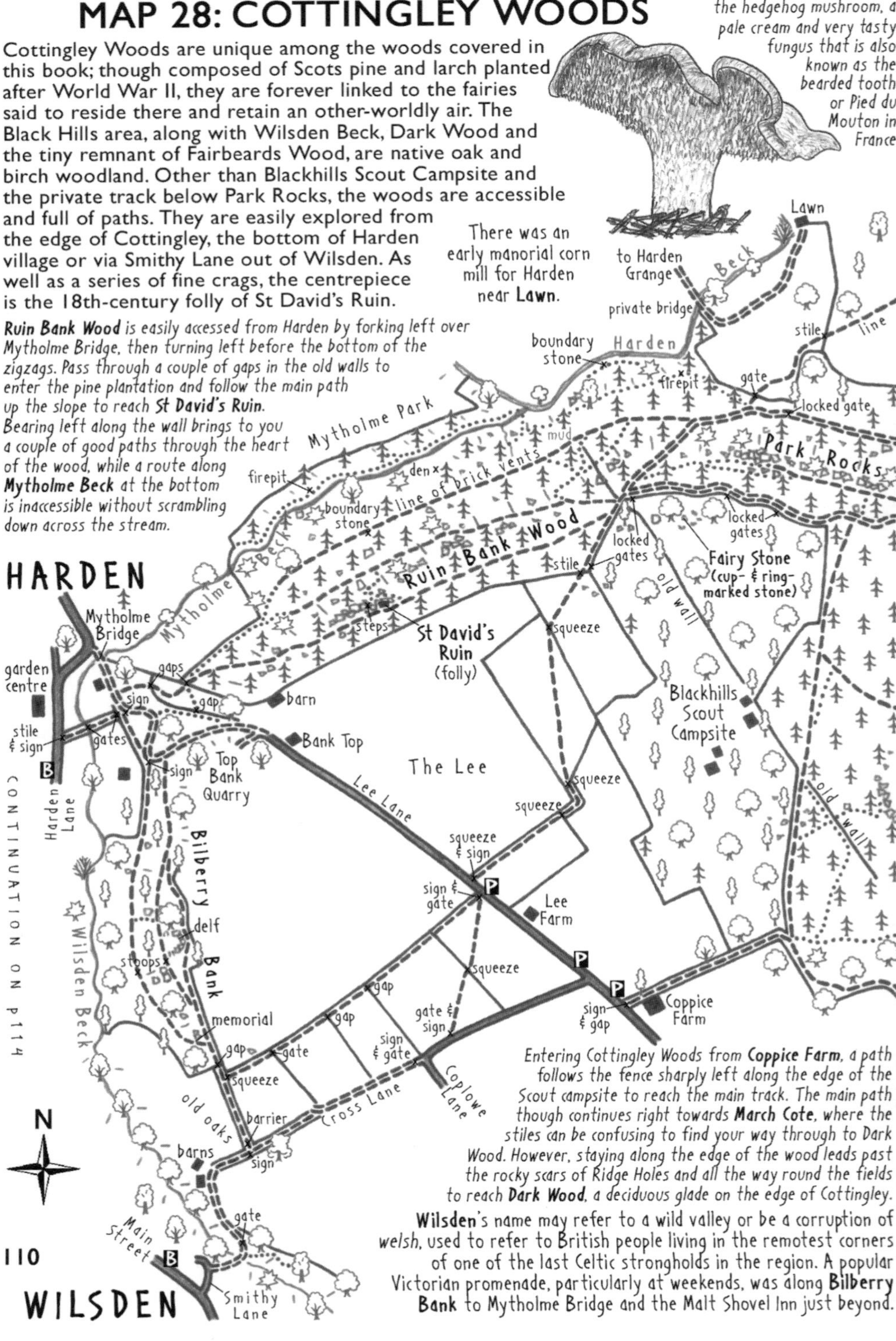

Lawn
to Harden Grange
Beck
private bridge
Harden
boundary stone
firepit
stile
line
gate
locked gate
Mytholme Park
mud
Park Rocks
den
line of brick vents
firepit
boundary stone
Ruin Bank Wood
locked gates
locked gates
stile
Fairy Stone (cup- & ring-marked stone)
old wall
HARDEN
Mytholme Beck
Mytholme Bridge
steps
St David's Ruin (folly)
squeeze
garden centre
gaps
sign
gap
barn
stile & sign
gates
Bank Top
Blackhills Scout Campsite
sign
Top Bank Quarry
The Lee
Harden Lane
Lee Lane
squeeze
squeeze
old wall
Bilberry Bank
squeeze & sign
sign & gate
Lee Farm
delf
stoops
Wilsden Beck
squeeze
gap
gap
gate & sign
memorial
gap
gate
sign & gate
sign & gap
Coppice Farm
squeeze
Coplowe Lane
Cross Lane
old oaks
barrier
barns
sign
N
gate
Main Street
Smithy Lane
WILSDEN


CONTINUATION ON p114

*Entering Cottingley Woods from **Coppice Farm**, a path follows the fence sharply left along the edge of the Scout campsite to reach the main track. The main path though continues right towards **March Cote**, where the stiles can be confusing to find your way through to Dark Wood. However, staying along the edge of the wood leads past the rocky scars of Ridge Holes and all the way round the fields to reach **Dark Wood**, a deciduous glade on the edge of Cottingley.*

***Wilsden**'s name may refer to a wild valley or be a corruption of welsh, used to refer to British people living in the remotest corners of one of the last Celtic strongholds in the region. A popular Victorian promenade, particularly at weekends, was along **Bilberry Bank** to Mytholme Bridge and the Malt Shovel Inn just beyond.*

CONT. ON p119

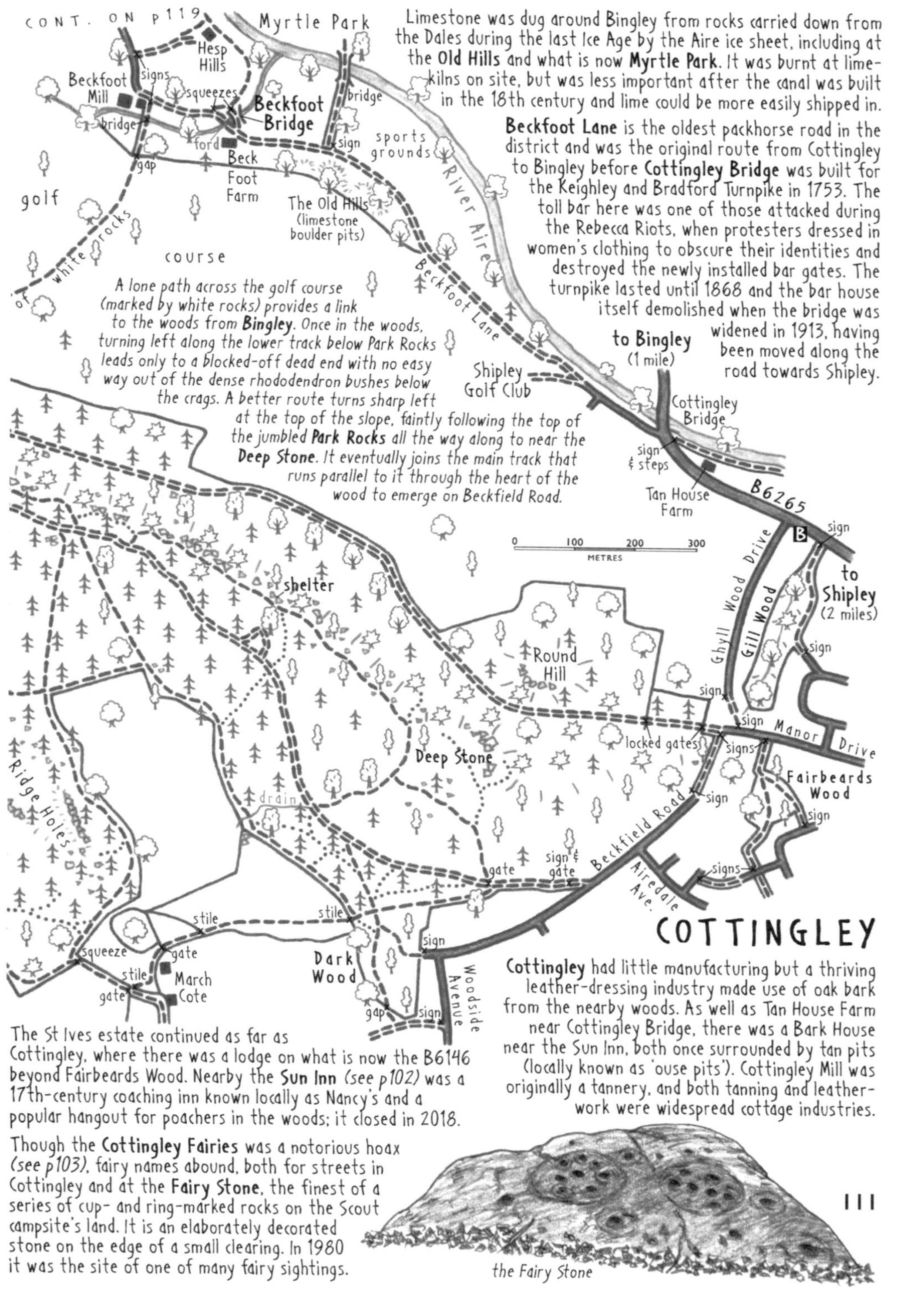
Myrtle Park
Hesp Hills
Beckfoot Mill
signs
squeezes
Beckfoot Bridge
bridge
bridge
ford
sign
sports grounds
gap
Beck Foot Farm
golf
The Old Hills (limestone boulder pits)
River Aire
of white rocks
course
Beckfoot Lane
to Bingley (1 mile)
Shipley Golf Club
Cottingley Bridge
sign & steps
Tan House Farm
B6265
0 100 200 300 METRES
sign
to Shipley (2 miles)
Ghyll Wood Drive
Gill Wood
shelter
Round Hill
sign
sign
sign
Manor Drive
locked gates
signs
Deep Stone
Fairbeards Wood
Ridge Holes
drain
sign
sign
Beckfield Road
Airedale Ave.
gate
sign & gate
signs
stile
stile
squeeze
gate
March Cote
stile
gate
sign
Dark Wood
gap
sign
Woodside Avenue

Limestone was dug around Bingley from rocks carried down from the Dales during the last Ice Age by the Aire ice sheet, including at the **Old Hills** and what is now **Myrtle Park**. It was burnt at lime-kilns on site, but was less important after the canal was built in the 18th century and lime could be more easily shipped in.

**Beckfoot Lane** is the oldest packhorse road in the district and was the original route from Cottingley to Bingley before **Cottingley Bridge** was built for the Keighley and Bradford Turnpike in 1753. The toll bar here was one of those attacked during the Rebecca Riots, when protesters dressed in women's clothing to obscure their identities and destroyed the newly installed bar gates. The turnpike lasted until 1868 and the bar house itself demolished when the bridge was widened in 1913, having been moved along the road towards Shipley.

*A lone path across the golf course (marked by white rocks) provides a link to the woods from* ***Bingley****. Once in the woods, turning left along the lower track below Park Rocks leads only to a blocked-off dead end with no easy way out of the dense rhododendron bushes below the crags. A better route turns sharp left at the top of the slope, faintly following the top of the jumbled* ***Park Rocks*** *all the way along to near the* ***Deep Stone****. It eventually joins the main track that runs parallel to it through the heart of the wood to emerge on Beckfield Road.*

# COTTINGLEY

**Cottingley** had little manufacturing but a thriving leather-dressing industry made use of oak bark from the nearby woods. As well as Tan House Farm near Cottingley Bridge, there was a Bark House near the Sun Inn, both once surrounded by tan pits (locally known as 'ouse pits'). Cottingley Mill was originally a tannery, and both tanning and leather-work were widespread cottage industries.

The St Ives estate continued as far as Cottingley, where there was a lodge on what is now the B6146 beyond Fairbeards Wood. Nearby the **Sun Inn** *(see p102)* was a 17th-century coaching inn known locally as Nancy's and a popular hangout for poachers in the woods; it closed in 2018.

Though the **Cottingley Fairies** was a notorious hoax *(see p103)*, fairy names abound, both for streets in Cottingley and at the **Fairy Stone**, the finest of a series of cup- and ring-marked rocks on the Scout campsite's land. It is an elaborately decorated stone on the edge of a small clearing. In 1980 it was the site of one of many fairy sightings.

*the Fairy Stone*

# ROUTE 18: COTTINGLEY WOODS FROM BINGLEY

**Distance:** 6½ miles (10.5km)

**Ascent:** 190m

**Parking:** Pay car parks in Bingley near station and on Queen Street.

**Public Transport:** Bingley is on the main Airedale bus and train routes.

**Character:** A lovely circuit of the many magical corners of Cottingley Woods from the centre of Bingley. These distinctive conifer plantations are surprisingly varied and the route takes in St David's Ruin, Park Rocks and Beckfoot Bridge, as well as Bilberry Bank and Giles Stone. The paths are largely clear, dry and easy underfoot.

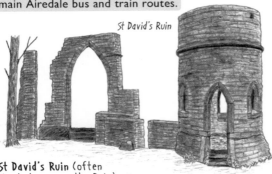

St David's Ruin

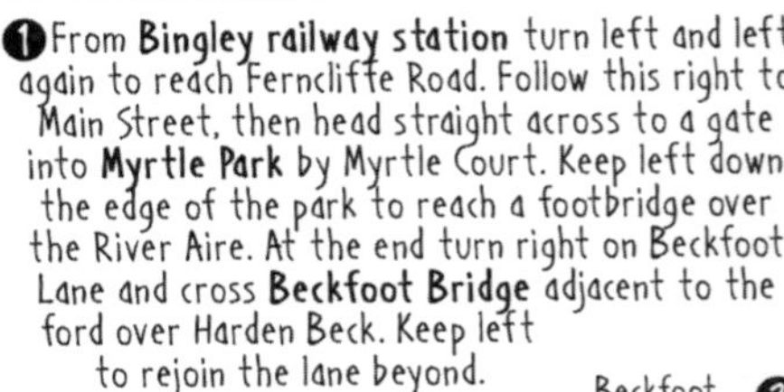

**1** From **Bingley railway station** turn left and left again to reach Ferncliffe Road. Follow this right to Main Street, then head straight across to a gate into **Myrtle Park** by Myrtle Court. Keep left down the edge of the park to reach a footbridge over the River Aire. At the end turn right on Beckfoot Lane and cross **Beckfoot Bridge** adjacent to the ford over Harden Beck. Keep left to rejoin the lane beyond.

**2** Just before the buildings of **Beckfoot Mill** turn left and recross Harden Beck. A path continues across the middle of the golf course, marked by a line of white rocks. It eventually leads into the larch and pine of **Cottingley Woods**, where you join a vehicle track heading right. On the next bend bear right on a path for 200m, then fork left before it gets muddy. This fainter path winds up the steep slope near an old wall. After the path zigs back left, turn right and follow a wonderful path beneath the rocky parapets in **Ruin Bank Wood**. Before a huge wedge of rock, pick up a faint path winding up the slope to emerge on the crest by the impressive folly of **St David's Ruin**.

**St David's Ruin** (often simply known as the Ruin) was built as a Gothic ruin in 1796 by Benjamin Ferrand of nearby Harden Grange *(see p122)*. It has a circular tower that looks like a chess piece connected to an archway, and would have been visible from his home across the valley before the pine trees were planted in the 20th century. It was used as St Clair Folly in John Braine's novel *Room at the Top*.

**3** From **St David's Ruin** a good path continues right along the top of Ruin Bank Wood before dropping down through a couple of gaps to reach a track by **Bank Bottom Cottage.** Follow it left, then go right up the wall; where you rejoin the track, bear right on a signed path through the oak and birch trees of **Bilberry Bank**. Turn right at the end to leave the wood, and turn left when you reach a T-junction, ascending to join a vehicle track.

**4** At the road continue straight ahead, then turn right at the end. After 100m follow a signed path left back into **Cottingley Woods**. Keep right along the wall around the edge of the woods, ignoring a path through a squeeze out of the trees. The path continues round the perimeter past the rocks of **Ridge Holes** to reach a junction, where you head straight on, finally leaving the boundary wall.

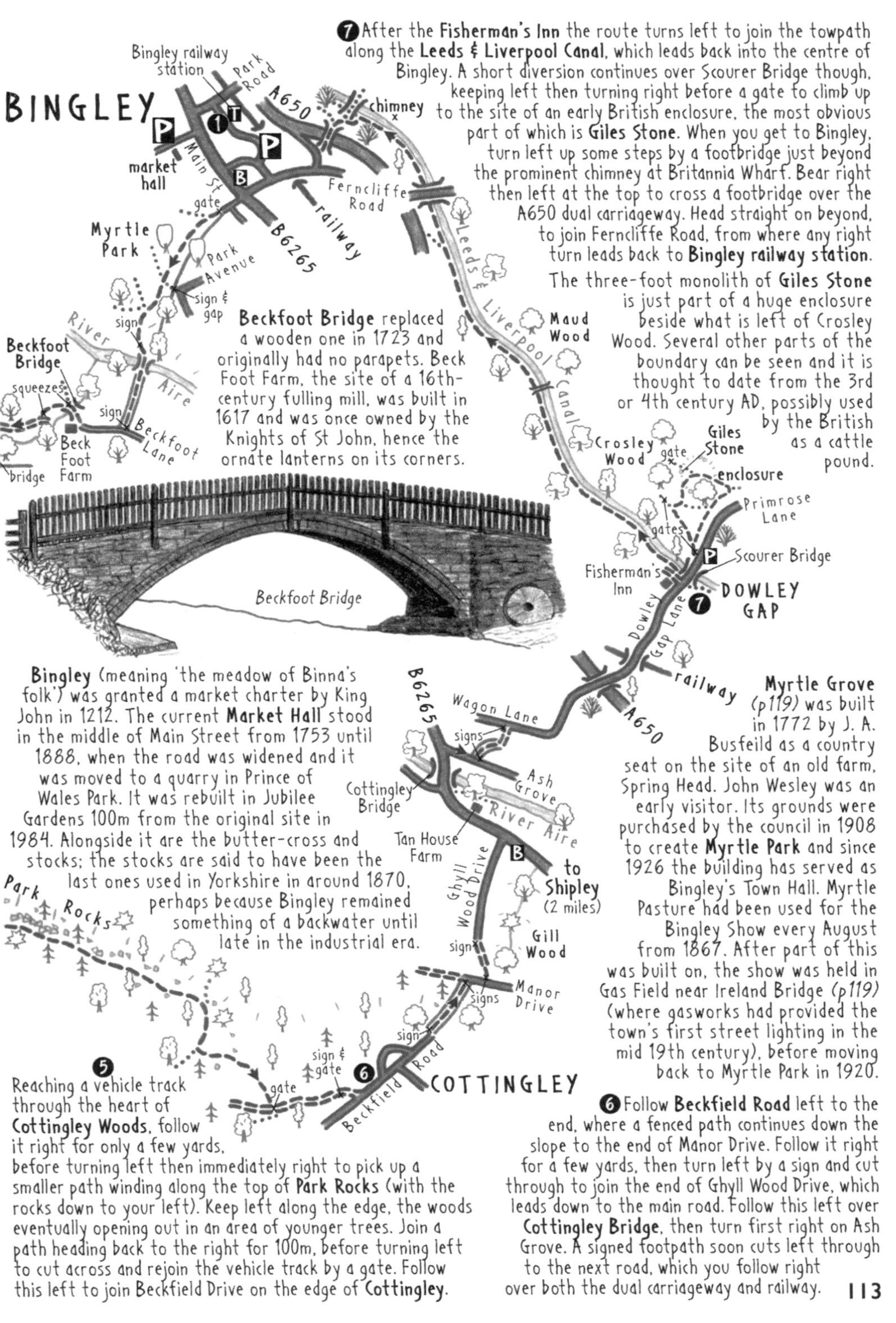
BINGLEY
Bingley railway station
Park Road
A650
chimney
market hall
Main St
Ferncliffe Road
railway
gate
Myrtle Park
Park Avenue
B6265
Leeds & Liverpool Canal
sign & gap
sign
River Aire
Beckfoot Bridge
squeezes
sign
Beckfoot Lane
Beck Foot Farm
bridge
Maud Wood
Crosley Wood
gate
Giles Stone
enclosure
Primrose Lane
gates
Scourer Bridge
Fisherman's Inn
DOWLEY GAP
Dowley Gap Lane
railway
A650
B6265
Wagon Lane
signs
Ash Grove
Cottingley Bridge
River Aire
Tan House Farm
Ghyll Wood Drive
to Shipley (2 miles)
Gill Wood
sign
Manor Drive
signs
sign
sign & gate
Beckfield Road
COTTINGLEY
Park Rocks
gate
Beckfoot Bridge

**7** After the **Fisherman's Inn** the route turns left to join the towpath along the **Leeds & Liverpool Canal**, which leads back into the centre of Bingley. A short diversion continues over Scourer Bridge though, keeping left then turning right before a gate to climb up to the site of an early British enclosure, the most obvious part of which is **Giles Stone**. When you get to Bingley, turn left up some steps by a footbridge just beyond the prominent chimney at Britannia Wharf. Bear right then left at the top to cross a footbridge over the A650 dual carriageway. Head straight on beyond, to join Ferncliffe Road, from where any right turn leads back to **Bingley railway station**.

The three-foot monolith of **Giles Stone** is just part of a huge enclosure beside what is left of Crosley Wood. Several other parts of the boundary can be seen and it is thought to date from the 3rd or 4th century AD, possibly used by the British as a cattle pound.

**Beckfoot Bridge** replaced a wooden one in 1723 and originally had no parapets. Beck Foot Farm, the site of a 16th-century fulling mill, was built in 1617 and was once owned by the Knights of St John, hence the ornate lanterns on its corners.

**Bingley** (meaning 'the meadow of Binna's folk') was granted a market charter by King John in 1212. The current **Market Hall** stood in the middle of Main Street from 1753 until 1888, when the road was widened and it was moved to a quarry in Prince of Wales Park. It was rebuilt in Jubilee Gardens 100m from the original site in 1984. Alongside it are the butter-cross and stocks; the stocks are said to have been the last ones used in Yorkshire in around 1870, perhaps because Bingley remained something of a backwater until late in the industrial era.

**Myrtle Grove** *(p119)* was built in 1772 by J. A. Busfeild as a country seat on the site of an old farm, Spring Head. John Wesley was an early visitor. Its grounds were purchased by the council in 1908 to create **Myrtle Park** and since 1926 the building has served as Bingley's Town Hall. Myrtle Pasture had been used for the Bingley Show every August from 1867. After part of this was built on, the show was held in Gas Field near Ireland Bridge *(p119)* (where gasworks had provided the town's first street lighting in the mid 19th century), before moving back to Myrtle Park in 1920.

**5** Reaching a vehicle track through the heart of **Cottingley Woods**, follow it right for only a few yards, before turning left then immediately right to pick up a smaller path winding along the top of **Park Rocks** (with the rocks down to your left). Keep left along the edge, the woods eventually opening out in an area of younger trees. Join a path heading back to the right for 100m, before turning left to cut across and rejoin the vehicle track by a gate. Follow this left to join Beckfield Drive on the edge of **Cottingley**.

**6** Follow **Beckfield Road** left to the end, where a fenced path continues down the slope to the end of Manor Drive. Follow it right for a few yards, then turn left by a sign and cut through to join the end of Ghyll Wood Drive, which leads down to the main road. Follow this left over **Cottingley Bridge**, then turn first right on Ash Grove. A signed footpath soon cuts left through to the next road, which you follow right over both the dual carriageway and railway.

# MAP 29: GOIT STOCK WOODS & HEWENDEN RESERVOIR

Goit Stock Woods is a generic name for the narrow but richly wooded valley of the Hallas Beck between Harden, Cullingworth and Wilsden, which was once aptly known as 'the Hidden Valley'. The gorge centres on the spectacular Hallas Lumbs waterfalls, but the whole valley is wonderful to explore as it continues upstream to further woodlands around Hewenden Viaduct and Reservoir.

*The beautiful path along* **Hallas Beck** *past the waterfalls is well used, while a pleasant path stays west of the stream through* **Little Ridge Wood** *(one of its forks climbing over the knoll of Little Ridge). Before a stile into the open ground, you can follow the old walled track left to pick up a path that continues along the top of* **Pellon Wood**. *At Woodfield Road bear right to pick up another path through* **Royd Wood** *that climbs steeply above the rocky Dell to emerge near the centre of* **Cullingworth**.

Timothy Horsfall ran a tannery at Cow House in the late 18th century, before moving to take up residence in the newly built **Goit Stock Mill** (now the site of a caravan park). In 1815 it became one of John White's tanneries, producing leather belts and combing leather until the 20th century. The company still produces leather stirrups and saddles in Bingley.

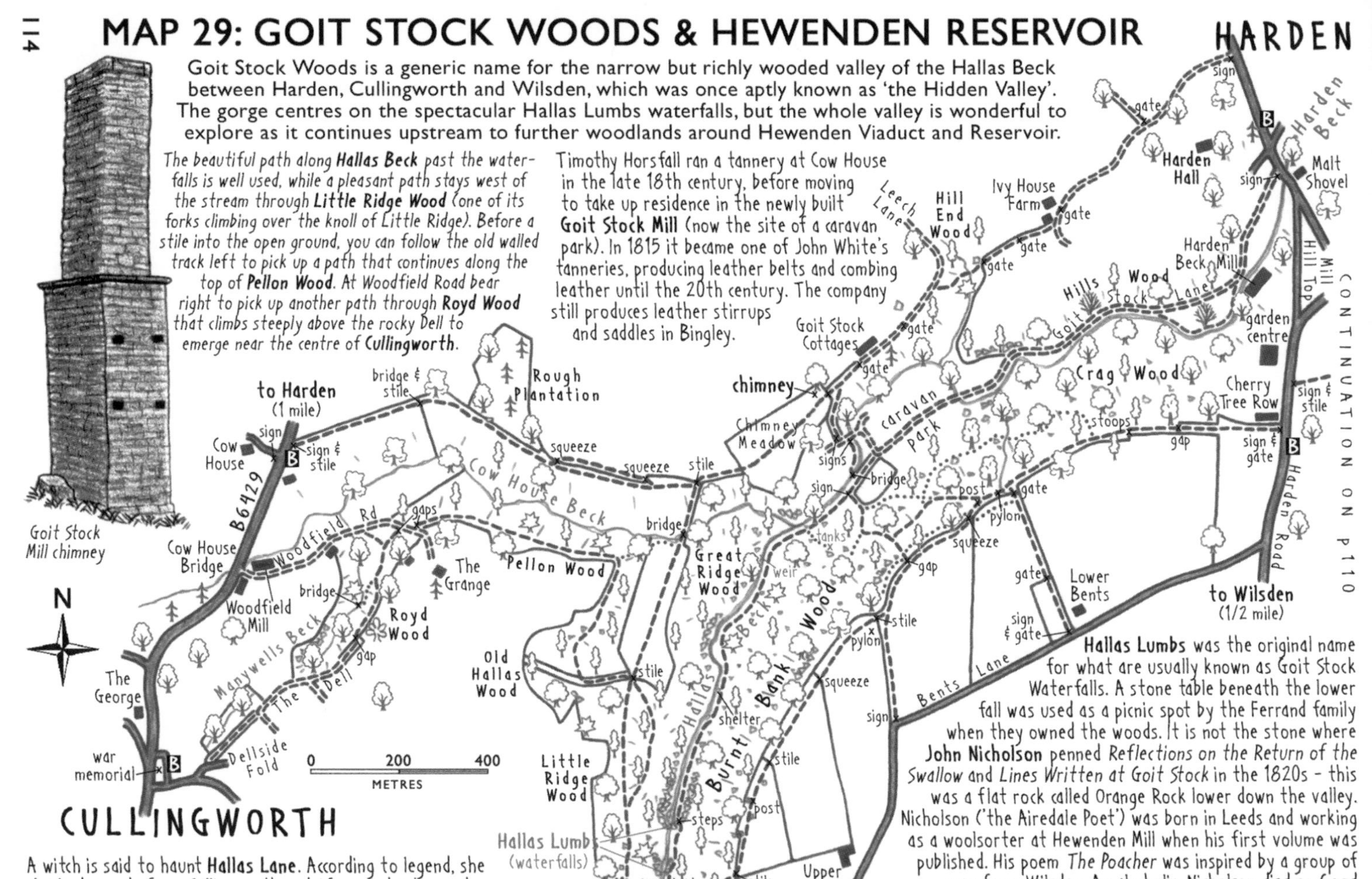
HARDEN
CULLINGWORTH
Harden Beck
Malt Shovel
Mill Hill Top
Harden Hall
Ivy House Farm
Hill End Wood
Leech Lane
Harden Beck Mill
Hills Wood
Goit Stock Lane
garden centre
Crag Wood
Cherry Tree Row
Harden Road
to Wilsden (1/2 mile)
Lower Bents
Bents Lane
Upper Bents
Goit Stock Cottages
chimney
Chimney Meadow
caravan park
stoops
pylon
tanks
weir
Great Ridge Wood
Burnt Bank Wood
Hallas Beck
shelter
steps
Hallas Lumbs (waterfalls)
Hallas Hall Farm
Little Ridge Wood
Old Hallas Wood
Pellon Wood
Rough Plantation
Cow House Beck
The Grange
Royd Wood
Woodfield Rd
Woodfield Mill
Manywells Beck
The Dell
Dellside Fold
to Harden (1 mile)
Cow House
B6429
Cow House Bridge
The George
war memorial
sign
gate
stile
squeeze
gap
gaps
bridge
bridge & stile
sign & stile
sign & gate
post
signs
0 200 400
METRES
N
Goit Stock Mill chimney

CONTINUATION ON p110

**Hallas Lumbs** was the original name for what are usually known as Goit Stock Waterfalls. A stone table beneath the lower fall was used as a picnic spot by the Ferrand family when they owned the woods. It is not the stone where **John Nicholson** penned *Reflections on the Return of the Swallow* and *Lines Written at Goit Stock* in the 1820s – this was a flat rock called Orange Rock lower down the valley. Nicholson ('the Airedale Poet') was born in Leeds and working as a woolsorter at Hewenden Mill when his first volume was published. His poem *The Poacher* was inspired by a group of men from Wilsden. An alcoholic, Nicholson died on Good Friday 1843 after falling drunkenly into the river at Saltaire.

A witch is said to haunt **Hallas Lane**. According to legend, she slowly descends from Cullingworth and, if were she to reach Hallas Bridge, all of the houses on the hillside would vanish.

**Hewenden Mill** was one of the first worsted mills in Bradford when it was built in 1792 alongside the site of a medieval corn mill. It fell into disuse as it was hard to access, but was popular as a roller-skating rink in the early 20th century, before being converted into apartments in recent years.

**Manywells Spring** discharges up to half a million gallons of clear water a minute through a broad fissure in the rock and was known locally as Seth's Spring, as the land was owned by Seth Wright. In 1838 Bradford Corporation compulsorily purchased Trooper's Farm and built an aqueduct from the spring to the water treatment plant at Chellow Heights to provide drinking water for the city. **Hewenden Reservoir** was built in the 1840s as compensation to the mill owners in the valley for the loss of water from the spring. On June 11th 1956, 155mm rain fell in two hours, still the most anywhere in Britain.

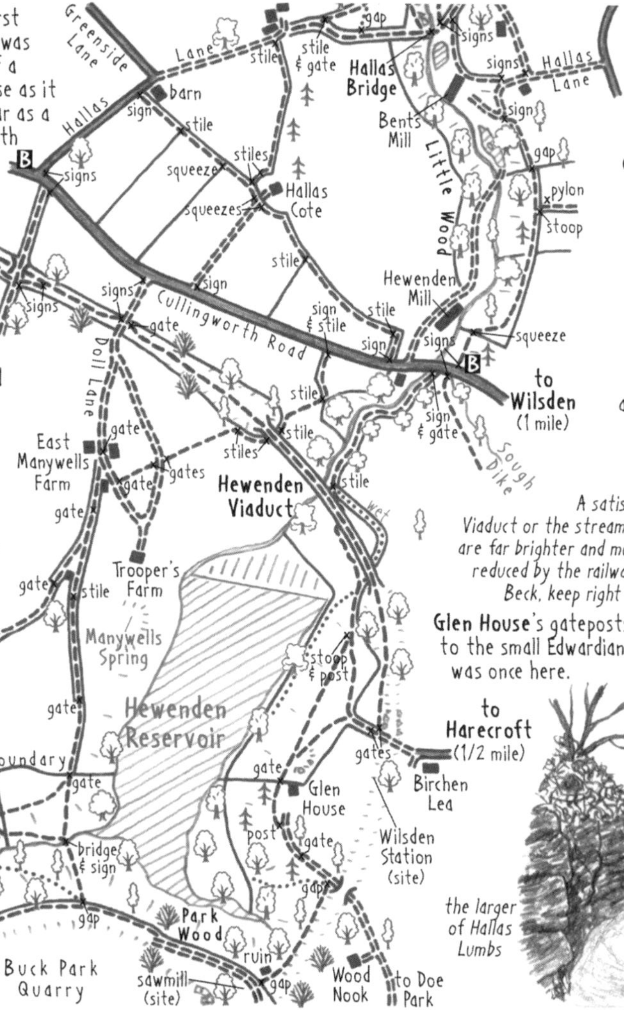

**Goit Stock Mill** (now the site of a caravan park) was built in 1802 and was one of the first mills in the area to use steam rather than water power, hence the striking chimney stack on the hillside above.

Cotton was spun here until 1848, after which Harry Beldon, a successful poultry breeder, used it for rearing chickens. The mill had become run down when it was converted into **Happy Valley Pleasure Grounds** in 1919. A ballroom was built on the top floor of mill, with a 1,000-seat café below. Outside there was an al fresco tea pavilion modelled on an outback hotel, putting greens, miniature golf, an aviary, toboggan run, monkey house and boating on the mill pond.

Entry was 6d and charabancs ferried visitors to and from the stations at Cullingworth and Bingley. Kiosks in the wood served passing ramblers and it was a far cry from the days when the Ferrands had made anyone apply for permission to visit the valley.

During its 1920s heyday, boxing matches, concerts, festivals and firework displays were held here. Late on Easter Monday in 1927, after 20,000 people had visited, a fire razed the mill to the ground. Despite attempts to refurbish it, the business never recovered and Happy Valley closed in 1932, since when plans to fell the trees and build a large housing estate have been mercifully shelved.

*A satisfactory circuit of* ***Hewenden Reservoir*** *is straightforward from Hewenden Viaduct or the stream below. It is worth the short diversion up* ***Milking Hole Beck****, whose woods are far brighter and more appealing than dingy Park Wood (once home to a saw mill, but now much reduced by the railway, reservoir and quarry). Before Doctor's Bridge at the top of Milking Hole Beck, keep right and double back to return across the fields past the site of* ***Castle Stead****.*

**Glen House**'s gateposts proclaim it as Porky Park, a reference to the small Edwardian pleasure garden that was once here.

The indiscernible outline of **Castle Stead** was thought to be a Roman encampment, but is now considered more likely to be an Iron Age or British earthwork.

**Buck Park**, like nearby Doe Park, is a remnant of Denholme Park, a 13th-century deer park created by the monks of Byland Abbey. The deer park boundary followed what is now the parish boundary between Cullingworth and Denholme and stretched for several miles. The park was broken up after Richard Tempest gambled away the family's money in the 17th century and the estate was sold to the Saviles.

*the larger of Hallas Lumbs*

# ROUTE 19: GOIT STOCK WOODS & HEWENDEN VIADUCT FROM HARDEN

**Distance:** 8 miles (12.9km)

**Ascent:** 300m

**Parking:** Free street parking along Wilsden Road in Harden, or small lay-by on B4269 at Manywells Brow.

**Public Transport:** Harden is on the 616 & 619 buses from Bradford to Eldwick, and the K17 & K19 from Keighley and Bingley.

**Character:** A fine exploration of the Harden/Hallas Beck, taking in the dramatic Hallas Lumbs waterfalls, Hewenden Viaduct and Reservoir and a glimpse of the prehistoric sites of Harden Moor. As a rough figure-of-eight loop it can easily be shortened at Hallas Bridge, but the route never feels convoluted. There are some steep and narrow paths, but navigation is reasonably straightforward.

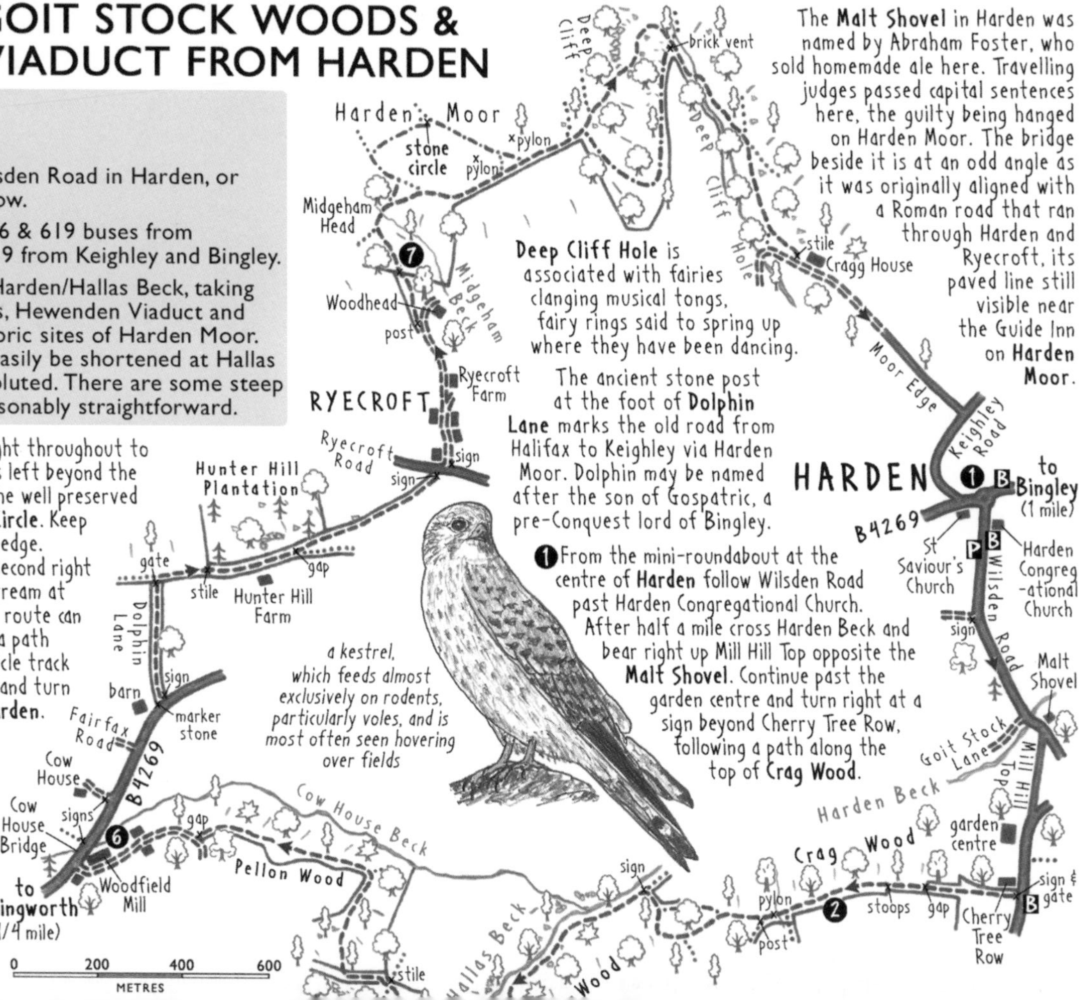

❼ On **Harden Moor** the simple route keeps right throughout to follow the moor edge, but an alternative turns left beyond the hollow of Midgeham Head, then right to pass the well preserved Bronze Age ring cairn of **Harden Moor Stone Circle**. Keep right to rejoin the main route along the moor edge. Reaching trees at the top of Deep Cliff, bear second right to descend steeply through the oaks to the stream at **Deep Cliff Hole** (a more gentle but overgrown route can be followed first right). At the bottom follow a path down the stream, forking right to reach a vehicle track near Cragg House. Follow this left to the road and turn right at the end to return to the centre of **Harden**.

❻ Turn right along the **B4269** for a quarter of a mile and turn left at a bridleway sign just beyond the bend, following the grassy track of Dolphin Lane up the hill. Turn right at the top and skirt below **Hunter Hill Plantation**. Keep left along the wall to reach Ryecroft Road, heading straight across to pass through the beautiful hamlet of **Ryecroft**. Follow the track past Ryecroft Farm, then bear left on a path just before Woodhead to reach the edge of **Harden Moor**.

The **Malt Shovel** in Harden was named by Abraham Foster, who sold homemade ale here. Travelling judges passed capital sentences here, the guilty being hanged on Harden Moor. The bridge beside it is at an odd angle as it was originally aligned with a Roman road that ran through Harden and Ryecroft, its paved line still visible near the Guide Inn on **Harden Moor**.

**Deep Cliff Hole** is associated with fairies clanging musical tongs, fairy rings said to spring up where they have been dancing.

The ancient stone post at the foot of **Dolphin Lane** marks the old road from Halifax to Keighley via Harden Moor. Dolphin may be named after the son of Gospatric, a pre-Conquest lord of Bingley.

❶ From the mini-roundabout at the centre of **Harden** follow Wilsden Road past Harden Congregational Church. After half a mile cross Harden Beck and bear right up Mill Hill Top opposite the **Malt Shovel**. Continue past the garden centre and turn right at a sign beyond Cherry Tree Row, following a path along the top of **Crag Wood**.

*a kestrel, which feeds almost exclusively on rodents, particularly voles, and is most often seen hovering over fields*


Harden Moor
stone circle
pylon
Deep Cliff
brick vent
Deep Cliff Hole
stile
Cragg House
Moor Edge
Keighley Road
HARDEN
to Bingley (1 mile)
B4269
St Saviour's Church
Harden Congregational Church
Wilsden Road
sign
Malt Shovel
Goit Stock Lane
Mill Hill Top
Harden Beck
garden centre
Crag Wood
sign & gate
Cherry Tree Row
stoops
gap
post
Hallas Beck
Wood
stile
Midgeham Head
Midgeham Beck
Woodhead
post
Ryecroft Farm
RYECROFT
Ryecroft Road
Hunter Hill Plantation
Hunter Hill Farm
gate
Dolphin Lane
barn
marker stone
Fairfax Road
Cow House
Cow House Bridge
signs
Woodfield Mill
to Cullingworth (1/4 mile)
Pellon Wood
Cow House Beck
0 200 400 600
METRES

❷ Just beyond a pylon, fork right and soon join a large path descending steeply down to the stream. Turn left at the bottom and follow the beautiful gorge of Hallas Beck up to the waterfalls at **Hallas Lumbs**. Continue up the steps and soon emerge by **Hallas Bridge**, where there is an obvious short-cut right if you want to shorten the walk. Otherwise the route continues left then immediately right, passing above Bents Mill. Turn right at the top of the steps, then left on the next bend, picking your way along the top of **Little Wood** to emerge on the B6144.

**Hallas** may be a corruption of 'hallowes', a reference perhaps to monastic ownership of the land by Harden Grange.

**Hewenden Viaduct** was built in 1884 and, at 128-feet high, was one of the highest in England. It was part of a very expensive railway between Queensbury and Keighley whose hilly nature delayed construction and earned it the nickname 'the Alpine route'. Wilsden station was built near the south end of the viaduct in 1886, but it was so far from the village it was used mostly as a goods yard moving local coal and stone. It closed to passengers in 1955 and the last train crossed the viaduct on November 8th 1963. Parts of the line, including this section over the viaduct, have recently been reopened as part of the Great Northern Railway Trail.

This fine little bridge was part of an aqueduct built in the 1870s between Stubden Reservoir and Manywells Spring that was soon superseded by a pipeline via Thornton.

*aqueduct bridge on Milking Hole Beck*

❸ Follow the road right for a few yards to the second sign on the left, joining a path alongside the stream towards the towering **Hewenden Viaduct**. Beyond a stile follow the edge of the viaduct's feet, first on the left then the right, to reach a grassy track. Follow this right and fork right at a stoop to cross the hillside above **Hewenden Reservoir**. In the trees, join a vehicle track by Glen House, before turning right off it just before it cuts beneath the old railway. Turn right at a concrete track and continue along the fenceline where it ends by Buck Park Quarry. At a gap on the right, turn right and descend the steep grassy slope to **Milking Hole Beck** (don't follow a path diagonally into the woods). Over the stream turn left and, just after the second broken-down wall, bear right up the slope to join a clearer path higher up. This leads left through a beautiful mixed plantation studded with crags. Keep left before a striking **aqueduct bridge** to reach the A629.

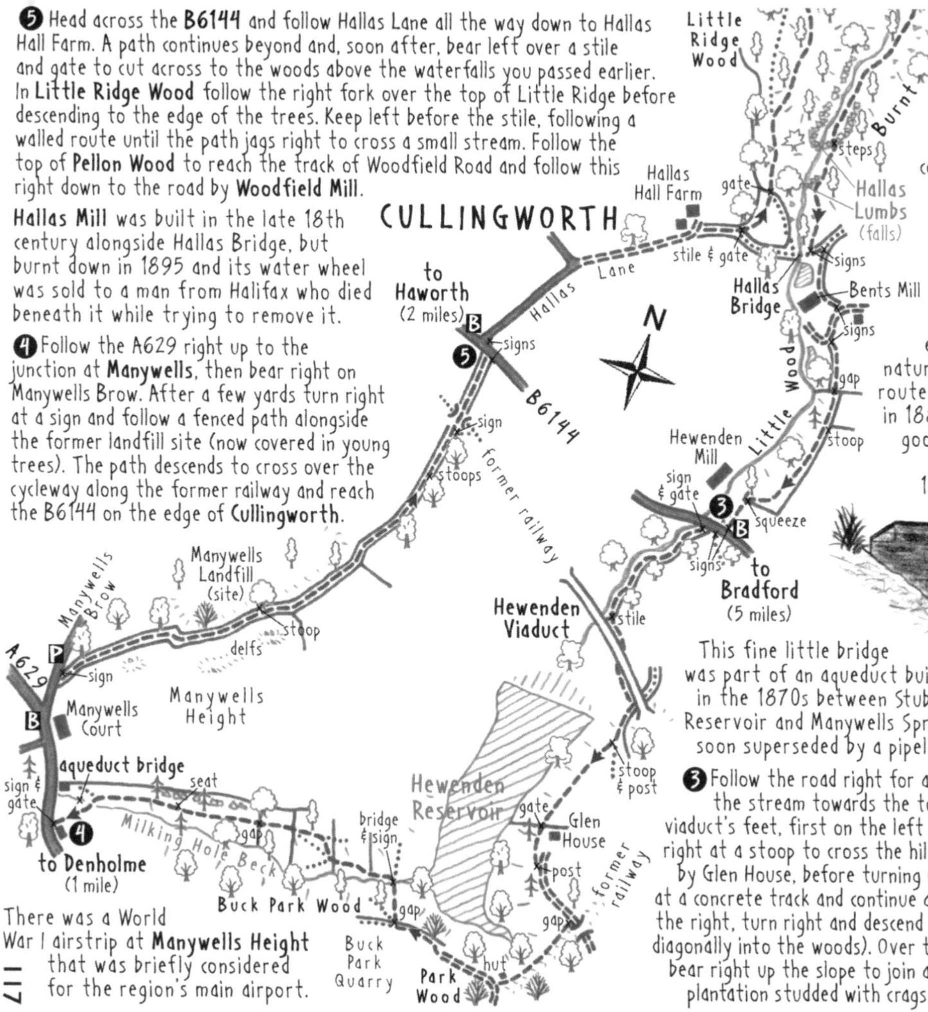

❹ Follow the A629 right up to the junction at **Manywells**, then bear right on Manywells Brow. After a few yards turn right at a sign and follow a fenced path alongside the former landfill site (now covered in young trees). The path descends to cross over the cycleway along the former railway and reach the B6144 on the edge of **Cullingworth**.

❺ Head across the **B6144** and follow Hallas Lane all the way down to Hallas Hall Farm. A path continues beyond and, soon after, bear left over a stile and gate to cut across to the woods above the waterfalls you passed earlier. In **Little Ridge Wood** follow the right fork over the top of Little Ridge before descending to the edge of the trees. Keep left before the stile, following a walled route until the path jags right to cross a small stream. Follow the top of **Pellon Wood** to reach the track of Woodfield Road and follow this right down to the road by **Woodfield Mill**.

**Hallas Mill** was built in the late 18th century alongside Hallas Bridge, but burnt down in 1895 and its water wheel was sold to a man from Halifax who died beneath it while trying to remove it.

There was a World War I airstrip at **Manywells Height** that was briefly considered for the region's main airport.

# MAP 30: BINGLEY & THE ST IVES ESTATE

The St Ives estate is a well-used park around the Ferrand family's mansion at St Ives House. Easily reached from the centre of Bingley, it is particularly busy around the Coppice Pond, Lady Blantyre's Rock and Elm Crag Wood, but quieter further up the hill, where the woods are shaped around the golf course. The fine and varied woods continue down from the Druid's Altar towards the River Aire, providing many wonderful corners to explore.

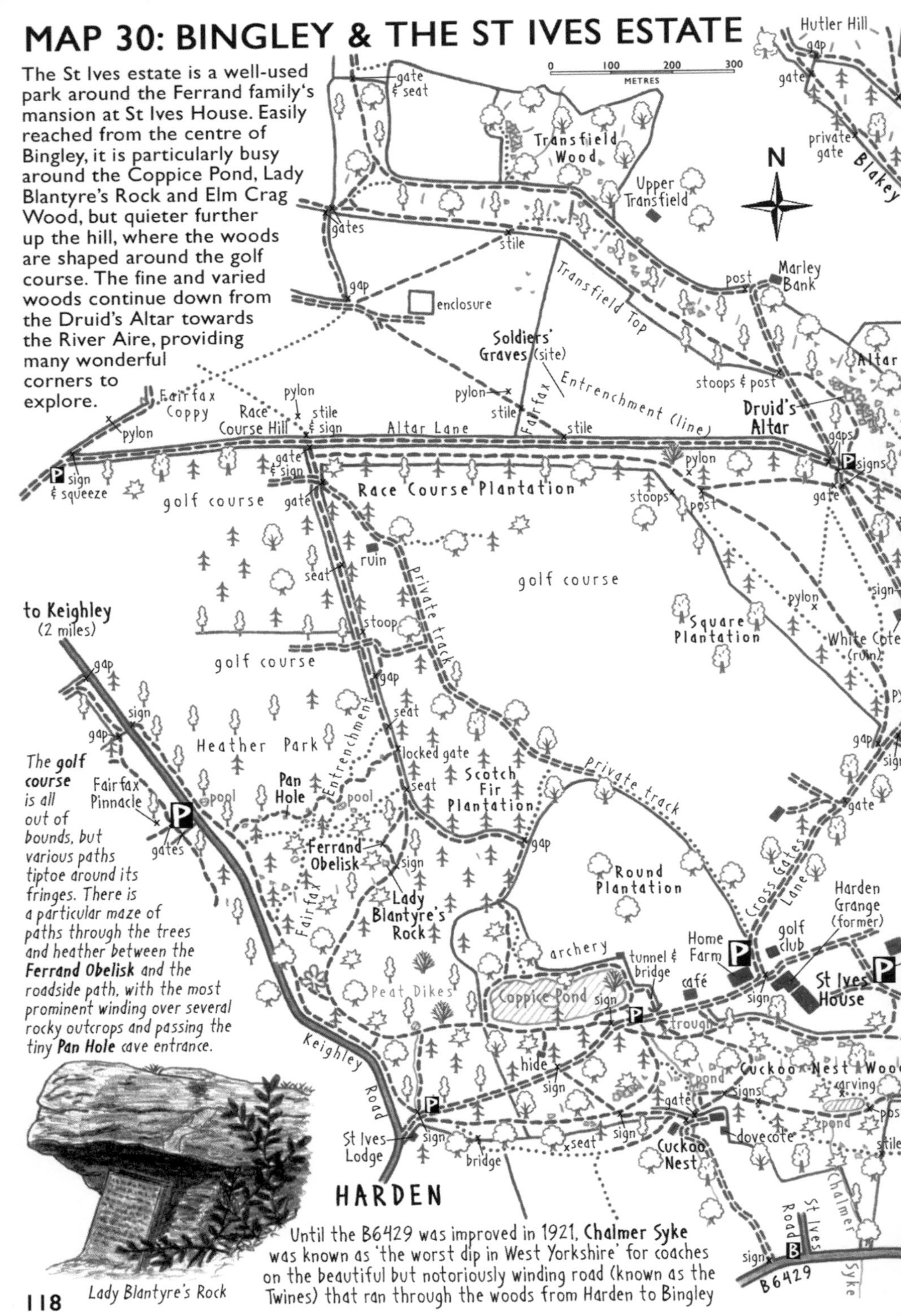

0
100
200
300
METRES
N
Hutler Hill
gap
gate
private gate
Blakey
gate & seat
Transfield Wood
Upper Transfield
gates
stile
Transfield Top
Marley Bank
post
gap
enclosure
Soldiers' Graves (site)
Fairfax Entrenchment (line)
stoops & post
Altar
Druid's Altar
pylon
stile
Fairfax Coppy
Race Course Hill
stile & sign
Altar Lane
gaps
signs
sign & squeeze
gate & sign
golf course
gate
Race Course Plantation
stoops
post
ruin
seat
private track
stoop
golf course
to Keighley (2 miles)
Square Plantation
White Cote (ruin)
golf course
gap
sign
seat
Entrenchment
Heather Park
locked gate
Scotch Fir Plantation
private track
gate
Pan Hole
pool
Fairfax Pinnacle
gates
Ferrand Obelisk
sign
gap
Round Plantation
Cross Gates Lane
Lady Blantyre's Rock
Fairfax
Harden Grange (former)
golf club
Home Farm
archery
tunnel & bridge
café
St Ives House
Peat Dikes
Coppice Pond
sign
trough
Keighley Road
hide
sign
pond
Cuckoo Nest Wood
carving
signs
gate
post
pond
dovecote
stile
St Ives Lodge
sign
bridge
seat
sign
Cuckoo Nest
HARDEN
Chalmer Syke
St Ives Road
B6429
sign


*The* ***golf course*** *is all out of bounds, but various paths tiptoe around its fringes. There is a particular maze of paths through the trees and heather between the* ***Ferrand Obelisk*** *and the roadside path, with the most prominent winding over several rocky outcrops and passing the tiny* ***Pan Hole*** *cave entrance.*

Until the B6429 was improved in 1921, **Chalmer Syke** was known as 'the worst dip in West Yorkshire' for coaches on the beautiful but notoriously winding road (known as the Twines) that ran through the woods from Harden to Bingley

*Lady Blantyre's Rock*

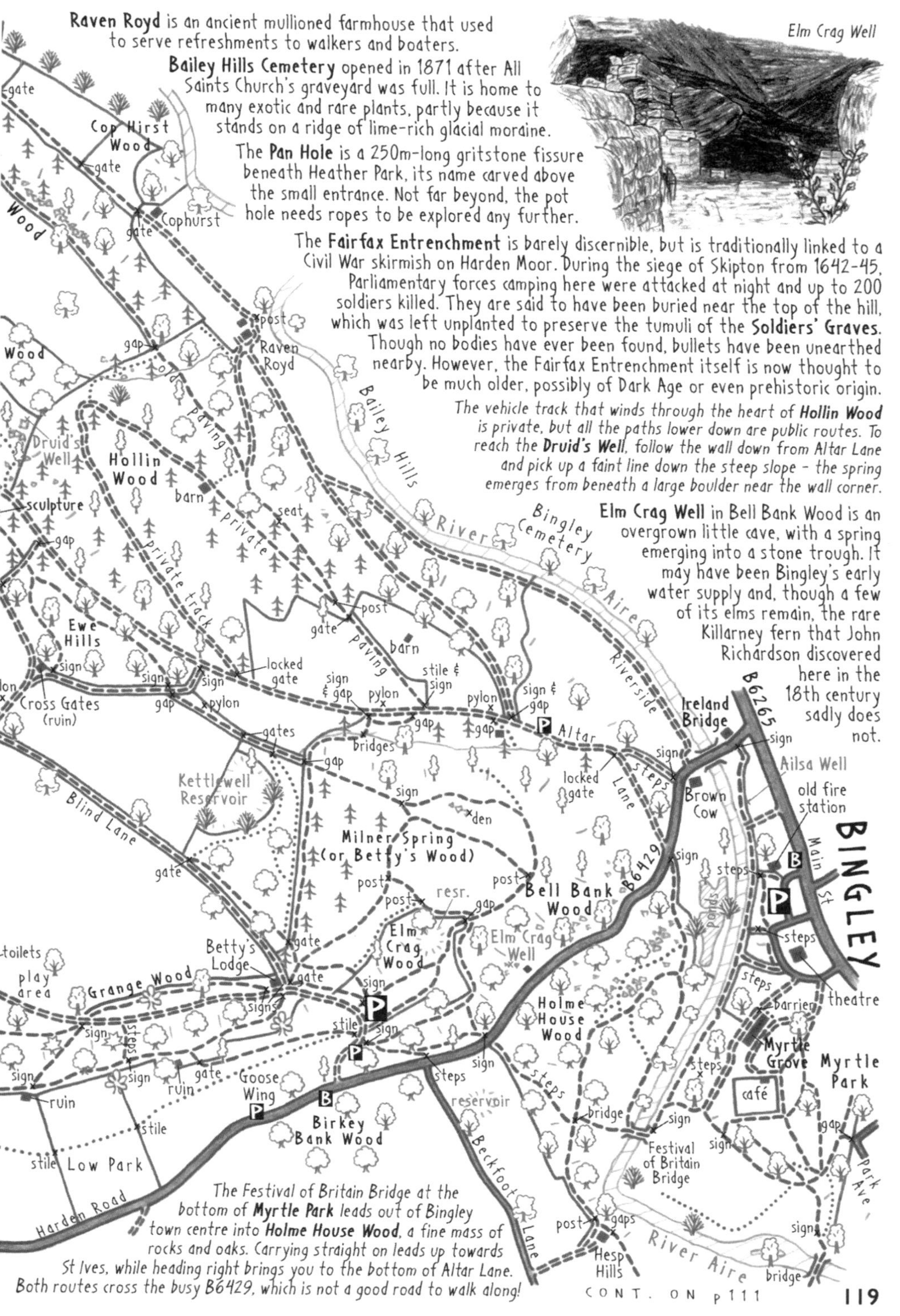
Elm Crag Well
gate
Cop Hirst Wood
gate
Cophurst
gate
Wood
post
Raven Royd
gap
Wood
paving
Bailey Hills
Druid's Well
Hollin Wood
barn
sculpture
seat
private
private track
River
Bingley Cemetery
Aire
gap
Ewe Hills
post
gate
paving
barn
sign
locked gate
stile & sign
Riverside
Cross Gates (ruin)
sign
sign
gap
pylon
sign & gap
pylon
pylon
sign & gap
Ireland Bridge
B6265
sign
gates
gap
bridges
gap
gap
Altar
sign
Ailsa Well
gap
Kettlewell Reservoir
steps
locked gate
Lane
Brown Cow
old fire station
sign
den
Blind Lane
Milner Spring (or Betty's Wood)
B6429
sign
BINGLEY
gate
post
post
resr.
post
Bell Bank Wood
steps
Main St
gap
ponds
toilets
gate
Betty's Lodge
Elm Crag Wood
Elm Crag Well
steps
play area
Grange Wood
gate
sign
steps
theatre
signs
barrier
stile
sign
Holme House Wood
Myrtle Grove
Myrtle Park
sign
steps
sign
sign
gate
steps
steps
café
sign
ruin
Goose Wing
ruin
steps
reservoir
bridge
sign
gap
stile
Birkey Bank Wood
sign
Festival of Britain Bridge
stile
Low Park
Beckfoot Lane
Park Ave
Harden Road
post
gaps
sign
Hesp Hills
River Aire
bridge

**Raven Royd** is an ancient mullioned farmhouse that used to serve refreshments to walkers and boaters.

**Bailey Hills Cemetery** opened in 1871 after All Saints Church's graveyard was full. It is home to many exotic and rare plants, partly because it stands on a ridge of lime-rich glacial moraine.

The **Pan Hole** is a 250m-long gritstone fissure beneath Heather Park, its name carved above the small entrance. Not far beyond, the pot hole needs ropes to be explored any further.

The **Fairfax Entrenchment** is barely discernible, but is traditionally linked to a Civil War skirmish on Harden Moor. During the siege of Skipton from 1642-45, Parliamentary forces camping here were attacked at night and up to 200 soldiers killed. They are said to have been buried near the top of the hill, which was left unplanted to preserve the tumuli of the **Soldiers' Graves**. Though no bodies have ever been found, bullets have been unearthed nearby. However, the Fairfax Entrenchment itself is now thought to be much older, possibly of Dark Age or even prehistoric origin.

*The vehicle track that winds through the heart of **Hollin Wood** is private, but all the paths lower down are public routes. To reach the **Druid's Well**, follow the wall down from Altar Lane and pick up a faint line down the steep slope – the spring emerges from beneath a large boulder near the wall corner.*

**Elm Crag Well** in Bell Bank Wood is an overgrown little cave, with a spring emerging into a stone trough. It may have been Bingley's early water supply and, though a few of its elms remain, the rare Killarney fern that John Richardson discovered here in the 18th century sadly does not.

*The Festival of Britain Bridge at the bottom of **Myrtle Park** leads out of Bingley town centre into **Holme House Wood**, a fine mass of rocks and oaks. Carrying straight on leads up towards St Ives, while heading right brings you to the bottom of Altar Lane. Both routes cross the busy B6429, which is not a good road to walk along!*

# ROUTE 20: DRUID'S ALTAR

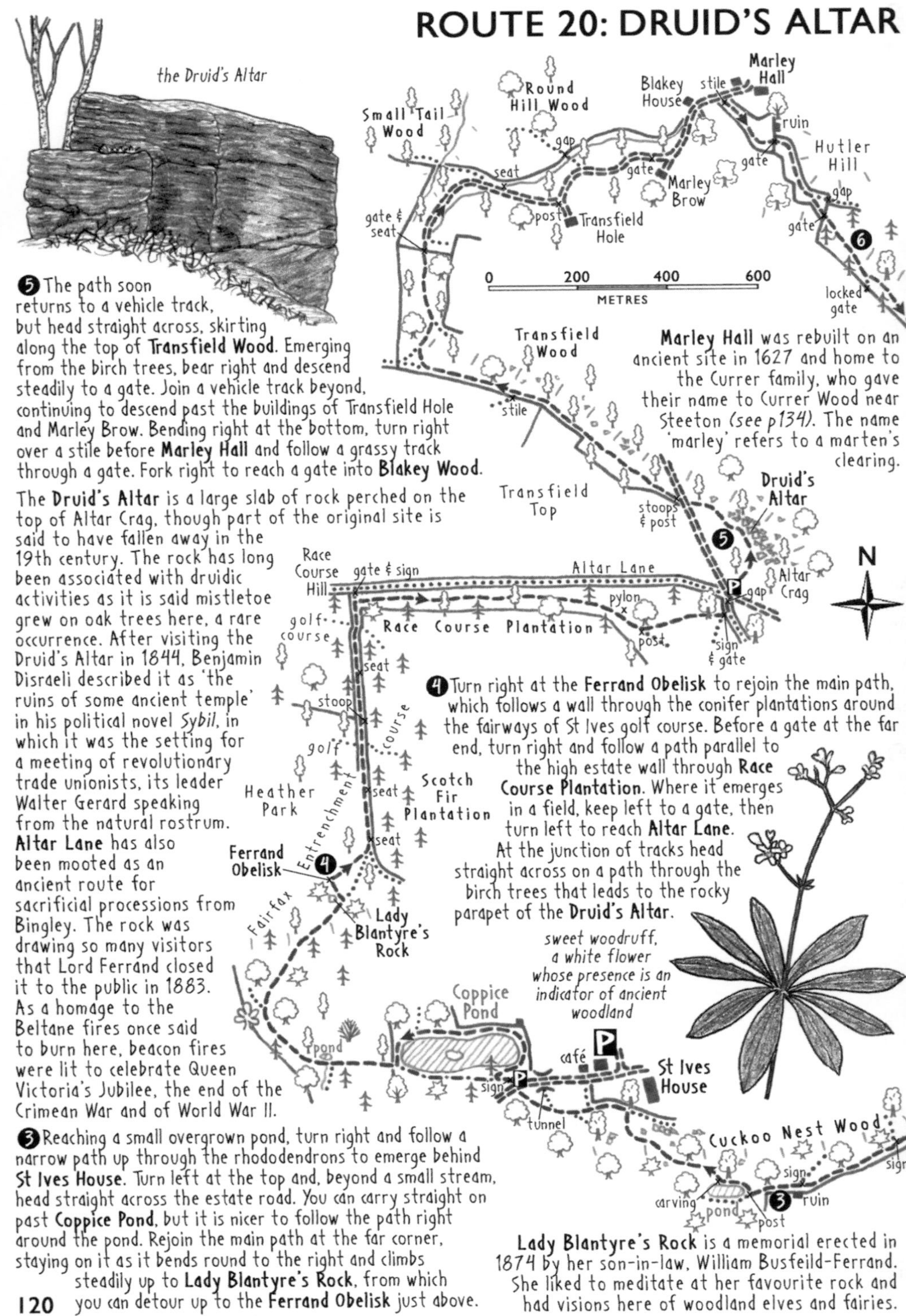

Marley Hall
Blakey House
stile
Round Hill Wood
Small Tail Wood
ruin
Hutler Hill
gap
gate
seat
Marley Brow
gate & seat
post
Transfield Hole
gap
gate
6
0 200 400 600
METRES
locked gate
Transfield Wood
stile
Transfield Top
stoops & post
Druid's Altar
5
N
Race Course Hill
gate & sign
Altar Lane
P
gap
Altar Crag
pylon
golf course
Race Course Plantation
post
sign & gate
seat
stoop
golf
course
seat
Heather Park
Scotch Fir Plantation
Entrenchment
seat
Ferrand Obelisk
4
Fairfax
Lady Blantyre's Rock
Coppice Pond
pond
café
P
St Ives House
sign
P
tunnel
Cuckoo Nest Wood
sign
sign
carving
pond
3
ruin
post


the Druid's Altar

❺ The path soon returns to a vehicle track, but head straight across, skirting along the top of **Transfield Wood**. Emerging from the birch trees, bear right and descend steadily to a gate. Join a vehicle track beyond, continuing to descend past the buildings of Transfield Hole and Marley Brow. Bending right at the bottom, turn right over a stile before **Marley Hall** and follow a grassy track through a gate. Fork right to reach a gate into **Blakey Wood**.

**Marley Hall** was rebuilt on an ancient site in 1627 and home to the Currer family, who gave their name to Currer Wood near Steeton *(see p134)*. The name 'marley' refers to a marten's clearing.

The **Druid's Altar** is a large slab of rock perched on the top of Altar Crag, though part of the original site is said to have fallen away in the 19th century. The rock has long been associated with druidic activities as it is said mistletoe grew on oak trees here, a rare occurrence. After visiting the Druid's Altar in 1844, Benjamin Disraeli described it as 'the ruins of some ancient temple' in his political novel *Sybil*, in which it was the setting for a meeting of revolutionary trade unionists, its leader Walter Gerard speaking from the natural rostrum. **Altar Lane** has also been mooted as an ancient route for sacrificial processions from Bingley. The rock was drawing so many visitors that Lord Ferrand closed it to the public in 1883. As a homage to the Beltane fires once said to burn here, beacon fires were lit to celebrate Queen Victoria's Jubilee, the end of the Crimean War and of World War II.

❹ Turn right at the **Ferrand Obelisk** to rejoin the main path, which follows a wall through the conifer plantations around the fairways of St Ives golf course. Before a gate at the far end, turn right and follow a path parallel to the high estate wall through **Race Course Plantation**. Where it emerges in a field, keep left to a gate, then turn left to reach **Altar Lane**. At the junction of tracks head straight across on a path through the birch trees that leads to the rocky parapet of the **Druid's Altar**.

sweet woodruff, a white flower whose presence is an indicator of ancient woodland

❸ Reaching a small overgrown pond, turn right and follow a narrow path up through the rhododendrons to emerge behind **St Ives House**. Turn left at the top and, beyond a small stream, head straight across the estate road. You can carry straight on past **Coppice Pond**, but it is nicer to follow the path right around the pond. Rejoin the main path at the far corner, staying on it as it bends round to the right and climbs steadily up to **Lady Blantyre's Rock**, from which you can detour up to the **Ferrand Obelisk** just above.

**Lady Blantyre's Rock** is a memorial erected in 1874 by her son-in-law, William Busfeild-Ferrand. She liked to meditate at her favourite rock and had visions here of woodland elves and fairies.

# & ST IVES ESTATE FROM BINGLEY

❻ Angle up to the top of **Blakey Wood** (a sea of bluebells at the right time of year) and bear left along a lovely path before the locked gate at the top. The path continues along an ancient route through the heart of **Hollin Wood**, before joining a larger track to reach a gate out into the field the far end. Follow the wall up to **Altar Lane**, then turn left as far as the bend, where some steps lead down to the left to emerge on the road opposite the Brown Cow. Cross **Ireland Bridge** then turn right at a sign, the narrow footpath soon rejoining the riverbank. After 300m turn left through an arch and climb the steps to pass the old fire station and return to the car park and main road in **Bingley**.

**Distance:** 6 miles (9.8km)

**Ascent:** 300m

**Parking:** Free parking in St Ives estate and pay car parks in Bingley, including on Queen Street.

**Public Transport:** Bingley is on the main Airedale bus and train routes.

**Character:** A simple circuit of the charming woodland of the St Ives estate, taking in the Druid's Altar, Lady Blantyre's Rock and St Ives House, as well as the quieter bowers of Hollin, Blakey and Transfield Woods. The route is on good paths throughout.

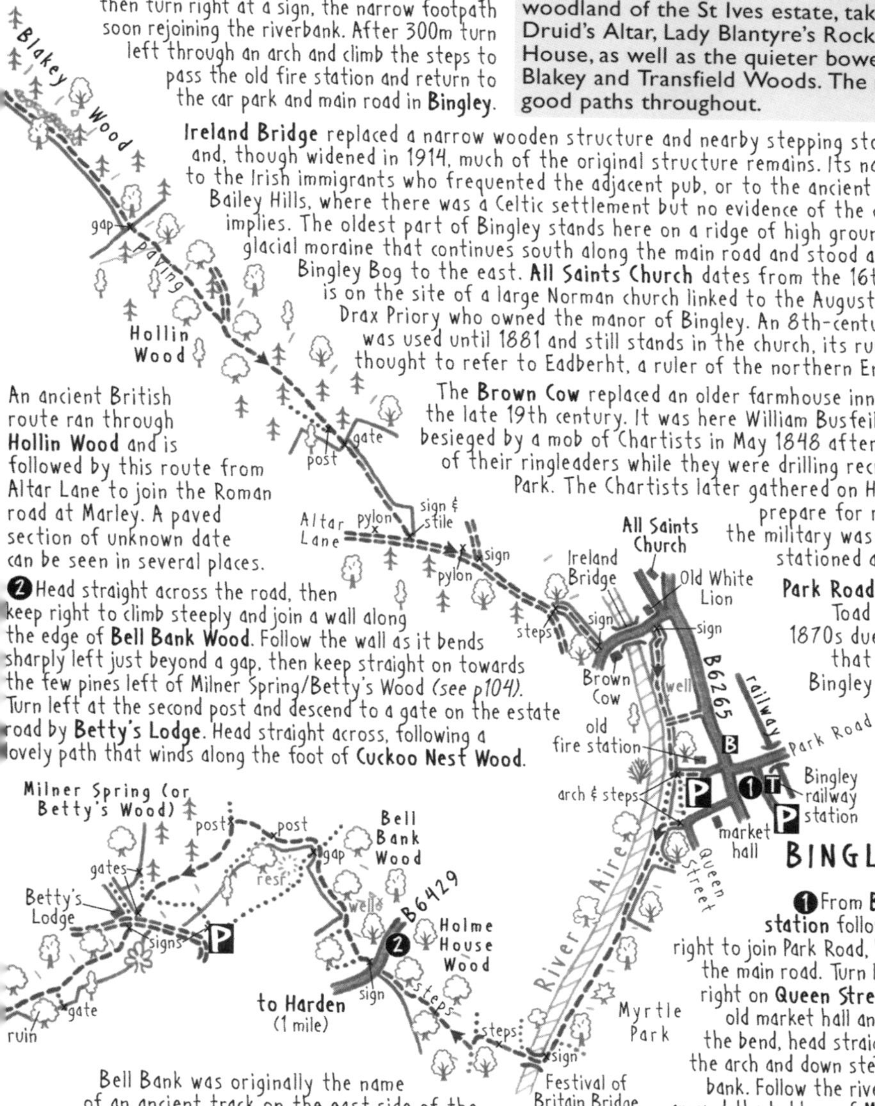

**Ireland Bridge** replaced a narrow wooden structure and nearby stepping stones in 1685/6 and, though widened in 1914, much of the original structure remains. Its name may relate to the Irish immigrants who frequented the adjacent pub, or to the ancient 'island' site of Bailey Hills, where there was a Celtic settlement but no evidence of the castle its name implies. The oldest part of Bingley stands here on a ridge of high ground composed of glacial moraine that continues south along the main road and stood above what was Bingley Bog to the east. **All Saints Church** dates from the 16th century, and is on the site of a large Norman church linked to the Augustinian monks of Drax Priory who owned the manor of Bingley. An 8th-century Saxon font was used until 1881 and still stands in the church, its runic inscriptions thought to refer to Eadberht, a ruler of the northern English kingdom.

The **Brown Cow** replaced an older farmhouse inn on the site in the late 19th century. It was here William Busfeild-Ferrand was besieged by a mob of Chartists in May 1848 after capturing two of their ringleaders while they were drilling recruits in Myrtle Park. The Chartists later gathered on Harden Moor to prepare for revolution, and the military was called in to be stationed around Bingley.

An ancient British route ran through **Hollin Wood** and is followed by this route from Altar Lane to join the Roman road at Marley. A paved section of unknown date can be seen in several places.

❷ Head straight across the road, then keep right to climb steeply and join a wall along the edge of **Bell Bank Wood**. Follow the wall as it bends sharply left just beyond a gap, then keep straight on towards the few pines left of Milner Spring/Betty's Wood (see p104). Turn left at the second post and descend to a gate on the estate road by **Betty's Lodge**. Head straight across, following a lovely path that winds along the foot of **Cuckoo Nest Wood**.

**Park Road** was known as Toad Lane until the 1870s due to the toads that emerged from Bingley Bog on either side, which was partly filled in to allow the railway to be built.

❶ From **Bingley railway station** follow the approach right to join Park Road, heading left to the main road. Turn left, then first right on **Queen Street**, passing the old market hall and a car park. At the bend, head straight on through the arch and down steps to the river bank. Follow the riverside trail left around the bottom of **Myrtle Park** and cross the Festival of Britain Bridge. Go straight on up some steps into **Holme House Wood**, keeping straight on to continue climbing to the B6429.

Bell Bank was originally the name of an ancient track on the east side of the river past All Saints Church and over Bailey Hills. The name *bel* was a Celtic word for a ford, referring to the ancient crossing in Bingley below **Bell Bank Wood**, so perhaps it makes sense that the name was used on both sides of the river.

# ST IVES HOUSE & HARDEN GRANGE

Researching the history of St Ives and Harden Grange, my mind was frazzled by the apparently interchangeable nature of the two names. In fact they have only switched names once, in 1854, but that is enough to cause plenty of confusion.

The original Harden Grange was established in the early 13th century on lands granted to Rievaulx Abbey by Thomas de Birkin. The monks operated an ironworks near Harden Beck and worked the surrounding woods. A forester here was recorded as being shot by an arrow during a confrontation with neighbouring farmers in 1267. The grange continued to provide a good income until the Dissolution of the Monasteries in the 16th century, after which it fell into ruin.

In 1616 a house was built at St Ives half a mile away from the grange on the other side of the road from Harden to Bingley. St Ives (like its namesake near Pontefract) may be named after a holy well to St Hilda, the 7th-century founding abbess of Whitby Abbey. St Ives Well was just one of a number of holy wells in the area whose waters were revered; St Anthony's Well in Harden was dedicated to the protector of lower animals, especially pigs, and its site is marked by a plaque on Anthony Lane.

By 1636 Robert Ferrand, a wealthy cloth merchant, had acquired a large estate around Harden, including Harden Grange, St Ives and the ancient site of Harden Hall. He built a house on the site of the former grange, reusing some of the old masonry and retaining the name Harden Grange for his new family seat. A self-made tradesman and non-conformist, Ferrand sided with the Parliamentarians during the Civil War, and their commander in the north, Sir Thomas Fairfax, stayed at Harden Hall in 1644. While his troops camped on nearby Harden Moor, he is said to have written dispatches and casualty lists from Fairfax Table, a stone table that was moved to the summer house at St Ives in 1841 by William Ferrand, who also erected Fairfax Pinnacle on Harden Moor *(p118)*.

Benjamin Ferrand moved to St Ives on the death of his father in 1712 and this became the family seat. The original St Ives was rebuilt in 1759, but little remains of this fine house except for the domestic offices, which were incorporated into its third incarnation, built in 1859 by William Busfeild Ferrand.

As there was no male heir on the Ferrand side of the family, William Busfeild inherited the estate from his mother in 1854 on the proviso that he append Ferrand to his name. He had been an MP for Knaresborough and a leading member of the Ten-Hour Factory Reform movement, campaigning to improve child labour conditions, though he also crushed opposition to the establishment at every turn (including the Chartists). His predecessor, William Ferrand, had extended the original house at Harden Grange and laid out an ornamental garden, making the old grange the family seat again. Busfeild Ferrand continued this work, extending the mansion greatly according to plans drawn up by his wife and her mother, Lady Blantyre. It was at this point that the names St Ives and Harden Grange were switched around. The new St Ives House was surrounded by a vast parkland, with lodges at every corner, a home farm and walled kitchen garden, two ponds with cascades in between inspired by the Italian artist Salvator Rosa, a summer house, romantic walkways through the woods and a monumental packhorse bridge. Beech, pine, larch, sycamore and rhododendron were planted to create what was now four hundred acres of woodland on the estate. Busfeild Ferrand entertained his friend Benjamin Disraeli and many notable artists at his new country pile.

After World War I the St Ives estate was broken up and its farms sold off. Bingley Urban Development Council bought St Ives House and its immediate parkland in 1928 for £39,500 and it was opened to the public, with an entrance fee of 2d/3d chargeable until 1936. The house and its outhouses have since been used as a hotel, café, riding school, residence and industrial units, with a golf course being created on the former parkland.

monk carving, Cuckoo Nest Wood

# CHAPTER 10 - KEIGHLEY & SURROUNDS

**Map Sheet:** Explorer OL21 (South Pennines)

**Public Transport:** Railway stations at Keighley, and Steeton & Silsden. The Keighley & Worth Valley Railway serves Oakworth, Haworth and Oxenhope.

**Parking:** Free car park at Oxenhope station. Pay car parks in Keighley, Silsden and Haworth.

At the furthest reaches of West Yorkshire, the River Aire winds through a broad valley with high moors rising steeply beyond. It is a definitively glacial landscape more reminiscent of the Yorkshire Dales, the bare slopes scattered with rocks and the few trees huddled together. Its woodlands are concentrated on the east bank between Riddlesden and Silsden and a few disparate areas around Steeton, and include the savage gorges of Holden and Steeton Gills.

Keighley is the gateway to this area, a large town near where the River Worth flows into the Aire. Included in the Domesday Book as Chichelai, it was granted a market charter by Edward I in 1305. Its name means 'Cyhha's clearing' and Kicheburn (the older name for North Beck) was derived from the same root. Park Wood gives the town a wooded backdrop, but other than this there are only a few piecemeal woodlands along the River Worth, Bridgehouse Beck and North Beck as they reach high up onto the moors around Haworth, Oakworth and Oxenhope. Only Newsholme Dean, a secluded beauty spot upstream of Goose Eye, and parts of North Beck can be said to be defined by their trees. I have included a linear route from Oxenhope to Keighley, which links several smaller parcels of woodland and allows for a return along the Keighley and Worth Valley Railway, the finest way to experience this valley.

*Dean Bridge, Newsholme Dean*

# MAP 31: NEWSHOLME DEAN

Newsholme Dean is a beautiful wooded valley leading down from Keighley Moor towards Keighley. Now rather overlooked, it was a playground for the town in the early 20th century. The lower parts around Teapot Dam and Dean Bridge are easily explored from Goose Eye or Newsholme, but much of the upper valley is impossible to access. The steep-sided cloughs are dominated by birch and alder woodlands with several impressive quarry scars, but the main footpath up the valley stays out of the trees on the north side. Access is not helped by several Public Rights of Way on the OS map being non-existent on the ground.

**Baily Hall Quarry** is the largest of several quarries in Newsholme Dean and is said to be named after the Duke of Devonshire's bailiff. The Duke owned the land on which Todley Hall was built by the Green Family in 1771 (there is nothing now but rubble behind Todley Hall Farm). There is a paved stone track from Dean Lane down to the quarry, which was used until the 1930s and stone from it is said to have been used to build Burnley Town Hall.

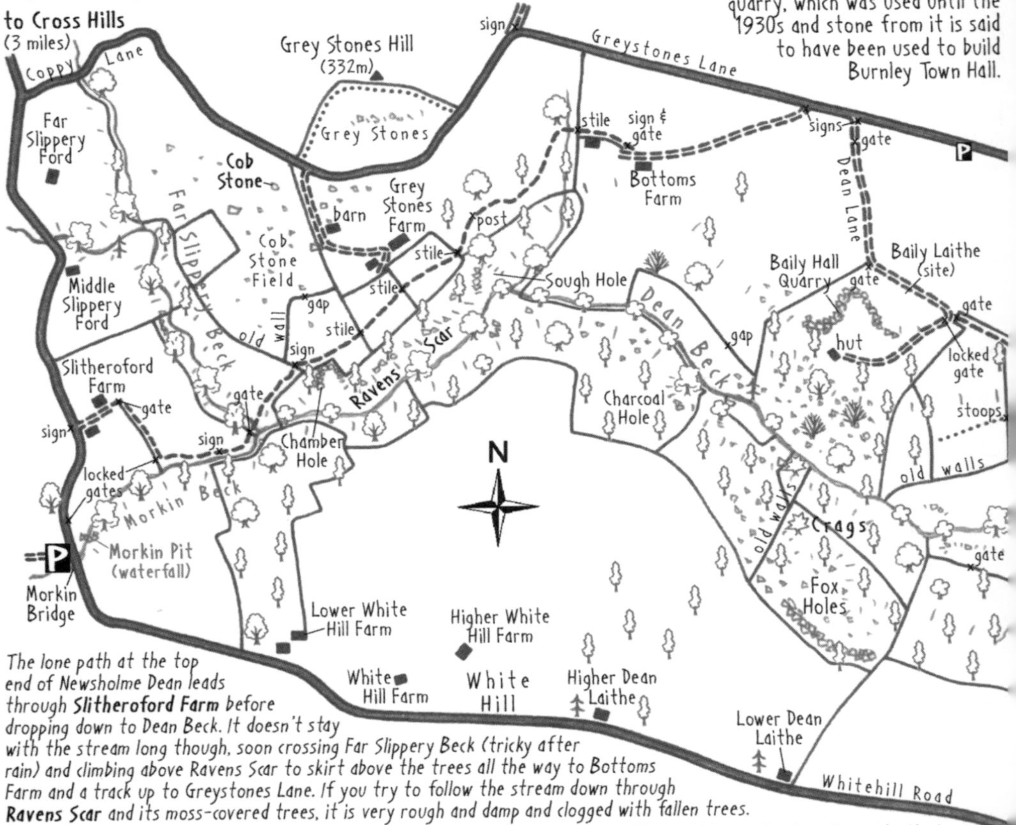

to Cross Hills
(3 miles)
Coppy Lane
Grey Stones Hill
(332m)
Greystones Lane
sign
Grey Stones
stile
sign & gate
signs
gate
P
Far Slippery Ford
Cob Stone
Bottoms Farm
Dean Lane
Grey Stones Farm
barn
post
Far Slippery Beck
Cob Stone Field
stile
stile
Sough Hole
Baily Hall Quarry
gate
Baily Laithe (site)
Middle Slippery Ford
gap
old wall
stile
sign
Ravens Scar
Dean Beck
gap
gate
hut
locked gate
Slitheroford Farm
gate
gate
sign
Chamber Hole
Charcoal Hole
stoops
sign
N
old walls
locked gates
Morkin Beck
old walls
Crags
gate
P
Morkin Pit (waterfall)
Fox Holes
Morkin Bridge
Lower White Hill Farm
Higher White Hill Farm
White Hill Farm
White Hill
Higher Dean Laithe
Lower Dean Laithe
Whitehill Road


*The lone path at the top end of Newsholme Dean leads through **Slitheroford Farm** before dropping down to Dean Beck. It doesn't stay with the stream long though, soon crossing Far Slippery Beck (tricky after rain) and climbing above Ravens Scar to skirt above the trees all the way to Bottoms Farm and a track up to Greystones Lane. If you try to follow the stream down through **Ravens Scar** and its moss-covered trees, it is very rough and damp and clogged with fallen trees.*

**Dean Bridge** is a precarious looking cantilever bridge of unknown origin, with a packhorse bridge alongside that was built by a local farmer alongside. The older bridge is often referred to as a clapper bridge, though I call these clam bridges as clapper bridges typically have two stones side by side that clap up to each other. It is surprising so little is known about this striking feature, but there has been plenty of speculation. It is thought to stand on a major pack-horse route into Lancashire which forded the Aire at Utley, and is known locally as the Roman Bridge as there are unsubstantiated connections with a Roman route.

*stoops in Cat Clough*

The **Cob Stone** is a glacial erratic boulder near the north-east corner of Cob Stone Field and has a series of impressive cup marks along its crest. Its name (like hob) may relate to a local word for the devil. There is a larger stone a little to the south-west, which along with several others in the vicinity may have fainter cup markings. Though a footpath theoretically crosses this field, it is obstructed and the best way to the stone is via to the south.

**Newsholme Dean** was a popular day trip in the early 20th century, when there seemed to be more access than today. The 17th-century farmhouse at **Rose Cottage** had a tea room and pleasure gardens (known as Judson's), with swings and roundabouts down by the beck, as did Hoyle Farm (now Far Dene Farm). People paddled in the stream and played cricket, rounders and knurr & spell on the grass, and there was even a football field near Dean Bridge at one point. The tea rooms continued until the late 1950s and offered dances on summer evenings.

*The easiest part of this area to explore is* ***Dean Wood****, along Dean Beck from* ***Goose Eye****, with paths passing either side of* ***Teapot Dam*** *then spreading through the oak woods beyond. All paths lead right up to Fallow Lane, which can be followed down past Newsholme Dean Farm to the beautiful clam bridge at* ***Dean Bridge****. The only path from here leads up Cat Clough to* ***Newsholme*** *and, since the footpath over Brown Hill shown on the OS map is obstructed, the best way back to Goose Eye is via Yew Lane.*

**Laycock** is mentioned in the Domesday Book as an agricultural manor, but **Goose Eye** hamlet only sprang up at the meeting of two streams during the Industrial Revolution. The origin of Goose Eye's name is unclear, possibly a corruption of either *height* or *ae* (an Old English word for a stream). **Turkey Mill** was a huge paper mill, producing much of the paper on which the Indian rupee was printed, as well as Australian 'fivers' and the Queen Mother's writing paper. Watermarks were added using water from **Teapot Dam** (named after its shape, but officially Harry Holme Dam). The raw materials were sorted at Rag Mill (originally Brow End Mill) and the Turkey Inn car park is on the site of a millpond, the chimney alongside originally standing 200ft high.

Johnny Wood
Todley
Glen Bridge Farm
Nettle Hole
Royd Quarry
Green Sykes Lane
to Laycock (1/4 mile)
sign & stile
Clough
Royd (site)
guide stoop
sign
stile
sign & gate
Game Scar Lane
Game Scar Farm
Todley Hall Road
stile
Todley Hall Farm
stoop
Clough Bank Farm
Dob Field
0 100 200 300 400
METRES
Dean Lane
post
delf
gates
Far Dene Farm
gap
old walls
Rose Cottage
gate
post
Fallow Lane
Brow End Farm
Lund Lane
GOOSE EYE
Turkey Inn
Turkey Mill
Dean Wood
bridges
mill
sign & steps
pool
Goose Eye Wood
Newsholme Dean Farm
Stony Lane
barn
Dean Bridge (clam bridge)
Dean Beck
Teapot Dam
aqueduct
wet
squeeze
K1 telephone box
stoop
stoops
Cat Clough
fold (site)
memorial stone
trough
Cat Clough Spring
Newsholme Beck
Holme House Lane
Carr Laithe
steps
stoops
True Well Hall Farm
Holme House
sign & stile
Brown Hill
Green Top
Hill Top Farm
Fieldhead
NEWSHOLME
to Oakworth (1 mile)
St John's Church
Gill Lane
Yew Lane
pond
Lower Laithe Farm
Green Bottom
to Oakworth (1/2 mile)
Pro Bono Publico
1707


**True Well Hall Farm** was the site of a venerated spring, while the public water trough at Holme House still bears the inscription 'pro bono publico'.

*Holme House public water trough*

**Newsholme** is a corruption of Newhouse. Church Farm was built in 1670, with **St John's Church** appended to it as a chapel of ease and Sunday school in 1843, having made use of two of the farm's rooms. The Old Bobbin Mill on Gill Lane was the higher of two bobbin mills on Newsholme Beck (known locally as Cuckoo Beck).

# MAP 32: PARK WOOD

Park Wood is a fine wooded hillside rising right up from the centre of Keighley, its ancient woodland given to the people of the town by the Duke of Devonshire in 1928. Although extensively quarried, the whole slope is dominated by beech trees and full of paths that are easily accessed from the roads on all sides.

*Park Wood is easy to reach from **Keighley railway station**. Turn left outside, then left again down Low Mill Lane. Beyond the railway turn right up a path to Parkwood Street. Turn left then right up any of the roads to access the woods from Kendal Street.*

*The main path runs diagonally up through **Park Wood** from unsurfaced Kendal Street to the edge of Long Lee estate; its surface is made of setts and it was once lit by gas lamps. All of the other paths lie above this, linking to Park Lane and Parkwood Rise, though a faint line does head down towards Parkside Works only to become lost in the soggy mulch of beech leaves.*

Remains of an **earth bank** in the lower part of Park Wood are thought to be part of an ancient woodland boundary.

The **nuthatch** is a common woodland bird that doesn't tend to stray far from its nest. It has a distinctive black stripe around its eyes, a blue-grey back and pinkish underbelly. Uniquely it scuttles up and down tree trunks (unlike the treecreeper, which can only climb up), and cracks open nuts in clefts in the tree, its name being a corruption of 'nut hacker'.

There was a 19th-century **tannery** on Parkwood Street that may have made use of bark from trees in Park Wood. Certainly the few veteran trees in the wood show signs of having been coppiced during their lifetime.

East of the wall through the middle of the wood, the land is private, although a good path follows the edge above the quarries to emerge on **Spring Avenue**. Another path below the quarries descends uncertainly towards the far corner of the wood, but a fence prevents access to **Parkwood Street** via Clover Rise. The ruined walls indicate that parts of what is now woodland were fields until the early 20th century, and this end of the wood is more of a mixture of trees.

There are few obvious features in Park Wood; apart from the old gate stoops and 19th-century quarries, there are several old **wells** and **springs**. Some emerge in stone troughs, another in an old cistern, and many were formal springs now lost beneath the leaves. The clearest lies below the ruined site of Parkwood Top, but it is fun to go looking for others among the trees.

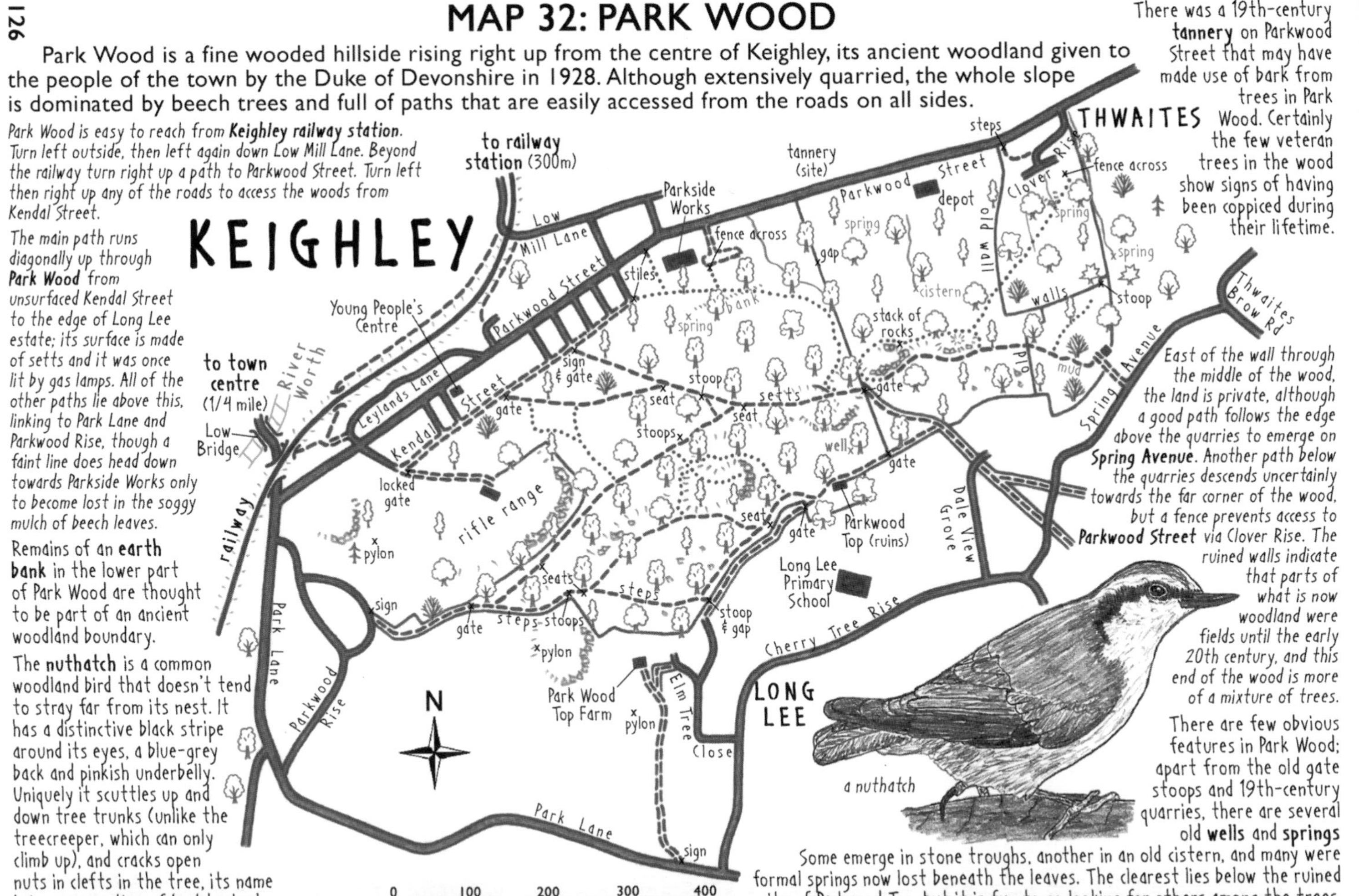
KEIGHLEY
to railway station (300m)
to town centre (1/4 mile)
Low Bridge
River Worth
railway
Low Mill Lane
Leylands Lane
Young People's Centre
Parkwood Street
Kendal Street
Parkside Works
fence across
stiles
sign & gate
gate
locked gate
rifle range
pylon
sign
Park Lane
Parkwood Rise
N
bank
spring
stoop
seat
setts
stoops
seats
steps
steps-stoops
stoop & gap
tannery (site)
gap
depot
cistern
stack of rocks
well
Parkwood Top (ruins)
Long Lee Primary School
Park Wood Top Farm
Elm Tree Close
Cherry Tree Rise
LONG LEE
Dale View Grove
Spring Avenue
Thwaites Brow Rd
THWAITES
steps
Clover Rise
old wall
walls
old
mud
a nuthatch
0
100
200
300
400

# ROUTE 21: OXENHOPE TO KEIGHLEY (Part 1)

**Route details overleaf**

CONTINUED OVERLEAF

he **Keighley and Worth Valley Railway** opened in April 367 as a single-track branch line, funded initially by cal businessmen but soon becoming part of Midland ailway. As well as a passenger service, it provided n invaluable link with the mainline in Keighley, ringing coal to the valley's mills and sending nished products the other way. Despite local pposition it was closed in 1962 following the eeching Report, but a Preservation Society was uickly formed and set about saving the railway. fter six years a sale was agreed with British ail, payable in instalments over 25 years, the rst rail privatisation in Britain. The line eopened as a heritage railway on 29th June 968, ironically a day of strikes elsewhere on e railways. Several steam locomotives were used n the line and it was used as the location for onel Jeffries' 1970 film of *The Railway Children*.

**2** Follow Brow Road down to the bottom, then bear ght along Station Road past **Haworth station** (an ternative starting point). Continue up the hill, then ar left down Ebor Lane by a stone plaque in e wall. After crossing the River Worth, rn right on a path alongside the ilway then stream to emerge at e foot of **Murgatroyd Wood** Vale Farm. Follow the track ght, then turn left along the road to the nd (Hoot Corner) by **Vale Mill**, where a th heads up the steps and under the ilway. Turn right at the top and keep ght to reach another Station Road on the ge of **Oakworth** *(map continues overleaf)*.

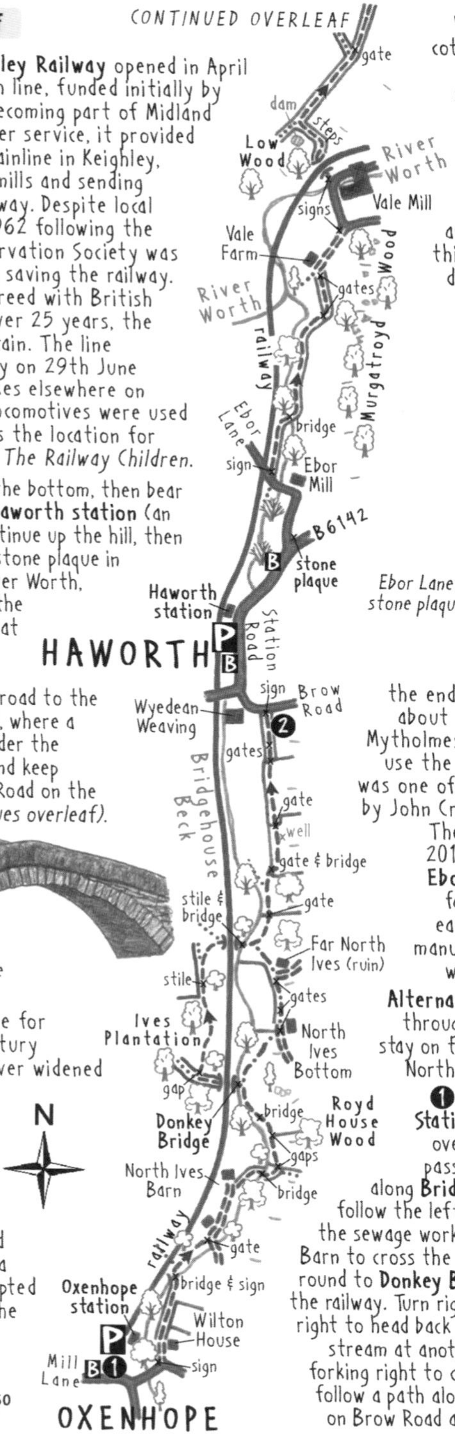

*Donkey Bridge*

nkey Bridge was a nickname for rth Ives Bridge, a 17th-century ckhorse bridge that was never widened replaced as it became elatively minor route.

ther than one village, **enhope** is really a nglomeration of several mlets, including Uppertown, wertown, Leeming, Shaw and rsh. Oxenhope only became a lage when its name was adopted the new station, built as the rminus of the Keighley and rth Valley Railway in 1867.

**Vale Mill** was built in 1785 as a cotton-spinning mill, but has been greatly expanded since, even spreading over the road beyond what locals call Hoot Corner. The railway line originally crossed the millpond on the upstream side via a trestle bridge, but it proved unsafe and the line was rerouted round this, requiring a new tunnel to be dug at Mytholmes (which coincidentally became a vital feature in *The Railway Children* film).

*Ebor Lane stone plaque*

The **stone plaque** at the end of Ebor Lane is a public notice about the private road from here to Mytholmes Lane. Others were allowed to use the road for certain fees, and this was one of three notices erected in 1843 by John Craven of Dockroyd in Oakworth. The plaque was only reinstated in 2013 after the wall was damaged. **Ebor Mill** was built by the Craven family in 1819 on the site of an earlier mill and used for worsted manufacture. Many of the buildings were destroyed by fire in 2010.

**Alternative route:** If the informal path through Ives Plantation is ever blocked, stay on the right side of the stream past North Ives Bottom and Far North Ives.

**1** From the entrance to **Oxenhope Station** car park, follow the road left over the stream, then turn left to pass Wilton House. A path continues along **Bridgehouse Beck**, soon crossing to follow the left bank. Bear left on a track past the sewage works, then bear right by North Ives Barn to cross the stream again. Follow the stream round to **Donkey Bridge**, crossing to duck beneath the railway. Turn right at a gap soon after and keep right to head back under the railway and rejoin the stream at another bridge. Follow it left, before forking right to cross a bridge into the fields and follow a path along their foot to emerge on Brow Road at the edge of **Haworth**.

**Holme House Woods** were known locally as Old Mouse Woods and during the 19th century a hermit known as Lucky Luke lived in the wood for twenty years. He was said to change his clothes with scarecrows and plunder nearby fields and gardens for vegetables.

On 22nd May 1936, the Hindenburg airship flew over Keighley, dropping a parcel that was found by two Boy Scouts. A letter attached requested the flowers and crucifix inside be placed on the grave of a Lieutenant Franz Schulte, who was buried in the town (at Morton Cemetery) after being shot down in World War I and dying of Spanish flu.

❺ Continue past most of the buildings of **Newsholme**, then fork left along a muddy track. Fork right and, at the end, descend steeply into the birch trees of **Cat Clough**, part of beautiful **Newsholme Dean**. The path emerges at a gate, beyond which you can see to the right a **K1 telephone box** by the stream. Head across the packhorse bridge adjacent to the ancient and precarious clam bridge of **Dean Bridge**, then follow the track up past Far Dene and Newsholme Dean Farm. At a waymark post above the latter bear right onto a path that follows the wall down through **Dean Wood**. Fork left before dropping down to the bridge and wind through the trees to pass above **Teapot Dam**. Join the path alongside the stream to emerge on the road opposite **Goose Eye Mill**.

❻ Follow the road left into **Goose Eye**, then turn right before crossing the stream unless you want to visit the Turkey Inn. Follow the old setts through **Goose Eye Wood**, then turn left either through a gap just before a small mill pond or a gate beyond it. Both join a fenced path along the edge of the field above **Higher Holme House Wood**. Continue along the south side of North Beck into **Lower Holme House Wood**, then fork left beyond a small bridge to rejoin the river bank. Climbing back up the slope, keep left to emerge at a gate the far end, then follow the sometimes soggy path down to **Intake Bridge**.

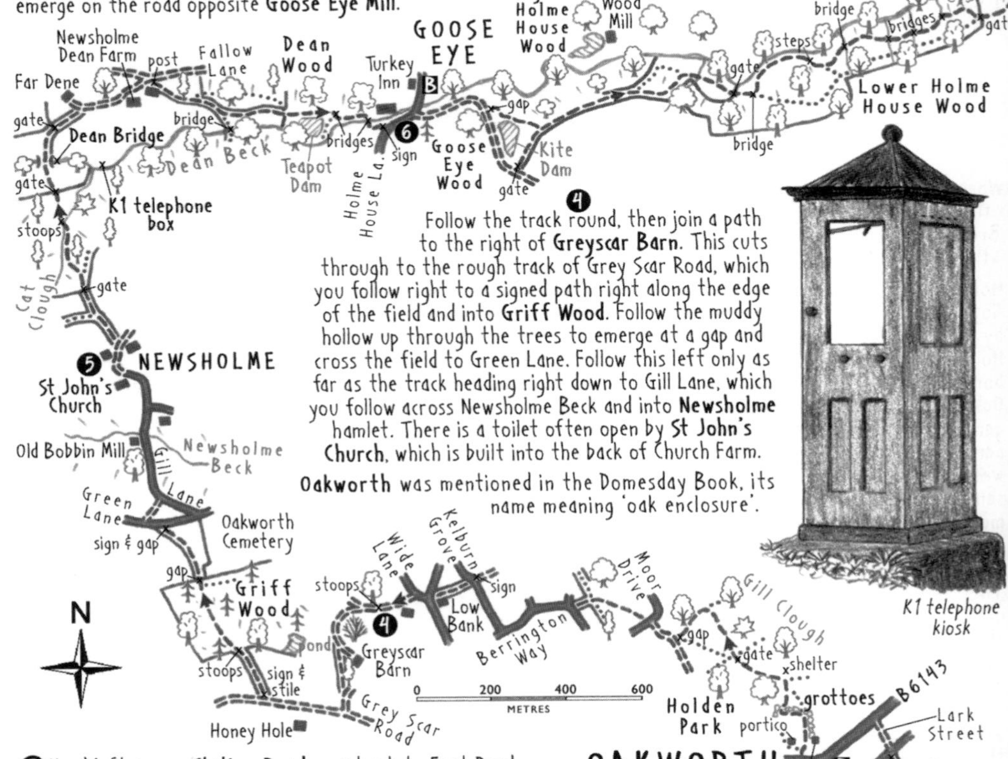

Higher Holme House Wood
Wood Mill
GOOSE EYE
Newsholme Dean Farm
post
Fallow Lane
Dean Wood
Turkey Inn
Far Dene
gate
bridge
Dean Bridge
Dean Beck
Teapot Dam
bridges
sign
Goose Eye Wood
Kite Dam
gap
K1 telephone box
stoops
Cat Clough
NEWSHOLME
St John's Church
Old Bobbin Mill
Newsholme Beck
Gill Lane
Green Lane
Oakworth Cemetery
sign & gap
Griff Wood
pond
Greyscar Barn
Honey Hole
Grey Scar Road
sign & stile
Wide Lane
Kelburn Grove
Low Bank
Berrington Way
Moor Drive
Gill Clough
shelter
grottoes
Holden Park
portico
B6143
Lark Street
OAKWORTH
summer house
Park Ave.
Low Eas Royd
gates
signs
sign & gates
Station Road
steps
Lower Holme House Wood
North
0 200 400 600
METRES
N


K1 telephone kiosk

❹ Follow the track round, then join a path to the right of **Greyscar Barn**. This cuts through to the rough track of Grey Scar Road, which you follow right to a signed path right along the edge of the field and into **Griff Wood**. Follow the muddy hollow up through the trees to emerge at a gap and cross the field to Green Lane. Follow this left only as far as the track heading right down to Gill Lane, which you follow across Newsholme Beck and into **Newsholme** hamlet. There is a toilet often open by **St John's Church**, which is built into the back of Church Farm.

**Oakworth** was mentioned in the Domesday Book, its name meaning 'oak enclosure'.

❸ Head left across **Station Road** on a track to East Royd, then turn left at a sign and follow a path across the fields to join Lark Street and reach the B6143 through **Oakworth**. Turn left to reach the entrance into **Holden Park** just beyond the mini-roundabout and keep right to head into the remarkable maze of grottoes. All paths through this lead up to an open grassy area; cross to a path leading left before the shelter and follow it up to the top of the woods, then turn left to reach a gap beyond another open area. Follow the track right, then bear left across the road and open ground beyond to cut straight through the band of trees and join Berrington Way. Head straight down to the bottom, then turn right on Kelburn Grove. Opposite a signpost, follow a narrow footpath left through to **Low Bank**. Head straight on into Wide Lane, then immediately bear left on an unsigned vehicle track.

CONT. OVERLEAF

# ROUTE 21: OXENHOPE TO KEIGHLEY (Part 2)

**Keighley Shared Church** was built as St Andrew's Church in 1807 after the medieval church there was deemed too small for the expanding town. Evidence of a 12th-century church on the site was uncovered during its demolition. It adopted its current name in 2000 after merging with Temple Street Methodist Church.

**Keighley Town Hall** was built in 1902 and the library was the first Carnegie library in England in 1904.

**7** Unfortunately there is no official route along North Beck beyond **Tinker Bridge**, so you have to follow a path over the bridge and up past Intake Farm. Turn right at the top along North Dean Road then turn right again at a signed path opposite Broster Avenue to join **Cat Steps** below the play area. At the bottom turn left along the stream for a bit before bearing left up to join a larger track through the allotments. Where this bends left, keep straight on, then keep right of the school grounds, dropping down some steps to **North Brook Mills**. Turn left and, at the end, follow a path right through the trees to emerge on the **B6143** in Keighley.

**Holden Park** was once the grounds of Oakworth House, an Italianate mansion built from 1864 by French and Italian craftsmen for Sir Isaac Holden. Holden was a former MP for Knaresborough and known as the Grand Old Man of Oakworth. A huge glass dome covered a winter garden, whose grottoes and mosaic floor is partly retained. The fascinating **grottoes** were made of limestone at the front and sandstone and hypertufa (a mix of peat and mortar) elsewhere. The summer house was made to look like tree branches and the portico was the original entrance to the grounds. There was a string of five dams in Gill Clough, which fed the mills, as well as a series of cascades and fountains. The house made Oakworth more popular with Victorian tourists than nearby Haworth. After Holden died in 1897 the house lay empty and was demolished following a serious fire in 1909. The grounds were given to the people of Oakworth and are well worth exploring.

*Holden Park grottoes*

**8** Head straight across the **B6143** on a road past the Royal Oak. Turn left on the main road at the end, then go right into Church Street. To reach the bus station continue straight on to rejoin the main road, or to reach the railway station head round either side of **Keighley Shared Church**. Follow the road to the left of the supermarket, then turn right on the A6035 and immediately left along Long Croft. At the end turn right over **Low Bridge**, then bear left on a path under the railway. Beyond a bridge, turn left and follow a tarmac path back under the railway and along its side to Low Mill Lane. Follow this left up to the A6035 by the entrance to **Keighley railway station**.

The **K1 telephone kiosk** is one of only six surviving examples of Britain's first national phone boxes, of which just 500 were introduced by the General Post Office from 1922. Though the familiar red K2 boxes were introduced in cities from 1924 after a design competition, this simpler and cheaper model was still used in rural areas. A listed building, it is made of concrete and would have originally been painted cream. It was moved to its current location by the stream in the 1960s to house equipment for monitoring flow over the weir.

**Distance:** 9 miles (14.2km)

**Ascent:** 260m

**Parking:** Free parking at Oxenhope station. Various pay car parks in the centre of Keighley.

**Public Transport:** Keighley is on the main Airedale railway line. The Keighley & Worth Valley railway runs regularly at weekends, school holidays and most of the summer from Keighley to Oxenhope and has its own ale bar. The B3 Brontë Bus runs hourly year round from Keighley bus station to Oxenhope station.

**Character:** A linear route along the length of the Keighley & Worth Valley Railway, following the railway at first but then exploring Holden Park in Oakworth, Newsholme Dean and the fine woods along North Beck. The perfect return is a journey back on the steam train from Keighley with a pint of local ale.

# MAP 33: HOLDEN PARK & GILL

In the 1650s Lady Anne Clifford of Skipton Castle erected a corn mill on the east side of **Holden Bridge**, which separated the townships of Silsden and Holden. There was already a soke mill on Silsden Beck and the tenants of Silsden were promptly forbidden to use Lady Anne's new mill. Litigation between the neighbouring landowners dragged on for 15 years and, when the court ruled against her (partly because evidence was destroyed during the Civil War siege on her castle), Holden Mill quickly disappeared, leaving only faint traces of the millpond on Mill Ing.

***Spring Crag Wood*** *is the largest woodland in this area, with all its paths running north-south across the slope and little linking them. The highest two routes lead only to a locked gateway on Holden Lane, though the higher path in particular is a lovely route. The lower paths both lead to stiles out of the wood, as well as giving access to fainter routes through* ***Alder Carr Wood****. This is a fascinating wet woodland, with dense holly higher up. A reasonable path skirts all the way round its perimeter, though there is no way to cross the private Lodge hill Bridge. The paths through the middle are harder to follow but it is a charming wood to explore.*

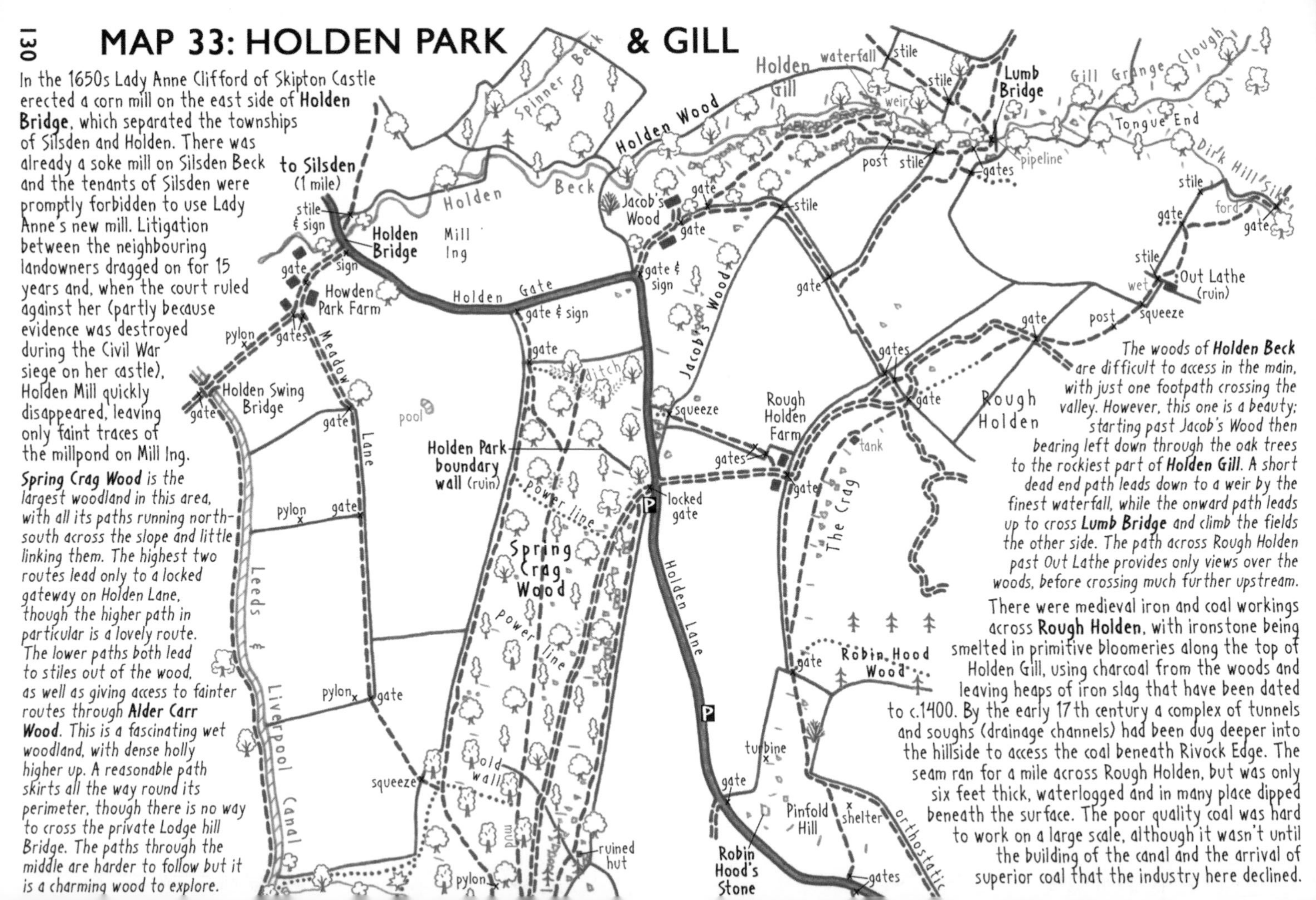
to Silsden
(1 mile)
stile & sign
Holden Bridge
sign
gate
Howden Park Farm
gates
pylon
Meadow
Holden Swing Bridge
gate
Lane
pylon
Leeds & Liverpool Canal
squeeze
pylon
Holden
Mill Ing
Spinner Beck
Beck
Holden Gate
gate & sign
pool
ditch
Holden Park boundary wall (ruin)
power line
Spring Crag Wood
old wall
mud
ruined hut
Holden Wood
Jacob's Wood
gate & sign
Jacob's Wood
squeeze
locked gate
Holden Lane
Holden Gill
waterfall
weir
stile
post
Lumb Bridge
gates
pipeline
Gill Grange Clough
Tongue End
Dirk Hill Sike
ford
Out Lathe (ruin)
wet
squeeze
Rough Holden Farm
Rough Holden
tank
The Crag
Robin Hood Wood
turbine
Pinfold Hill
shelter
orthostatic
Robin Hood's Stone

*The woods of* ***Holden Beck*** *are difficult to access in the main, with just one footpath crossing the valley. However, this one is a beauty; starting past Jacob's Wood then bearing left down through the oak trees to the rockiest part of* ***Holden Gill****. A short dead end path leads down to a weir by the finest waterfall, while the onward path leads up to cross* ***Lumb Bridge*** *and climb the fields the other side. The path across Rough Holden past Out Lathe provides only views over the woods, before crossing much further upstream.*

There were medieval iron and coal workings across **Rough Holden**, with ironstone being smelted in primitive bloomeries along the top of Holden Gill, using charcoal from the woods and leaving heaps of iron slag that have been dated to c.1400. By the early 17th century a complex of tunnels and soughs (drainage channels) had been dug deeper into the hillside to access the coal beneath Rivock Edge. The seam ran for a mile across Rough Holden, but was only six feet thick, waterlogged and in many place dipped beneath the surface. The poor quality coal was hard to work on a large scale, although it wasn't until the building of the canal and the arrival of superior coal that the industry here declined.

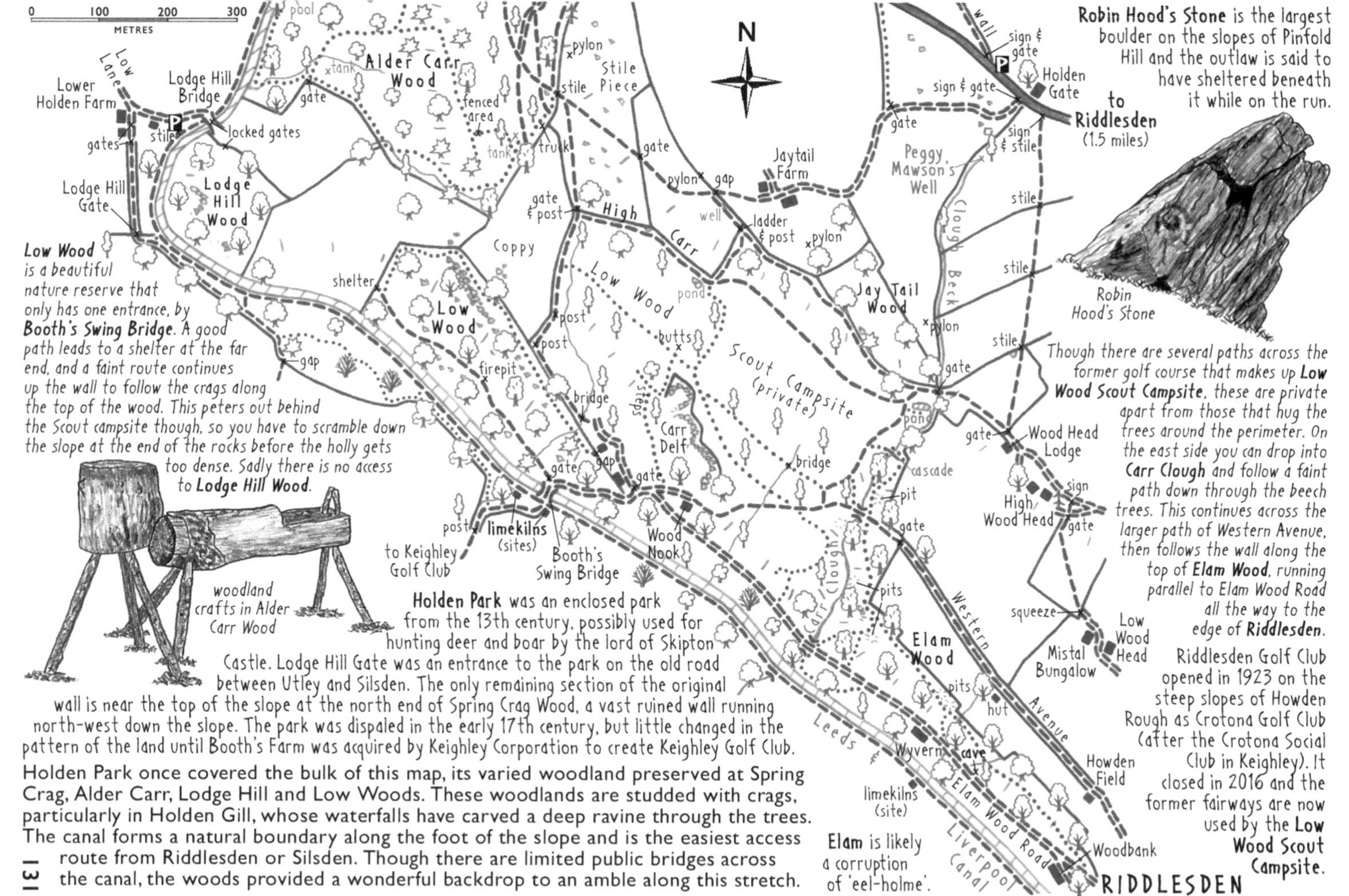
0 100 200 300
METRES
N
Robin Hood's Stone is the largest boulder on the slopes of Pinfold Hill and the outlaw is said to have sheltered beneath it while on the run.
Low Wood is a beautiful nature reserve that only has one entrance, by Booth's Swing Bridge. A good path leads to a shelter at the far end, and a faint route continues up the wall to follow the crags along the top of the wood. This peters out behind the Scout campsite though, so you have to scramble down the slope at the end of the rocks before the holly gets too dense. Sadly there is no access to Lodge Hill Wood.
Though there are several paths across the former golf course that makes up Low Wood Scout Campsite, these are private apart from those that hug the trees around the perimeter. On the east side you can drop into Carr Clough and follow a faint path down through the beech trees. This continues across the larger path of Western Avenue, then follows the wall along the top of Elam Wood, running parallel to Elam Wood Road all the way to the edge of Riddlesden.
Riddlesden Golf Club opened in 1923 on the steep slopes of Howden Rough as Crotona Golf Club (after the Crotona Social Club in Keighley). It closed in 2016 and the former fairways are now used by the Low Wood Scout Campsite.
Holden Park was an enclosed park from the 13th century, possibly used for hunting deer and boar by the lord of Skipton Castle. Lodge Hill Gate was an entrance to the park on the old road between Utley and Silsden. The only remaining section of the original wall is near the top of the slope at the north end of Spring Crag Wood, a vast ruined wall running north-west down the slope. The park was dispaled in the early 17th century, but little changed in the pattern of the land until Booth's Farm was acquired by Keighley Corporation to create Keighley Golf Club.
Holden Park once covered the bulk of this map, its varied woodland preserved at Spring Crag, Alder Carr, Lodge Hill and Low Woods. These woodlands are studded with crags, particularly in Holden Gill, whose waterfalls have carved a deep ravine through the trees. The canal forms a natural boundary along the foot of the slope and is the easiest access route from Riddlesden or Silsden. Though there are limited public bridges across the canal, the woods provided a wonderful backdrop to an amble along this stretch.
Elam is likely a corruption of 'eel-holme'.
woodland crafts in Alder Carr Wood
Robin Hood's Stone
to Riddlesden (1.5 miles)
Low Lane
Lower Holden Farm
gates
stile
Lodge Hill Bridge
locked gates
Lodge Hill Gate
Lodge Hill Wood
pool
tank
Alder Carr Wood
gate
fenced area
tank
truck
stile
Stile Piece
pylon
gate & post
High Carr
Coppy
shelter
gap
Low Wood
firepit
post
post
Low Wood
pond
butts
steps
Carr Delf
bridge
gate
gap
gate
gate
Scout Campsite (private)
limekilns (sites)
post
to Keighley Golf Club
Booth's Swing Bridge
Wood Nook
gate
pylon
gap
well
ladder & post
pylon
Jaytail Farm
Jay Tail Wood
pylon
gate
pond
cascade
pit
gate
Carr Clough
pits
Elam Wood
pits
hut
cave
Wyvern
limekilns (site)
Leeds Liverpool Canal
Elam Wood Road
Western Avenue
wall
sign & gate
Holden Gate
sign & gate
sign & stile
Peggy Mawson's Well
Clough Beck
gate
stile
stile
stile
gate
Wood Head Lodge
sign
High Wood Head
gate
squeeze
Mistal Bungalow
Low Wood Head
Howden Field
Woodbank
RIDDLESDEN

# ROUTE 22: HOLDEN GILL & SPRING CRAG WOOD FROM SILSDEN

The aqueduct bridge in **Swartha Wood** and the pipe by Lumb Bridge in Holden Gill are both part of the Nidd Aqueduct, bringing drinking water to Bradford from Angram and Scar House Reservoirs since the 1850s.

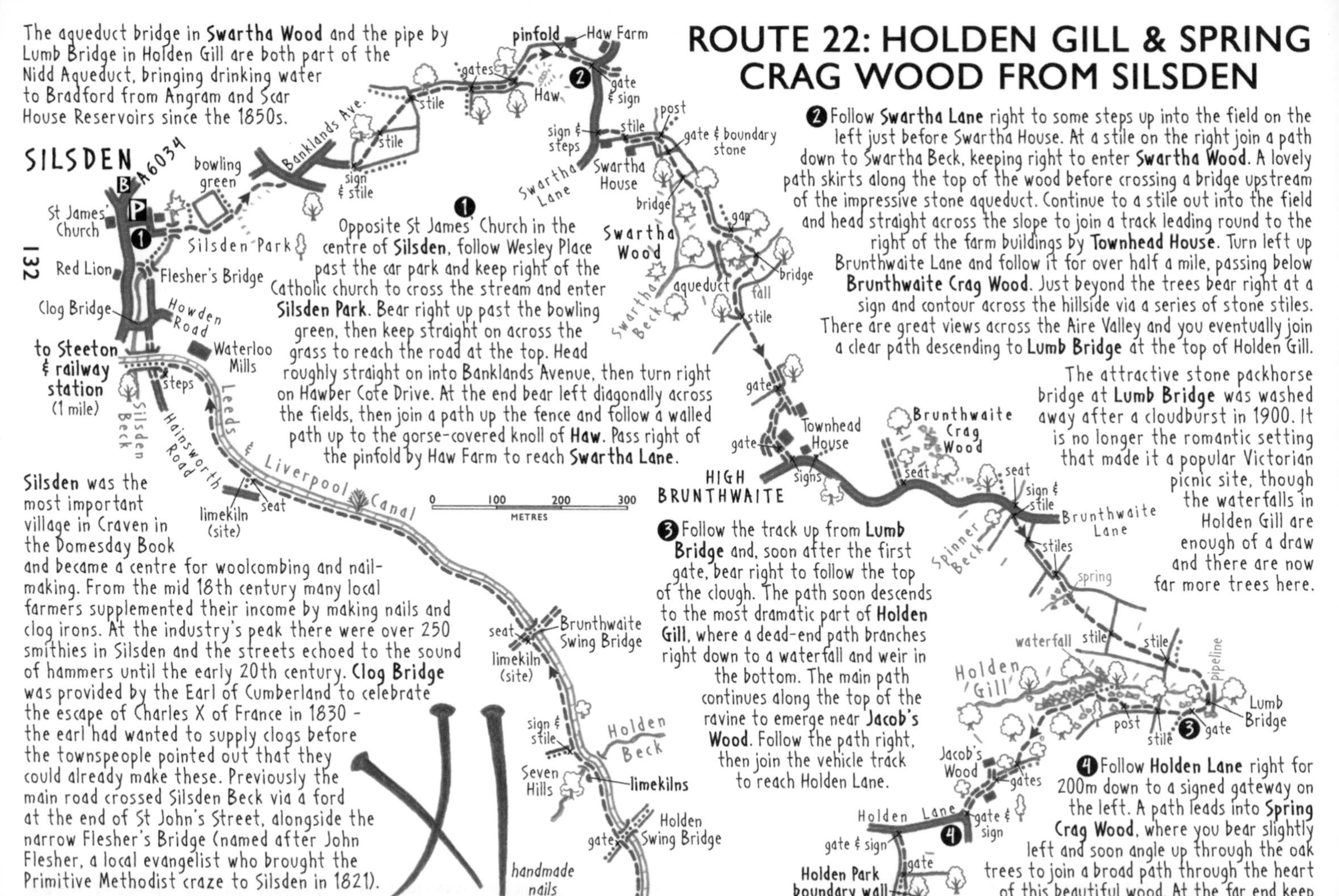
SILSDEN
B
P
A6034
St James' Church
Red Lion
Clog Bridge
Flesher's Bridge
Howden Road
Waterloo Mills
to Steeton & railway station (1 mile)
steps
Silsden Beck
Hainsworth Road
Leeds & Liverpool Canal
limekiln (site)
seat
bowling green
Silsden Park
Banklands Ave.
sign & stile
stile
gates
pinfold
Haw Farm
Haw
gate & sign
sign & steps
Swartha Lane
Swartha House
post
gate & boundary stone
bridge
Swartha Wood
gap
aqueduct
fall
Swartha Beck
gate
Townhead House
HIGH BRUNTHWAITE
signs
Brunthwaite Crag Wood
seat
Spinner Beck
sign & stile
Brunthwaite Lane
stiles
spring
waterfall
Holden Gill
pipeline
Lumb Bridge
post
Jacob's Wood
gates
gate & sign
Holden Lane
Holden Park boundary wall
0 100 200 300
METRES
Brunthwaite Swing Bridge
Seven Hills
limekilns
Holden Beck
Holden Swing Bridge
handmade nails

❶ Opposite St James' Church in the centre of **Silsden**, follow Wesley Place past the car park and keep right of the Catholic church to cross the stream and enter **Silsden Park**. Bear right up past the bowling green, then keep straight on across the grass to reach the road at the top. Head roughly straight on into Banklands Avenue, then turn right on Hawber Cote Drive. At the end bear left diagonally across the fields, then join a path up the fence and follow a walled path up to the gorse-covered knoll of **Haw**. Pass right of the pinfold by Haw Farm to reach **Swartha Lane**.

❷ Follow **Swartha Lane** right to some steps up into the field on the left just before Swartha House. At a stile on the right join a path down to Swartha Beck, keeping right to enter **Swartha Wood**. A lovely path skirts along the top of the wood before crossing a bridge upstream of the impressive stone aqueduct. Continue to a stile out into the field and head straight across the slope to join a track leading round to the right of the farm buildings by **Townhead House**. Turn left up Brunthwaite Lane and follow it for over half a mile, passing below **Brunthwaite Crag Wood**. Just beyond the trees bear right at a sign and contour across the hillside via a series of stone stiles. There are great views across the Aire Valley and you eventually join a clear path descending to **Lumb Bridge** at the top of Holden Gill.

The attractive stone packhorse bridge at **Lumb Bridge** was washed away after a cloudburst in 1900. It is no longer the romantic setting that made it a popular Victorian picnic site, though the waterfalls in Holden Gill are enough of a draw and there are now far more trees here.

❸ Follow the track up from **Lumb Bridge** and, soon after the first gate, bear right to follow the top of the clough. The path soon descends to the most dramatic part of **Holden Gill**, where a dead-end path branches right down to a waterfall and weir in the bottom. The main path continues along the top of the ravine to emerge near **Jacob's Wood**. Follow the path right, then join the vehicle track to reach Holden Lane.

❹ Follow **Holden Lane** right for 200m down to a signed gateway on the left. A path leads into **Spring Crag Wood**, where you bear slightly left and soon angle up through the oak trees to join a broad path through the heart of this beautiful wood. At the far end keep

**Silsden** was the most important village in Craven in the Domesday Book and became a centre for woolcombing and nail-making. From the mid 18th century many local farmers supplemented their income by making nails and clog irons. At the industry's peak there were over 250 smithies in Silsden and the streets echoed to the sound of hammers until the early 20th century. **Clog Bridge** was provided by the Earl of Cumberland to celebrate the escape of Charles X of France in 1830 – the earl had wanted to supply clogs before the townspeople pointed out that they could already make these. Previously the main road crossed Silsden Beck via a ford at the end of St John's Street, alongside the narrow Flesher's Bridge (named after John Flesher, a local evangelist who brought the Primitive Methodist craze to Silsden in 1821).

straight on where another path crosses, then bear left steeply up to a stone stile out of the wood. Fork right down the field to a gate, then turn left along the edge of the trees of **High Carr**. Where this opens out, turn left on a path up the wall, then turn right to skirt along the edge of **Jay Tail Wood** with the former golf course below.

**5** At the far end of **Jay Tail Wood** turn right 50m before the next gate and descend down the edge of the former golf course. A faint path descends left after 150m and follows **Carr Clough** below a cascade. Cross the stream and descend through the beech trees, heading straight across a larger path to join the edge of the wall high above the clough (these paths can be hard to make out after fresh leaf fall). Keeping left along the wall, the path becomes clearer through **Elam Wood**, running parallel to the wall for some distance before finally emerging on **Elam Wood Road**.

**6** Double back right on **Elam Wood Road** and follow it along the foot of the wood parallel to the **Leeds and Liverpool Canal** for half a mile. Reaching the Scout campsite, keep left down the track to cross the canal at **Booth's Swing Bridge**. Just before the bridge, a gate on the right gives access to Low Wood, a beautiful ancient oak woodland, but there is no way out the far end so if you want to explore this you need to return to the bridge. If you continue 50m beyond the bridge you can see one of the many **limekilns** that once lined this canal.

There were over 40 **limekilns** along the Leeds & Liverpool Canal between Skipton and Bradford, one of the primary purposes in this area being to transport limestone from the Yorkshire Dales. It could then be burned here using local charcoal and spread on the fields to sweeten the acidic soil.

**Seven Hills** was a popular picnic site beside Holden Beck. It was an area previously known as Penny Lands or Sour Lands for its poor soil.

**7** Join the towpath alongside the **Leeds & Liverpool Canal** and follow it for two miles all the way back into Silsden. Early on you pass along the edge of Low Wood, Lodge Hill Wood and **Alder Carr Wood**, although all these appealing woods are frustratingly inaccessible across the water. The landscape then opens out, crossing fields to reach the edge of Silsden and its waterside estates. Soon after passing **Waterloo Mills**, the first obvious mill buildings, turn left down some steps and join Hainsworth Road to pass under the canal. Head straight across Howden Road, following St John's Street to its end before cutting left over **Silsden Beck** to join the main road through **Silsden**. St James' Church and the car park are reached 100m to the right.

This part of the Aire Valley was once generously strewn with **limestone** boulders and rubble deposits from the Aire glacier. These were dug out and burnt in small field kilns, producing quicklime to be used as a soil improver and in building mortar. When this source was exhausted, local farmers had to send packhorses to distant limekilns near Skipton until the canal was built in the 1770s.

*limekilns by Holden Beck*

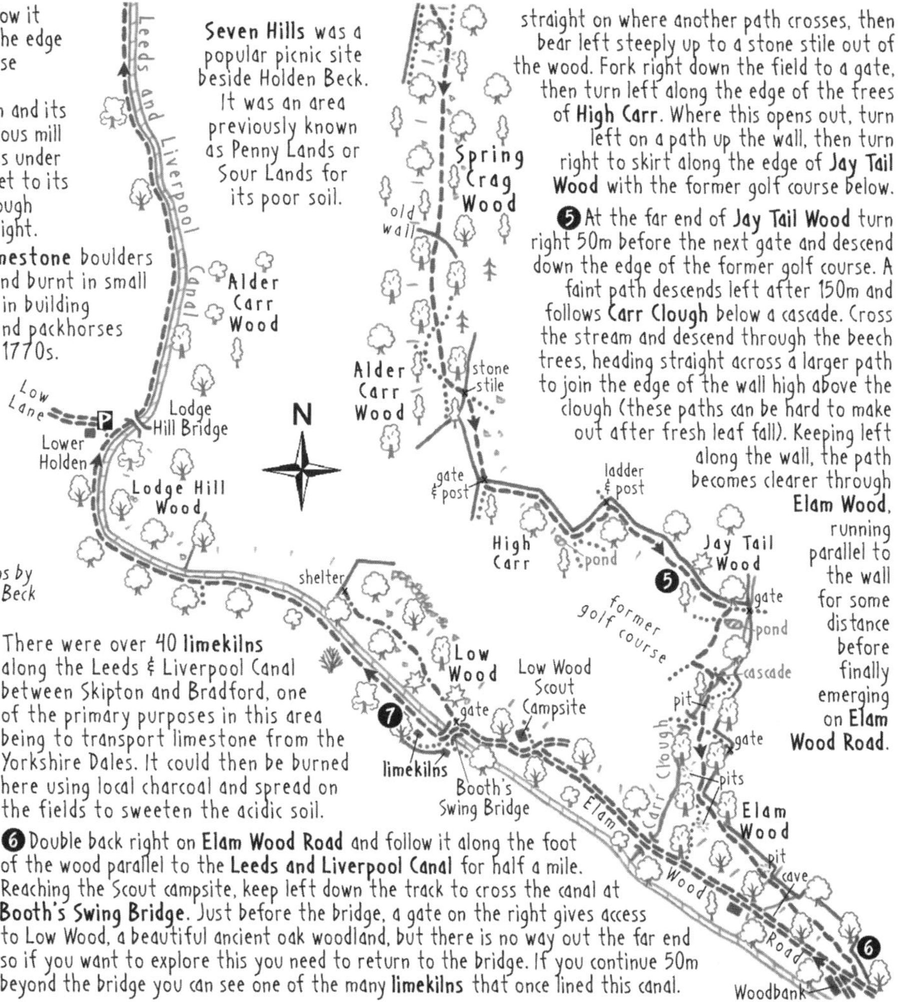

**Distance:** 7½ miles (12.3km)

**Ascent:** 270m

**Parking:** Pay car park in the centre of Silsden and small parking area by Lower Holden at the end of Low Lane.

**Public Transport:** Silsden is on various bus routes from Keighley. Steeton & Silsden railway station (on the main Airedale line) is 1 mile from the route along the A6034.

**Character:** A lovely exploration of the piecemeal woodlands dotted across the hillside between Silsden and Riddlesden. The route takes in the dramatic rocky gorges of Holden Gill and Swartha Beck and the varied trees of Spring Crag, Alder Carr and Elam Woods before a sedate return along the Leeds & Liverpool Canal. Largely on good paths throughout.

# MAP 34: CURRER WOOD & STEETON BECK

At the furthest extent of West Yorkshire, the wooded slopes above Steeton and Eastburn house the remarkable waterfalls of Steeton Beck, the great gulf of Eastburn Quarry and the ancient Currer Wood. Though there are only a few public paths here, it still provides a fine short circular exploration from either village.

*There is little option for exploring here other than following the footpath up past Steeton Manor and through* ***Currer Wood****, then keeping right along Intake Lane before following the bridleway of Moor Lane back down past* ***Eastburn Quarry*** *to Eastburn. It is a fine little walk, but unfortunately Currer Wood and Eastburn Quarry are both private, and signs let you know as much.*

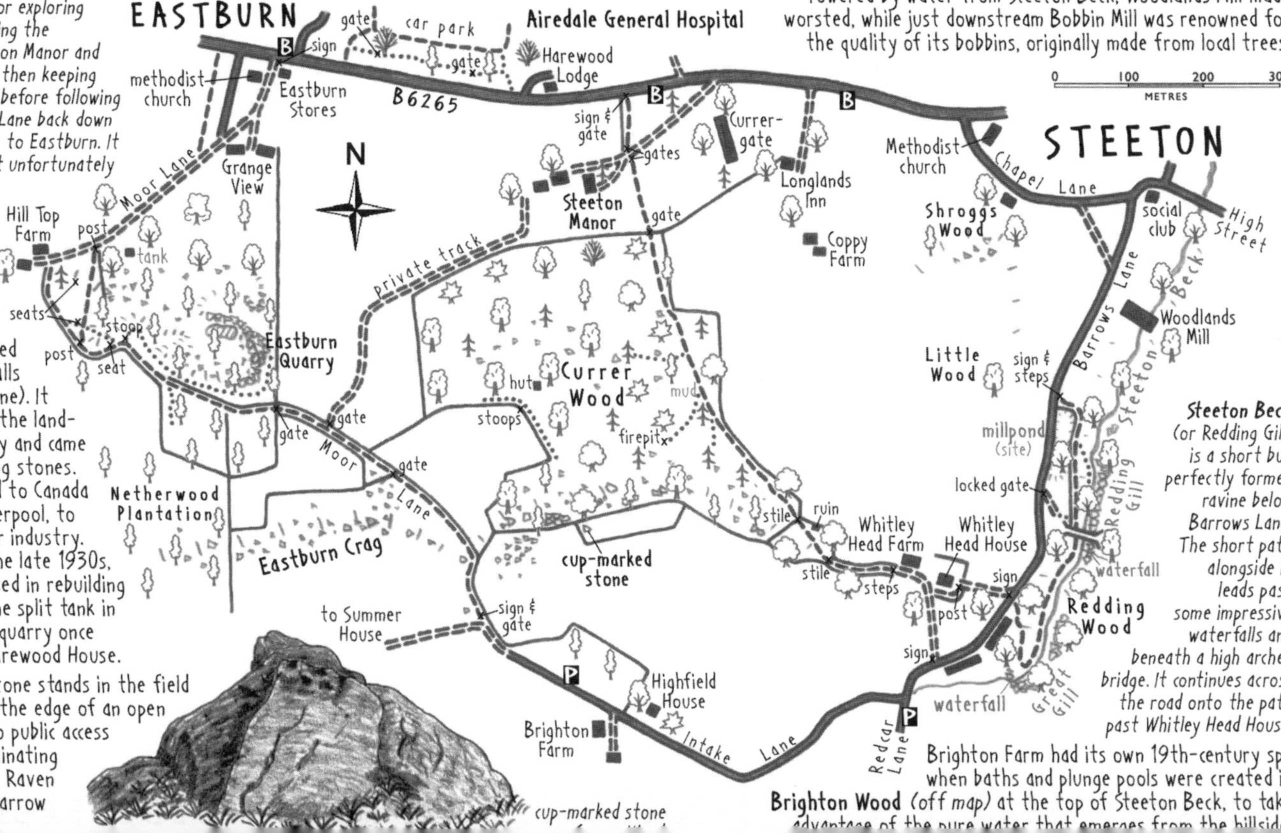

**Eastburn Quarry** is a vast hole surrounded by overgrown judd walls (stacks of waste stone). It was used initially by the land-owning Barrett family and came to specialise in pulping stones. These were exported to Canada via the canal and Liverpool, to be used in the lumber industry. Before it closed in the late 1930s, its stone was also used in rebuilding Heysham Harbour. The split tank in the trees below the quarry once provided water to Harewood House.

A lone cup-marked stone stands in the field above **Currer Wood**, the edge of an open landscape that has no public access but is covered in fascinating names; Dragon Stone, Raven Stones, Kirk Rocks, Barrow Fields and Hawk Cliff.

**Steeton** is a contraction of Stiveton (Stephen's town) and is an ancient manorial settlement. However, the current **Steeton Manor** house was only built in 1894 by Sir Swire Smith, a textile manufacturer who later became MP for Keighley. Powered by water from Steeton Beck, Woodlands Mill made worsted, while just downstream Bobbin Mill was renowned for the quality of its bobbins, originally made from local trees.

**Steeton Beck** *(or Redding Gill) is a short but perfectly formed ravine below Barrows Lane. The short path alongside it leads past some impressive waterfalls and beneath a high arched bridge. It continues across the road onto the path past Whitley Head House.*

Brighton Farm had its own 19th-century spa when baths and plunge pools were created in **Brighton Wood** *(off map)* at the top of Steeton Beck, to take advantage of the pure water that emerges from the hillside

# THE LEEDS & LIVERPOOL CANAL

Construction of the Leeds and Liverpool Canal was first proposed in 1764 to provide a direct link from the Aire Valley across the Pennines to Liverpool Dock, creating a passage between the North Sea and Irish Sea. Inspired by the need to trade wool, cotton, lime and coal across the Pennines, it was approved by an Act of Parliament in May 1770, following a survey of its 127-mile course. Costing £1.2 million, it had 91 locks and would be the longest canal built by a single company in the UK.

Construction began immediately after the Act. Small sections, often just one mile long, were built by local contractors, who employed a travelling workforce of navvies, about whose behaviour there were many local complaints. In Silsden, John Tickle was accused of not properly supervising his workers or the standard of their workmanship. Some of his unfinished work had to be passed to others and, only a few years after being built, the bridge over Silsden Beck started to weaken and had to be reinforced with buttresses.

The canal's construction also created problems by dividing existing areas of woodland and farmland and blocking access routes. Several swing bridges were needed to preserve existing rights of way and allow access for landowners whose land was now split. However, the compensation was good for landowners and there was generally little problem acquiring land for the canal.

By July 1771 the section from Liverpool to Newburgh was open in Lancashire, but it was the Yorkshire side that generally progressed more quickly, as its route was more straightforward, following the Aire Valley all the way up to the Aire Gap. Industrialists in Lancashire wanted it to link in as many places as possible, hence its large loop through Chorley and Wigan and its journey through Burnley and Blackburn rather than along the Ribble Valley. This required tunnelling at the canal's highest point near Foulridge, and the construction of several compensation reservoirs, in spite of which the canal would often close during dry summers.

The 18-mile section from Bingley to Skipton was opened by 1773 as there was no need for any locks. The next section was delayed by protracted negotiations with local landowners and the difficult terrain around Bingley, where the broad valley floor is complicated by large deposits of glacial moraine. Bingley's famous Five Rise and Three Rise Locks were designed by John Longbotham of Halifax and their completion enabled the section to Thackley to open in March 1774. The whole stretch from Leeds to Gargrave was open by 1777.

Though the Leeds and Liverpool Canal was started earlier, it was actually the third trans-Pennine canal to be opened; the Rochdale Canal was completed in 1802 and Huddersfield Narrow Canal in 1804. Financial difficulties delayed the completion of the Leeds and Liverpool Canal and it wasn't opened fully until 1816, when a flotilla of decorated boats sailed its whole length to celebrate. However, money had started to come in quickly in the form of goods tolls, particularly for limestone, coal and stone. The canal's greater width of 27' meant it carried far larger barges and consequently better payloads. Passenger traffic was also significant, with regular packet services the whole width of the Pennines. Passenger traffic operating, some covering the whole route in four days.

The canal was its peak in the 1820s. With the arrival of the railways in the 1840s and 50s, the importance of many canals began to decline, but the Leeds and Liverpool remained buoyant until World War II. It was bombed in Bootle and was in poor condition when it was breached near Riddlesden in 1952, spewing a torrent of water across Keighley Golf Course. After narrowly avoiding closure in the 1970s, it became one of the Aire Valley's best amenities, as well as a focal point for regeneration in the centre of Leeds.

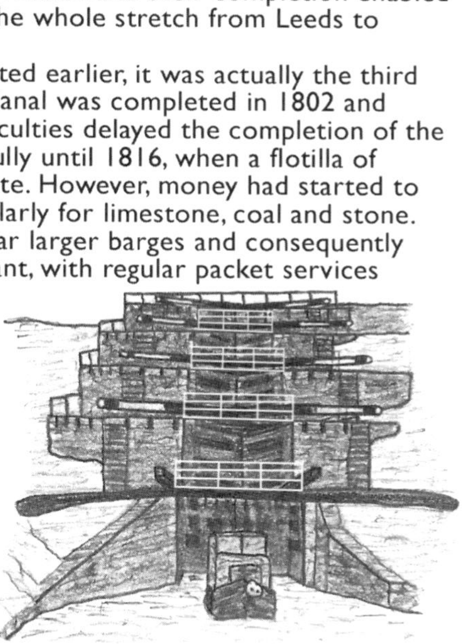

*Five Rise Locks in Bingley*

# BIBLIOGRAPHY


Adams, Vera – *Drighlington in Times Past* (Chorley: Countryside Publications Limited, 1985)

Aireborough & Horsforth Museum Society – *The Esholt Estate: A Brief History* (Leeds: Aireborough & Horsforth Museum Society, 1991)

Alvin, N.A. – *Buck Wood, Thackley: Survey of Archaeological Features* (unpublished)

Alvin, N.A. – *Charcoal Burning in Buck Wood* (unpublished)

Baildon Local History Society – *In Celebration of Tong Park* (Saltaire: ASAP, 1995)

Baldwin, Heather & Mills, Helen – *Bingley* (Stroud: Chalford, 1995)

Beamon, Sylvia & Roaf, Susan – *The Ice Houses of Britain* (London: Routledge, 1990)

Belfield, Wilbye & Gilleghan, John – *Templenewsam Nature Trail* (Leeds: City of Leeds Parks and Museums Department)

Belle Isle Study Group – *Belle Isle* (Leeds: Belle Isle Study Group, 1985)

Bewell, Peter (ed.) – *Meanwood in Pictures: Volume 1* (Leeds: MVA Publications, 2004)

Bogg, Edmund – *Round About Leeds and the Old Villages in Elmete* (Leeds: Old Hall Press, 1987)

Bogg, Edmund – *The Old Kingdom of Elmet: the Land 'twixt Aire and Wharfe* (Leeds: The Old Hall Press, 1987)

Boughey, K. – *Sermons in Stones: Buck Wood and the Prehistoric Rock Art of the Former West Riding of Yorkshire* (unpublished)

Bramley History Society – *Bramley: The Village that Disappeared* (Bramley History Society, 1984)

Branston, Graham – *Alwoodley, Leeds: The History of a Twentieth Century Suburb* (Leeds: Graham Branston, 2004)

Branston, Graham – *The Commons, Waste Lands and Urban Moors of Leeds* (Leeds: Graham Branston, 2005)

Broadhead, Helen – *Shipley Glen: Woodland Management* (unpublished)

Brooke, Dennis, Brooke, Mary, Hirst, Bernard & Thorp, John – *Oulton: Village Church Estate* (St John's Press, 1979)

Bulmer, Simon & Brown, Albert – *Around Rothwell* (Stroud: Tempus, 1999)

Burrows, Dorothy – *Baildon: A Look at the Past* (Pudsey: Allanwood Press Ltd, 1986)

Burt, Steven – *An Illustrated History of Roundhay Park* (Leeds: Steven Burt, 2000)

Burt, Steven & Grady, Kevin – *The Illustrated History of Leeds* (Derby: Breedon Books, 2002)

Burt, Steven – *An Illustrated History of Alwoodley* (Leeds: Steven Burt, 2005)

Bushell, J. – *The World's Oldest Railway* (Sheffield: Turntable Publications, 1975)

Casperson, Frederic P. & Hopwood, Arthur W. – *Meanwood: Village, Valley, Industry and People* (Otley: Smith Settle, 2004)

Cattell, Alan – *Bingley and Surrounds: Forgotten Moments from History* (Bradford: Overt Marketing Ltd, 2011)

Cattey, William Neil – *Silsden in Old Picture Postcards* (Zaltbommel, European Library, 1992)

Chaffer, Kenneth – *Victorian Village: Guiseley Yorkshire, an Intimate View* (Harrogate: Kenneth Chaffer, 1988)

City of Bradford – *Esholt: Conservation Area Assessment* (City of Bradford, 2002)

Cockcroft, Alan & Young, Matthew – *Horsforth* (Stroud: Chalford, 1995)

Cole, Don – *Cookridge: The Story of a Yorkshire Township* (Leeds: D&J Thornton, 1980)

Cole, Don – *An Early 20th Century Housing Estate in a Yorkshire Parish* (Leeds: Impressive Characters, 2003)

Cooper, Wallace – *Bygone Guiseley* (Guiseley: M.T.D. Rigg Publications, 1995)

Crompton, Val – *History of Adel, Yorkshire* (Leeds: Val Crompton, 2009)
Cruikshank, John Louis – 'Surveying the administrative boundaries of Lancs & Yorks after 1841 OS Act' in *Sheetlines 50* (1997)
Cruikshank, John Louis – 'The Maps of the Ordnance Survey as They Are and as They Ought to Be' in *Sheetlines 92* (2011)
Cruikshank, John Louis – *Headingley-cum-Burley C.1544-C.1784: Volume 22* (Leeds: Thoresby Society, 2013)
Cudworth, William – *Round About Bradford* (Queensbury: Mountain Press, 1968)
Darbyshire, Revd Hubert Stanley & Lumb, George Denison (ed.) – *The History of Methley* (Leeds: Thoresby Society, 1937)
Dewhirst, Ian – *A History of Keighley* (Keighley Corporation, 1974)
Dodd, E.E. – *Bingley* (Guiseley: M.T.D. Rigg Publications, 1958)
Doherty, Edward – *Bygone Middleton* (Chorley: Countryside Publications, 1987)
Douglas, Janet, Hammond, Chris & Powell, Ken – *Leeds: Three Suburban Walks* (London: The Victorian Society, 1987)
Eccleshill Local History Group – *A Ramble Around Fagley* (Bradford: Eccleshill Local History Group, 1995)
Entwistle, Norman – *Pictures of Old Baildon* (Chorley: Countryside Publications, 1985)
Evans, Lucy – *Celebrating the Roundhays* (Leeds: L. Evans, 2002)
Eyres, Patrick – *St Ives, Bingley* (Leeds: New Arcadians, 1982)
Fairburn Village Book Group – *Fairburn: A Part of its History* (Fairburn Village Book Group, 1983)
Fiennes, Peter – *Oak and Ash and Thorn: The Ancient Woods and New Forests of Britain* (London: Oneworld, 2017)
Firth, Gary – *Bingley History Trail* (Nelson: Hendon Publishing Co, 1977)
Firth, Gary – *Wilsden in Times Past* (Chorley: Countryside Publications, 1985)
Firth, Gary – *Shipley and Windhill* (Stroud: Chalford, 1996)
Firth, Gary – *Salt and Saltaire* (Stroud: Tempus, 2001)
Firth, Gary & Hitt, Malcolm – *Bingley Past and Present* (Stroud: The History Press, 2009)
Ford, Margaret & Throp, Christine – *Rodley: Both Sides of the Beck* (Pudsey Civic Society, 2012)
Gardener, Christopher – *From Acorn to Oak: A History of Headingley* (Leeds: Christopher Gardener, 1985)
Garnett, Edward – *The Story of the Calverley Murders: A Yorkshire Tragedy* (Calverley: Edward Garnett, 1991)
Gill, Lucy I. – *Baildon Memories* (Guiseley: M.T.D. Rigg Publications, 1986)
Gill, Walter – *Woodhouse in Leeds* (Leeds: D&J Thornton, 1984)
Gilleghan, John – *The Story of Temple Newsam Park* (unpublished)
Goodall, Armitage – *Place-names of South-West Yorkshire* (Cambridge University Press, 1914)
Hall, David – *Far Headingley: Weetwood and West Park* (Leeds: Far Headingley Village Society, 2000)
Hannam, Dr Ruth – *The Hidden History of the Land: Geology and Landscape in Calverley, Farsley and Pudsey* (Pudsey Civic Society, 1984)
Hanson, Malcolm – *Bingley's Secret History* (Skipton: Malcolm Hanson, 2013)
Heaton Woods Trust – *Heaton Woods Guide* (Bradford: Lund Humphries, 2006)
Hindley, Reg – *Oxenhope: The Making of a Pennine Community* (Oxenhope: Reg Hindley, 2004)
Illingworth, T (ed.) – *Yeadon Yorkshire* (Guiseley: M.T.D. Rigg Publications, 1980)
James, David – *Bradford* (Halifax: Ryburn, 1990)

Kent, Alana – *What's that Chimney up There?* (Harden: Harden & Bingley Caravan Park Publications, 1993)
Kippax & District Historical Society – *A History of Kippax* (Manningtree: Heritage House Press, 2007)
Laurence, Alastair – *A History of Menston and Hawksworth* (Otley: Smith Settle, 1991)
Laurence, Alastair – *Horsforth History Tour* (Horsforth Village Historical Society, 2005)
Lee, J.D. & Davies, K. – *Riddlesden Reflections* (Keighley: Raiseprint, 1994)
Mabey, Richard – *The Ash and the Beech: The Drama of Woodland Change* (London: Vintage, 2013)
McDermott, Michael – *Allerton in Bygone Days* (Bradford: M. McDermott, 1989)
McDonald, A.S. – *Tong Hall, Tong, Bradford* (Bradford: A.S. McDonald, 2002)
Melvin, James H. – *Methley 2000* (Roberttown: James H. Melvin, 2000)
Mitchell, W.R. – *A History of Leeds* (Chichester: Phillimore, 2000)
Morfitt, J.M. – *Horsforth and its History* (Heysham: J.M. Morfitt)
Morkill, John W. – *The Manor and Park of Roundhay* (Leeds: Richard Jackson, 1893)
Newlay Conservation Society History Group – *Newlay: A Pictorial History* (Leeds: Newlay Conservation Society, 1989)
Oakwood & District Historical Society – *Oak Leaves: Part Four* (Leeds: Oakwood & District Historical Society, 2003)
Oakworth Village Society – *Oakworth Handbook* (Oakworth Village Society, 2007)
Ogden, John – *Yorkshire's River Aire* (Lavenham: Terence Dalton, 1976)
Owen, David E. – *Kirkstall Abbey* (Leeds: E.J. Arnold & Son Ltd, 1955)
Padgett, Lorenzo – *Castleford & District in the Olden Time* (London: Simpkin Marshall, Hamilton, Kent & Co & Alfred Wilson, 1904)
Parker, James – *Illustrated Rambles from Hipperholme to Tong* (Bradford: The Country Press, 1904)
Peck, Alice – *The Green Cure* (London: CICO Books, 2019)
Pickles, Edgar N. – *Kippax in Old Picture Postcards* (Zaltbommel: European Library, 1993)
Pudsey Civic Society – *Walks Around Pudsey, Farsley and Calverley* (Pudsey Civic Society, 1981)
Pudsey Civic Society – *Calverley in Old Picture Postcards* (Zaltbommel: European Library, 2005)
Raynor, Simeon – *The History & Antiquities of Pudsey* (London: Longman, Green & Co, 1887)
Rigg, Martin – *Round and About Aireborough: A Glimpse of the Past* (Guiseley: M.T.D. Rigg Publications, 1988)
Riley, Peter – *Esholt: A Bygone Era* (Runcorn: P. & D. Riley, 2008)
Roberts, I. & Richardson, J. – *Iron Age Enclosures at Moss Carr, Methley* (Leeds: West Yorkshire Archaeology Service, 2002)
Roe, Martin – *Coal Mining in Middleton Park* (Halifax: Meerstone, 2008)
Ruston, Cynthia – *Meanwood Quarries & Quarrymen* (Leeds: Propagator Press, 2006)
Senior, Janet C. – *Some Bits of Bradford's History* (Bradford Historical & Antiquarian Society, 2018)
Senior, Lee – *Walking in the Aire* (Airedale: Trig Point Publications, 2017)
Sheeran, George – *Village to Mill Town: Shipley and its Society 1600-1870* (Bradford: Bradford Libraries, 1984)
Shelton, Tony – *Leeds' Golden Acres* (Leeds: Age Concern Leeds, 2000)
Smith, Albert Hugh – *The Place-names of the West Riding of Yorkshire* (Cambridge University Press, 1959)

Speight, Harry – *Chronicles and Stories of Old Bingley* (London: Elliot Stock, 1898)
Stead, Geoffrey – *The Moravian Settlement at Fulneck 1742-1790* (Leeds: The Thoresby Society, 1999)
Stevens, F.N. – *The History of Horsforth* (Horsforth: F.N. Stevens, 1974)
Taylor, Rev. Richard Vickerman – *The Biographia Leodiensis* (London: Simpkin, Marshall & Co, 1865)
Thornton, David – *Leeds: The Story of a City* (Ayr: Fort Publishing Ltd, 2002)
Thurlow, William – *Yorkshire Place-Names* (Clapham: Dalesman Publishing, 1979)
Turner, Joseph Horsfall – *Ancient Bingley* (Bingley: Thomas Harrison & Sons, 1897)
Turner, Joseph Horsfall – *Historical Notices of Shipley, Saltaire, Idle, Windhill, Wrose, Baildon, Hawksworth, Eccleshill, Calverley, Rawdon and Horsforth* (Idle: Shipley Express, 1901)
Van den Daele, Richard Lee & Beale, R. David – *Milner Field: The Lost Country House of Titus Salt Jnr* (Barleybrook Ltd, 2011)
Waddington, David – *One Road In, One Road Out: A People's History of Fryston* (Sheffield: Hallam University Press, 1988)
Ward, A.J. & Ashton, T. (eds.) – *The History of Cookridge Hospital 1867-1972* (Leeds: Cookridge Hospital, 1997)
Warren, Denise – *Those First Affections* (Saltaire: ASAP, 1987)
Wilders, David G. – *History of Castleford* (Castleford: Briton Press, 1995)
Willcock, D.C. – *A History of Rawdon: Persons, Places and Prejudices* (Leeds: D.C. Willock, 2000)
Wilson, Benjamin Jr. – *Our Village: A Sketch of History and Progress of Bramley During Seven Centuries* (Bramley: J. Dawson, 1860)
Winter, W.P. – 'Shipley Glen' in *Bradford Scientific Journal, Volume III, Issue 2* (1910)
Wood, Steven & Palmer, Ian – *Oxenhope and Stanbury Through Time* (Stroud: Amberley, 2009)

## WEBSITES

Bradford & District Local Studies – *bradfordlocalstudies.wordpress.com*
Bradford Unconsidered Trifles – *bradfordunconsideredtrifles.wordpress.com*
Castleford – *www.castleford.org*
Fabulous Follies – *www.fabulousfollies.net*
Friends of Middleton Park – *www.fomp.co.uk*
Friends of Northcliffe – *www.friendsofnorthcliffe.org.uk*
Friends of Park Wood – *www.park-wood.co.uk*
Fryston Memories – *www.frystonmemories.co.uk*
The History of Gildersome – *www.gildersome.net*
A History of Rawdon – *a-history-of-rawdon.co.uk*
The Lagentian – *castlefordhistory.wordpress.com*
Laycock Village – *village.laycock.com*
Leeds Coppice Workers – *leedscoppiceworkers.co.uk*
Middleton Life – *middletonlife.wordpress.com*
The Northern Antiquarian – *megalithix.wordpress.com*
Secret Leeds – *www.secretleeds.com*
Silsden.net – *www.silsden.net*
Steeton with Eastburn Village – *steetonandeastburn.co.uk*
The Thoresby Society – *www.thoresby.org.uk*
Urban Tree Cover – *urbantreecover.org*
West Yorkshire Archive Service – *wytithemaps.org.uk*

# INDEX / GAZETTEER

# LIST OF OTHER WOODS IN THE AIRE VALLEY

*(These woods all fall within the catchment of the River Aire in West Yorkshire, but are not included in this book, either because they are too small, too far from other woods, do not have public access, or a combination of the above.)*

Barrowby Wood, Garforth (GR 386334)
Batcliff Wood, Headingley (GR 271361)
Beeston Spring, Wortley (GR 267310)
Boggart Wood, Thornton (GR 113331)
Brecks Wood, Kippax (GR 401314)
Bull Greave Wood, Clayton (GR 132325)
Burke Wood, Horsforth (GR 228374)
Calfhole Wood, Guiseley (GR 206428)
Carr Wood, Wibsey (GR 153304)
Clubbed Oaks, Morley (GR 256290)
Clumpcliffe Wood, Methley (GR 374269)
Cockshot Wood, Farsley (GR 210356)
Cote Hill Wood, Oxenhope (GR 038359)
Cottingley Spring, Wortley (GR 265305)
Cunliff Wood, Armley (GR 276341)
Dean Wood, Morley (GR 254287)
Deep Car, Guiseley (GR 205424)
Dunkirk Wood, Riddlesden (GR 069430)
Elm Close Wood, Keighley (GR 082407)
Elm Wood, Guiseley (GR 177408)
Gab Wood, Cookridge (GR 246407)
Green Hill Wood, Bingley (GR 108408)
Hainworth Wood, Keighley (GR 059394)
Hanging Fall Wood, Clayton (GR 110318)
Haugh Hill Plantation, Ledsham (GR 460283)
Hawkcliffe Wood, Steeton (GR 042440)
Hawkstone Wood, Guiseley (GR 179409)
Heald Wood, Castleford (GR 441256)
Hell Wood, Kirkstall (GR 262368)
High Birks, Queensbury (GR 099318)
Hollins, the, Keighley (GR 044432)
Holywell Wood, Castleford (GR 444244)
Intake Wood, Eldwick (GR 121415)
Jer Wood, Bingley (GR 113394)
Kirkstall Wood, Keighley (GR 064396)
Lime Pits Wood, Seacroft (GR 350373)
Little Fall, Bramley (GR 254358)
Lord Wood, Haworth (GR 032377)
Low Wood, Seacroft (GR 346372)
Marley Brow Wood, Keighley (GR 084408)
Morris Wood, Kirkstall (GR 263364)
Newfield Plantation, Ledsham (GR 453284)
Old Harrisons Wood, Guiseley (GR 202432)
Ox Moor Wood, Headingley (GR 272369)
Parks Wood, Bowling (GR 170306)
Ponden Wood (was Clogger Wood), Haworth (GR 989369)
Ramshead Wood, Seacroft (GR 352370)
Reck Wood, Silsden (GR 044474)
Red Hall Wood, Roundhay (GR 344387)
Ridge Wood, Armley (GR 266343)
Sheepcote Wood, Kippax (GR 436306)
Shuttocks Wood, Kippax (GR 418311)
Sough Wood, Horsforth (GR 226374)
Stony Hill Wood, Alwoodley (GR 323397)
Stony Ridge Plantation, Cottingley (GR 123362)
Thackley West Wood, Thackley (GR 167385)
The Plantation, Drighlington (GR 217291)
The Rein, Farsley (GR 210358)
Wetstone Plantations (GR 233397)
Whins Wood, Keighley (GR 052384)
Winter Wood, Methley (GR 377274)
Wormstall Wood, Ledsham (GR 464294)

# LOST WOODS OF THE AIRE VALLEY

*(These woods all fall within the catchment of the River Aire in West Yorkshire, but no longer exist. They are either marked on old Ordnance Survey maps or have been referenced elsewhere in my research, hence the unknown locations.)*

Alder Wood, Keighley (GR 060399)
Appleton Wood, Wrose (unknown)
Arthur's Rein, Fearnville (GR 340362)
Bailey's Rein, Seacroft (GR 347366)
Barker Wood, Gledhow (GR 324367)
Barry Leys Wood, Kippax (GR 412308)
Birks Wood, Farnley (GR 259313)
Brown's Wood, Thackley (unknown)
Burley Wood, Kirkstall (GR 272349)
Butler's Spring, Kirkstall (GR 259366)
Conyer's Spring, Middleton (GR 309287)
Cowgill Wood, West Park (GR 266372)
Daffill Wood, Morley (GR 267295)
Dan Wood, Pudsey (GR 213341)
Farnley Wood, Farnley (GR 260306)
Fox Wood, Seacroft (GR 346361)
Grimewell Banks, Weetwood (GR 263381)
Hawk Cliff Plantation, Haworth (GR 039363)
Head Wood, West Park (GR 266381)
High Royds Wood, Castleford (GR 458257)
Hog Holes Wood, Keighley (GR 068399)
Houghton Carr Wood, Castleford (GR 427237)
Ivy Royd Spring Wood, East Ardsley (GR 314256)
Langley Wood, Lofthouse (GR 327253)
Little Wood, Wortley (GR 263327)
Long Wood, Tinshill (GR 246389)
Low Wood, Steeton (GR 023443)
Lower Springs Wood, Riddlesden (GR 086421)
Major Wood, Gildersome (GR 242299)
March Intake Wood, Bingley (GR 112404)
Moseley Wood, Cookridge (GR 248402)
North Wood, Tyersal (GR 202329)
Nursery Wood, Halton Moor (GR 341324)
Nut Head Wood, Steeton (GR 031432)
Owlcotes Wood, Pudsey (GR 212343)
Parkinson's Wood, Newsam Green
Pearce Close Wood, Keighley (GR 051385)
Pollard Wood, Haworth (GR 005365)
Pontefract Wood, Weetwood (GR 271383)
Poverty Spring, Newsam Green
Rein Wood, Middleton (GR 305288)
Rye Loaf Wood, Bingley (GR 120378)
Seacroft Wood, Seacroft (unknown)
Shaw Wood, Guiseley (GR 203423)
Spring Wood, Bradford (GR 167314)
Spring Wood, Garforth (GR 395333)
Stump Cross Plantation, Haworth (GR 048369)
The Alders, Farnley (GR 259317)
Tinshill Plantation, Tinshill (GR 250397)
Upper Springs Wood, Riddlesden (GR 087422)
Wadlands Wood, Farsley (GR 207353)
Well Green Wood, Garforth (GR 393320)
Wet Close Plantation, Farnley (GR 254314)
Whitebirkes, Weetwood (unknown)
Windhill Wood, Windhill (GR 160381)
Wood House Wood, Keighley (GR 062398)

Many thanks for reading this book. I have realised over the past seven years, since publishing the first of these guidebooks, just how hard it is to get everything right. Things change fast too, so routes and maps can become out of date within a short time. To this end I have added a new Updates section to my website, which details where there are problems on the routes in my books; some of these may be temporary (such as a bridge closed for repairs), but others can be more permanent (such as informal access being closed off).

I often find out about these only because readers have got in touch with me through my website, so please do send me your feedback, suggestions, corrections and updates through the contact form, and do check the Updates page regularly. All of these are gratefully received.

**www.christophergoddard.net**